THE GALE
ENCYCLOPEDIA
OF THE UNUSUAL
AND
UNEXPLAINED

BRAD STEIGER

AND

SHERRY
HANSEN
STEIGER

THE GALE
ENCYCLOPEDIA
OF THE UNUSUAL
AND
UNEXPLAINED

GALE®

THOMSON
GALE

Detroit • New York • San Diego • San Francisco • Cleveland • New Haven, Conn. • Waterville, Maine • London • Munich

THOMSON

GALE

Gale Encyclopedia of the Unusual and Unexplained

Brad E. Steiger and Sherry Hansen Steiger

Project Editor
Jolen Marya Gedridge

Editorial
Andrew Claps, Lynn U. Koch, Michael Reade

Permissions
Lori Hines

Imaging and Multimedia
Dean Dauphinais, Lezlie Light

Product Design
Tracey Rowens

Manufacturing
Rhonda A. Williams

LIBRARY OF CONGRESS CATALOGING-IN-PUBLICATION DATA

Steiger, Brad.
　　Gale encyclopedia of the unusual and unexplained / Brad E. Steiger and Sherry Hansen Steiger.
　　　　p. cm.
Includes bibliographical references and index.
　　ISBN 0-7876-5382-9 (set : hardcover : alk. paper) — ISBN 0-7876-5383-7 (v. 1 : alk. paper) — ISBN 0-7876-5384-5 (v. 2 : alk. paper) — ISBN 0-7876-5385-3 (v. 3 : alk. paper)
　　1. Parapsychology—Encyclopedias. 2. Occultism—Encyclopedias. 3. Supernatural—Encyclopedias. I. Title: Encyclopedia of the unusual and unexplained. II. Steiger, Sherry Hansen. III. Title.
　　BF1025.S79 2003
　　130'.3—dc21

2003003995

This title is also available as an e-book
ISBN 0-7876-7764-7
Contact your Gale representative for ordering information

Printed in the United States of America
10 9 8 7 6 5 4 3 2 1

TABLE OF CONTENTS

VOLUME 2

PREFACE

The Gale Encyclopedia of the Unusual and Unexplained (GEUU) presents comprehensive and objective information on unexplained mysteries, paranormal abilities, supernatural events, religious phenomena, magic, UFOs, and myths that have evolved into cultural realities. This extensive three-volume work is a valuable tool providing users the opportunity to evaluate the many claims and counterclaims regarding the mysterious and unknown. Many of these claims have been brought to the forefront from television, motion pictures, radio talk shows, best-selling books, and the Internet.

There has been a conscious effort to provide reliable and authoritative information in the most objective and factual way possible, to present multiple viewpoints for controversial subject topics, and to avoid sensationalism that taints the credibility of the subject matter. The manner of presentation enables readers to utilize their critical thinking skills to separate fact from fiction, opinion from dogma, and truth from legend regarding enigmas that have intrigued, baffled, and inspired humankind over the centuries.

ABOUT THE AUTHORS AND ADVISORS

Brad E. Steiger has written over 150 books with over 17 million copies in print. His vast writing experience includes biographies, books of inspiration, phenomenon and the paranormal, spirituality, UFO research, and crimes. His first articles on the paranormal appeared in 1954 and, today, he has produced over 2,000 articles on such themes. Steiger has appeared on such television programs as *Nightline with Ted Koppel, ABC Evening News with Peter Jennings, NBC Evening News with Tom Brokaw, This Week* (with David Brinkley, Sam Donaldson, and Cokie Roberts), *The Mike Douglas Show, The David Susskind Show, The Joan Rivers Show, Entertainment Tonight, Haunted Hollywood, Inside Edition, The Unexplained,* and *Giants: The Myth and the Mystery.* Sherry Hansen Steiger is a co-author of 24 books on a variety of topics on the unusual and unexplained with her husband Brad. Her continual studies in alternative medicine and therapies led to the 1992 official creation of The Office of Alternative Medicine under the Institutes of Health, Education and Welfare in Bethesda, Maryland. Both Steigers have served as consultants for such television shows as *Sightings* and *Unsolved Mysteries*.

The advisors for *GEUU* are Judy T. Nelson, the Youth Services Coordinator for the Pierce County Library System in Tacoma, Washington; Lee Sprince, former Head of Youth Services for the Broward County Main Library in Fort Lauderdale, Florida; and Brad E. Steiger, author of Gale's former Visible Ink Press title *The Werewolf Book: The Encyclopedia of Shape-Shifting Things*. For *GEUU*, both Nelson and Sprince were consulted on *GEUU*'s subject content, its appropriateness, and format; Steiger advised on the content's organization before he became the author of *GEUU*.

FORMAT

The *Gale Encyclopedia of the Unusual and Unexplained* consists of fourteen broad-subject chapters covering a wide range of high-interest topics: Afterlife Mysteries; Mediums and Mystics; Religious Phenomena; Mystery Religions and Cults; Secret Societies; Magic and Sorcery; Prophecy and Divination; Objects of Mystery and Power; Places of Mystery and Power; Ghosts and Phantoms; Mysterious Creatures; Mysteries of the Mind; Superstitions, Strange Customs, Taboos, and Urban Legends; and Invaders from Outer Space. Each chapter begins with an **Overview** that summarizes the chapter's concept in a few brief sentences. Then the **Chapter Exploration** provides a complete outline of the chapter, listing all topics and subtopics therein, so that the user can understand the interrelationships between the chapter's topics and its subtopics. An **Introduction** consisting of 6 to 12 paragraphs follows; it broadly describes the chapter's theme. Then each topic is

explored, along with each subtopic, developing relevant concepts, geographic places, persons, practices, etc. After each topic, a **Delving Deeper** section provides complete bibliographical citations of books, periodicals, television programs, Internet sites, movies, and theses used, and provides users with further research opportunities. **Boldfaced cross-references** are used to guide users from the text to related entries found elsewhere in the three volumes. Sidebars supplement the text with unusual facts, features, and biographies, as well as descriptions of web sites, etc.

Each chapter contains photographs, line drawings, and original graphics that were chosen to complement the text; in all three volumes, over 250 images enliven the text. Many of these images are provided by Fortean Picture Library—"a pictorial archive of mysteries and strange phenomena"—and from the personal archives of the author, Brad Steiger. At the end of each chapter, a glossary, called **Making the Connection**, lists significant terms, theories, and practices mentioned within the text. A comprehensive glossary of the terms used throughout all three volumes can be found at the end of each volume.

Each volume has a cumulative **Table of Contents** allowing users to see the organization of each chapter at a glance. The **Cumulative Index**, found in each volume, is an alphabetic arrangement of all people, places, images, and concepts found in the text. The page references to the terms include the volume number as well as the page number; images are denoted by italicized page numbers.

USER COMMENTS ARE WELCOME

Users having comments, corrections, or suggestions can contact the editor at the following address: *Gale Encyclopedia of the Unusual and Unexplained*, The Gale Group, Inc., 27500 Drake Rd., Farmington Hills, MI 48331-3535.

Introduction

Understanding the Unknown

The belief in a reality that transcends our everyday existence is as old as humanity itself and it continues to the present day. In fact, in recent years there has been a tremendous surge of interest in the paranormal and the supernatural. People speak freely of guardian angels, a belief in life after death, an acceptance of extrasensory perception (ESP), and the existence of ghosts. In a Gallup Poll released on June 10, 2001, the survey administrators found that 54 percent of Americans believe in spiritual or faith healing; 41 percent acknowledge that people can be possessed by the devil; 50 percent accept the reality of ESP; 32 percent believe in the power of prophecy; and 38 percent agree that ghosts and spirits exist.

What are the origins of these age-old beliefs? Are they natural phenomenon that can be understood by the physical sciences? Some scientists are suggesting that such mystical experiences can be explained in terms of neural transmitters, neural networks, and brain chemistry. Perhaps the feeling of transcendence that mystics describe could be the result of decreased activity in the brain's parietal lobe, which helps regulate the sense of self and physical orientation. Perhaps the human brain is wired for mystical experiences and the flash of wisdom that illuminated the Buddha, the voices that Mohammed and Moses heard in the wilderness, and the dialogues that Jesus had with the Father were the result of brain chemistry and may someday be completely explained in scientific terms.

Perhaps the origin of these beliefs is to be found in psychology? Humankind's fascination with the unknown quite likely began with the most basic of human emotions—fear. Early humans faced the constant danger of being attacked by predators, of being killed by people from other tribes, or of falling victim to the sudden fury of a natural disaster, such as flood, fire, or avalanche. Nearly all of these violent encounters brought about the death of a friend or family member, so one may surmise that chief among the mysteries that troubled early humans was the same one that haunts man today: What happens when someone dies?

But belief in the unknown may be more than brain chemistry or a figment of our fears. Perhaps there is some spiritual reality that is outside of us, but with which one can somehow communicate? Perhaps the physical activity of the brain or psychological state (the two are of course related) may be only a precondition or a conduit to a transcendent world? The central mystery may always remain.

GHOSTLY ENTITIES AND URBAN LEGENDS

There is not a single known culture on planet Earth that does not have its ghost stories, and one can determine from Paleolithic cave paintings that the belief that there is something within the human body that survives physical death is at least 50,000 years old. If there is a single unifying factor in the arena of the unknown and the unexplained it is the universality of accounts of ghostly entities. Of course, not everyone agrees on the exact nature of ghosts. Some insist that the appearance of ghosts prove survival after death. Others state that such phenomena represent other dimensions of reality.

And then there are the skeptics who group most ghost stories in the category of "Urban Legends," those unverifiable stories about outlandish, humorous, frightening, or supernatural events. In some instances, the stories are based on actual occurrences that have in their telling and retelling been exaggerated or distorted. Other urban legends have their origins in people misinterpreting or misunderstanding stories that they have heard or read in the media or from actual witnesses of an event. There is usually some distance between the narrator and his tale; all urban legends claim that the story always happened to someone else, most often "a friend of a friend."

THE ROOTS OF SUPERSTITION

Whatever their basis in reality, certain beliefs and practices of primitive people helped ease their fear and the feeling of helplessness that arose from the precariousness of their existence. Others in the community who took careful note of their behavior ritualized the stories of those who had faced great dangers and survived. In such rituals lies the origin of "superstition," a belief that certain repeated actions or words will bring the practitioner luck or ward off evil. Ancient superstitions survive today in such common practices as tossing a pinch of salt over the shoulder or whispering a blessing after a sneeze to assure good fortune.

The earliest traces of magical practices are found in the European caves of the Paleolithic Age, c. 50,000 B.C.E. in which it seems clear that early humans sought supernatural means to placate the spirits of the animals they killed for food, to dispel the restless spirits of the humans they had slain, or to bring peace to the spirits of their deceased tribal kin. It was at this time that early humans began to believe that there could be supernatural powers in a charm, a spell, or a ritual to work good or evil on their enemies. Practices, such as imitating the animal of the hunt through preparatory dance, cutting off a bit of an enemy's hair or clothing to be used in a charm against him, or invoking evil spirits to cause harm to others, eventually gained a higher level of sophistication and evolved into more formal religious practices.

As such beliefs developed, certain tribal members were elevated in status to shaman and magician because of their ability to communicate with the spirit worlds, to influence the weather, to heal the sick, and to interpret dreams. Shamans entered a trance-like condition separating them from life's mundane existence and allowing them to enter a state of heightened spiritual awareness. According to anthropologists, shamanic methods are remarkably similar throughout the world. In our own time, Spiritualist mediums who claim to be able to communicate with the dead remain popular as guides for contemporary men and women, and such individuals as John Edward, James Van Praagh, and Sylvia Browne issue advice from the Other Side on syndicated television programs.

Monsters and Night Terrors

Stone Age humans had good reason to fear the monsters that emerged from the darkness. Saber-tooth tigers stalked man, cave bears mauled them, and rival hominid species—many appearing more animal-like than human—struggled against them for dominance. The memories of the ancient night terrors surface in dreams and imagination, a kind of psychic residue of primitive fears. Anthropologists have observed that such half-human, half-animal monsters as the werewolf and other werecreatures were painted by Stone Age artists more than 10,000 years ago. Some of the world's oldest art found on ancient sites in Europe, Africa, and Australia depict animal-human hybrids. Such "therianthropes," or hybrid beings, appear to be the only common denominator in primitive art around the planet. These werewolves, were-lions, and were-bats belonged to an imagined world which early humans saw as powerful, dangerous, and frightening.

Images of these creatures persisted into the historical period. The ancient Egyptians often depicted their gods as human-animal hybrids. Pharaoh identified himself with the god Horus, who could be represented as a falcon or a falcon-headed human. Anubis, the god of the necropolis, can be shown as a jackal-headed man, probably because such carrion-eating jackals prowled Egyptian cemeteries. Many other civilizations felt the power of these kinds of images. For example, the ancient Greeks fashioned the minotaur (half-human, half-bull), the satyr (half-human, half-goat), the harpy (half-woman, half-bird) and a host of other hybrid entities—the vast majority unfavorably disposed toward humankind. Examples could be found in other cultures as well.

Customs and Taboos

In 2001, scientists were surprised when bits of stone etched with intricate patterns found in the Blombos Cave, east of Cape Town on the southern African shores of the Indian Ocean, were dated at 77,000 years old, thereby indicating that ancient humans were capable of complex behavior and abstract thought thousands of years earlier than previously believed. In Europe, numerous sites have been excavated and artifacts unearthed that prove that structured behavior with customs and taboos existed about 40,000 years ago.

Customs are those activities that have been approved by a social group and have been handed down from generation to generation until they have become habitual. When an action or activity violates behavior considered appropriate by a social group, it is labeled a "taboo," a word borrowed from the Polynesians of the South Pacific. An act that is taboo is forbidden, and those who transgress may be ostracized by others or, in extreme instances, killed.

However, customs vary from culture to culture, and customary actions in one society may be considered improper in another. While the marriage of near-blood relations is prohibited in contemporary civilization, in earlier societies it was quite common. The ancient brother and sister gods of Egypt, Osiris and Isis, provided an example for pharaohs, who at times married their sisters. Polygamy, the marriage of one man and several women or one woman and several men, is prohibited in modern civilization, but there are still religious groups in nearly every nation who justify plural marriages as being ordained by the deity they worship. Adultery, an act of infidelity on the part of a married individual, is one of the most universal taboos. The code of Moses condemned both parties involved in the act to be stoned to death. Hindu religious doctrines demand the death, mutilation, or humiliation of both men and women, depending upon the caste of the guilty parties.

Taboos can change within a society over time. Many acts that were once considered forbidden have developed into an acceptable social activity. While some of the old customs and taboos surrounding courtship and marriage, hospitality and etiquette, and burials and funerals may seem amusing or quaint, primitive or savage, certain elements of such acts as capturing one's bride have been preserved in many traditions that are still practiced in the modern marriage ceremony.

BELIEF IN AN AFTERLIFE

Belief in the survival of some part of us after death may also be as old as the human race. Although one cannot be certain the earliest members of man's species (*Homo sapiens* c. 30,000 B.C.E.) conducted burial rituals that would qualify them as believers in an afterlife, one does know they buried their dead with care and consideration and included food, weapons, and various personal belongings with the body. Anthropologists have also discovered the Neanderthal species (c. 100,000 B.C.E.) placed food, stone implements, and decorative shells and bones with the deceased. Because of the placement of such funerary objects in the graves, one may safely conjecture that these prehistoric people believed death was not the end. There was some part of the deceased requiring nourishment, clothing, and protection in order to journey safely in another kind of existence beyond the grave. This belief persisted into more recent historical times. The ancient Egyptians had a highly developed concept of life after death, devoting much thought and effort to their eternal well-being, and they were not the only early civilization to be concerned about an afterlife.

With all their diversity of beliefs, the major religions of today are in accord in one essential teaching: Human beings are immortal and their spirit comes from a divine world and may eventually return there. The part of the human being that survives death is known in Judaism, Christianity, and Islam as the soul—the very essence of the individual person that must answer for its earthly deeds, good or bad. Hinduism perceives this spiritual essence as the divine Self, the *Atman,* and Buddhism believes it to be the summation of conditions and causes. Of the major world religions, only Buddhism does not perceive an eternal metaphysical aspect of the human personality in the same way that the others do. However, all the major faiths believe that after the spirit has left the body, it moves on to another existence. The physical body is a temporary possession that a human has, not what a person is.

The mystery of what happens when the soul leaves the body remains an enigma in the teachings of the major religions; however, as more and more individuals are retrieved from clinical death by the miracles of modern medicine, literature describing near-death-experiences has arisen which depicts a transition into another world or dimension of consciousness wherein the deceased are met by beings of light. Many of those who have returned to life after such an experience also speak of a life-review of their deeds and misdeeds from childhood to the moment of the near-death encounter.

PROPHECY AND DIVINATION

The desire to foresee the future quite likely began when early humans began to perceive that they were a part of nature, subject to its limitations and laws, and that they were seemingly powerless to alter those laws. Mysterious supernatural forces—sometimes benign, often hostile—appeared to be in control of human existence.

Divination, the method of obtaining knowledge of the future by means of omens or sacred objects, has been practiced in all societies, whether primitive or civilized. The ancient Chaldeans read the will of the gods in the star-jeweled heavens. The children of Israel sought the word of the Lord in the jewels of the Ephod. Pharaoh elevated Joseph from his prison cell to the office of chief minister of Egypt and staked the survival of his kingdom on Joseph's interpretation of his dreams. In the same land of Egypt, priests of Isis and Ra listened as those deities spoke through the unmoving lips of the stone Sphinx.

Throughout the centuries, soothsayers and seers have sought to predict the destiny of their clients by interpreting signs in the entrails of animals, the movements of the stars in the heavens, the reflections in a crystal ball, the spread of a deck of cards, and even messages from the dead. All of these ancient practices are still being utilized today by those who wish to know the future.

Objects and Places of Mystery and Power

Objects of mystery and power that become influential in a person's life can be an everyday item that an individual has come to believe will bring good fortune, such as an article of clothing that was worn when some great personal success was achieved or an amulet that has been passed on from generation to generation. In addition to such items of personal significance, some individuals have prized objects that reportedly brought victory or good fortune to heroes of long ago. Still others have searched for mysterious relics filled with supernatural attributes that were credited with accomplishing miracles in the past. No physical evidence is available to determine that such an object as the Ark of the Covenant ever existed, but its present location continues to be sought. The Holy Grail, the cup from which Jesus drank at the Last Supper, is never mentioned in the Bible, but by medieval times it had been popularized as the holiest relic in Christendom.

In addition to bestowing mystery and power upon certain objects, humans have always found or created places that are sacred to them—sites where they might gather to participate in religious rituals or where they might retreat for solitude and reflection. In such places, many people claim to experience a sense of the sublime. Others, while in a solemn place of worship or in a natural setting, attest to feeling a special energy that raises their consciousness and perhaps even heals their physical body.

Mysterious megaliths (large stones) were those placed at a special location by ancient people. Such sites include the standing stones of Brittany, the Bighorn Medicine Wheel in Wyoming, and the monuments of Easter Island. All of these places were ostensibly significant to an ancient society or religion, but many were long abandoned by the time they became known to today's world and their significance remains unexplained.

The most well-known megalithic structures are Stonehenge in Great Britain and the complex of pyramids and the Great Sphinx in Egypt. Like many such ancient places, those sites have been examined and speculated upon for centuries, yet they still continue to conceal secrets and occasionally yield surprising information that forces new historical interpretations of past societies.

There are other places that have become mysterious sites because of unusual occurrences. The claimed miraculous healing at Lourdes, France, the accounts of spiritual illumination at Jerusalem and Mecca, and the sacred visions at Taos, New Mexico, provide testimonies of faith and wonder that must be assessed by each individual.

There are also the "lost" civilizations and mysterious places that may never have existed beyond the human imagination. More than 2,500 years ago, legends first began about Atlantis, an ideal society that enjoyed an abundance of natural resources, great military power, splendid building and engineering feats, and intellectual achievements far advanced over those of other lands. This ancient society was described as existing on a continent-sized area with rich soil, plentiful pure water, abundant vegetation, and such mineral wealth that gold was inlaid in buildings. In the ensuing centuries, no conclusive evidence of Atlantis has been found, but its attributes have expanded to include engineering and technological feats that enhance its legendary status.

Sometimes legends come to life. The Lost City of Willkapanpa the Old, a city rumored to consist primarily of Incan rulers and soldiers, was not discovered until 1912 when a historian from Yale University found the site now known as Machu Picchu hidden at 8,000 feet in altitude between two mountains, Huayana Picchu ("young mountain") and Machu Picchu ("ancient mountain") in Peru.

Mystery Schools and Cults

Once a religion has become firmly established in a society, dissatisfied members often will break away from the larger group to create what they believe to be a more valid form of religious expression. Sometimes such splinter groups are organized around the revelations and visions of a single individual, who is recognized as a prophet by his or her followers. Because the new teachings may be judged as heretical to the original body of worshippers, those who follow the new revelations are branded as cultists or heretics.

Even in ancient times, the dissenters were forced to meet in secret because of oppression by the established group or because of their desire to hide their practices. Since only devotees could know the truths of their faith, adherents were required to maintain the strictest silence regarding their rites and rituals. The term "mysteries" or "mystery religion" is applied to these beliefs. The word "mystery" comes from the Greek word *myein,* "to close," referring to the need of the *mystes,* the initiate, to close his or her eyes and the lips and to keep secret the rites of the cult.

In ancient Greece, postulants of the mystery religions had to undergo a rigorous initiation that disciplined both their mind and body. In order to attain the self-mastery demanded by the priests of the mysteries, the neophytes understood that they must restructure their physical, moral, and spiritual being to gain access to the hidden forces in the universe. Only through complete mastery of oneself could one see beyond death and perceive the pathways of the after-life. Many times these mysteries were taught in the form of a play and were celebrated in sacred groves or in secret temples away from the cities.

In contemporary usage, the word "cult" generally carries with it negative connotations and associations. In modern times, a number of apocalyptic cults, such as the Branch Davidians and the People's Temple, have alarmed the general population by isolating themselves and preparing for Armageddon, the last great battle between good and evil. The mass suicides carried out by members of Heaven's Gate, People's Temple, and Order of the Solar Temple have also presented alarming images of what many believe to be typical cultist practice. Recent statistics indicate that there are 2,680 religions in the United States. Therefore, one must be cautious in labeling any seemingly unorthodox religion as a cult, for what is regarded as anti-social or blasphemous expression by some may be hailed as sincere spiritual witness by others.

SECRET SOCIETIES AND CONSPIRACIES

There will always be envious individuals who believe that wealthy and powerful members of society have been able to acquire their position only because of secret formulas, magical words, and supernatural rituals. Rumors and legends of secret societies have fueled the imaginations, fears, and envy of those on the outside for thousands of years. Many secret societies, such as the Assassins, the Garduna, the Thuggee, and the Tongs, were made up of highly trained criminals who were extremely dangerous to all outsiders. Others, such as the Knights Templar, the Illuminati, and the Rosicrucians, were said to possess enough ancient secrets of power and wealth to control the entire world.

Conspiracy enthusiasts allege that there are clandestine organizations which for centuries have remained a threat to individual freedoms, quietly operating in the shadows, silently infiltrating political organizations, and secretly manipulating every level of government and every facet of society. One of the favorites of conspiracy theorists, the Freemasons, while once a powerful and influential group throughout the Western world, is today regarded by many as simply a philanthropic and fraternal organization. Another secret society, the Illuminati, deemed by many conspiracy buffs to be the most insidious of all, faded into obscurity in the late eighteenth century. However, there is always a new secret society that seeks to divine arcane and forbidden avenues to wealth and power.

SORCERY, ALCHEMY AND WITCHCRAFT

Although Christianity affirms the existence of a transcendent reality, it has always distinguished between *religio* (reverence for God) and *superstitio*, which in Latin means "unreasonable religious belief." Christianity became the state religion of the Roman Empire in 395 C.E., and in 525 the Council of Oxia prohibited Christians from consulting sorcerers, diviners, or any kind of seer. A canon passed by the Council of Constantinople in 625 prescribed excommunication for a period of six years for anyone found practicing divination or who consulted with a diviner.

Although the Church had issued many canons warning against the practice of witchcraft or magic, little action was taken against those learned men who experimented with alchemy or those common folk who practiced the old ways of witchcraft. In 906 C.E., Abbot Regino of Prum recognized that earlier canon laws had done little to eradicate the practices of magic and witchcraft, so he issued his *De ecclesiaticis disciplinis* to condemn as heretical any belief in witchcraft or the power of sorcerers. In 1,000 C.E., Deacon Burchard, who would later become archbishop of Worms, published *Corrrector* which updated Regino's work and stressed that only God had the power to transform matter. Alchemists could not change base metals into gold, and witches could not shapeshift into animals.

In spite of such decrees, a lively belief in a world of witches and ghosts persisted throughout the Middle Ages and co-existed in the minds of many of the faithful with the miracle stories of the saints. To the native beliefs were added those of non-Christian peoples who either lived in Europe or whom Europeans met when they journeyed far from home, as when they went on the Crusades. By the twelfth century, magical practices based upon the arcane systems of the Spanish Moors and Jewish Kabbalah were established in Europe. The Church created the Inquisition in the High Middle Ages in response to unorthodox religious beliefs that it called heresies. Since some of these involved magical practices and witchcraft, the occult also became an object of persecution. The harsh treatment of the Manichaean Cathars in southern France is an example of society's reaction to those who mixed arcane practice with heterodox theology.

In spite of persecution, the concept of witchcraft persisted and even flourished in early modern times. At least the fear of it did, as the Salem witch trials richly illustrate. In the early decades of the twentieth century, schools of pagan and magical teachings were reborn as Wicca. Wiccans, calling themselves "practitioners of the craft of the wise," would resurrect many of the old ways and infuse them with modern thoughts and practices. Whatever its origin, the occult seems to be an object of permanent fascination to the human race.

Are We Alone?

Is the earth the only inhabited planet? Imagine the excitement if contact is made with intelligent extraterrestrial life forms and humankind discovers that it is part of a larger cosmic community. It would change the way we think of ourselves and of our place in the universe. Or is the belief in extraterrestrials a creation of our minds? The universe is so vast we may never know, but the mysteries of outer space have a grip on the modern psyche, since it seems to offer the possibility of a world that may be more open to scientific verification than witchcraft.

Purpose of Book

Whatever the origin and veracity of the unusual, these beliefs and experiences have played a significant role in human experiences and deserve to be studied dispassionately. These volumes explore and describe the research of those who take such phenomena seriously; extraterrestrials, ghosts, spirits, and haunted places are explored from many perspectives. They are part of the adventure of humanity.

Acknowledgements

Compiling such an extensive work as a three-volume encyclopedia of the unusual and unexplained proved many times to be a most formidable task. During those moments when I felt the labor pains of giving birth to such a large and exhausting enterprise might be beyond me, I was able to rely upon a number of wonderful midwives. My agent Agnes Birnbaum never failed to offer encouragement and support; my remarkably resourceful and accomplished editor Jolen Marya Gedridge continued to assure me that there truly was light at the end of the tunnel and that the great enterprise would one day be completed; the always pleasant and helpful staff at Gale—

Julia Furtaw, Rita Runchock, Lynn Koch, and Nancy Matuszak—stood by to offer assistance; and most of all, I am forever indebted to my wife Sherry Hansen Steiger for her tireless compiling of the glossaries, her efforts in writing sidebars, her invaluable talents as a researcher, her patience and love, and her always providing a shoulder to cry on during the all-night writing sessions.

—*Brad E. Steiger*

CHAPTER 1
AFTERLIFE MYSTERIES

Humankind's obsession with the unknown and the unexplained begins with the greatest question of all: Do humans survive physical death? And if so, are they born again? The mystery of what lies on the other side of death has given birth to humankind's magic, mysticisms, religions, and all the diverse creatures of Light and Darkness that populate the mysterious regions in between.

INTRODUCTION

Children take the continuity of life for granted. It is the fact of death that has to be taught. Self-preservation is one of humankind's most powerful instincts, transcending the grave itself, for the desire for immortality, an afterlife, is nothing else than one form of the search for self-preservation.

In the inner-self, humans visualize themselves as observers of all that can be seen or can be imagined. Consciousness is experienced as a ever-flowing stream which, in spite of its temporary breaks in sleep, still seems to be continuous and without a conscious beginning or end. One goes to sleep many times, but always to wake once more. Humans have gotten into the habit of being alive. To think of oneself as non-being is difficult. People can accept the mortality of others, but not of themselves.

One of the earliest recorded expressions of desire for a future life was written thousands of years ago by an Egyptian scribe for whom the expectation of personal immortality was connected with the belief that his body would avoid the horrors of disintegration if it were to be mummified. This prayer of a hopeful soul contains a cry of immediately recognizable human longing. To the god Osiris, the king and judge of the dead, he prays,

> Grant thou that I may enter into the land of everlastingness, according to what was done for thee, whose body never saw corruption…Let not my body become worms, but deliver me as thou didst thyself….Let life come from the body's death and let not decay…make an end of me…I shall have my being; I shall live; I shall live! (from the Egyptian Book of the Dead, translated by E. A. W. Budge, 1901)

The belief in an afterlife coincides with the innate conviction that present life has significance and purpose. And because humans believe their earthly existence has meaning and they therefore have a reason for being, it seems imperative that at least some part of them must somehow continue in a future life. While an afterlife may be difficult to prove in a material sense, various world religions promise to provide a spiritual link between a person's actions in this life and his or her continued existence in a future life.

Conceptions of the world beyond death vary considerably among the world religions, but in every religious expression known to history or anthropology, the question of the afterlife in store for the individual believer has been of prime importance. This chapter will offer summaries of the beliefs of the Buddhist, Christian, Hindu, Islamic, and Jewish faiths concerning the fate of the soul after death.

Belief in an afterlife, like belief in a Supreme Being, creates in those who affirm such faith a way of regarding themselves in relation to the future life. These individuals need not view the possibility of an afterlife in the abstract. Those whose faith has trained them to believe completely in an afterlife can easily imagine what the future life will be. For them, life after death is a definable concept, a genuine and real result of how they have lived their present life. To religious individuals, faith in an afterlife becomes increasingly part of their existence, a source of courage and strength as the years go by. And once physical death overtakes them, for the great majority of these individuals, the most significant feature of an afterlife will be their union with the Divine.

For those individuals who hold Christian, Islamic, or Jewish religious beliefs, the soul is generally conceived as coming into existence with the birth of the body, and it would perish when the body perished if it were not for the supernatural intervention of God, who confers upon the soul an immortality that it could not otherwise attain. Those whose view of the afterlife includes the possibility of reincarnation, past lives, and future incarnations have no doubt that the soul is immortal by its very nature. In their view, the existence of the soul did not begin when the body was born, so there is no reason to believe that it will cease to exist when the body dies. According to various doctrines of reincarnation, there are immutable spiritual laws which will determine whether the soul will be born again into another physical body or will be merged in eternal unity with the Absolute.

The earliest discovered burial sites are those of Neanderthal man, though according to researcher George Constable, they "were not credited with deliberate meaningful burial of their dead until more than a half-century after their discovery." The well-known anthropologist and archaeologist Louis Leaky said of the discoveries that their grave sites were intentional and thus indicates the Neanderthals displayed a keen self-awareness and a concern for the human spirit.

Many burial sites have been discovered in Europe and the Near East. The placement of the remains reveals ritualistic elements, as the cadavers were found in a sleeping or fetal position. Some remains have also been found with plants or flowers, placed in the hands or the body, and sometimes with red pigment, possibly used in a symbolic rite. Some Neanderthals were found buried together in a group, meaning that entire family groups remained united after death.

One of the most interesting burial sites contained remains that had been carefully placed in the fetal position on a bedding of woody horsetail, a regional plant. This particular Neanderthal was also buried with several varieties of flowers. Leaky stated that the flowers were arranged deliberately as the body was being covered. Apparently the family and friends of the deceased gathered the distinct species of flowers, carried them to the grave, and carefully placed them on the body.

An analysis of the flower specimens revealed them to be cornflowers, St. Banaby's thistle, and grape hyacinths, among other plants. Many of the plants found have curative qualities that range from pain relief to inflammation suppression. It is not known if Neanderthals were advanced enough to realize the exact medicinal properties of the plants to their specific uses, or if this was only a coincidental placement of flowers and herbs. Or perhaps they were honoring a special person of the tribe, such as a medicine man or shaman. Regardless, it is evident that Neanderthal man was much more complex than he was given credit for.

⊙LDEST DISCOVERED BURIAL SITE

According to anthropologist F. Clark Howell the flexed position of the body, and discoveries of other sites where stone slabs were placed over the Neanderthal graves, along with food and tools, suggests that Neanderthal man believed in life after death. Their concept of the afterlife must not have been that much different than the life they experienced on earth; they provided the dead with food, tools, and other everyday items, much like the Egyptians did for their journey to the next life. Death to the Neanderthals may have even been regarded as a kind of sleep, perhaps like a rest before a rebirth, as corpses were carefully positioned in the fetal state.

SOURCES:

Burial, Ritual, Religion, and Cannibalism. http://thunder.indstate.edu/~ramanank/ritual.html. 10 July 2001.

While many people consider the belief in reincarnation to be held primarily by the adherents of Hinduism and some Buddhist sects, the concept of past lives is by no means confined to these Eastern religions. This chapter will examine many Western philosophers, clerics, medical doctors, and scholars who have expressed an individual acceptance of a prior and continued existence in an earthly body, in addition to certain Christian, Islamic, and Jewish sects that have also suggested that reincarnation may be one of the forms of survival after death.

Down through the centuries, the physical act of passage from one world to another at the moment of death has remained a mystery for the living. From time to time, one who had been resuscitated and brought back to life returned with an account of having stood at the edge of some vast unknown and uncharted world and having witnessed the activity of ethereal beings within. In recent decades, there have been an increasing number of well-documented accounts of people who have been resuscitated from clinical death and returned with reports of passing through a darkened tunnel to emerge into a place of light, and therein, meeting beings of light. Such **near-death experiences** (NDEs) demonstrate the inherent desire for a conscious life beyond the grave and for an endless continuation of spiritual opportunities. This longing for an unobstructed life, for life in the fullest sense that the individual can conceive, is an essential element in the earnest desire for immortality.

A belief in an afterlife may be essentially humanity's belief in itself. Within the vast majority of human beings exists a fundamental longing for the continuance of conscious and rational life. In centuries past, a desire for a future life was confined to affirmations of faith in the teachings or the scriptures of one's religious belief. Today, the hopes of the common person, the saint, and the mystic that an afterlife is truly a reality have been joined by many scientists, who are proving that the scientific desire to know and to keep on knowing is but another form of the same demand for a continuation of a conscious and rational life.

HOW THE MAJOR RELIGIONS VIEW THE AFTERLIFE

With all their diversity of beliefs, the major religions are in accord in one great teaching: Human beings are immortal and their spirit comes from a divine world and may eventually return there. Since the earliest forms of spiritual expression, this is the great promise and hope that religions have offered to their followers. It is the believer's eternal answer to the cynicism of the materialist who shouts that there is no afterlife, that death is the end.

Anthropologists can only guess whether or not the earliest members of the *Homo sapiens* species (c. 30,000 B.C.E.) conducted burial rituals of a quality that would qualify them as religious. However, it is known that they buried their dead with care and consideration and included food, weapons, and various personal belongings with the body. Even the Neanderthal species (c. 100,000 B.C.E.) placed food, stone implements, and decorative shells and bones in the graves with the deceased, which they often covered with a red pigment. Since there are no written scriptures describing the purpose of including such funerary objects in the graves (writing was not developed until the fourth millennium B.C.E.), one must presume the placement of weapons, food, and other utilitarian items beside the dead indicates that these prehistoric people believed that death was not the end. The member of the tribe or clan who was no longer among the living still required nourishment, clothing, and protection to journey safely in another kind of existence beyond the grave. Somehow, there was some part of the person that survived death.

That part of the human being that survives death is known in Christianity, Islam, and Judaism as the soul, the very essence of the individual person that must answer for its earthly deeds, good or bad. Hinduism perceives this spiritual essence as the divine part of a living being, the atman, which is eternal and seeks to be united with the Universal Soul, or the Brahman. Buddhism teaches that an individual is but a transient combination of the five aggregates (*skandhas*)—matter, sensation, perception, predisposition, and consciousness—and has no permanent soul. Of the major world religions, only Buddhism does not perceive an eternal metaphysical aspect of the human personality in the same way that the others do. However, all the major faiths believe that after the spirit has left the body, it moves on to another existence. Some faiths contend that it ascends to a paradise or descends into a hell. Others believe it may achieve a rebirth into another physical body, or may merge with the Divine in an eternal unity. Traditional Christianity, Islam, and Judaism envision a resurrection of a spiritual body at a time of final judgment, but generally speaking, the soul is of greater value and purpose than the physical body it inhabited while on Earth. The material shell within which humans dwell during their lifetime is nothing other than clay or ashes into which God has breathed the breath of life. The physical body is a temporary possession that a human has, not what a person is.

All the major world religions hold the belief that how a person has conducted himself or herself while living on Earth will greatly influence his or her soul's ultimate destiny after physical death. In fact, many teachings state that the only reason for birth into the material world is the opportunity to prepare for the soul's destiny in the immaterial worlds. And what is more, how one meets the challenges of life on Earth, whether or not one chooses to walk a path of good or evil, determines how that soul will be treated after death. All the seeds that one has sown throughout his or her lifetime, good or bad, will be harvested in the afterlife.

When an individual dies, according to many world religions, the soul is judged or evaluated, then sent to what is perceived as an eternal place—heaven or hell. The Hindu or Buddhist expects to encounter Yama, the god of the dead. In the Hindu scriptures, Yama holds dominion over the bright realms and can be influenced in determining a soul's admission by offerings made for the benefit of the deceased by relatives and friends. In the Buddhist tradition, Yama is the lord of hell who administers punishment according to each individual's karma, the cause and effect of his or her actions on Earth. In neither religious expression is Yama at all comparable to Satan, who in Christian belief is both the creator of evil and the accuser of human weaknesses.

EARLIEST *members of the* Homo sapiens *species (c. 30,000 B.C.E.) conducted burial rituals of a quality that would qualify them as religious.*

In Christianity, Islam, and Judaism, the soul's arrival at either heaven or hell is made somewhat confusing by the teachings of a great, final Judgment Day and the Resurrection of the Dead. And when Roman Catholic Christianity added the doctrine of purgatory in the sixteenth century, the matter became all the more complex because now certain souls were given an opportunity to atone for their sins while residing in a kind of interim area between heaven and hell. While many Christians, Jews, and Muslims believe that the dead lie sleeping in their graves until the Last Judgment, others in those same faiths maintain that judgment is pronounced immediately after death. Likewise, the concept of the World to Come in Jewish writings may refer to a present heaven or foretell of a future redemption on Earth.

BUDDHISM

While the Buddhist text recognizes the existence of a self as a being that distinguishes one person from another, the Buddhist teachings state that the Christian, Hindu, Jewish, and Muslim concept of an eternal metaphysical soul is inaccurate. To Buddhists, the human person is but a temporary assemblage of various elements, both physical and psychical, and none of these individual aspects of a whole person can be isolated as the essential self; nor can the sum of them all constitute the self. Everything, all of reality, is in a constant state of change and decay. Because a human is composed of so many elements that are always in a state of flux, always dissolving and combining with one another in new ways, it is impossible to suggest that an individual could retain the same soul-self for eternity. Rather than atman, Buddhist doctrine teaches anatman/or, "no-self."

*"*W H E N *a son of the Buddha fulfills his course, in the world to come, he becomes Buddha."*

Although the Buddha (c. 567–487 B.C.E.) denied the Hindu concept of an immortal self that passes through a series of incarnations, he did accept the doctrines of karma ("actions," the cause-and-effect laws of material existence) and *samsara* (rebirth). If the Buddha recognized rebirth into another lifetime but did not believe in an essential self or soul, then what would be reborn? The Buddhist answer is difficult to comprehend; the various components in the perpetual process of change that constitute human beings do not reassemble themselves by random chance. The karmic laws determine the nature of a person's rebirth. Various aspects which make up a functioning human during his or her lifetime enter the *santana*, the "chain of being," whose various links are related one to the other by the law of cause and effect. While there is no *atman* or individual self that can be reincarnated, the "contingent self" that exists from moment to moment is comprised of aggregates that are burdened with the consequences of previous actions and bear the potential to be reborn again and again. Because the aggregates of each living person bear within them the fruits of past actions and desires, the moment of death sets in motion an immediate retribution for the consequences of these deeds, forcing the individual to be reborn once again into the unceasing cycle of karma and *samsara*. However, dharma, the physical and moral laws that govern the universe, flow through everything and everyone, thereby continually changing and rearranging every aspect of the human. Although driven by karma, the dharma rearranges the process of rebirth to form a new individual.

In his first sermon, the Noble Truth of Suffering (Dukha), the Buddha presented his views on the aggregates that constitute the human condition:

> The Noble Truth of Suffering is this: Birth is suffering; aging is suffering; sickness is suffering; death is suffering; sorrow and lamentation, pain, grief, and despair are suffering; association with the unpleasant is suffering; dissociation with the pleasant is suffering; not to get what one wants is suffering—in brief, the five aggregates of attachment are suffering.

In the Dhammapada (147:51) the Buddha speaks further of the destiny of all human flesh in quite graphic terms:

> Behold this beautiful body, a mass of sores, a heaped up lump, diseased, much thought of, in which nothing lasts, nothing persists. Thoroughly worn out is this body, a nest of diseases, perishable....Truly, life ends in death....Of bones is this house made, plastered with flesh and blood. Herein are stored decay, death, conceit, and hypocrisy. Even ornamented royal chariots wear out. So too the body reaches old age. But the Dhamma of the Good grows not old. Thus do the Good reveal it among the Good.

The Buddha's advice to all those who wish to rise above the karmic laws of death and rebirth is to live a contemplative, religious life:

> Men who have not led a religious life and have not laid up treasure in their youth, perish like old herons in a lake without fish. Men who have not led a religious life and have not laid up treasure in their youth lie like worn-out bows, sighing after the past. (Dhammapada 155:56)

The counsel of the Buddha is quite similar to the words of Jesus in Matthew 6:19–21 when he admonished those who would follow him not to expend their energies accumulating treasures on Earth where moth and rust consume and where thieves break in and steal, but lay up for yourself treasure in heaven, where neither moth nor rust consumes and where thieves do not break in and steal. For where your treasure is, there will your heart be also.

Dharma is the path to the goal of nirvana, which in Buddhist teachings can represent the final extinction of the desire to exist, or can also suggest a high level of mystical experience achieved through deep meditation or trance. It never means the complete annihilation of the self, only the squelching of the wish to be reborn. Most often, nirvana is meant to indicate a transformed state of human consciousness which achieves a reality independent of the material world.

Once the desire to continue existence in a material flesh form has been extinguished, and "when a son of the Buddha fulfills his course, in the world to come, he comes Buddha." To achieve one's Buddhahood in Buddhism is comparable to realizing Brahma, the Absolute and Ultimate, in Hinduism. Once those levels have been attained, it is believed that one is freed forever from material reality and becomes one with eternal reality.

There are many schools of historical Buddhism—Hinayana, Mahayana, Tantric, and Pure Land—and it is difficult to find consensus among them concerning the afterlife. Tibetan Buddhism's Book of the Dead provides an important source for an understanding of their concept of the afterlife journey of the soul. A lama (priest) sits at the side of the deceased and recites texts from the Book, a ritual which is thought to revive the *bla*, the life force within the body, and give it the power to embark upon a 49-day journey through the intermediate stage between death and rebirth. Such a recitation by the priest at the bedside of the deceased might include these words from the Tibetan Book of the Dead:

> Since you [no longer] have a material body of flesh and blood, whatever may come—sounds, lights, or rays—are, all three, unable to harm you; you are incapable of dying. It is quite sufficient for you to know that these apparitions are your own thought-forms. Recognize this to be the *bardo* [the intermediate state after death].

If there is to be no rebirth for the soul, it appears before Yama, the god of the dead, to be judged. In Tibetan Buddhism, there is a direct link between one's earthly lifetimes and inter-

The Fourteenth Dalai Lama. (AP/WIDE WORLD PHOTOS)

mediate stages of existence in the various spheres of paradise, extending to the appearance of the soul remaining the same as the one it assumed when living as a human on Earth.

Both Buddhism and Hinduism place Yama, god of the dead, in the position of judge in the afterlife, and these passages from the Rig-Veda depict the special reverence with which he was held:

> Yama was the first to find us our abode, a place that can never be taken away, a place where our ancient Fathers have departed; all who are born go there by that path, treading their own. Meet the Fathers, meet Yama, meet

with the fulfillment of wishes in the highest heaven; casting off imperfections, find anew your dwelling, and be united with a lustrous body.

Regardless of one's religious background, it is in the presence of death that all humans find themselves face to face with the single greatest mystery of their existence: Does life extend beyond the grave? Whether one believes in a supernatural heavenly kingdom, the inescapable laws of karma, or a state of eternal bliss, death remains a dreadful force beyond one's control. For untold millions of men and women the ceremonies of religion provide their only assurance that life goes on when the darkness of physical death envelops them.

✤ DELVING DEEPER

Carter, John Ross and Mahinda Palihawadana, trans. *Buddhism: The Dhammapada*. New York: Oxford University Press for the Book of the Month Club, 1992.

Crim, Keith. *The Perennial Dictionary of World Religions*. San Francisco: Harper Collins, 1989.

Eerdmans' Handbook to the World's Religions. Grand Rapids, Mich.: Wm. B. Eerdmans Publishing Co., 1994.

Larousse Dictionary of Beliefs and Religions. New York: Larousse, 1994.

Rosten, Leo, ed. *Religions of America*. New York: Simon & Schuster, 1975.

Sullivan, Lawrence E., ed. *Death, Afterlife, and the Soul*. New York: Macmillan, 1989.

Wilson, Andrew, ed. *World Scripture: A Comparative Anthology of Sacred Texts*. New York: Paragon House, 1995.

CHRISTIANITY

The core of the Christian faith is the belief in the resurrection of Jesus (c. 6 B.C.E.–c. 30 C.E.) after his death on the cross and the promise of life everlasting to all who accept his divinity and believe in him. Because Christianity rose out of Judaism, the teachings of Jesus as recorded in the gospels reflect many of the Jewish beliefs of the soul and the afterlife, primarily that a reunion of body and soul will be accomplished in the next world. The accounts of the appearance of Jesus to his apostles after his resurrection show how completely they believed that they beheld him in the flesh, even to the extreme of the skeptical Thomas placing his fingertips into the still-open wounds of the crucifixion. "A spirit does not have flesh and bones as you see that I have," Jesus told them. Then, to prove his physicality still further, he asks if they have anything for him to eat.

Paul (?–c. 68 C.E.), the apostle and once avid persecutor of Christians, received his revelation from the voice of Jesus within a blinding light while he was traveling on the road to Damascus. He discovered it to be a challenge to convince others in the belief in the physical resurrection of the dead when he preached in Athens. Although the assembled Athenians listened politely to his message of a new faith, they mocked him and walked away when he began to speak of dead bodies standing up and being reborn. To these cultured men and women who had been exposed to Plato's philosophy that the material body was but a fleshly prison from which the soul was freed by death, the very notion of resurrecting decaying bodies was repugnant. Paul refused to acknowledge defeat. Because he had been educated as a Greek, he set about achieving a compromise between the resurrection theology being taught by his fellow apostles and the Platonic view of the soul so widely accepted in Greek society.

Paul knew that Plato had viewed the soul as composed of three constituents: the *nous*, (the rational soul, is immortal and incarnated in a physical body); the *thumos* (passion, heart, spirit); and *epithumetikos* (desire). After many hardships, imprisonments, and public humiliation, Paul worked out a theology that envisioned human nature as composed of three essential elements—the physical body; the psyche, the life-principle, much like the Hebrew concept of the *nephesh*; and the *pneuma*, the spirit, the inner self. Developing his thought further, he made the distinction between the "natural body" of a living person that dies and is buried, and the "spiritual body," which is resurrected.

In I Corinthians 15:35–44, Paul writes:

> But some will ask, "How are the dead raised? With what kind of body do they come?" You foolish man! What you sow

does not come to life unless it dies. And what you sow is not the body which is to be, but a bare kernel....God gives it a body as He has chosen, and to each kind of seed its own body. For not all flesh is alike....There are celestial bodies and there are terrestrial bodies; but the glory of the celestial is one, and the glory of the terrestrial is another....So it is with the resurrection from the dead. What is sown is perishable, what is raised is imperishable. It is sown in dishonor, it is raised in glory. It is sown in weakness, it is raised in power. It is sown in the physical body, it is raised in a spiritual body. If there is a physical body, there is also a spiritual body.

Although he had begun to mix Platonic and Jewish philosophies in a manner that would be found acceptable to thousands of new converts to Christianity, Paul could not free himself completely from the Hebrew tradition that insisted upon some bodily form in the afterlife. However inconsistent it might appear to some students of theology, Paul and his fellow first-century Christian missionaries taught that while the immortal soul within was the most essential aspect of a person's existence, in order for a proper afterlife, one day there would be a judgment and the righteous would be rewarded with reconstituted bodies.

The early church fathers began more and more to shape Christian doctrines that reflected Plato's metaphysical philosophy, but they remained greatly divided over the particular nature of the immortal soul. The Platonists saw the soul as supraindividual and remaining within the universal cosmic soul after its final ascent to oneness with the Divine. The Christian philosophers could not be shaken from their position that each soul was created by God to be immortal and individual, irrevocably connected to the afterlife. Among them was Tertullian (c. 160 C.E.–220 C.E.), who defined the soul as having sprung directly from the breath of God, thereby making it immortal. The body, in the Platonic view, was merely the instrument of the *anima*—the soul. The highly respected Alexandrian scholar Origen (c. 185 C.E.–254 C.E.) theorized that in the beginning, God had created a certain number

of spirit entities who received physical bodies or spiritual bodies as determined by their respective merits. Some might be appointed human forms, while others, according to their conduct, would be elevated to angelic status, or relegated to the position of demons.

EACH *soul was created by God to be immortal and individual, irrevocably connected to the afterlife.*

Such a concept of the preexistence of souls seemed too close to reincarnation for those learned Christian scholars assembled for the First Council of Constantinople in 543. By then, church doctrine had decreed that it was given each soul to live once, to die, and then to await the Day of Judgement when Christ returned to Earth. Despite his prestige as a learned and wise church father, Origen's views were condemned as heretical. The prevailing view of the early Christian church was the one espoused by Jerome (c. 342 C.E.–420 C.E.), who envisioned God as creating new souls as they were required for the new bodies being born to human parents on Earth. Essentially, orthodox contemporary Christianity continues to maintain the position that each new person born receives a new soul that has never before existed in any other form. In Christian doctrine, the soul is superior to the body because of its divine origin and because it is immortal, but belief in a resurrection of the physical body is also an essential aspect of both the Apostles' Creed and the Nicene Creed, which declare that after the Last Judgment Jesus shall once again appear to "judge the living and the dead."

In Chapter 25 of Matthew, Jesus tells a parable of how the Son of Man is to come and sit on his throne as the people of all nations gather before him so that he might separate them as a shepherd separates the sheep from the goats. Those individuals who loved their neighbors as themselves will be rewarded with eternal life, but those who have chosen greed and self-interest will be sent away into eternal punishment.

In Acts 17:31, it is stated that God has appointed Jesus Christ to judge the world; Acts 10:42 again names Christ as the one "ordained by God to be judge of the living and the dead."

HELL, *in traditional Christian thought, is a place of eternal torment for those who have been damned after the Last Judgment.*

The early Christian Church believed that the Second Coming of Jesus was imminent and that many who were alive in the time of the apostles would live to see his return in the clouds. When this remarkable event occurred, it would signal the end of time and Jesus Christ would raise the dead and judge those who would ascend to heaven and those who would suffer the everlasting torments of hell. The delay in the Second Coming forced the Church to adjust its theology to acknowledge that the time of judgment for each individual would arrive at the time of that person's death.

For the traditional Christian, heaven is the everlasting dwelling place of God and the angelic beings who have served him faithfully since the beginning. There, those Christians who have been redeemed through faith in Jesus as the Christ will be with him forever in glory. Liberal Christians acknowledge that, as Jesus promised, there are many mansions in his father's kingdom where those of other faiths may also dwell. For more fundamental and conservative Christians, the terrifying graphic images depicted over the centuries of the Last Judgment have been too powerful to be eliminated from doctrinal teachings, so they envision a beautiful place high above the Earth where only true believers in Jesus may reign with him.

Hell, in traditional Christian thought, is a place of eternal torment for those who have been damned after the Last Judgment. It is generally pictured as a barren pit filled with flames, the images developed out of the Hebrew Sheol and the Greek Hades as the final resting places for the dead. Roman Catholic Christianity continues to depict hell as a state of unending punishment for the unrepentant, but over five centuries ago, the councils of Florence (1439) and Trent (1545–63) defined the concept of purgatory, an intermediate state after death during which the souls have opportunities to expiate certain of their sins. Devoted members of their families can offer prayers and oblations which can assist those souls in purgatory to atone for their earthly transgressions and achieve a restoration of their union with God.

Protestant Christianity does not offer its followers the opportunities for afterlife redemption afforded by purgatory or any other intermediate spiritual state, but it has removed much of the fear of hell and replaced it with an emphasis upon grace and faith. While fundamentalist Protestants retain the traditional views of heaven and hell, there are many contemporary Protestant clergy who have rejected the idea of a place of eternal torment for condemned souls as incompatible with the belief in a loving God of forgiveness. Hell has been transformed from a place of everlasting suffering to an afterlife state of being without the presence of God. For liberal Christian theologians, the entire teaching of a place of everlasting damnation has been completely rejected in favor of the love of Jesus for all humanity.

✤ **DELVING DEEPER**

Brandon, S. G. F. *Religion in Ancient History.* New York: Charles Scribner's Sons, 1969.

Clifton, Charles S. *Encyclopedia of Heresies and Heretics.* New York: Barnes & Noble, 1992.

Crim, Keith, ed. *The Perennial Dictionary of World Religions.* San Francisco: Harper Collins, 1989.

Pelikan, Jaroslav, ed. *Christianity: The Apocrypha and the New Testament.* New York: Oxford University Press and Cambridge University Press for the Book of the Month Club, 1992.

Rosten, Leo, ed. *Religions of America.* New York: Simon & Schuster, 1975.

HINDUISM

In India's religious classic work, the Bhagavad Gita ("Song of the Lord"), the nature of the soul is defined: "It is born not, nor does it ever die, nor shall it, after having been brought into being, come not to be hereafter. The unborn, the permanent, the eternal, the ancient, it is slain not when the body is slain."

The oldest collection of Sanskrit hymns is the Rig-Veda, dating back to about 1400 B.C.E. Composed by the Aryan people who invaded the Indus Valley in about 1500 B.C.E., the early Vedic songs are primarily associated with funeral rituals and perceive the individual person as composed of three separate entities: the body, the *asu* (life principle), and the *manas* (the seat of the mind, will, and emotions). Although the *asu*, and the *manas* were highly regarded, they cannot really be considered as comprising the essential self, the soul. The facet of the person that survives the physical is yet something else, a kind of miniature of the living man or woman that resides within the center of the body near the heart.

During the period from about 600 B.C.E. to 480 B.C.E., the series of writings known as Upanishads set forth the twin doctrines of *samsara* (rebirth) and karma (the cause and effect actions of an individual during his or her life). An individual has a direct influence on his or her karma process in the material world and the manner in which the person deals with the difficulties inherent in an existence bound by time and space; the individual determines the form of his or her next earthly incarnation. The subject of the two doctrines is the *atman*, or self, the essence of the person that contains the divine breath of life. The *atman* within the individual was "smaller than a grain of rice," but it was connected to the great cosmic soul, the Atman or Brahma, the divine principle. Unfortunately, while occupying a physical body, the atman was subject to *avidya*, an earthly veil of profound ignorance that blinded the *atman* to its true nature as Brahma and subjected it to the processes of karma and *samsara*. *Avidya* led to *maya* the illusion that deceives each individual *atman* into mistaking the material world as the real world. Living under this illusion, the individual accumulates karma and continues to enter the unceasing process of *samsara*, the wheel of return with its succession of new lifetimes and deaths.

The passage of the soul from this world to the next is described in the Brihadarankyaka Upanishad:

The Self, having in dreams enjoyed the pleasures of sense, gone hither and

thither, experienced good and evil, hastens back to the state of waking from which he started. As a man passes from dream to wakefulness, so does he pass from this life to the next.... Then the point of his heart, where the nerves join, is lighted by the light of the Self, and by that light he departs either through the eye, or through the gate of the skull, or through some other aperture of the body.... The Self remains conscious, and, conscious, the dying man goes to his abode. The deeds of this life, and the

In Hinduism, Vishnu is considered one of the main gods of worship. (ST. LOUIS ART MUSEUM)

Hindu holy man or *Sadhu.* (AP/WIDE WORLD PHOTOS)

impressions they leave behind, follow him. As a caterpillar, having reached the end of a blade of grass, takes hold of another blade and draws itself to it, so the Self, having left behind it [a body] unconscious, takes hold of another body and draws himself to it.

"IT *is born not, nor does it ever die, nor shall it, after having been brought into being, come not to be hereafter. The unborn, the permanent, the eternal, the ancient, it is slain not when the body is slain.*"

By the third century B.C.E. Hinduism had largely adopted a cyclical worldview of lives and rebirths in which the earlier concepts of heaven and hell, an afterlife system of reward and punishment, were replaced by intermediate states between lifetimes. Hindu cosmology depicted three *lokas,* or realms—heaven, Earth, and a netherworld—and 14 additional levels in which varying degrees of suffering or bliss awaited the soul between physical existences. Seven of these heavens or hells rise above Earth and seven descend below. According to the great Hindu teacher Sankara, who lived in the ninth century, and the school of Advaita Vedanata, the eventual goal of the soul's odyssey was *moksa,* a complete liberation

from *samsara,* the cycle of death and rebirth, which would lead to nirvana, the ultimate union of *atman* with the divine Brahma. In the eleventh century, Ramanjua and the school of Visitadvaita saw the bliss of nirvana as a complete oneness of the soul with God.

In the last centuries before the common era, a form of Hinduism known as *bhakti* spread rapidly across India. *Bhakti* envisions a loving relationship between God and the devout believer that is based upon grace. Those devotees who have prepared themselves by a loving attitude, a study of the scriptures, and devotion to Lord Krishna may free themselves from an endless cycle of death and rebirth. Eternal life is granted to the devotees who, at the time of death, give up their physical body with only thoughts of Lord Krishna on their minds.

❋ DELVING DEEPER

Brandon, S. G. F. *Religion in Ancient History.* New York: Charles Scribner's Sons, 1969.

Crim, Keith, ed. *The Perennial Dictionary of World Religions.* San Francisco: Harper Collins, 1989.

Pelikan, Jaroslav, ed. *Hinduism: The Rig Veda.* Trans. by Ralph T. H. Griffith. New York: Motilal Banarsidass Publishers for the Book of the Month Club, 1992.

Sullivan, Lawrence E., ed. *Death, Afterlife, and the Soul.* New York, Macmillan, 1989.

Wilson, Andrew, ed. *World Scripture: A Comparative Anthology of Sacred Texts.* New York: Paragon House, 1995.

Zaehner, R. C., ed. *Encyclopedia of the World's Religions.* New York: Barnes & Noble, 1997.

ISLAM

In regard to the concept of a soul, Islam envisions a human as a being of spirit and body. The creation of Adam as described in the Qur'an (or Koran) is reminiscent of Genesis in the Judeo-Christian Bible as the Lord announces to the angels that he is going to create a human of clay and that he will breathe his spirit into him after he has given him form. "And He originated the creation of man out of clay, then He fashioned his progeny of an extraction of mean water, then He shaped him, and breathed His spirit in him." (Qur'an 32:8–9)

Muhammed (570 C.E.–632 C.E.) appears to have regarded the soul as the essential self of a human being, but he, adhering to the ancient Judeo-Christian tradition, also considered the physical body as a requirement for life after death. The word for the independent soul is *nafs*, similar in meaning to the Greek *psyche*, and the word for the aspect of the soul that gives humans their dignity and elevates them above the animals is *ruh*, equivalent to the Greek word *nous*. These two aspects of the soul combine the lower and the higher, the human and the divine.

As in the other major religions, how one lives on Earth will prepare the soul for the afterlife, and there are promises of a paradise or the warnings of a place of torment. The Qur'an 57:20 contains an admonition concerning the transient nature of life on Earth and a reminder of the two possible destinations that await the soul after death: "Know that the present life is but a sport and a diversion, an adornment and a cause of boasting among you,

and a rivalry in wealth and children. It is as a rain whose vegetation pleases the unbelievers; then it withers, and you see it turning yellow, then it becomes straw. And in the Hereafter there is grievous punishment, and forgiveness from God and good pleasure; whereas the present life is but the joy of delusion."

Muhammed speaks of the Last Judgment, after which there will be a resurrection of the dead which will bring everlasting bliss to the righteous and hellish torments to the wicked. The judgment will be individual. No soul will be able to help a friend or family member, he warns; no soul will be able to give satisfaction or to make intercession for another.

While the doctrine of the resurrection of the body has never been abandoned in Islam, later students of the Qur'an sought to define the soul in more metaphysical terms, and a belief in the preexistence of souls was generally established. In this view, Allah kept a treasure house of souls in paradise available for their respective incarnations on Earth.

Muslims pray in the direction of Mecca during an Islamic holiday at Coney Island, New York. (AP/WIDE WORLD PHOTOS)

The Islamic paradise is in many ways an extension of the legendary Garden of Eden in the Bible. It is a beautiful place filled with trees, flowers, and fruits, but it really cannot be expressed in human terms. It is far more wonderful than any person could ever imagine. "All who obey God and the Apostle are in the company of those on whom is the grace of God—of the Prophets who teach, the sincere lovers of Truth, the witnesses [martyrs] who testify, and the righteous who do good: Ah! What a beautiful fellowship!" (Qur'an 4:69)

MUHAMMED *says the Last Judgment will bring everlasting bliss to the righteous and hellish torments to the wicked.*

Hell is a place of torment, and, like the image held by many Christians, a place of fire and burning. In the Islamic teachings, neither heaven nor hell last throughout eternity. Infinity belongs to Allah alone, and there may exist various stages of paradise and hell for those souls who dwell there.

✤ DELVING DEEPER

Ali, Ahmed, trans. *The Qur'an*. New York: Akrash Publishing Karachi for the Book of the Month Club, 1992.

Crim, Keith, ed. *The Perennial Dictionary of World Religions*. San Francisco: Harper Collins, 1989.

Larousse Dictionary of Beliefs and Religions. New York: Larousse, 1994.

Sullivan, Lawrence E., ed. *Death, Afterlife, and the Soul*. New York: Macmillan, 1989.

Wilson, Andrew, ed. *World Scripture: A Comparative Anthology of Sacred Texts*. New York: Paragon House, 1995.

JUDAISM

"Then the Lord God formed man out of the dust of the ground, and breathed into his nostrils the breath of life; and man became a living being" (Genesis 2:7). In the second chapter of Genesis, Yahweh, the god of Israel, shapes the form of Adam from the clay, then breathes into him the "breath of life," so that Adam becomes *nephesh*, or a "living soul."

Interestingly, Yahweh also bestows the breath of life into the animals that flourished in the Garden of Eden, and they, too, are considered living souls. *Nephesh* is closely associated with blood, the life-substance, which is drained away from the body at death, thus establishing in Hebrew tradition the recognition that a living person is a composite entity made up of flesh and *nephesh*, the spiritual essence. "The body is the sheath of the soul," states the Talmud, Sanhedrin 108a.

The early Hebrews believed that after death the soul descended to Sheol, a place deep inside the Earth where the spirits of the dead were consigned to dust and gloom. "All go unto one place; all are of the dust, and all turn to dust again" (Ecclesiastes 3:20). By the time the Book of Daniel was written, in about 165 B.C.E., the belief had been established that the dead would be resurrected and receive judgment: "Many of those who lie dead in the ground will rise from death. Some of them will be given eternal life, and others will receive nothing but eternal shame and disgrace. Everyone who has been wise will shine bright as the sky above, and everyone who has led others to please God will shine like the stars" (Daniel 12: 2–4).

While the verses from Daniel are the only ones in Jewish scripture that specifically mention the afterlife of the soul, the subject is widely discussed in Rabbinic literature, the Kabbalah, and Jewish folklore. Generally, the soul is believed to have its roots in the world of the divine, and after the physical death of the body, the soul returns to the place of its spiritual origin. Some Jewish thinkers refer to the soul's sojourn on Earth as a kind of exile to be served until its reunion with God.

By the second century B.C.E., many Jewish teachers had been exposed to the Greek concept of the soul as the essential self that exists prior to the earthly body into which it is born and which survives the body's physical death. However, the old traditions retained the view that, an existence in the afterlife requires the restoration of the whole person. As Jewish thinking on the afterlife progressed from earlier beliefs, a school of thought arose maintaining that during the arrival of the Messiah, God would raise the dead to life again and pass judgment upon them—rewarding the righteous and punishing the wicked. Such a resurrection was viewed as a restoration of persons who would possess both physical bodies and spirits, thus reinforcing the traditional philosophy that to be a living person was to be a psycho-physical unit, not an eternal soul temporarily inhabiting a mortal body. More often, however, the references to a judgment of the dead in Judaism recall the scene in the seventh chapter of the Book of Daniel in which the Ancient of Days opens the books of life and passes judgment on the kingdoms of the Earth, rather than on individuals.

According to some circles of Jewish thought, the actual Day of Judgment, *yom hadin*, the resurrection of the dead, will occur when the Messiah comes. On that fateful day, both Israel and the Gentile nations will be summoned to the place of judgment by the blowing of the great *shofar* (ram's horn) to awaken the people from their spiritual slumber. Elijah the prophet will return and set about the task of reconciling families who have become estranged. The day when the Lord judges "will be dark, very dark, without a ray of light" (Amos 5:20). Those who have maintained righteous lives and kept their covenant with God will be taken to the heavenly paradise. Those who have been judged as deserving of punishment for their misdeeds will be sent to Gehenna, to stay there for a length of time commensurate with the seriousness of their transgressions.

🔹 DELVING DEEPER

Jewish Publication Society Translation. *The Tanakh.* New York, 1992.

Sullivan, Lawrence E., ed. *Death, Afterlife, and the Soul.* New York: Macmillan, 1989.

Unterman, Alan. *Dictionary of Jewish Lore and Legend.* New York: Thames and Hudson, 1997.

Wilson, Andrew, ed. *World Scripture: A Comparative Anthology of Sacred Texts.* New York: Paragon House, 1995.

A white-bearded rabbi reading the Talmud.
(CORBIS CORPORATION)

ANCIENT EGYPT AND THE AFTERLIFE

The ancient Egyptians were preoccupied with the specter of death and the problem of how best to accomplish passage to the other side. There was never an ancient people who insisted upon believing that death was not the final act of a human being, that "it is not death to die," with more emphasis than the Egyptians.

In the cosmology of the early Egyptians, humans were considered the children of the gods, which meant that they had inherited many other elements from their divine progenitors than physical bodies. The *ba*, or soul, was portrayed on the walls of tombs as a human-headed bird leaving the body at death. During a person's lifetime, the *ba* was an intangible essence, associated with the breath. In addition to the *ba*, each person possessed a *ka*, a kind of ghostly double

MANKIND'S HISTORY OF BURIAL PRACTICES

TIMELINE

70,000 B.C.E.

Earliest discovered burial sites of Neanderthal man.

3600 B.C.E.

Earliest known attempts to mummify bodies in Egypt.

3000 B.C.E.

Ancient Chileans mummify bodies.

1000 B.C.E.

Ancient Greeks cremate their dead.

625 B.C.E.

Mourners in Ancient Greece place metal coins under the tongues of the dead.

600 B.C.E.

Romans cremate their dead.

SOURCES:

Weathersby, Trudy. *About Death and Dying.* http://dying.about.com/blchron1.htm. 9 July 2001.

ial possessions were made. Those priests who were ordained to carry the offerings to the dead were called "servants of the *ka*."

Upon an Egyptian's death, although the body became inert, no longer capable of motion, the body did not decay, for the greatest care was taken to preserve it as a center of individual spirit manifestation. The body was carefully embalmed and mummified and placed in a coffin, on its side, as if it were only asleep. In the tomb with the mummy were brought all the utensils that a living person might need on a long journey, together with toilet articles, vessels for water and food, and weapons and hunting equipment to protect against robbers and to provide food once the initial supply was depleted.

Based on their writings concerning their concepts of goodness, purity, faithfulness, truth, and justice, beginning in the **Pyramid Texts** and extending onward, most scholars agree that the ancient Egyptians were a highly moral people. The gods Osiris and Isis were exalted as the ideal father and mother, and Set (god of chaos) became the personification of evil. During the time of the Middle Kingdom (c. 2000 B.C.E.,) the story of Osiris became a kind of gospel of righteousness, and justice was exalted in a manner found in few periods of history.

EGYPTIAN BOOK OF THE DEAD

As early as the Eighteenth Dynasty, which began about 1580 B.C.E., most of the religious literature of ancient Egypt, including the **Pyramid Texts**—the oldest extant funerary literature in the world, dating back to as early as the fourth millennium B.C.E.—and certain revised editions of those texts, called the Coffin Texts, were brought together, reedited, and added to, and painted on sarcophagi and written on papyrus. This massive literary effort, the work of many authors and compilers, is now known as the Book of the Dead; its creators called it The Chapters of Coming Forth by Day. Although many known copies of this ancient work exist, no one copy contains all the chapters, which are thought to number around 200. The subject matter of each chapter is the beatification of the dead, but the chapters are as independent of one another as are the psalms in the Old Testament.

which was given to each individual at the moment of birth. As long as people kept control of their *ka*, they lived. But as soon as they died, it began a separate existence, still resembling the body that it formerly occupied, and still requiring food for sustenance. Each person also had a *ren*, or name, which could acquire a separate existence and was once the underlying substance of all one's integral aspects. Other facets include the *khu*, or intelligence; the *ab*, or heart (will); the *sakkem*, or life force; the *khaybet*, or shadow; the *ikh*, or glorified spirit; and the *sahu*, or mummy. But the most important of all these facets of a human being was the *ka*, which became the center of the cult of the dead, for it was to the *ka* that all offerings of food and mater-

The Egyptians did not believe that mummifying a body would enable it to come back to life in the next world. They knew the physical body would remain in this world, but they preserved it, believing that the spirit of the person needed its body as a kind of base or reference point. If a body could not be recovered, had it, for example, been destroyed by fire or lost at sea, it was a serious matter. In cases such as these, a statue or a kind of reconstruction or artistic portrait would be used for the departing spirit.

An important ritual was performed at the funeral service of the departed, called *The Opening of the Mouth*. This ceremony was a "magical treatment" of the mouth and other apertures of the body to ensure the spirit's ability to continue to hear, see, eat, and so forth, should it need to in the spirit world. The Egyptians also performed this ceremony over statues and paintings, to endow them with a form in the afterworld.

EGYPTIAN JOURNEY TO THE NEXT WORLD

SOURCES:

Ruffle, John. "Ancient Egypt: Land of the Priest-King; Egyptian Temples: Houses of Power." In *Eerdman's Handbook to the World's Religions*. Edited by R. Pierce Beaver. Grand Rapids, Mich.: William B. Eerdman's Publishing Co., 1982.

One of the most curious aspects of the Egyptian Book of the Dead is that while the work is filled with realistic and graphic scenes of the preparation of the deceased for mummification, there are no illustrations depicting death and dying. For a people obsessed with the mortuary and funerary aspects of death, the Egyptians seldom dealt with the actual ways in which people lost their lives. Some scholars have observed that it was not so much that the ancient Egyptians wished to avoid the unpleasant topic of death and dying; it was rather that they never really formulated any clear conception of the nature of death or of its cause.

By the time the text of the Book of the Dead was being copied on rolls of papyrus and placed in the tombs of the dead, a great social and religious revolution had taken place. Whereas the Pyramid Texts were meant only to be inscribed on the sarcophagi of the royals,

it was now decreed that anyone who could afford the rituals would be entitled to follow the god Osiris into the afterlife. The cult of Osiris had now been extended so that any deceased human, commoner or noble-born, who had the means could become an "Osiris."

UPON an Egyptian's death the greatest care was taken to preserve the body as a center of individual spirit manifestation.

The most important ceremony associated with the preparation of the dead was the opening of the eyes, mouth, ears, and nose of the deceased. This rite was thought to guarantee

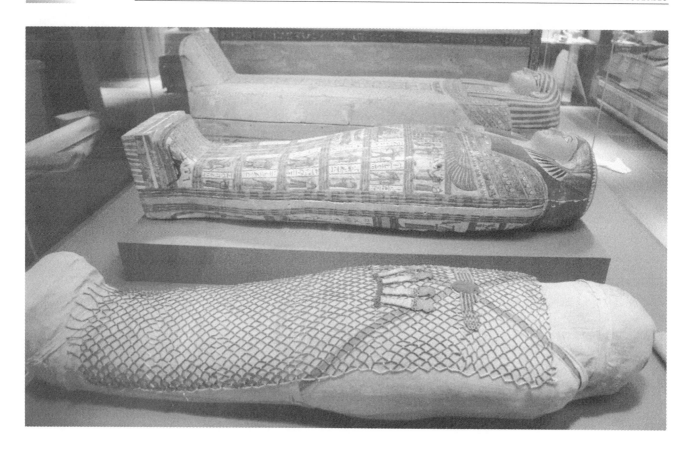

life to the body and make it possible for the *ba* to reenter its former dwelling. If the deceased's budget allowed, it was also customary to bring into the tomb a number of small figures called *ushabtiu*, whose duty was to speak up and give character witness when the entombed stood before Osiris and the 42 divine judges.

THE *Pyramid Texts were the oldest extant funerary literature in the world, dating back to as early as the fourth millennium* B.C.E.

The Book of the Dead also contained certain holy incantations that were designed to free the *ka* from the tomb and allow it to be incarnated again. The spirit might experience an existence as a hawk, a heron, or even a plant form, such as a lotus or a lily, moving along through various expressions of the life force until, after about 3,000 years, it could once again achieve rebirth as a human.

✤ DELVING DEEPER

Gaster, Theodor H., ed. *The New Golden Bough*. New York: Criterion Books, 1959.

Larousse Dictionary of Beliefs and Religions. New York: Larousse, 1994.

OSIRIS: DEATH AND RESURRECTION

Osiris was called Lord of Lords, King of Kings, and God of Gods by the Egyptians. According to the scholar E. A. W. Budge, "[Osiris] was the god-man who suffered, and died, and rose again, and reigned eternally in heaven. They [the Egyptians] believed that they would inherit eternal life, just as he had done."

The ancient myths proclaim that Osiris first received renown as a peaceful leader of a higher culture in the eastern Delta, then as a powerful ruler over all the Delta, a veritable god of the Nile and its vegetation, growth, life, and culture. He was the husband of Isis, goddess of enchantment and magic; father of the great war god Horus; and finally conqueror of northern Upper Egypt with his principal city at Abydos. It was then that he came into conflict with Set, who killed and dismembered him. The dark mists of death didn't eliminate Osiris. Quite the opposite, in fact, for Isis, incarnation of the divine mother goddess, used her magic to put him back together. Osiris rose from the dead and became for all of his followers a god of resurrection. The cult of Osiris was established at Abydos, where he became known as the Lord of the Death or Lord of the West, referring to his mastery over all those who had traveled "west" into the sunset of death. The theology of Osiris, which promised resurrection, soon overshadowed that of the sun god Ra and became the dominant feature of all Egyptian religion.

Ra was a creator god, fundamentally solar, a king by nature, whose theology concerned itself with the world, its origin, creation, and the laws that governed it. Osiris and his doctrines were concerned with the problems of life, death, resurrection, and an afterlife. The connection between the two deities was Horus, who was a sky god of the heavens and also the dutiful son and heir of Osiris. The general influence of Ra and Osiris can be traced back to the time of the **Pyramid Texts** and forward to the decline of Egyptian religious history. The cosmology of Osiris may be divided into two periods. The earlier one extended up until the time of the Pyramid Texts, during which he was a peaceful political power, an administrator of a higher culture, the unifying factor in bringing the Delta and northern Upper Egypt into one realm, the ideal husband and father, and after his death, the god of resurrection. The second period extended from the time of the Pyramid Texts to the common era, when he was primarily god of the dead and king of the underworld.

When an ancient Egyptian died, the deceased expected to appear before Osiris, who would be sitting upon his throne, waiting to pass judgment on him or her. The deceased would be led in by the jackal-headed god Anubis, followed by the goddess Isis, the divine enchantress, representing life, and the goddess of the underworld, Nephthys, representing death. There were 42 divine judges to assess the life of the one who stood before them, and the deceased would be allowed to deny 42 misdeeds. Once the deceased had presented his or her case, Osiris indicated a large pair of balances before them with the heart of the deceased and the feather of truth, one in each

Osiris, God of the Underworld. (AP/WIDE WORLD PHOTOS)

of the pans. The god Thoth read and recorded the decision. Standing in the shadows was a monstrous creature prepared to devour the deceased, should the feather of truth outweigh his or her heart. In those instances when the heart outweighed the feather—and few devout Egyptians could really believe that their beloved Osiris would condemn them—the deceased was permitted to proceed to the Fields of Aalu, the world, where the gods lived. Because humans were the offspring of the gods, the Fields of Aalu offered an eternal association and loving companionship with the deities. This, the ancient Egyptians believed, was the natural order of things. They had no doubts about immortality. In their cosmology, a blessed afterlife was a certainty.

✦ **DELVING DEEPER**

Ferm, Vergilious, ed. *Ancient Religions*. New York: The Philosophical Library, 1950.

Gaster, Theodor H., ed. *The New Golden Bough*. New York: Criterion Books, 1959.

Larousse Dictionary of Beliefs and Religions. New York: Larousse, 1994.

MUMMY FACTS

1. Mummification was not limited to Egyptians. Greeks and Romans who resided in Egypt were also mummified in Egyptian fashion.

2. The process of mummification continued in Egypt as late as the fifth century C.E., then slowly tapered off when Christianity took hold.

3. From 400 to 1400 C.E. there was a common belief that *mummia* was a potent medicine with curative powers. This mummia was obtained by grinding up actual mummies.

4. Many travelers who visited Egypt from Europe in the 1600s and 1700s took mummies home and displayed them as centerpieces or in curio cabinets.

5. The study of Egyptian antiquities, known as *Egyptology,* became a popular academic discipline in the 1800s. The event of "unwrapping a mummy" became a most popular attraction and draw to European museums.

6. In 1896, British archaeologist William Flinders Petrie began using X-ray techniques to examine mummies without unwrapping them.

7. In the early 1970s, scientists began using computed tomography, or CAT scans, to create images of the insides of mummies. This aided them in determining information about the embalming and wrapping processes the Egyptians used.

8. During the 1980s and 1990s, scientists extracted DNA from mummies in hopes of gathering information about ancient Egyptian patterns of settlement and migration, as well as information on diseases and genetic characteristics.

9. Recent approaches to studying mummies involve the interdisciplinary cooperation of Egyptologists, physicians, radiologists, physical anthropologists, and specialists in ancient languages.

10. Recent discoveries of mummies in the Sinai Peninsula, the desert oases, and the eastern delta of the Nile River are providing abundant information about the regional mummification styles.

SOURCES:

Teeter, Emily. *Presentation of Maat: Ritual and Legitimacy in Ancient Egypt and Scarabs, Scarboids, Seals and Seal Impressions from Medinet Habu.* N.p., n.d.

PYRAMID TEXTS

The Pyramid Texts recorded some of humankind's earliest written insights concerning its concepts about the soul and the afterlife. The texts were inscribed on the stone walls of five pyramids at Saccara during the later part of the Old Kingdom, 2400–2240 B.C.E., and were compiled by priestly scholars from a variety of sources, some dating earlier than the beginning of the historical period, about 3000 B.C.E. Beginning with the Middle Kingdom, about 2000 B.C.E., priests began to copy large portions of the Pyramid Texts onto the sarcophagi of pharoahs and nobles.

Although the texts deal only with the manner in which to guarantee the safe passage of deceased nobility to the other world, they also reflect the general thinking of the common people toward the next world, as well as that of the priesthood and the royal heads of state. It is clear that the Egyptians, even during this remote and long-ago period, thought of themselves as being more than a physical body, but what is not easily understood is exactly what their conception of death might have been. From what can be ascertained from the earliest mortuary texts is that the entire culture was in denial of death and refused to accept it as a natural and inevitable event. In fact the texts allude to a time when death did not exist, but there is no account of how death entered the world, as there are in many other cultures.

All pharaohs were considered to be divine, a belief that had its roots in the myths that gods had ruled Egypt in prehistoric times and that the earliest human rulers were the actual children of these divine beings. Therefore, when a pharaoh died, he could be prepared for death and become an "Osiris," the god of resurrection.

The Egyptians of this period conceived of two nonphysical entities, the *ka* and the *ba,* that made up the whole self and were of equal value to the physical body. Although it is difficult to ascertain a precise understanding of the cosmology of the Egyptian people of such a faraway time, it would appear that the *ka,* often represented in hieroglyphs as two arms upstretched in a gesture of protection, was believed to have been a kind of spiritual double of a living person that also served as his or her guardian spirit. A

HONGSHAN PYRAMID DISCOVERED IN CHINA

I n the Inner Mongolia Autonomous Region in northern China, Chinese archeologists have discovered a pyramid which they have dated to be more than 5,000 years old. Archaeologist Guo Dashun stated that the three-stepped pyramid belongs to the Hongshan culture period of 5,000 to 6,000 years ago, during the Stone Age.

At the top of the pyramid, the archeologists found seven tombs and the ruins of an altar. Also found were many fragments of broken pottery carved with the Chinese character *mi* (rice). They also discovered a bone flute, a stone ring, and a life-sized sculpture of a goddess.

Archeologists believe that the discovery of these relics, as well as of the pyramid itself, will be crucial in learning more about both the spiritual and earthbound life of the peoples of the Hongshan culture.

SOURCES:

"Xinhua." *China Daily.* http://www.chinadaily.net/cndy/2001-07-10/19256.html. 10 July 2001.

person's tomb was called the *het ka*, the "house of the *ka*," suggesting that the Egyptians not only considered the *ka* an essential aspect of a human being, but understood that a provision for it, as well as for the physical body, must be made at the time of death.

The *ba* is generally understood by modern scholars as representing that aspect of the essential self that is commonly referred to as the soul. Often depicted in ancient Egyptian art and hieroglyphs as a bird with a human head—male or female, corresponding to the sex of the person represented—the *ba* hovers near its physical counterpart. In cultures throughout the world, the bird is often utilized as a symbol for the soul. And certainly, in the Egypt of thousands of years ago, the high-flying, free-moving creature of the air would have seemed an obvious representation of the aspect of the self that separates from the body at the time of death.

THE *Pyramid Texts were inscribed on the stone walls of five pyramids at Saccara.*

While there seems no question that the ancient Egyptian view of the nature of each individual human included both the physical and nonphysical aspects of the whole person, the spiritual, nonmaterial representations were not valued above the material body. Such an assertion is easily demonstrated by the lengthy process of embalmment and the elaborate process of mummification conducted on the physical body of the deceased. The magical rit-

uals and ceremonies carefully performed to prepare the dead for the afterlife journey indicate that the body was as important an aspect of the complete entity as were the *ka* and the *ba*. Nor can it truly be known if the *ka* and the *ba* were viewed strictly as spiritual entities, for they, as well as their mummified human-self, were left food and drink in the mortuary offerings so they might live on in their roles of overseers.

❖ DELVING DEEPER

Brandon, S. G. F. *Religion in Ancient History*. New York: Charles Scribner's Sons, 1969.

Ferm, Vergilius, ed. *Ancient Religions*. New York: Philosophical Library, 1950.

INDIVIDUAL HUMAN EXPERIENCE WITH DEATH AND THE AFTERLIFE

For the past three hundred years, Western science has been fixated upon the concept that everything in the universe is subject to physical laws and exists only in terms of mass and energy—matter being transformed by energy into a variety of conditions and shapes that come into existence only to pass away eventually in time and space. Death, therefore, is the end of existence for all who succumb to its ultimate withdrawal of the life force.

From time to time, however, highly regarded scientists have protested that such a view of the universe leaves out a sizable portion of reality. British philosopher and mathematician Alfred North Whitehead (1861–1947) observed that a strictly materialistic approach to life completely ignored the subjective life of humans—or that area of existence which is commonly called the spiritual. It in no way accounted for emotions—the manner in which human beings experience the feelings of love between a woman and a man, between parents and children; the joy upon hearing a magnificent symphony; the sense of beauty and awe in sighting a rainbow; the inspiration of religious thought.

But the major tenets of Western science hold fast. Such human experiences, material scientists insist, are mere transient illusions—things that people imagine for themselves or dream for themselves—while the only true reality consists in the movement of atoms blindly obeying chemical and physical laws.

This soulless "world machine" was created three centuries ago by the genius of Rene Descartes (1596–1650), Sir Isaac Newton (1642–1727), and their predecessors; and it has proved useful for the development of physical science. The attempts of Whitehead and others to construct an approach to science that could include the experiences of people's inner lives within the framework of reality has made little impression in contemporary science, which remains rigidly devoted to the seventeenth century "world machine." Everything must be explained in terms of the physical action of material bodies being acted upon by external forces.

But even the most rigid disciple of the materialistic religion of test tubes, chemical compounds, and mathematical formulas still cannot answer the ultimate question—what lies beyond physical death?

Some scientists compromise because their instincts or desires prompt them to hope that life goes on, and they point to the research being done with those men and women who have survived the near-death experience (NDE) and the testimonies of medical personnel who have observed individuals undergoing deathbed visions. While some scientists may argue that the answers that come forth from those who have experienced NDE are subjective, other researchers insist that such reports do provide valuable clues to the dimensions of reality that lie beyond physical death.

Throughout history there have been men and women who have been somehow brought back to life after accidents, severe injuries, surgeries, and other physical traumas, and they have related their own accounts of life beyond death, the journey of the soul, and the process of judgment that awaits the spirits of the deceased on the other side. While the various representatives of religious orthodoxy may often look upon such stories as visions wrought by the severity of a painful ordeal and a subsequent misinterpretation of accepted religious teachings, and while the proponents of the material sciences may consider these experiences delusions, those who have survived such near-death encounters cannot be shaken from the testimony of their own personal experiences, regardless of the accepted dogmas and doctrines taught by the various religious bodies or the physical sciences concerning the afterlife.

Father Andrew Greeley (1928–   ), who has a Ph.D. in sociology and is a best-selling novelist as well as a Roman Catholic priest, has been keeping tabs on the spiritual experiences of Americans since 1973. Together with colleagues at the University of Chicago, Greeley, a professor of sociology at the University of Arizona, released the following data in the January/February 1987 issue of *American Health:* Seventy-three percent of the adult population in the United States believe in life after death; 74 percent expect to be reunited with their loved ones after death.

In the fall of 1988, the editors at *Better Homes and Gardens* drew more than 80,000 responses when they surveyed their readership regarding their spiritual lives. Eighty-nine percent believed in eternal life; 30 percent believed in a spirit world; and 86 percent believed in miracles.

DEATHBED VISIONS

For thousands of years, many individuals have received personal proof of survival by observing their fellow humans at the moment of death. Reports of deathbed experiences have long intrigued physical researchers, but systematic investigations of such accounts were not attempted until the pilot study of Dr. Karlis Osis (*Deathbed Observations by Physicians and Nurses,* 1961) sought to analyze the experiences of dying persons in search of patterns.

Because of their specialized training, ability to make accurate medical assessments, and proximity to dying patients, Osis selected doctors and nurses as informants. Each of the 640 respondents to Osis's questionnaires had observed an average of 50 to 60 deathbed patients—a total of over 35,000 cases. The

The Near-Death Experiences and the Afterlife website (http://www.near-death. com) presents a comprehensive overview of the near-death experience and views of the afterlife from the standpoint of all world religions including Christian, New Age, Jewish, Hindu, Atheist, Buddhist, and Muslim. There are also NDEs, (near-death experiences) of children, of those who are blind and those who committed suicide.

Research, analysis, and support are among the many other features on the website. There are interesting and related topics including scientific or psychic research, informative news, books, documentaries, audio, television shows, and films available within the fields of study of the afterlife and the near-death experience. Links are provided to many of the researchers in the field, such as Dr. P. M. H. Atwater and Dr. George Ritchie, as well as to those who have widely written about their own transformative near-death events, such as Bettie Eadie and Dannion Brinkley.

NEAR-DEATH EXPERIENCES AND THE AFTERLIFE

Also, a section called *Films with Afterlife Themes* provides a list of more than 30 films that were made from 1939 to the present. A brief overview and description of the plot is given, in addition to the rating and length of the film.

SOURCES:

Near Death Experiences and the Afterlife. http://www.near-death.com. 15 October 2001.

---

parapsychologists followed up the initial questionnaire with telephone calls, additional questionnaires, and correspondence.

A total of 385 respondents reported 1,318 cases wherein deathbed patients claimed to have seen apparitions or phantasms. Fifty-two percent of these apparitions represented dead persons who were known to the patients; 28 percent were of living persons; and 20 percent were of religious figures. Visions that either gave the dying patient a view of the traditional heaven or depicted scenes of wondrous beauty and brilliant color were reported by 248 respondents to have been observed in 884 instances. Mood elevation—that is, a shift in the patient's emotions from extreme pain and fear to tranquility—was reported by 169 respondents in 753 cases.

About half of the apparitions reported by the dying patients seemed to have appeared for the purpose of guiding them through the transition from death to the afterlife. One distinct observation emerging from Osis's study was that few patients appeared to die in a state of fear.

Age and sex showed no correlation with the phenomena of deathbed apparitions, visions, or mood elevations. Interestingly enough, the more highly educated patients evidenced more deathbed phenomena than the less well educated, thus contradicting the allegation that the more superstitious are likely to experience deathbed phenomena.

Religious beliefs correlated in a positive manner, as might be expected. Only those patients who believed in life after death experienced visions depicting scenes in the other world. Religious figures were sometimes reported by those with no religious affiliation, but those with strong beliefs most often identified a biblical or saintly figure.

Another interesting statistic revealed by the study is that visions, apparitions, and mood elevations are reported more often in cases where the dying patient is fully conscious and appears in complete control of his senses. Sedation, high fever, and painkilling drugs seem to decrease, rather than to increase, the ability to experience these phenomena. By the same token, cases of brain damage or brain disease were found unrelated to the kinds of deathbed experiences relevant to Osis's study.

The questionnaire and subsequent follow-up also uncovered some intriguing areas for additional research. There were cases, for example, in which collective viewings of apparitions were reported by those who had gathered around the patient's deathbed. There were numerous instances of "extrasensory" interaction between patients and attending physicians and nurses; and many cases wherein observers underwent a change in their own personal philosophy after witnessing the experience of the dying person.

Among the many patterns disclosed by the study, Osis feels that one of the most consistent was that phenomena relevant to the survival hypothesis occurred most often when the physiological and psychological balance of the patient was not greatly disturbed. According to the research project's findings as reported by Osis, "Trends in line with the survival hypothesis occurred predominantly in patients whose mentality was not disturbed by sedatives or other medications, who had no diagnosed hallucinogenic pathology, and who were fully conscious as well as responsive to their environment." The study found that experiences irrelevant to the survival hypothesis occurred more often in those patients who were generally prone to hallucinate, "such as the sedated patients, those whose pathology was diagnosed as hallucinogenic, or those whose consciousness and contact with the environment was impaired."

Dr. Elisabeth Kubler-Ross (1926–) has said that the turning point in her work as a medical doctor occurred in a Chicago hospital in 1969 when a deceased patient appeared before her in fully materialized form. Kubler-Ross had been feeling discouraged about her research with the dying because of the opposition that she had encountered among her colleagues, but the apparition of Mary Schwartz appeared to her to tell her not to abandon her work because life after death was a reality.

"DEATH *is simply a shedding of the physical body, like the butterfly coming out of a cocoon.*"
—DR. ELISABETH KUBLER-ROSS

"Death is simply a shedding of the physical body, like the butterfly coming out of a cocoon," Kubler-Ross has told her lecture audiences in presentations which she had conducted around the world. "Death is a transition into a higher state of consciousness where you continue to perceive, to understand, to laugh, to be able to grow, and the only thing you lose is something that you don't need anymore—and that is your physical body."

The thousands of case histories that Kubler-Ross has studied have demonstrated to her that while, in some cases, dying may be painful, death itself—as described by those who have survived near-death experiences (NDE)—is a completely peaceful experience, free of pain and fear. Kubler-Ross also found that when one of her patients died, someone was always there to help in the transition from life to death, often a deceased family member or friend. Those who had experienced a "comeback" from death to life assured her that to die was to experience a feeling of "peace, freedom, equanimity, a sense of wholeness," and they told her that they were no longer afraid to die.

While the great majority of today's scientists may consider the quest to discover the world beyond death a waste of time and energy when there are so many physical challenges awaiting humankind in the twenty-first century, Dr. Karlis Osis has spoken to this issue and advised his more materialistic colleagues to take a "wider look toward the far horizons which have attracted the best minds through the centuries." There is, of course, greatness in defeating humankind's diseases and in conquering new worlds in outer space, but, Osis wonders "how the age-old problem, 'What happens when someone dies?,' compares with these material challenges? Is it not equally important to know the certain answer to such a basic question of human existence?"

> "To fear death, gentlemen, is nothing other than to think oneself wise when one is not; for it is to think one knows what one does not know. No man knows whether death may not even turn out to be the greater of blessings for a human being, and yet people fear it as if they knew for certain that it is the greatest of evils."
>
> —SOCRATES

In his *A Practical Guide to Death and Dying,* (1988) author John W. White, a founding member of the International Association for Near-Death Studies, quotes the philosopher Socrates' (c. 470–399 B.C.E.) statement just before drinking the hemlock that would kill him: "To fear death, gentlemen, is nothing other than to think oneself wise when one is not; for it is to think one knows what one does not know. No man knows whether death may not even turn out to be the greater of blessings for a human being, and yet people fear it as if they knew for certain that it is the greatest of evils."

White states that, in his opinion, the current research on death and dying indicates that one's personality will survive death of the body and, in all likelihood, will be reincarnated. "Death challenges us to find the meaning of life," he writes, "and with it, genuine happiness. It is nature's way of goading us to discover our true condition, our real self—beyond the transience and ephemerality of this material world. And not only this world, but all worlds."

✤ DELVING DEEPER

Kubler-Ross, Elisabeth. *Living with Death and Dying.* New York: Macmillan, 1997.

Morse, Melvin. *Parting Visions: Uses and Meaning of Pre-Death.* New York: Villard Books, 1994.

White, John. *A Practical Guide to Death and Dying.* Wheaton, Ill.: Theosophical Publishing House, 1988.

Willis-Brandon, Carla. *One Last Hug Before I Go: The Mystery and Meaning of Deathbed Visions.* Deerfield Beach, Fla.: Health Communications, 2000.

NEAR-DEATH EXPERIENCES (NDEs)

In the mid-1970s, the work of such noted researchers as Drs. Raymond Moody, Melvin Morse, Kenneth Ring, and Elisabeth Kubler-Ross (1926–   ) brought the subject of the near-death experience (NDE) to the attention of the general public. As accounts of men and women who had been brought back to life and told of having witnessed scenes from the other side received wide circulation, more near-death experiencers felt confident in sharing their own stories of having come back from other-dimensional journeys outside of their bodies. As medical science became increasingly sophisticated and successful in terms of its ability to resuscitate those individuals who might otherwise have died from heart attacks, automobile accidents, and other physical traumas, the more men and women came forward to tell of having perceived the spirits of deceased friends and relatives, guardian angels, and beings of light that met them in a heavenly kind of place and communicated with them before returning them to their bodies.

In 1983, an extensive survey conducted by George Gallup, Jr., found that eight million Americans—5 percent of the adult population—said that they had undergone a near-death experience. A survey conducted in 1991 by Dr. Colin Ross, associate professor of psychiatry at the University of Manitoba in Winnipeg, suggests that as many as one in three people have left their bodies and returned—most often during times of crisis, extreme pain, and near-death. In 1992, a new Gallup Poll survey revealed that around 13 million Americans claimed to have undergone at least one NDE. While such statistics and inspirational stories were new to many men and women, accounts of people who came back to life after clinical death and who told of experiencing proof of life after death had been recorded by researchers for hundreds of years.

In *Memories, Dreams, Reflections,* psychoanalyst Dr. Carl G. Jung (1875–1961) describes a near-death experience he underwent after he had broken a foot and suffered a heart attack. "It seemed to me that I was high up in space," he wrote. "Far below I saw the globe of Earth, bathed in a gloriously blue light.... Below my feet lay Ceylon, and in the distance ahead… the subcontinent of India. My field of vision did not include the whole Earth, but its global shape was plainly distinguishable."

The psychoanalyst described the reddish-yellow desert of Arabia, the Red Sea, and the Mediterranean. "The sight of the Earth from this height was the most glorious thing I had ever seen," Jung said, estimating that his consciousness would have had to have been at least a thousand miles up to have perceived such a panoramic view of the planet. He was most emphatic in stressing his belief that the experiences he had during his heart attack were not the products of imagination or a fevered brain. "The visions and experiences were utterly real," he wrote. "There was nothing subjective about them; they all had a quality of absolute objectivity."

Ernest Hemingway (1899–1961), the American author of such works as *The Sun Also Rises* and *The Old Man and the Sea,* wrote of his near-death experience while serving in the trenches near Fossalta, Italy. It was about midnight on July 8, 1918, when a mortar shell exploded near the 19-year-old Hemingway, badly wounding him in the legs. Later, he said that he experienced death at that moment. He had felt his soul coming out of his body "like you'd pull a silk handkerchief out a pocket by one corner. It flew around and then came back and went in again and I wasn't dead any more."

Hemingway used his own near-death experience in *A Farewell to Arms* when he has his fictional hero, Frederick Henry, undergo a similar experience. The novel's protagonist is also positioned in the Italian trenches when

"…a blast-furnace door is swung open and a roar that started white and went red…in a rushing wind." Henry feels his spirit rush out of himself and soar with the wind. He believes himself to be dead and realizes that there is an existence beyond physical death. Then "…instead of going on, I felt myself slide back. I breathed and I was back."

Dr. Robert Crookall, a British biologist and botanist, was one of the great pioneers in the clinical study of near-death experiences. Crookall theorized that what metaphysicians had labeled the astral or the etheric body—the soul—is normally "enmeshed in" the physical body so that most people are never aware of its existence. During out-of-body or near-death experiences, however, the Soul Body separates or projects from the physical body and is used temporarily as an instrument of consciousness. According to Crookall, this Soul Body consists of matter "…but it is extremely subtle and may be described as 'superphysical.'"

Crookall perceived the physical body as animated by a semiphysical "vehicle of vitality," which serves as a bridge between the physical body and the Soul Body. This, he believed, was the "breath of life" mentioned in Genesis. In some people, he speculated "…especially (though not necessarily) saintly people," the Soul Body may be less confined to the physical flesh than it is in persons of a more physical or material nature, thus making it easier for the aesthetic to achieve out-of-body experiences.

Among the hundreds of cases of near-death and out-of-body experiences that Crookall collected, he found numerous references to a kind of psychic "umbilical cord" that appears to connect the nonphysical Soul Body to the physical body. Citing such cases from his research, Crookall wrote:

> With regard to form, several [experiencers] have described seeing merely a "cord" and said that it was about half an inch wide. T. D. compared his to a "thread." H. considered, "I am sure that, had a feeble thread between soul and body been severed, I would have remained intact" (i.e., the soul would

have survived the death of the body). The Tibetans also observed that "a strand" subsisted between the [Soul Body] and the [physical] body. Like H., Miss K. realized that once [the cord] was "loosed" the reentry…into the body would have been impossible. She said, "This is what death means."

Those men and women of a Judeo-Christian belief construct who have undergone the near-death experience (NDE) sometimes quote Ecclesiastes 12:5–7 as scriptural testimony to the reality of the spiritual body and its ability to separate itself from the flesh: "Or ever the silver cord be loosed, or the golden bowl be broken, or the pitcher be broken at the fountain, or the wheel be broken at the cistern: Then shall the dust return to the earth as it was; and the spirit shall return to God who gave it."

One frequently observed quality of the silver cord which appears to connect the Soul Body to the physical body is its elasticity. Numerous persons who have undergone near-death experiences have remarked upon this quality in their descriptions of the experience. Crookall wrote of a man named Edwards who stated that from the pull of his silver cord he would characterize it as being made of some kind of substance similar to "stout elastic." Another of his subjects, a Mrs. Leonard, noted that as her Soul Body neared her physical body, the cord not only became shorter and thicker, as would be expected, but also less elastic, agreeing with the often reported statements that when the Soul Body approaches very near the physical body, it tends to reenter it—in fact it is often "sucked" back.

In the late 1970s, the popular acceptance of the work of Dr. Elisabeth Kubler-Ross brought sharp scientific focus to bear on the question of what happens to humans after the experience of physical death. In her book *Death, the Final Stages of Growth* Kubler-Ross declares that "beyond a shadow of a doubt, there is life after death."

Far from an evangelical tract, Kubler-Ross's publication is actually a textbook that is based on more than a thousand interviews with terminally ill persons, many of whom had recovered from near-death experiences. They describe such sensations as floating above their own physical bodies and being able to transcend the normally accepted limitations of time and space. Nearly all of the near-death survivors told of a sense of euphoria and peace, and many had been confronted by angels and spirit beings who told them that it was not yet time for them to make the final transition to the other side. When the dying do accomplish that ultimate change of dimensions, according to Kubler-Ross's observations, they are "…at peace; they are fully awake; when they float out of their bodies they are without fear, pain, or anxiety; and they have a sense of wholeness."

Dr. Raymond Moody, who is both a medical doctor and the holder of a doctorate in philosophy, discovered an enormous number of similar reports when he became curious about what happened to his patients in the period of time in which they "died" before being revived and returned to life through medical treatment. After interviewing many men and women who had survived near-death experiences, for his book *Life after Life*, Dr. Moody discovered what Dr. Kubler-Ross and numerous other researchers had found: The near-death experiencers had the sensation of moving rapidly through a long, dark tunnel before "popping" outside of their physical bodies. If they were in hospital rooms or other enclosures, they often floated near the ceiling and watched medical teams attempting to revive their physical bodies. Many reported their life literally "flashing" before their eyes, and others said that they were welcomed to the other world by previously deceased relatives or friends. Whether or not they were of a religious background, they often reported an encounter with a brilliant, intense white light that assumed the form of an angel, a guide, a teacher, Father Abraham, or a Christ-figure.

In 1977, Dr. Kenneth Ring, professor of psychology at the University of Connecticut, began a scientific investigation of 102 men and women who had undergone the near-death experience. In his *Life at Death*, published in 1980, Ring released the results of the data that he had compiled. According to his assessment of his subjects' experiences, Ring tabulated that

60 percent of them found that the near-death experience had brought them a sense of peace and well-being; 37 percent reported a separation of consciousness from the physical body; 23 percent mentioned the process of entering a dark tunnel; 16 percent said that they had seen a bright light; and 10 percent claimed that they had entered the light.

Ring concludes his book by dropping his scientific demeanor and admitting that he, personally, believes that humankind has a "conscious existence after our physical death and that the core experience does represent its beginning, a glimpse of things to come." Ring further states that he considers the near-death experience to be a teaching, revelatory experience. In his observation, both those who undergo a near-death experience and those who hear about them from others receive "an intuitive sense of the transcendent aspect of creation." To Ring, the near-death experience clearly implies that "there is something more, something beyond the physical world of the senses, which, in the light of these experiences, now appears to be only the mundane segment of a great spectrum of reality."

Ring has also given some thought to the question of why the study of death became so prominent in the late 1970s and early 80s: "One reason...is to help us to become globally sensitized to the experience of death on a planetary scale which now hangs like the sword of Damocles over our heads. Could this be the universe's way of 'innoculating' us against the fear of death?"

A consensus among those who investigate the near-death experience yields a number of features commonly described by those who have undergone NDE:

- They usually see their physical bodies apart from their spiritual bodies. They experience a soaring sensation, a definite movement out of the body and discover that their consciousness is free of time and space and all prior physical limitations.

- There is often a sense of disorientation and confusion when family, friends, medical personnel, and other people seem unaware of their nonphysical presence.

- The sensation of moving down a tunnel toward a bright light is frequently mentioned.

- A great number of those who have undergone NDE state that they encountered an angelic being, a spirit guardian, or the spirit of someone known by them to have been deceased, such as a friend or a relative.

- Many report having witnessed a kind of life review of their Earth-plane existence.

- A glimpse of paradise or even a guided tour of heaven conducted by an angelic host is recalled by many.

- An extreme reluctance to leave this beautiful state of existence and return to their physical bodies is commonly expressed.

- Upon their return to their bodies, many near-death experiencers discover that their awareness has been expanded far beyond what it was before the NDE. Some report heightened extrasensory abilities, such as **telepathy, clairvoyance,** and **precognition.**

Dr. Antonio Aldo Soldaro, chief surgeon at Rome's main public hospital and a professor of surgery at Rome University, has observed that all NDE subjects "improve their spiritual and social lives. They become more generous, optimistic, and positive."

Dr. Melvin Morse, clinical associate professor of pediatrics at the University of Washington, is another NDE researcher who has found that certain survivors of the near-death experience return with enhanced abilities. Morse, author of such books as *Transformed by the Light,* noted that some of the people he interviewed came back to life with "an increase in the amount of electrical energy their bodies emit," an acceleration of intellect and/or psychic abilities, and even the power to heal themselves.

In one of his investigations, Morse spoke to a 45-year-old woman named Kathy who said that she had been afflicted with incurable thyroid cancer and had been given six months to live. It was at that awful moment that she also developed pneumonia. After she was rushed to a hospital, her heart stopped; and as doctors worked desperately to revive her,

Kathy stated that the real her was "high on top of a beautiful ridge overlooking a beautiful valley. The colors were extremely vivid, and I was filled with joy." A being of light touched her spirit body, and her entire essence was "filled with light."

Later, when she was revived, Kathy's pneumonia had disappeared. A few weeks later, her cancer, too, had inexplicably left her. Morse theorized that Kathy's NDE had a direct influence on healing the cancer. He also stated that he had studied instances in which near-death survivors had returned to life more intelligent than they had been before the experience.

DR. Susan Blackmore of Bristol University in England claims all the phenomena associated with an NDE are manifestations of the "winding down" of brain functions as a person nears death.

Dr. P. M. H. Atwater, of Charlottesville, Virginia, nearly died after hemorrhaging in 1977. After her own dramatic experience, she began to investigate other cases of NDE in which ordinary men and women had survived near-death. By 1988, she had interviewed more than 200 NDE survivors and found that their experiences had triggered something in them that had enhanced certain abilities. She has written a number of books on the subject, such as *Beyond the Light* (1997). In one of her case studies, she tells of a truck driver who had survived a near-fatal crash and who subsequently began to display advanced mathematical abilities. Literally overnight he demonstrated a gift for higher mathematics. He was able to write down complicated mathematical equations about which he had no prior knowledge. Gradually, the man began to understand his new abilities and was eventually able to use them in practical applications.

In those cases in which near-death survivors claim to have been left with after effects, Atwater states that her research indicates that 80 to 90 percent exhibit physiological changes as well as psychological alterations. Among the most frequent after effects reported to Atwater are the following: The near-death experiencer looks and acts more playful. His or her skin brightens, and eyes sparkle. There is an increased sensitivity to any form of light, especially sunlight, and to any form of sound and to noise levels. Boredom levels decrease or increase. He or she has substantially more or less energy. He or she can handle stress easier and heal quicker from hurts and wounds. His or her brain begins to function differently.

If it is true that near-death survivors are physically as well as psychologically changed by their experiences, what does this say about the real power of the experience? Atwater suggests ever larger questions: "Since the part of us that has this experience 'separates' from the body to the extent that it does, is that an indication that not only do we have a soul, we are a soul-resident in a lifeform? If that is true, what else is true about life, about death, about purpose and mission and Source and Creation?"

While skeptics ridicule the "will to believe" in an afterlife as religious wishful thinking, it might be suggested that many of them embrace a "will to disbelieve" with what also amounts to a kind of religious fervor. For many scientists, there can be no consciousness after the physical body dies. The universe is comprised exclusively of material realities, and without the physical organism there can be no mind, no consciousness—and certainly no life after death. Many believe near-death experiences are but hallucinations caused by reasons that may be psychological, pharmacological, or neurological. According to the material scientists, those men and women who claim to be survivors of a near-death experience and who report that their soul left their body and began a journey into an afterlife before being revived are suffering from delusions. Science has proved that there is no aspect of personality within a human being that could travel anywhere without a physical body to propel it.

Dr. Susan Blackmore of Bristol University in England has spent many years investigating the near-death experience and is convinced that all the phenomena associated with an NDE are manifestations of the "winding down" of brain functions as a person nears death. Blackmore explains the oft-mentioned "tunnel of light" seen by near-death experiencers as a result of the turmoil occurring in the section of the brain that controls vision. As the brain continues to shut down and is increasingly deprived of sensory input, it begins to draw upon memory to answer such questions as "who am I?" and "where am I?" and information stored in the memory supplies images based upon the individual's perception of self and expectations of an afterlife.

In October 2000, the results of a year-long research project that was described as the "first scientific study of near-death experiences" were released by Dr. Peter Fenwick, a consultant and neurophysicist at the Institute of Psychiatry in London, and Dr. Sam Parnia, a clinical research fellow and registrar at Southampton Hospital. Although the doctors were initially skeptical of reports in which people close to death had encounters with bright lights and heavenly beings, their new study concludes that a "number of people have almost certainly had these experiences after they were pronounced clinically dead." By carefully examining medical records, the researchers ruled out the collapse of brain functions caused by low levels of oxygen or that drugs might be responsible for the experiences.

"These people were having these experiences when we wouldn't expect them to happen, when the brain should be able to sustain lucid processes or allow them to form memories that would last," Parnia said. "So [the study] might hold an answer to the question of whether mind or consciousness is actually produced by the brain or whether the brain is a kind of intermediary for the mind, which exists independently."

Fenwick commented, "If the mind and brain can be independent, then that raises questions about the continuation of consciousness after death. It also raises the question about a spiritual component to humans and about a meaningful universe with a purpose rather than a random universe."

✦ DELVING DEEPER

Atwater, P. M. H. *Beyond the Light*. New York: Avon, 1997.

———. *The Complete Idiot's Guide to Near-Death Experiences*. New York: Alpha Books, 2000.

Crookall, Robert. *More Astral Projections: Analysis of Case Histories*. London: Aquarian Press, 1964.

Eadie, Betty J. *Embraced by the Light*. New York: Bantam Books, 1994.

Kubler-Ross, Elisabeth. *On Death and Dying*. New York: Macmillan, 1969.

Moody, Raymond A., Jr. *Life After Life*. New York: Bantam Books, 1981.

Morse, Melvin. *Closer to the Light*. New York: Ivy Books, 1991.

Muldoon, Sylvan, and Hereward Carrington. *The Projection of the Astral Body*. New York: Weiser, 1981.

Ring, Kenneth. *Life at Death*. New York: Coward, McCann and Geoghegan, 1980.

Steiger, Brad. *Minds Through Space and Time*. New York: Award Books, 1971.

Steiger, Brad and Steiger, Sherry Hansen. *Children of the Light*. New York: Signet, 1995.

THE MYSTERY SCHOOLS

The great Epic of Gilgamesh, which dates back to the early part of the second millennium B.C.E., portrays an ancient Mesopotamian king's quest for immortality and his despair when he learns that the gods keep the priceless jewel of eternal life for themselves. From clay, the gods shaped humankind and breathed into their nostrils the breath of life. What a cruel trick, then, to snatch back the wind of life at the time of physical death and permit the wonderful piece of work that is man to return once again to dust. The destiny of all humans, regardless of whatever greatness they may achieve or however low they might sink, is the same—death.

Throughout all of humankind's recorded history, there have been those who have sought to guarantee a dignified way of death and to ensure a stylish and safe passage into the afterlife. Many of these individuals who sought to approach death on their own terms formed secret societies and cults which are known by the general name of "mysteries," which comes from the Greek *myein*, "to close," referring to the need of the *mystes*, the initiate, to close the eyes and the lips and to keep secret the rites of the cult.

All of the early mysteries and mystical traditions appear to center around a kind of mystery play or ritual reenactment of the life of such gods as Osiris, Dionysus, and Demeter, divinities most often associated with the underworld, the realm of the dead, the powers of darkness, and the process of rebirth. Because of the importance of the regenerative process, the rites of the mysteries were usually built around a divine female as the agent of transformation and regeneration. While the initiates of the mystery cult enacted the life cycle of the gods who triumphed over death and who were reborn, they also asserted their own path of wisdom that would enable them to conquer death and accomplish resurrection in the afterlife, with rebirth in a new body in a new existence.

THE *rites of Dionysus often featured animal sacrifice. This was meant to symbolize the incarnation, death, and resurrection of the divinity.*

The origin and substance of the state religion of ancient Greece was a sophisticated kind of nature worship wherein natural elements and phenomena were transformed into divine beings who lived atop Mount Olympus. If the Judeo-Christian tradition proclaimed that humans were fashioned in the image of God, their creator, then it must be said that the gods of ancient Greece were created in the image of humans, their creators. Like the humans who worshipped them, the Olympians lived in communities and had families, friends, and enemies and were controlled by the same emotions, lusts, and loves. The pantheon of the gods of ancient Greece were not cloaked in the mysterious, unfathomable qualities of the deities of the East, but possessed the same vices and virtues as the humans who sought their assistance. Although the Olympians could manifest as all-powerful entities—especially when a rival

god wasn't interfering—none of them were omnipotent. Although they were capable of exhibiting wisdom, none of them were omniscient. And they often found themselves as subject to the whims of Fate as the humans who prayed for their guidance.

The Olympians were worshipped by the Greeks most often in small family groups. There existed no highly organized or formally educated priesthood, no strict doctrines, no theologians to interpret the meaning of ambiguous scriptural passages. The followers of the state religion could worship the god or gods of their choosing and believed that they could gain their favor by performing simple ritual acts and sacrifices.

In addition to the state religion into which every Greek belonged automatically at birth, there were also the "mystery religions," which required elaborate processes of purification and initiation before a man or woman could qualify for membership. The mystery religions were concerned with the spiritual welfare of the individual, and their proponents believed in an orderly universe and the unity of all life with God. The relationship of the *mystes*, the initiate, was not taken lightly, as in the official state religion, but was considered to be intimate and close. The aim and promise of the mystical rites was to enable the initiate to feel as though he or she had attained union with the divine. The purifications and processions, the fasting and the feasts, the blazing lights of torches and the musical liturgies played during the performances of the sacred plays—all fueled the imagination and stirred deep emotions. The initiates left the celebration of the mystery feeling that they were now superior to the problems that the uninitiated faced concerning life, death, and immortality. Not only did the initiates believe that their communion with the patron god or goddess would continue after death, but that they would eventually leave Hades to be born again in another life experience.

✤ **DELVING DEEPER**

Cotterell, Arthur, ed. *Encyclopedia of World Mythology*. London: Dempsey Parr, 1999.

Ferm, Vergilius, ed. *Ancient Religions*. New York: The Philosophical Library, 1950.

Fox, Robin Lane. *Pagans and Christians*. New York: Alfred A. Knopf, 1989.

Gordon, Stuart. *The Encyclopedia of Myths and Legends*. London: Headline Book Publishing, 1994.

Walker, Barbara G. *The Woman's Encyclopedia of Myths and Secrets*. San Francisco, Harper & Row, 1983.

DIONYSIAN MYSTERIES

Next to the Eleusinian mysteries in importance and popularity were the Dionysian, which were centered around Dionysus (Bacchus), a god of life, vegetation, and the vine who, because all things growing and green must one day decay and die, was also a divinity of the underworld. Those initiates who entered into communion with Dionysus drank large amounts of wine and celebrated with feasts that encouraged them to dress themselves in leaves and flowers and even to take on the character of the god himself, in an attempt to achieve his power. Once the god had entered into union with the initiates, they would experience a new spiritual rebirth. This divine union with Dionysus marked the beginning of a new life for the initiates, who, thereafter, regarded themselves as superior beings. And since Dionysus was the Lord of Death, as well as the Lord of Life, the initiates believed that their union with him would continue even after death, and that immortality was now within their grasp.

The rites of Dionysus were conducted on a much lower level than those of Eleusis, and often featured the sacrifice of an animal—usually a goat—that was torn to pieces by the initiates, whose savagery was meant to symbolize the incarnation, death, and resurrection of the divinity. Although the cult was not looked upon with high regard by the sages and philosophers of the day, amulets and tablets with fragments of Dionysian hymns upon them have been found dating back to the third century B.C.E. These magical symbols were buried with the dead and meant to protect the soul from the dangers of the underworld.

✤ DELVING DEEPER

Brandon, S. G. F. *Religion in Ancient History*. New York: Charles Scribner's Sons, 1969.

Ferm, Vergilious ed. *Ancient Religions*. New York: Philosophical Library, 1950.

ELEUSINIAN MYSTERIES

The sacred Eleusinian mysteries of the Greeks date back to the fifth century B.C.E. and were the most popular and influential of the cults. The rites took place in the city of Eleusis, a small community 14 miles west of Athens, but it was the ruler of Athens, together with a specially selected committee, who was in charge of the general management of the annual event. Although the Dionysian and Orphic rites could be celebrated at any time, the Eleusinian rites were held at a fixed time in the early fall after the seeds had been entrusted to the fields, and were conducted by a hereditary priesthood called the Eumolpedie.

THE *Eleusinian rites were held at a fixed time in the early fall after the seeds had been entrusted to the fields, and were conducted by a hereditary priesthood called the Eumolpedie.*

Sometime in the month of September, the Eumolpedie removed the Eleusinian holy objects from Eleusis and carried them to the sacred city of Athens, where they were placed in the Eleusinion temple. Three days after the holy relics had been transported, the initiates gathered to hear the exhortations of the priests, who solemnly warned all those who did not consider themselves worthy of initiation to leave at once. Women and even slaves were permitted to join the mysteries of Eleusis, providing that they were either Greeks or Romans, but it was required that all those wishing to be considered as initiates had first undergone the lesser mysteries held in Agrae, a suburb of Athens, six months before. After the rites of purification had been observed, the initiates bathed in the sea and were sprinkled with the blood of pigs as they emerged. A sacrifice was offered to the gods, and a procession began the journey to Eleusis, where, upon the arrival of the priests and the initiates, a midnight feast was celebrated and the new members of the cult were made one with the gods and goddesses by partaking of holy food and drink and enacting the ritual drama.

The Eleusinian drama reenacted the myth of the rape, abduction, and marriage of Kore (Persephone) by Hades, god of the underworld, and her separation from her mother, Demeter, the goddess of grain and vegetation. When, in her despair, Demeter refuses to allow the earth to bear fruit and brings about a time of blight and starvation that threatens to extinguish both humans and the gods, Zeus recalls Persephone from Hades. Filled with joy at the reunion with her daughter, Demeter once again allows the Earth to bear fruit. Persephone, however, will now divide the days of each year between her husband, Hades, in the underworld, and her mother, ensuring a bountiful harvest.

Essentially, the rites imitated the agricultural cycles of planting the seed, nurturing its growth, and harvesting the grain, which, on the symbolical level, represented the birth of the soul, its journey through life, and its death. As the seed of the harvest is planted again and the agricultural cycle is perpetuated, so is the soul harvested by the gods to be resurrected. Membership in the mysteries of Eleusis was undertaken to ensure initiates a happy immortality.

❋ DELVING DEEPER

Ferm, Vergilious, ed. *Ancient Religions*. New York: Philosophical Library, 1950.

Gaster, Dr. Theodor H., ed. *The New Golden Bough*. New York: Criterion Books, 1959.

Larousse Dictionary of Beliefs and Religions. New York: Larousse, 1994.

HERMETIC MYSTERIES

The **Hermes Trismegistus** (the thrice greatest Hermes), who set forth the esoteric doctrines of the ancient Egyptian priesthood, recognized the reincarnation of "impious souls" and the achievement of pious souls when they know God and become "all intelligence." Hermes was the name the Greeks gave to the Egyptian god Thoth, the god of wisdom, learning, and literature. To Hermes was given the title "scribe of the gods," and he is said to have authored 42 sacred books, the Hermetic Mysteries, which contained a wide assortment of secret wisdom. These divine documents were divided into six categories. The first dealt with

the education of the priesthood; the second, temple ritual; the third, geographical knowledge; the fourth, astrology; the fifth, hymns in honor of the gods and a guide for the proper behavior of royalty; the sixth, medical commentary. Legend has it that these sacred texts contain all the accumulated wisdom of ancient Egypt, going back in an unbroken tradition to the very earliest time.

As the Hermetic texts continued to influence the growth of European alchemy, astrology, and magic, the author of the books was said to have been Adam's grandson, who built the great pyramids of Egypt; or an Egyptian magician who lived three generations after Moses; or a magus from Babylonia who instructed **Pythagoras.** The Hermetic text decrees against transmigration, the belief that the souls of humans may enter into animals: "Divine law preserves the human soul from such infamy."

❋ DELVING DEEPER

Gordon, Stuart. *The Encyclopedia of Myths and Legends*. London: Headline House, 1993.

ORPHIC MYSTERIES

Orpheus may have been an actual historic figure, a man capable of charming both man and beast with his music, but god or human, he modified the Dionysian rites by removing their orgiastic elements. Dionysus Zagreus, the horned son of Zeus (king of the Gods) and Persephone (daughter of Zeus and Demeter), was the great god of the Orphic mysteries, who was devoured by the evil Titans while Zeus was otherwise distracted. Athena managed to save Dionysus Zagreus's heart while the enraged Zeus destroyed the Titans with his thunderbolts. Zeus gave the heart of his beloved son to the Earth goddess Semele who dissolved it in a potion, drank thereof, and gave birth to Dionysus, the god of vegetation, whose cycle of birth, death, and rebirth reflects the cycle of growth, decay, and rebirth seen in nature. Orpheus preached that humankind was created from the ashes of the Titans who devoured Dionysus Zagreus; therefore, the physical bodies of humans are formed from the evil of the Titans, but they also contain within them a tiny particle of the divine essence. Within this duality a constant war rages, so it is the duty of each human to repress the Titanic element and allow the Dionysian an opportunity to assert itself. The final release of the divine essence within, the redemption of the soul, is the utmost goal of the Orphic process. This process may best be obtained by the soul reincarnating in a number of physical bodies in different life experiences.

While other schools of reincarnation see the process of rebirth as an evolving of the soul ever higher with each incarnation, the Orphic concept introduces the aspect of the soul being gradually purged or purified through the sufferings incurred during each physical rebirth. As the soul inhabits the body, it is really doing penance for previous incarnations, a process which gradually purifies the soul. Between lifetimes, when the soul descends to Hades, it can enjoy a brief period of freedom that can be pleasant or unpleasant. Then it must return to the cycle of births and deaths. How many lifespans must the soul endure before the process of purification is completed and its final release is obtained? Plato (c. 428–348 B.C.E.) envisioned three periods of a thousand years each as a possible answer.

According to Orphic teachings, the only way out of the "wheel of birth," the "great circle of necessity," was through an act of divine grace that could possibly be obtained by the supplicant becoming immersed in the writing, ritual acts, and teachings of Orpheus and receiving initiation into the mysteries of the cult. Although there are no available texts clearly setting forth the process of initiation, it likely included fasting, rites of purification, and the reciting of prayers and hymns. It also seems quite certain that the initiates would have enacted a play depicting the life, death, and resurrection of Dionysus Zagreus. In addition, records suggest that a horned bull was sacrificed and the initiates partook of a sacramental feast of its raw flesh as a holy act that brought them in closer union with the god. Once this had been accomplished, the initiates were given secret formulas which would enable them to avoid the snares awaiting the unwary soul as it descended to Hades and would ensure them a blissful stay while they awaited a sign that their participation in the "great circle of necessity" had ended.

❋ Delving Deeper

Ferm, Vergilius, ed. *Ancient Religions*. New York: Philosophical Library, 1950.

Gaster, Dr. Theodor H., ed. *The New Golden Bough*. New York: Criterion Books, 1959.

Dionysus, *the god of vegetation, whose cycle of birth, death, and rebirth reflects the cycle of growth, decay, and rebirth seen in nature.*

Pythagoras (c. 590–c.520 b.c.e.)

Pythagoras, one of the greatest philosophers and mathematicians of the sixth century B.C.E., is reported to have been the first of the Greeks to teach the doctrine that the soul, passing through the "great circle of necessity," was born at various times to various living bodies. Pythagoras believed in the soul as a "thought of God," and he considered the physical body to be simply one of a succession of "receptacles" for the housing of the soul. Many of his followers became vegetarians, for he taught that the soul might live again in animals.

Because of his importance to early Greek culture, Pythagoras is among those individuals given the status of becoming a myth in his own lifetime. Therefore, the philosopher was said to have been born of the virgin Parthenis and fathered by the god Apollo. Pythagoras's human father, Mnesarchus, a ring merchant from Samos, and his mother consulted the **Delphic Oracle** and were told that he would be born in Sidon in Phoenicia and that he would produce works and wonders that would benefit all humankind. Wishing to please the gods, Mnesarchus demanded that his wife change her name from Parthenis to Pythasis, in order to honor the seeress at Delphi. When it was time for the child to be born, Mnesarchus devised "Pythagoras" to be a name in which each of the specially arranged letters held an individual sacred meaning.

Pythagoras is said to have traveled the known world of his time, accumulating and absorbing wisdom and knowledge. According to the legends surrounding his life, he was taught by Zoroaster (c. 628–c. 551 B.C.E.), the Persian prophet, and by the Brahmans of India. Although his teachings on past lives formed the essence of so many of the mystery religions, he was initiated into the **Orphic,** Egyptian, Judaic, Chaldean, and many other mystery schools.

At last Pythagoras formed his own school at Crotona in southern Italy. An unyielding taskmaster, he accepted only those students whom he assessed as already having established personal regimens of self-discipline. To further stress the seriousness of his study program, Pythagoras lectured while standing behind a curtain, thereby denying all personal contact with his students until they had achieved progress on a ladder of initiatory degrees that allowed them to reach the higher grades. While separated from them by the curtain, Pythagoras lectured his students on the basic principles of music, mathematics, astronomy, and philosophy.

Pythagoras called his disciples mathematicians, for he believed that the higher teachings began with the study of numbers. From his perspective, he had fashioned a rational theology. The science of numbers lay in the living forces of divine faculties in action in the world, in universal macrocosm, and in the earthly microcosm of the human being. Numbers were transcendent entities, living virtues of the supreme "One," God, the source of universal harmony.

Devoted to his studies, his travels, and his school, Pythagoras did not marry until he was about 60. The young woman had been one of his disciples, and she bore him seven children. The legendary philosopher died while exercising authority over his strict standards of admittance to his school. He denied a man acceptance because it was apparent that the would-be student had an unruly temper that could easily become violent. The rejected follower fulfilled Pythagoras's negative evaluation by angrily leading a mob against the school and burning down the house where the teacher and 40 students were gathered. Some accounts state that Pythagoras died in the fire; others have it that he died of grief, sorrowing over how difficult a task it was to elevate humanity.

✢ DELVING DEEPER
Schure, Edouard. *The Great Initiates.* Trans. by Gloria Raspberry. New York: Harper and Row, 1961.

TRIBAL RELIGIONS

The legends of the dead told by ancient or tribal people are perhaps the most accurate indicators of their religious thought. And from what can be assumed from the burial rites of early humans, they pondered the same kinds of questions concerning the afterlife as humans do today. Where had their friends gone? What do they do and see when they disappear into the unknown? Will they live again? Can their spirits return to communicate? Or are they just gone—forever? Early humans could not answer these great questions, and so, to temper their fear of death, they created rituals, rites, and religions to comfort them.

Although the process of death and the reasons why the once animated body became lifeless were puzzles, aboriginal tribal societies understood that there was something in their departed friends and family members that survived somehow in another existence. The reason for this belief can be easily imagined. As they slept, early humans saw those persons whom they knew to be dead, alive and well in their dreams. Perhaps they themselves had witnessed their friends being killed in a dispute with another tribe or mangled by a predator, yet now they saw them and spoke with them, just as they had before their death. These vivid dreams of the dead undoubtedly led to the belief that there existed an immaterial aspect of human beings, a part that managed to survive the dissolution of the body.

Many Native American tribes believed that the physical body housed two or more souls, which became separated at death. The ancient Chinese affirmed three souls set free at death: one remained in the family house to serve as a kind of protector; another watched over the grave site as "guardian of the tomb"; and the third passed into the invisible realm. The aboriginal people of New Zealand, the Maori, believe that each of the eyes of the deceased is given a separate immortality: the spirit of the left eye ascends to heaven and is seen as a new dark star in the sky, and the spirit of the right takes flight to *Reinga*, a place beyond the sea.

The Fang people of Gabon envision seven types of souls:

1. a vital principle that resides in the brain until death, when it disappears;

2. the heart, the seat of the conscience, which inspires action during the life experience, but also disappears at the time of death;

3. the person's name, which achieves a kind of individuality after death;

4. the essence of the person, which perpetuates itself after death;

5. the active principle of the soul as long as the body lives;

6. the blending of shadow and soul;

7. the spiritual residue, which can appear to living humans as a ghost.

The aboriginal inhabitants of the Fiji Islands believe that a human has two souls: the "dark spirit" and the "light spirit." The Nootkas of British Columbia regarded the soul as a tiny facsimile of the person that lived in the crown of the head.

Early humans generally did not accept death as due to natural causes. Death was either the result of acts of violence caused by human or animal enemies, or it was caused by evil and unseen demons. To the primitive mind, if a man or a woman, without wound or injury, fell silently asleep and never awakened, they had to have been the victim of malevolent spirits.

Some of the earliest rituals revolving around death concerned the interaction between the living and the body of the newly dead. Some tribal cultures believed that an evil spirit inhabited the corpse, and it should not be touched for fear of providing the malevolent entity with a living body to possess. Some anthropologists have theorized that it was fear of the dead body that led early humans to dispose of it. Since evil spirits had caused the "long sleep," they must undoubtedly still be lurking near the body to seize new

victims. Therefore, the practical thing to do was to bury or burn or otherwise dispose of the body, thereby removing both the dead and the demons at the same time.

The Australian aborigines showed their fear of the dead by burning all the deceased's property and running away to establish a new village. They believed that the demon resided not only in the dead body, but in all the deceased's belongings. Early tribes in Greenland threw everything out of the house that had been owned by the dead person. At Batta funerals, the natives marched behind the body, brandishing swords to frighten away the death demons. The Galibis of Guiana dance on the newly covered grave to stamp down the spirits. The Winnebago tribe had a fear of evil spirits troubling the corpses of their deceased loved ones, so they swept the grass around the grave in a circle from six to 20 feet in diameter, a ritual that they believed prevented the evil spirits from approaching the departed's final earthly resting place.

The cosmology of certain eastern Native American tribes placed two powerful manitous, representatives of the Great Spirit, on duty in the Land of the Departed. One of the manitous, Chibiabos, like the Egyptian god Osiris and the Hindu judge of the dead, Yama, was master over the realm of the dead and escorted the newly arriving souls into their new environment. Sometimes there was a process of judgment involved, in which the worthy souls would be allowed to dwell in the Land of the Departed and the unworthy would be set adrift in space. The other manitou, Pauguk, protected the realm of the dead from unwelcome intruders with his bow and arrows.

Many Native American tribes believed that spirits of the dead lingered among the living until certain rites had been performed that would aid the spirits in their passage to the other world. Among the Ogallala Sioux, it was maintained that the spirit of the dead passed into the spirit world, by degrees, at the completion of necessary rituals that became the duty of the deceased person's family. Like fleeting shadows, the spirits of the dead slowly migrated to the **Land of the Grandparents,** gaining strength for their journey from the energy received from their living relatives, who performed a long and demanding rite known as the Shadow or Ghost Ceremony. The time needed to complete the ritual successfully could amount to as long as two years, during which period the immediate family and close relatives endured great privation to ensure the safe passage of the departed spirit.

These extensive rites were conducted in special Ghost Lodges, and it was here that the body of the deceased was kept prior to burial and where the ceremonies on the part of the deceased were held long after his or her interment. The Ogallala most often kept Ghost Lodges when the death was a particularly sad one, such as the passing of a child by accident or illness.

AMONG *most tribal cultures, it is customary to dance and feast at the time of death to please the spirit of the departed and to stamp upon the ground to frighten away evil spirits.*

Among the Ojibway people it is customary to cut the hair of a child who has died and make a little doll of it, which they call the "doll of sorrow." This doll takes the place of the deceased child, and the mother carries it with her everywhere for a year. They believe that during this period of time, the soul of the child is transferred through the hair from the dead body to the doll.

The ghost land or spirit land of tribal people is equivalent to the concept of a heaven or a paradise: It is a place free from worry, illness, war, and the fear of death. It seems a general belief among many different tribal cultures that the afterlife of the soul is concerned with the same kind of pursuits that the entity followed as a living person. The spirit land would feature good hunting and fishing, beautiful new lands to explore, and no warfare or tribal rivalries.

Because the deceased individuals would be continuing a life similar to their life on Earth,

they would need their valuables, their tools and weapons, and, of course, food and drink. Therefore, in nearly all tribal religions, it was customary to bury material things with the body. For the Papuans, Tahitians, Polynesians, Malanans, ancient Peruvians, Brazilians, and countless others, food and drink was left with the corpse. In Patagonia, it was the annual custom to open the burial chambers and reclothe the dead. Each year the Eskimo take clothes as a gift to the dead. Among the Kukis, the widow is compelled to remain for a year beside the tomb of her deceased husband, while other members of the family bring food daily for her and the spirit of the deceased. In the Mosquito tribe, the widow is obligated to supply the grave of her husband with provisions for a year.

It has been suggested that the religious aspects of funerals grew out of the belief that death was nothing more than a journey to another world and that the newly dead expect to have ceremonies performed for them to hasten their travels and to lessen the dangers of the journey. Among most tribal cultures, therefore, it is customary to dance and feast at the time of death for purposes of pleasing the spirit of the departed and to stamp upon the ground to frighten away evil spirits.

🔹 DELVING DEEPER

Steiger, Brad. *Medicine Power.* New York: Doubleday, 1974.

Sullivan, Lawrence E., ed. *Death, Afterlife, and the Soul.* New York: Macmillan, 1989.

BURIAL MOUNDS

Rising out of the earth in Ohio, Minnesota, Wisconsin, Iowa, and other states are the huge earthworks of the mysterious Mound Builders. The earthworks, also known as "effigy mounds" because of their bird and animal shapes, are scattered throughout the Midwest and were apparently raised by the same unknown people. Along with skeletal remains, the earthworks contain weapons, pottery, and numerous other artifacts, thus indicating that the Mound Builders believed that the dead buried in these earthworks were beginning a journey into the afterlife.

The burial mounds that depict animals quite likely represent the **totem animal** of the deceased buried within the earthwork. To the Native American tribes, the totems were sacred beings to which great importance was attributed. To have the mound shaped in such a design would ensure a positive afterlife destiny for the deceased. There are also ancient mounds shaped in a combination of animal and human forms, very likely indicating the name of a great chief, such as Standing Bear or Strong Eagle.

Excavation of certain mounds indicate that one or several bodies were buried at various levels, either on the floor, above it, or in a pit beneath it. In the effigy mounds shaped as birds or animals, the placement of the bodies was in the head or heart region. In the round mounds, the bodies were interred in the center; and in the linear earthworks, they were found along the central axis. The most common burial position was the flexed, with arms and legs over the chest.

Early settlers in the Ohio Valley in the 1700s were greatly impressed by the Great Serpent Mound on Brush Creek in Adams County, Ohio. The mound is approximately five feet high, and its length is 30 feet, diminishing in height toward the head and the tail of the "serpent." Near the open jaws of the serpent is another much smaller, oval mound. There are other such serpentine mounds near the Mississippi River at McGregor, Iowa; another structure in Licking County, Ohio, resembles an alligator.

At Prairie du Chien, Wisconsin, there is a circular mound enclosing a pentagram. The outer circle measures 1200 feet, and the pentagon is 200 feet on each side. The mound is 36 feet in diameter and 12 feet high. Its summit is composed of white pipe-clay, beneath which has been found a large quantity of mica. Four miles away, on the low lands of the Kickapoo River, is a mound with eight radiating points, very likely representing the sun. This mound is 60 feet in diameter at the base and three feet high, the points extending about nine feet. Surrounding this mound are five crescent-shaped mounds, arranged in a circle.

The size and number of the earthworks suggest that the construction of the burial mounds was a community project. Hundreds of tribespeople had to dig soil from nearby areas, then over a period of weeks or months carry innumerable baskets or buckets, and dump them on the growing mound. The work may have been directed by a **shaman,** for it appears from the presence of fire pits in some of the mounds that religious ceremonies were conducted and funeral rites were observed.

THE *construction of the burial mounds was a community project.*

In Pike County, Ohio, on the banks of the Scioto River, there is a mound consisting of a circle and square, constructed with great geometric accuracy. In Native American pictography, the ring or circle is generally an emblem of the sun, the stars, and the Great Spirit, the divine being. The oval also represents the Creator or the act of creation. The square designates the four cardinal directions. If it is assumed that the ancient Mound Builders had similar religious philosophies, then some insight may be gained into their beliefs about destiny and life after death.

One of the largest of the effigy mounds is a huge bird earthwork that is located on the Mendota Hospital grounds near Madison, Wisconsin. The bird is six feet high with a wingspread of 624 feet. A panther mound at Buffalo Lake in Marquette County, Wisconsin, is 575 feet in length, including its remarkably long tail. The largest of all earthworks yet discovered is Cahokia Mound (c. 1000) near St. Louis, Missouri, which is 998 feet long, 721 feet wide, and 99 feet high. Archaeologists have also discovered 45 mounds of smaller dimensions in the same area.

Who the Mound Builders were and why they stopped constructing their massive earthworks may never be known. There is nothing to point to their destruction by enemies or catastrophes. The most likely theory of their destiny is that their descendants were eventually absorbed into the Native American tribes that greeted the European explorers in the fifteenth and sixteenth centuries.

※ DELVING DEEPER

Emerson, Ellen Russell. *Indian Myths*. Minneapolis: Ross & Haines, 1965.

Steiger, Brad. *Worlds Before Our Own*. New York: G. P. Putnam, 1978.

LAND OF THE GRANDPARENTS

It was a general belief among most Native American tribes that the world of spirit, the Land of the Grandparents, was similar to the physical world in its tasks and pursuits, hence the common reference to the "happy hunting ground," a place where all needs would be easily met. In this respect, the ghost land, the Land of the Grandparents, is equivalent to the Elysian Fields of the ancient Greeks, the Valhalla of the Vikings, and the general concept of a heaven or a paradise that awaits the virtuous soul after death.

Some tribes believed that their eternal abode would be in the stars. To these people, the Milky Way was known as the Pathway of the Dead; and it was their custom to light fires upon the graves of the dead for four days to give the spirits ample time to arrive safely on the glorious path in the sky.

For other tribes, the Land of the Grandparents, the Place of the Souls, was located under the earth, where the sun would shine during the time of its disappearance from the topside world at night. Others believed the place of the departed spirits was far away in the south.

Medicine priests among the Algonquin people taught that two souls resided in the physical body. One of the souls kept the body animate and remained with it during sleep. The other, less attached to the material plane, moved about at will, free to travel to faraway places and even to the spirit world. It was for the soul that remained with the physical body that the tribespeople left food beside their dead.

The Dakota, among other tribes, believed that each person possessed four souls: One animated the body and required food; a second watched over the body, somewhat like a guardian spirit; a third hovered around the village; the fourth went to the Land of the Grandparents at the time of physical death.

In the Chippewa cosmology, the soul passed to another world immediately after death. Once in the dimension of the afterlife, the soul would arrive in a beautiful lake and be ferried across by a spirit ancestor in a stone canoe. In the middle of the lake was a magic island of good spirits, and the soul must remain in the stone canoe to await judgment for its conduct during life. If its good actions predominated, the soul would be permitted to reside on the island of good spirits. If the soul in its physical incarnation had spent a life seeking only carnal and material satisfactions, the stone canoe would sink at once and leave only the soul's head above the water. This imagery is reminiscent of the Greek belief that after death the soul must have ready its fee for Charon, ferryman of the Styx, to transport it to the afterlife.

Among many of the eastern tribes, there was a tendency to believe that the spirit stayed near the body for a time before it went to the paradise of the happy hunting grounds. The Iroquois left small holes in the grave so that the spirit could go in and out as it pleased until it left for the Land of the Grandparents. The tribes of the Ohio followed a similar custom of boring holes in the burial casket to allow the spirit to leave at a time of its own choosing.

For the Native American tribes, the color black was the symbol of death, evil, and mourning, as it seems to be so often throughout the world. In Native American tribal art or sign-writing, a black circle signified the departure of the soul, whose travel to the Land of the Grandparents occurred at night, after the sun had gone down.

The human soul was represented among some tribes as a dark and somber image, complete with feet, hands, and head. Because the soul still existed in human shape, it, like the *ka* of the ancient Egyptians, still needed to be provided with nourishment. Some tribal members burned the best part of their food as an offering to the souls of the departed.

※ DELVING DEEPER

Emerson, Ellen Russell. *Indian Myths*. Minneapolis: Ross & Haines, 1965.

Gill, Sam D., and Irene F. Sullivan. *Dictionary of Native American Mythology.* New York: Oxford University Press, 1992.

Pope John Paul II places a signed note into a crack in the Western Wall in Israel. (AP/WIDE WORLD PHOTOS)

HOW THE MAJOR RELIGIONS VIEW REINCARNATION

Reincarnation, the belief that the soul of a man or woman who has died will later be born again into another physical body, is an ancient doctrine, ancient even at the time of the Greek and Roman empires. Plato (c. 428–348 B.C.E.) alludes to reincarnation in many of his essays, and he seems to be speaking of the law of karma, the spiritual balance of cause and effect, in Book X of *Laws* when he says: "Know that if you become worse, you will go to the worst souls, or if better, to the better; and in every succession of life and death you will do and suffer what life may fitly suffer at the hands of life."

Cicero's (106–43 B.C.E.) *Treatise on Glory* concedes that "the counsels of the Divine Mind had some glimpse of truth when they said that men are born in order to suffer the penalty for some sins committed in a former life." Plotinus (205–270 C.E.), in the *Second Ennead,* writes that reincarnation is "a dogma recognized throughout antiquity…the soul expiates its sins in the darkness of the infernal regions and…afterwards…passes into new bodies, there to undergo new trials."

Reincarnation is not an approved doctrine in any of the orthodox Christian, Islamic, or Judaic religions, which all hold fast to the belief that there is but one lifetime, one Day of Judgment, and a heavenly resurrection of the body for the righteous. Reincarnation, the great Wheel of Return set in motion by one's karma, is accepted as a reality in the Hindu and Buddhist religions, as well as certain mystical sects in Judaism and Islam.

In the early days of Christianity, however, even the Church's greatest leaders, such as St. Clement of Alexandria (150–215 C.E.) in his *Exhortations to the Pagans,* stated their beliefs in the soul's preexistence: "We were in being long before the foundation of the world. We existed in the eye of God, for it is our destiny to live in Him. We are the reasonable creatures of the Divine Word; therefore, we have existed from the beginning, for in the beginning was the Word.… Not for the first time does He show pity on us in our wanderings; He pitied us from the very beginning."

The Christian philosopher St. Augustine (354–430 C.E.) asked the eternal question in his *Confessions:* "Say, Lord…did my infancy succeed another age of mine that died before it? Was it that which I spent within my mother's womb?…and what before that life again, O God…was I anywhere or in any body?"

REINCARNATION *is not an approved doctrine in any of the orthodox Christian, Islamic, or Judaic religions.*

Even though the majority of Eastern cultures maintain a belief in reincarnation as an integral element in their religious faiths, people—young children, in particular—are not encouraged to "remember" past lives. Regardless of such admonitions against pursuing the

The Chinese Taoists believe that after death, the soul crosses a bridge to the next life where it undergoes a process of judgment. Once on the other side of the bridge, judges in ten courts decide whether the deceased person has lived a good or bad life. If the person has lived a good life, the soul is allowed to pass through the courts and go to heaven. If the person was judged to have been bad, a punishment is ordered before the soul can go any further.

Following the burial of the coffin, paper models of houses, cars, and money are burned to assist the soul in the afterlife. It is believed that these items will help the deceased "pay his or her way" through the courts of judgment. The son of the deceased burns the most important and "influential" paper models.

Ten years after the burial, the coffin is then dug up. The remains, or the bones of the deceased are taken to be cleaned and then placed in a pot which is then sealed by a priest. The priest finds the "right place" to bury the pot in a special ceremony called

CHINESE TAOIST JOURNEY TO THE NEXT LIFE

feng-shui. They believed it important to bury the bones in a place where the dead person will be happy, or else his or her ghost might return to punish the family. Annually, the Chinese festival, *Ching-Ming,* is held to pay tribute to and honor the deceased.

SOURCES:

Mayled, John. *Death Customs.* Morristown, N.J.: Silver Burdett Press: 1987.

knowledge of karma acquired from prior life experiences, the holy books of Eastern faiths teach reincarnation with none of the reluctance of the West.

The chief theological work of the Hindus, the Upanishads, expresses the doctrine of rebirth in the poetic imagery of a goldsmith who takes a raw piece of gold and shapes it into another more beautiful form. "So verily, the Self, having cast off this body and having put away ignorance, makes another new and more beautiful form."

The Anguttara Nikaya, a Buddhist text, observes that "the wise priest knows he now must reap the fruits of deeds of former births. For be they many or but few, deeds done in covetousness or hate, or through infatuation's power, [he] must bear their needful consequence."

Although the Qur'an, the holy book received by the prophet Muhammed, doesn't really address the concept of past lives and rebirth, Sufism, a mystical sect of Islam, accepts transmigration of souls as a reality. In the words of the Sufi teacher Sharf-U'D Din-Maneri: "O Brother, know for certain that this work has been before thee and me in byone ages....No one has begun this work for the first time."

Orthodox Judaism also rejects reincarnation as doctrine, but the Hasidic sect and those who follow the teachings of the Kabbalah, a collection of mystical texts first published in 1280, accept the belief in the transmigration of souls as a firm and infallible doctrine. Rabbi Manasseh ben Israel (1604–1657), the revered theologian and English statesman, said that reincarnation was a fundamental point of their religion: "We are therefore duty bound to obey and accept this dogma with acclamation…as the truth of it has been incontestably demonstrated by the Zohar, and all the books of the Kabbalists."

In *Religion and Immortality*, G. Lowes Dickinson presents his view that reincarnation offers "…a really consoling idea that our present capacities are determined by our previous actions and that our present actions again will determine our future character." Such a philosophy, Dickinson observes, liberates people from the bonds of an external fate and places them in charge of their destiny: "If we have formed here a beautiful relationship, it will not perish at death, but be perpetuated, albeit unconsciously, in some future life. If we have developed a faculty here, it will not be destroyed, but will be the starting point of later developments. Again, if we suffer…from imperfections and misfortunes, it would be consoling to believe that these were punishments of our own acts in the past, not mere effects of the acts of other people, or of an indifferent nature over which we have no control."

✤ DELVING DEEPER

Goring, Rosemary, ed. *Larousse Dictionary of Beliefs and Religions*. New York: Larousse, 1994.

Head, Joseph, and S. L. Cranston. *Reincarnation: An East-West Anthology* . Wheaton, Ill.: Quest Books, 1968.

May, Robert M. *Physicians of the Soul: The Psychologies of the World's Great Spiritual Teachers*. Warwick, N.Y.: Amity House, 1988.

Smith, Huston. *The World's Religions*. New York: Harper San Francisco, 1991.

Sullivan, Lawrence E., ed. *Death, Afterlife, and the Soul*. New York: Macmillan, 1989.

Zaehner, R. C. *Encyclopedia of the World's Religions*. New York: Barnes & Noble, 1997.

BUDDHISM

The Buddha (563–483 B.C.E.) believed in the karmic laws that gripped and held those who did not understand the true nature of life and death. But because the universe and reality are always in a state of flux, forever changing and reshaping themselves, there can be no single, unique soul of any individual that is caught up in the cycle of death and rebirth. The various components that make up a human being are in a perpetual process of change but always

held by the laws of karma, which determine the nature of a person's rebirth.

THE *Buddha believes the laws of karma determines the nature of a person's rebirth.*

There are many schools of Buddhism, and certain scholars point out that the so-called "Northern Buddhism" of Tibet, China, and Japan, emphasizes the doctrine of a permanent identity which serves to unite all the incarnations of a single individual. Such an emphasis is closer to the Hindu interpretation of a continuity of a soul linked to its karma than the strict Buddhist teaching that only psychic residues remain of an individual's traits of personality and character. As might be expected, Northern Buddhism claims to have preserved the true teaching given by the Buddha to his initiated disciples. Since karma is one of the key teachings of the Buddha, they insist that the concept becomes virtually meaningless unless it is applied to the idea of a single reincarnating ego. The teachers of Northern Buddhism also recall that according to tradition, the Buddha's dying words were: "All compounds are perishable. Spirit is the sole, elementary, and primordial unity, and each of its rays is immortal, infinite, and indestructible. Beware of the illusions of matter."

CHRISTIANITY

Although many of the great minds who have shaped the intellectual and religious climate of the West held firm beliefs in reincarnation, historically, at least since the fourth century, Christian theologians have spoken out against the doctrine of rebirth. Reincarnation is not taught in any of the mainstream Christian churches, and most denominations condemn the concept.

Origen (185–254 C.E.) devoted his life to the preservation of the original gospels and is considered by many scholars to have been the most prominent of all the church fathers, with the possible exception of Augustine (354–430

C.E.). A prolific Christian writer and leader, Origen preached a relationship between faith and knowledge and explained the sinfulness of all men and women by the doctrine of the pre-existence of all souls. In *Contra Celsum* he asked, "Is it not rational that souls should be introduced into bodies in accordance with their merits and previous deeds, and that those who have used their bodies in doing the utmost possible good should have a right to bodies endowed with qualities superior to the bodies of others?" In response to the query, Origen continues: "The soul, which is immaterial and invisible in its nature, exists in no material place without having a body suited to the nature of that place; accordingly, it at one time puts off one body, which is necessary before, but which is no longer adequate in its changed state, and it exchanges it for a second."

In the *Des Principiis*, Origen states that every soul comes into this world strengthened by the victories or weakened by the defeats of its previous life. The soul's place in this world in terms of dwelling within a physical body of honor or dishonor is determined by its previous merits or demerits. Its work in this world determines its place in the world to follow.

At the Council of Nicaea in 325, Origenism was excluded from the doctrines of the Christian Church and 15 anathemas were proposed against Origen himself. The Origenists, those who favored including the ethics of karma and the doctrine of preexistence in the official Church teachings, had lost by only one vote. But, as stated by Head and Cranston in *Reincarnation: An East-West Anthology* (1968), "Catholic scholars are beginning to claim that the Roman church never took any part in the anathemas against Origen....However, one disastrous result of the mistake still persists, namely, the exclusion from the Christian creed of the teaching

I n England, until the fourteenth century, the Christian Bible was considered the preserve of the priestly classes. *The Vulgate* was a Latin translation by Saint Jerome, read and interpreted only by the clergy, as the Church deliberately discouraged common people from reading vernacular bibles. They believed those outside the Church would misinterpret the text in the Bible, which would then lead to heresy. In fact, it was a crime to possess a vernacular bible.

In the centuries that followed, however, the efforts of men who challenged the Church, and the invention of the printing press, made the Bible available in plain English, to ordinary men and women.

In his *New York Times* article "Where Is it Written? Right Here," Simon Winchester discusses the men who sought to put the Bible in commoners' hands. Among them is William Tyndale, who was strangled and burned at the stake for "such a heretical presumption." Winchester also comments on two interesting books, which go into detail about how the Bible revolutionized England: *Wide as the Waters: The Story of the English Bible and the Revolution It Inspired,* by Benson Bobrick, and *In the Beginning: The Story of the King James Bible and How It Changed a Nation, a Language and a Culture,* by Alister McGrath.

Winchester states that the more important points in these books are about the realizations that came from the brave actions taken to make the Bible available to all, and how the popularization of the Bible led to the establishment of the individual's inviolable rights and the formation of equal government, for and of the people. "In other words, the essentials of popular democracy were inspired by writings first set down on papyrus and in manuscript two millenniums ago in Hebrew, Aramaic, and Greek—words since translated and then printed for the benefit of all, by the courageous and long-suffering heroes," Winchester said.

THE CHRISTIAN BIBLE

SOURCES:

Bobrick, Benson. *Wide as the Waters: The Story of the English Bible and the Revolution It Inspired.* New York: Simon & Schuster, 2001.

McGrath, Alister. *In the Beginning: The Story of the King James Bible and How it Changed a Nation, a Language and a Culture.* New York: Doubleday, 2001.

Winchester, Simon. "Where Is It Written? Right Here." *New York Times,* http://www.nytimes.com/books/01/04/08/reviews 010408.winchet.html. 8 April 2001.

of the preexistence of the soul, and, by implication, reincarnation."

REINCARNATION *is not taught in any of the mainstream Christian churches, and most denominations condemn the concept.*

While the official position of the Christian churches still holds with those anathemas against reincarnation, a more liberal attitude exists among many Christian laypeople, who, in modern times, need not fear being branded as heretics and threatened with burning at the stake. A 2001 Gallup poll of public opinion indicate that nearly 25 percent of the people in the United States, including Christians, believe that they may have past-life memories of their own. Those Christians who accept at least the possibility of reincarnation insist that there are many passages in the New Testament that imply a belief on the part of Jesus (c. 6 B.C.E.–30 C.E.) and his disciples in the reality of past lives.

In his *Lux Orientalis* (c. 1670), Joseph Glanvil states that the preexistence of humankind was a philosophy commonly held by the Jews; and he maintains that such a theological position is illustrated by the disciples' ready questioning of Jesus when they asked (John 9:1–4): "Master, was it for this man's sin or his father's that he was born blind?" If the disciples had not believed that the blind man had lived another life in which he might have sinned, Glanvil argues, the question would have been senseless and impertinent.

When Jesus asked his disciples who the crowds said he was, they answered that some said John the Baptist, others Elijah, others Jeremiah or one of the prophets (Matthew 16:13–14). Again, Glanvil reasons that such a response on the part of the disciples demonstrates their belief in preexistence.

At another time, Jesus' disciples asked him why the scribes had said that Elijah must come first before the Messiah, to which Jesus answered (Matthew 17:10–13), "Elijah truly shall first come and restore all things. But I say unto you that Elijah has already come, and they knew him not!" The disciples then understood that Jesus was referring to John the Baptist.

Information gained from the Dead Sea Scrolls, which were discovered near Qumran in 1947 and are slowly being translated and released to the public, may have a great effect on both the Jewish and Christian religions. These scrolls refer often to a great Teacher of Righteousness and a great warfare between the Sons of Light and the Sons of Darkness. The Qumran sect, known as the Essenes, forms a definite link between Judaism and Christianity, and many scholars have suggested that Jesus was a member of the group. The Nag-Hammadi scrolls, discovered in Egypt in 1945, also give a strong indication that Jesus may have been an Essene, a student of the Essenes, or at least closely associated with this apocalyptic sect during the so-called "silent years of Jesus," ages 12 to 30. It is generally believed that the Essenes incorporated certain aspects of reincarnation in their teachings. Certain scholars have also speculated that Jesus may have studied various mystical traditions in Egypt, India, and Tibet, all of which would have introduced him to the teachings of reincarnation.

✦ DELVING DEEPER

Eerdman's Handbook to the World's Religions. Grand Rapids, Mich.: William B. Eerdman's Publishing, 1994.

Fox, Robin Lane. *Pagans and Christians*. New York: Alfred A. Knopf, 1989.

Head, Joseph, and S. L. Cranston. *Reincarnation: An East-West Anthology*. Wheaton, Ill.: Quest Books, 1968.

McDannell, Colleen, and Bernard Lang. *Heaven: A History*. New York: Vintage Books, 1990.

HINDUISM

The Bhagavad-Gita, the holy text of the Hindus, observes that "…as the dweller in the body experiences childhood, youth, old age, so passes he on to another body." In 2:19–25, the holy book declares that a man who regards himself as a slayer, or another who thinks he is the slain, are both ignorant:

You are never born; you will never die. You have never changed; you can never change. Unborn, eternal, immutable, immemorial, you do not die when the body dies. Realizing that which is indestructible, eternal, unborn, and unchanging, how can you slay or cause another to be slain? As a man abandons his worn-out clothes and acquires new ones, so when the body is worn out a new one is acquired by the Self, who lives within. The Self cannot be pierced with weapons or burned with fire; water cannot wet it, nor can the wind dry it. The Self cannot be pierced or burned, made wet or dry. It is everlasting and infinite, standing on the motionless foundation of eternity. The Self is unmanifested, beyond all thought, beyond all change. Knowing this, you should not grieve.

Paramahansa Yogananda (1893–1952), the founder of the Self-Realization Fellowship, which seeks to blend Hindu and Christian concepts, once presented three truths to be employed by those who wished to rise above karma. The first truth, the Yogi said, is that when the mind is strong and the heart is pure, we are free. "It is the mind that connects you with pain in the body," he said. "When you think pure thoughts and are mentally strong, you can endure the painful effects of evil karma." The second truth is that in subconscious sleep, we are free. Truth number three, he revealed, is when we are in ecstasy, identified with God, we have no karma. "This is why the saints say, 'Pray unceasingly.' When you continuously pray and meditate, you go into the land of superconsciousness, where no troubles can reach you."

Krishna, one of the main gods in Hinduism, represented in a thirteenth-century relief. (CORBIS CORPORATION)

Understanding Hinduism. http://www.hinduism.co.za. 28 September 2001.

ISLAM

The Qur'an (or Koran), the holy book of Islam, has no direct reference to reincarnation, and there are only a few passages that may suggest a concept of rebirth, such as the following: "God generates beings and sends them back over and over again, 'til they return to Him." Orthodox Islamic scholars generally frown upon the concept of transmigration.

THE *Qur'an, the holy book of Islam, has no direct reference to reincarnation.*

However, the Islamic mystical sect of Persia, the Sufis, carries on the ancient teachings of rebirth as espoused by Moorish and Saracenic philosophers in the schools of Baghdad and Cordova. The Sufis claim to keep alive the Islamic esoteric philosophies and

❊ DELVING DEEPER

Brunton, Paul. *A Search in Secret India.* New York: Samuel Weiser, 1972.

Crim, Keith, ed. *The Perennial Dictionary of World Religions.* San Francisco: Harper Collins, 1989.

Head, Joseph, and S. L. Cranston. *Reincarnation: An East-West Anthology.* Wheaton, Ill.: Quest Books, 1968.

Hinduism Today. http://www.hinduism-today.com. 28 September 2001.

maintain that reincarnation is an important doctrine. The Sufi poet Jalalu 'D-Din Rumi (1207–1273) wrote these lines that are often quoted as containing the essence of transmigration: "I died as mineral and became a plant; I died as plant and rose to animal; I died as animal and I was Man.…Yet once more I shall die as Man, to soar with angels blest; but even from angelhood I must pass on.…"

JUDAISM

The Hebrew term for the passage of a soul after death into another physical form—human, animal, or inanimate—is *gilgul neshamot*. Although reincarnation as a doctrine is generally renounced by Jewish theologians and philosophers, the Karaites, a Jewish sect which rejected Rabbinism and Talmudism, taught transmigration of the soul. Anan ben David, who founded the Karaites in Baghdad about 765, said that all human souls have a common origin in the primordial human, Adam Kadmon, whose spiritual essence sends forth sparks which form individual souls. When the later Adam of Genesis committed sin in the Garden of Eden, his fall brought about confusion among higher and lower souls throughout creation, which resulted in the need for every soul to pass through a series of incarnations. Although Anan ben David's teachings were severely criticized as contrary to Orthodox belief, *gilgul* became a part of the Kabbalah, the compilation of mystical works collected in thirteenth-century Spain. Transmigration of souls is also a universal belief in Hasidism.

TRANSMIGRATION *of souls is a universal belief in Hasidism.*

According to Alan Unterman in his *Dictionary of Jewish Lore and Legend* (1994): "Transmigration gave a new meaning to many aspects of life.…The deaths of young children were less tragic, since they were being punished for previous sins and would be reborn in a new life.…Proselytes to Judaism were Jewish souls which had been incarnated in Gentile bodies. [Transmigration] also allowed for the gradual perfection of the individual souls through different lives."

The Zohar (Hebrew for "Splendor"), the main work of the Kabbalah, describes the esoteric reality that lies behind everyday experience, and insists that the real meaning of the Torah lies in its mystical secrets. Although tradition declares Rabbi Simeon ben Jochai (c. 80 C.E.) as its author, later scholarship acknowledges the contribution of Rabbi Moses De Leon (1240–1305) and other Hebrew scholars in the thirteenth century. The Zohar states that since the human soul is rooted in the divine, the redemption of the world will be achieved when each individual has undergone the process of the transmigration of souls and completes his or her task of unification. Because humans cannot know the Most High's plans for each individual, they cannot know how they are being judged at all times, both before and after coming into the world and when they leave it. Because the goal of all human souls is to reenter the absolute from which they originally emerged, it is necessary for them to develop the level of perfection that will find them worthy of reunion with God. Since it is unlikely that such perfection can be achieved in one lifetime, the souls must continue their spiritual growth from lifetime to lifetime until they are fit to return to the divine.

Although the study of the Kabbalah undergoes cycles of popularity and esteem, reincarnation is not generally taught today in the three main branches of Judaism—Reform, Conservative, and Orthodox—but is accepted by those in the Hasidic sect. Rabbi Yonassan Gershom, a neo-Hasidic rabbi, has said that although Jews are generally reluctant to speak of their personal spiritual experiences in public, it doesn't mean that some of them aren't having memories of past lives.

"There are many teachings about reincarnation in Jewish mysticism," Gershom said. "The Hebrew word *gilgul* comes from the same root as the Hebrew word for 'circle' or 'cycle.' So the essence of its meaning is similar to the ideal of the Wheel of Karma."

✦ Delving Deeper

Crim, Keith, ed. *The Perennial Dictionary of World Religions*. San Francisco: Harper Collins, 1989.

Eerdmans' Handbook to the World's Religions. Grand Rapids, Mich.: Wm. B. Eerdmans Publishing Co., 1994.

Head, Joseph, and S. L. Cranston, S.L., eds. *Reincarnation: An East-West Anthology*. Wheaton, Ill.: Theosophical Publishing House, 1968.

Larousse Dictionary of Beliefs and Religions. New York: Larousse, 1994.

Unterman, Alan. *Dictionary of Jewish Lore and Legend*. London: Thames and Hudson, 1991.

Contemporary Mystery Schools and Reincarnation

Since the earliest days of organized religious expression there have always been those who preferred seeking the individual mystical experience as their personal doorway to other dimensions of reality and the world beyond death. These mystics found the doctrines and dogmas of structured religion to be too inhibiting, too restrictive, and not at all conducive to the kind of personal relationship with the holy which they so desperately sought. Regardless of the religion or the culture from which they sprang, all mystics have as their goal the transcendence of the earthly self and union with the Absolute.

While the ancient mystery schools were built upon the worship of a particular god or goddess, the contemporary mystery schools have been built around the charisma and the spiritual teachings of a psychic sensitive, a **medium,** or a prophet. Since the latter part of the nineteenth century, in Europe, Great Britain, Canada, and the United States, the men and women who are most often attracted to the modern mystery schools are those who have grown dissatisfied with the teachings of Christianity and what they consider to be its restrictive religious doctrines concerning the afterlife and rebirth. Each of the contemporary mystery schools examined in this section—Anthroposophy, the Association for Research and Enlightenment, and Theoso-

phy—accept the concept of reincarnation and blend many of the beliefs of Christianity and Judaism with traditional teachings of Hinduism and Buddhism.

In his classic work, *The Varieties of Religious Experience,* **William James** (1842–1910) has this to say regarding the oneness and unity of the mystical traditions: "This overcoming of all the usual barriers between the individual and the Absolute is the great mystic achievement. In mystic states we both become one with the Absolute and we become aware of our oneness. This is the everlasting and triumphant mystical tradition, hardly altered by differences of climate or creed. In Hinduism, in Neoplatonism, in Sufism, in Christian mysticism…we find the same recurring note, so that there is about mystical utterances an eternal unanimity…perpetually telling of the unity of man with God."

CONTEMPORARY *mystery schools have been built around teachings of a psychic sensitive, a medium, or a prophet.*

Many scholars of the early Christian church believed strongly that the various church councils had erred in removing reincarnation from official doctrine. The **Gnostics,** who strongly influenced early Christian doctrine, believed in reincarnation, and when the teachings of Origen (185 C.E.–254 C.E.), who championed preexistence, was anathematized in 553, they, along with other believers in reincarnation, were condemned as heretics. In later centuries, those who held Gnostic views were forced to remain silent regarding their beliefs in reincarnation, so they very often formed their own sects and schools of thought, such as the **Cathars,** the **Knights Templar,** the **Rosicrucians,** and the Albigenses.

Because many serious-minded Christians believe that there is evidence in the gospels that Jesus (c. 6 B.C.E.–30 C.E.) himself believed in reincarnation, they are comfortable with

Hindu and Buddhist concepts of past lives and karma and see no conflict with their traditional belief in Christianity. Dr. Gladys McGarey is a member of the Association for Research and Enlightenment, the contemporary mystery school based on the medical and past-life readings of **Edgar Cayce** (1877–1945). The daughter of Christian missionaries and a medical doctor who employs the concepts of past lives in her practice, McGarey has expressed her belief that Jesus came to offer humankind the law of grace to supersede the law of karma.

"I believe sincerely that when Jesus said that he came to fulfill the law and not destroy it, he was referring to the law of karma, the law of cause and effect, which is superseded by the law of grace," she said. "If we are functioning under the law of karma, it is as if we are walking away from the Sun and walking into our own shadow—which means we are walking into darkness. But if we turn around and walk toward the Sun, then we are walking toward the Light, and that is great. To me, the light of the Sun—whether you spell it *son* or *sun* is a symbol of moving in the law of grace. The law of grace does not take away the karmic pattern, it just makes it so I don't have to hurt myself as I move through the karma that I have created."

In A *Psychological and Poetic Approach to the Study of Christ in the Fourth Gospel* (1923), Eva Gore-Booth explains the role of Jesus the Christ from the perspective of a reincarnationist and states that he is the way-shower in God's Great Plan, the intercessor who offers humankind release from the cycle of rebirth, the "circle of wanderings." In this view, Jesus became the anointed one who achieved Christ consciousness and thereby was allowed to offer eternal life to all people, a "deliverance from reincarnation, from the life and death circle of this earthly living."

In the latter part of the nineteenth century, Charles Fillmore (1854–1948) and his wife founded what eventually became known as Unity School of Christianity. Fillmore once observed that a large part of the Western world looked upon reincarnation as a heathen doctrine and that many people closed the doors of their mind without waiting to find

out what message it may have for them, interpreted in the Light of Truth. According to Fillmore's view, Christ released humanity from the bondage of karmic law, thereby allowing each individual to make the most of each incarnation.

Edgar Cayce (1877–1945), the famous "sleeping prophet" of Virginia Beach, was a solid Baptist and a Sunday school teacher, but while in a trance, he gave past-life readings to thousands of men and women. Cayce believed that each soul enters the material plane not by chance, but through grace and the mercy of a loving Father-God. As to whether the soul is developed or retarded during these various incarnations is left to the free will of the individuals as they live through the errors incumbent in the life process or rise above them in their journey toward Oneness.

Rudolf Steiner (1861–1925) was the head of the German Theosophical Society until 1912, when he broke away to form his Anthroposophical Society. Steiner's objections with the Theosophists were mainly that they didn't revere Jesus and Christianity as special. However, he had no problem incorporating reincarnation and karma into his beliefs.

Helena Petrovna Blavatsky (1831–1891), the founder of Theosophy in collaboration with Henry Steele Olcott (1832–1907), had no problem with Christianity, but she preferred focusing on its esoteric traditions, which united it with all other religions. She popularized the study of reincarnation and past lives in Europe and the United States and introduced many occult and metaphysical concepts which flourished in the New Age Movement of the 1970s.

The contemporary mystery schools accept the doctrine of reincarnation as completely as did the ancient mystery religions. And just as the ancient mysteries departed from the state religions to form secret groups that required special initiations to ensure oneness with the gods, so have the contemporary mysteries departed from the organized religions of their cultures to form groups that require special memberships to establish a mystical union with the Absolute.

Akashic Records

Some metaphysicians believe that they have the ability to perceive and to read the Akashic Records, eternal accountings of individual human life patterns which have been somehow impressed on the celestial ether or astral light that fills all of space. These records are said to detail each lifetime and are perpetuated like vast computer-like memory banks in the collective unconscious. Certain psychic sensitives claim to enter altered states of consciousness, such as **trance** or meditation, and thereby achieve the ability to read the past lives of individuals who seek such knowledge. When these seers return to the mundane world, they may recount these memories in such a way as to aid men and women to avoid certain errors in their present life experience which were committed in earlier lifetimes.

According to many readers of the Akashic Records, they possess an accounting of the divine laws of debt (karma) and duty (dharma). It is as the Christian gospels declare; they say, "whatsoever a man soweth, that shall he also reap." So do the psychic forces that emanate from an individual also come full circle and return to that person.

Most readers of the Akashic Records will present their clients with the events of certain past lives that are affecting them today in their present lives. It depends on the judgment of the Akashic readers to give whatever lives and whatever events they think may be causing the present problems and to offer suggestions on how to resolve them.

Paul Twitchell (d. 1971) the modern exponent of **Eckankar,** once explained that to read the Akashic Records, he had to project himself via his soul body so that he might rise above the time track and study the lives of whomever had requested a reading. Twitchell said that it didn't make any difference where his subjects might be, Australia or the Arctic Circle: "Once I rise above the time track in my soul body, I can read the lives of anyone. I must look at the lives of my clients, spread out like a fan of hundreds of playing cards. And I must look at the millions of little file cards, which are memories of past lives, in order to select what I believe to be most important to my

clients and the problems that they are facing today. Next, it is up to me to make suggestions about how they might go about dissolving the karmic debts that they have accumulated."

ACCORDING to readers of the Akashic Records, they possess an accounting of the divine laws of debt (karma) and duty (dharma).

❈ Delving Deeper

Gaynor, Frank, ed. *Dictionary of Mysticism*. New York: Philosophical Library, 1953.

Steiger, Brad. *Returning from the Light*. New York: Signet Inspiration, 1996.

Anthroposophy

When he was in his late 30s, **Rudolf Steiner** (1861–1925), the founder of Anthroposophy, received a revelation of what he believed was the turning point in human spiritual history, the incarnation of the divine being known as the Christ. In the twentieth century, Steiner said, humankind began to enter the "fullness of time" when the Christ principle, cosmic consciousness, might once again become manifest. Steiner defined "Christ consciousness" as a transformative energy that greatly transcended orthodox Christianity. In Steiner's view, the Master Jesus became "christed" and thereby was able to present humankind with a dramatic example of what it means to achieve a complete activation of the spiritual seed within all human souls and to rise above all material considerations.

Steiner was born in Krajevic, Austria-Hungary (now Serbia-Montenegro), on February 27, 1861. Although he had experienced encounters with the mystical and the unknown as a young child and was introduced to the occult by an adept he would only refer to as the "Master," Steiner's early academic accomplishments were in the scientific fields. His father wanted him to become a railway engineer, so that had led Steiner into a study of mathematics, which seemed only to whet his appetite for

the material sciences, leading him to pursue studies in medicine, chemistry, and physics, as well as agriculture, architecture, art, drama, literature, and philosophy. Fascinated by the works of Johann Wolfgang von Goethe (1749–1832), Steiner began the extensive task of editing Goethe's scientific papers, and from 1889 to 1896 worked on this project. It was also during this period that Steiner wrote his own highly acclaimed *The Philosophy of Freedom.*

RUDOLF *Steiner defined "Christ consciousness" as a transformative energy that transcended orthodox Christianity.*

Steiner grew increasingly interested in the occult and mystical doctrines, and he later claimed to be endowed with the ability to read the **Akashic Records,** from which he had been able to envision the true history of human evolution. According to his interpretation of humankind's prehistory, many present-day men and women were descended from the people of the lost continent of **Atlantis,** who had been guided to achieve illumination by a higher order of beings. Eventually, the smartest,

strongest, and most intellectually flexible of the Atlanteans evolved into demigods, semidivine beings, who were able to relay instructions from higher intelligences. Consequently, within the contemporary mass of evolving humans are individuals who are descendants of those divine human-hybrid beings, men and women who are animated by higher ideals and who regard themselves as children of a universal power. Steiner perceived these individuals as members of the emerging "Sixth Post-Atlantean Race," who, imbued with divine universal power, would be able to initiate the more advanced members of the larger mass of humankind. The catalyst for this acceleration of humanity, in Steiner's vision, was the Christ energy, which the rest of the species must begin to imitate.

At the turn of the twentieth century, Steiner found that his lectures were well-received by those in the audience who were members of the **Theosophical Society,** so he began to make himself more familiar with their philosophy. In 1902, he became the general secretary of the German Section of the society, but he began to feel uncomfortable with what he perceived to be their lack of enthusiasm about the place of Jesus and Christ consciousness in the overall scheme of spiritual evolution. Although he accepted most of their teachings on reincarnation and highly approved of meditation, he came to believe that **Helena Petrovna Blavatsky** (1831–1891) and other high-ranking Theosophists were distorting many of the Eastern doctrines that they claimed to espouse.

In 1913, Steiner made a formal break with the Theosophical Society and set about forming his own group, which he declared would be about the utilization of "human wisdom" (anthro ' man; sophy ' wisdom) to achieve contact with the spiritual world. The human intellect, Steiner insisted, could be trained to rise above material concerns and to perceive a greater spiritual reality. The human consciousness had the ability to activate the seed that the great Spirit Beings had implanted within their human offspring.

Steiner recognized that while the physical seeds of male and female intermingled to produce the whole human being, there was also something in each human that did not arise from the blending of two physical seeds. Something ineffable and indescribable somehow flowed into the process of germination of the seed of the Spirit Beings within, something that could be accessed by human consciousness and directed by the Christ principle.

Steiner emphasized that the path to such contact might best be attained by a proper application of meditation. When human consciousness had been raised to the spiritual level, where it can experience the eternal element that is limited by neither birth nor death, then it can comprehend its own eternality and its ability to be born again in subsequent life existences. Steiner taught that the process of spiritual evolution enabled those who died in one period of history to be reborn in other epochs to experience various levels of Earth-existence.

In *Lecture V, Earthly and Cosmic Man* (1948) Steiner stated that in rejecting the doctrine of reincarnation, Christian thought had lost something vital that the East had always possessed, and he urged that such knowledge be reacquired. Western religion and culture is in the process of passing through a period during which individuals were "split up" into separate personalities, Steiner said, but now men and women of the West "…stand on the threshold of a deepening of thought and experience…they will themselves be aware of a longing to find the thread uniting the fragments which make their appearance in the life of a human being between birth and death…."

In 1914, Steiner married Marie von Sievers, an actress, who had been secretary of the German Section of the Theosophical Society. Together they established a school for esoteric research near Basel, Switzerland, and developed new approaches to the teaching of speech and drama, which led to "eurythmy," an art of movement. Later, Steiner originated the Waldorf School Movement, an innovative educational system, which still maintains 80 schools in Europe and the United States. Rudolf Steiner died on March 30, 1925, in Dornach, Switzerland.

✛ Delving Deeper

Melton, J. Gordon, Jerome Clark, and Aidan A. Kelly. *New Age Almanac*. Detroit: Visible Ink Press, 1991.

Shepherd, A. P. *Rudolf Steiner: Scientist of the Invisible*. Rochester, Vt.: Inner Traditions International, 1983.

Steiner, Rudolf. *Lecture V, Earthly and Cosmic Man*. Rudolf Steiner Publishing, 1948.

ASSOCIATION FOR RESEARCH AND ENLIGHTENMENT

When **Edgar Cayce** (1877–1945) died at the age of 67, he had given nearly 9,000 medical readings while in a state of clairvoyant **trance.** In addition, the "sleeping prophet" also gave life readings dealing with the vocational, psychological, and human-relations problems of individuals. It was through these life readings that the concepts of reincarnation and the possibility of past lives were introduced. All together, more than 14,000 Cayce readings have been recorded on 200,000 permanent file cards and cross-referenced into 10,000 major subjects.

In 1931, the Association for Research and Enlightenment (ARE) was chartered in Virginia as a nonprofit organization to conduct scientific and psychical research.

In 1931, the Association for Research and Enlightenment (ARE) was chartered in the state of Virginia as a nonprofit organization to conduct scientific and psychical research. In 1947, two years after Cayce's death, the Edgar Cayce Foundation was established. The original ARE has become the membership arm of the Cayce programs. The foundation is the custodian of the original Cayce readings, and the memorabilia of the great contemporary seer's life and career. Both are headquartered in Virginia Beach, Virginia, and there are more than 1,500 ARE study groups around the world.

Since the establishment of the ARE, thousands of people from every corner of the

Edgar Cayce (1877–1945).
(CORBIS CORPORATION)

nation, as well as from around the world, have journeyed to Virginia Beach to attend lectures and conferences and to investigate the information in the Cayce readings. Many of the skeptics who came to expose Cayce stayed on to support his work. Among these have been Jess Stearn, author of *Edgar Cayce: the Sleeping Prophet* (1967), and Thomas Sugrue, author of *There Is a River: The Story of Edgar Cayce* (1942), both of which are important books about the life and work of Edgar Cayce.

Cayce's son, Hugh Lynn Cayce (1907–1982), once commented that his father had said that everyone was psychic, "but for many people manifestation of this ability can be very disturbing, very upsetting, and in fact, it can even destroy the personality if it runs rampant in the person's life. This can be very damaging if the individual does not use these abilities constructively. If he takes ego trips with it, or begins to fake it, the result can be very destructive to the personality, particularly that of young children."

With these concerns in mind, before he died Edgar told Hugh Lynn that the Association for Research and Enlightenment had better make certain that they were doing the research before they did too much enlightening. To fulfill Edgar's wish, the ARE maintains an extensive library of information concerning the entire field of psychical research and metaphysics, as well as the Cayce materials. It also sponsors regular seminars, publishes a journal, and established Atlantic University as an environment in which various psychic attributes can be examined and developed.

Cayce believed that in an earlier incarnation, he had been wounded in battle and left in the field for dead. However, he had managed to live for several days, conscious and in extreme pain. He was not able to help himself in any way, having only his mind as a weapon against pain. Just prior to his physical death, he had been able to elevate his mind beyond the reach of his body and its suffering. Since no achievement, good or bad, is ever lost, the ability to subdue the body and its feelings became part of the pattern of his individuality—and he was able to use this ability in his physical incarnation as Edgar Cayce.

In a trance state, Cayce was able to give complete medical diagnoses, prescribe remedies, and review the past lives of his clients. Cayce learned that each existence on Earth is a purposeful experience, and the place in which people find themselves provides them with the opportunities to use their present-life abilities, weaknesses, or virtues in fulfilling the purpose for which their souls decided to manifest in the three-dimensional plane of Earth. In Cayce's opinion, no soul is placed here accidentally. Humans are all where they are today because they have "chosen" to be there in an effort to work out their soul development.

"My father's unconscious mind was able to tap the unconscious minds of other people and draw information from them," Hugh Lynn Cayce said. "He insisted that there is a river of thought forms and intelligence at another level of consciousness, and that this was the source of his information. This procedure apparently had nothing to do with **medi-**

umship as we understand it. He had no guides or anything like that. He had to do his own legwork, so to speak."

Hugh Lynn Cayce died on July 4, 1982, in Virginia Beach. Posthumously, a collection of his speeches concerning Edgar Cayce's teachings on Jesus and Christianity was published under the title *The Jesus I Knew* (1982). Hugh Lynn's son Charles Thomas Cayce (1942–) became the president of the ARE in 1976 after his father suffered a heart attack, and he still serves the organization in that position.

Dr. Gina Cerminara, a trained psychologist with a specialty in semantics, conducted an extensive study of the Edgar Cayce past-life readings while she was residing in Virginia Beach. In Chapter XXIV, "A Philosophy to Live By," in her book *Many Mansions* (1950), Cerminara presented the ethics of karma as delineated in the Cayce readings. In outline form, the pattern that she discovered is as follows:

- God exists, and every soul is a portion of God. (You are a soul; you inhabit a body.)
- Life is purposeful and continuous.
- All human life operates under the law of karma and reincarnation.
- Love fulfills that law.
- The will of all humans creates their destiny.
- The mind of all humans has formative powers.
- The answer to all problems is within the Self.

In accordance with the above postulates, humankind is enjoined as follows:

- Realize first your relationship to the Creative Forces of the Universe: God.
- Formulate your ideas and purpose in life. Strive to achieve those ideals.
- Be active. Be patient. Be joyous. Leave the results to God.
- Do not seek to evade any problem.
- Be a channel of good to other people.

Dr. Gladys McGarey is a medical doctor who employs various concepts from the Edgar Cayce material in her practice at the Association for Research and Enlightenment Clinic in Phoenix, Arizona. McGarey gave new life to the Temple Beautiful program as it was described in Cayce's readings of the lost continent of **Atlantis.** The daughter of Christian missionaries, McGarey has said that her work with the Cayce readings had not changed her basic attitude toward life and death, religion and immortality. "It is still Christ-centered with a basic Christian foundation. The part that has changed is the addition of reincarnation and the concept that comes from the Cayce material that gives impact and reality to the importance of us as ongoing beings. We are as rays of light and love that are involved in this three-dimensional world."

Rather than taking her away from the church, McGarey stated that the concepts of reincarnation had actually given her a deeper understanding of Christian ritual and the belief structures of the Christian faith. She also said that the concept of past lives had helped her to be a better physician, because they had enabled her to share responsibility with her patients, "rather than take responsibility from them."

✤ **DELVING DEEPER**

Cayce, Hugh Lynn. *Venture Inward.* New York: Paperback Library, 1966.

Cerminara, Gina. *Many Mansions.* New York: William Morrow, 1950.

Stearn, Jess. *Edgar Cayce: The Sleeping Prophet.* New York: Doubleday, 1967.

Steiger, Brad. *Returning from the Light.* New York: Signet Inspiration, 1996.

Sugrue, Thomas. *There Is a River: The Story of Edgar Cayce.* New York: H. Holt and Co., 1942.

THEOSOPHY

Theosophy (divine wisdom) is an eclectic blend of many earlier philosophies and cult teachings, all of which claim to have been handed down to contemporary seekers of spiritual truth by disciples of ancient wisdom. The Theosophical Society, cofounded by **Helena Petrovna Blavatsky** (1831–1891) in New York in 1875, is an esoteric blend of Zoroastrianism, **Hinduism, Gnosticism, Manichaeism,** the Kabbalah, and the philosophy of Plato (c. 428 B.C.E.–c. 348 B.C.E.) and other mystics, combined with the teachings of mysterious masters who dwell in secret places in the Himalayas and communicate with their initiates through their psychic abilities and their projected astral bodies. Whereas **Edgar Cayce (1877–1945)** and **Rudolf Steiner (1861–1925)** evolved their spiritual teachings primarily through their own revelations, inspirations, and psychic abilities, Blavatsky claimed to be able to draw upon the ancient wisdom of the Masters Koot Hoomi and Morya to abet the considerable knowledge that she had distilled from various mystery schools, Hindu religious thought, Jewish mysticism, and Christian sects. Many of the concepts and the spiritual eclecticism professed by Blavatsky in the 1880s would be revised on a large scale in the 1970s, in what has loosely been called the New Age Movement. In addition to such contributions as occult masters and guides, Blavatsky introduced the legend of the lost continent of Lemuria, the return of the Maitreya (world savior), and was greatly responsible for popularizing the concepts of reincarnation and past lives in Europe and the United States.

T H E *Theosophical Society is an esoteric blend of Zoroastrianism, Hinduism, Gnosticism, Manichaeism, the Kabbalah, and the philosophy of Plato.*

At the time of her death in 1891, Blavatsky's detractors considered her to have been a hoaxster, a fraud, and a deceiver, while her followers revered her as a genius, a veritable saint, and a woman of monumental courage who had struggled against an incredible array of adversities and adversaries to fashion a modern mystery school without equal. Foe and follower alike conceded that she was a unique, sometimes overpowering, personality who had apparently traveled the world in search of spiritual truths and who had survived physical crises and challenges that would certainly have discouraged—or killed—a less indomitable individual.

Born Helena Petrovna Hahn on July 30, 1831, in Ekaterinoslav (now Dnepropetrovsk) in the Ukraine, she began displaying mediumistic abilities as a young girl. Just before her seventeenth birthday, she married the much older General Nicephore Blavatsky, a Russian official in Caucasia. Three months later, she left her husband and her homeland to travel freely and widely throughout the world, exploring the occult wisdom and teachings of many traditions.

In 1858, Blavatsky arrived in Paris, where she met the famous spirit medium **Daniel Dunglas Home (1833–1886)**. By this time, she had herself acquired a modest reputation for **mediumship,** and she began to practice these talents more openly. In Cairo, Egypt, in 1871, Blavatsky founded a spiritualist group that was forced to disband after accusations of having produced fraudulent phenomena to deceive its patrons. In 1873, she settled in New York City and resumed the practice of her mediumship in association with the brothers William and Horatio Eddy, two well-known materialization mediums. Her participation in numerous seances in New England brought her to the attention of Henry Steel Olcott (1832–1907), a newspaperman fascinated with psychic phenomena, who established a group centered around her mediumship.

In 1875, Blavatsky, Olcott, and William Q. Judge (1851–1896), an attorney, made the decision to move beyond the precepts of **Spiritualism** and create a more sophisticated approach to spirit contact and mysticism, which they named the Theosophical Society. The threefold purpose of the society was

1. to form a universal brotherhood of man;

2. to study and make known the ancient religions, philosophies, and sciences;

3. to investigate the laws of nature and develop the divine powers latent in humankind.

In 1877, Blavatsky published her worldview of the occult, *Isis Unveiled*. In this work, she argues that the reason metempsychosis (reincarnation) has been ridiculed by scientists and orthodox theologians in the West is because it has never been properly understood. While learned individuals accept the indestructibility of energy, she reasons, how can they believe that

> "man, the living, thinking, reasoning entity, the indwelling deity of our nature's crowning masterpiece, will evacuate his casket and be no more! Would the principle of continuity which exists even for the so-called inorganic matter, for a floating atom, be denied to the spirit, whose attributes are consciousness, memory, mind, *love!* Really, the very idea is preposterous....If the Pythagorean metempsychosis should be thoroughly explained and compared with the modern theory of evolution it would be found to supply every 'missing link' in the chain of the latter. There was not a philosopher of any notoriety who did not hold to this doctrine, as taught by the Brahmans, Buddhists, and later by the Pythagoreans."

In 1878, Blavatsky and Olcott moved to Bombay, India, to be nearer the mahatmas and masters, the members of the Great White Brotherhood who appeared to her in their astral bodies to relay metaphysical teachings. After a turbulent period in India, which she left under charges of fraud to settle in London in 1887, Blavatsky began work on her magnum opus, *The Secret Doctrine* (1888), a massive statement of her theosophical philosophy, including her views on reincarnation.

Only a constant series of rebirths of one and the same individual, passing through the "Circle of Necessity," can fully explain the age-old problems of good and evil and the apparent injustices of life, Blavatsky argues. Only a system wherein one is rewarded or punished for the deeds or crimes committed in a former life can explain the inequalities of "birth and fortune, of intellect and capacities." When a person's life is beset by injustice and misfortune, only the "blessed knowledge of Karma" can prevent one "from cursing life and men, as well as their supposed Creator." Those individuals who believe in karma have to believe in destiny, which, Blavatsky states in *The Secret Doctrine*, "from birth to death, every man is weaving, thread by thread,

around himself, as a spider does his cobweb....Karma creates nothing, nor does it design. It is man who plants and creates causes, and karmic law adjusts the effects, which adjustment is not an act but universal harmony....Karma has never sought to destroy intellectual and individual liberty....On the contrary, he who unveils through study and meditation its intricate paths, and throws light on those dark ways...is working for the good of his fellow men...."

✤ **DELVING DEEPER**
Blavatsky, H. P. *Collected Writings.* 16 vols. Wheaton, Ill: Theosophical Publishing House, 1950–85.

Spence, Lewis. *An Encyclopedia of Occultism.* New Hyde Park, N.Y.: University Books, 1960.

EXPERIENTIAL QUESTS INTO PAST LIVES

Some speculate that the phenomenon of past lives can answer troubling questions in the present and explain deja vu, a feeling that one has seen or heard something before. Many people report that they have walked down a street in a strange city and been overwhelmed with the sudden familiarity of its shop windows, sidewalks, and store fronts. Others say that hidden memories have been stimulated by witnessing a dramatic reenactment of some scene from the past in a motion picture or television production.

In recent years, men and women in Western cultures have begun to explore the possibility that reincarnation is a spiritual reality.

Throughout the centuries, millions of individuals, especially those who live in India and Asia, believe that they have lived before, and in recent years increasing numbers of men and women in the Western cultures have begun to explore the possibility that reincarnation is a spiritual reality.

Accomplished Broadway lyricist Alan Jay Lerner (1918–1986) said that the first-act ending of his musical *Brigadoon* (1946), which features an outdoor wedding ceremony in seventeenth-century Scotland, seemed at first to have sprung spontaneously from his mind. Several years later, when Lerner was in London, he came into possession of a book entitled *Everyday Life in Old Scotland* and found "his" marriage ceremony word for word. Lerner's later musical success, *On a Clear Day You Can See Forever,* openly declared his fascination with the subject of reincarnation. The storyline tells of a Brooklyn model who is hypnotically regressed to an earlier life in eighteenth-century England.

British psychiatrist Dr. Denys Kelsey believed that his acceptance of the cycle of rebirth enabled him to show his patients how they might begin anew at any given moment. He was also convinced that it was occasionally possible for subjects to recall experiences that were felt centuries before their present incarnation. Belief in the doctrine of rebirth may have come somewhat easier to Kelsey than it might to the average psychiatrist because he was married to Joan Grant, an

author who claimed to be 25,000 years old and to have soul memories of 30 prior-life experiences. Grant wrote seven popular historical novels without doing a bit of research, yet none of the material in her books has ever been successfully challenged by skeptical scholars. To the contrary, a good deal of the material in her books that was considered controversial at the time of publication has since been validated by archaeologists and historians. Every time, when queried how she could have acquired such knowledge, she attributed her accuracy to memories of her past lives.

Winged Pharaoh, the novel that Joan Grant wrote in 1937, described her life as a woman pharaoh in the first dynasty of Egypt, 4,000 years ago. On those frequent occasions when she was asked to comment on the book's almost biblical style, she replied that the words had just come out that way. She insisted that she never did any research at all and that she had previously known nothing of Egypt on the conscious level, yet Egyptologists had been unable to fault the book. Grant stated that even her critics had said that she couldn't possibly have made it all up, so she must have experienced it all to write in such detail.

Yonassan Gershom, a neo-Hasidic rabbi who lives in Minnesota, tells in his book *Beyond the Ashes: Cases of Reincarnation from the Holocaust* (1992) of hearing the terrible memories of concentration camps, gas chambers, barbed wire, swastikas, and the sadistic henchmen of Nazi Germany not from elderly Jewish survivors of the Holocaust, but from young people, many of them blonde, blue-eyed Gentiles of Nordic descent, who were being forced to deal with what appeared to be past-life memories of having died as victims of Hitler's "final solution" to the "Jewish problem." At the time he was writing his book, Gershom stated that out of the hundreds of people who had told him their dreams, visions, regressions, or intuitions of having died as Jews in the Holocaust, two-thirds had been reborn as non-Jews. Later samplings, however, indicated that many more Jews have also experienced such past-life memories. Gershom's later book, *From Ashes to Healing* (1996), focused on stories about the acts of physical or spiritual healing that have resulted from the act of recalling a Holocaust lifetime.

The aspect of physical and spiritual healing that accompanies a past-life recall is one of the principal motives in regression into prior-life experiences for therapeutic reasons. Benjamin Smith of Port Orchard, Washington, has been involved in past-lives therapy for over 25 years, and he stated that when he first began doing regressions, he was concerned with establishing dates, names, and locations associated with the past-life personality of his clients. "Then I discovered that they didn't really care if they would be able to trace and to prove a particular lifetime. All they were interested in was removing the personal problem that they had come to me for help in solving. I quit worrying whether reincarnation was real or not. The important thing to my clients was whether or not they discovered the origins of their pains, their traumas, and their problems. If the solution came from their previous lifetime or from their Higher Self, it really didn't make any difference to them."

In Volume 9 of *Collected Works* (1981) Dr. Carl G. Jung (1875–1961) expressed his opinion that "the mere fact that people talk about rebirth and that there is such a concept at all, means that a store of psychic experiences designated by that term must actually exist. Rebirth is an affirmation that must be counted among the primordial affirmations of mankind."

Benjamin Franklin (1706–1790) saw the whole matter of past lives and rebirth as a practical cosmic recycling: "When I see nothing annihilated [in the works of God] and not a drop of water wasted, I cannot suspect the annihilation of souls, or believe that He will suffer the daily waste of millions of minds ready-made that now exist, and put Himself to the continual trouble of making new ones. Thus, finding myself to exist in the world, I believe I shall…always exist; and with all the inconveniences human life is liable to, I shall not object to a new edition of mine, hoping, however, that the errata of the last may be corrected."

❋ Delving Deeper

Gershom, Yonassan. *Beyond the Ashes: Cases of Reincarnation from the Holocaust*. Virginia Beach, Va.: A.R.E. Press, 1992.

Goldberg, Dr. Bruce. *The Search for Grace*. Sedona, Ariz.: In Print Publishing, 1994.

Guirdham, Arthur. *We Are One Another*. Wellingborough, Northamptonshire, Great Britian: Turnstone Press Ltd., 1982.

Jung, Carl Gustav, and Herbert Read, eds. *Archtypes and the Collective Unconscious (Collected Works of C. G. Jung, Vol. 9, Part 1)*. 2nd edition. Princeton, N. J.: Princeton University Press, 1981.

Lane, Barbara. *Echoes from Medieval Halls*. Virginia Beach, Va.: A.R.E. Press, 1997.

Stearn, Jess. *The Search for the Girl with the Blue Eyes*. New York: Bantam Books, 1969.

Sutphen, Richard. *You Were Born Together to Be Together*. New York: Pocket Books, 1976.

Hypnotic Regression into Past Lives

Richard Sutphen (1937–   ) began his hypnosis and past-lives regression work in 1972 and was probably the first to develop a technique whereby a hypnotist might regress large numbers of men and women to alleged former lifetimes at the same time and in the same room. Sutphen began fine-tuning his style in his Phoenix, Arizona, home with a roomful of people at a time. He continued perfecting his technique in area colleges and high schools and at metaphysical gatherings in the Southwest. In 1973, he founded and directed a hypnosis/metaphysical center in Scottsdale, Arizona. The convenience of working at an established center provided him with the structure that he needed to experiment extensively with both individual and group techniques and the opportunity to amass a large number of case histories for comparison and contrast.

In 1976, Sutphen created and marketed the first prerecorded hypnosis tapes through his Valley of the Sun publishing company. In 1978, Pocket Books published Sutphen's *You Were Born Again to Be Together*, case histories of men and women who had found themselves and their loves once again after the separation of many lifetimes. The book became a national best-seller, and soon thousands of people wanted to be regressed by Sutphen and explore the possibilities of their past lives. To meet the sudden demand for his hypnotic abilities, he began holding past-life seminars in major cities throughout the United States and hosting an annual Super Seminar in Scottsdale. By the 1990s, over 100,000 people had attended a Sutphen seminar; his inventory had grown to include 380 audio and video titles; and he had written 18 books, including *Past Lives, Future Loves* (1978), *The Master of Life Manual* (1980), and *Unseen Influences* (1982).

"Past-life hypnotic regression can be used as an extremely valuable therapeutic tool to explore the cause of unconscious anxiety, repressed hostilities, hidden fears, hangups, and interpersonal relationship conflicts," Sutphen said. He cautioned, however, that past-life therapy is not a magic wand, and the past-life causes don't always surface immediately. "But it does work," he stated, "and it can be for many the first stop in letting go of a problem. Psychiatrists often spend months or even years searching for the cause of their patient's problem. They are aware that in understanding the cause they can begin to mitigate and, eventually, eliminate the effect. Yet by limiting their search to the time frame of only one lifetime, they may never find the origin of the present-life problem."

During one of his seminars, Sutphen spoke with a woman named Barbara who had driven hundreds of miles to be in attendance because it was important to her to experience past-life regression. She told Sutphen that she had several problems, some he could see plainly, others he couldn't. He could see that Barbara was obviously referring to her excessive weight when she spoke of some of her problems being easily visible. The attractive 29-year-old woman weighed 225 pounds.

As the seminar sessions progressed, Sutphen observed Barbara during two group regressions, trying to be comfortable in two chairs because her weight made lying down on the floor with everyone else too difficult. He could see, though, that she was a good deep-level hypnotic subject, for she had practically fallen off the chairs almost immediately after he had begun the process. During an evening session, Sutphen asked Barbara to join 11 other subjects on the platform for a demonstration of individual regression work.

During the group hypnosis of the 12 volunteers, Sutphen instructed them to think about something in their life that they would like to change—any kind of problem, habit, or personal situation. As he counted backward from three to one, they would move back in time to the cause of their present problem, whether it should be in their past, in their present life experience or in any of their previous lives. They would see clearly and relive the situation before their inner eyes, thereby understanding the problem and be able to release it.

That night a man cried out as he relived an ancient battle. A young woman relived the fear of being lost in the woods as a small child. A middle-aged woman was recalling starving to death in an African village. But when Sutphen came to Barbara, she cried out, screamed, and began to shake. Her voice became that of a young girl on the edge of panic. The hypnotist quickly redirected her from the alarming memory to a state of peaceful sleep. Later, after all the other subjects had been awakened, Sutphen asked if Barbara wished to explore in greater detail the prior life on which she had touched so emotionally. She eagerly agreed, and Sutphen once again induced the trance state.

In a few moments, Barbara was speaking in the voice and persona of a 12-year-old French girl, describing her luxurious home and her perfect life in eighteenth-century France at the time of the Revolution. When the hypnotist moved her forward in time, she experienced the arrival of soldiers who had orders to take her family to prison. Numerous humiliations followed, and the young girl was eventually killed by the revolutionaries.

After her death experience in that lifetime, Sutphen directed a question to Barbara's Higher Self: How had events from the past life in France related to her present life problems? From the depths of her hypnotic sleep, Barbara cried out that pretty people got hurt. She had been very pretty in that life in France and the soldiers had humiliated and killed her. "The only way to be safe is to remain ugly in the world," she said."

After she was once again awakened from the trance state, Barbara provided additional information about her weight problems. She explained how she had attended the best and most highly recommended weight-loss centers, but she could never shed the pounds. In some cases, she had begun to lose a little, then she would go on an eating binge and bring her weight right back to 225. One well-known specialist had told her that once she found out why she psychologically needed to retain weight, then she would be able to keep it off.

"You know you can do that now, don't you, Barbara?" Sutphen asked. She answered with a smile that now she knew that she could.

Sutphen has never been dogmatic in his definition of what reincarnation may be, but he remains convinced that regardless of how the question of rebirth is viewed philosophically, it would appear that which is perceived as the past is somehow affecting the present. And once one has pondered the significance of one's past lives, one learns how to transform the present into a meaningful growth experience and in this manner prepare for as significant a future as possible.

One of the best documented cases of reincarnation in recent times had another incarnation of its own when, on May 17, 1994, CBS presented a television movie "inspired by an actual case history," *Search for Grace*, starring Lisa Hartman and Ken Wahl. As fictionalized for mass viewing, the television drama is a thriller about an attractive young woman named Ivy who becomes ensnared by an overwhelming attraction for a powerful, suspicious stranger who turns physically abusive. When Ivy seeks psychological therapy for this irrational compulsion and for related nightmares, she is hypnotically regressed and begins to relive the events leading to the brutal death of a woman, Grace Lovel, which had taken place more than 60 years before. In her waking state, Ivy has never heard of the woman, and she has never been to the city in which her murder occurred. Ivy's confusion and terror grow as she learns that Grace Lovel actually did live and die exactly as she relived in the hypnotic trance. Even more frightening is the uncomfortable awareness that Ivy's violent new lover, John, bears an eerie resemblance to Grace's murderous boyfriend, Jake.

All of the above makes for an exciting evening in front of the television set, but it was based on an actual case researched and documented by renowned hypnotherapist Dr. Bruce Goldberg and reported in detail in his book *The Search for Grace: A Documented Case of Murder and Reincarnation* (1994). "Ivy's past-life regression revealed an eternal love triangle, a terrifying karmic dance of passion and murder, culminating in the short tragic career of one Grace Doze, a headstrong flapper from Buffalo, New York, whose reckless love life ended in murder," Goldberg states in his book. Exhaustive research enabled Goldberg to discover that even the smallest details of Grace's life and death could be explicitly documented through contemporary newspapers and police reports.

In Goldberg's actual transcript of the regression in which Ivy/Grace recalled the details of the murder that took place on Tuesday night, May 17, 1927, Grace had ditched her "boring" husband Chester and gone shopping. Although her new bobbed hairstyle, short skirt, and red shoes might be everything that dull old Chester hates, Jake finds them magnetically appealing. When he picks her up that night, Jake has already had a few too many drinks.

As Goldberg listened to Ivy/Grace altering her voice to speak both parts, Jake's foul temper is displayed, and the two of them get into a heated argument as they drive. Jake is angry that she dresses so cheaply and is still flirting with other men, and he punches her on the jaw. Although she is in pain, Grace is still conscious when Jake stops the car, threatening to teach her a lesson. He beats her badly, strangles her, and dumps her body in Ellicott Creek.

Goldberg guided Ivy/Grace to the superconscious mind level and asked her if she knew Jake in her current lifetime. She answered without hesitation that he was John.

As a therapist, Goldberg was not particularly interested in obtaining documentation for his various patients' claims to past lives, but a search of old files from Buffalo, New York, newspapers for May 19–21, 1927, produced accounts of a "handsome bob-haired woman found floating in Ellicott Creek," who had been strangled to death "before she was thrown in the water." At first there was doubt that the identity of "the beautiful young woman" would ever be determined. And then, on June 1, 1927, the *Buffalo Courier* reported the find of a "small black suitcase owned by *Mrs. Grace Doze* and carried by her the night she was thrown into the Ellicott Creek." When the police showed the suitcase to "*Chester Doze*," husband of the murdered woman, he identified the bag and contents as the property of his wife.

Goldberg's book contains an astonishing 54 pages of documentation—death and birth certificates, newspaper accounts, police reports, and so forth—that prove to any reasonable person that Grace Doze, the victim of a murder in 1927, did most certainly exist. Exactly how Ivy's psyche gained that information remains a mystery. "Could it have been the unquiet spirit of the murdered young woman, working through her reincarnation as Ivy, that demanded at long last public resolution of the mystery of her death?" Goldberg asks.

One more eerie "coincidence" regarding the case must be mentioned. When *Search for Grace* was telecast on that Tuesday night in May 1994, it was 67 years to the hour since Grace Doze was murdered.

✤ DELVING DEEPER

Gershom, Yonassan. *Beyond the Ashes: Cases of Reincarnation from the Holocaust*. Virginia Beach, Va.: A.R.E. Press, 1992.

Goldberg, Bruce. *The Search for Grace: A Documented Case of Murder and Reincarnation*. Sedona, Ariz.: In Print Publishing, 1994.

Sutphen, Richard. *Past Lives, Future Loves*. New York: Pocket Books, 1978.

Sutphen, Richard. *You Were Born Again to Be Together*. New York: Pocket Books, 1976.

BRIDEY MURPHY

To a great number of Americans, the name Bridey Murphy has become synonymous with reincarnation and accounts of past lives. The story of the Pueblo, Colorado, housewife who remembered a prior incarnation as a nineteenth-century Irish woman while under hypnosis made a dramatic impact upon the public imagination. Newspapers, magazines, and scholarly journals debated the validity of the "memory," and the controversy surrounding this alleged case of reincarnation has not resolved itself to this day.

William J. Barker of the *Denver Post* published the first account of this now-famous case in that newspaper's *Empire* magazine. Barker told how Morey Bernstein, a young Pueblo business executive, first noticed what an excellent subject "Mrs. S." was for deep trance when he was asked to demonstrate hypnosis at a party in October of 1952. It was some weeks later, on the evening of November 29, that Bernstein gained the woman's consent to participate in an experiment in age-regression.

The amateur hypnotist had heard stories of researchers having led their subjects back into past lives, but he had always scoffed at such accounts. He had been particularly skeptical about the testimony of the British psychiatrist Sir Alexander Cannon, who reported that he had investigated over a thousand cases wherein hypnotized individuals had recalled past incarnations.

Mrs. S., who later became identified as Ruth Simmons (and many years later by her actual name, Virginia Tighe), was not particularly interested in hypnotism, either, nor in becoming a guinea pig for Bernstein's attempt to test the theses of those psychical researchers who had claimed the revelation of past lives. She was, at that time, 28 years old, a housewife who enjoyed playing bridge and attending ball games with her husband.

With Rex Simmons and Hazel Bernstein as witnesses, the hypnotist placed Simmons in a trance and began to lead her back through significant periods of her childhood. Then he told her that she would go back until she found herself in another place and time and that she would be able to talk to him and tell him what she saw. She began to breathe heavily and her first words from an alleged previous memory were more puzzling than dramatic. She said that she was scratching the paint off her bed because she was angry over having just received an awful spanking. She identified herself by a name that Bernstein first heard as "Friday," then clarified as "Bridey," and the

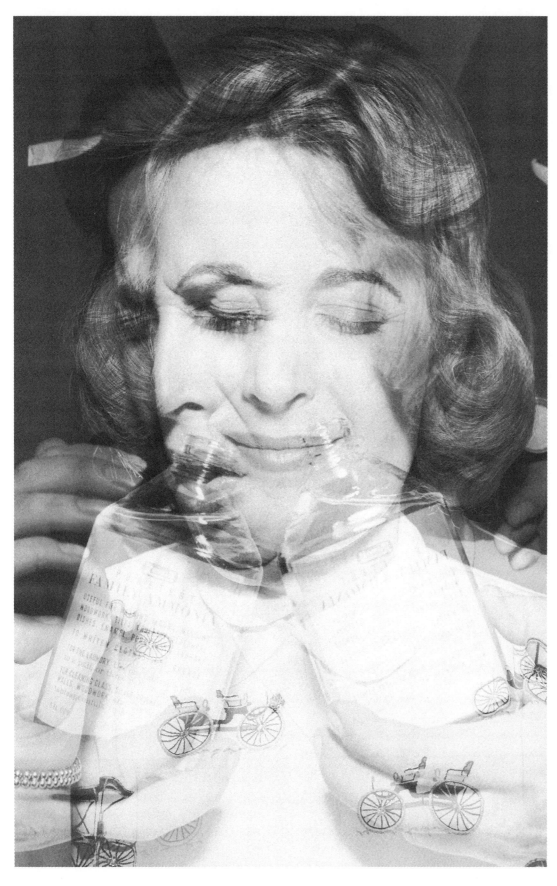

Under hypnotism, Virginia Tighe claimed to be the incarnation of an Irish woman named Bridey Murphy. (CORBIS CORPORATION)

strange search for evidence of a former incarnation had begun.

Bridey—short for Bridget—Murphy began to use words and expressions that were completely out of character for Ruth Simmons. Bridey told of playing hide'n'seek with her brother Duncan, who had reddish hair like hers (Simmons was a brunette). She spoke of attending Mrs. Strayne's school in Cork where she spent her time "studying to be a lady." With sensitivity she recreated her marriage to Brian MacCarthy, a young lawyer, who took her to live in Belfast in a cottage back of his grandmother's house, not far from St. Theresa's Church.

To a number of Americans, "Bridey Murphy" has become synonymous with reincarnation and accounts of past lives.

In her melodic Irish brogue, Bridey told of a life without children, a life laced with an edge of conflict because she was Protestant while Brian was Catholic; then in a tired and querulous voice, she told how she had fallen down a flight of stairs in 1864 when she was 66. After the fall, she was left crippled and had to be carried about wherever she went.

Then one Sunday while her husband was at church, Bridey died. Her death upset Brian terribly, she said. Her spirit lingered beside him, trying to establish communication with him, trying to let him know that he should not grieve for her. Bridey told the astonished hypnotist and the witnesses that her spirit had waited around Belfast until Father John, a priest friend of her husband's, had passed away. She wanted to point out to him that he had been wrong about purgatory, she said, and added that he admitted it.

The spirit world, Bridey said, was one in which "you couldn't talk to anybody very long…they'd go away." In the spirit realm, one did not sleep, never ate, and never became tired. Bridey thought that her spirit had

resided there for about 40 Earth years before she was born as Ruth Simmons. (Ruth/Virginia had been born in 1923, so Bridey's spirit had spent nearly 60 years in that timeless dimension.)

At a second session, Bridey again stressed that the afterlife was painless, with nothing to fear. There was neither love nor hate, and relatives did not stay together in clannish groups. Her father, she recalled, said he saw her mother, but she hadn't. The spirit world was simply a place where the soul waited to pass on to "another form of existence."

Details of Bridey Murphy's physical life in Ireland began to amass on Morey Bernstein's tape recorders. Business associates who heard the tapes encouraged Bernstein to continue his experiments, but to allow someone else, a disinterested third party, to check Bridey's statements in old Irish records or wherever such evidence might be found. Ruth Simmons was not eager to continue, but the high regard that she and her husband had for Bernstein led her to consent to additional sessions.

Utilizing her present-life incarnation as Ruth Simmons, Bridey Murphy demonstrated a graceful and lively rendition of an Irish folk dance which she called the "Morning Jig." Her favorite songs were "Sean," "The Minstrel's March," and "Londonderry Air." Ruth Simmons had no interest in musical activities.

William Barker of the *Denver Post* asked Bernstein if the case for Bridey Murphy could be explained by genetic memory which had been transferred through Simmons's ancestors, for she was one-third Irish. Bernstein conceded that such a theory might make the story more acceptable to the general public, but he felt the hypothesis fell apart when it is remembered that Bridey had no children. He also pointed out that other researchers who have regressed subjects back into alleged previous-life memories have found that blood line and heredity have nothing to do with former incarnations. Many have spoken of the afterlife as a kind of "stockpile of souls." When a particular type of spirit is required to inhabit and animate a body that is about to be born, that certain spirit is selected and introduced into that body. Bernstein observed that a person who boasts of having noble French ancestry might have been a slave or a concubine on his or her prior visit to the physical plane of existence.

In Bernstein's opinion, one could take only one of two points of view in regard to the strange case of Bridey Murphy. One might conclude that the whole thing had been a hoax without a motive. This conclusion would hold that Ruth Simmons was not the "normal young gal" she appeared to be, but actually a frustrated actress who proved to be a consummate performer in her interpretation of a script dreamed up by Bernstein because he "likes to fool people." Or if one did not accept that particular hypothesis, Bernstein said, then the public must admit that the experiment may have opened a hidden door that provided a glimpse of immortality.

Doubleday published Morey Bernstein's *The Search for Bridey Murphy* in 1956. Skeptics and serious investigators alike were interested in testing the validity of Bernstein's experiments and in determining whether or not they might demonstrate the reality of past lives.

In mid-January of 1956, the Chicago *Daily News* sent its London representative on a three-day quest to check out Cork, Dublin, and Belfast and attempt to uncover any evidence that might serve as verification for the Bridey Murphy claims. With only one day for each city, it is not surprising that the newsman reported that he could find nothing of significance.

In February, the *Denver Post* sent William Barker, the journalist who first reported the story of the search for Bridey Murphy, to conduct a thorough investigation of the mystery. Barker felt that certain strong supportive points had already been established by Irish investigators and had been detailed in Bernstein's book. Bridey (Irish spelling of the name is Bridie) had said that her father-in-law, John MacCarthy, had been a barrister (lawyer) in Cork. The records revealed that a John MacCarthy from Cork, a Roman Catholic educated at Clongowes School, was listed in the Registry of Kings Inn. Bridey had mentioned a "green-grocer," John Carrigan, with whom she had traded in Belfast. A Belfast librarian attested to the fact that there had been a man of that name and trade at 90 Northumberland

during the time in which Bridey claimed to have lived there. The librarian also verified Bridey's statement that there had been a William Farr who had sold foodstuffs during this same period. One of the most significant bits of information had to do with a place that Bridey called Mourne. Such a place was not shown on any modern maps of Ireland, but its existence was substantiated through the British Information Service.

While under hypnosis, Ruth Simmons had "remembered" that Catholics could teach at Queen's University, Belfast, even though it was a Protestant institution. American investigators made a hasty prejudgment when they challenged the likelihood of such an interdenominational teaching arrangement. In Ireland, however, such a fact was common knowledge, and Bridey scored another hit. Then there were such details as Bridey knowing about the old Irish custom of dancing at weddings and putting money in the bride's pockets. There was also her familiarity with the currency of that period, the types of crops grown in the region, the contemporary musical pieces, and the folklore of the area.

When Barker dined with Kenneth Besson, a hotel owner who was interested in the search, the newsman questioned Bridey's references to certain food being prepared in "flats," an unfamiliar term to Americans. Besson waved a waiter to their table and asked him to bring some flats. When the waiter returned, Barker saw that the mysterious flats were but serving platters.

Some scholars believed that they had caught Bridey in a gross error when she mentioned the custom of kissing the Blarney Stone. Such a superstition was a late nineteenth-century notion, stated Dermot Foley, the Cork city librarian. Later, however, Foley made an apology to Bridey when he discovered that T. Crofton Cronker, in his *Researches in the South of Ireland* (1824), mentions the custom of kissing the Blarney Stone as early as 1820.

Bridey was correct about other matters that at first were thought to be wrong by scholars and authorities. For example, certain authorities discredited her statement about the iron bed she had scratched with her fingernails after the "awful spanking" on the grounds that iron beds had not yet been introduced into Ireland during the period in which Bridey claimed to have lived. The *Encyclopedia Britannica*, however, states that iron beds did appear in Bridey's era in Ireland and were advertised as being "free from the insects which sometimes infect wooden bedsteads." Bridey's claims to have eaten muffins as a child and to have obtained books from a lending library in Belfast were at first judged to be out of proper time context. Later, her challengers actually uncovered historical substantiation for such statements.

Throughout the regressions conducted by Morey Bernstein, one of the most convincing aspects of the experiments had been the vocabulary expressed by the hypnotized subject. The personality of Bridey Murphy never faltered in her almost poetic speech, and of the hundreds of words of jargon and colloquial phrases she uttered, nearly all were found to be appropriate for the time in which she claimed to have lived. The songs that Bridey sang, her graphic word pictures of wake and marriage customs, were all acclaimed by Irish folklorists as being accurate. Her grim reference to the "black something" that took the life of her baby brother probably referred to famine or disease. The Irish use of "black" in this context means "malignant" or "evil" and would have nothing to do with the actual color of the pestilence.

Bridey Murphy did not always score hits, though. Numerous Irish historians and scholars felt that she must have been more Scottish than Irish, especially when she gave the name Duncan for her father and brother. Certain experts sympathetically suggested that she may have been attempting to say Dunnock, rather than Duncan.

William Barker could find no complete birth data for either Bridey or her kin, and he learned that she had shocked most Irish researchers with her crude term "ditched" to describe her burial. The Colorado journalist was informed that the Irish are much too reverent about the dead to employ such a brutal word.

Bridey demonstrated little knowledge of Ireland's history from 1800 to 1860. Bridey and Brian's honeymoon route was hopelessly untraceable and appeared to be confused with the trip that she had made to Antrim as a child of 10. The principal difficulty in accepting the whole of Bridey's story lay in the fact that so much of the testimony was unverifiable.

While most psychical researchers agree that the Bridey Murphy case is not a consciously contrived fraud, they will not rule out the role that some psychic or extrasensory ability may have played in the "memory" of the Irish woman allegedly reborn in a Colorado housewife. Other investigators have suggested that Mrs. S., Virginia Tighe, could have had several acquaintances throughout her life who were familiar with Ireland and who may each have imparted a bit of the memory of Bridey Murphy as it was mined from her subconscious by the hypnotic trance induced by Morey Bernstein.

As other researchers explored the claims of *The Search for Bridey Murphy*, the phenomenon of cryptomensia was also applied to the case when reporters for the *Chicago American* discovered that a woman named Bridie Murphey Corkell had lived across the street where Virginia Tighe had grown up. To say that cryptomensia was responsible for Tighe's alleged memories of a nineteenth-century Irishwoman is to propose that she had forgotten both the source of her "memory" and the fact that she had ever obtained it. Then, under hypnosis, such memories could be recalled so dramatically that they could be presented as a past-life memory.

The attempts to discredit Bridey Murphy as a manifestation of cryptomensia fail in the estimation of researchers C. J. Ducasse and Dr. **Ian Stevenson** (1918–   ). In Stevenson's estimation, the critics of the Bridey Murphy case provided only suppositions of possible sources of information, not evidence that these had been the sources.

The controversy over Bridey Murphy and the value of past-life regressions still rages. Those who champion the case state that it cannot be denied that Bridey/Virginia possessed a knowledge of nineteenth-century Ireland that contained a number of details that were unfamiliar even to historians and authorities. Such details, when checked for accuracy after elaborate research, were found to be correct in Bridey's favor. Others insist that such data could have been acquired paranormally, through extrasensory means, and therefore does not prove reincarnation. Skeptics dismiss the evidence of Bridey Murphy's alleged past-life memories by stating that they originated in her childhood, rather than in a prior incarnation.

On July 12, 1995, Virginia Tighe Morrow died in her suburban Denver home. She had never again submitted to hypnosis by any researcher seeking to test her story. Although she never became a true believer in reincarnation, she always stood by the entranced recollections as recorded in *The Search for Bridey Murphy*.

✤ DELVING DEEPER

Bernstein, Morey. *The Search for Bridey Murphy*. New York: Doubleday and Co., 1956.

Steiger, Brad. *You Will Live Again*. Nevada City, Calif.: Blue Dolphin Publishing, 1996.

PAST-LIFE THERAPY

In past-life therapy, subjects arrive at the office of a past-life therapist with a phobia, an obsession, or a compulsion that seems unrelated to anything they can remember in their present life experience. Their problem has increasingly begun to become awkward, stressful, or embarrassing. When they relive a past life during a hypnotic regression or in a dream or a vision, they view a scenario in which they see themselves setting in motion that karma, the initial action or deed that created their phobia, obsession, or compulsion. Dissociated from their present life experience, they become capable of accepting responsibility for a past action that was performed in a prior existence. Once the subjects have made the transfer of responsibility to the present life and have recognized that the "fault" or the trauma lies in a time far removed from current concerns, they are able to deal with the matter with a new perspective and without embarrassment or shame.

Today, a great number of past-life therapists have learned that it really doesn't matter whether past-life recall is pure fantasy or the actual memory of a prior existence. What does

Dr. Brian Weiss with his book on reincarnation. One of his patients in his book claims to have 86 past lives. (AP/WIDE WORLD PHOTOS)

matter to the therapists is their claim that thousands of men and women have obtained a definite and profound release from a present pain or phobia by reliving the origin of their problems in some real or imagined former existence.

While skeptics may scoff at men and women who claim to recall past lives while under hypnosis, and even question their mental balance, psychiatrist Reima Kampman of the University of Oulu in Finland has said that her research demonstrates that people who are able to display multiple personalities or alleged past lives under hypnosis are actually healthier than those who cannot. According to Kampman, one of her subjects, a 28-year-old woman, revealed eight different personalities in progressive chronological order, ranging from a young woman who lived in Russia during the Bolshevik Revolution to an eighteenth-century titled English lady to a girl named Bessina who said that she lived in Babylonia. Contrary to what the established psychiatric literature would lead one to believe, Kampman stated, these were not troubled minds on the verge of fragmentation.

Compared with those who could not rise to the hypnotist's challenge, the multiple-personality group had greater stress tolerance, more adaptability, and far less guilt. Internal identity diffusion—a neurotic quality defined as the discrepancy between what one feels about oneself and how one feels that others perceive one—was also greater in the nonre-sponsive group.

Kampman suggests that in the ego-threat-ening situation induced by the hypnotist's request for other personalities, only the men-tally healthy can afford to respond creatively: "Creating multiple personalities is evidence of a highly specialized ability of the personality to extricate itself adaptively by a deep regres-sion of the conflict situation created by the hypnotist" (*Human Behavior*, May 1977).

Bettye B. Binder, former president of the Association for Past-Life Research and Thera-pies, has conducted over 3,600 individual past-life regressions and has taught nearly 20,000 students in workshops and classes since 1980. The author of six books on past lives, her *Past Life Regression Guidebook* (1992) has become a popular textbook in the field. When asked to provide a case history demonstrating the benefits of past-life regression, she often makes reference to the case of "Darrell," whose story was featured on the television programs *Sightings* and *20/20*.

A native of Toronto who has lived in Southern California for many years, Darrell came to Bettye Binder with a terror of drown-ing in the middle of the ocean. He was not frightened of seashores, swimming pools, or other bodies of water, but he would not ven-ture far into the ocean because of a morbid fear of drowning there. In three separate regressions with Binder, Darrell discovered that he drowned in the middle of the ocean in three previous lifetimes. In one, he was a black slave in the South, about 1840, who tried to escape in a small boat that sank due to an explosion on board. In 1940, before the United States entered World War II, he was a young man from Pennsylvania who joined the Canadian Air Force and was shot down over the Pacific Ocean. His death on the *Titanic*, however, was the most important experience related to his phobia.

In regression, Darrell experienced being a crew member on the *Titanic*, which sank after striking an iceberg in the middle of the Atlantic Ocean in April 1912. He was asleep in his bunk when the crisis began. He was awakened and told to go to the boiler room where he worked. It was flooded, so he went to the next available boiler room that was still free of seawater. He and his workmates did their best to get the ship moving, but it soon became evident that the huge ship was sink-ing. Darrell's last memory in that lifetime was being tangled up in ropes as the ship began to lurch and dive into the depths of the sea.

Binder has had Darrell undergo this partic-ular regression on many different occasions, both as a demonstration before students and for television. Each time, she has observed, Darrell receives more resolution from such explorations of his past life as a victim of the *Titanic* disaster. In June 1992, when she regressed him for a television crew, Darrell saw his angels leading him away from the body that was entangled in heavy ropes and being pulled down into the ocean. He felt peace and light come over him as he rose toward the heavens, and he also experienced great com-passion for the man that he had been.

What is most significant about Darrell's case, Binder pointed out, is how the experi-ence of past-life regression has turned his life around. When he had first come to her, she said, he was a timid, withdrawn, fearful young man, whose life and career were going nowhere. He had dreams of becoming an ani-mator for a major movie or television studio, but those aspirations were not being realized. After a series of regressions in 1992, Darrell's career began to move in an exciting new direction. He began to exhibit a sense of peace and happiness that he had never before known. He became poised and self-assured. He was hired as an animator on a major fea-ture film, and at Christmas in 1994, he was hired to direct an animated feature film, a huge career breakthrough.

According to Binder, "Darrell has learned lessons that he was unable to learn in his pre-vious past lives in which he drowned, and he is no longer phobic about the ocean. Today, Darrell is a man who smiles easily and who is doing what he loves most in life. He has gained a spiritual peace for the first time in several lifetimes."

In her view of past-life exploration, Binder believes that the key to making reincarnation acceptable in the Western world lies in the culture learning to acknowledge individuals' true identities as souls that exist in a multi-dimensional universe where time is not limited to a linear construction. Through the altered states of consciousness available in meditation or hypnosis, one can experience what "multi-dimensionality" and "simultaneous time" feel like even if one does not yet understand what the words mean.

A teacher of reincarnation since 1980, Binder frequently emphasizes in her classes that individuals don't *have* souls, they *are* souls. "All of us are souls who chose to become human beings, but our human identity is limited to being in this body," she said. "The soul is pure energy, and energy cannot be destroyed. The soul's existence is independent of the body it occupies. It is the soul that continues to exist after the human body dies, and it is the soul that reincarnates lifetime after lifetime."

Dr. Russell C. Davis was editor of *The Journal of Regression Therapy* and practiced past-life therapy for 40 years before his death in 1998. According to Davis, the concept of an eternal part of oneself that moves from lifetime to lifetime is fundamental to conducting past-life regressions. Whether one chooses to call this "eternal part" the soul or the Higher Self, it is "the very core of the person that is accessed during the experience and in which is stored that collective awareness of what is and what was. Over the years, I have come to call this 'the part of us that knows and understands,' and it is this element of the person that I address during the regression experience. In essence, in conducting a past-life regression, this 'part [of the subject] which knows and understands,' the 'Higher Self,' is asked to reveal to the client's conscious awareness information and understanding about a past life (or lives) and what its meaning is to the present."

❋ DELVING DEEPER

Binder, Bettye B. *Discovering Your Past Lives and Other Dimensions*. Culver City, Calif.: Reincarnation Books & Tapes, 1994.

Binder, Bettye B. *Past Live Regressions Guidebook*. Torrance, Calif.: Reincarnation Books, 1992.

Moody, Raymond A., Jr. *Life After Life*. New York: Bantam Books, 1985.

Sutphen, Richard. *Past Lives, Future Loves*. New York: Pocket Books, 1978.

Wambaugh, Helen. *Reliving Past Lives: The Evidence Under Hypnosis*. New York: Harper & Row, 1978.

Weiss, Brian. *Many Lives, Many Masters*. New York: Simon & Schuster, 1988.

Whitton, Joel, and Joe Fisher. *The Case for Reincarnation*. New York: Bantam Books, 1984.

IAN STEVENSON (1918–)

Dr. Ian Stevenson is the former head of the Department of Psychiatry at the University of Virginia, and now is director of that school's Division of Personality. In the more than 40 years that he has devoted to the documentation of past-life memories, Stevenson has done a great deal to put a serious study of reincarnation on a scientific basis. His classic work, *Twenty Cases Suggestive of Reincarnation*, which was published by the American Society for Psychical Research in 1966, is an exhaustive exercise in research in which Stevenson dons the mantle of historian, lawyer, and psychiatrist to gather evidence from as many percipients as possible.

Stevenson has now collected over 3,000 cases of past-life memories of children from all over the world, and in 1997 published *Reincarnation and Biology: A Contribution to the Etiology of Birthmarks and Birth Defects*. In the first volume of this massive work, he primarily describes the various kinds of birthmarks, those uniquely distinguishing marks on a newborn's skin cannot be explained only by inheritance. The second volume focuses on deformities and other anomalous markings with which certain children are born and cannot be traced back to inheritance, prenatal, or perinatal (formed during birth) occurrences.

Although Stevenson concedes that nobody has "as yet thought up a way that reincarnation could be proved in a laboratory test tube," he argues that even in the laboratory the scientist cannot escape from human testimony of one kind or another. In his essay "The Evidence for Survival from Claimed Memories of Former Incarnations," which won the American **Society for Psychical Research**'s 1960 contest in honor of **William James** (1842–1910), Stevenson discussed a number of hypotheses that he feels deserve consideration in attempting to comprehend data from cases suggestive of reincarnation. Among these hypotheses are the following:

Unconscious Fraud. In some cases, other individuals have attributed statements to the subjects alleging past lives that they never made, and in this way have permitted the initial claim to grow out of proportion. Stevenson terms this a kind of "collective hallucination" in which further statements are imaginatively attributed to the subjects.

Derivation of the "Memories" through Normal Means with Subsequent Forgetting of the Source. Stevenson holds this hypothesis to be most often responsible for the many cases of pseudo-reincarnation. He quotes from the work of E. S. Zolik, who studied the ability of students to create fictitious former lives while under hypnosis. These fantasy personalities were the products of bits and pieces of characters in novels, motion pictures, and remembered childhood acquaintances. Because of the remarkable ability of the human mind to acquire paranormal information and to create fantasy personalities all its own, Stevenson cites another difficulty in serious research into cases suggestive of reincarnation: "We need to remember that items normally acquired can become mingled with those paranormally derived in the productions of persons apparently remembering past lives."

Racial Memory. Stevenson, a medical doctor as well as a psychiatrist, is well aware that science has not yet discovered the parameters of genetic transmission. He feels, however, that such a theory applied to the alleged memories of previous lives will encounter serious obstacles. While he concedes that the hypothesis of "remembering" our ancestors' lives might apply in those instances where it can be shown that the subject having the past-life memories belongs to a genetic line descending from the personality whom he or she claims to be, in most cases, Stevenson believes that the separation of time and place makes "…impossible any transmission of information from the first to the second person along genetic lines."

Extrasensory Perception of the Items of the Apparent Recollections in the Minds of Living Persons. Stevenson finds it difficult to accept the theory that an individual gifted with paranormal talents should limit the exercise of such abilities only to communication with the specific living persons who might have relevant bits of information about the deceased personalities from whom the subjects claim to derive their memories.

Retrocognition. Stevenson is receptive to the notion that the psychic ability known as retrocognition could be responsible for some cases suggestive of reincarnation. The subjects in such cases could be stimulated by being at the scene of historical events, by some object connected with the events themselves or persons who participated in them, or in an altered state of consciousness, such as staring at a crystal ball or being in a trance.

Possession. The doctor recognizes the plausibility of temporary possession as an explanation for some apparent memories of former incarnations. But he makes a very important distinction: In cases of possession, the entity that has accomplished the transformation of personality usually does so solely for the purpose of communication with its loved ones on the physical plane, and it never claims to be a former incarnation of the subject who has temporarily provided a physical body. In true cases suggestive of reincarnation, there is no other personality claiming to occupy the body of the subject and the entity speaks of a former life, not of communication with surviving loved ones.

✷ DELVING DEEPER

Stevenson, Ian. *Twenty Cases Suggestive of Reincarnation.* 2d ed. Charlottesville: University Press of Virginia, 1974.

MAKING THE CONNECTION

anthroposophy A spiritual or religious philosophy that Rudolph Steiner (1861–1925), an Austrian philosopher and scientist, developed, with the core belief centering around the human accessibility of the spiritual world to properly developed human intellect. Steiner founded the Anthroposophical Society in 1912 to promote his ideas that spiritual development should be humanity's foremost concern.

clairvoyance The ability to see, visualize, or sense things beyond the normal range of human vision or senses.

cosmology The philosophical study and explanation of the nature of the universe or the scientific study of the origin and structure of the universe.

cryptomensia A state of consciousness in which the true source or origin of a particular memory is forgotten or is attributed to a wrongful source or origin.

ephemerality Refers to the state of something living or lasting for a markedly short or brief time. The nature of existing or lasting for only a day, such as certain plants or insects.

hieroglyphs A system of writing which uses symbols or pictures to denote an object, concept, sound, or sequence of sounds. The word comes from an ancient Greek term meaning "sacred carving," to describe the characters carved on Egyptian tombs.

incantations Ritual chanting or recitation of verbal charms or spells to produce a supposed magic effect.

Kabbalah (Cabala, Cabbala, Kabala, or Kabbala) A body of mystical Jewish teachings based on an interpretation of hidden meanings contained in the Hebrew scriptures. Kabbalah is Hebrew for "that which is received," and also refers to a secret oral tradition handed down from teacher to pupil. The term Kabbalah is generally used now to apply to all Jewish mystical practice.

karmic law Karma is the Sanskrit word for "deed." In the Eastern religions of Buddhism and Hinduism all deeds of a person in this life dictate an equal punishment or reward to be met in the next life or series of lives. In this philosophy, it is a natural moral law rather than a divine judgment which provides the process of development, enabling the soul into higher or lower states, according to the laws of cause and effect to be met.

manitou A supernatural force, or spirit that suffuses various living things, as well as inanimate objects, according to the Algonquian peoples. In the mythology of the Ojibwa of the eastern United States, Manitou is the name of the supreme deity, or God, and means "Great Spirit."

precognition The direct knowledge of the ability to foresee what is going to happen in the future, especially if this perception is gained through other than the normal human senses or extrasensory.

retrocognition The mental process or faculty of knowing, seeing, or perceiving things, events, or occurrences of things in the past, especially through other than the normal human senses as in extrasensory.

Sanskrit Sanskrit is an ancient Indo-European language and the language of traditional Hinduism in India. Spoken between the fourteenth and fifth centuries B.C.E., it has been considered and maintained as a priestly and literary language of the sacred Veda scriptures and other classical texts.

shaman A religious or spiritual leader, usually possessing special powers, such as that of prophecy, and healing, and acts as an intermediary between the physical and spiritual realms.

shofar A trumpet made of a ram's horn, blown by the ancient and modern Hebrews during religious ceremonies and as a signal in battle.

soul The animating and vital principal in human beings, credited with the faculties of will, emotion, thought and action and often conceived as an immaterial entity, separate from the physical body. The spiritual nature of human beings, regarded as immortal, separable from the body at death, and susceptible to happiness or misery in a future state. The disembodied spirit of a dead human being.

telepathy Communication of thoughts, mental images, ideas, feelings, or sensations from one person's mind to another's without the use of speech, writing, signs, or symbols.

transience A state of impermanence, or lasting for only a brief time. Remaining in a place only for a short time, or the brief appearance of someone or something.

CHAPTER 2

Mediums and Mystics

Throughout history, certain men and women have claimed that they can speak to the deceased on the other side and relay messages to those who yearn for such confirmation that there is life after death. In this chapter, the colorful and controversial lives of such mystics and mediums will be examined and their philosophies, techniques, and spiritual tools identified.

Introduction

The belief in an afterlife in which the soul continues a conscious and rational existence is an intensely powerful human longing. While even those of deep religious faiths may still have apprehensions when it comes to facing death and standing on the edge of the boundaries of the unknown, throughout history there have been those men and women who claim that they can not only conceive of a future life, but also directly experience it and communicate with those souls who have died and gone there. These individuals who claim such extraordinary abilities are known as mystics, mediums, or channels, and they are as sought after by those who seek reassurance of the afterlife in the twenty-first century as they were in the days of the pharaohs.

For traditional shamans in aboriginal cultures throughout the world, the barrier between the world of spirits and the world of humans was a very thin one, and the ability to communicate with the spirits and to travel in their dimension of reality was an essential facet of the shamans' responsibility to their people. It was also true of the medicine people and shamans of the various Native American tribes, and a belief in a total partnership with the world of spirits and the ability to make personal contact with those who had changed planes of existence was a basic tenet in their spiritual practice.

Whether the man or woman who claims contact with the spirit world is a traditional shaman or a contemporary channeler, he or she will most likely establish that communication through the ethereal services of a spirit guide or spirit control. This entity serves the medium as a link between the worlds of flesh and spirit. It is said to have the ability to usher the spirits of the departed to a level of the medium's consciousness that permits him or her to relay messages to those who have come to hear words of comfort and inspiration.

While most of the major religions condemn those who claim to be able to speak to the dead or deny their abilities, mediums have countered by questioning the lack of logic displayed by members of orthodox faiths who say that it is all right to hope for survival after death but wrong to prove it. For centuries, various investigators of mediumistic phenomena have argued that if it could be proved that sincere and honest mediums were able to contact the dead, then the mysteries of the afterlife could be answered, and organized religion's hope of the future life would be transformed from an ethereal promise to a demonstrable guarantee.

Those scientists who have been intrigued enough by spiritistic phenomena to study it in a serious manner under laboratory conditions are known as psychical researchers, and they have been examining mediums and mystics in a structured and determined process since the establishment of the British Society of Psychical Research in 1882 and the American Society in 1885.

Most mediums, however, feel that they can get along well without psychical researchers. Successful mediums do not need to prove anything to their followers, who already believe in their abilities. The tests of the psychical researchers are often tedious and set up to be administered by objective and unemotional personnel. The mediums argue that the laboratory certainly does not offer the mood and atmosphere to be found in the seance parlor, and the bright lights are not as conducive to the trance state as the dimly lighted room. Psychical researchers counter such arguments by pointing out that laboratory controls are necessary to unmask the charlatans, because there are those who deceive people during their period of grieving for a deceased loved one.

This chapter will introduce some extraordinarily colorful and fascinating men and women and explore the remarkable claims of mediums who insist that they can summon spirits from the world beyond death. There are passionate believers, determined debunkers, and individuals who believe that they have proved scientifically and conclusively that a future existence awaits the soul of each human who passes from life to death.

A Native American Indian medicine man, spiritual leader, philosopher, and acknowledged spokesman and intertribal shaman for the Cherokee and Shoshone tribes, Rolling Thunder, served as a consultant to the popular films *Billy Jack* (1971), and its sequel, *Billy Jack II* (1972). His way of life as a powerful healer, teacher, and activist gave him widespread fame following the films. Internationally known, Rolling Thunder's spiritual counsel and tribal skills were sought on a regular basis by many in the entertainment industry.

Rolling Thunder was among the first ever to be studied by mainstream institutions and undergo many laboratory tests to determine the authenticity of his shamanic skills. It had been said that his powers over the elements of nature surpassed any seen in recent times. Reports of Rolling Thunder's ability to "make rain" on a clear day, to heal disease and wounds, to transport or teleport objects through the air, and his telepathic skills were legendary until he agreed to submit himself to testing. His abilities have been investigated and documented by such organizations as the Menninger Foundation.

An advocate for Native American rights, as well as for ecological harmony, Rolling Thunder traveled widely and was in great demand worldwide for his insight and teachings. He himself joked that he had to make it rain and thunder "in order to clean the polluted air" before he spoke in a new city. Speaking before spiritual, ecological, psychological, and healing gatherings, Rolling Thunder participated in conferences sponsored by the Association for Research and Enlightenment (Edgar Cayce's Foundation), the Menninger Foundation, the East West Academy of the Healing Arts, the Stockholm United Nations Conference on the Environment, the World Conference of Spiritual Leaders of the United Nations, and the World Humanity Conference in Vancouver, B.C., among others.

Often controversial, and regarded even militant at times, Rolling Thunder was known for being outspoken and "telling it like it is." "The Great Spirit guides me to tell people what they need to know, not what

ROLLING THUNDER

they want to know," he often said. Never making claims for his special powers, he reminded those who called him a medicine man, or who spoke of his healing abilities, that "All power belongs to the Great Spirit." Then he would add, "You call him God." In response to the charges of being militant, Rolling Thunder said, "Yes, I'm a militant. So was your great healer they call Jesus Christ."

SOURCES:

Boyd, Doug. *Rolling Thunder.* New York: Dell Publishing Co., Inc.: 1974.

Steiger, Brad, and Sherry Hansen Steiger. *Indian Wisdom And Its Guiding Power.* West Chester, Penn.: Whitford Press: 1991.

Steiger, Sherry Hansen, and Brad Steiger. *Hollywood and the Supernatural.* New York: St. Martin's Press: 1990.

Shaman's headdress.

Shamanism

A shaman is one who serves his people by acting as an intermediary to the spirit world. The claimed ability to communicate with the world beyond death is at least as old as the time when early humans first conceived the idea that some part of them somehow survived physical death and existed in some other place in spirit form. The grief that came with the sorrowful thought of losing all contact with a loved one was lessened by the assertion of a fellow tribesperson that he or she could still communicate with the spirit of the one who lay in the grave. Among early humans, those individuals who claimed to be able to visit the place of the dead were known as shamans, and the messages that they relayed from the spirit world were sought by the elders regarding every major tribal decision. Originally, the term "shaman" was applied to the spirit doctors and exorcists of the Tungus of Siberia, but in recent years the title has been applied as well to the medicine men and women of the various North American tribes who also serve as mediums, healers, and visionaries for their people. Many tribal traditionalists still revere the wisdom that is shared by those men and women who maintain the shamanic traditions and who travel to the other side in the company of their spirit helper.

In the introduction to his book *The Way of the Shaman* (1982) anthropologist Michael Harner writes that shamans "...whom we in the 'civilized' world have called 'medicine men' and 'witchdoctors' are the keepers of a remarkable body of ancient techniques that they use to achieve and maintain well-being and healing for themselves and members of their communities." Harner states that shamanic methods are remarkably similar throughout the world, "even for those peoples whose cultures are quite different in other respects, and who have been separated by oceans and continents for tens of thousands of years."

The anthropologist Ivar Lissner, who spent a great deal of time among the Tungus of Siberia, as well as native peoples in North America, defines a shaman as one "...who knows how to deal with spirits and influence them....The essential characteristic of the shaman is his excitement, his ecstasy and trancelike condition....[The elements which constitute this ecstasy are] a form of self-severance from mundane existence, a state of heightened sensibility, and spiritual awareness. The shaman loses outward consciousness and becomes inspired or enraptured. While in this state of enthusiasm, he sees dreamlike apparitions, hears voices, and receives visions of truth. More than that, his soul sometimes leaves his body to go wandering."

It is believed that during those times when the souls of shamans go wandering, they project their consciousness to faraway places on Earth as well as to the shadow world of spirits. These soul journeys may inform those who seek their shaman's counsel of everything from where to find the choicest herds of game to how to banish a troublesome spirit from their home. Those men and women who aspire to learning such techniques for themselves may pay a shamanic practitioner for the privilege of undergoing an arduous course of training that would include periods of fasting, going on vision quests, and encounters with the world of spirits—a regimen that may take the student many years to accomplish.

In 1865, the great warrior Roman Nose, who had studied under the tutelage of White Bull, an elderly Cheyenne medicine man, lay on a raft for four days in the midst of a sacred lake. Roman Nose partook of no food or water, and he suffered a relentless sun by day and a pouring rain by night. But he felt none of these distractions, for Roman Nose was in a **trance** so deep that he appeared to be dead.

When he returned from the **Land of the Grandparents,** the place of spirits, Roman Nose had obtained the necessary vision teachings to attack the white man's cavalry who were invading the Powder River country. On the day of battle, Roman Nose mounted his white pony and told the assembled warriors not to accompany his charge until the Blue Coat soldiers had emptied their rifles at him. The power that he had received from the spirits during his "little death" had rendered him impervious to their bullets.

Roman Nose broke away from the rest of the war party and urged his pony into a run toward the ranks of white soldiers standing behind their wagons. When he was so near that he could see their faces, Roman Nose wheeled his mount and rode parallel to their ranks and their rifles. He made three or four passes before volley after volley from the soldiers' Springfield rifles. He remained untouched, unscratched. Finally a musket ball knocked his pony out from under him, but Roman Nose rose untouched and signaled his warriors to attack. They believed that magic he had received from the spirits kept him safe that day from all the bullets.

While one can pursue the path of becoming a medicine man or woman by undergoing a **vision quest,** receiving a **spirit guide,** and serving an apprenticeship under the direction of an established medicine person, traditionally, it seems, the greatest shamans are created by spiritual intervention in the shape of a sudden and severe illness, spells of fever, epileptic seizures, or possession by tutelary spirits. It would appear that those who become the most effective intermediaries between the worlds of flesh and spirit must have their physical bodies purged and nearly destroyed before they can establish contact with spirits.

Twylzh selecting medicine stones. (ARCHIVES OF BRAD STEIGER)

Black Elk (1863–1950), the respected medicine practitioner/shaman of the Oglala Sioux, became a "hole," a port of entry for spirits to enter the physical world, when he fell terribly ill as a boy of nine. He heard voices telling him that it was time for him to receive his first great vision, and he was taken out of his body by two spirit guides who informed him that they were to take him to the land of his grandfathers. Here, in the land of the spirits, Black Elk received the great vision that was to sustain him all of his life. When he was returned to his body, his parents greeted the first flutterings of his eyelids with great joy. The boy had been lying as if dead for 12 days.

A shaman is one who acts as an intermediary to the spirit world.

As he grew to maturity and learned to focus his healing and **clairvoyant** energies, Black Elk never failed to credit the other world for his accomplishments and to explain that he was but a "hole" through which the spirits entered this world. Rather than the

term "hole," today's counterparts of the shamanic mission might say that they are **spirit mediums** or channels through which the power from the spirit world might flow.

In many tribal societies, the pseudo-death, or **near-death experience,** appears to be nearly a precondition that must be met by those who aspire to the role of the most prestigious of shamans.

A crucial element in shamanism is the ability to rise above the constrictions and restraints of linear time.

In 1890, Jack Wilson, a Paiute who worked as a hired hand for a white rancher, came down with a terrible fever. His sickness became so bad that for three days he lay as if dead. When he returned to consciousness, he told the Paiutes who had assembled around

his "corpse" that his spirit had walked with God, the Old Man, for those three days; and the Old Man had given him a powerful vision to share with the Paiute people.

His vision proclaimed that the dead of many tribes were all alive, waiting to be reborn. If the native peoples wished the buffalo to return, the grasses to grow tall, and the rivers to run clean, they must not injure anyone; they must not do harm to any living thing. They must not make war. They must lead lives of purity, cease gambling, put away strong drink, and guard themselves against all lusts of the flesh.

Jack Wilson's grandfather had been the esteemed prophet Wodziwob. His father had been the respected holy man Tavibo. Among his own people, Wilson was known as Wovoka; and now he, too, had spent his time of initiation in death and had emerged as a holy man and a prophet.

The most important part of the vision that the Great Spirit had given to Wovoka was the

Ghost Dance. The Paiute prophet told his people that the dance had never been performed anywhere on Earth. It was the dance of the spirit people of the Other World. To perform this dance was to insure that the Great Mystery's blessings would be bestowed upon the tribe. Wovoka said that the Old Man had spoken to him as if he were his son and assured him that many miracles would be worked through him. The native people had received their shamanic messiah.

A crucial element in shamanism is the ability to rise above the constrictions and restraints of linear time. In his text for *American Indian Ceremonial Dances* (1972), John Collier comments upon the shaman's and the traditional native people's possession of a time sense that is different from the present societal understanding of the passages of minutes, hours, and days. At one time everyone possessed such freedom, Collier says, but the mechanized world took it away. If humans could exist, as the native people in their whole lives affirmed, "in a dimension of time, a reality of time—not linear, not clock-measured, clock-controlled, and clock-ended," Collier suggests that they should gladly enter it, for individuals would expand their consciousness by being there. "In solitary, mystical experience many of ourselves do enter another time dimension," he continues. But the "frown of clockwork time" demands a return to chronological time. The shaman, however, recognizes that this other time dimension originated "within the germ plasm and the organic rhythms…of moveless eternity. It is life's instinct and environment and human society's instinct and environment. To realize it or not realize it makes an enormous difference."

Achieving a deep **trance** state appears to be the most effective way that shamans regularly abandon linear time restrictions in order to gain entrance to that other dimension of time. By singing their special songs received in vision quests or dreams, shamans put themselves into trances that permit them to travel with their spirit helpers to the Land of the Grandparents, a place free of "clockwork time," where they gain the knowledge to predict the future, to heal, and to relay messages of wisdom from the spirit people.

Shaman's mask. *(Archives of Brad Steiger)*

✤ DELVING DEEPER

Harner, Michael. *The Way of the Shaman*. New York: Bantam Books, 1982.

Hirschfelder, Arlene, and Paulette Molin. *The Encyclopedia of Native American Religions*. New York: MJF Books, 1992.

Lissner, Ivar. *Man, God and Magic*. New York: G. P. Putnam's Sons, 1961.

Steiger, Brad. *Medicine Power*. New York: Doubleday, 1972.

SPIRIT GUIDE

When **spirit mediums** speak of their control or guide, they are referring to the entity from the world beyond physical death who assists them in establishing contact with deceased humans. The spirit guides of mediums usually claim to have lived as humans on Earth before the time of their death and their graduation to higher realms of being.

In the shamanic tradition, the spirit guide or spirit helper is usually received by those who choose to participate in a vision quest. Before initiates embark upon this ordeal, tribal elders and shamans tutor them for many weeks on what to expect and what is expected of them. In many shamanic traditions, the

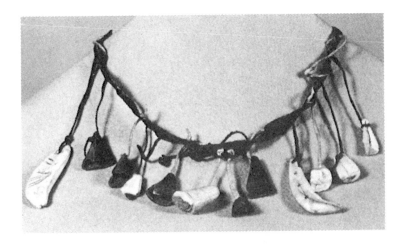

Shaman's necklace.
(ARCHIVES OF BRAD
STEIGER)

spirit helper serves as an ambassador from the world of spirits to the world of humans and often manifests in animal form to serve as a kind of chaperone during visits to other dimensions of reality.

A spirit guide or spirit helper is received by those who choose to participate in a vision quest.

For the more contemporary spirit mediums, who often prefer to call themselves "channels," the guide may represent itself as a being who once lived as a human on Earth or as a Light Being, an extraterrestrial, or even an angel. Regardless of the semantics involved, today's mediums and channels follow the basic procedures of ancient shamanic traditions.

✦ DELVING DEEPER

Fodor, Nandor. *Between Two Worlds*. New York: Paperback Library, 1969.

Garrett, Eileen. *Many Voices: The Autobiography of a Medium*. New York: G. P. Putnam's Sons, 1968.

Murphy, Gardner, and Robert O. Ballou, eds. *William James on Psychical Research*. New York: Viking Press, 1960.

Paranormal News. http://paranormal.about.com/science/paranormal/library/blnews.htm. 1 October 2001.

Post, Eric G. *Communicating with the Beyond*. New York: Atlantic Publishing, 1946.

TOTEM ANIMAL

Among the shamanic or medicine teachings of the traditional Native Americans, the totem animal represents the physical form of one's spirit helper, the guide, who will lead the shaman into the spirit world and return him or her safely to the physical world. Contrary to the misinterpretations of early missionaries, the native people did not worship these animal representations of their guides as gods.

Latvian ethnologist Ivar Lissner stated in his *Man, God, and Magic* (1961) that his 17 years of expeditions among the shamans and people of the Tungus, Polynesians, Malaysians, Australian Aborigines, Ainus, Chinese, Mongols, and North American tribes demonstrated to him quite clearly that totemism is not religion. While all these diverse people lived in a world filled with animate beings, they all believed in a single supreme deity.

Aside from a few Venus-type mother-goddess statuettes, there remains a rather strange collection of ghostly creatures and a great variety of two-legged beings with the heads of animals and birds. Why, so many anthropologists have wondered, did these cave painters, despite their remarkable artistic gifts, never pass on an accurate idea of their features? Why did they confine themselves to portraying beings that were half-human, half-animal?

And then Lissner has an inspiration. It is quite possible that the Stone-Age artists really were portraying themselves, but in something more than in human shape. Perhaps they were depicting themselves "...in the guise of intermediary beings who were stronger than common men and able to penetrate more deeply into the mysteries of fate, that unfathomable interrelationship between animals, men, and gods." Lissner suggests that what the ancient cave painters may have been relaying is that the "road to supernatural powers is easier to follow in animal shape and that spirits can only be reached with an animal's assistance." The ancient artists may have been portraying themselves after all, but in animal guise, shamanistically.

The **spirit guides,** appearing as totemic animals, guide the shamans to the mysterious, transcendent reality beyond the material world and lead them into another dimension of time and space wherein dwell the inhabitants of the spirit world. It is through such a portal that mediumistic shamans must pass to gain their contact with the grandfathers and grandmothers who reside there. With their spirit guide at their side in the form of a totem animal, they can communicate with the spirits and derive wisdom and knowledge which will serve their tribe or those who have come to seek specific information from the world beyond death.

✤ DELVING DEEPER

Bennett, Hal Zina. *Spirit Animals and the Wheel of Life*. Charlottesville, Va.: Hampton Roads Publishing, 2000.

Steiger, Brad. *Totems: The Transformative Power of Your Personal Animal Totem*. San Francisco: HarperSanFrancisco, 1997.

VISION QUEST

The personal revelatory experience and the contact with the spirit world received during the vision quest becomes the fundamental guiding force in the shaman's power (medicine). In addition to those who would be shamans, all traditional young men and women may partake of the vision quest, setting out alone in the wilderness to fast, to exhaust the physical body, to pray, to establish their own contact with the dimension of spirit, and to receive their individual "medicine" power. The dogma of tribal rituals and the religious expressions of others become secondary to the guidance that one receives from his or her own personal visions.

"The seeker goes forth solitary," writes Hartley Burr Alexander in *The World's Rim* (1967) "carrying his pipe and with an offering of tobacco. There in the wilderness alone, he chants his song and utters his prayers while he waits, fasting, such revelation as the Powers may grant."

The vision quest is basic to all traditional Native American religious experience, but one may certainly see similarities between the youthful tribal members presenting themselves to the Great Mystery as helpless, shelterless, and humble supplicants and the initiates of other religious traditions who fast, fla-

gellate, and prostrate themselves before their concept of a Supreme Being. In Christianity, the questing devotees kneel before a personal deity and beseech insight from the Son of God, whom they hope to please with their example of piety and self-sacrifice. In the Native American tribal traditions, the power granted by the vision quest comes from a vast and impersonal repository of spiritual energy; and those who partake of the quest receive their personal guardian spirit and a great vision that will grant them insight into the spiritual dimensions beyond physical reality.

T⊙TEM *animals represent the physical form of one's spirit helper, the guide, who will lead a shaman into the spirit world and return him or her safely to the physical world.*

For the traditional Native American, the vision quest may be likened to the first Communion in Christianity. Far from being a goal achieved, the vision quest marks the beginning of the traditionalist's lifelong search for knowledge and wisdom. Nor are the spiritual mechanics of the vision quest ignored once the youths have established contact with their guardian spirit and with the forces that are to aid them in the shaping of their destiny. At any stressful period of their life, the traditionalists may go into the wilderness to fast and to seek insight into the particular problems that beset them.

Hartley Burr Alexander saw the continued quest for wisdom of body and mind—the search for the single essential force at the core of every thought and deed—as the perpetually accumulating elements in medicine power. The reason the term "medicine" became applied to this life-career function is simply because those attaining stature as men and women who had acquired this special kind of wisdom were so often also great healers. The true meaning of "medicine" extends beyond the arts of healing to **clairvoyance, precognition,** and the control of weather elements.

The power received in the vision quest enables the practitioner to obtain personal contact with the invisible world of spirits and to pierce the sensory world of illusion which veils the Great Mystery.

✦ DELVING DEEPER

Harner, Michael. *The Way of the Shaman*. New York: Bantam Books, 1982.

Hirschfelder, Arlene, and Paulette Molin. *The Encyclopedia of Native American Religions*. New York: MJF Books, 1992.

SPIRIT MEDIUMSHIP

A spirit medium is a person who has become qualified in some special way to form a link between the living and the dead. Through the physical agency of the medium, the spirits of the deceased may speak to their family and friends and relay messages of comfort, support, and personal information. While some mediums gain impressions from the spirit world in a fully conscious state, others place themselves into a trance, which is often accompanied by manifestations that appear to defy known physical laws, such as moving objects without touching them, levitating the mediums' own body, and materializing spirit forms of the deceased.

A spirit medium is a person who has become qualified in some special way to form a link between the living and the dead.

The essential attribute that qualifies one to be a medium is an extreme or abnormal sensitivity which seemingly allows the spirits more easily to control the individual's psyche. For this reason, mediums are often referred to as "sensitives."

During **seances,** spirit mediums, often working in a **trance** state, claim to be under the direction of a spirit control or **spirit guide** that serves as an intermediary between themselves and the spirits of deceased men and women. Once contact has been made with particular spirits in the other world, the guide speaks through the medium and relays messages to the sitters, those men and women who have assembled in the seance room for the opportunity of hearing words of comfort or guidance from their departed loved ones.

Spirit mediums argue that while Christianity, Judaism, and Islam promise their followers a life eternal whose reality must be taken on faith alone, for thousands of years those who visit mediums have been able to base their hope for a life beyond the grave on the tangible evidence provided by the phenomena provided in the seance room. Although they have been condemned as cultists, scorned as **satanists,** and reprimanded for communing with evil spirits by most of the major religions, mediums have remained thick-skinned toward their critics among the various clergy.

In addition to any religious objections one might have toward the kind of evidence that spirit mediums present as proof of life after death, an important factor that has long contributed to the layperson's skepticism toward mediums is the fact that few areas of human relationships are so open to cruel deceptions. It has taken neither scientific training nor orthodox religious views to expose many spirit mediums as charlatans preying upon such human emotions as grief and sorrow over the loss of a loved one.

Beginning in the latter decades of the nineteenth century, **Spiritualists** and spirit mediums began to contend with an increasingly materialistic and mechanistic science that did a great deal to obliterate the idea of a soul and the duality of mind and body. The concept of an eternal soul was being steadily eroded by an emphasis on brain cells, conditioned responses, and memory patterns that could exist only while the body remained alive.

When the British Society for Psychical Research (BSPR) was established in 1882 and the American Society for Psychical Research (ASPR) was formed in 1885, leading spirit mediums such as **Florence Cook** (1856–1904), **Mina "Margery" Crandon** (1888–1941), **Leonora E. Piper** (1857–1950), and **Daniel**

S pooky phenomena like levitating tables and ghostly goings-on that occur at seances are most likely manifestations of the power of suggestion, say some researchers.

At *Fortean Times* conventions in London, paranormal investigator Dr. Richard Wiseman arranged two fake seances in which participants were told they would be taking part in a reenactment in which the "medium" would be an actor. Even though they were told it was not a "real" seance, 30 percent of those who participated were convinced they saw a luminous-edged table levitate in the air —when it was suggested by the staged medium that it would do so.

The "seance" was filmed in infrared light so they had proof that the table did not move, yet 30 percent of people believed it had levitated, Wiseman stated. Wiseman said, "These seances are pretty spooky. We're arguing that some seance phenomena are down to the power of suggestion." Conceding that there might indeed be other explanations, and sometimes even an element of fraud or trickery, Wiseman expressed there were no supernatural forces at work.

The experiments were carried out with Emma Greening, also from the University of Hertfordshire, and Dr. Matthew Smith from Liverpool Hope University College.

In another study, with people who claimed to be highly intuitive, Wiseman and his colleague, Dr. Paul Rogers, produced results to show their claims might be something else. Their findings indicated that being highly intuitive may be a result of their simply being good at assessing strangers' personality traits.

Wendy Snowden and Kei Ito, both researchers from the University of Buckingham, reported in another study that the feeling of having been there before, known as "deja vu," was a very common experience associated with the particular personality traits of extroversion and emotional disorders.

The researchers' findings were presented at the European Congress of Psychology, organized by the British Psychological Society in London.

ARE SPOOKY THINGS ALL IN THE MIND?

SOURCES:

British Psychological Society. http://www.bps.org.uk/index.cfm. 15 October 2001.

British Psychological Society Report to European Congress of Psychology. N.p., 2001.

C. P. Webster's Paranormal Photography

Researcher and artist Dr. Christopher Webster presents an interesting website of paranormal photography (especially the relationship between the crisis in belief and spirit photographs in the nineteenth century). Webster describes his work as being "to some degree a visual equivalent of automatic writing." He explores photography as a tool for recording the paranormal.

Sources:

C. P. Webster's Homepage and Paranormal Photography. http://users.aber.ac.uk/cpw/mainpage.html. 15 October 2001.

Dunglas Home (1833–1886) allowed themselves to be subjected to extensive tests conducted by psychical researchers, most of whom at least believed that man and mind were something more than physical things. However, as the experiments progressed year after year with spirit guides, materialized beings, and levitated objects, the researchers came more to believe in the enormous reach and abilities of the human psyche. They began to see the medium's spirit control as evidence that the human mind was capable of projecting a segment of itself unhampered by time and space, that one level of mind might be able to give "birth" to new personalities, that one level of the subconscious might telepathically gain knowledge of a departed individual from a sitter's memories while yet another level dramatized that knowledge into an imitation of the deceased's voice. In other words, the more the psychical researchers learned about the range and power of the human mind, the less credence they tended to grant to the spirit medium's "proof" of survival.

Spirit mediums have never felt that the phenomena of the seance room can be properly or fairly transferred to the sterile environment of the laboratory with any degree of success. In answering the criticism that spiritistic phenomena cannot be repeated again under individually controlled conditions as demanded of a scientific experiment, Maurice Barbanell (1902–1981) wrote in *This Is Spiritualism* (1966) that such was not possible "because mediumship involves the use of human beings. Whenever you deal with human beings, the human factor can be wayward and liable to upset the most intricate calculations."

Sometime in the 1940s, Dr. **J. B. Rhine** (1895–1980) summarized the research on survival evidence provided by spirit mediums in the laboratory to be a draw. While hardly anyone would claim that all the investigations conducted by psychical researchers since the 1880s could disprove the claim that "if a man shall die he shall in some manner or other be capable of living again," Rhine stated, "On the other hand, no serious scientific student of the field of investigation could say that a clear, defensible, scientific confrontation has been reached."

However, in March of 2001, scientists involved in a unique study of spirit mediums at the University of Arizona announced that their findings were so extraordinary that they raised fundamental questions about the survival of human consciousness after death. Professor Gary Schwartz, who led the team of researchers, concluded that highly skilled spirit mediums were able to deal directly with the dead, rather than merely with the minds of the sitters. In the opinion of the scientists, all the data they gathered was "consistently in accord with survival of consciousness after death." Based on all their data to date, Schwartz said, "The most parsimonious explanation is that the mediums are in direct communication with the deceased."

OUIJA BOARD

A Ouija board is used by some **spirit mediums** for purposes of contacting the other side. The instrument has two parts: a large smooth board, approximately 22 by 15 inches, and a three-legged triangular or heart-shaped pointer called a planchette, which slides easily across the face of the board. On the board the letters of the alphabet are arrayed in large, easily read characters in two curved lines; above to the right and left, respectively, are the words "yes" and "no." At the bottom are the words "Good Bye" (on some boards the word "Maybe" is added). During a **seance,** spirit mediums who use a Ouija board will place their fingers lightly on the planchette, and the spirits will provide the energy to move it to answer yes or no questions or to spell out names and more detailed information. On certain occasions, mediums may invite one or more sitters to place their own hands on the planchette so that they may feel the spiritual force controlling its movements and determine that the medium is not responsible for its actions.

Spirit mediums and certain psychical researchers maintain that the Ouija board has been instrumental in producing volumes of impressive communications from the other side and has also helped to develop hundreds of psychic-sensitives who have become adept at spirit contact.

The Ouija board was first available for the American public in 1890 and was marketed as a parlor game. According to its creators, E. C. Reiche, Elijah Bond, and Charles Kennard, the name of the board was derived from the ancient Egyptian word for good luck. Egyptologists flatly stated that "ouija" was not an ancient blessing, and William Fuld, a foreman at Kennard's company, agreed, protesting that he was the one who had really invented the board, fashioning its name by splicing together the German (ja) and the French (oui)

Ouija boards were created in the 1890s and used by spirit mediums to contact people in the afterlife. It was used in seances and as a parlor game. (CORBIS CORPORATION) words for "yes." In 1892, Kennard lost his company, and the selling of the Ouija boards was taken over by Fuld.

It seems likely that the Ouija board was inspired by the planchette that has been used by spirit mediums for centuries as they received automatic writing from their control. This planchette is a roughly triangular or heart-shaped object about four inches long and three inches wide, approximately one-eighth on an inch thick, and is mounted on two small legs which are generally padded with felt or equipped with small wheels or casters. At the tip of the planchette is a hole through which a soft pencil or ballpoint pen can be inserted point downward to serve as a third leg. When the planchette is placed on a plain sheet of paper and the medium places his or her fingers lightly on its surface, the planchette will move across the paper and write messages for those sitters in attendance at the seance.

THE *Ouija board was first available for the American public in 1890 and was marketed as a parlor game.*

The idea of the Ouija board may also be a modern adaptation of glass writing, a method still favored by some spirit mediums. In glass writing, a fairly large sheet of paper on which the letters of the alphabet are printed in a wide circle is placed on a table. On it, upside down, is placed a thin wine glass or a light water tumbler. Then the sitters, usually two and never more than four, place their finger-tips on the bottom of the upturned glass. After a while, spirit energy is believed to enter the glass. As the glass moves, it will come to rest over certain letters which, when written out on a separate sheet of paper, will spell out intelligent messages.

Skeptics believe that those mediums who use such devices as a Ouija board are not summoning spirits to provide the answers to questions put to the board, but are either consciously or unconsciously moving the planchette to spell

out the desired answers. The same thing is true of those persons who use the Ouija board as a kind of parlor game and who may receive "spirit communications" that appear on first examination to be baffling and indicative of unseen intelligences hovering nearby. These people may have permitted themselves to become suggestible by the mood provoked by seeking spirit contact and may have allowed the answers provided by the planchette to reflect their unconscious thoughts, fears, or wishes.

Both psychical researchers and skeptical investigators agree that impressionable children should not use the Ouija board as a game to be played late at night during slumber parties or sleep-overs. Often the messages relayed by the planchette—whether by spirits or the human unconscious—are of a profane and vile nature, revealing psychological weaknesses and primal fears.

❋ **DELVING DEEPER**

Gaynor, Frank, ed. *Dictionary of Mysticism*. New York: Philosophical Library, 1953.

Paranormal News. http://paranormal.about.com/science/paranormal/ library/blnews. htm. 1 October 2001.

Post, Eric G. *Communicating with the Beyond*. New York: Atlantic Publishing, 1946.

Skeptics Dictionary. http://skepdic.com. 1 October 2001.

SEANCE

Those who accept the teachings of **Spiritualism** believe that the varied phenomena associated with a seance, such as the levitation of objects, the materialization of spirit forms, or the acquisition of information beyond the normal sensory channels, emanate from spirits of the dead. Nonspiritualists who attend seances may hold a wide variety of religious and philosophical views, but they are likely to believe that some part of their being survives physical death, and they are willing to base their hope for life eternal on the phenomena of the seance room and the messages that they receive from discarnate beings.

After the sitters have been ushered into the seance room with its subdued lighting, they are invited to be seated, generally forming a circle around a large round table. The successful medium of an established reputa-

tion usually begins the seance in a friendly manner, making light conversation with each of the sitters. Such an approach relaxes the sitters and encourages them to express their wishes or any concerns that they might have about their communicating with the deceased. The medium is quite certain that their very presence at a seance indicates some degree of receptivity to the idea of communication with the dead. By the time the medium has entered the meditative state that induces the trance which summons the spirit guide, the sitters have been prepared by the medium's confidence and by their own beliefs and expectancy to accept the reality of an outside intelligence occupying the medium's physical body.

Mediums usually make it quite clear to neophyte sitters that the best manner in which

to secure a demonstration of genuine spiritistic phenomena is to assure the medium of one's good will. The sitter should also let the medium know that he or she is assured of the medium's honesty and abilities. The sitter should not hurry the medium, but keep in mind that the greatest guarantee of a successful seance is the medium's serene state of mind.

Often the spirit voices of the deceased speak through a metal trumpet that has been coated with luminous paint and which floats around the seance room. At trumpet seances—almost invariably conducted in complete darkness—the horn rises, apparently lifted by spirit hands, and the voices of the departed are heard speaking through the instrument. Theoretically, these voices manifest independently from the medium. Trumpet

A group of men and women levitating a table. (ARCHIVES OF BRAD STEIGER)

mediums are popular at Spiritualist camps, and husband and wife teams often travel the circle of summer camps giving demonstrations. Skeptics suggest that the reason for such male and female partnerships among trumpet mediums is the simple fact that many more voice tones may be imitated by the mediums during the course of a seance.

The materialization of an old coin, a ring, a bracelet, or a semiprecious stone from the spirit world to a sitter attending a seance is called an "apport" (from the French *apporter*, "to bring"). According to mediums, spirit friends bring these objects from great distances to lay before the sitters. Sometimes, according to mediums, these objects come from old treasure chests that have lain lost and forgotten beneath the land or sea for ages. On other occasions, the apports are said to be items lost by owners who are now dead and presented as gifts to their living relatives in attendance at the seance.

PSYCHIC *photography is nearly as old as photography itself.*

Spirit photography is one phenomenon of the seance room which seems to function as effectively in a spontaneous situation—such as snapping a photograph in a graveyard or a haunted house—as in the trappings of the sitting room. Psychic photography is nearly as old as photography itself. Since the earliest daguerrotypes, people have been taking pictures that have shown unexplainable objects and figures in the background. The idea that such figures and objects could have originated because of some paranormal influence has been rejected by the great majority of scientists. Hazy, spectral figures have been credited to the faulty processing of film. Clearly discernible and even recognizable features on the ghostly faces have been attributed to deliberate fakery.

In the early days of photography, such skepticism was understandable because of the many steps of processing that a photograph had to undergo before it could be examined. With loading and unloading of the film and darkroom operations that sometimes took hours, the opportunities for switching the plates were so great that even the most open-minded person could not help becoming suspicious if shown the photograph of spirit forms appearing over his or her shoulder after the portrait had been taken.

Technological advances in photography have managed to eliminate many such objections and, at the same time, created many more. With modern 10-second processing of film and the use of an observer's own camera, the opportunity for trickery in the seance room has been greatly lowered. But computer technology has been able to create seamless photographs of an endless array of ghosts, phantoms, and spirit forms. Ghost sites and spirit photographs are popular on the Internet and available for scrutiny by skeptic and believer alike.

Perhaps the ultimate in seance phenomena is the materialization of a spirit form that is in some way recognizable to one or more of the sitters. This is often accomplished through the utilization of a cabinet from which the materialized spirit emerges and communicates with those gathered around the medium. Spirit cabinets may be elaborate wooden structures or they may simply be blankets strung across wires in order to give the medium some privacy while in trance.

"The miracle of materialization," Maurice Barbanell (1902–1981) writes in *This Is Spiritualism* (1959), "is that in a few minutes there is reproduced in the seance room the birth which normally takes nine months in the mother's womb." Numerous researchers, as well as Spiritualists, have claimed to have seen a nearly invisible cord which links the materialized spirit figure to the medium and have all made the obvious comparison to an umbilical cord.

If, indeed, disembodied spirits are capable of fashioning temporary physical bodies for their ethereal personalities, just what kind of substance could be used for such a remarkable materialization? The name that Spiritualists give to such a substance is "ectoplasm," and they contend that it is drawn from the medium's body.

Maurice Barbanell claims that ectoplasm is ideoplastic by nature, which is to suggest that it may be molded by the psychic "womb" of the medium into a representation of the human body. Barbanell gives "spirit chemists" the credit for compounding ectoplasm until it assumes a human form that "breathes, walks, and talks, and is apparently complete even to fingernails."

French researcher Dr. Charles Richet (1850–1935) christened ectoplasm in the 1920s, but Baron Albert von Schrenck Notzing (1862–1929), a German investigator of the paranormal, gained a medium's permission to "amputate" some of the material and to analyze it. He found it to be a colorless, odorless, slightly alkaline fluid with traces of skin discs, minute particles of flesh, sputum, and granulates of the mucous membrane.

Few contemporary mediums attempt to produce ectoplasmic materializations in the seance room. Today, the vast majority of seances conducted by professional mediums fit into the categories of "direct-voice" communication, during which the spirit guide speaks directly to the sitters through a medium who appears in a deep state of trance; "twilight" communication, during which the medium in a very light altered state of consciousness relays messages from the guide in a conversational exchange with the sitters; or a "reading," in which the medium in a fully conscious state presents a series of images and messages that are "shown" or "told" by spirits who have some personal connection to the sitters.

Some **parapsychologists** who have witnessed a wide range of the phenomena of the seance room under test conditions state that all such manifestations may be the result of conscious or unconscious fraud on the part of the medium. These researchers also point out that the intelligence exhibited by the "spirits" appears to be always on a level with that of the medium through whom they manifest.

Such critics go on to state that the spirits can be controlled by the power of suggestion and can be made to respond to questions which have no basis in reality. Many investigators have discovered that they can as readily establish communication with an imaginary person as with a real one.

Other parapsychologists accept a great deal of the phenomena of the seance room, but they deny that the source of the manifestations comes from spirits. These investigators have found that in many seances conducted under controlled conditions, the information relayed often rises far above the medium's known objective intelligence, but they argue that there are a number of ways by which the subjective mind can be elevated above the threshold of ordinary consciousness to the point where various phenomena may be produced. When mediums induce the trance state which summons the spirit control, they may sincerely believe that their physical body is possessed by an outside intelligence. When the subjective mind is operating under the suggestion that it is being controlled by the spirit of a deceased person, it can become marvelously adept at filling in the details of that person's life on Earth.

For many individuals who hold certain religious views, it is abhorrent for anyone to claim the ability to talk to the dead. At best, in this view, such claimants are frauds and charlatans. At worst, they are committing a grave sin. And if the phenomena of the seance room is really due to as-yet unknown faculties of the human mind, then the sins of mediums are doubled if they claim that manifestations originating in their subconscious come from discarnate entities.

Spiritualists will answer such charges by stating that the more conservative religions promise their congregations a life eternal, but spirit mediums offer tangible proof that the human soul does survive the act of physical death. They will assert that millions of stricken hearts have been healed by the consolation afforded by the conviction that they have truly communicated with the spirits of loved ones who have gone on before. They will argue that the sincere medium is no more a fraud than the sincere pastor, priest, or rabbi. And when parapsychologists claim that the phenomena of the seance room are controlled by the subconscious of the medium, Spiritualists insist that these researchers are basing their conclusions on a hypothesis influenced by mechanistic psychology and a materialistic society.

Parapsychologists counter by stating that the subjective mind of the medium operates under the suggestion that it is being controlled by the spirit of a deceased person. The medium has conditioned his or her subjective mind to that pervading premise by a selective education, environment, and religious beliefs; therefore, any display of paranormal abilities, such as **clairvoyance, telepathy,** or **precognition,** will be attributed to the interaction of spirit entities.

⚜ **Delving Deeper**

Barbanell, Maurice. *This Is Spiritualism*. London: Herbert Jenkins, 1959.

Carrington, Hereward. *The Case for Psychic Survival*. New York: Citadel Press, 1957.

Fodor, Nandor. *An Encyclopedia of Psychic Science*. Secaucus, N.J.: Citadel Press, 1966.

Garrett, Eileen. *Many Voices: The Autobiography of a Medium*. New York: G. P. Putnam's Sons, 1968.

Hart, Hornell. *The Enigma of Survival*. London: Rider & Co., 1959.

Matthews, Robert. *Scientists Becoming Believers in Spiritualists' Paranormal Powers*. http://www.telegraph.co.uk. 6 March 2001.

Mysteries of the Unknown: Spirit Summonings. Alexandria, Va.: Time-Life Books, 1989.

Rhine, Louisa E. *ESP in Life and Lab: Tracing Hidden Channels*. New York: Collier-Macmillan, 1969.

Smith, Alson J. *Immortality: The Scientific Evidence*. New York: Prentice Hall, 1954.

Spence, Lewis. *An Encyclopedia of Occultism*. New Hyde Park, N.Y.: University Books, 1960.

Spirit Control

Spirit mediums believe that while they are in an entranced state of consciousness, they fall under the control of a particular spirit that has become their special guide and who speaks through them and works all manner of mysterious phenomena on their behalf. Although this spirit was once a living person, it has, since its time in the spirit world, become greatly elevated in spiritual awareness.

The concept of a spirit guide goes back to antiquity. The philosopher Socrates (c. 470 B.C.E.–399 B.C.E.) furnishes the most notable example in ancient times of an individual whose subjective mind was able to communicate with his objective mind by direct speech stimulus. Socrates referred to this voice as his daemon (not to be confused with **"demon,"** a fallen angel or a negative, possessing entity). Daemon is better translated as **guardian angel** or muse, and the philosopher believed that his guardian spirit kept vigil and warned him of approaching danger.

Parapsychologists have suggested that the spirit guide may be another little-known power of the mind which enables the medium's subjective level of consciousness to dramatize another personality, complete with a full range of personal characteristics and its very own voice. The subjective mind of the medium may clairaudiently contact its own objective level, as in the instances of those people, such as Socrates, who claim to hear the voice of a personal guide.

Mediums perceive the spirit guide in a very different manner. While they may admit that the action of the subjective mind is not entirely eliminated during trance and the arrival of the guide, they will insist that their subconscious mind is taken over and controlled by a spirit entity of great compassion and wisdom.

Psychical researchers will counter such a claim of communication with a spirit by stating that the intelligence exhibited by the spirit control appears to be always on a level with that of the medium through whom it manifests itself. Some investigators of mediumistic phenomena will admit that the information relayed during a seance often rises above the medium's known objective intelligence, but they are quick to point out that the limits of the human subjective mind are not yet known.

Critics of spiritualistic phenomena also point out that the "spirits" can often be controlled by the power of suggestion and can be made to respond to questions which have no basis in reality. Many investigators have discovered that one can as readily establish communication with an imaginary person as with a real one. Careless or mediocre mediums have found themselves the object of ridicule when they have relayed a message from a living person or even from a sitter who has given the medium a fictitious name.

The experienced and knowledgeable psychical researcher **Hereward Carrington** (1880–1958) devoted an entire book, *The Case for Psychic Survival* (1957), to his examination of **Eileen Garrett** (1892–1970), an English medium who is generally regarded as one of the greatest of the twentieth century, and her spirit control, Uvani. Carrington administered an extensive battery of personality tests to both Uvani and Garrett so that researchers might compare the two sets of responses. The spirit guide and the medium sat through sessions of the Bernreuter Personality Inventory, the Thurstone Attitude Scale, the Woodworth Neurotic Inventory, the Rorschach Test, and a seemingly endless number of word association tests. Carrington concluded that even though there existed only slight evidence for the genuinely supernatural character of spirit guides, "...they nevertheless succeed in bringing through a vast mass of supernormal information which could not be obtained in their absence." Spirit guides, he theorized, seem to act as some sort of psychic catalyst.

Carrington speculated that the function of a medium's spirit guide appears to be that of an intermediary—and whether the entity is truly a spirit or a personification of the medium's subconscious, it is only through the cooperation of the guide that authentic, verifiable messages are obtained.

The psychical researcher stressed in his report that an essential and significant difference between the secondary personality in pathological cases—such as multiple personality and schizophrenia—and the personality of the spirit guide in mediumship lay in the fact that in the pathological cases, the secondary personalities do not acquire supernormal information, while in mediumship, the guide does: "In the pathological cases, we seem to have a mere splitting of the mind, while in the mediumship cases we have to deal with a (perhaps fictitious) personality which is nevertheless in touch or contact, in some mysterious

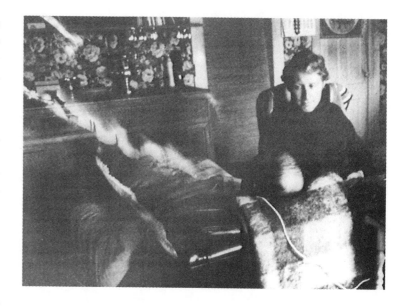

way, with another (spiritual) world, from which it derives information, and through which genuine messages often come."

Entranced medium and spirit phenomenon. (ARCHIVES OF BRAD STEIGER)

THE *concept of spirit control goes as far back as to Socrates's lifetime.*

In an interesting appendix to Carrington's book, he records a conversation with the spirit guide Uvani in which he questions him concerning the mechanics involved in the controlling of Eileen Garrett's "underconsciousness," his term for the unconscious. Uvani emphasizes that although he controls the medium's "underconsciousness," he has absolutely no control over her conscious mind—nor would he ever consider such control to be ethical or right. In answer to a direct question of whether or not he had any knowledge of the medium's thoughts, Uvani stressed that he had no interest in her thinking processes or in the activity of her conscious mind. It was that time when she was in the trance state that he could make the medium's unconscious become a means of expression not only for his ideas but for the concepts and thoughts of many other entities. Garrett's "underconsciousness" became an instrument that he could work "like notes on a piano."

Carrington touches on two questions that skeptics and believers alike have asked of many mediums and their alleged guides:

1. How do you know when the medium is ready for you to assume control of her unconscious?;

2. If in life you were a man from another culture speaking a different language, how is it that you now speak perfect English through the medium?

To the first question, Uvani responded that he received a "telegraphed impression" when the mediumistic instrument was ready. Then the medium's conscious mind becomes very low in energy, but her "soulbody" becomes more vibrant before he assumes command.

As to the question of speaking perfect English through their medium's mouths, Uvani answered bluntly that he does not speak English: "It is my Instrument who speaks. I impress my thought upon her, on that 'figment' which I must work up, but no word of mine actually comes to you. The Instrument is impressed by my personal contact."

Chicago psychic-sensitive **Irene F. Hughes** explained how she can tell when her spirit guide wishes to bring forth an impression or message from a discarnate entity on the other side. "I am quiet, completely relaxed, deep in meditation," she explained. "I may be alone at home or among friends in a prayer circle. A tingling sensation, similar to a chill, begins on my right ankle, then on my left. Slowly the tingling spreads to cover my entire body. It is as though a soft silken skin has been pulled over me, glove-tight—even over my face, changing its features—yet comfortable and protective. At this point I am on the way to that golden flow of consciousness that we earthlings term the Spirit Plane. I am in semi-trance. Were I in full trance, I could not recall a single detail."

As her involvement with the spirit plane progresses, Hughes says that her body becomes as "icy cold as death itself," yet a delightful warmth engulfs her inner self. Soon, Kaygee, her spirit teacher, appears, smiles, bows to her as a trusted friend, indicating approval of her incursion into the spirit world. By a slight waving of his hand, he ushers in those of the spirit plane who wish to speak through her. "I am bound to my spirit teacher by ties that are ethereal, yet mighty as a coaxial cable," she said. "Every thought that flashes through his consciousness becomes crystal clear also in my consciousness."

Critics of the spiritistic hypothesis remain unimpressed by the agile mental phenomena of the spirit guide and the medium's attempts to explain the levels of his or her interaction with this mysterious personality. Many parapsychologists agree that mediums may arrive at certain information through paranormal means, but they maintain that the knowledge was gained through extrasensory abilities rather than through the cooperation of spirits. And in those cases when the alleged spirit guide displays a prima donna's temperament at being questioned for further proof of identity, it would seem that all-too-human behavior finds its seat in the unconscious of the medium.

❀ Delving Deeper

Barbanell, Maurice. *Spiritualism Today*. London: Herbert Jenkins, 1969.

Bayless, Raymond. *The Other Side of Death*. New Hyde Park, N.Y.: University Books, 1971.

Carrington, Hereward. *The Case for Psychic Survival*. New York: Citadel Press, 1957.

Garrett, Eileen. *Many Voices: The Autobiography of a Medium*. New York: G. P. Putnam's Sons, 1968.

Uphoff, Walter and Mary Jo. *New Psychic Frontiers*. Gerrards Cross, Bucks, Great Britain: Colin Smythe, 1975.

Trance

Numerous researchers have noted the obvious parallels between hypnotic sleep and the trance state of the medium. In **hypnosis** the subject is controlled by the suggestions of the hypnotist. In the trance state, many investigators believe, the medium is controlled by autosuggestion—a kind of self-induced hypnotic state.

Good subjects for hypnosis can be made to assume any number of characterizations, from elderly people to babies, and will firmly appear to believe themselves to be the individuals they represent, complete with a set of habits and idiosyncrasies for the characters they are impersonating. Likewise mediums, through autosuggestion in the trance state, assume the guise of the spirit communicators who have come to speak to the sitters in the seance circle. Professional hypnotists have often claimed that all the phenomena of mediumship can be duplicated through their subjects by suggesting to them that they are under the control of discarnate entities.

A medium or a **Spiritualist** might counter such an assertion by saying that certain spirits may actually take possession of a hypnotic subject when they receive permission to do so, and that the subject may then truly be said to be in the control of the souls of the deceased.

Parapsychologists who have tested both the hypnosis hypothesis and the possibility of spirit **possession** have found that, in some instances, it is just as easy to obtain communication from a living person through a hypnotic subject or a medium as from a dead one, and from a fictitious person as from a real one, simply by making the proper suggestion to either entranced agent.

When mediums enter the trance state, they enter into a subjective condition that leaves them as open and amenable to the law of suggestion as is the subject of hypnosis. The potent suggestion that the spirit of a deceased person is about to enter their body and control them is ever present in the subjective mind of mediums. Such a suggestion has been a part of their educational development, and their religious beliefs are based on the "fact" of spirit survival and communication. All paranormal phenomena are considered by mediums to be a direct interaction of the spirit world with the material world. The trance state allows them to cooperate with spirit personalities and to become a vital link in communication between the two worlds. Since mediums believe so strongly in survival and their ability to establish contact with the departed, it is their mission to aid others in communicating with their beloved deceased.

Many parapsychologists theorize that with such a powerful autosuggestion constantly being directed to the transcendent or subjective level of the mind of a medium, all subjective knowledge gained by establishing telepathic rapport with the unconscious level of other minds will be immediately interpreted as information gained by the intercession of spirits. And so far as the transcendent mind of the medium is able to receive impressions of the "spirits," that mental image will be impersonated with all the creative abilities that reside in the almost limitless range of subjective intelligence.

✳ Delving Deeper

Barbanell, Maurice. *Spiritualism Today*. London: Herbert Jenkins, 1969.

Fodor, Nandor. *An Encyclopedia of Psychic Science*. Secaucus, N.J.: Citadel Press, 1966.

Mysteries of the Unknown: Spirit Summonings. Alexandria, Va.: Time-Life Books, 1989.

Uphoff, Walter and Mary Jo. *New Psychic Frontiers*. Gerrards Cross, Bucks, Great Britain: Colin Smythe, 1975.

Mediums and Channelers

The idea that humans survive physical death, that some part of the human being is immortal, profoundly affects the lives of those who harbor such a belief. While Christianity, Islam, Judaism, and many other religions promise their followers some form of a life after death, many thousands of men and women feel that they have proof of a life beyond the grave based on the evidence of survival that manifests through spirit mediums.

THE *idea that humans survive physical death, profoundly affects the lives of those who harbor such a belief.*

Some psychical researchers maintain that the principal difference between a psychic-sensitive and a trance medium is that the psychic attributes his or her talents to some manifestations of extrasensory ability, such as **clairvoyance, precognition,** or **telepathy,** whereas the medium credits his or her abilities to the interaction with spirits.

BERKELEY PSYCHIC INSTITUTE

Berkeley Psychic Institute (BPI), throughout California—with locations in Berkeley, Mountain View, Sacramento, and Santa Rosa—refers to itself as "a Psychic Kindergarten." The meaning of kindergarten, in this case, is the virtual playground in the psychic field, a place for exploring what it means to be psychic.

Since 1973, the BPI has taught students how to recognize and develop their own psychic abilities through classes in clairvoyance, meditation, healing, and male and female energy. Since that time, more than 100,000 students have taken classes, and an additional 4,000-plus have graduated from a one-year intensive clairvoyant training program.

SOURCES:

Berkeley Psychic Institute. http://www.berkeleypsychic.com/ BPI/bpi.html. 15 October 2001.

Mediums most often relay messages from the other side through the agency of a **spirit control** or **spirit guide,** an entity who claims to have lived on Earth and acquired certain skills, knowledge, and wisdom before its own physical death. The concept of a spirit guide dates back to antiquity, and serious scholars and researchers have been asking the same question for hundreds of years: Is this alleged entity, who claims to speak through the medium, really a spirit, or is it the voice of the medium's subconscious?

Some mediums would probably concede that the action of the subjective mind is not entirely eliminated during trance and the arrival of the spirit control, but from their viewpoint their subconscious is taken over by the guide. An aspect of mediumistic phenomena on which both psychical researchers and mediums will be likely to agree is that there is an intelligence that directs and controls them. Another area of agreement would probably be that this intelligence is a human intelligence. Once again, the area of dispute would be whether that human intelligence issues from the living or from the dead. Interestingly, spirit communication still requires both a soul and a body—the soul of an alleged deceased human personality and the physical body of the medium.

In the 1970s, after the publication of **Jane Roberts**'s (1929–1984) books *The Seth Material* and *Seth Speaks*, "channeling" became a more popular name for mediumship, and it remains so to the present day. Jane Roberts received contact with an entity named Seth after undergoing a **trance state** while Robert Butts, her husband, recorded the thought, ideas, and concepts communicated by the spirit in notebooks. The material dictated by Seth was literate and provocative, and especially well-suited to a generation of maturing sixties' flower children and baby boomers. It wasn't long before Seth discussion groups around the United States were celebrating such concepts as the following: 1) We all create our own reality; 2) Our point of power lies in the present; and 3) We are all gods couched in "creaturehood." Nor was it long before "channelers" were emerging in large numbers throughout the country, and individuals such as **Jach Pursel,** Kevin Ryerson (1953–), and **J. Z. Knight** (1946–) had attained national and international celebrity status.

Perhaps in the mind of the channelers, the designation of "mediums" conjured up images of the traditional darkened seance parlors and ectoplasmic spirit guides, imagery that had become unacceptable to the modern spirit communicator, who more often relays messages from guides and master teachers in the full light of a platform setting or a television studio and seldom claims to materialize anything other than an engaging performance for the assembled audience. Then, too, just as in the 1930s when mediums were often compared to radio receiving sets for transmissions from the spirit world, it likely occurred to someone that the contemporary medium might be thought of as being similar to a

Boundary Institute, in Los Altos, California, is a nonprofit scientific research center, focusing on the development and exploration of physics, quantum theories of physics, mathematics and their linked relationships.

Asserting they are beginning to understand and explain psi phenomena—without contradicting existing well-established physical laws—they use the standard tools of science, such as grounded theoretical development, carefully controlled experiments, statistical analyses and replication, and collaboration with other researchers.

One of the most popular features is the institute's *On-Line Experimental Program,* focusing in the areas of psi and the psychic. Also of interest is background information on psychic phenomena, profiles of the staff and research associates, and various papers and articles about the theories they are developing and the experimental evidence that has been accumulated.

BOUNDARY INSTITUTE—GOT PSI?

SOURCES:

Boundary Institute. http://www.boundaryinstitute.org. 15 October 2001.

human television channel, receiving thoughts and images from beyond. Whichever title is preferred by those who claim to relay messages from the spirits, the process of communication remains the same: Spirit entities occupy the physical body of the channelers or the mediums and speak through them.

Although the very idea of establishing contact with great spirit teachers from the beyond or from other dimensions of reality seemed new and exciting to the great masses of men and women in the 1970s, from the viewpoint of those individuals who research such matters it seemed only as though another cycle had once again reached its season and general public interest in spirit contact had returned. It was time again to recognize those sensitive men and women—modern-day shamans, so to speak—who were carrying on the tradition of spirit

communication first set in motion in the nineteenth century by such great mediums as **Daniel Dunglas Home** (1833–1886), **Mina "Margery" Crandon** (1889–1941), **Leonora E. Piper** (1857–1950), and **Eileen Garrett** (1892–1970)—all of whom were quite likely to be completely unknown to the general public and even, perhaps, to the contemporary crop of channelers themselves. In addition to the pioneer work accomplished by such long-forgotten spirit mediums as those named above, the entire New Age Movement of the late twentieth century owes a great debt to the controversial **Helena Petrovna Blavatsky** (1831–1891), who was the first to popularize "channeling" wisdom from ancient teachers and masters, as well as the mystique of past lives and lost worlds.

In 1987, the ABC television network presented a miniseries based on actress Shirley

Rhine Research Center

The Rhine Research Center is the successor to the Duke University Parapsychology Laboratory. It carries forward Duke's research mission to explore unusual experiences. Located adjacent to Duke University's East Campus in Durham, North Carolina, the center offers a variety of lectures, workshops, guest speakers, and conferences, in addition to courses.

Sources:

Rhine Research Center. http://www.rhine.org. 15 October 2001.

MacLaine's (1934–   ) book *Out on a Limb* (1987), which dealt with many subjects exciting to New Age enthusiasts, such as reincarnation, extraterrestrial visitation, ancient mysteries, and spirit communication. Perhaps the most captivating segments of the miniseries depicted MacLaine receiving spirit communication through channeler Kevin Ryerson. The actress and the channeler played themselves in the five-hour dramatization on prime-time television, and an international audience of millions were able to see for themselves how Tom McPherson, the 400-year-old spirit of an Irishman, spoke through Ryerson to advise MacLaine. Due to the popularity of *Out on a Limb* as a book and as a miniseries, channeling became a kind of craze throughout North America. The actress herself conducted a series of seminars in which she openly discussed her

beliefs in past lives, UFOs, and spirit communication. Channeling and the claimed accessibility of the world beyond death achieved a peak of popularity which led to an outpouring of television programs, motion pictures, books, New Age expos, psychic fairs, and the "birth" of new channelers in a virtual cosmic population explosion. The interest in channelers and after-death communication continues to find its expression in such individuals as **Sylvia Browne** (1936–   ), **James Van Praagh** (ca. 1960–   ), and **John Edward.**

Even in this day of mass communication, Skylabs, the Internet, and increasingly sophisticated technology people are still fascinated by mediumship, channeling, and contacting the spirit world. According to J. Z. Knight (1946–   ), another of Shirley MacLaine's favorite channelers, through her guide, Ramtha, believes the reason for their continued popularity is that there really aren't any mysteries left in humankind's material journey. Millions of people have reached a kind of peak in their evolution. Knight explained: "This has nothing to do with class distinction. Rich and poor, superstars and mediocrity alike feel that there must be more to life than this. The rich ask if there isn't more to life than material things. They also ask, 'Who am I?' 'Why am I doing this?' The poor ask if there isn't more to life than strife and suffering."

Knight says that Ramtha, the 35,000-year-old warrior from **Lemuria** who speaks through her, calls this point in people's lives the "time of fantastic realism." Ramtha also said that the human journey has reached a point when the self seeks to turn inward to self-examination. "In this age of communication and travel and the media, we have all been brought so close together," Knight said. "There really isn't much left to discover about our binary-thinking world. The next step will have to be that the analogical mind takes things into a different perspective, and we find ourselves in an 'unknown mind,' discovering what the ultimate journey is all about."

✦ DELVING DEEPER

Christopher, Milbourne. *Mediums, Mystics & the Occult.* New York: Thomas Y. Crowell, 1975.

Klimo, Jon. *Channeling: Investigations on Receiving Information from Paranormal Sources*. Los Angeles: Jeremy P. Tarcher, 1987.

Maclaine, Shirley. *Out on a Limb*. New York: Bantam Books, 1983.

Paranormal News. http://paranormal.about.com/ science/paranormal/library/blnews.htm. 1 October 2001.

Weinberg, Steven Lee, ed. *Ramtha*. Eastsound, Wash.: Sovereignty, Inc., 1986.

Kevin Ryerson, channeler. (ARCHIVES OF BRAD STEIGER)

SYLVIA BROWNE (1936–   )

Spiritual advisor, trance medium, and psychic detective Sylvia Brown has proclaimed that her goals are to prove that the soul survives death, that God is a real and loving presence, and that there is a divine plan to everyone's life.

Browne is an example of the modern channel/medium who has become a media personality, thanks to her 27 years of making television and radio talk show appearances, 47 years of giving psychic readings, and 25 years of conducting paranormal research. Slowly building a reputation as a psychic-sensitive and trance channeler in California throughout the sixties, seventies, and eighties, Browne arrived upon the national scene in December of 1998 when she appeared on the *Montel Williams Show* to promote her biography, *Adventures of a Psychic*. The best-selling book was quickly followed in 1999 by *The Other Side and Back: A Psychic's Guide to Our World and Beyond*. These books, coupled with her appearances on *Larry King Live*, the *Montel Williams Show,* and *Unsolved Mysteries*, soon increased her popularity quotient to celebrity status.

Born Sylvia Shoemaker in Kansas City, Missouri, in 1936, she first gave evidence of her psychic ability at the age of five when she experienced frightening premonitions of the deaths of her two great-grandmothers just weeks before their passing. Fortunately for the sensitive child, she had her grandmother, Ada Coil, an established and respected psychic counselor and healer, to guide her and to help her to understand her paranormal talents, including the ability to communicate with those in the spirit world. Developing as a deep trance medium, Browne learned to allow her

guide "Francine" to enter her body and communicate directly with people.

For many years Sylvia Browne quietly shared her insights with family and friends and became well known in the Kansas City area for her talent in helping people foresee their future. Even after moving to California in 1964, she continued assisting people on a private basis.

About 10 years after making the move to the West Coast, Browne decided that after having spent 18 years as a Catholic schoolteacher, she now wished to research the paranormal and her own psychic abilities through a professionally established and legally sanctioned organization. In 1974, she incorporated the Nirvana Foundation for Psychic Research, a nonprofit organization known today as the Sylvia Browne Corporation. Soon the readings in her home with a dozen or so friends in attendance had grown to gatherings of two or three hundred people in churches and town halls. Although she was raised predominantly a Roman Catholic, she was familiar with the Jewish, Episcopalian, and Lutheran backgrounds of her extended family. In 1986, she established a church called the Society of Novus Spiritus (New Spirit), which, though based essentially upon Christian Gnostic the-

ology, rejects the concepts of sin, guilt, and retribution and is devoted to the building of a spiritual community that loves both the Father and Mother God.

While many spirit mediums reject reincarnation as contradictory to their concept of the divine program of spiritual evolution for the spirits of the deceased on the other side, Sylvia Browne accepts past lives as a central theme in her philosophy. She states that she has conducted thousands of **hypnotic regressions** and hundreds of trance sessions, which have convinced her that to understand the laws of karma/reincarnation is to possess one of the keys to understanding the true meaning of life. Browne is not dogmatic regarding any of her personal views, however, and she makes a point not to force her beliefs on anyone else.

There are hazards in establishing a high profile as a medium or a psychic-sensitive. Orthodox religionists condemn them as satanic; skeptics accuse them of exaggerating their claims of success; and nearly everyone charges them with being in the "spooky" business only to take money from the gullible and the grieving. In addition, various research groups often demand to conduct their own tests to decide whether or not the medium or the psychic has what they deem true paranormal abilities.

Brill's Content (2001) claimed to have examined 10 of the Montel Williams programs that featured Browne's work with the police as a "psychic detective," dealing with 35 cases. According to their analyses, in 21 the details were too vague to be verified. Of the 14 cases remaining, interviews with the law-enforcement officers involved in the investigations or family members of the victims produced comments that Browne had contributed nothing of value to the solving of the cases.

Regardless of the skeptics and the critics who seek to undermine her reputation, Sylvia Browne has counseled hundreds of men and women who will attest to the value and accuracy of her psychic readings. According to her supporters, Browne has been able to help thousands of men and women gain control of their lives, understand the deeper meaning of life, and find God in their own individual way.

❖ DELVING DEEPER

Browne, Sylvia. *Life on the Other Side: A Psychic's Tour of the Afterlife.* New York: E. P. Dutton, 2000.

Browne, Sylvia, and Lindsay Harrison. *The Other Side and Back: A Psychic's Guide to Our World and Beyond.* New York: Signet, 2001.

Browne, Sylvia, and Lindsay Harrison. *Past Lives, Future Healing: A Psychic Reveals the Secrets to Good Health and Great Relationships.* New York: Penguin, 2001.

FLORENCE COOK (1856–1904)

In his book *Researches into the Phenomena of Spiritualism* (1874), **Sir William Crookes** (1832–1919), the famous and respected British scientist, states that he walked with a materialized spirit form, talked with it, and took more than 40 flashlight photographs of the entity. The lively and charming spirit form was named Katie King, and she materialized through the mediumship of a teenager named Florence Cook.

When she was 15, Cook began sitting in seances with her mother in their home in Manchester, England, and she soon found that she was capable of producing writing she claimed was dictated by spirits from the other side. Her mediumship progressed rapidly, and within a short period of time, she was conducting dramatic demonstrations of spirit phenomena at meetings of the Dalston Society, a Spiritualist group. At some of these meetings the phenomena became so powerful that Cook was levitated above the heads of the sitters.

It was at this time that the teenaged medium met the spirit personality of "Katie King," who claimed to be the daughter of John King, alias Henry Owen Morgan, the infamous buccaneer. King promised to be Cook's spirit control and to produce many types of remarkable phenomena for a period of three years.

Cook was conducting her seances only at her parental home, and her father, mother, two sisters, and their household maid served as her steady circle of sitters. The teenager's reputation as a medium of remarkable talents had spread, and wealthy citizens of Manchester were offering retainers that would guarantee their attendance at her spirit circles whenever they required them.

In April of 1872, Katie King made an attempt to materialize, and she appeared only as a deathlike face between the gauze curtains of a seance cabinet. As spirit and medium strengthened their spiritual bond, King's ability to materialize became more and more advanced. Then, after a year's time, the spirit being could step out of the cabinet and show herself in full body to those who had gathered for Cook's seances. Sitters were allowed to touch her and even to photograph her.

As the spirit responded to questions concerning her life before death, she told a story of having been in the crowd that watched King Charles I of England lose his head at the chopping block in 1649. She had been but 12 then, and within a few more years, she was married. King confessed, however, to having been a violent, rather than a domestic, type; and she related with a macabre kind of eagerness how she had herself "done in" many people with her own hands before her death at the age of 23.

In a letter written February 3, 1874, Sir William Crookes described a seance in which Cook entered the spirit cabinet and slipped into trance. Moments later, Katie King emerged to say that the medium was not well enough that night to permit her to materialize

to the level where she might wander very far from the cabinet. The spirit form did come a short distance amidst the sitters, but all the while they could hear the moanings and sobbings of Florence Cook.

Crookes stated that he sat in a position where he could clearly see the entranced form of Florence Cook and the materialized form of Katie King at the same time. Although he was impressed by the lifelike quality of the spirit control and by the fact that he could both see and hear Florence Cook while Katie King moved elsewhere in the seance room, the scientist was not firmly convinced by the demonstration.

At a later sitting, when Cook was feeling better, Katie King materialized for nearly two hours. Crookes reported that the charming spirit took his arm as she walked, and he found it hard to believe that his lovely companion could indeed be a visitor from beyond the grave. He asked permission to clasp King in his arms and was astonished when his request was granted.

During that same seance when he was allowed to touch the materialized spirit form, Crookes was also able to compare the features of the young medium and the spirit when King stood behind the form of the entranced Florence Cook. The medium lay in her customary black velvet dress, and the spirit form stood behind the couch in her flowing white drapery. Then, holding one of the medium's hands in one of his, Crookes knelt before the spirit and passed a lamp slowly up and down the whole figure of Katie King. Such a meticulous and brightly illumined examination thoroughly satisfied the eminent scientist that he had beheld a materialized spirit being and not "the phantasm of a disordered brain."

Crookes repeated the process three times, in each instance pausing to examine yet another aspect of either the spirit or the medium, whose psychic energy had manifested the spirit form. Later, in addition to a number of decided differences between the medium and the spirit, he listed various points of physical dissimilarities that he had observed between Florence Cook and Katie King: King was a good four and one-half inches taller than the medium. The skin of the spirit form's neck was very smooth both to touch and to sight, while Florence had a large blister on her neck that was distinctly visible and rough to the touch. Katie's ears were unpierced, while Florence habitually wore earrings. King's complexion was very fair, while Cook's was very dark. The spirit entity's fingers were much longer than the medium's, and King's face was also much larger.

For a period of over six months, Crookes studied the phenomena of Florence Cook at close hand. For as long as a week at a time, the young medium would be a guest at the Crookes's residence, constantly in the presence of some member of his family. Crookes became so familiar to the spirit that Katie King would allow him to enter the seance cabinet whenever he wished or to touch her at any time. The scientist wrote that it was a common thing for the seven or eight workers in his laboratory to view the materialized King in full glare of the electric lights.

After he had seen the spirit many times in the full light of his laboratory environment, Crookes added to the points of difference between the medium and the spirit form. In an article for a newspaper, he stated that he had the most absolute certainty that Florence Cook and the materialized entity were two separate individuals, so far as their physical bodies were concerned. There were several small blemishes on Cook's face which were absent on King's. The medium's hair was a very dark brown, whereas the spirit's hair was a rich golden auburn.

On the evening of Katie King's final appearance in the seance cabinet, she gave each of the members of the circle a farewell message and relayed a few general directions for the future well-being of Florence Cook. Crookes stated that after the spirit being had closed the curtains of the cabinet, she conversed with him for some time, then walked across the room to where the medium was lying on the floor in a state of deep trance. Stooping over her, King touched Cook and said, "Wake up, Florrie. Wake up! I must leave you now."

Crookes testified that the medium and the materialized spirit conversed with one another for several minutes, as Cook begged King to

stay with her a little longer. "My work is done," King told her. "God bless you."

Sir William Crookes was outspoken in his defense of the validity of the phenomena produced by the young medium Florence Cook and her spirit control, Katie King. "Every test that I proposed [Florence Cook] agreed to," he told his scientific colleagues in the Royal Society. "She is open and straightforward in speech....Indeed, I do not believe she could carry on a deception if she wished to try....And to imagine that an innocent schoolgirl of fifteen should be able to conceive and then successfully carry out for three years so gigantic an imposture as this, and in that time should submit to any test which might be imposed upon her, should bear the strictest scrutiny, should be willing to be searched at any time, either before or after a seance, and should meet with even better success in my own house...does more violence to one's reason and common sense than to believe [Katie King] to be what she herself affirms."

The controversy over the scientist and his "pet ghost" has not been quieted to this day. One of the most common theories proposed by the detractors of the phenomena produced by Florence Cook is that Sir William Crookes fell in love with the 15-year-old medium and thereby became blinded to her trickery. Although the issue has been muddied by such charges, the experiments and reports of an illustrious scientist with the courage to bring his knowledge and training to psychic research stand as a matter of public record.

Florence Cook married Elgie Corner in 1874 and about the same time acquired a new spirit control named Marie, who followed in Katie King's ghostly footsteps by stepping out of the spirit cabinet, even singing and dancing to the delight of those clients assembled for a seance. At a sitting on January 9, 1880, during a materialization seance, Sir George Sitwell reached into the spirit cabinet and grabbed Marie. When the lights came up, the lively spirit Marie was found to be the medium Cook clad only in her corsets and petticoat and wrapped in white drapery.

Apologists for the medium argue that all of the incredible phenomena produced by Florence Cook Corner and witnessed by numerous psychical researchers, including the eminent scientist Sir William Crookes, should not be dismissed because of one incident of cheating. Skeptics counter that all of Cook's mediumistic materializations of Katie King and Marie were really dramatic impersonations for true believers in **Spiritualism** and that Crookes had become too infatuated with the young medium to be effectively objective.

Cook withdrew from public mediumship until 1899, when she accepted an invitation from the Sphinx Society in Berlin to sit under test conditions and demonstrate her abilities. According to many observers, the remarkable phenomena that Cook produced during those tests went a long way toward clearing her somewhat tarnished reputation.

Sir William Crookes stoutly maintained that Florence Cook had produced genuine spirit phenomena under the strictest of controls imposed upon her. When he learned of her death, he expressed his deepest sympathy for her family in a letter dated April 24, 1904, and declared that for many people their belief in an afterlife was strengthened because of the mediumship of Florence Cook.

✵ DELVING DEEPER

Brandon, Ruth. *The Spiritualists*. New York: Alfred A. Knopf, 1983.

Fodor, Nandor. *These Mysterious People*. London: Rider & Co., 1935.

MINA "MARGERY" STINSON CRANDON (1888–1941)

Mina "Margery" Stinson Crandon ranks as one of the most thoroughly investigated and controversial mediums of the twentieth century. Psychical researchers put the ever-cooperative woman in uncomfortable situations, encased her in awkward contraptions, and sometimes wound her in enough adhesive tape to make her look like a mummy. In spite of such laborious efforts to disprove the validity of her phenomena, Margery Crandon again and again materialized spirits and performed astounding feats of **psychokinesis,** or mind over matter.

Mina Stinson was born in Canada in 1888 and moved to Boston when she was quite

Mrs. Mina "Margery" Crandon (1888–1941).
(FORTEAN PICTURE LIBRARY)

young. In 1918, after an unsuccessful marriage, she became the wife of a senior Boston surgeon, Dr. Le Roi Goddard Crandon, whose family dated back to the Mayflower. They bought the house at Number 11 Lime Street on Beacon Hill, and became popular in Boston society. Crandon was a highly respected instructor at Harvard Medical School, and Mina was known as a lady with a sharp and lively wit.

In 1923, Crandon became extremely interested in psychical research, and he convinced Mina and a number of their friends to begin to explore the possibilities of contacting the dead. The group began with the customary attempts at table-tipping and spirit raps, and Crandon was astonished when it became evident that Mina was a powerful medium. After a few sessions Mina's deceased brother Walter, who had died in a train crash in 1911, announced his presence as her spirit control and within a brief period of time he began speaking through Mina and demonstrating a wide variety of spirit phenomena. Walter, speaking in down-to-earth language, often colored with profanity, stated that it was his mission to perform the process of mind over matter, rather than delivering flowery inspirational messages from the other side.

Although Mina was regularly producing dramatic phenomena, attendance to the seances were by invitation only in order to protect Crandon's standing at Harvard. Within a few months after they had begun the private seances, the Crandons submitted to the first formal investigation of Mina's mediumship under the auspices of Professor William McDougall, head of Harvard's Department of Psychology, and a committee from the university. After five months of observation, the committee declared its opinion that the spiritistic mind over matter phenomena were produced through fraudulent means.

Mina "Margery" Stinson Crandon ranks as one of the most thoroughly investigated and controversial mediums of the twentieth century.

In November of 1923, J. Malcolm Bird (1886–1964) of *Scientific American* magazine attended one of the Crandons' seances and was impressed with the spiritistic manifestations he witnessed. At that time, *Scientific American* was offering a prize of $2,500 to anyone who could provide conclusive proof that psychic phenomena truly existed, and Bird asked Mina to submit to a series of their tests. The investigating committee for the magazine included **Harry Houdini** (1874–1926), **Hereward Carrington** (1880–1958), Dr. Walter Franklin Prince (1863–1934), Dr. D. F. Comstock, Dr. William McDougall (1871–1938), and J. Malcolm Bird, secretary of the committee. To protect Mina Crandon's social standing as the wife of a prominent Boston surgeon and Harvard professor, Bird gave her the pseudonym of "Margery," which is how she shall

always be remembered in the annals of psychical research.

The tests began in January 1924 under the general supervision of Crandon. The strictest of control conditions were enforced to ensure that fraud of any kind, conscious or unconscious, on the part of the medium could not go undetected. The most controversial aspect of the tests has to do with the role of the famous magician Harry Houdini in the experiments. Houdini was outspoken in his declarations that he had exposed Margery as a fraud. The medium's defenders proclaim that the greatest myth in the history of psychical research is that Houdini caught Margery cheating and exposed her. On one point there is agreement: Houdini seemed determined to expose Margery as a fake by whatever means necessary.

During one night of tests, Houdini brought an electric doorbell into the seance room and said that he would challenge the spirit to ring it for the circle. Once Margery was in a trance state, a low voice, that of Walter, the medium's deceased brother and her spirit control, bemoaned the presence of Houdini. "Still trying to get some publicity by haunting seance rooms, eh?" the spirit voice taunted the magician.

Walter then directed Malcolm Bird, secretary of the committee, to take Houdini's doorbell out of the room so that he might examine it and see what kind of trickery the magician had planned. Bird hesitated for a moment, then picked up the apparatus and left the room. When he returned a few moments later, Bird frowned in displeasure at the magician, accusing him of having placed pieces of rubber on the contact points of the bell so that it could not possibly ring. Houdini offered no defense of his actions, and he was admonished that dishonesty would do the committee no service.

The words of admonishment were scarcely out of Bird's mouth when the electric bell began to ring in vigorous spurts of clanging sound, and Walter's booming voice filled the seance room. "How does that suit you, Mr. Houdini?" the spirit control mocked.

Houdini's tricks to confuse Margery were methodically uncovered by the all-seeing spirit guide Walter, and the magician's attendance at the sessions in the medium's seance room became more and more infrequent. When the committee demanded that the magician make good his boast that he could duplicate all the effects that the medium had manifested during her seances, Houdini found that he had suddenly been called away on business.

The investigating committee from the *Scientific American* never seemed to exhaust their list of inventive tests by which they might challenge the abilities of the patient Margery. For one experiment, the medium allowed herself to be encased in a wooden compartment which would permit only her arms and legs to protrude. With her limbs grasped firmly by the researchers, Margery was still able to ring bells, snuff out candles, and set in motion rocking chairs on the opposite side of the room.

In order to better investigate the spirit voices that seemed to be under Margery's control, the committee carefully measured an amount of colored water that would easily fill her mouth. With her mouth full of the colored water, the voices of Walter and other entities were still able to speak freely and to answer all questions put to them. After the experiment's completion, the water was removed from the medium's mouth and remeasured. The color remained the same and the amount of water withdrawn varied not more than a teaspoonful.

The water test had not adequately impressed all the investigators, however, so they devised a balloon which could be placed in the medium's mouth and inflated while the seance was in progress. Once again, the voices were able to engage in free discourse, even though Margery's larynx was completely blocked off. A number of the spirit voices expressed their scorn with the feeble attempts that the investigators were making in an attempt to mute them.

Although Margery was always remarkably patient and good-humored regarding the tests that the committee devised, there were some overeager members among the researchers who did not return her good will. Before the research seances had begun, each of the investigators had signed an affidavit stating that none of them would touch the ectoplasm that streamed forth from the medium's body, but on one occasion, a committee member seized the substance as it moved over his wrist. Margery emitted a terrible shriek of pain, and later she became ill and hemorraged for several days. Another time when she was in deep trance, a researcher drove a thick needle into her flesh. Although the medium did not flinch while entranced, she suffered greatly from the wound when she awakened. On still another occasion, Margery was badly burned by corrosive chemicals which a zealous investigator had designed for an experiment.

After six weeks of tests, the committee remained undecided as to the validity of the phenomena produced by Margery, but an enthusiastic J. Malcolm Bird began writing positive articles concerning the authenticity of the medium's abilities. When it seemed apparent that there was no general consensus accepting or rejecting Margery's mediumship as providing proof of survival, Houdini became furious, fearing that they were about to hand over the prize money of $2,500 to the Crandons. Because of his open and much publicized skepticism of spirit mediums and Spiritualists, Houdini felt that his very reputation as a master magician was being challenged and insulted, so he wrote his own report, *Houdini Exposes the Tricks Used by the Boston Medium Margery*, and had it published as a booklet in 1924. As should be obvious from the title, Houdini presented his own explanations of how each of the phenomena manifested by Margery had been accomplished through trickery. The angry magician even went so far as to accuse two of his fellow committee members, Hereward Carrington and J. Malcolm Bird, of having assisted Margery in perpetrating her fraudulent mediumship.

In spite of crude and careless acts on the part of certain members of the committee throughout the grueling tests, Margery Crandon retained her goodwill toward the persistent investigators and produced a remarkable variety of phenomena, ranging from breezes, raps, spirit writing in several languages, independent voice manifestations, apports, and the imprint of spirit fingerprints in paraffin. Many members of the committee made public declarations that Margery Crandon had control of forces beyond the present knowledge of twentieth-century science. Hereward Carrington went on record as stating that after attending more than 40 sittings with Margery he had arrived at the "…definite conclusion that genuine supernormal would frequently occur. Many of the observed manifestations might well have been produced fraudulently…however, there remains a number of instances when phenomena were produced and observed under practically perfect control."

Unfortunately for Margery and her many friends and supporters, it was discovered that a fingerprint that had been allegedly left in wax by Walter was found to be that of a Boston dentist, Dr. Frederick Caldwell, who admitted that he had given Margery a bit of wax in which his own print had been pressed. One such exposure of fraud could not prove that all of Margery's spirit phenomena had been produced as products of clever deception, as Houdini had declared, but the falsification of her spirit control's fingerprint caused the majority of researchers who had examined and tested her mediumship to decide that perhaps she had, after all, been too good to be true.

Mina Crandon herself remains a mystery. The most famous medium of the 1920s has become a martyr in the minds of Spiritualists, a courageous woman who submitted to test after complex test for the sake of demonstrating the truth of survival after death. For psychical researchers, she stands as a classic example of a talented medium who, though capable of occasionally producing genuine phenomena, from time to time resorted to trickery. For the skeptics, she is simply another clever fraud who deceived the gullible until she was exposed by the harsh light of scientific investigation.

Mina Stinson Crandon died in her sleep on November 1, 1941. Although she was said to have spent her final years unhappy and disillusioned, tending to her husband during a long convalescence, then succumbing herself to illness, her supporters never ceased to remind her that her fame as a medium was known throughout the world.

❋ Delving Deeper

Fodor, Nandor. *These Mysterious People*. London: Rider & Co., 1935.

Steiger, Brad. *Voices from Beyond: Do They Prove Survival?* New York: Award Books; London: Tandem Books, 1968.

Tietze, Thomas R. *Margery*. New York: Harper & Row, 1973.

JOHN EDWARD

John Edward is an internationally acclaimed psychic medium. At the age of 31, he has attained the ability to touch the deepest aspects of the human spirit: longing and curiosity.

The debut of his highly rated cable TV show, *Crossing Over with John Edward*, on the Sci Fi Channel, went from a large audience of 275,000 households to more than 614,000 households within a year and was moved from late-night to prime-time, five days a week. His overwhelming popularity bought him syndication and a network spot on CBS.

Born and raised John MaGee Jr. in Long Island, New York, to a father who was a policeman, Edward remembers exhibiting at a very young age an uncanny ability to "know" family history and events that took place before he was even born.

It wasn't, however, until Edward had a reading with Lydia Clar, a famed psychic from New Jersey, that he embarked on developing his abilities. At age fifteen, it was Clar who made him aware that his psychic abilities were extraordinary and should be used to help and assist others. Before his reading with her, despite being somewhat aware of his childhood abilities, Edward said he was actually quite skeptical. He did not believe Clar when she said his destiny was to be a medium.

Attributing the nourishing environment and acceptance of his family to "psychic phenomena," Edward found it easy to flourish and eventually fine tune his gifts. Graduating from college with a degree in public administration and health care administration, he was able to maintain a management position in a health care facility in the Northeast, while continuing his research in the field of parapsychology. He also made time for lecturing, teaching, writing, and doing readings for others, until the demand for his time and ability grew to such a point that he decided to devote himself exclusively to "speaking to the dead."

In a June 18, 1998, interview with Larry King on *Larry King Live*, Edward explained:

> Basically, I act as a bridge, I go between the physical world and the non-physical world. And what I do—I'm somewhat of a waiter—I go to the other side, not literally go there, but I go to the other side and get information and I bring it out and I serve my client the information and hope that they understand it.

Elaborating on "how" the energy comes from the "other side," Edward says it comes in different ways: "clairvoyance" (clear-seeing), "clairaudience" (clear-hearing), "clairsentience" (clear-sensing), "clairalience" (clear-smelling), and "clairhambience" (clear-tasting). Then it is up to him to interpret what is being communicated through these various senses, or what the loved ones on the other side are trying to communicate.

Detractors such as James Randi, a.k.a. "Amazing Randi" (of the James Randi Educational Foundation in Fort Lauderdale, Florida), say that Edward does nothing more than do "cold readings"—using the same technique that has been long used by magicians to entertain and mediums. The technique involves posing a series of questions and suggestions, each shaped by the subject's previous response. For example, a generic statement might be uttered, such as, "I sense a father-figure here," and when that gets a response, adding something like, "I'm getting that his death resulted from a problem in his chest" (which Randi says can be anything from a heart attack to emphysema to lung cancer). If the subjects answers "no," then the response is normally, "Well, I'll get back to that...."

Others say Edward's show benefits from the use of "creative editing." They argue that many of the "misses" are left out of the final airing and the successes "enhanced." Some even suggest that a lot of information comes from detailed questionnaires filled out by the audience members, who go through a stringent selection process before being accepted on the set.

The skeptics haven't deterred the vast numbers of people who feel that John Edward has helped them deal with loss, grief, and closure, and given them the ability to move on with their lives. Edward's book *One Last Time*, released in November 1999, hit number one on the *L.A. Times'* best-seller list. Edward has also been featured in the HBO documentary *Life Afterlife* and appeared not only on *Larry King Live*, but on *Leeza*, *Roseanne*, *Maury*, *Sally*, *Entertainment Tonight*, *The Crier Report*, and *Charles Grodin*—among others.

✦ **DELVING DEEPER**

About John Edward. http://www.johnedward.net/aboutjohn.htm. 15 October 2001.

"Can the Living Talk to the Dead? Psychics say They Connect with the Spirit World, but Skeptics Respond: 'Prove It.'" *USA Today.* http://www.usatoday.com/usatonline/20010620/3415680s.htm. 18 October 2001.

Edward, John. "After Death Communication." *The Psychic Reader*, June 1999. http://www.berkeleypsychic.com/Reader/archive/june99/afterdeathcommunication.html. 18 October 2001.

Entertainment Weekly. http://www.ew.com/ew/article/commentary/0,6115,104073~3~0~scifispsychictalk,00.html 28 March 2001.

Leon Jaroff. "Talking To The Dead." *Time* Magazine, Vol. 157, No. 9: (March 5, 2001).

ARTHUR AUGUSTUS FORD (1896–1971)

In his autobiography written in collaboration with Marguerite Harmon Bro, the highly respected medium Arthur Ford, an ordained minister of the Disciples of Christ Church, explained the working relationship that he enjoyed with his **spirit guide,** Fletcher. When Ford wished to enter **trance,** he would lie down on a couch or lean back in a comfortable chair and breathe slowly and rhythmically until he felt an in-drawing of energy at the solar plexus. Then he focused his attention on Fletcher's face, as he had come to know it, until gradually he felt as if his guide's face had pressed into his own "at which instant there is a sense of shock," as if he were fainting or "passing out." At this point, Ford says, he loses consciousness—and when he awakens at the completion of a seance, it is as if he has had a "good nap."

Born into a Southern Baptist family on January 8, 1896, in Titusville, Florida, young Arthur had no real psychic experiences as a child, other than the occasional instances when he seemed to know what people were about to say. He was drawn to the religion, but he annoyed the local clergy with his persistence in asking questions about church doctrines, especially those concerning life after death. Although he was excommunicated from the Baptist church at the age of 16, in 1917 Ford entered Transylvania College in Lexington, Kentucky on a scholarship, with the intention of becoming a minister. His education was interrupted when the United States entered the First World War that same year, and Ford joined the army in 1918.

Ford advanced to the rank of second lieutenant, but he was not among the doughboys who served in the trenches overseas. Although he never saw action in Europe (the war ended soon after he enlisted), Ford observed firsthand the ravages of the terrible influenza epidemic as it struck the army camps. He began to have visions concerning those who would die of influenza, and at the same time, he heard the names of the soldiers who would be killed in action in Europe. For several frightening months, Ford thought that he was going insane. It was not until he had returned to his studies at Transylvania College that Dr. Elmer Snoddy, a psychology professor, suggested that Ford might be experiencing some kind of extrasensory phenomena, rather than insanity.

In 1922, Ford married Sallie Stewart and was ordained a minister of the Disciples of Christ Church in Barbourville, Kentucky. He began to gain immediate attention as a powerful presence in the pulpit, but his developing mediumistic abilities were creating an increasing amount of friction with his conventional ministry and his personal relationships. After five years of marriage, he divorced his wife and left the church to begin lecturing about life after death. It was not long before his lecture appearances included his entering self-induced states of trance and relaying messages from the spirit world to members of his audi-

ences. Ford's spiritistic talents were rather spontaneous and undisciplined, however, until he made the acquaintance of the great Hindu Yogi Paramhansa Yogananda (1893–1952), who taught him how to achieve a Yogic trance state and establish control of his burgeoning psychic abilities.

In 1924, Ford encountered another important influence in his life, the entity Fletcher, who would become his **spirit control.** In this particular instance, it was more a matter of reacquaintance, for Fletcher was a boyhood friend of Ford's who had been killed in action in Europe during World War I. With the advent of Fletcher as his spirit guide, Ford began a lifepath that would soon lead to world fame. In the late 1920s, Ford established the First Spiritualist Church of New York, the first of numerous churches and spiritual organizations that he would found or lead. Such luminaries as **Sir Arthur Conan Doyle** (1859–1930) called him one of the most amazing mental mediums of all times.

In 1929, Ford received a message that he believed to have originated from the spirit of the late master magician **Harry Houdini** (1874–1926) and conveyed it to Mrs. Houdini's attention. Immediately a storm of fierce arguments pro and con erupted in the media. It was well known that before his death Houdini had left a coded message with his wife that he would attempt to send her from beyond the grave to prove life after death. Some feature writers championed the authenticity of Ford's relayed after-death communication from Houdini, while others quoted his widow as saying that the message was not correct.

On February 9, 1929, however, according to Ford's supporters, Beatrice (Bess) Houdini wrote the medium to state with finality: "Regardless of any statement made to the contrary: I wish to declare that the message, in its entirety, and in the agreed upon sequence, given to me by Arthur Ford, is the correct message prearranged between Mr. Houdini and myself."

Eventually it came to be widely known that the various words in the Houdini code spelled out the secret message: "Rosabelle, believe." Ford's detractors argued that there was nothing paranormal involved in the medium's providing the secret message to Mrs. Houdini. Houdini's spirit had not whispered the words to Ford, they insisted. Rather, Ford had carefully studied an interview that Bess Houdini had given the year before in which she had inadvertently revealed the code to several reporters when she explained that the message her late husband would pass on from the world beyond was based on their old vaudeville mind-reading routine that used a secret spelling code.

Arthur Ford was at the center of another great afterlife controversy when Fletcher brought forth Bishop James A. Pike's son James A. Pike, Jr., who had committed suicide in February 1966, at the age of 22, as well as other communicating entities during a seance on September 3, 1967. This particular seance, which took place in Toronto, Ontario, was unique in that it was not limited to a drape-darkened room, but was taped and televised on CTV, the private Canadian television network. Allen Spraggett, the religion editor of the *Toronto Star* and a former pastor of the United Church of Canada, arranged the seance and later told the Associated Press that he believed that during the seance there had been strong evidence for communication with the dead or of **extrasensory perception** at the least.

At the beginning of the seance, Ford placed a dark handkerchief over his eyes, commenting that it was easier to go into trance if he did not have light, and the bright lights of the television studio would make the reception of the trance state that much more difficult. Once he had attained the trance state, Fletcher soon made an appearance. Fletcher said that he had two people eager to speak. The first communicating entity was that of a young man who had been mentally disturbed and confused before he departed. He revealed himself as James A. Pike, Jr. He said how happy he was to speak with his father. Next Fletcher brought forward George Zobrisky, a lawyer who had taught history at Virginia Theological Seminary. Zobrisky said that he had more or less shaped Bishop Pike's thinking, a point which the clergyman readily conceded. Louis Pitt then sent greetings to the bishop, who recognized Pitt as having been

acting chaplain at Columbia University before Pike had become chairman of the Department of Religion.

Fletcher next described an "old gentleman," who, after some discussion, Bishop Pike recognized as Donald McKinnon, a man who had been the principal influence on his thinking at Cambridge. The last spirit to come forward told Fletcher that he had called himself an "ecclesiastical panhandler" in life. Bishop Pike appeared to know at once what man had carried such a humorous self-described title. Allen Spragget, serving as moderator, asked Fletcher for a precise name. "Oh," said the spirit control, "something like Black. Carl. Black. Block."

"Carl Block," Bishop Pike agreed, "the fourth bishop of California, my predecessor." Then addressing the spirit directly, Bishop Pike said, "I admired and respected you, and yet I hoped you weren't feeling too badly about some changes."

Speaking through Fletcher, Bishop Block told his successor that he had done a "magnificent job" and that he had "magnificent work yet to do."

Bishop Pike said later that he did not see how any research done by Arthur Ford could have developed such intimate details about his life and such facts about the roles that certain individuals had played in shaping his thinking. He felt that the details had been "quite cumulative…not just bits and pieces, an assortment of facts." Bishop Pike stated that the information provided through Fletcher had formed a pattern. "Also, the persons who purportedly communicated had one thing in common—they were in varying ways connected with the development of my thought. They knew me at particularly significant times in my life, turning-points."

In many ways, the life of Arthur Ford was quite tragic. In 1930, a truck went out of control and struck the car in which he was driving with his sister and another woman as passengers. The two women were killed outright, and he suffered serious internal injuries, a broken jaw, and crushed ribs. During his long hospitalization, he became addicted to morphine and attempted to free himself of the resultant insomnia by drinking heavily. While at the height of his popularity, he was also an alcoholic, suffering blackouts and failing to appear for scheduled demonstrations.

In 1938, Ford married an English widow, Valerie McKeown, whom he had met while on tour, but in spite of their initial happiness together, his bouts with alcoholism doomed the marriage from the beginning. His public displays of drunkenness had become so humiliating that his faithful spirit control, Fletcher, threatened to leave Ford unless he began to exercise some degree of self-control. Ford continued to drink and Fletcher left the medium. Soon thereafter, Ford entered a deep depression and suffered a complete physical breakdown.

The Twelve-Step Program of Alcoholics Anonymous managed to help Ford attain a level of control over his drinking problem, though he was never able to give up alcohol completely. In the 1950s, Fletcher returned as his spirit control, and Ford began once again to provide demonstrations of afterlife communications that many individuals found provided proof of survival of the spirit after death. Among Ford's many positive accomplishments during this period of revival was his participation in the founding of Spiritual Frontiers Fellowship in 1956. Arthur Ford spent the final years of his life in Miami, Florida, where he died of cardiac arrest on January 4, 1971.

❈ Delving Deeper

Ford, Arthur (as told to Jerome Ellison). *The Life Beyond Death*. New York: G. P. Putnam's Sons, 1971.

Ford, Arthur, with Marguerite Harmon Bro. *Nothing So Strange: The Autobiography of Arthur Ford*. New York: Harper & Brothers, 1958.

Spraggett, Allen. *Arthur Ford: The Man Who Talked with the Dead*. New York: New American Library, 1973.

Steiger, Brad. *The World Beyond Death*. Norfolk, Va.: Donning, 1982.

Tribbe, Frank C., ed. *An Arthur Ford Anthology*. Nevada City, Calif.: Blue Dolphin, 1999.

Eileen Garrett (1893–1970)

Eileen Garrett, who became one of the most respected mediums of the twentieth century, continued to study the phenomena of her **mediumship** throughout her long career, and she consistently questioned the source of the power that guided her for so many years.

Both of her parents committed suicide shortly after her birth in 1893 in Beauparc, County Meath, Ireland, and she was adopted by an aunt and uncle. Garrett had what many researchers recognize as a typical medium's childhood: She was ill a great deal, suffered many family tragedies at a young age, and began to experience visions and to see "people" who weren't there. Little Eileen had imaginary playmates, saw various forms of light and energy around people and animals, and became aware at an early age that life did not end with physical death when she saw a kind of grayish smoke rising up from the bodies of pets after they died.

Garrett was plagued by tuberculosis and other respiratory illnesses throughout her childhood, and when she was 15 she left Ireland for the milder climate of England. She lived there with relatives for only a short time when an older gentleman named Clive began to call on her. After a courtship of a few months, she married him, and during the course of their brief marriage, she bore him three sons, all of whom died at young ages. She eventually gave birth to a daughter, Eileen, and succumbed once again to ill health. By the time she had recovered, the marriage had ended in divorce.

During World War I, Garrett opened a hostel for convalescent soldiers. While she was caring for the wounded men, she attracted the attention of a young officer who asked her to marry him. Although she had a premonition that their life together would be very short, she agreed to a marriage just before he left for the front. Within a brief period of time apart, she had a vision of his dying, and two days later she received word that he was missing in action. Shortly thereafter, she was notified that he had been killed in Ypres. She was recuperating from yet another illness when she met a young man whom she married one month before the armistice in 1918—in spite of the fact that her intuitive abilities informed her that this union would not become any more permanent than her previous states of matrimony.

Eileen Garrett did not learn that she was a trance medium until shortly after the armistice in November, when she accidentally fell asleep at a public meeting in London and the spirits of deceased relatives of the men and women seated around her began to speak through her. One gentleman present was familiar with the phenomenon of mediumship, and he explained to the young woman what had happened to her. He went on to say that he had communicated with an Asian spirit named Uvani that had manifested through her while she was entranced, and the entity had informed him that henceforth he would serve as Eileen Garrett's guide and **spirit control.** Uvani had declared that together they would do serious work to prove the validity of the survival of the human spirit after physical death.

At first Garrett was horrified at the prospect of a spirit sharing her subconscious and eavesdropping on her private thoughts and her private life. For weeks she slept with the light burning in her bedroom, fearful that Uvani might put in a materialized appearance. Such stress contributed to another bout of illness, and her developing mediumship contributed to the breakup of her third marriage. Until she sought advice from James Hewat McKenzie (1869–1929), founder of the British College of Psychic Science, she was troubled by fear of the unknown and doubts about her sanity. Under the guidance of McKenzie and his wife, Barbara, Garrett was assured that her spirit guide would not be at all interested in her daily life and that his whole purpose was based on a sincere wish to be of service to humanity. Garrett concentrated on developing her mediumship and studied with the college until McKenzie's death in 1929.

Although she had another of her premonitions concerning the transient nature of her role as wife in the state of marriage, Garrett had fallen in love and planned to be married for a fourth time. As strange as it might seem, both Garrett and her fiance became ill on the same day. She barely survived a mastoid operation, and he died of pneumonia. Confused

Eileen Garrett (1893–1970). (FORTEAN PICTURE LIBRARY)

about the course in life she was to follow, Eileen Garrett decided to come to the United States and devote herself to the process of understanding mediumship and survival after death by submitting to an intense barrage of tests at the hands of academic parapsychologists and psychical researchers.

Hereward Carrington (1880–1958), one of the leading researchers during that period, had devoted decades to psychical investigations, with a special emphasis on the various phenomena of mediumship. After years of scrupulous tests and experiments, he had concluded that 98 percent of all such phenomena are fraudulent. But when he began a series of tests with Eileen Garrett, he declared her to be a "medium's medium." He found that she was a generous woman who had always been "on the fence" with regard to her own highly acclaimed mediumship and who had offered herself to science in a sincere effort to learn more about the spirits who communicated through her.

During the years in which she perfected her ability to communicate with the spirits of the deceased through her spirit guide, Eileen Garrett often expressed doubts about Uvani's spiritual independence and frequently voiced her suspicions that he might only be a segment of her own subconscious mind. Eventually, she had four trance communicators. Uvani, a fourteenth-century Arab soldier, remained always as the control, but there was also Abdul Latif, a seventeenth-century Persian physician, who dealt primarily with healing, and Tahotah and Ramah, who claimed no prior earthly incarnations and who spoke only seldom and then on philosophical and spiritual matters. Such indecisiveness about the source of her abilities dismayed the Spiritualists, who in her developmental years in London, had tutored her with the utmost seriousness.

To⊙ Eileen Garrett, mediumship was not a "breaking-down of the personality," but a state of wholeness.

Eileen Garrett became a persistent and highly qualified researcher in her own right. In 1951, she founded the Parapsychology Foundation, Inc., in New York City, and in 1952 reestablished her magazine *Tomorrow* as a quarterly journal of psychic science. In 1959, the foundation began publishing the *International Journal of Parapsychology* and in 1970, the *Parapsychology Review*. She also authored such books as *Adventures in the Supernormal* (1949), *The Sense and Nonsense of Prophecy* (1950), and *Many Voices: The Autobiography of a Medium* (1968).

In an article entitled "The Ethics of Mediumship" for the Autumn 1960 issue of *Tomorrow*, Eileen Garrett stated that she was not one who "assumes that the gift of mediumship necessarily brings with it greater insight into the phenomena of that mediumship." She goes on to advise the serious medium to "withdraw herself from the ideas thrown out by the inquirer" and regard herself "as a mechanism, clear and simple, through which ideas flow." According to an accomplished medium such

as Garrett, those who had similar gifts should put themselves into a "receptive mood" which will enable them to "accept the flow of events and ideas to be perceived and known."

Continuing with this line of thought, she wrote:

> If the medium allows herself to be thus used, things will happen of themselves—a technique old as wisdom itself, and not contradictory to Zen. One allows the feminine perceptive principle of the unconscious to emerge and thus one is not swamped by the demanding consciousness of the self or the inquirer. This instructive feminine element is, according to Jung, the common property of all mankind. It cannot be coerced. It must be respected and nurtured.

To Eileen Garrett, mediumship was not a "breaking-down of the personality," but a state of wholeness. She regarded the tendency of "enthusiastic sitters to regard the medium as priest or priestess" as the "major danger area in mediumistic activities." She wisely concluded that "…communication with the 'other world' may well become a substitute for living in this world. Understanding that this world in which we live has priority in this existence is the core of mediumship ethics."

Eileen Garrett died on September 15, 1970, in Nice, France, following a period of declining health.

✤ DELVING DEEPER

Angoff, Allan. *Eileen Garrett and the World Beyond the Senses*. New York: William Morrow, 1974.

Carrington, Hereward. *The Case for Psychic Survival*. New York: Citadel Press, 1957.

Garrett, Eileen. *Many Voices: The Autobiography of a Medium*. New York: G. P. Putnam's Sons, 1968.

LeShan, Lawrence. *The Medium, the Mystic, and the Physicist*. New York: Viking Press, 1974.

DANIEL DUNGLAS HOME (1833–1886)

The clientele of Daniel Dunglas Home was one of the most exclusive that ever gathered around any one medium: Elizabeth Barrett Browning, Mark Twain, Napoleon III, the Empress Eugenie, Tolstoy, and many other notables on both sides of the Atlantic. Home was poked and probed and examined by dozens of scientists, and he graciously submitted to hundreds of tests by psychical researchers. No skeptical investigator ever succeeded in exposing him, and two of the most prestigious scientists of the day, **Sir William Crookes** (1832–1919) and Dr. Robert Hare (1781–1858), stated that, in their opinion, the phenomena manifested by Home was genuine. Home conducted over 1,500 seances and produced phenomena at all times, under all manner of conditions, in broad daylight, under artificial lighting, indoors, outdoors, in private homes, in hotel rooms, and on public lecture platforms.

Born near Edinburgh, Scotland, on March 20, 1833, Home was said to have been rocked in his cradle by unseen entities. His mother was also said to have had the gift of "second sight," as **clairvoyance** was called in those days, and Mary McNeal Cook, an aunt who adopted Home when he was but a year old, began noticing clairvoyant impressions from the child almost as soon as he began to speak. At the age of four he began having visions which proved to be accurate. A frail child who contracted tuberculosis at an early age, Home's early childhood was marked by long periods of convalescence. When he was nine, his aunt and uncle moved to the United States, where they settled in Greeneville, Connecticut.

Home was 17 when the physical phenomena which was to direct the course of his life began to occur around him. In his memoirs, Home writes that he first heard "…three loud blows on the head of the bed as if it had been struck by a hammer." His first impression was that someone had hidden in his bedroom to frighten him, but the next morning at breakfast, the table at which he had seated himself was shaken nearly to pieces by a wild flurry of rappings.

His aunt, near hysteria, left the home to summon three clergymen from the village to drive the devil out of her house. Unable to make the rappings cease with their prayers, the ministers advised Cook to ignore the disturbances.

While it may have been possible to heed the ministers' advice regarding the mysterious rapping sounds, Cook found it impossible to ignore the activity of the furniture when tables and chairs began to move about the rooms. As the townspeople gathered to watch the strange, unexplainable occurrences, Home gave his first impromptu seance. According to an account in the local newspaper, scores of people from Greeneville and nearby communities came to ask questions of the "talking table" in the Cook residence. The table would raise or lower a leg and tap out answers to queries put to it by the astonished villagers, and even a strong man could not make the heavy table duplicate such movements when Home was not there to control it.

By the early 1850s, his fame had spread, and the teenager was soon beleaguered by scientists, clergymen, and medical doctors, each seeking to be the first to explain his mysterious talents. Home's powers began to grow stronger, and numerous individuals testified to instantaneous healings accomplished by the young medium. At the same time, Home displayed an amazing ability to divine the future and to clairvoyantly determine happenings at great distances.

DANIEL *Dunglas Home conducted over 1,500 seances and produced phenomena at all times.*

In 1852, when, at the age of 19, he made his first trip to New York, Home was eagerly received by those who had been awaiting an opportunity to see firsthand the various wonders that had been attributed to the youthful medium. Dr. Robert Hare, professor emeritus of chemistry at the University of Pennsylvania, attested to the absolute authenticity of Home's strange talents, but the American Association for the Advancement of Science refused to hear the report of its distinguished member. Although the association declined even to examine Home or to witness any phenomena produced by him firsthand, the elite of New York society outdid themselves in bidding for the medium's appearance at their homes.

In 1855, after three years of exhaustive tests with those scientists who were not fearful of risking their reputations by examining his mediumistic talents, Daniel Dunglas Home set out for England and France. The overseas press had been awaiting the medium's arrival, and so had the greatest hostesses of London society. Home soon captivated England as thoroughly as he had the United States. Those who attended his seances could expect to see spirit lights, to hear raps and the voices of disembodied spirits, and perhaps even to experience the thrill of being lifted into the air by unseen hands.

The English novelist Sir Edward Bulwer-Lytton (1831–91), who was well versed in the occult, reported a series of seances held in his home in which the medium had set heavy tables rolling like hoops, and invisible musicians had played familiar melodies on accordions. Spirit hands and arms materialized, and Bulwer-Lytton claimed to have seen objects being transported about the room by ethereal fingers.

In Florence, Italy, Home is reported to have caused a grand piano, at which the Countess Orsini was seated, to rise into the air and to remain levitated until she had completed the musical number that she had been playing. Home's mediumship was witnessed by such members of the aristocracy as Prince Murat, Napoleon III, and the Empress Eugenie. During one seance, Napoleon Bonaparte appeared and signed his name, and his grandson attested to its authenticity. The young medium's demonstrations in Florence were of such a dramatic nature that frightened whispers began to circulate that Daniel Dunglas Home was one of Satan's own. Public fervor became so heated that Home was attacked and wounded by an unknown assailant.

As he lay in pain recovering from his wound, the spirits appeared to deal Home a psychological blow. They informed him that they would remove his powers for a period of one year, beginning on February 10, 1856. True to their word, Home found that he was unable to summon any spirit control or to produce any phenomena whatsoever after that date.

The 23-year-old medium traveled to Rome, where he sought consolation in the Roman Catholic Church. He was without funds, ill, and sorely disillusioned with his spirit guides for having deserted him. Home expressed a wish to shun everything pertaining to the material world, and for a time he considered entering a monastery. Although the church became a mainstay to Home during his period of despondency, the relationship was terminated at the stroke of midnight on February 10, 1857, when Home's bedstead resounded with hearty spirit raps, and a voice from the other side announced the return of his powers of mediumship.

Father Ravignan, who had been Home's confessor and close friend, was convinced that the young man had been sincere about his embracing the church, but the Roman Catholic clergyman could in no way sanction mediumship and the contacting of spirits. Although Home was grateful to the church that had ministered to him during his hour of greatest need, he saw clearly that there could be no more harmony between them.

The wealthy and powerful of Europe had been waiting to see if the medium's powers would truly return to him after their year of desertion. When Home reappeared on the scene, once again materializing spirit forms and producing raps on the walls, his elite clientele immediately restored him to celebrity status. He demonstrated his dramatic control of unseen forces before the courts of Napoleon III, Empress Eugenie, and Prince Murat, and won hundreds of new supporters.

Back in Rome, Home married Alexandrina, the wealthy sister-in-law of a Russian nobleman. Alexander Dumas (1802–1870), the French novelist, was Home's best man. The marriage ceremony was performed with both Roman Catholic and Greek Orthodox rites—a gesture that Home intended as an expression of his good will toward the church, in spite of the interminable religious controversies in which he was embroiled.

It was in the presence of the Russian novelist Count Leo Tolstoy that Home first produced the phenomenon with which he has come to be most commonly associated in the annals of psychical research. In full view of several sitters and with Tolstoy's hands firmly clasping his feet, Home levitated from his chair until he was seen floating above the heads of the members of the seance circle.

Home's wife died in London in 1862, and without her contributions to their upkeep from her family's wealth, he was forced to give lectures and other public demonstrations that proved to be exhausting. He decided to return to Rome and express his creativity through sculpturing, rather than mediumship, but he was ordered to leave Italy on the charge of sorcery. He promised once again to abandon the summoning of spirits, but Italian officials put little faith in such vows. Home was forced to leave the country, and he returned to Britain in 1864.

The single event in Home's remarkable psychic career that is most remembered occurred on the evening of December 13, 1868, when he was seen to float out of the window of a third-floor home in Ashley House and return through another window to rejoin the men who witnessed the extraordinary act of levitation. Among those who observed the feat were Captain Wynne, the Earl of Dunraven, and the Earl of Crawford, all men of solid character and integrity. Ever since the phenomenon was first reported, skeptics have insisted that the witnesses themselves helped to perpetuate a fraud. Others have suggested that Home merely hypnotized the illustrious men into believing that he floated in and out of the windows on the third floor or that he had discovered nasty secrets about all of them and used blackmail to pressure them into going along with his account.

In 1869, William Thackeray's publication *The Cornhill Magazine* printed an article which created a sensation in all of England. The author told of another seance in which Daniel D. Home levitated from his chair to a height of about four feet, then assumed a horizontal position and floated about the room.

By then the controversy over the "Wizard Home" had reached such proportions that the press was demanding a scientific investigation of such remarkable feats. Sir William Crookes seemed to be the scientist most likely to succeed in revealing Home's alleged wonders as hoaxes, if he was a hoaxster. Crookes, a member of the Royal Society, was a chemist and physicist, inventor of the X-Ray tube, and a scientist eager to test the medium under the strictest of laboratory conditions. Home did not shrink from the challenge. On the contrary, he appeared as eager as Crookes to enter into a full series of experiments and tests. He imposed no restrictions on Crookes's probings, and he voiced no objection to producing all spiritistic phenomena in a bright light.

Crookes found that Home's strange talents were strong enough to resist the antagonistic influence of the laboratory. In one of his reports on the medium, Crookes stated that he was prepared to attest that the phenomena he had witnessed "are so extraordinary and so directly oppose the most firmly-rooted articles of scientific belief—[such as]…the ubiquity and invariable action of gravitation—that even now, on recalling the details of what I witnessed, there is an antagonism in my mind between reason, which pronounces it to be scientifically impossible, and the consciousness that my senses both of touch and sight—and these corroborated, as they were, by the senses of all who were present—are not lying witnesses when they testify against my preconceptions."

Crookes studied firsthand the full gamut of Home's phenomena, from levitation to the movement of objects. The physicist noted that the movements were generally preceded by "…a peculiar cold air, sometimes amounting to a decided wind. I have had sheets of paper blown about by it, and a thermometer lowered several degrees." Crookes also observed luminous points of light and glowing clouds that formed and often settled on the heads of various investigators. In some instances, the scientist saw these luminous clouds form hands which carried small objects about the laboratory.

On one occasion, Crookes watched while a beautifully formed small hand rose up from an opening in a dining table and handed him a flower before it disappeared. The scientist testified that the materialization occurred in the light of his own room while he was securely holding the medium's hands and feet. During another such experiment when a hand materialized before him, Crookes reached out to clasp it, firmly resolving not to allow it to escape. He stated that there was no struggle on the part of the spirit hand, but it gradually seemed to become vaporous and slowly faded from his grasp.

A spirit form materialized in a corner of the laboratory during the course of one experiment, took up an accordion into its hands, and glided about the room playing the instrument. Crookes's report of the incident indicated that the phantom was visible for several minutes before it disappeared at a slight cry from one of the female sitters. Intrigued by this particular demonstration, Crookes designed a special cage wherein he placed an accordion which he invited the spirit to play. During the laboratory-controlled experiment, the accordion floated about the "spook-proof" cage and unseen fingers played a variety of melodies on the keyboard of the instrument.

In addition to his famous feats of levitation—a phenomenon that Crookes personally witnessed on three different occasions—Daniel Dunglas Home was well known for his ability to handle fire without being burned or incurring any ill effects. During one demonstration, Crookes watched in astonishment as "…Home went to the fire, and after stirring the hot coals about with his hand, took out a red hot piece nearly as big as an orange, and putting it on his right hand, covered it over with his left hand so as to almost completely enclose it, and then blew into the small furnace that extemporized until the lump of charcoal was nearly white-hot.…"

Sir William Crookes took extensive notes on all phases of Home's abilities, and a number of his reports were published in the *Quarterly Journal of Science*. However, his colleagues in the Royal Society of Science were immensely disappointed in his affirmation that the phenomena produced by Home were genuine. Most of the members of the prestigious society of scientists had long before made up their minds that Daniel Dunglas Home was a faker, and they had set Sir William Crookes to the task of exposing him. The chemist and physicist who had only a short time before been acclaimed as one of Great Britain's most brilliant scientists was

now being viciously attacked by his colleagues as a gullible simpleton who had been taken in by Home's parlor magic tricks.

Crookes stood firm, and he challenged his fellow members of the Royal Society to prove his errors by showing him where the errors lay, by showing him how the medium's tricks had been performed. "Try the experiment fully and fairly," Crookes answered his critics. "If then fraud be found, expose it; if it be truth, proclaim it. This is the only scientific procedure, and this it is that I propose steadily to pursue."

Although the Royal Society stood as one in refusing to witness a new series of tests with Home, the ridicule that was heaped upon Crookes was not enough to greatly damage his solid reputation. Twenty years later, when Sir William Crookes was president of the British Association for the Advancement of Science, he publicly reaffirmed that his previous assessment of the experiments with Daniel Dunglas Home had been valid and that he found nothing to retract or to alter in his original findings.

In 1871, Home married for the second time, and once again his wife, Julie de Gloumeline, came from a wealthy Russian family. He ceased giving mediumistic demonstrations for the public or for science during the 1870s, and on June 12, 1886, Daniel Dunglas Home died from the tuberculosis that had first assailed him in his youth. Home remains one of the most remarkable figures of the nineteenth century, and if one of the most respected scientists of that era is to be believed, he was one of the most amazing spirit mediums who ever lived.

Although Home was accused many times of fraudulent mediumism, in 1907 the respected psychical researcher Hereward Carrington stressed in his book *The Physical Phenomenon of Spiritualism* (1907) that in spite of such persistent accusations, Daniel Dunglas Home was never exposed as a fraud. Such prominent magicians as **Harry Houdini** (1874–1926) and John Mulholland, well known for their efforts to expose mediums as charlatans, claimed that they could duplicate Home's phenomena, but they never actually did so. Houdini even announced that he could duplicate the famous Home feat of levitating in and out of the third-floor windows at Lord Adare's home, but he canceled the event without explanation.

❋ DELVING DEEPER

Brown, Slater. *The Heyday of Spiritualism*. New York: Hawthorn Books, 1970.

Edmonds, I. G. *D. D. Home, the Man Who Talked with Ghosts*. Nashville, Tenn.: Thomas Nelson, 1978.

Fodor, Nandor. *An Encyclopedia of Psychic Science*. Secaucus, N.J.: Citadel Press, 1966.

———. *These Mysterious People*. London: Rider & Co., 1935.

J. Z. KNIGHT (1946–)

J. Z. Knight channels "Ramtha," or "the Ram," for the purpose of presenting his message to humankind. The Ram says that he lived only one time on Earth, 35,000 years ago, as a young man from **Lemuria** who grew up in the port city of Onai in **Atlantis.** Through the vehicle of J. Z. Knight, who was his daughter in that existence, he claims that he did not die a physical death during that lifetime but learned to harness the power the of mind so that he could take his body with him to an unseen dimension of life. Ramtha states that he is now a part of an unseen brotherhood that loves humankind. He is, therefore, fulfilling a mission of aiding and preparing humankind for a great event that has already been set in motion.

Entertainers such as Shirley MacLaine, Linda Evans, and Richard Chamberlain have been in the audiences of Ramtha, along with throngs of people around the United States and Canada. Since 1978, thousands have studied the Ramtha videos, cassettes, and books. For a period of time, it seemed impossible to pick up a weekly tabloid without finding an article about Ramtha and his high-profile disciples in its pages. In 1988, Ramtha founded the School of Enlightenment on J. Z. Knight's ranch in Yelm, Washington, which continues to hold teaching seminars. Knight and her followers make clear that the school is neither a church nor a nonprofit organization. They pay business taxes and run the school as a business.

Born Judith Darlene Hampton on March 16, 1946, in Dexter, New Mexico, Knight

Shirley MacLaine.
(CORBIS CORPORATION)

grew up in poverty and married Caris Hensley, a gas station attendant, soon after attending Lubbock Business College in Lubbock, Texas. The marriage produced two sons, but ended in divorce. It was while she was working as a cable television salesperson in Roswell, New Mexico, and Tacoma, Washington, that she began using the initials "J. Z.," signifying her first name and her nickname, "Zebra," derived from her penchant for wearing black-and-white clothing.

It all began for J. Z. Knight one day in 1977 when she and her second husband, Jeremy Wilder, a dentist, were cutting out and putting together small pyramids and experimenting with "pyramid energy." She jokingly put a pyramid on her head, and as it slipped down over her eyes, Ramtha appeared physically before them in their kitchen in Tacoma.

In the beginning, Knight said that she believed that the power of the pyramid may have induced the manifestation of the spirit entity, but she grew to understand that it was a combination of the student being ready and the teacher appearing, plus her own spiritual energy and her willingness to take a step into

J. Z. Knight with Linda
Evans. (AP/WIDE
WORLD PHOTOS)

the unknown. "I feel I may have created a state of readiness in my mind," she said. "Part of my mind said, 'Girl, here you are doing something really bizarre.' Another part of my mind said, 'This is wonderful—you are starting to reach out and explore.' I think by virtue of that process alone, the entity's consciousness was able to become visual to me at that time."

AFTER *her period of study with Ramtha,*
J. Z. Knight gave her first public channeling in
November 1978.

It took two years of Ramtha's working with J. Z. Knight before she got used to his presence. Frankly, she stated, it was her persistent love of God that maintained her. "To have gone through the two-year study with Ramtha and his teachings, then to have the courage to

change my life and to allow myself to be used as an instrument and to face a critical world and go on with the teachings led to a very beneficial personal growth and depth for me," she said. "I have been nailed to the cross of the media, and yet nothing will keep me from progressing because I know the truth."

After her period of study with Ramtha, Knight gave her first public channeling in November 1978, and word of the content and the mystique spread quickly and gained a wide following for the 35,000-year-old entity and his channel. Knight's increased popularity and the demand for public appearances placed a strain on her marriage, and in 1981, she divorced Wilder to marry Jeff Knight, a trainer of Arabian horses. In the late 1980s she underwent a series of financial and legal stresses, and she filed for divorce from Knight in 1989.

Knight has said that Ramtha occurs in her life in three different ways. The first is when she leaves the body in trance. She claims to have no conscious recollections of what transpires when Ramtha takes over. In her personal assessment, he is a consciousness that works through her brain and mind and manipulates her body in order for that to occur. "We both cannot occupy the same space," she said, "so I was afraid of letting go because that meant death, in a sense, to me. It took me two years to get over that fear."

In her opinion, Ramtha is a "channeled consciousness," rather than a spirit. "As a consciousness that has hyperlucidity, Ramtha can be considered superconsciousness that affects itself through physical mass," Knight said.

Secondly, Ramtha appears separate from her. The channeler said that she had come to understand that his visual appearance "may be a hologram of his consciousness that was actually working through my brain to create that vision."

The third manner that Ramtha can manifest is that he can answer J. Z. Knight when she has a question. "I can actually hear the answer that is translated in my head," she said. "I hear that as a vocal voice. Ramtha has never imposed by taking over my body. Regardless of what anybody says, I am not being possessed. It is of my own free will."

Ramtha told the thousands of men and women who gathered for the series of popular lectures and seminars that they were gods, possessed of a divine nature, fully capable of creating and realizing whatever goals they desired. When answering questions from individuals, he addresses them as "master," thereby indicating that he considers them on the path of self-mastery. Consistent with other New Age teachers, Ramtha teaches that all those who meditate upon the vital life-force within will be directed to the path of self-realization.

Although J. Z. Knight has been criticized by those who point out that there is no substantial evidence that Ramtha's Lemuria or Atlantis ever existed and that 35,000 years ago, humankind was still at the hunter and gatherer stage of development, she has received the harshest criticism for the high prices she charges for her seminars. The channeler admitted that at first she had difficulty with Ramtha's insistence that she must charge people for the teachings, but the entity told her that people did not appreciate knowledge that they receive for free.

"The only way we ever gain wisdom is when we interact and experience life," she explained. "We pay the price of experiencing life in order to gain wisdom, the virtue of which is the prize of evolution. So the price people pay to attend the teachings is equal to the price they pay in life to gain knowledge and wisdom. It is equal and relative to personal experience, which always comes with a price."

❁ Delving Deeper

Klimo, Jon. *Channeling: Investigations on Receiving Information from Paranormal Sources*. Los Angeles: Jeremy P. Tarcher, 1987.

Knight, J. Z. *A State of Mind*. New York: Warner Books, 1987.

Steiger, Sherry Hansen, and Brad Steiger. *Hollywood and the Supernatural*. New York: St. Martin's Press, 1990.

Weinberg, Steven Lee, ed., with Randall Weischedell, Sue Ann Fazio, and Carol Wright. *Ramtha*. Eastsound, Wash.: Sovereignty, 1986.

Carlos Mirabelli (1889–1951)

Cesar (Carlos) Augusto Mirabelli was born in 1889 in Botucatu in the state of Sao Paulo, Brazil. From his earliest childhood, he demonstrated a strong interest in religion. He hoped to enter into the service of the Roman Catholic Church, but these aspirations were never realized, and he took employment with a commercial firm in Rio de Janeiro.

Things did not go smoothly for Mirabelli on the job, and the strange happenings that had begun to occur around the place of business were soon attributed to the peculiar young man. While some of his fellow employees were drawn to the short man with the light-blue eyes, others found him arrogant and conceited and complained that his eyes seemed to look right through them. And then there were the eerie manifestations that seemed always to take place around him.

Mirabelli was examined by medical doctors and sent to the Juqueri Asylum where the director, Dr. E. Costa, recognized the young man's peculiarities to be due to psychism

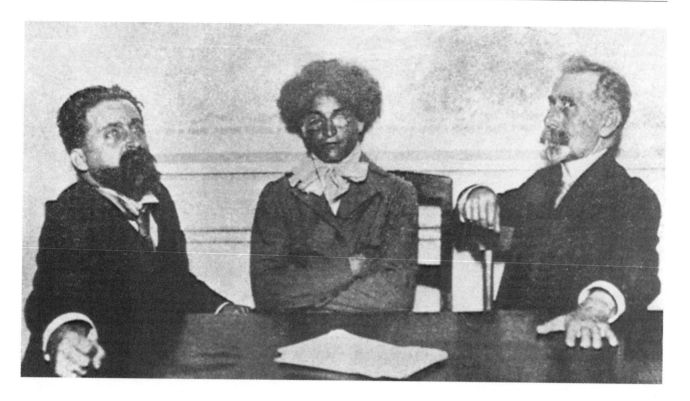

rather than insanity. Costa conducted a number of tests with his patient and became the first doctor to verify the reality of Mirabelli's mediumship. Costa returned Mirabelli to Rio de Janeiro, where he arranged for the young medium to demonstrate his abilities. Under the strictest of controls, Mirabelli confounded an assembly of doctors by utilizing apparent **teleportation** to send a painting over a distance of several miles from one house to another. This experiment was reported in sensational detail in the Brazilian newspapers, and the career of the medium Mirabelli had been launched.

As an automatic-writing medium, Mirabelli produced lengthy and erudite written dissertations in 28 languages.

By 1926 Mirabelli had produced phenomena before a total of nearly 600 witnesses, most of whom had been recruited from the ranks of Brazil's leading scientists, medical doctors, administrators, and writers, with an occasional learned visitor from abroad. As a trance-speaking medium, Mirabelli particularly excelled in xenoglossy, the ability to speak in languages unknown to him in his normal state. Not only did he speak in foreign tongues, but he gave spontaneous lectures on philosophy, astronomy, sociology, politics, medicine, history, and the natural sciences. These speeches were delivered alternately in German, French, Dutch, English, Greek, Polish, Syrian, Albanian, Czech, four Italian dialects, Arabic, Turkish, Hebrew, Chinese, Japanese, and several African dialects, in addition to Latin, Ancient Greek, and his native tongue, Portuguese.

As an automatic-writing medium, he produced lengthy and erudite written dissertations in 28 languages, in a speed impossible to achieve under normal writing conditions. While entranced, it is said that Mirabelli wrote treatises in the style of Lombroso, Kepler, Voltaire, and Galileo. These works included an essay on evil written in Hebrew and signed by Moses, a tract on the instability of empires by Alexander the Great, and an essay on the mysterious things between heaven and Earth by Shakespeare. Although unable to verify such prestigious authorship,

linguists were said to be amazed at the masterful control that the medium exercised over each of the languages employed in these treatises. Such accomplishments are made the more impressive by noting that Mirabelli's formal education ended with primary school.

As a physical medium, Mirabelli once materialized the spirit bodies of a marshal and a bishop, both long deceased, and both of whom were instantly recognizable to many who had assembled for the seance. Levitation seemed almost to be a specialty of the medium, and witnesses once observed him levitate an automobile to a height of six feet, where it was suspended for a period of three minutes. Once when Mirabelli visited a pharmacy, a skull rose from the back of the laboratory and came to rest on the cash register. Before a gathering of doctors, who lent their names to a deposition, Mirabelli caused a violin to be played by spirit hands. To exhibit spirit control, Mirabelli caused billiard balls to roll and stop at his command.

At a party with more than a thousand guests in attendance, the medium conducted an invisible orchestra of trumpets and drums which entertained the astonished partygoers with a lively march. During numerous seances, Mirabelli caused such inanimate objects as books, bells, chairs, and chandeliers to move at his command. The list of doctors and other witnesses who attested to Mirabelli's psychic abilities include the names of many well-known persons. Time and again, psychical researchers subjected the medium to the most rigorous examinations, but none ever caught him in an act of trickery.

While he was undergoing examination by the members of the Lombroso Academy, Mirabelli was bound to a chair in which he raised himself to a height of more than six feet and hung suspended for over two minutes. Several members of the academy walked beneath the levitated medium and satisfied themselves that they were witnessing an authentic phenomenon and not a magician's trick.

During one seance held for the academy at the unlikely hour of 9:00 A.M., the dead daughter of Dr. de Souza materialized. The doctor recognized his daughter and the dress in which she had been buried. He was allowed to embrace the spirit form and numerous photographs were taken of the scene. The spirit being remained in material form for a period of 36 minutes. This seance was witnessed by a large assembly, including 20 medical doctors and seven professors. Investigated by scientists and psychic researchers from all over the world, the mediumship of Mirabelli offered yet another question mark to the skeptical mind and another source of reassurance to the believer.

In 1990, Dr. Gordon Stein found a picture in the collection of the London Society for Psychical Research that depicted Mirabelli in a white laboratory coat levitating to a height of several feet in the air. The photograph was inscribed to Theodore Besterman, an SPR researcher who was known to have visited the medium in August of 1934. At the time, Besterman had prepared a contradictory report about Mirabelli's paranormal abilities which, according to Mirabelli's defenders, reflected more upon Besterman's inexperience as a psychical researcher than the medium's ability to produce genuine phenomena. In 1992, Guy Lyon Playfair published an illustrated article about the incident in the *Journal of the American Society for Psychical Research* in which he points out that the famous levitation photograph reveals signs of careful retouching which eliminated the ladder under Mirabelli's feet. Proponents of Mirabelli's mediumship argue that if the photograph was deliberately faked by Mirabelli, it would be the first evidence of trickery on his part ever discovered by any investigator.

✤ DELVING DEEPER

Mello, Da Silva A. *Mysteries and Realities of This World and the Next.* Trans. by M. B. Fierz. London: Weidenfeld & Nicolson, 1950.

EUSAPIA PALLADINO (1854–1918)

At the time of her death in 1918, Eusapia Palladino had been both the most thoroughly investigated physical medium in the history of psychical research and the most controversial and startling personality ever to confront a team of investigators into the unexplained. She could be at once flirtatious and so suggestive in her conversation that some researchers were embarrassed by her frank sexuality; and at the same time, she dominated her husband so completely that the beleaguered man had to take her maiden name as his own when they were married. Palladino could hardly sign her own name and reading was beyond her knowledge, but the world's leading scientists and psychical researchers testified that this enigmatic woman was somehow able to tap into strange powers as yet unnamed by conventional science.

Born in Bari, Italy, in 1854, Palladino's mediumship was discovered by a family who employed her as a maid when she moved to Naples as a young girl. The quality of the phenomena that she produced brought her to the attention of Professor Chiaia, who, in turn, introduced her to the professor Cesare Lombroso (1835–1909). When the great psychologist's initial reports on Eusapia Palladino were published, it was not long before she was sitting with research groups in Paris, St. Petersburg, Turin, Genoa, London, and New York. As far as the audacious Eusapia was concerned, it mattered little where she conducted her seances. Her mysterious talents were not bound by geographical locations. She was able to produce incredible psychic effects whenever and wherever she sat.

In 1908, a special committee was selected by the British Society for Psychical Research (BSPR) for the sole purpose of investigating the claims that had been made by a number of celebrated scientists on behalf of the medium. The committee was especially chosen for their skepticism and was composed of Everard Feilding, Mrs. W. W. Baggally, and **Hereward Carrington** (1880–1958), each of whom had exposed many fraudulent mediums in the course of their investigations. Previous test results with the medium at Cambridge in the summer of 1895 had been contradictory, with some of the researchers convinced of her abilities, and others equally certain that they had caught her in acts of trickery. Subsequent examinations of Palladino by psychical researchers in Paris in 1898 and various cities in Italy during the years 1901–7 had produced the same mixture of acceptance and doubt.

Between November 21 and December 19, 1908, the team of professional skeptics spent several weeks in the Hotel Victoria in the medium's native city of Naples and were able to observe an incredibly wide range of spiritistic phenomena. Each of the members published lengthy reports on the remarkable Palladino, and each of them came away from the exhaustive series of seances quite convinced that the medium had the ability to release an extremely potent paranormal force. They also noted that Palladino would cheat if she were allowed to do so, but because of their strict controls, she was forced to abandon the easier path of trickery and produce genuine phenomena.

Working under the strictest control the investigators could exert upon her, Palladino allowed the committee to examine both her person and her room as thoroughly as they might wish. She utilized a spirit cabinet that was formed by stretching two black curtains across one of the corners of the room. Inside this makeshift affair, the investigators placed musical instruments and a variety of other small, movable objects. The medium sat directly in front of the closet with at least a foot of space between her chair and the curtains.

After warming up with simple displays of table levitation, Palladino would call for a dimming of the lights. Almost instantly, the medium would summon her **spirit control,** John King, who would subsequently cause the objects behind the curtain to come floating out. Musical instruments would be played by unseen hands, and the sound would be easily heard by all sitters in the room. The highlight of every seance was the materialization of spirit hands and bodies. These materializations always came last in any seance, as if the woman's inborn sense of the dramatic knew how best to leave an audience wanting more.

Hereward Carrington, who published a great deal of material about the medium, relat-

Eusapia Palladino in 1907. (FORTEAN PICTURE LIBRARY)

ed one incident wherein Palladino had asked him to replace a small table that had been levitated from the closet behind her. Carrington pushed aside the curtains and attempted to place the table on the floor where it had been situated. He was startled when some powerful force resisted his doing so.

Outside the cabinet, the other members of the committee had observed Carrington's difficulty in replacing the small table. One of the psychical investigators crouched under the table and clamped both of his hands around the medium's feet. Two other researchers were stationed at her side. They all assured Carrington that the medium had not moved since she had asked him to replace the table and that they would prevent her from making any moves at all. Once these precautions had been taken, Carrington resolutely tried again to replace the stubborn table behind the curtain of the spirit cabinet—but each time some unknown force repelled his efforts. At last the invisible entity seemed to grow tired of the game, and with a considerable burst of energy, sent both Carrington and the table tumbling out of the cabinet and sprawling to the floor.

In 1909, at a later sitting in New York where Palladino had been brought by great demand on the part of American psychical researchers, the medium capped her usual repertoire of paranormal feats by materializing a small hand in the air. Carrington later reported that the hand appeared white in the dim light of the laboratory and that its arm was visible up to a ghostly elbow. The wrist was encased in a lacy cuff. The hand and forearm were clearly seen by all the researchers in the room, and Palladino's own limbs were tied to two men, one on either side of her. While the investigators watched as if mesmerized, the ghostly hand moved to the medium's bonds and deftly untied the knots. When the spirit had undone the ropes, it threw one of the bonds at an observer and struck him in the chest. The other rope was thrown against the far wall of the sitting room.

The good-natured medium laughed at the antics of the ambitious spirit hand and bade the researchers to bind her once again. The men had no sooner fastened the knots a second time when the spirit hand rematerialized and quickly untied them.

The mystery of Eusapia Palladino's mediumship is a many-faceted one. Carrington wrote, for example, that she was often caught attempting the most crude kind of trickery—pranks that even the most inexperienced psychical researcher would be certain to catch. Her nature was permeated with mischief and guile, and she would try to cheat at card games or even croquet. Carrington felt that she did these things to those who would test her to see how far she might go in taunting them—or because she was basically a lazy person, to see if she could fool them with a few tricks so that she might be spared the effort of going into trance. When she found that she could not deceive the knowledgeable investigators from the various research committees—most of whom were accomplished amateur magicians—Palladino would settle down to producing some of the most remarkable psychic phenomena ever recorded and witnessed by an investigating body of skeptics.

✤ Delving Deeper

Carrington, Hereward. *Eusapia Palladino and Her Phenomena*. New York: B. W. Dodge, 1909.

Dingwall, E. J. *Very Peculiar People*. London: Rider & Co., 1950.

Tabori, Paul. *Pioneers of the Unseen*. New York: Taplinger, 1973.

Leonora E. Piper (1857–1950)

Psychical researcher **Hereward Carrington** (1880–1958) considered Leonora E. Piper to be the greatest psychical medium of her time. Piper was a resident of Boston, as was **Margery Crandon** (1888–1941), but her **mediumship** had already won the endorsement of such luminaries as **William James** (1842–1910), Dr. Richard Hodgson (1855–1905), and **Sir Oliver Lodge** (1851–1940) before Crandon had really begun her psychic career. Piper was a direct-voice medium, who while entranced, would allow her body to be taken over by spirits who would use her voice to speak and, on occasion, to write messages to those persons assembled for her seances.

Eight-year-old Leonora (often spelled Leonore) had been playing in the family garden when she suddenly felt a stinging blow on her right ear and heard a kind of hissing sound that gradually became a voice repeating the letter "S." Once this had been resolved, Leonora clearly heard the same voice tell her that her Aunt Sara had died, but her spirit remained near. Leonora's mother made note of the day and the hour in which she had received the spirit communication, and a few days later the family learned that Sara had died at the very hour on the very day that Leonora received the message.

Although this event signaled the advent of Leonora's mediumship, her mother wisely insisted on the young girl enjoying a normal childhood and the dramatic impact of any subsequent paranormal phenomena was underplayed. When Leonora was 22, she married William Piper of Boston, and shortly thereafter developed a friendship with a blind clairvoyant named Dr. J. R. Cocke, who had been attracting a substantial following as a result of his accurate medical diagnoses and cures. At their first meeting, Leonora Piper had fallen into a **trance,** walked in such a state across the room, where she sat at a table, picked up pencil and paper, and began to write messages from spirit entities. Prominent Bostonians were often seated in the seance circle at Cocke's home, the remarkable accuracy of Piper's trance communications soon spread throughout the city, and she was soon being pursued by men and women who wished to sit with her in her own seances.

At the beginning of her mediumship, Piper's **spirit control** claimed to be a young Native American girl, but within a short time, Cocke's guide, Phinuit, a French doctor, had switched his allegiance to Piper. Phinuit remained the medium's principal spirit control from 1884 to 1892, although other entities spoke or wrote through her, notably the spirit of George Pelham, a friend of the well-known psychical researcher Dr. Richard Hodgson. Pelham communicated through automatic writing until sometime in 1897 when both he and Phinuit essentially retreated back into the spirit world upon the arrival of a powerful control known simply as the Imperator.

Harvard University psychologist William James, author of *The Varieties of Religious Experience*, was brought to Piper's seance room by some rather astonishing reports which he had heard from his mother-in-law and his sister-in-law. The elder woman had heard the medium give the names, both first and last, of distant relatives. Later, James's sister-in-law had approached Piper with a letter written in Italian that had been sent to her by a writer who was known only to two people in the entire United States. The medium placed the letter to her forehead and gave details of its contents and described the physical appearance of the writer.

As he entered Piper's seance room, James identified himself with a false name in order not to provide the medium with even the slightest clue on which to work. In spite of his precautions, the psychologist came away from the sitting completely baffled as to how Piper had been able to give accurate information on all of the subjects about which he had queried.

James soon returned to Leonora Piper's seance room. He was uninterested in the spirit hypothesis, but he was convinced that the woman could only be obtaining her information through some paranormal means. Piper became William James's "one white raven." In a well-known passage from his works, James writes that the phenomena that he witnessed

through the mediumship of Piper had weakened his orthodox beliefs. "To use the language of logic," he states, "I will say that a universal supposition may become false because of one particular example. If you are taught that all crows are black, and you wish to destroy this belief, it is sufficient to you to present to your teacher one white raven. My only white raven is Mrs. Piper."

It became the psychologist's conviction that, while in the state of trance, Piper was able to reveal knowledge that she could not have acquired through the normal sensory channels. "Science, like life, feeds itself on its own ruins," James said. "New facts break old rules."

Sir Oliver Lodge, after a series of experiments with Piper, told how the medium from Boston had completely convinced him "…not only of human survival but also of the faculty possessed by disembodied spirits to communicate with people on earth."

Hereward Carrington related that Piper's procedure during a seance was to make herself comfortable on a pile of cushions, then gradually pass into the trance state. Once entranced, the medium was impervious to pain and oblivious to everything that happened around her. After a few moments of trance, her right hand would reach out and accept the pencil that a sitter would place in her hand. At this point, automatic writing was produced and spirit communications were relayed to the members of the seance circle.

Professor James Hervey Hyslop (1854–1920) wished to observe this remarkable woman for himself and contacted Richard Hodgson, who at that time was conducting extensive tests with Piper, to make arrangements for his attendance at a seance. Hyslop was a stickler for taking extreme precautions. He drove up to the medium's house in a closed carriage, wearing a black mask which completely covered his face. After Piper had entered into the trance state, Hodgson motioned for Hyslop to take his place in a chair behind the medium.

From the time he entered the seance room until the moment the sitting was completed and he was out the door and back in his closed carriage, Hyslop did not utter a word. Even if the medium had not been in a trance state, she would not have been able to determine the identity of the silent man who sat behind her with his face completely covered. But in spite of these extreme precautions, Piper had mentioned Professor Hyslop's name several times during the course of the seance and had given the names of so many of his family members that it took him more than six months of correspondence with his kin back in the small Ohio town where he was born to verify all the information told him during the sitting.

Piper died on July 3, 1950. The majority of researchers who sat with Leonora Piper were more than willing to agree with William James when he said of her: "I wish to certify here and now the presence of a supernatural knowledge; a knowledge the origin of which cannot be attributed to ordinary sources of information, that is, to our physical senses."

❖ DELVING DEEPER

Fodor, Nandor. *These Mysterious People*. London: Rider & Co., 1935.

Gauld, Alan. *Mediumship and Survival*. London: William Heinemann, 1982.

Piper, Alta L. *The Life and Works of Mrs. Piper*. London: Kegan Paul, 1929.

JAMES VAN PRAAGH

Born in Bayside, New York, and the youngest of four children, James Van Praagh, remembers himself as being an average child, but having a tremendous fascination with death. Raised a devout Catholic, James served as an altar boy and entered the seminary at the age of 14. It was while he was attending the seminary that his "interest in Catholicism ended and his sense of spirituality began."

Although Van Praagh graduated from public high school and went on to graduate from San Francisco State University with a degree in broadcasting and communications, his direction would change slightly. He soon moved to Los Angeles and became deeply involved in the study of metaphysics and psychic phenomena. He was invited to a session with a medium who told Van Praagh that within two years he would be doing the same kind of work; that is, talking to the dead. At that time, Van Praagh claims he didn't even know what a medium was. His first reaction was that he had a hard enough time dealing with the living; why would he want to talk with the dead? Van Praagh would soon realize he would indeed continue in broadcasting and communications, just a bit less conventionally than what he studied at the university level.

At the young age of eight, while Van Praagh was fervently praying for God to reveal Himself to him, an open hand appeared through the ceiling of his room emitting radiant beams of light. Incredibly, he recounted, "I wasn't scared. It was actually very peaceful."

Perhaps this experience was an early sign that Van Praagh had an unusual sensitivity and gift to share between worlds. Often called a survival evidence medium, Van Praagh explained his discovered ability to bridge the gap between two planes of existence—that of the living and that of the dead—and has done so by providing evidential proof of life after death through detailed messages. "I'm clairsentient," he has said of himself, "which simply means clear feeling. I feel the emotions and personalities of the deceased. I am also clairvoyant," he added, clarifying that, "the first is feeling, the second is seeing, very much like Whoopi Goldberg in *Ghost*."

When Van Praagh began doing psychic readings for his friends, although it seemed strange to him, he couldn't deny that the detailed messages he received were on target. Personality traits of the deceased come through as well as physical traits and death conditions or circumstances to validate the connection, he said. The true essence of the messages he receives from the departed are the "feelings behind them" and the actual "love bond" between the living and the dead—not words. "No words exist in the English language, or any other for that matter, which can describe the intense sensations," Van Praagh explained.

Learning how to fine tune and refine this gift into understanding what the emotions of the spirits wished to convey and how to relay those messages to the living, earned Van Praagh the status as one of the most recognized and foremost mediums in the world. His message has been broadcast on numerous appearances on such shows as *Oprah, Larry*

King Live, Maury Povich, 20/20, and *48 Hours.* A CBS television miniseries is being produced on Van Praagh's first book, *Talking to Heaven* (1997). Also in production is a television talk show, *Beyond With James Van Praagh.*

Humble in his success, Van Praagh said, "If I convey recognizable evidence along with even a fraction of the loving energy behind the message, I consider the reading successful." He said of his work: "When someone is alone and overwhelmed by grief, life seems over. But, when someone is able to make contact with a loved one by utilizing the information…grief and loneliness disappear and proper closure can take place." His message is that "our personalities do indeed survive death."

There are, of course, skeptics. Michael Shermer of *Skeptic* magazine called Van Praagh "the master of cold-reading in the psychic world." Marcello Truzzi of Eastern Michigan University said he has studied "characters" like Van Praagh for more than 35 years and described his demonstrations as "extremely unimpressive."

❖ DELVING DEEPER

James Van Praagh Biography. http://www.vanpraagh. com/bio.cfm. 15 October 2001.

Maryless, Daisy. "A Medium Becomes Large." *Publishers Weekly,* 19 January 1998.

Rubin, Sylvia. "Spirit of Success," *San Francisco Chronicle,* 24 April 1998.

Sefton, Dru. "A Spirited Debate." *The San Diego Union-Tribune,* 10 July 1998, p. E1.

Van Praagh, James. *Talking To Heaven.* New York: Dutton: 1997.

Witchel, Alex. "Gone, Perhaps, but No Less Chatty: A Visit With Friendly Spirits." *New York Times–Sunday Styles,* February 22, 1998.

JACH PURSEL

Jach Pursel grew up in Lansing, Michigan. And after marrying his high school sweetheart, Peny, he graduated from University of Michigan with degrees in international business and political science.

In 1974, that was to change forever. Pursel, then a young corporate business executive with State Farm Insurance, was on the fast track in an accelerated program to move up the corporate ladder. But, while out of town and halfway through a five-day conference and training session, Jach would encounter "a teacher from another realm" who was about to take him on a long journey unlike any other, and one that would change the direction of his entire life forever.

Late one evening, after the day's events, Pursel sat on his bed, alone in the hotel room, closed his eyes, and began to relax. Using the routine he learned for meditation, he "breathed the tension out of his body" and thought he felt himself drifting off to sleep. Several years before, Peny had urged him to take a meditation course. Many times he had tried meditating, and although he observed great benefits from meditation in the lives of others, he saw little or no benefits in his own life. "Glorified napping" is what Jach called meditation, until, for whatever reason, he decided to give it another try.

Suddenly he realized he had not fallen asleep after all, as something strange and real began happening. He started "seeing things" in visualizations so vivid in detail that the colors, smells, sights, and sounds came to life. He felt the images bursting with a reality that caused his mind to race with excitement and anticipation.

Following a path through ferns, lush trees, and sweet smells, he was beckoned to a cabin with a thatched roof that was nestled among tall pines and sequoia trees. Feeling almost like he could hear the cabin breathe he started to reach for the latch on the door, when the door opened on its own. Stepping into the room, he saw a man standing in front of him. A warm light seemed to pour through the windows and doors, as the kind man spoke to Jach, identifying himself as Lazaris. Just then, Jach's meditation ended abruptly, but he furiously recorded every detail, writing as fast as he could, lest he forget. Excited, he called his wife to tell her about his successful meditation and that he hadn't fallen asleep.

Jach said he all but forgot about the experience for a time, but many months later, he decided to try meditating again, this time with Peny present. She asked him questions while he was in the meditative state, but the answers he gave to the questions "bored him," so he fell asleep—or so he thought. Two hours later, Jach started to apologize to Peny for sleeping, but barely got the words out. Peny was exhilarated as her words tumbled out to tell him that she had thought he was asleep too, until an "entity" had spoken through him, in a deep, resonant voice, saying he was "Lazaris"—the same one from months before.

Actually, Lazaris took over answering the questions, and lengthy dialogues took place between Peny and Lazaris. Peny recorded every word, and although Jach had a difficult time believing what he was hearing, and wished to avoid even talking about it, he did agree to sit and close his eyes and take what he called his "after-dinner nap" while Lazaris channeled through him. Over time, the words "just keep moving" continued to go through Jach's mind, as Peny and Michaell, a friend knowledgeable in Eastern philosophy and metaphysics, helped interpret what was being said. They experienced an overwhelming spirit of love as they witnessed the channeled messages. It would be two years, however, before Jach himself felt the compassion, concern, and wisdom of Lazaris, and when it came, he broke down sobbing, as he was filled with a perfect peace.

From that point on, Jach devoted his life to allowing Lazaris "to borrow his vocal chords" while he went into a deep trance, in order to teach and heal others. Lazaris explained that by Jach going into a "full-trance state," the information coming through him would not be colored or tainted with Jach's personality or personal interpretation, but it would come through as a pure message from Lazaris. Clarifying that Jach's energy field acts merely as an antenna—his body an amplifier for the "vibratory frequencies" that end up as sound—Lazaris was emphatic that there is no taking over or possessing of Jach's body any more than a news anchor on TV is *really* in the television set. Stating that Lazaris has never been in a physical body, nor do "they" desire to ever be, one of the main messages "they" wish to make known is that a consciousness exists far beyond what one could imagine or believe.

Since 1974, tens of thousands, including celebrities, have found friendships with what they describe as the loving, humorous, and witty Lazaris, who offers them emotional and spiritual guidance on a wide range of topics.

❖ DELVING DEEPER

Kautz, William H. and Melanie Branson. *Channeling: The Intuitive Connection*. San Francisco: Harper and Row, 1987.

Lazaris. http://www.lazaris.com/lmintromf.htm. 15 October 2001.

———. *Lazaris Interviews, Book 1*. Beverly Hills: Concept: Synergy Publishing, 1988.

———. *The Sacred Journey: You and Your Higher Self*. Beverly Hills: Concept: Synergy Publishing, 1987.

Zuromski, Paul. "A Conversation with Jach Pursel and Lazaris." *Body, Mind Spirit* 7, no. 1: (January/February 1988).

JANE ROBERTS (1929–1984)

On September 9, 1963, 34-year-old Jane Roberts had finished her dinner and was sitting down to her usual evening session of poetry writing. Her husband, Robert F. Butts, was in his art studio, three rooms away, working on his painting. Roberts picked up her pen and stared at the blank piece of paper, waiting for the creative juices to begin flowing. She had no reason to suspect that this night would be any different from others in her life.

All at once she found herself in the throes of an experience she could only liken to a drugless trip. "Between one normal minute and the next, a fantastic avalanche of radical, new ideas burst into my head, with tremendous force, as if my skull were some sort of receiving station, tuned up to unbearable volume," she wrote later, describing the experience. "Not only ideas came through this channel, but sensations, intensified and pulsating. I was...connected to some incredible source of energy."

The startled young woman had no time to call out to her husband, but her pen began feverishly to cover the page before her with a multitude of thoughts and feelings. Consciousness and reality were all turned around, and the thoughts that she was receiving seemed to be invading her mind, taking up permanent residence. Feeling and knowing became one and the same thing, and the importance of intellectual knowledge paled before the sensation of wisdom gained beyond the power of reasoning. At the same time all this was happening, a small part of Roberts seemed to remember that this same scenario had been enacted the night before in a dream, but she had forgotten it. Somehow, though, she knew the two experiences were connected.

When she returned to full consciousness, Roberts found herself giving a title to the barrage of words that had streamed across the paper in front of her: *The Physical Universe of Idea Construction*. The title seemed to fit the hastily scribbled notes, but none of the material fit anywhere into Roberts's previous convictions regarding life and the human psyche. The sudden paranormal experience had turned her world upside-down and would eventually lead to a series of dramatic events that forever changed her life.

Jane Roberts and Rob Butts bought a book on **extrasensory perception,** and they decided to try some experiments with an old **Ouija board** that their landlady had found in the attic. The first two times they tried to move the planchette, nothing happened. Neither of them were surprised, for they had little faith in the board's capabilities. On the third try, they were both amazed when the planchette began to move across the board and spell out answers to their questions. The couple found out that they had contacted an entity calling itself Frank Withers, who claimed to have lived in their New York town of Elmira and died there in the 1940s. The spirit provided other details of his life on Earth, and Jane Roberts and Rob Butts were surprised when the information actually checked out in the town records.

On December 8, 1963, the spirit of Frank Withers said while he had lived a "rather colorless" existence by that name, he preferred to be addressed as Seth, because it better suited the whole self that he was trying to be. He went on to say that from his perspective, Rob would better be named Joseph, and Jane, Rupert.

After that session, which lasted until after midnight, Roberts was convinced that Seth was an aspect of either her or Butts's subcon-

scious. She could not accept the idea that Seth might represent a separate entity that had survived death. In subsequent sessions, she was determined to resist the development of mediumship that was apparently growing stronger within her each time they sat down at the Ouija board. Then, on the evening of December 15, Roberts felt a great rush of words welling up within her. She felt nearly choked up with "piles of nouns and verbs" in her head. And then, "without really knowing how or why, I opened my mouth and let them out." Seth was no longer restricted to the Ouija board. He was now able to speak through Jane and to deal with complex subjects that changed their response to the universe and their own role within it.

There seemed little in either Roberts's or Butts's early lives to which a psychical researcher might point and reach a clear conclusion that a spirit medium or channel was in the making. Growing up in Saratoga Springs, New York, as far as Roberts could remember, she had never demonstrated any extrasensory abilities before Seth's arrival. She had begun writing poetry as a child, and she had always been creative, but there was nothing to indicate that the girl would grow into a psychic of substantial ability. Her parents divorced, and Roberts had lived with her mother as they struggled to make ends meet. It had been a poetry scholarship that got Roberts into Skidmore College and out of her relentlessly poor life.

Butts was a product of what Jane called middle-class American "social Protestantism." A talented painter, Butts's role in accumulating what would later come to be called "The Seth Material" was from the first that of scribe and questioner. They seldom used a tape recorder during their twice-a-week sessions, but Butts maintained meticulous notes. He observed the subtle changes in Roberts or Seth as he carefully transcribed Seth's words verbatim, and he had the pleasure of conversing with Seth, something that Roberts at times wished that she were able to do.

At first Roberts had been reluctant to give in too much to Seth, and she insisted on being able to keep her eyes open while she paced around the room. Later, she liked to sit in a rocker while in trance, and though she went through a period of closing her eyes for a couple of years, she returned to open, though half-lidded, eyes. Seth usually announced his presence by taking off Roberts's glasses and casting them to the floor or a nearby piece of furniture. The volume of his voice went through various stages of development. It was resonant and conversational, but on occasion, boomed out at an extraordinary volume.

Both Butts and Roberts were greatly affected personally by the lessons learned from their sessions with Seth. Butts benefitted from what Seth termed "inner visual data," and he even received a few useful art instructions from his unusual friend. Roberts saw her latent psychic abilities flower under Seth's tutelage. She received specific instructions from Seth on how to develop **telepathy, clairvoyance,** and **precognition.** Of particular interest to her were her **out-of-body experiences,** which sometimes occurred under curious circumstances while she was in trance with Seth.

Through such books as *The Seth Material,* Jane Roberts essentially created a renewed interest in contemporary spirit mediumship, which was now updated as "channeling," likening the psychic-sensitive to a television set receiving channels telecast to it. Central to an understanding of the Seth Material is an awareness of the entity's basic teaching that all reality is created by thought and emotions. Specifically, what a person thinks and feels forms his or her surrounding reality. This process of reality-building is not static, however. It is dynamic. Therefore, reality is constantly changing, and it follows that a conscious awareness of this process can change any reality for the better. No one is at the mercy of past events. An individual cannot blame his or her parents, church, schooling, or any other person or event for making him or her the way he or she is. In ignorance, one may have made oneself unhappy, but with conscious awareness that person can make himself or herself a happy, productive individual. Because individuals create their own reality, they can therefore change it.

Seth's belief in mind as the builder expands the concept of human personality in a unique way. Since thoughts and emotions are believed to create reality, then dreams, too, have a separate reality. When individuals dream of themselves, they are seeing a fragment of their own personality, such as the probable self identified by Seth. According to the spirit entity, each individual has a counterpart in other systems of reality. These are not identical selves or twins, but other selves who are part of the whole person, developing ideas in a different way. Each of these probable selves represents a portion of the whole self existing in a different dimension, yet all are a part of the whole self. According to Seth, these various realities "merge in the overall perceptions of the whole self" and "ultimately the inner ego must bring about comprehension on the parts of the simultaneous selves. Each portion of the whole self must become aware of the other parts." Seth also maintained that all layers of the whole self continually exchange information on a subconscious level.

In such terms, Jane Roberts may then have been a physical manifestation of the personality Seth; she may even have been one of his probable selves. She could have been part of a completely other whole self, separate from the whole self of which Seth was a part. Roberts continually attempted to better understand the relationship she had with Seth and to explain the true nature of their connection.

On February 26, 1982, Roberts was hospitalized for an underactive thyroid gland, severe arthritis, and other complications. Through the years of their spiritual interaction, Seth had provided suggestions to ease certain of her physical conditions, but nevertheless, she died on September 5, 1984. Butts has continued disseminating the Seth Material and completed two books on which they had been working before his wife's death.

It is difficult to place Jane Roberts in a category, for she herself refused any attempts to analyze either her trance abilities or the phenomenon of Seth in the old traditional medium/spirit guide relationship. The material that Seth imparted to her was not often seen in traditional examples of mediumship and spirit guides. It may take years before the Seth Material can be appropriately evaluated.

✴ DELVING DEEPER

Roberts, Jane. *The Afterdeath Journal of an American Philosopher: The World View of William James.* Englewood Cliffs, N.J.: Prentice-Hall, 1978.

———. *Dialogues of the Soul and Mortal Self in Time.* Englewood Cliffs, N.J.: Prentice-Hall, 1975.

———. *Seth Speaks: The Eternal Validity of the Soul.* Englewood Cliffs, N.J.: Prentice-Hall, 1972.

Steiger, Brad. *Exploring the Power Within.* West Chester, Penn.: Whitford Books, 1989.

RUDI SCHNEIDER (1908–1957)

Rudi (Rudolf) Schneider was one of four brothers who produced mediumistic phenomena in the family's hometown of Branau, Austria. Although his older brothers—Willy, Hans, and Karl—demonstrated somewhat impressive abilities when they were children, it was Rudi who gained the greatest attention from scientific investigators.

Willy was the first of the Schneider brothers to receive more than a local reputation when a skeptic, a man named Kogelnik, witnessed one of Willy's seances and was convinced that he was observing genuine phenomena. Kogelnik brought Willy to the attention of the active psychical researcher Baron Albert von Schrenck-Notzing (1862–1929), who immediately tested and monitored the young medium. However, shortly after the tests had begun in earnest, "Olga," Willy's **spirit control,** asked that eleven-year-old Rudi be present. Although at that time Rudi's **mediumship** was only in the early process of development, von Schrenck-Notzing was intrigued by the fact that while Willy insisted upon complete darkness in which to produce phenomena, the younger Schneider felt contented to work under at least partially lighted conditions.

In January of 1926, a seance was held in the headquarters of the British Society for Psychical Research (BSPR) with Willy Schneider. The meeting had been organized by researcher Dr. E. J. Dingwall (1890–1986) and was attended by Douglas Dexter, a professional magician, and Dr. C. G. Lamb of the Engineering Laboratory at Cambridge. Schneider was carefully inspected by Dingwall the moment he set foot on the society's premises. The clothing that Schneider changed into before the seance—a set of pajamas and a dressing jacket—was the property of the society. Every precaution was taken to assure the investigators that whatever they might witness that night would be the result of psychic ability and not trickery.

The medium was led to a seat, and luminous strips were taped around both his ankles and his wrists so that his slightest movement could easily be seen by the members of the society. During the seance, as an added precaution, the medium's hands would be held by two researchers.

Enclosed in a gauze cage were a luminous cardboard ring and a tambourine. The cage itself was set on a table several feet in front of Schneider. As the seance progressed, the investigators were astonished to see the two enclosed objects float about in the gauze enclosure and dance like snowflakes through the air. The researchers found the phenomenon inexplicable, and Dingwall concluded his report with the statement that "…the only reasonable hypothesis is that some supernormal agency produced the result."

AFTER *Rudi Schneider had entered a trance, Olga, his spirit contact, manifested and the medium levitated several times. The investigators were astounded to record an increase in his respiration rate to 250 to 300 times a minute.*

But even more impressive was the showing that Willy's brother Rudi made for the society six years later, on December 8, 1932. Days before he was to conduct the seance, representatives from a firm of building contractors inspected the seance room to assure the society that no hidden apparatus of any kind existed that might in some way simulate psychic effects. With the assistance of society member Lord Rayleigh and the Imperial College of Science, infrared equipment was installed in the seance room so that the slightest movement of Rudi's limbs could be detect-

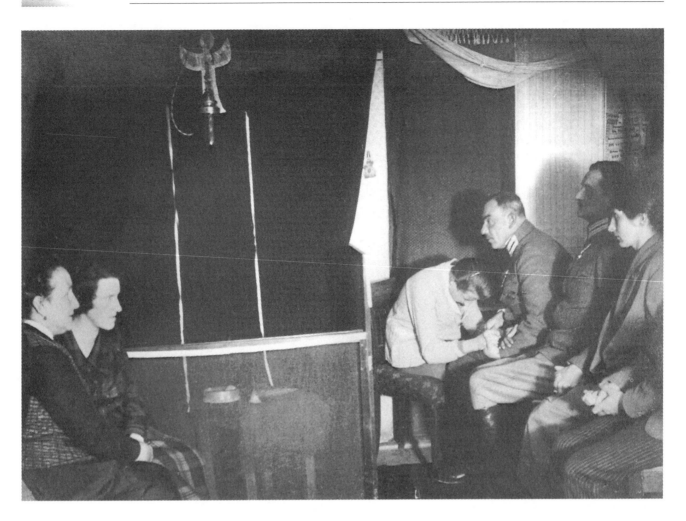

ed. Before the sitting began, Rudi was trussed up in much the same manner as his brother had been.

After Schneider had entered a **trance,** Olga, his spirit contact, manifested and the medium levitated several times. The investigators were astounded to record an increase in his normal respiration rate of 14–26 times a minute to 250 to 300 times a minute. The medium maintained this rate for two hours, a feat that the researchers considered almost as remarkable as his ability to rise into the air and to flutter the curtains across the room.

The installation of the infrared equipment enabled the researchers to be assured that Rudi Schneider had not moved his limbs. However, C. V. C. Herbert, the man behind the controls, did report that the medium seemed to generate a mysterious force that had made the infrared beam oscillate at exactly twice the rate of his respiratory pattern.

In an intensive series of sittings conducted under the auspices of the Institute Metaphysique of Paris in 1930, Rudi Schneider had submitted to the experiments of Dr. Eugen Osty (1874–1938) and his son, Marcel. Osty enthusiastically confirmed the paranormal abilities of the medium and presented the results of his findings in a pamphlet entitled *Unknown Power of the Spirit Over Matter* in which he concluded that Rudi Schneider possessed the ability to move objects by sheer power of will. In Osty's assessment, the medium could not have produced such phenomena by fraudulent means because his hands and feet had been controlled by electrical apparatus and his body had been held down by researchers, who had prevented any movement on his part.

Between February and May of 1932, Rudi Schneider began another series of experiments in London with Harry Price (1881–1948), a psychical researcher who was attempting to have his National Laboratory for Psychical Research integrated into the Society for Psychical Research. Earlier, Price had been a champion of Willy's psychic abilities, and he appeared equally enthusiastic about Rudi's mediumistic talents. Price arranged for a complicated array of photographic equipment to photograph the resultant phenomena from every possible angle. While some of the sessions produced such manifestations as ghostly winds, the movement of objects, and the materialization of various forms, other tests were unsuccessful and left the observing scientists sharply divided in their opinions over the genuineness of Schneider's mediumship.

Price continued to proclaim the authenticity of Schneider's paranormal abilities, writing various articles insisting that he had passed every major test set before him and emerged unscathed from the ordeals of intense scientific investigation. Then on March 5, 1933, Price puzzled both his many admirers and detractors when he published an article in the *Sunday Dispatch* claiming that Rudi Schneider was a fraud. One of the photographs taken in April of the previous year, during the period of exhaustive experiments, revealed Schneider freeing a hand at the time that spiritistic phenomena had occurred. Why Price reversed himself so dramatically after having so publicly championed Schneider remains a mystery, though some psychical researchers felt that Price had become jealous of other investigators who appeared to have taken Schneider away from him to conduct their own tests. When other researchers who had examined Schneider began to waffle and backpeddle on their prior positive endorsements of his mediumship, proponents of Spiritualism denounced the psychic investigators as deceitful individuals who could not handle the truth of confronting genuine spirit phenomena. The renowned Swiss psychologist Carl G. Jung (1875–1961), who had attended one of Schneider's seances in 1925, said, "I shall not commit the fashionable stupidity of regarding everything I cannot explain as a fraud."

In *The Strange Case of Rudi Schneider* (1985), Anita Gregory concludes that any objective person who studied Schneider's life and his mediumship would form the impression that he was possessed of remarkable psychic abilities. Since he was a boy of 11, he had permitted himself to be thoroughly investigated by psychical researchers and had willingly accepted whatever strenuous conditions they chose to impose. In Gregory's assessment, "there is not one iota of evidence to suggest that he was ever in his life anything other than transparently honest." Today, psychical researcher John Beloff has decreed Rudi Schneider's mediumship to be rightly considered among the most authenticated in the annals of psychical research.

Until his death on April 28, 1957, at the age of 49, Rudolf Schneider continued to indulge various researchers who wished to test his mediumship, and he generously shared his talents with his friends and neighbors in Meyer, Austria, where he had supported his family by starting his own driving school.

✤ DELVING DEEPER

Gregory, Anita. *The Strange Case of Rudi Schneider.* Metuchen, N.J.: Scarecrow Press, 1985.

Inglis, Brian. *Science and Parascience: A History of the Paranormal.* London: Hodder and Stoughton, 1984.

Tabori, Paul. *Companions of the Unseen.* New Hyde Park: N.Y.: University Press, 1968.

WITCH OF ENDOR (C. 1025 B.C.E.)

The Witch of Endor receives her indelible moments in the spiritual history of the Judeo-Christian traditions in Chapter 28: 4–28 of I Samuel. Saul, King of Israel, had begun his reign with a great military victory over the Ammonites, but he, who had once been a humble man, allowed his early successes to go to his head. When it becomes apparent to King Saul that David, once a mere shepherd boy whose musical talents eased his troubled mind, has found favor in God's eyes and will soon claim the throne of Israel, Saul tries to kill him. But David has evolved from the boy who slew the giant warrior Goliath with a sling-shot and the giant's own sword to a capable leader with his own army. Thoroughly frightened and confused, King Saul wishes that he would once again be able to seek the advice of the great and wise Samuel, who, before his death, had served Israel as the last of the judges, the first of the prophets, and the founder of the monarchy, the sole ruler between Eli and Saul.

Receiving no answer to his prayers to God, Saul tells one of his servants to find him a woman who has a **familiar spirit** (i.e., a **spirit medium**) who can speak to the dead. The servant reminds Saul that he had passed laws that forced all such mediums and wizards out of the land under penalty of death, but, he admits, he does know of such a woman who lives at Endor.

Saul disguises himself and, accompanied by two loyal men, comes to see the Witch of Endor after it is dark. Getting directly to the point, Saul asks the woman to ask her spirit control to summon someone from the dead so that he might speak with him. No fool, the medium plays it very carefully, and reminds the stranger that Saul has driven all such men and women who claim to have familiar spirits out of the land of Israel. If she even acknowledges that she has such abilities, she could be put to death.

THE *Witch of Endor has become the prototype for the spirit medium as a necromancer, a magician who raises the spirits of the dead.*

Saul, desperate for counsel from the spirit of Samuel, swears to her by the Lord that no punishment will come to her if she will perform this favor for him. He promises that he will tell no one. Satisfied with her client's oath of secrecy, the witch asks whom she shall ask her spirit control to summon from the land of the dead. Saul answers, "Bring me Samuel."

When the woman sees the spirit of Samuel materialize before her, it is also given to her to know that her client is King Saul, none other than the very ruler who had banished all mediums and conjurors from Israel. Saul once again reassures her that no harm will come to her, but he can see nothing and asks her what it is that has startled her. She describes the

elderly man covered with a mantle who has appeared, and Saul, knowing that it is the spirit of Samuel, bows before him.

Although it seems Saul cannot see the form of his mentor, he can clearly hear the prophet's words of distress at being disturbed and brought back to the land of the living. "Why are you bothering me by bringing me up like this?" a querulous Samuel demands. When Saul explains how worried he is—the Philistines are preparing to attack his forces and God appears to have turned his back on him—Samuel goes on to say that there is nothing he can do or say to help him, because the Lord has departed from him and will turn the kingdom of Israel over to David. Moreover, Saul and his sons will soon be with Samuel among the spirits of the dead, slain in battle by the Philistines.

Saul trembles and falls to the ground in a faint. He is weak because of fear and because he has not eaten a single bit of food all that day or night. The Witch of Endor prevails upon him to eat something, and Saul's two bodyguards agree with her insistence that he needs nourishment. The woman kills a calf that she has been fattening for a special occasion, prepares its meat along with some unleavened bread that she bakes, and Saul dines with her and his men before he takes his leave to meet his destiny on the battlefield.

The *Dictionary of Jewish Lore and Legend* states that the Witch of Endor was able to raise Samuel from the spirit world because he had been dead less than 12 months, "and the soul stays close to the body for this period." Certain traditional accounts of the incident state that other spirits, including Moses, came with Samuel because when they saw his spirit arise, they thought that the Resurrection of the Dead had begun. Other scholars are divided in their opinions whether the apparition of Samuel was real or fraudulent, some stating that the Witch of Endor only placed Saul into a **trance** and deceived him into believing that he had seen Samuel. The Witch of Endor has become the prototype for the spirit medium as a necromancer, a magician who raises the spirits of the dead.

✦ DELVING DEEPER

Holy Bible: Contemporary English Version. New York: American Bible Society, 1995.

Unterman, Alan. *Dictionary of Jewish Lore and Legend*. London: Thames and Hudson, 1991.

SPIRITUALISM

Modern Spiritualism began in the late winter months of 1847 with the mysterious knocking and window rattling at the John Fox residence in Hydesville, New York. Fox spent an entire day securing everything that looked as if it might shake or vibrate, only to have the night resound with even louder knockings and rappings. After a time, the Fox family began to observe that the center of the disturbances seemed to be the bedroom shared by 12-year-old Catherine (Katie) and 15-year-old Margaretta (Maggie).

One night in March 1848, when John Fox was once again attempting to discover a cause for the rappings, the family was startled to hear mysterious sounds imitating those that their father was making as he went hammering about the room. Katie excitedly challenged the unseen presence, which she laughingly personified as "Old Splitfoot," to follow the snappings of her fingers. When the sounds responded in a precise manner, other members of the family began to test the mysterious invisible agency.

As word spread that the John Fox family had a knocking ghost that could respond to any question answerable with a "yes" or "no" (one rap for yes; two for no), people from all over Hydesville came to test the spirit's knowledge. Although the invisible agency responsible for the initial knockings claimed to be the spirit of a peddler who had been murdered and buried in the basement of the Fox home (some accounts have it that investigation produced a skeleton interred in the basement), other spirit entities soon manifested themselves. Young Katie and her older sister Maggie seemed especially suited for the role of medium, for they seemed pleased and excited by the phenomena and did not appear to fear the invisible communicators as did the other Fox children. Serious investigators who were attracted to the phenomena soon worked out codes whereby in-depth communication with the spirits might be possible. Committees of researchers tracked through the Fox home and did considerable knocking and rapping of their own.

In order to give their parents a respite from the knocking spirits and the crowds of the curious, Katie and Maggie were sent to their older sister Leah's home in Rochester, New York. It was soon apparent that the spirits had followed them, and Leah encouraged her sisters to hold seances to contact other entities. When these initial attempts at spirit contact proved successful, Leah arranged for Maggie and Katie to give a public demonstration of the spiritistic phenomena, which brought an audience of 400. According to witnesses, the spirit knockings did not seem confined to the stage, but rapped from numerous areas in the hall.

After they had played to that enraptured audience in Rochester, it seemed clear to Leah that the spirits were telling her that she should act as a manager for Maggie and Katie and arrange demonstrations in other cities. Following her other-worldly guidance, Leah set up a tour that made her sisters a sensation wherever they appeared. Soon the two young girls were being routinely hailed as modern prophets or as frauds and deceivers, depending upon the biases of the witnesses. Maggie and Katie were examined by scientific investigators on both sides of the Atlantic and were "exposed" when they purportedly confessed that they produced the knocks and raps by cracking their toe joints. In the skeptic's casebook, this has become the accepted disclaimer for the phenomena produced by the Fox sisters.

Official cynicism had little effect on the budding Spiritualist movement, however. Some authorities fix the membership of the Spiritualist church as nearly two million by the height of the American Civil War in 1864. This seems high when one notes that the total population of the United States at this time was about 30 million. (The Spiritualist church today—International General Assembly of Spiritualists, National Spiritual Alliance of the U.S.A., and Nationalist Spiritualist Association of Churches—numbers about 200,000 members.) In the second half of the nineteenth century, though, several important Americans were either members of a Spiritualist church or were in sympathy with its philosophy of spirit contact. Shortly after Abraham Lincoln's (1809–1865) election to the presidency, Cleveland's *Plain Dealer* dealt the president-elect some harsh criticism for having "consulted spooks." Lincoln's honest reply was that the only falsehood in the story was that "the half of it has not been told. The article does not begin to tell of the wonderful things I have witnessed."

SHORTLY after Abraham Lincoln's (1809–1865) election to the presidency, Cleveland's Plain Dealer dealt the president-elect some harsh criticism for having "consulted spooks."

Lincoln made no secret of having consulted backwoods "granny women" in his youth, and once he moved to Washington, D.C., he invited some of the most noted mediums of the day to conduct seances in the White House. Lincoln had received a strong spiritual heritage from his mother, and he had been reared in an atmosphere in which one did not reject advice from "the other side." Although Lincoln never became dependent upon mediums to guide his administration, he was by no means a skeptic, and he stated that spirit messages had enabled him to survive crisis after crisis during his presidency. The president became so outspoken in praise of the guidance he received from the spirit world that it is said that it was Lincoln's influence that prompted Union general Ulysses S. Grant (1822–1885) to turn to Spiritualism.

In December of 1862, when the Union cause was on the brink of defeat, Lincoln was under great pressure from all sides to drop the rigid enforcement of the forthcoming Emancipation Proclamation. Mary Lincoln, aware of the terrible strain on her husband, called several trusted individuals together in the Red Parlor and called for one of the president's favorite mediums, Nettie Colburn (b. ca. 1841), to conduct a seance.

The medium went into **trance** and her **spirit control** spoke of matters which only the president seemed to understand. Then the entranced Nettie Colburn's spirit control charged President Lincoln not to compromise the terms of the Emancipation Proclamation, but resolutely to carry out all the implications of the announcement he had made.

When the medium came out of the trance, she found the president looking soberly at her. One of the gentlemen present asked Lincoln if he had recognized anything about the voice and the message of the delivery. Nettie Colburn recalled later that the president "raised himself as if shaking off a spell," then glanced at the full-length portrait of Daniel Webster that hung over the piano. "Yes," the president admitted, "and it is very singular, very."

In his *Miracles and Modern Spiritualism* (1975), Alfred Russell Wallace writes that the hypothesis of Spiritualism is the only one that can at all commend itself to the modern philosophical mind. "The main doctrines of this religion are: That after death man's spirit survives in an ethereal body, gifted with new powers, but mentally and morally the same individual as when clothed in flesh. That he commences from that moment a course of apparently endless progression, which is rapid just in proportion as his mental and moral faculties are cultivated when on earth. That his comparative happiness or misery will depend entirely upon himself….Neither punishments nor rewards are meted out by an external power, but each one's condition is the natural and inevitable sequence of his condition here.…"

Spiritualists contend that they have proof of survival after death and the existence of an afterlife that other churches only promise on faith. Many orthodox clergypersons do not deny the occurrence of genuine spiritual phenomena, but they are in sharp disagreement with Spiritualists as to the source of the manifestations. Some of the disagreement stems from the accusation that Spiritualism may be treading dangerously close to demonology. Religious orthodoxy, which believes survival after death to be assured, holds that contact with departed mortals cannot be established and warns that those who attempt to establish communication with the dead may find themselves involved with deceptive evil spirits. The oft-quoted allegation that Spiritualists consort with demons goes a long way toward preventing any sort of ecumenical movement between Spiritualists and the conventional religious groups from developing.

In an effort to clarify their theological position, the National Spiritualist Association adopted these following definitions of its belief in October 1914:

1. Spiritualism is the science, philosophy, and religion of a continuous life, based on the demonstrated fact of communication, by means of mediumship, with those who live in the spirit world.

2. A spiritualist is one who believes, as the basis of his or her religion, in the communication between this and the spirit world by means of mediumship, and who endeavors to mold his or her character and conduct in accordance with the highest teaching derived from such communication.

3. A medium is one whose organism is sensitive to vibrations from the spirit world and through whose instrumentality intelligences in that world are able to convey messages and produce the phenomena of spiritualism.

4. A spiritualist healer is one who, either through his own inherent powers or through his mediumship, is able to impart vital, curative force to pathologic conditions.

"Spiritualism is a science" because it investigates, analyzes, and classifies facts and manifestations demonstrated from the spirit side of life.

"Spiritualism is a philosophy" because it studies the laws of nature both on the seen and unseen sides of life and bases its conclusions upon present observed facts. It accepts statements of observed facts of past ages and conclusions drawn therefrom, when sustained by reason and by results of observed facts of the present day.

Many orthodox clergypersons do not deny the occurrence of genuine spiritual phenomena, but they are in sharp disagreement with Spiritualists as to the source of the manifestations.

"Spiritualism is a religion" because it strives to understand and to comply with the physical, mental, and spiritual laws of nature, which are the laws of God.

✳ Delving Deeper

Barbanell, Maurice. *This Is Spiritualism*. London: Herbert Jenkins, 1959.

Brown, Slater. *The Heyday of Spiritualism*. New York: Pocket Books, 1972.

Moore, R. Laurence. *In Search of White Crows: Spiritualism, Parapsychology and American Culture*. New York: Oxford University Press, 1977.

Moore, Raymond C., and Paul Perry. *Reunions: Visionary Encounters with Departed Loved Ones*. New York: Villard Books, 1993.

Mysteries of the Unknown: Spirit Summonings. Alexandria, Va.: Time-Life Books, 1989.

Post, Eric G. *Communicating with the Beyond*. New York: Atlantic Publishing, 1946.

Andrew Jackson Davis (1826–1910)

Andrew Jackson Davis is often referred to as the "John the Baptist" of modern Spiritualism, for he preached the advent of spirit communication in the United States with an evangelical fervor. Davis grew up in extreme poverty in Blooming Grove, New York, a small hamlet along the Hudson River, the only son in a family of six. His mother was illiterate, but highly religious, and quite likely encouraged her frail, nervous son to receive visions and to hear voices early in life. Davis's father was afflicted with alcoholism and barely managed to provide any sustenance for his family in his trade as a weaver and shoemaker. Only one of the family's five daughters survived to adulthood.

When he was 12, Davis's clairvoyant impressions and spirit voices manifested convincingly enough to persuade his father to move the family to Poughkeepsie. Five years later, in 1843, Davis attended a demonstration on mesmerism conducted by Dr. J. Stanley Grimes. Mesmerism, usually defined as an old-fashioned term for hypnotism, developed out of the theories of certain physicians in the sixteenth century that humans could project and control their animal magnetism, sometimes inducing **trance** states in themselves or in others. In the 1760s, Dr. Franz Anton Mesmer (1734–1815) began healing patients with what he believed was the result of animal magnetism's effect on a kind of "universal fluid" that flowed between the stars, the human body, and everything on the planet, but which today would likely to be attributed to light trance states and the power of suggestion.

With Davis's childhood experiences of hearing spirit voices, it is not surprising that he was found to be a good subject by a local tailor named William Levingston, who had decided to experiment with mesmerism on his own. Once Davis had entered an altered state of consciousness, he seemed to have the ability to see through the human body and to diagnose the cause of illnesses and medical disorders. Within a short period of time, Andrew Jackson Davis was being proclaimed as the "Poughkeepsie Seer." Men and women were coming from miles around to draw from his magnetic powers, and Levingston abandoned his tailor shop to devote all of his time to overseeing Davis's healing ministry.

On the evening of March 6, 1844, Davis experienced a life-altering event that would direct the course of his personal destiny. All he claimed to remember was being overcome by some power that made him feel as though he were literally flying through the air. When he regained consciousness the next morning, he found himself in the Catskill Mountains, 40 miles away from Poughkeepsie. Had the spirits transported him through the air and deposited him there in the mountains? Or had he walked 40 miles in one evening while in a trance? And why did he suddenly awaken to find himself in this particular spot?

While Davis claimed never to learn the answer as to how he got to that particular setting in the Catskills, he soon learned the reason why. He said that first the spirit of the Greek philosopher Galen (129 C.E.–C. 199 C.E.) materialized before him, then the spirit of the Swedish seer **Emanuel Swedenborg** (1688–1772), both of whom provided him with mental illumination and spiritual revelation. From that day onward, Andrew Jackson Davis set forth on an extensive lecture schedule, proclaiming the advent of spirit communication for humans everywhere. He claimed a great cosmic doorway was being opened, and ministers from the spirit world would soon be making themselves available for contact with those individuals who wished to gain from their wisdom and inspiration.

While on tour, Davis met Dr. S. Silas Lyons, an experienced mesmerist, who was able to induce a deep trance state in the Poughkeepsie seer. In November of 1845, with Lyons as the mesmerist, Davis as the prophetic voice, and Reverend William Fishbough as the stenographer, dictation was begun on *The Principles of Nature: Her Divine Revelations and a Voice to Mankind*. The process lasted for 15 months, and often small crowds of enthusiastic men and women, including such luminaries as American writer Edgar Allan Poe (1809–1849), bore witness to the words as they poured forth from the entranced Davis.

In 1847, the book was published and was received eagerly by a public seeking new revelations from a modern prophet. Although some critics pointed out many similarities to the writings of Swedenborg concerning creation, philosophy, and religion, Davis' champions replied that the seer was a man of modest education who had never read the works of the great Swedish mystic. Davis had, in fact, only five months of formal schooling. However, there should be little mystery if the *Principles of Nature* contained echoes of Swedenborg, for it was his spirit who had manifested with Galen to inspire Davis. Due to the success of his book, Davis began issuing *Univercoelum*, a periodical which was published from 1847 to 1849 and was devoted to **clairvoyance,** trance phenomena, and his Harmonial Philosophy.

On March 31, 1848, it is said that Davis predicted the coming of modern **Spiritualism** when he reported that he had awakened that morning hearing a voice telling him that the good work had begun: "About daylight this morning a warm breathing passed over my face, and I heard a voice, tender and strong, saying, 'Brother, the good work has begun. Behold, a living demonstration is born.' I was left wondering what could be meant by such a message." Although Davis and his followers would not ally themselves with the Spiritualist cause until 1850, it would often be pointed out that the **Fox sisters** first challenged "old Splitfoot" on March 31, 1848, and that the "voice, tender and strong," had obviously been referring to their "living demonstration" of spirit communication.

In July 1848, after creating a bit of scandal for the conservative times, Andrew Jackson Davis married Catherine Dodge, a wealthy heiress, who was 20 years his senior. Their union was unhappy and brief, and she died in 1853, leaving her estate to Davis. Davis continued to lecture and teach his Harmonial Philosophy for many years. At the age of 60, he acquired a medical degree, but soon thereafter he retired to Boston, where he ran a bookshop and prescribed herbal remedies to his patients. Andrew Jackson Davis died amidst his books and herbs in 1910, a quiet ending to the full life of the "John the Baptist" of the Spiritualist movement.

✳ DELVING DEEPER

Brown, Slater. *The Heyday of Spiritualism.* New York: Pocket Books, 1972.

Fodor, Nandor. *An Encyclopedia of Psychic Science.* Secaucus, N.J.: Citadel Press, 1966.

———. *These Mysterious People.* London: Rider & Co., 1936.

Moore, R. Laurence. *In Search of White Crows: Spiritualism, Parapsychology and American Culture.* New York: Oxford University Press, 1977.

SIR ARTHUR CONAN DOYLE (1859–1930)

When many first learn that Sir Arthur Conan Doyle, author of the Sherlock Holmes mystery series, was fascinated with psychical research and an investigation of life after death, they make the immediate assumption that he may well have been allied with the likes of the great magician **Harry Houdini** (1874–1926) (especially when it is learned that the two men were friends), devoting his intellect and his experience to exposing fraudulent **spirit mediums.** They may visualize the author much like Holmes, his famous fictional detective, unveiling the trickery by which a charismatic, but phony, medium has deceived the unwary, then climaxing his explanation of the deception with the casual utterance of, "elementary, my dear Watson." In fact, nothing could be further from the truth. Doyle was an ardent believer in the reality of spirit communication, and he became such a missionary for **Spiritualism** that he came to be known as the "St. Paul" of the movement. While Holmes, the quintessential proponent of deduction, and his creator did not share the tendencies to be unfailingly skeptical, extremely rational, and shrewd, there were other aspects of the fictional detective which did manifest in Doyle. Arthur Conan Doyle was tall, upper-class, thoroughly English, self-confident, and successful at his chosen profession, which, like that of Holmes's loyal associate, Dr. Watson, was the practice of medicine.

Doyle was first invited to witness mediumistic phenomena while he was a physician at Southsea in 1885. For the next three years, he participated in a number of sittings in the home of one of his patients, who was a teacher at the Greenwich Naval College. The medium at the center of these experiments was a railway signalman who seemed capable of producing a wide range of astonishing phenomena. So astonishing, that Doyle, the young man of science and medicine, eventually concluded that the man was occasionally faking the manifestations, and that the other sitters either chose to ignore the trickery in the hope that more genuine phenomena would manifest—or else were too gullible or too eager to accept the miraculous to protest.

While his early encounters with mediumship were not greatly impressive, Doyle's interest in exploring the unknown was stirred, and he joined the **Society for Psychical Research** (SPR) shortly thereafter. In 1902 he met **Sir Oliver Lodge** (1851–1940), and the experiences and research of this highly respected scientist had a great impact upon him.

Doyle became convinced that **telepathy** was a genuine phenomenon that could also account for a great deal of apparent mediumistic knowledge of the deceased. Perhaps, he theorized, the medium was picking up thoughts about the dead from the various sitters in the seance circle who had lost loved ones. During the same period of time, Doyle read **Fredric W. H. Myers**'s (1843–1901) *Human Personality and Its Survival of Bodily Death* (1903), which had a great effect on his acceptance of mediumship and spirit communication.

In 1916, after 30 years of intense study, Doyle accepted the phenomena of Spiritualism as genuine. He was 58, at the height of his literary career, and filled with self-confidence, so he openly associated himself with the cause of modern Spiritualism in two books, *The New Revelation* (1918) and *The Vital Message* (1919). In that same year, with World War I creating turmoil in both the physical and spiritual worlds, his second wife, Jean, lost her brother at the Battle of Mons. In the midst of her grief, she began experimenting with automatic writing, a mediumistic technique whereby one allows the pen to flow across the page under the guidance of spirit writers. When her early attempts at spirit communication proved successful, Sir Arthur and Lady Doyle became convinced that their earthly mission was in large part to be devoted to relaying messages from those who had fallen in battle to their bereaved families.

In 1918, Doyle's oldest son, Kingsley, died of pneumonia during the Battle of the Somme. A year after his son's death, Doyle attended a seance held by a Welsh medium who spoke in Kingsley's voice and referred to matters that would have been completely unknown to the medium. Shortly after the remarkable direct voice communication, the medium materialized Doyle's mother and nephew. Contemptuously brushing aside the efforts of those who attempted to explain the phenomena, Doyle declared that he saw his loved ones as plainly and as clearly as he had ever seen them in life.

After the war ended in 1918, Sir Arthur and Lady Doyle began the first of their extensive lecture tours. For the next 12 years, they were seldom at home for very long periods of time as they traveled throughout Great Britain, Australia, New Zealand, northern Europe, South Africa, and the United States. Among the members of the large crowds that gathered were those who were eager to meet the author of their favorite detective fiction and those who wished to hear words of comfort from the Doyles concerning the kind of existence that their deceased loved ones were living on the other side.

The December 1920 issue of *Strand* magazine contained several allegedly authentic photographs of fairies that had been taken with an inexpensive camera by two young girls, Elsie Wright and her cousin Frances Griffiths, in a little valley through which ran a narrow stream near the village of Cottingley. One snapshot taken by Elsie in the summer of 1917, when she was 16, captured her 10-year-old cousin seated on the grass surrounded by four dancing fairies. Another, taken a few months later, showed Elsie with a tiny gnome.

Doyle managed to obtain the negatives and brought them to one of England's most eminent photographic analysts. At first the expert dismissed the very notion of fairy photographs, but he ended up staking his professional reputation by saying that not only were the pictures all single exposures, but he said that he could detect that the tiny beings had actually been moving while having their images snapped by the girls' camera. Furthermore, he stated firmly, he could not detect the slightest evidence of any fakery in the photographs. Doyle wisely sought another opinion, so he took the negatives to the Kodak Company's offices in Kingsway. While these experts declined to acknowledge that the photographs actually depicted fairies, they did issue a statement that they could find no evidence of trick photography or any tampering with the film. Yet a third analyst expressed his opinion that the most significant factor in the Cottingley photographs was that the fairy figures seemed clearly to have been caught in motion as they hovered over the flowers and the girls.

As the British press spread the charming story of the Cottingley fairy photographs, numerous individuals came forward to testify that they, too, as children had played with the little people. Fortified by the photographic analyses of several experts that the photographs were genuine, Doyle obtained the services of one of Great Britain's most gifted clairvoyants to see if he might be able psychically to verify the girls' accounts of fairies near Cottingley. The psychic sat down with Elsie and Frances in the little valley and found that he was able to see even more of the fairy realm because of his mediumistic abilities. According to his great sensitivity, the entire glen was alive with many types of elemental spirits—wood elves, gnomes, fairies, and graceful water sprites around the valley and stream. Try as he might, though, the clairvoyant was unable to project to the fairies the amount of psychic energy necessary to allow them to materialize. It appeared that only the young girls had the unique blend of innocence and wonder that could somehow supply the fairies with the necessary energy to permit them to attain a material form.

Doyle issued his summation of the case of Elsie and Frances and their fairy photographs, along with his interpretation of the phenomena, in which he stated that while the proof offered by the Cottingley experience was not as "overwhelming" as in the case of spiritualistic phenomena, "there is enough already convincing evidence [for the authenticity of fairies] available." Later, the photographs were exposed as fakes, and Doyle was embarrassed by his having endorsed both the girls and their pictures in his book *The Coming of the Fairies* (1922) as being authentic examples of the ability of certain sensitive individuals to take genuine spirit photographs.

Sir Arthur and Lady Doyle had met Harry Houdini after one of the famous magician's performances at the Hippodrome in Brighton, England, in 1920, and while many have pondered how Doyle, a true believer in Spiritualism, and Houdini, the determined nemesis of spirit mediums, could ever have become friends, a bond of friendship was formed between the two families. Some writers and researchers contend that Houdini didn't disbelieve in survival after death, but, rather, was seeking proof that he could find completely acceptable by his standards. His attack against certain spirit mediums may have been inspired by his feeling that their evidence for the afterlife had been faked. Indeed, the friendship between Doyle and Houdini may have been inspired by the entertainer's sincere desire that the Doyles might somehow be instrumental in providing him with the proof of the afterlife that he so desired. Sadly, their friendship ended quite explosively after Lady Doyle conducted a seance in the United States.

In 1922, Sir Arthur and Lady Doyle were lecturing in the United States, and Houdini asked them to join him and his wife Beatrice (Bess) for a brief vacation in Atlantic City on June 17. That particular date was sacred to Houdini because it was his beloved mother's birthday. Expressing the belief that she could establish contact with his mother on that special day, Lady Doyle entered a light **trance** and began producing lovely and sentimental messages from the magician's mother in the spirit world. Although Houdini was grateful for the kind sentiments, he later publicly expressed his strong doubts that the spirit of his mother had written such words, especially since she had never learned to write English. Also, since the Weiss family (Houdini's birthname) was Jewish, Houdini doubted that his mother would have begun the message by drawing a cross at the top of the page of automatic writing. Houdini's public denials of Lady Doyle's mediumship created a breach between the friends which never healed.

Doyle was nominated honorary president of the International Spiritualist Congress that was held in Paris in 1925. In 1927, he published *Pheneas Speaks,* revelations relayed through automatic writing to Lady Doyle from her **spirit control** Pheneas. Sir Arthur Conan Doyle died on July 7, 1930.

✢ **DELVING DEEPER**

Brandon, Ruth. *The Spiritualists.* New York: Alfred A. Knopf, 1983.

Doyle, Sir Arthur Conan. *The Edge of the Unknown.* New York: Berkley Medallion Books, 1968.

Fodor, Nandor. *An Encyclopedia of Psychic Science.* Secaucus, N.J.: Citadel Press, 1966.

THE FOX SISTERS

On one of the last days of her life, in February of 1893, Margaretta Kane managed to prop herself into a sitting position and demanded a pencil and paper from Dr. Mellin, the doctor who had been commissioned to care for her. Kane began writing at an incredible pace, and before she had finished she had filled 20 sheets with clear handwriting. After handing the written sheets back to the doctor, she fell into a coma and died.

When Mellin had the opportunity to examine what Kane had written, she was astonished to discover that her patient had filled the sheets with an accurate and detailed biography of the doctor's own life. It included many events that Mellin had not divulged to anyone. Some time later, Mellin described the incident to the Medico-Legal Society of New York. She concluded her remarks about the manuscript by saying: "To my surprise, I found she had written down a detailed story of my life. The most startling thing did not appear until near the end where Mrs. Kane mentioned the missing will of my mother and the names of several people back home in Manchester, Indiana. I wrote at once to my brother. He sent a friend to Manchester and mother's missing will was recovered."

The story of the dying woman who somehow knew intimate details about her doctor that could not have been known through ordinary means takes on tragic significance when Kane's history is revealed. Kane was born Margaretta Fox, and it was she and her sister Catherine who were credited with the founding of modern Spiritualism. They were later discredited by certain investigators as being clever deceivers with no paranormal or mediumistic abilities whatsoever.

Mysterious knocking and window rattling began in the John Fox home in Hydesville, New York, shortly after they had moved into the house on December 11, 1847. After the first night, Fox spent the next day securing everything that looked as though it might make knocking or rattling sounds, but the following night the knockings and rappings were even louder. One of the family members ventured a guess that it was a prankster playing a trick on them or some neighbor trying to frighten them away, but as much as they tried to catch the supposed joker in the act, they never saw him.

Then Fox, the local blacksmith, began to hear talk about the complaints of some of the previous tenants in the house, who, as early as 1843, had also complained of mysterious rappings, footsteps, and dragging sounds. Michael Weekman, who had rented the house just prior to their occupancy, moved out when he could no longer stand the eerie night sounds.

By March 31, 1848, John and Margaret Fox gave up chasing after the rappings and resolved to live with the disturbances. After all, no real damage had ever occurred. The sounds were just annoying. They would go to bed early that evening and try to get a good night's sleep.

But that night when the disturbances began, the five children—John, David, Maria, Margaretta (Maggie), and Catherine (Katie)—seemed to be more frightened than ever before by the continual knocks and thuds echoing throughout the house. Observing that the strange noises were centering around 12-year-old Katie and 15-year-old Maggie, Fox closed the window in the girls' bedroom with a loud thump. His thump was immediately followed by two others, and Katie cried out that "they" were answering him.

For a few moments, no one moved. Then Fox cautiously knocked on the window sill. There came an answering knock from somewhere in the room. Katie was more excited than frightened. As if it were all some thrilling game, she commanded the sounds to follow the snaps of her fingers and called out: "Here, Mr. Splitfoot, do as I do." The unseen prankster did so perfectly, even when she only held up a certain number of fingers to prompt an appropriate number of raps. "It can see as well as hear!" she laughed in childlike triumph.

Soon other members of the family had entered the game with the mysterious unseen visitor and were asking it to pound out number sequences or to sound one rap for yes, two raps for no. Mrs. Fox was no stranger to psychic phenomena, for although they were respected members of the Methodist Church, three prior generations of women in her family (Rutan) had the ability to predict deaths, births, and other local occurrences.

As his daughters' communication with the spirit progressed, Fox wanted to determine whether or not his entire family was deluded. He went next door and brought a neighbor, Mrs. Redfield, into the children's bedroom. Although the woman laughed at the thought of a knocking spirit, she went away greatly disturbed by the fact that she had not only heard the knocks, but whatever invisible source was making them knew a great deal about her past, also.

As word spread about the curious phenomena that was occurring in the Fox home, people from all over Hydesville came to hear the mysterious rappings. A committee composed of 20 friends and neighbors and directed by William Duesler set about a program of investigation. Shortly after the committee had reached its conclusions regarding the authenticity of the phenomena, E. E. Lewis published a 40-page pamphlet of their findings entitled, "A Report on the Mysterious Noises Heard in the House of John D. Fox at Hydesville, Arcadia, Wayne County. Authenticated by the certificates and confirmed by the statements of the citizens of that place and vicinity."

After Katie and Maggie had experimented with the phenomena for several weeks, a code of rappings had been developed and intelligent communication with the entity had been established. The spirit revealed itself as Charles B. Rosna (Rosa in some accounts), a 31-year-old itinerant peddler who had been murdered in the house and buried in the basement. Charles became the **spirit control** for Katie and Maggie, and he revealed a great deal of personal information about his life on Earth through their mediumship.

On April 3, 1848, David Fox and some neighbors began digging in the cellar and discovered charcoal, quicklime, strands of human hair, and portions of a human skull. Based on the evidence provided by the spirit of the murdered man, a former tenant was accused of having perpetrated the deed, but the authorities refused to arrest or prosecute on such testimony.

The Fox family was growing weary of all the attention that they were receiving both from the spirit world and from the populace of Hydesville and the surrounding area. John and Margaret thought they might be able to get rid of the ghostly noises if they sent Maggie and Katie away from the house for a while. The girls were sent to their older sister Leah, 34, who was living in poverty in Rochester after her husband had deserted her. Loud, resounding raps broke out in Leah's home when the girls arrived, indicating that the spirits had followed them to Rochester, and they received the following message from the spirits: "You must proclaim this truth to the world. This is the dawning of a new era. You must not try to conceal it any longer. When you do your duty, God will protect you and good spirits will watch over you."

SPIRITUALISTS *believe that death is only a change of worlds, and communication with those who have passed to the other side is possible.*

With this message from the spirit world, modern Spiritualism was born. Spiritualists believe that death is only a change of worlds, and communication with those who have passed to the other side is possible. For the Fox sisters, their declaration of this message from the spirits placed them in the center of a tumultuous storm that raged throughout their lifetimes. Leah, who according to some sources is also said to have demonstrated some mediumistic abilities, became the manager for Maggie and Katie and arranged during numerous stage presentations for them to demonstrate their interaction with spirits, first in Rochester, then in many other cities throughout New England. The sisters were tested and exposed, tested and authenticated, tested and humiliated, over and over again—damned or praised, depending upon the biases of the investigators. They succumbed to such continual stresses by resorting to heavy drinking. They fought among themselves.

In 1857, Leah married a wealthy insurance man named Underhill and retired from her position as her sisters' manager. Maggie had been wooed by the famous Arctic explorer Dr. Elisha Kane (1820–1857), who died tragically before they could be married. Undeterred by such a sorrowful change of plans, Maggie considered herself a widow and called herself Margaretta Kane. In 1861, Katie went to England to be tested by such active psychic researchers as **Sir William Crookes** (1832–1919) and became the wife of H. D. Jencken, an attorney. She bore Jencken two sons before he died in 1885, leaving her despondent and once again dependent upon alcohol. In 1888, Katie's lifestyle had become so destructive that Leah managed to have the Society for the Prevention of Cruelty to Children assume custody of her two children.

Outraged by what she considered a traitorous act, Maggie allied herself with her younger sister and vowed to ruin Leah. This she sought to accomplish by writing a letter to the *New York Herald* denouncing Spiritualism and promising revelations of the frauds that the sisters had employed to deceive their audiences. Maggie made good her threat to Leah and her promise to the *New York Herald* by giving a lecture at the New York Academy of Music, where she confessed to being a fraud and offered explanations as to how she and Katie had produced various aspects of the phenomena. An angry Katie joined her sister and endorsed her exposure of spirit communication. They had been able to crack their toes and certain joints to make the sound of the spirit raps, the two sisters said. It had begun as a joke on their parents, but Leah had seen a way to make money from their unique talents. Plus, Maggie and Katie said, Leah had wanted to establish a new religion.

A year later, after passions had cooled among the sisters, Maggie completely retracted her confession of trickery and fraud. She explained that she had been under great mental stress and suffering severe financial difficulties. For five dollars, she declared, she would have sworn to anything. The demonstration at the New York Academy of Music only revealed how such phenomena could be faked, she swore, not how she and her sisters had actually engaged in fraudulent activity. Maggie swore now that they had served as mediums for genuine spirit manifestations.

The phenomena produced by the Fox sisters were important to psychical research. Professor Charles Richet (1850–1935), world-famous physiologist at the Sorbonne, stated that spirit rappings were of "primary importance" as demonstrations that "there are in the universe human or nonhuman intelligences that can act directly on matter." Sir William Crookes (1832–1919), the renowned British chemist and physicist, concluded after a full investigation of Katie Fox that she only had to place her hand on any substance to produce "raps loud enough to be heard several rooms off. In this manner, I have heard them in a living tree, on a sheet of glass, on a stretched iron wire, on a stretched membrane, a tambourine, on the roof of a cab, and on the floor of a theatre. Moreover, actual contact is not always necessary. I have heard these sounds proceeding from the floors, walls, etc., when the medium's hands were held, when she was standing on a chair, when she was suspended from the ceiling, when she was enclosed in a wire cage...."

Psychical researcher Robert Dale Owen observed Leah Fox Underhill in a seance during which she manifested a "light about as large as a small fist, that rose and fell as a hammer would, striking the floor. At each stroke, a loud rap was heard." In over 400 seances sponsored by investigators in New York, Katie Fox, whose hands were held by the researchers, materialized phantom human forms that produced flowers, glowing lights, and written messages in the handwriting of deceased individuals.

Katie worked as a medium and conducted seances until, at the age of 56, she drank herself to death on July 2, 1892. Leah had passed away the year before, November 1, 1891. Maggie died ill and destitute on March 8, 1893, at the age of 59.

Whether the majority of Americans accepted the exposure of the Fox sisters as deceivers and frauds or believed the more positive appraisals by certain psychical researchers that Maggie and Katie were capable of producing genuine spirit phenomena, the Spiritualist movement had been born, and with the help of sensationalistic articles in the press, word of the controversial mediums spread around the world. **Andrew Jackson Davis** (1826–1910) and Emma Vera Brittain began to deliver trance lectures in the major cities of the eastern seaboard of the United States. In 1859, Dr. Phelps, a Presbyterian minister in Stratford, Connecticut, produced spirit manifestations and developed a following. Soon, trance mediums from the United States were visiting Scotland, England, and being embraced in the Scandinavian countries, where the teachings of **Emanuel Swedenborg** (1688–1772) had prepared them to expect such messages from the spirit world. Within months, the movement had taken root in Germany, France, Russia, and many other countries on the continent—all the result of the rappings and knockings of Maggie and Katie Fox, two little girls who, in the eyes of their supporters, had broken down the dividing wall between the worlds of life and death.

❉ DELVING DEEPER

Brandon, Ruth. *The Spiritualists*. New York: Alfred A. Knopf, 1983.

Brown, Slater. *The Heyday of Spiritualism*. New York: Hawthorn Books, 1970.

Fodor, Nandor. *These Mysterious People*. London: Rider & Co., 1936.

Jackson, Herbert G., Jr. *The Spirit Rappers*. Garden City, N.Y.: Doubleday, 1972.

ALLEN KARDEC (1804–1869)

Allen Kardec, known as the father of Spiritism, distinct from **Spiritualism,** was born in Lyons, France, in 1804, with the birth name Hypolyte Leon Denizard Rivail. The names "Allen" and "Kardec" were names from prior lifetimes that he chose to use in his present life experience. The son of an attorney, Kardec decided to become a medical doctor, but he soon became intrigued by the enthusiasm for experiments in mesmerism and spirit communication that were spreading throughout Europe.

In 1850, he began sitting with Celina Bequet, a professional somnambulist (hypnotist) who, for family reasons, assumed the name of Celina Japhet. Japhet not only placed others in **trance** states, but was assisted in achieving a somnambulistic state by M. Roustan. While in trance, Japhet was under the **spirit control** of her grandfather, M. Hahne-

mann, and the spirit of Franz Anton Mesmer (1734–1815) spoke from the spirit world to give medical advice through her mediumship. Many other spirit entities manifested themselves and explained to the assembled sitters that the process of **reincarnation** was not only possible, but that it was compulsory for all souls to be reborn and receive new life experiences. Because Kardec was recognized as a proficient writer as well as a medical doctor, the spirits urged him to author what would be considered his classic work, *Le Livre des Esprits* (known today as *The Spirits' Book*), first published in 1856.

TRADITIONAL *Spiritualists reject the concept of reincarnation.*

The 1857 revised edition of Kardec's book, based on the trance communications of Celina Japhet, became the guidebook for those wishing information regarding mediumship, life in spirit, and the evolution of the soul. *The Spirits' Book* went into more than 25 editions and became popular throughout Europe and South America. However, because traditional Spiritualists reject the concept of reincarnation, conflict developed between the established dogma and the writings of Kardec. Kardec remained firm in his belief in what the spirits had told him: Reincarnation was necessary for the soul to progress and to better understand and heal current physical or mental illnesses, which had been caused by the deeds and misdeeds of prior life experiences. Because of his resolve in these matters, "Spiritism" or "Kardecism" became distinguished from Spiritualism.

Other books written by Allen Kardec include *The Gospel as Explained by Spirits* (1864); *Heaven and Hell* (1865); and *Experimental Spiritism and Spiritualist Philosophy* (1867). Although Spiritism was gradually reabsorbed back into Spiritualism in Europe, it remains popular as a separate philosophy throughout South America, especially in Brazil, where its members see no conflict in being nominal Roman Catholics and practicing *espiritas*.

❀ Delving Deeper

Fodor, Nandor. *An Encyclopedia of Psychic Science*. Secaucus, N.J.: Citadel Press, 1966.

Playfair, Guy Lyon. *The Unknown Power*. New York: Pocket Books, 1975.

Mystics

Mysticism is the attempt of humans to attain ultimate knowledge of the true reality of things and to achieve communion with a hierarchy of spiritual beings and with God, not through the ordinary religious paths, but by means of personal revelation and interaction with the divine. Whereas the major religions teach submission of the individual will and adherence to various creeds and dogmas, the mystic desires to realize a union with the Supreme Being free of all ecclesiasticisms and physical limitations. While the faithful member of the orthodox religious bodies seeks to walk the doctrinal spiritual path and obey the will of God according to accepted dogma, the mystic wishes to become one with the Divine Essence itself.

In other words, for the conventional, unquestioning member of a religious faith, revealed truths come from an external source, such as God and his selected prophets and teachers. For the mystic, however, truth comes from the god-self within and with the union of the human mind and the Divine.

Many mystics speak of having received "cosmic consciousness," or illumination, a sense of oneness with all-that-is. In his classic study of the experience, Dr. Raymond Bucke (1837–92) studied a number of individuals whom he considered recipients of cosmic consciousness, such as Gautama the Buddha (c. 563 B.C.E.–c. 483 B.C.E.), Jesus the Christ (6 B.C.E.–c. 30 C.E.), Paul (?–c. 62 C.E.), Plotinus (205 C.E.–270 C.E.), Muhammed (570–632), Dante (1265–1321), Moses (c. 1400 B.C.E.), Isaiah, **Emanuel Swedenborg** (1688–1772), Ralph Waldo Emerson (1803–1882), and Ramakrishna Paramahansa. Bucke concluded that the recipient of such illumination must be a person of high intellectual, moral, and physical attainment and express a "warm heart, courage, and strong and religious feeling." He considered the approximate age of 36 as the most propitious time in one's life to achieve this elevated state of consciousness.

In *Varieties of Religious Experience* (1902) **William James** (1842–1910) cites four features that he feels may distinguish a mystical state of consciousness from other states of consciousness:

1. *Ineffability*. When one receives an illumination experience, James comments, it defies expression; "no adequate report of its contents can be given in words." The mystical experience, he suggests, must be directly experienced; "it cannot be imparted or transferred to others." Mystical states are, therefore, more like states of feeling. "Lacking the heart or ear, we cannot interpret the musician or the lover justly," James writes, "and are even likely to consider him weak-minded or absurd. The mystic finds that most of us accord to his experiences an equally incompetent treatment."

2. *Noetic quality*. Although the mystical states are similar to states of feeling, to those who experience them they seem also to be states of knowledge. "They are states of insight into depths of truth" that evade the intellect; they are revelations "full of significance and importance" that carry with them a "curious sense of authority."

3. *Transiency.* James observes that mystical states cannot be sustained for lengthy periods of time. "Often, when faded, their quality can but imperfectly be reproduced in memory; but when they recur it is recognized."

4. *Passivity.* Although the onset of a mystical state may be facilitated by entering a self-induced state of meditation or trance, James comments that once the "characteristic sort of consciousness" has set in, "the mystic feels as if his own will were in abeyance, and indeed sometimes as if he were grasped and held by a superior power. This latter peculiarity connects mystical states with certain definite phenomena of secondary or alternative personality, such as prophetic speech, automatic writing, or the mediumistic trance....Mystical states...are never merely interruptive. Some memory of their content always remains, and a profound sense of their importance."

In a chapter on "Basic Mystical Experience" in his *Watcher on the Hills* (1959), Dr. Raynor C. Johnson, Master of Queens College, University of Melbourne, lists seven characteristics of illumination:

1. *The appearance of light.* "This observation is uniformly made, and may be regarded as a criterion of the contact of soul and Spirit."

2. *Ecstasy, love, bliss.* "Directly or by implication, almost all the accounts refer to the supreme emotional tones of the experience."

3. *The approach to one-ness.* "In the union of soul with Spirit, the former acquires a sense of unity with all things."

4. *Insights given.*

5. *Effect on health and vitality.*

6. *Sense of time obscured.*

7. *Effects on living.* Johnson quotes a recipient of the illumination experience who said: "Its significance for me has been incalculable and has helped me through sorrows and stresses which, I feel, would have caused shipwreck in my life without the clearly remembered refreshment and undying certainty of this one experience."

The British marine biologist Sir Alister Hardy (1896–1985), D.Sc., Emeritus Professor

THE PARAPSYCHOLOGICAL ASSOCIATION, INC.

The Parapsychological Association provides readers with *Parapsychology FAQ* which is a three-part document compiled by researchers who are leaders in the field, offering a basic introduction to and explanation of the basics in parapsychology; *Available FYI*—books, audio and video tapes, CDs, etc.; and *Parapsychology Online*—science papers and articles.

SOURCES:

The Parapsychological Association, Inc.
http://www.parapsych.org. 15 October 2001.

at Oxford, came to believe that the nonmaterial side of life was of extreme importance in providing science with a complete account of the evolutionary process. Contending that spiritual experiences could be subject to scientific scrutiny, Hardy established the Religious Experience Research Unit at Manchester College in England. "A biology based upon an acceptance of the mechanistic hypothesis is a marvelous extension of chemistry and physics," Hardy remarked. "But to call it an entire science of life is a pretense. I cannot help feeling that much of man's unrest today is due to the widespread intellectual acceptance of this mechanistic superstition when the common sense of his intuition cries out that it is false."

In April 2001, research funded by the Alister Hardy Trust being conducted at the

University of Wales revealed that Christians, Muslims, and Jews have similar mystical experiences in which they describe intense light and a sense of encompassing love. Since 1969, the trust has collected accounts of 6,000 religious experiences from people of all ages and backgrounds. Christians most often described the light as an encounter with Jesus or an angel, and Muslims also often interpreted the light to be an angel. Jews perceived it as a sign of inspiration or an experience of God.

Writing in *Fields Within Fields* (1971), Reza Arasteh, a transcultural developmental psychologist and author of *Final Integration in the Adult Personality,* speaks of the role that mysticism has played in all major cultures by permitting individuals to transcend cultural reality. Whether one examines Judaic, Christian, or Muslim mysticism in the Near East; humanism and modern psychoanalysis in the West; or Zen Buddhism and Taoism in Far Eastern cultures, "the interesting point is that all these mechanisms have come to us as a 'path' rather than as logic, as experience rather than rationality." Regardless of language or cultural or temporal differences, Arasteh says, "all these styles of life have adopted the same goal of experiencing man in his totality, and the reality of all is cosmic reality." The common denominator of mystical experience "comes with encounter and inner motivation, and the result is inner freedom for a cosmic trip and outer security for the release of unbound energy for future creativity. "The Cosmic Self," he states, "is the manifestation of transcending the earthly and cultural self."

Although there are many schools of mysticism associated with the major world religions, the kind of mystic who focuses upon establishing a meaningful relationship with spirits and the afterlife is also a person who is likely to incorporate the secret teachings of ancient brotherhoods, mysterious mahatmas and masters from secret monasteries in hidden cities, and even tutelary entities from Atlantis and other lost civilizations. While such mystics as **Helena Petrovna Blavatsky** (1831–1891), Alice Bailey (1880–1949), Annie Besant (1847–1933), **Rudolf Steiner** (1861–1925), and **Emanuel Swedenborg** (1688–1772) may have seemed out of touch with reality to those

members of their societies who judged them as mad, they believed themselves to be exercising the power of their intellects to establish a truer connection with the actual powers of the universe than their contemporary scholars and clergy could ever hope to achieve. For those professors and scientists who assessed the claimed ability of Swedenborg to communicate with angels and spirits as heresy at worst and insanity at best, he barely noticed such criticism and continued to write book after book and do God's work as it was specially revealed to him. While critics of Steiner were astonished by the depths of his scholarship, they were appalled by his belief in Atlantis and his suggestions that the seeds of the giants of old are ripening in certain modern humans, and that he went on to establish a model of scholastic education that thrives to this day. When Blavatsky, Bailey, and Besant insisted that their wisdom was being astrally communicated to them by great mahatmas and masters in India, they ignored the psychical researchers who cried fraud, and continued to build the Theosophical Society, which still flourishes today.

In his *Mystics as a Force for Change* (1981), Dr. Sisirkumar Ghose writes that the mystic's real service to humankind is not so much to help people solve material problems as it is to show them how to "transcend secular and humanistic values, to transfigure them in the light of the spiritual ideal or the will of God. The mystic brings not peace, but the sword of discrimination and a sense of the holy....The mystics have played an important part in the making of...civilization. Most early civilizations owe a good deal to this creative minority....The early mystics would also be among the priests and medicine men of the tribe."

❋ **DELVING DEEPER**
Bach, Marcus. *The Inner Ecstasy.* New York-Cleveland: World Publishing, 1969.

Bancroft, Anne. *Twentieth Century Mystics and Sages.* Chicago: Henry Regnery Co., 1976.

James, William. *Varieties of Religious Experience.* Garden City, N.Y.: Masterworks Program, 1963.

Johnson, Raynor C. *The Imprisoned Splendour.* New York: Harper & Brothers, 1953.

Otto, Rudolf. *Mysticism East and West.* New York: Macmillan, 1970.

Stace, Walter T. *The Teachings of the Mystics.* New York: New American Library 1960.

Steiger, Brad. *Revelation: The Divine Fire.* Englewood Cliffs, N.J.: Prentice-Hall, 1973.

Talbot, Michael. *Mysticism and the New Physics.* New York: Bantam Books, 1981.

Underhill, Evelyn. *Mysticism.* New York: E. P. Dutton & Co., 1961.

Helena Petrovna Blavatsky (1831–1891)

Helena Petrovna Blavatsky, founder of the Theosophical Movement, was born in Ekaterinoslav (now Dnepropetrovsk), in the Ukraine, on July 30, 1831, the daughter of Colonel Peter Hahn. As a child, she loved mystery and fantasy and claimed supernatural companions that kept her safe from harm. She appeared to demonstrate this paranormal protection when she fell from the saddle while horseback riding and caught her foot in the stirrup. According to young Helena, she would surely have been dragged to death before the horse was stopped if it weren't for the unseen entities that kept her from falling to the ground.

At the age of 17 she married Nicephore Blavatsky, a Russian official in Caucasia, who was 40 years older than she. She separated from her husband after three months and spent over a year traveling in Texas, Mexico, Canada, and India. All the time she was wandering, she was developing her mediumistic abilities, secure in the confidence that her phantom protector watched over her. Twice she attempted to enter Tibet, and on one occasion she managed to cross its frontier in disguise, but she lost her way and after various adventures was found by horsemen and escorted out of the country.

Blavatsky described the 10-year period between 1848 and 1858 as the "veiled" time in her life, refusing to divulge anything specific that happened to her during that period, but making mysterious allusions to spiritual retreats in Tibet or in the Himalayas. In 1847, shortly after she had "escaped" from her husband, she fled to Egypt, where she said that she became adept in the art of snake-charming and was initiated in the secrets of Oriental

magic by a Coptic magician. In 1851, according to her account, she was in New Orleans, studying the rites and mysteries of voodoo. She traveled to Paris in 1858 and was introduced to the internationally famous medium **Daniel Dunglas Home** (1833–1886) and was so impressed by his paranormal abilities that she became a **Spiritualist.** When Blavatsky, in turn, sought to impress him with her own mediumistic talents, Home ignored her and informed her that she was a cheat.

In 1858 she returned to Russia, where she soon gained fame as a **spirit medium.** Always a mesmerizing storyteller, Blavatsky claimed to have disguised herself as a man and fought under Garibaldi during the battle of Mentana when she was wounded and left for dead. After about five years spent perfecting her **mediumship** in Russia, Blavatsky entered another "veiled" period in her life when, from 1863 to1870, she was allegedly in retreat in Tibet, studying with the mahatmas Koot Hoomi and Morya, and a secret brotherhood of adepts.

In 1870, back in Europe, Blavatsky was en route to Greece when the vessel on which she was traveling exploded, and she lost all her earthly possessions, including whatever money she had managed to save. Rescued at sea and brought to Cairo, she supported herself through her mediumship, and in 1871, she founded the Spirit Society, which was quickly disbanded after accusations of fraud.

In 1873, after two months in Paris, she traveled to the United States and settled in New York, where she remained for six years and, according to some accounts, became a naturalized citizen. She resumed the practice of her mediumship in association with the brothers William (1832–1932) and Horatio Eddy (1842–1922), two well-known materialization mediums. As she became more prominent in Spiritualist circles in America, Blavatsky came to the attention of Henry Steel Olcott (1832–1907), a journalist, who established a study group around her unique style of mediumship, a blend of Spiritualism and Buddhistic legends about Tibetan sages. She professed to have direct spiritual contact with two Tibetan mahatmas, Koot Humi and Morya, who communicated with her on the astral plane and who provided her with wonderful teachings of wisdom and knowledge.

On November 17, 1875, with the aid of Henry Olcott and William Q. Judge (1851–1896), an attorney, Blavatsky founded the Theosophical Society in New York. The threefold purpose of the society was: 1) to form a universal brotherhood of man; 2) to study and make known the ancient religions, philosophies, and sciences; 3) to investigate the laws of nature and develop the divine powers latent in humankind. **Theosophy** (divine wisdom) is a vigorous blend of many earlier philosophies, all of which claim to have been handed down to modern students of the occult by disciples of ancient wisdom. Theosophy combines teachings from Zoroastrianism, **Hinduism, Gnosticism, Manichaeism,** the Kabbalah, and numerous other philosophies.

Sometime during that same year, (1875), Blavatsky entered into a brief marriage of two or three months with a merchant in Philadelphia named M. C. Betanelly. At about the same time, she was partially responsible for breaking up the marriage of Olcott, who left his wife and children for her.

Disappointed by Blavatsky's lack of enthusiasm for the day-to-day administration of a growing movement, Olcott became responsible for the management of the Theosophical Society. In 1877, he began to speak of moving the headquarters of the society to India, where they might be closer to the mahatmas, the occult brotherhood, and sincere practicing Hindu adepts. A year later, Olcott, Blavatsky, and a handful of the faithful left New York for India because the masters wished them to do so. By 1879, the central headquarters of the society had been established in Adyar, India, and an amalgamation with the Arya Samaj sect founded by Swami Dayanand Saraswati had also been accomplished. By April 1882, however, the swami realized that he had been exploited by the leaders of the Theosophists and he denounced the group.

By that time, the influence of the swami in India was no longer required, for in 1880, Blavatsky had visited northern India and observed phenomena manifested especially for her by the mahatmas. It was also at this time that she met A. P. Sinnett, journalist and editor of *The Pioneer,* and Allen O. Hume, of the Indian Civil Service, her two most important converts in India. Shortly after reports had spread of the wondrous phenomena the masters had created for her benefit in northern India, Theosophy began to attract students and followers from around the world who came to observe for themselves the miracles centered around the spiritual teachings of Morya and Koot Hoomi as channeled through Blavatsky's mediumship.

In order to gain converts to Theosophy, Blavatsky felt obliged to perform such miraculous manifestations as the written letters from Koot Hoomi and Morya that would materialize in midair. Eventually such reports reached the attention of England's **Society for Psychical Research** (SPR), which dispatched Dr.

Richard Hodgson (1855–1905), one of its most formidable researchers, to investigate. It didn't take long for Hodgson to assess the followers of Theosophy to be extremely gullible men and women who had arrived in India with expectations of finding in Blavatsky a modern miracle worker. The psychical researcher quite easily detected the sliding panels, the dummy head and shoulders of Koot Hoomi, and the cracks in the ceiling from which the letters from Mahatmas Koot Hoomi and Morya dropped down from "midair" to the astonishment of the true believers assembled around the medium. The script in which these documents was written were shown to be an amateurish attempt on the part of Blavatsky to disguise her handwriting.

Regardless of the expose published by the Society for Psychical Research (SPR), Theosophy continued to grow to become a worldwide movement. In 1877, Blavatsky published *Isis Unveiled,* and in 1887, her monumental *The Secret Doctrine,* which was alleged to have been written in an altered state of consciousness while attuned to higher powers. In spite of a barrage of attacks and exposures, Blavatsky's commanding personality secured a large following, and when she died in 1891 she was at the head of a large body of believers, numbering about 100,000 persons. Annie Besant (1847–1933) became her successor and actively preached the wisdom and insights provided in *The Secret Doctrine* and shepherded the movement into steadily larger growth.

❋ DELVING DEEPER

Blavatsky, H. P. *Collected Writings.* 16 vols. Wheaton, Ill.: Theosophical Publishing House, 1950–1985.

Harris, Iverson L. *Mme. Blavatsky Defended.* Santa Fe Springs, Calif.: Stockton Trade Press, 1971.

Meade, Marion. *Madame Blavatsky: The Woman Behind the Myth.* New York: G. P. Putnam's Sons, 1980.

Murphet, Howard. *When Daylight Comes: A Biography of Helena Petrovna Blavatsky.* Wheaton, Ill.: Theosophical Publishing House, 1975.

RUDOLF STEINER (1861–1925)

Rudolf Steiner was born in Krajevec Austria-Hungary (now Yugoslavia), on February 27, 1861, the son of a minor railway official. By the age of eight, Steiner had experienced the unseen worlds, the invisible reality within the everyday world. Once he even perceived the apparition of a deceased relative. Because of his tendencies toward the spiritual aspects of life, it was thought for a time that Steiner might become a clergyman; but his freethinking father argued that he was a bright boy, and he envisioned him following a more practical and materially rewarding occupation as a railway engineer.

When he was 15, Steiner met Felix Kotgutski, an herbalist and metaphysician, who, when Steiner was 19, introduced him to an adept in the occult to whom Steiner referred only as "the Master." Steiner never revealed the man's identity, in keeping with occult tradition. The Master informed him of his spiritual mission in life and foretold that Steiner would develop a system of knowledge that would blend science and religion.

Wishing to please his father, Steiner took a degree in mathematics, physics, and chemistry, from the Technische Hochschule in Vienna, but he wrote his doctoral thesis, "Truth and Science," at the University of Rostock in 1891. In 1894, he published the book *The Philosophy of Spiritual Activity,* which he described as "a biographical account of how one human soul made the difficult ascent to freedom." In the work, Steiner sought to help others discover the reality of spiritual experience and demonstrate how it could function side by side with the world of ordinary thought and experience. In his worldview, it was possible to have a spiritual science that would be an outgrowth of the true spirit of natural science.

In his thirties, Steiner awakened to an inner recognition of what he believed was the turning point in time in human spiritual history—the incarnation of the Divine Being known as the Christ. In his "Tenth Lecture on the Gospel of St. Luke," he reflects that just as a plant cannot unfold its blossom immediately after the seed has been sown, so has humankind had to progress from stage to stage until the right knowledge could be brought to maturity at the right time. Steiner is among those mystics who state that in the twentieth century humankind began to enter the "fullness" time

when the Christ principle, cosmic consciousness, might once again become manifest. "Christ consciousness" is defined as a transformative energy that transcends orthodox Christianity. According to Steiner, the Master Jesus became "christed" and thereby presented humankind with an example of what it means to achieve a complete activation of the spiritual seed within all souls.

Following the example of the Master Jesus, Steiner told his students that the rest of humanity must now in imitation of Christ gradually develop "what was present for thirty-three years on the Earth in one single personality." Jesus, the Christed One, was able to implant into humanity a seed which must now unfold and grow. To Steiner, the Christ energy is the catalyst that germinates the seed that great spirit beings implanted within their human offspring. The physical seeds of male and female intermingled to produce the whole human being, but Steiner believed there was also something within each human that did not arise from the blending of the two physical seeds: a "virgin birth," something ineffable, which somehow flowed into the process of germination from a different source.

Steiner also claimed to be able to read the **Akashic Records,** from which he had been able to ascertain the true history of human evolution. He set forth the hypothesis that the people of prehistory, the Atlanteans, had been largely guided and directed by a higher order of beings who interacted and communicated with certain humans—the smartest, the strongest, the most intellectually flexible. Eventually, these select humans produced what might be called demigods, semidivine human beings, who, in turn, could relay instructions from higher intelligences. In effect, Steiner may have presented another definition of the children of humans and the "sons of God" referred to in the book of Genesis, the hybrids that the ancient Hebrews named "Nephilim," which does, in fact, mean demigods, men of "great renown."

Steiner went on to speculate that within the larger evolving human race were the descendents of those divine-human hybrid beings, men and women who are animated by higher ideals, who regard themselves as children of a divine, universal power. He also believed that within what he termed the emerging "Sixth Post-Atlantean Race" would be children of the divine universal power who could be able to initiate those men and women who have developed their facility of thought so that they might better unite themselves with the divine. The children of the divine universal power, those who have the "seed" within them, would be able to initiate the more advanced members of humankind. People so initiated would be able to receive revelations and perform what others would consider miracles. The initiates would go on to become the mediators between humankind and the higher intelligences. The whole point of the efforts of these higher intelligences was to enable humankind to become more inde-

pendent, more able to stand on its own feet without having to rely on the higher order of beings that directed humans in ancient times.

In 1902, Steiner became the general secretary of the German Section of the **Theosophical Society.** His lectures had found great reception among Theosophical audiences, so Steiner felt confident that he would be comfortable joining the movement. It wasn't long, however, before he became disappointed with the society's emphasis on Eastern mysticism, for he had become convinced that the passive Eastern doctrines were incapable of satisfying the spiritual needs of the Western consciousness. Steiner also believed that its founders had distorted a number of basic metaphysical and occult truths and did not place enough emphasis on the role of the Christ and the Christian Church in humankind's spiritual evolution. In 1913, Steiner left the Theosophists and formed his own group, the Anthroposophical Society, dedicated to constructing a path for spiritual growth established on four levels of human nature—the senses, imagination, inspiration, and intuition.

In 1914, Steiner married Marie von Sievers, an actress, who had been secretary of the German Section of the Theosophical Society. His first marriage, to Anna Eunicke, had ended in divorce some years previously. Between 1910 and 1914, he had written four mystery plays and he intended to stage these, together with the dramas of Goethe, in the Goetheanum, a school for esoteric research that he founded in Dornach, near Basel, Switzerland. Together with the talents of his wife, Steiner began to develop new approaches to speech and drama, which led to the beginnings of "eurythmy," an art of movement that makes visible those inner forms of language and music formerly revealed only in the unseen levels of artistic expression. After the First World War, an international group of volunteers, together with local craftsmen, constructed the unique building designed by Steiner. The Goetheanum was opened in 1920, to serve the "awareness of one's humanity" and to support the developing work of anthroposophy. On December 31, 1922, an arsonist burned the wooden building to the ground. A new building was designed and constructed in 1923, which still serves as the international headquarters of the Anthroposophical Society.

Among Steiner's greatest legacies is his work in education and the establishment of the Waldorf School Movement, which originated from a request made by Emil Molt, director of the Waldorf-Astoria cigarette factory, for a school to which his employees could send their children. Steiner died on March 30, 1925, in Dornach.

✤ Delving Deeper

McDermott, Robert A., ed. *The Essential Steiner*. San Francisco: Harper & Row, 1984.

Shepherd, A. P. *Rudolf Steiner: Scientist of the Invisible*. Rochester, Vt.: Inner Traditions International, 1983.

Steiner, Rudolf. *An Autobiography*. Blauvelt, N.Y.: Rudolf Steiner Publications, 1977.

Emanuel Swedenborg (1688–1772)

Emanuel Swedenborg was perhaps the last of the Renaissance men—he was fluent in nine languages, wrote 150 works in 17 sciences, was expert in numerous crafts, and was a musician, a politician, and an inventor with dozens of major contributions attributed to his name. When his name is recalled today, it is usually as a Swedish mystic and medium who courted angels and cursed demons. Swedenborg claimed daily communications with the inhabitants of the unseen world, and his manifestations of remarkable psychic phenomena are well documented.

Emanuel Swedberg was born in Stockholm, Sweden, on January 29, 1688. His father was a professor of theology at the University of Upsala, who later became the Lutheran Bishop of Scara in spite of certain opinions which appeared to challenge orthodox religious views. Emanuel completed his university education at Upsala in 1710, then traveled abroad in England, Holland, France, and Germany. In 1715, he returned to Upsala and gained a solid reputation as an engineer, leading to his appointment by Charles XII to the Swedish Board of Mines in 1716. In addition to his engineering duties, Emanuel published numerous works on mathematics, as well as mechanical engineering. Shortly thereafter, he was elevated to the rank of nobility by Queen Ulrica, and changed his name to Swedenborg.

As he sat in the House of Nobles, Swedenborg was much admired for his political views. Some of his opinions were a bit unsettling to his royal benefactors, however, for Swedenborg was openly in favor of a democratic form of government. Hardly content to pontificate in the House of Nobles, he published works on the nature of the universe, as well as papers on geology, physics, anatomy, zoology, and astronomy which were decidedly ahead of their time. In 1734, he published *Prodomus Philosophia Ratiocinatrio de Infinite*, which explores the relationship of the finite to the infinite and of the soul to the body. In spite of his mastery of the material sciences and mechanical engineering, it was becoming obvious to all his readers that Swedenborg's concept of the supreme effort of humankind was an intense study of the spiritual and the divine.

In 1743, when he was 56, Swedenborg had a vision in which he believed that "Our Lord" initiated him into the deeper spiritual meaning of the scriptures. The Bible was the word of God, he was told, but its true meaning differed greatly from its more apparent teachings. Only Swedenborg, with the help of ministering angels, could translate the actual message of scripture. After a series of dreams and visions, Swedenborg abandoned his life of politics and science to spend all of his considerable energy delving into the mysteries of the spiritual world. He immediately resigned all of his appointments and retired at half his pension. Not only had God revealed himself and the true spiritual essence of the scriptures to him, but Swedenborg felt that God wanted him to develop a new church. Swedenborg said that he could hear the conversations of angelic beings and could even participate in such otherworldly discussions. In time, he was given visions of both heaven and hell, and he developed the habit of lying in trance for several days and nights. His arguments with the evil spirits, the fallen angels, terrified his servants, but the gentle conversations with the benign angelic beings soothed their fears.

In 1759, Swedenborg had the vision of the great fire at Stockholm, which has been recorded as one of the first completely documented cases of **clairvoyance** in history and which has become well known throughout the

Western world. In September, at about four o'clock on a Saturday afternoon, Swedenborg arrived in Gotenburg, Sweden, from England, and was invited by a friend to spend some time at his house before returning to his home in Stockholm. While there, Swedenborg became restless and went outside for about two hours. When he came back inside, he informed his host and other guests that a terrible fire had just broken out in Stockholm (which was about 300 miles from Gotenburg) and that it was spreading rapidly. His friends did not know how to respond to such news, for they had no idea how Swedenborg could possibly know that such a dreadful conflagration was occurring at such a distance away.

Swedenborg remained agitated and restless and went outside often that day, only to return with additional dire news, as if he were somehow viewing the disaster as it occurred. Alarmed, he told the company that the house of a friend was already in ashes and that the fire was fast approaching his own home. At eight o'clock in the evening, he came back inside to announce joyfully that the awful fire had been extinguished—and that it had been stopped just three doors away from his house.

By Sunday morning, word had spread of Swedenborg's remarkable vision, and he was summoned to the governor, who questioned him about the disaster. The seer described the fire precisely, telling exactly how it had begun and precisely how it had at last been squelched. On Monday evening, a messenger dispatched by the Board of Trade during the time of the fire arrived in Gotenburg. In letters the courier had brought with him, the fire was described exactly as stated by Swedenborg, and the next morning the news was further confirmed by messages brought to the governor by royal courier. As the seer had proclaimed, the fire had been extinguished at exactly eight o'clock in the evening.

Swedenborg's conversations with the angels and spirits of the dead had informed him that humans possess two receptacles for the containment of God—the will for divine love and the understanding for divine wisdom. Before the Fall, the flow of these virtues from God into the human spirit was perfect, but the

Emanuel Swedenborg (1688–1772).

intervention of evil and the sins of humankind itself had interrupted this once-perfect communion. The purpose of religion is to accomplish good and to establish a connection between God and the human spirit. Swedenborg came to recognize that even though he had become an apostle of God for whom no mysteries were hidden, it was not necessary for him to form a new church. All sincere members of all existing religious systems were connected as one in a spiritual sense. In spite of this apparent change of focus, Swedenborgianism did become a religion, with churches established in England in 1778 and in the United States in 1792.

Swedenborg believed strongly in what he termed the Doctrine of Correspondence: that everything in the visible, material world has a counterpart in the unseen, nonmaterial world. To those who questioned the validity of his journeys and conversations in the spiritual world, Swedenborg responded firmly that his observations of these other dimensions had been recorded as strictly as any man of science among his detractors. It had been given to him, as a scientist and as a man of spirit, to be able to reach into two worlds—one of spirit, the other of matter.

From the time he was 55 until his death, Swedenborg spoke to spirits of the deceased and to angelic beings. According to his constant dialogues with such entities, he said that the spirit world was comprised of a number of concentric spheres, each with its own density and inhabitants. The existence of the spirits was quite similar to that of Earth, with houses, trees, parks, schools, and so forth. Those who died of disease or old age regained their youth and health in the spirit world. Everyone who arrived on those ethereal planes after death rested for a few days before regaining full consciousness. Because on Earth it takes a man and a woman to form a complete human unit, marriage continues to exist as a spiritual union on the other side. There is no such thing as hell or eternal punishment. Those spirits who find themselves in a hellish place after death can evolve toward a higher spiritual plane.

In spite of it being granted to him "to be constantly and uninterruptedly in company with spirits and angels," Swedenborg did issue a caution in regard to receiving counsel from just any spirit that might manifest with an alleged personal message. "When spirits begin to speak," he wrote in *Miscellaneous Theological Works* (1996), "care should be taken not to believe them, for nearly everything they say is made up by them....They love to feign. Whatever be the topic spoken of, they think they know it, and if man listens and believes, they insist, and in various ways deceive and seduce."

From 1747 onward, Swedenborg lived at various times in Stockholm, Holland, and London, where he died on March 29, 1772. He was first buried in the Swedish Church in Prince's Square, then, later, at the request of the Swedish government, his body was sent to Stockholm for reinterment.

🕈 DELVING DEEPER

Brown, Slater. *The Heyday of Spiritualism*. New York: Hawthorn Books, 1970.

Swedenborg, Emanuel. *Divine Providence*. New York: The Swedenborg Foundation, 1972.

———. *Heaven and Its Wonders and Hell*. New York: Citadel Press, 1965.

Wilson, Colin. *The Occult*. New York: Vintage Books, 1973.

RESEARCHERS INTO THE MYSTERY OF SPIRIT CONTACT

To the uninformed layperson, psychical researchers who investigate individuals who claim to be able to make contact with the spirits of the departed are sometimes thought of as gullible men or women who go to **seances** in order to converse with the ghost of their late Uncle Henry. To be certain, mediums and their paranormal abilities are studied and tested, but not in an attitude of open acceptance. Such investigations are conducted in all earnestness and seriousness and under the strictest laboratory conditions possible. And rather than being gullible, the researchers are more likely to be skeptical and cautious observers, ever on the watch for trickery and evidence of charlatanism.

Many of those who research spirit contact believe that the difference between the genuine medium or channel and the great majority of humankind lies in the fact that the medium's threshold of consciousness may be set lower than that of others. In other words, the medium has access to levels of awareness that lie beyond the normal "reach" of the subconscious. The spirit medium usually works in **trance,** and while in this state of consciousness, he or she claims to be under the direction of a **spirit guide** or **spirit control.** Spiritualists believe in the reality of the guide as a spiritual entity apart from the medium. Psychical researchers theorize that the control personality is but a secondary personality of the medium that is able to dip into the psychic abilities residing in the subconscious.

The physical phenomena of **mediumship** are among the strangest and most dramatic of all occurrences studied by psychical researchers. Under laboratory conditions, serious reports have been made of the materialization of

Americans are trying to communicate with spirits in record numbers; half of all Americans believe in extrasensory perception. A new 2000 Gallup poll reports that fully 28 percent of Americans believe people can hear from or communicate mentally with the dead.

Regardless of whether spirits are attempting to communicate with us, people are trying to communicate with them—spouses with deceased spouses; parents with deceased children; children with deceased parents—says Greg Barrett of the Gannett News Service. Skeptics and believers alike say it is this love—and love lost—that drives our undying desire to talk to the dead.

Longtime skeptic and magician James Randi, a.k.a. "Amazing Randi," says, "People not only want it to be true, they need it to be true. It's the feel-good syndrome," says the 72-year-old, who has standing offer of $1 million to psychics who can independently verify their "magic."

Between 1972 and 1995 U.S. taxpayer,s unbeknownst to them, supported the paranormal profession. Before the ties were severed to psychics in 1996, the CIA and various U.S. Defense Department intelligence agencies spent $20 million in an effort to turn psychics into spy satellites. Some of the details of the government program may soon be released, as they are in the process of being reviewed for declassification, according to CIA spokeswoman Anya Guilsher. Guilsher adds that the government's conclusion of the use of psychics was "unpromising."

Psychic Noreen Renier doesn't agree. She was lecturing on extrasensory perception at the FBI Academy in Quantico, Virginia, when she warned that President Reagan would soon receive an injury to the upper chest. Two months later, John Hinckley shot Reagan.

Skeptic Paul Kurtz says all of this medium stuff is "nincompoopery." "But for whatever reason, it's all the rage." Kurtz is chairman of the Committee for the Scientific Investigation of Claims of the Paranormal and he tackles claims of psychics and the like in his *Skeptic Inquirer* magazine.

Can the Living Talk to the Dead?

Gary Schwartz thinks he has evidence that the living can talk to the dead. Schwartz, Harvard-educated and head of the University of Arizona Human Energy Systems Laboratory, claims the lab, which is a psychic testing ground, is revealing some interesting data. Several years ago, five mediums that Schwartz refers to as the "Dream Team" were flown to Tucson and put through a battery of tests. Most psychics scored 83 percent in revealing personal details about others, when asking yes or no questions.

When asked if any of his "Dream Team" will take Amazing Randi's challenge for the $1 million prize, he answers that Randi is an eternal skeptic who will never convert, no matter what evidence confronts him, so it is unlikely.

Sources:

Barrett, Greg. *USA Today,* 20 June 2001.

THE ASPR

Based in New York, New York, the American Society for Psychical Research, Inc., (ASPR) , the oldest psychical research organization in the United States, seeks to advance the understanding of psychic phenomena, with emphasis on scientific research. With its laboratories, offices, library and archive, it offers extensive topics in Parapsychology, such as extrasensory perception, (ESP), telepathy, clairvoyance, precognition (PK), psychokinesis, out of body experiences (OBEs), near death experiences (NDE's), survival after death, reincarnation, and apparitions and poltergeists.

There is also an "On-line Research" section where one can fill out a questionnaire to participate in current research linked with the Department of Psychology at the State University of West Georgia.

SOURCES:

American Society for Psychical Research, Inc. http://www.aspr. com. 15 October 2001.

human heads, hands, and even complete bodies from a cloudy substance, known as ectoplasm, which somehow appears to issue from the medium's physical body. Mediums have been seen to levitate into the air, manifest **stigmata** on their bodies, and cause mysterious apports (arrivals) of flowers, medallions, and items of jewelry.

SPIRITUALISTS *believe in the reality of the guide as a spiritual entity apart from the medium.*

Some of the world's best minds have been vitally concerned with the mystery of survival, life after death, and whether or not it is possible to speak with the dead. The British states-man William E. Gladstone (1809–1898), who most of his life was an avowed skeptic of spirit contact and all paranormal occurrences, finally concluded that psychical research "is the most important work in the world today—by far the most important."

The famous statesman was not alone in his declaration of the importance of psychical research. Pierre Curie (1859–1906), who with his wife, Marie, discovered radium, stated shortly before his death that in his opinion psychical research had more importance for humankind than any other. Sigmund Freud (1856–1939), generally accepted as the "father of psychoanalysis," belonged to both the British and the American Societies for Psychical Research and once commented that he wished he had devoted more time to such study when he was younger. His colleague and sometimes rival, Carl G. Jung (1875–1961), remained actively interested in psychical experiments until his death.

Sir William Crookes (1832–1919), a British physicist, conducted many exhaustive studies of spirit contact and mediums. The German philosopher Arthur Schopenhauer (1788–1860) insisted that psychical research explored the most important aspects of human experience and that it was the obligation of every scientist to learn more about them. Julian Huxley (1887–1975), the biologist; Sir James Jeans (1877–1946), the astronomer; Arnold Toynbee (1889–1975), the historian; Alfred North Whitehead (1861–1947), the philosopher—all of these great thinkers urged that their fellow scientists seriously approach psychical research.

In spite of the attention of such commanding intellects and the painstaking research of such individuals as Sir William Crookes, **Sir Oliver Lodge** (1851–1940), Dr. Gardner Murphy (1895–1979), **Hereward Carrington** (1880–1958). **J. B. Rhine** (1895–1980), G. N. M. Tyrell (1879–1973), Dr. Karlis Osis (1917–1997), Dr. Stanley Krippner (1932–), and Dr. Harold Puthoff (1930–), psychical researchers are still regarded by a large section of the scientific community as being "spook chasers" and as outright rebels and heretics to the bodies of established knowledge. The basic reason for such disdain on the part of orthodox scientists is the understandable reluctance of the scientific establishment to grant a hearing to a body of knowledge that might very well reshape or revise many of the premises on which its entire structure is based.

Arthur Koestler (1905–1983), noted novelist and journalist, told of his visit with a leading mathematical logician and philosopher. Koestler expressed his interest in recent statistical work in psychical research. The logician loudly scoffed at such studies until Koestler, irritated by the man's closed mind, provided him with the name of the world-famous statistician who had checked the statistics. Upon hearing the statistician's name, the logician seemed completely nonplussed. After a few moments he said, "If that is true, it is terrible, terrible. It would mean that I would have to scrap everything and start from the beginning."

Orthodox scientists in the more conventional disciplines are not about to "scrap everything," and many of them feel that the best method of avoiding the research statistics compiled by psychical researchers is to insist upon the requirements demanded of all conventional sciences: (1) that they produce controlled and repeatable experiments; (2) that they develop a hypothesis comprehensive enough to include all psychic phenomena— from **telepathy** to **poltergeists,** from water **dowsing** to spirit contact.

The difficulties in fulfilling these requirements can be immediately grasped when one considers how impossible it would be to repeat, for example, the apparition of a man's father as it appeared to him at the moment of his father's death. This sort of crisis apparition occurs only at death, and the man's father is going to die only once. The great majority of psychic phenomena are almost completely spontaneous in nature, and ungovernable elements of mood and emotion obviously play enormously important roles in any type of paranormal experience. As G. N. M. Tyrell pointed out, people are never aware of a telepathic, clairvoyant, or precognitive process at work within them. They are only aware of the product of that process. In fact, it seems apparent from laboratory work that conscious effort

SOCIETY FOR PSYCHICAL RESEARCH (SPR)

During a lecture given to the Society for Psychical Research (SPR) in 1919, Carl G. Jung said, "I shall not commit the fashionable stupidity of regarding everything I cannot explain as fraud." Still located in Kensington, London, the society offers research and data available both in classrooms and lecture halls in London, or over the Internet. Its said purpose is to advance the understanding of events and abilities commonly described as "psychic" or "paranormal" in a scientific manner. Scheduled conferences and lectures are offered on the website in addition to paranormal review, journals, books, and research initiatives.

SOURCES:

Society for Psychical Research. http://www.spr.ac.uk. 15 October 2001.

at determining any psychic process at work within oneself will either completely destroy it or greatly diminish its effectiveness.

PSYCHICAL *researchers are still regarded by a large section of the scientific community as being "spook chasers" and as outright rebels and heretics to the bodies of established knowledge.*

Those men and women who devote themselves to researching the possibility of life beyond death and spirit contact insist that science must not continue to ignore that which is not directly perceivable. By the same token, it falls upon the psychical researchers to exercise the greatest caution and the strictest controls when conducting tests with those who claim to be able to contact the dead.

In his *Psychic Science and Survival* (1947) Hereward Carrington, who devoted a lifetime to psychical research, listed the following requirements of an ideal researcher:

1. a thorough knowledge of the literature of the subject;

2. a good grounding in normal and abnormal psychology, in physics, chemistry, biology, and photography;

3. keen powers of observation and an ability to judge human nature and its motives;

4. training in magic and sleight of hand;

5. shrewdness, quickness of thought and action, patience, resourcefulness, sympathy, and a sense of humor;

6. freedom from superstition;

7. the strength to stand out against bigotry, scientific as well as theological.

✸ Delving Deeper

Carrington, Hereward. *The Case for Psychic Survival.* New York: Citadel Press, 1957.

Murphy, Gardner. *Challenge of Psychical Research: A Primer of Parapsychology.* New York: Harper & Row, 1970.

Murphy, Gardner, and Robert O. Ballou, eds. *William James on Psychical Research.* New York: Viking Press, 1960.

Rhine, Louisa E. *Hidden Channels of the Mind.* New York: William Sloane Associates, 1960.

Steinour, Harold. *Exploring the Unseen World.* New York: Citadel Press, 1959.

Sudre, Rene. *Parapsychology.* New York: Citadel Press, 1960.

Hereward Carrington (1880–1958)

Hereward Carrington spent his childhood years in Jersey, one of Britain's Channel Islands, and received his early schooling in London. Although he would one day write over one hundred books in the field of psychical research, as a teenager, he was far more interested in becoming a stage magician than exploring the spirit world. If it weren't for a fascination with certain well-documented cases of the paranormal, such as those recorded by **Fredric W. H. Myers** (1843–1901) and other serious psychical researchers, his only interest in mediums would have been to seek to expose them in the manner of **Harry Houdini** (1874–1926).

Carrington moved to Boston when he was 20 and remained in the United States for the rest of his life. While at first he earned his living as a journalist, he began to spend more and more time continuing to research the unexplained, and in 1905, he joined the staff of the American Society for Psychical Research (ASPR) as an investigator.

In addition to such famous mediums as **Margery Crandon** (1888–1941), **Eusapia Palladino** (1854–1918), and **Eileen Garrett** (1893–1970), Carrington had a number of impressive sittings with William Cartheuser. Cartheuser appeared to have been representative of some of the many paradoxes with which serious researchers may find themselves confronted in paranormal investigations. The medium had a harelip and a cleft palate which caused a severe impediment in his speaking voice, yet at no time did any of the spirit voices produced by him give any evidence of unclear or unintelligible speech—although most of the visiting entities did speak in whispers. The female voices from beyond seemed obviously to be those of a male speaking in a falsetto. Many of the communicating spirits reflected the same opinions and temperament of the medium, but now and then Carrington felt that the alleged entities did make reference to information and the names of individuals that could only have been gained in some paranormal manner.

In assessing the **mediumship** of William Cartheuser, Carrington could only theorize that the alleged **spirit controls** upon which the medium relied to summon the departed were nothing other than the medium speaking in a number of different voices. On occasion, however, Cartheuser's simulated **spirit guides** enabled him, perhaps by the power of suggestion and a state of light trance, to come up with information that he could only have acquired through an unknown power of mind or through a surviving personality—and to relay those messages in voices free of his usual speech impediments.

Carrington devoted an entire book to his examination of the famous medium Eileen Garrett. In *The Case for Psychic Survival* (1957) he concluded that even though there existed only slight evidence for the genuinely spiritistic character of spirit guides, the alleged spirit personalities "…nevertheless succeed in bringing through a vast mass of supernormal information which could not be obtained in their absence." The mechanism of believing in a spirit control somehow seemed to act as some sort of psychic catalyst to bring about information acquired through paranormal means.

The psychical researcher went on to theorize that the function of a medium's regular spirit guide seems to be that of an intermediary; and whether the entity is truly a spirit or is a dramatic personification of the medium's subconscious, it is only through the cooperation of the guide that accurate and truthful messages are obtained. In Carrington's opinion, the essential difference between the kind of secondary personality in pathological cases and the spirit control personality in mediumistic cases is that in those instances of multiple personalities, the secondary selves acquire no supernormal information, while in the case of a medium's spirit control it does. "In the pathological cases," he said, "we seem to have a mere splitting of the mind, while in the mediumistic cases we have to deal with a (perhaps fictitious) personality which is nevertheless in touch or contact, in some mysterious way, with another (spiritual) world, from which it derives information, and through which genuine messages often come."

In his conversations with Uvani, Eileen Garrett's spirit control, Carrington learned that the entity claimed to have no control over the medium's conscious mind, nor would he feel that he would have the right to interfere with her normal thinking processes. During the trance state, however, Uvani said that he could work Garrett's subconscious like playing notes on a piano. When Carrington asked why a personality who claimed to have lived a life as an Asian could speak such excellent English through the medium, Uvani

Hereward Carrington (1880–1958). (FORTEAN PICTURE LIBRARY)

answered that he could not speak English, but as a spirit he had the ability to impress his thoughts upon his "instrument," Eileen Garrett, who thereby relayed the communication.

Carrington concluded, as a result of extensive analysis of mediumship techniques, that an intelligently influenced mechanism was somehow involved in producing the physical phenomena of spirit contact in the seance room. In an essay written in 1946, Carrington said that there appears to be a form of "unknown energy" that issues from the body of the medium, "capable of affecting and molding matter in its immediate environment. At times this is invisible; at other times it takes forms and becomes more or less solid, when we have instances of the formation of so-called ectoplasm. It is this semi-material substance which moves matter and even shapes it into different forms."

According to Carrington's observations, this ectoplasm issues from various parts of the medium's body—from the fingertips, the solar plexus, and the genitals. "It represents a psychic force," he claimed, "as yet unknown to science, but now being studied by scientific men as part and parcel of supernormal biology." Carrington was certain that this energy had a biological basis and was dependent upon the physical body of the medium for its production, regardless of whether it was directed by the subconscious mind of the medium or by the mind of an unseen, disembodied personality.

Although few psychical researchers had as much firsthand experience investigating instances of spirit contact and hauntings as Hereward Carrington, there were times when even he found himself dealing with something that affected him in a very primal, frightening way. It was on the night of August 13, 1937, that Carrington, his wife, Marie Sweet Smith, and a party of five others obtained permission to spend a night in a haunted house located some 50 miles from New York City. As he referred to the incident in his *Essays in the Occult* (1958), the summer tenant had been forced to move back to the city in the middle of July because neither he nor his wife could sleep uninterrupted and their servants had all left their employ because of the haunting.

Carrington insisted that he be told nothing of the history of the house until he had first had an opportunity to explore the place from cellar to attic. The house was lighted from top to bottom, and the party began its safari into the unknown. On the second floor, two or three of the group commented that they had sensed "something strange" in one of the middle bedrooms, especially in the area next to an old bureau. The tenant, whom Carrington identified only as "Mr. X," told the party that he and his wife had heard noises coming from that particular bedroom.

The group proceeded down a hallway until they came to the door that led to the servants' quarters. Carrington opened the door, glanced up, and saw that the top floor was brightly illuminated and that a steep flight of stairs lay just ahead of the investigators. With Carrington in the lead, the party ascended the stairs until they found themselves confronted by a series of small rooms. Carrington made a sharp turn to the right, and the moment he did so, he felt as though a sudden blow that been delivered to his solar plexus. His forehead broke out into profuse perspiration, his head swam, and he had difficulty swallowing. "It

was an extraordinary sensation," he said, "definitely physiological, and unlike anything I had ever experienced before."

The veteran investigator was gripped by terror and panic and only through a firm exercise of will was he able to stop himself from fleeing in horror. His wife, who was only a step or two behind him, had just finished commenting on the "cute little rooms," when she suddenly uttered a frightened cry, turned, and ran down the stairs. Two unemotional, hardnosed psychical researchers, completely accustomed to psychic manifestations of all kinds, had experienced "distinctly a bodily and emotional reaction—accompanied…by a momentary mental panic and sensation of terror" such as neither of them had ever known before.

Carrington saw to his wife, whom he found outside on the porch, breathing deeply of the fresh air; then he returned to the remainder of the group. Each of them had experienced identical sensations and had retreated to the lower floor, where they sat sprawled in chairs or leaned against walls, tears streaming down their cheeks.

Carrington made special note of the fact that two highly skeptical friends of the tenant had accompanied the group to the house out of boredom. Both of these skeptics experienced the same sensations as the other members of the group—a difficulty in swallowing, tears streaming from the eyes, and cold perspiration on the forehead.

A dog, belonging to a member of the party, resisted all manner of coaxing designed to lure it upstairs. It growled, planted its feet stubbornly, and the hair raised on its back. In short, Carrington commented, the dog behaved "very much as dogs are supposed to behave in the presence of ghostly phenomena."

Much later that evening, Carrington led another expedition up the stairs to the servants' quarters. This time, the atmosphere seemed to have purged itself of the poisonous influence, and no member of the party experienced any sensations similar to their previous excursion. The dog bounded up the stairs, poked its nose into all the corners, and behaved as if prowling around such a house were the most natural thing in the world. Carrington later sought to return to the house with a spirit medium and special apparatus for recording and testing sounds and atmosphere. He was denied permission to continue his investigation, because one of the friends of the tenant had given the story to the papers, and the owner of the house did not wish additional publicity about his haunted house.

Carrington broke with the American Society for Psychical Research (ASPR) over a disagreement concerning the mediumship of **Mina "Margery" Stinson Crandon** (1888–1941), and he formed his American Psychical Institute in 1933. His wife served as the institute's secretary, and their principal research area focused upon the testing of such spirit mediums as Eileen Garrett. Sometime in 1938, the Carringtons moved the institute to Southern California, where they continued to investigate claims of hauntings and spirit contact. Among his many books are such titles as *The Physical Phenomena of Spiritualism* (1907); *Your Psychic Powers and How to Develop Them* (1920); and *Psychic Science and Survival* (1947). Hereward Carrington died on December 26, 1958, in Los Angeles.

✣ Delving Deeper

Carrington, Hereward. *The Case for Psychic Survival.* New York: Citadel Press, 1957.

———. *Essays in the Occult: Experiences Out of a Lifetime of Psychical Research.* New York: Thomas Yoseloff, 1958.

Tabori, Paul. *Pioneers of the Unseen.* New York: Taplinger, 1973.

Sir William Crookes (1832–1919)

Sir William Crookes, a physicist and chemist of international reputation, was a professor at the University of London, editor of the *Quarterly Journal of Science,* president of the British Chemical Society, discoverer of the element thallium, and inventor of the radiometer and the Crookes tube, which made the later development of X-rays possible. In addition to these accomplishments, Crookes was one of the most thorough and exacting scientific investigators of spirit contact. After many years of painstaking research and experimentation with dozens of well-known mediums, he became convinced that a great deal of spiritis-

tic phenomena was real and indicated proof of an afterlife.

Born in London on June 17, 1832, Crookes was one of 16 children of a well-known and prosperous tailor and his second wife. William also had five stepbrothers and stepsisters from his father's first wife. Although the young man had little formal education, his keen mind and natural abilities allowed him to enroll in the Royal College of Chemistry when he was only 16. Upon graduation in 1854, Crookes became superintendent of the Meteorological Department at Radcliffe Observatory, Oxford. A year later, he gained a post at the College of Science in Chester, Cheshire.

In 1856, when he was 24, he married Ellen Humphrey, and because of the large fortune he had inherited from his father, Crookes was able to establish a private laboratory and devote himself entirely to scientific work of his own choosing. Three years later, in 1861, Crookes discovered the element thallium and the correct measurement of its atomic weight. In 1863, when he was only 31, he was elected a fellow of the Royal Society.

Just when it seemed Crookes faced only a life of one triumph after another, he was grief-stricken when his youngest brother, Phillip, died in 1867. Cromwell Varley, a close friend and fellow physicist who was also a practicing Spiritualist, convinced William and Ellen to attend a **seance** and attempt to communicate with Phillip. Whatever spirit messages Crookes and his wife received during a series of seances in 1867, it appears that they were convincing enough to inspire the brilliant physicist to turn his genius toward the exploration of spiritistic phenomena.

Some scholars of the psychic field have declared the series of experiments that Crookes conducted with the famous medium **Daniel Dunglas Home** (1833–1886) to be the first strictly scientific tests of mediumistic ability. Of one such test, Crookes stated that Home went to the fireplace and after stirring the hot coals around with his bare hands, took out a red-hot piece nearly as large as an orange, and "putting it on his right hand, so as to almost completely enclose it, he then blew

complexion that photography could not hope to capture," tongues began to wag that the great scientist had lost all form of objectivity and had grown much too attached to the spirit that he was supposed to be investigating. When such a man of stature as Crookes announced that he had judged medium **Florence Cook**'s (1856–1904) materializations of the spirit Katie King to be genuine, it was bound to spark controversy. Whether or not the "perfect beauty" with whom Sir William chatted and strolled about the seance room was a ghost or a hoax is a question that is still being debated to this day.

Florence Cook, the medium through whom Katie King materialized, first met the spirit in seances which she conducted when she was only 15. Katie promised to be Florence's **spirit control** for a period of three years and assist her in producing many types of remarkable phenomena. In April of 1872, Katie appeared only as a deathlike face between the gauze curtains of a seance cabinet, but as her control of the medium became more advanced, she could at last step out of the cabinet and show herself in full body to those sitters assembled for Cook's seances.

It has been said that the spirit of Katie King became almost as if she were a full-time boarder at the Cook household. When Florence Cook married, her husband complained that it was like being married to two women. Katie began to materialize at unexpected moments, and some nights she even went to bed with the medium and her long-suffering spouse.

Many people became thoroughly convinced of the validity of Katie King's existence because of Crookes' testimony. Others whispered scandal and made much of the many hours the physicist had spent alone with Florence Cook and her alleged spirit friend. Crookes, however, stood firm in his convictions that he had not been duped and summed up his investigations by stating that it was unimaginable to suggest that "an innocent schoolgirl of fifteen" should be able to devise and to carry out such a "gigantic imposture" so successfully for a period of three years. Crookes pointed out to his critics that in those same three years the fact that she sub-

into the small furnace" he had made of his hand "until the lump of charcoal was nearly white hot," and then drew Crookes's attention to the flame that was "flickering over the coal and licking round his fingers." A number of witnesses to the experiment were also able to handle the hot coal without burning themselves after Home had transferred his "power" to them. Those who handled the coal without the transference of energy from Home "received bad blisters at the attempt."

Crookes no doubt created quite a stir among his more orthodox scientific colleagues when he told them that he had walked with a ghost, talked with a ghost, and taken more than 40 flashlight photographs of the specter. And when he went on to describe the spirit as a "perfect beauty" with a "brilliant purity of mitted to any test that might be imposed upon her, was willing to be searched at any time, either before or after a seance, and visited his laboratory for the express object of submitting to the strictest scientific tests, certainly demonstrated her integrity. To insist further that the spirit Katie King was the result of deceit did more "violence to one's reason and common sense than to believe her to be what she herself affirms."

William Crookes's experiments in psychical research did little to prevent his receiving the Royal Medal from the Royal Society in 1875 or from being knighted in 1897. He supported the **Society for Psychical Research** (SPR) when it was founded in 1882 and even served as its president in 1886, but he conducted no tests of **mediumship** or any other paranormal phenomena after 1875. As a kind of summation of his views on the subject, Crookes once said: "The phenomena I am prepared to attest to are extraordinary and so directly oppose the most firmly rooted articles of scientific belief—amongst others, the ubiquity and invariable action of the force of gravitation—that even now, on recalling the details of what I witnessed, there is an antagonism in my mind between reason which pronounces it to be scientifically impossible, and the consciousness of my senses, both of touch and sight....It is absolutely true that connections have been set up between this world and the next!"

After Lady Crookes died in 1916, Sir William immediately began attempts to communicate with her. According to some sources, he did receive messages from her spirit that he felt constituted proof of contact with the other side. Others say that an alleged spirit photograph of Lady Crookes appeared to have been manipulated in the developing process. Crookes died on April 4, 1919, survived by four of his eight children.

❋ Delving Deeper

Gauld, Alan. *The Founders of Psychical Research*. London: Routledge & Kegan Paul, 1968.

Hall, Trevor. *The Spiritualists*. London: Duckworth, 1962.

Medhurst, R. G., and K. M. Goldney. *Crookes and the Spirit World*. New York: Taplinger, 1972.

Harry Houdini (1874–1926)

Although Harry Houdini died in 1926, his name remains synonymous with incredible demonstrations of stage magic and daredevil escapes. For **Spiritualists** and mediums, however, his name is also synonymous with the devil at worst, the Grand Inquisitor at the least. Houdini developed a strange kind of ambivalence, a love-hate attitude, toward the spirit world that, according to many of his biographers, developed after he failed to contact the spirit of his deceased mother through a medium. Others have commented that Houdini, known as a notorious self-promoter, initiated the highly publicized attempts to expose fraudulent mediums only because of the attention that such exploits would receive in the press.

Houdini was born Ehrich Weiss in Budapest, Hungary, on March 24, 1874, and he was only 13 weeks old when his family emigrated to the United States and settled in Appleton, Wisconsin. He was only a boy when he read the memoirs of the great French conjuror Robert-Houdin (1805–1871), who is today known as the "Father of Modern Magic." Ehrich became so impressed with the life and the talent of Robert-Houdin that he resolved to become a magician, and when he was 17, he added an "i" to his idol's name and became "Houdini."

Houdini practiced long hours with a childhood friend who also aspired to become a master conjuror. When his friend's interests drifted elsewhere, Houdini began playing carnivals and amusement parks with his brother, Theodore, billing themselves as the Houdini Brothers. Houdini also added the first name Harry, which was an adaptation of his family nickname, "Ehrie."

The Houdini Brothers' first major booking was at the World's Fair in Chicago in 1893, and Houdini found great audience response to their act when he spontaneously added a handcuff escape during an evening performance. After the fair ended, he billed himself in a solo act as the "Handcuff King" and played a successful run at the Kohl and Middleton Dime Museum in Chicago. When that engagement came to a close, he rejoined Theodore in their double-act and played vari-

Harry Houdini
(1874–1926) had himself
wrapped in chains as
part of his escape act.
(THE LIBRARY OF CONGRESS)

ous high schools and social events. It was when the Houdini Brothers were performing at a girls' school that Houdini met Beatrice (Bess) Rahner, who would soon become his wife. After they were married, the newlyweds began playing the theatrical circuit as "The Houdinis," and Theodore went solo under his new stage name, "Hardeen."

Until they decided to try their luck in England in July 1900, the Houdinis barely managed to survive in show business. There had been brief stints with a circus, a burlesque show, a traveling medicine show, and an ill-fated attempt to begin a school of magic. Houdini was featuring escapes more and more in their act, but even the publicity gained from such risky ventures as freeing himself from a prison cell under the watchful eye of law enforcement officers didn't bring customers to the theaters. Utilizing his bold personality to the utmost degree, Houdini managed to secure a contract with the Alhambra Theatre, one of the largest music halls in London. By July 1901, Houdini and his daring escapes were receiving top billing all over Europe—and it wasn't long before accounts of his dangling from tall buildings wrapped in chains, freeing himself from casks, kegs, and trunks submerged in rivers, and escaping from coffins, giant milk cans, and huge mail bags were creating a stir back in the States, where audiences had once been unmoved by the Great Houdini.

It is difficult to ascertain exactly when or why Houdini became the great nemesis of Spiritualist mediums—or even if he really did, in fact, set about instituting any sort of vendetta against them. Some writers and researchers believe that Houdini truly did believe in survival of the spirit after physical death, and his supposed vicious attacks against spirit mediums were but an expression of his great disappointment that he never really found any whom he felt had truly provided him with actual proof of his mother's afterlife existence. Others maintain that he only set out to expose mediums as a means of keeping himself in the headlines.

Houdini's friendship with **Sir Arthur Conan Doyle** (1859–1930), the creator of Sherlock Holmes and an avid supporter of

Spiritualism, suggests his sincerity in seeking to pierce the veil of death. During the Doyles' lecture tour of the United States in June 1922, Houdini and Beatrice joined Sir Arthur and Lady Doyle for a brief vacation in Atlantic City. On June 17, Houdini's mother's birthday, Lady Doyle said that she felt she could establish contact with her. Houdini later claimed that he had kept an open mind regarding the alleged communication, but he publicly renounced the messages that Lady Doyle had produced through automatic writing. Houdini doubted that his mother would have begun writing the message by making a cross, since she had been Jewish. And since she spoke only broken English and couldn't write the language at all, he was skeptical of the answers that she had written so perfectly. Doyle was outraged at what he felt was his friend's betrayal of trust and the belittling of a spirit communication. Their friendship ceased after Houdini's statement.

H ARRY *Houdini became the great nemesis of Spiritualist mediums.*

Houdini's attacks on Spiritualist mediums also draws a parallel in many researchers' minds to his strange vitriolic assault on his childhood hero, Robert-Houdin, who provided the source of young Ehrich Weiss's inspiration to be a magician as well as the origin of his professional name. As he was beginning his own rise to fame, Houdini wrote a book about Robert-Houdin in which he not only ceased praising him, but ruthlessly sought to destroy the great conjuror's reputation. In *The Unmasking of Robert-Houdin* (1908), Houdini twisted facts and fictionalized others in order to fit the accusations that he had contrived. Houdini's critics point out that this kind of underhanded procedure was what he appeared to do with so many mediums. While Houdini's admirers state that he exposed some of the most famous mediums of the day as being fraudulent, his critics protest that he resorted to trickery, then loudly claimed that he had caught them in deceit when it was truly he who was the deceiver.

Dr. Walter Franklin Prince, head of the American Society for Psychical Research (ASPR) at the time of Houdini's campaign against mediums, stated that the magician showed "considerable bias by his selection of mediums and phenomena." According to Prince, Houdini "only chose to investigate those [mediums] already deemed spurious or very dubious by careful researchers in America and Britain, and ignored psychics and phenomena generally treated with respect by the same people."

Houdini's most publicized encounter with a medium was his alleged exposure of the famous Boston medium **Mina "Margery" Crandon** (1888–1941) in 1924. The investigating committee, sponsored by *Scientific American* magazine, had sought Houdini's expertise as a magician, but many of the members soon became irate over his attempts to employ trickery against the medium. Although Houdini claimed that he had caught Crandon in fraudulent actions, certain committee members felt that the medium's **spirit guide,** Walter, had been the one who had exposed Houdini and the tricks that he used in his attempts to confuse Crandon.

The great magician's crusade against fraudulent mediums, as well as his career as a conjuror and escape artist, was cut short on October 22, 1926, when a student who was visiting backstage at a Montreal theater wished to test Houdini's much vaunted muscle control, and caught him off guard with a punch to the stomach that ruptured his appendix. Houdini died nine days later on Halloween.

The controversy over whether or not the Houdini after-death code was broken will no doubt continue to rage on for many years. Houdini pledged to his wife, Bess, that if at all possible he would communicate with her after his death, and in order to prove his identity beyond all doubt and to eliminate the possibility of deception, the magician's prearranged message was a secret known only to Bess. To add to the mystique, Houdini, the master showman, stated that a **seance** should be held each anniversary of his death in an attempt for him to transmit the code words to a medium.

The Reverend Arthur Ford (1896–1971), formerly an orthodox clergyman, had become a trance medium and had gained an international reputation for the accuracy of his spirit communication, receiving accolades from such luminaries as Sir Arthur Conan Doyle, who called him one of the most amazing mental mediums of all times. In 1929, Reverend Ford received a message that he believed to have originated from Houdini and conveyed it to Bess Houdini's attention. Immediately a storm of fierce arguments pro and con erupted in the media. Perhaps betraying their own personal prejudices, some feature writers championed the authenticity of Reverend Ford's relayed communication from Houdini, while others quoted the magician's widow as saying that the message was incorrect.

On February 9, 1929, however, Beatrice Houdini wrote Reverend Ford to state with finality: "Regardless of any statement made to the contrary: I wish to declare that the message, in its entirety, and in the agreed upon sequence, given to me by Arthur Ford, is the correct message prearranged between Mr. Houdini and myself."

Critics of the paranormal downplay Ford's having received the code from the spirit of Houdini. They insist that Bess Houdini had inadvertently revealed the code to several reporters the year before when she explained that the message her late husband would pass on from the world beyond was based on their old vaudeville routine that utilized a secret spelling code that would pass information from her to Houdini. The various words in the code spelled out Harry's and Bess's secret message: "Roseabelle, believe."

❈ DELVING DEEPER

Brandon, Ruth. *The Spiritualists*. New York: Alfred A. Knopf, 1983.

Houdini, Harry. *A Magician Among the Spirits*. New York: Arno Press, 1972.

Mysteries of the Unknown: Spirit Summonings. Alexandria, Va.: Time-Life Books, 1989.

WILLIAM JAMES (1842–1910)

William James is best known for his classic work on the mystical experience *The Varieties of Religious Experience* (1902). James had a career as a psychologist, a philosopher, and a teacher. His father, Henry James, Sr. (1811–1882), was a philosopher, a friend of the poet and essayist Ralph Waldo Emerson (1803–1882), and an ardent follower of the teachings of **Emanuel Swedenborg** (1688–1772). William's brother, Henry James (1843–1916), was the acclaimed novelist of such American classics as *Daisy Miller* (1879), *The Europeans,* and the psychological thriller *The Turn of the Screw* (1898). James studied both science and art before receiving a degree in medicine from Harvard University in 1869. Two years later, he began teaching courses at Harvard, first in physiology, then in psychology and philosophy.

James's interest in mediumship and the afterlife was closely allied with his research in the psychology of altered states of consciousness. In 1882, while in London, he met **Fredric W. H. Myers** (1843–1901), Henry Sidgwick (1838–1900), Edmund Gurney (1847–1888), and other founding members of the newly formed British Society for Psychical Research (BSPR). James was impressed by Myers, a fellow psychologist, and his theory of the subliminal self, a secondary consciousness containing a number of higher-level mental processes which might be responsible for phenomena otherwise attributed to spirits. Returning to Boston, James, together with Sir William Barret and others, helped establish the American Society for Psychical Research (ASPR) in 1885.

That same year, James was brought to the seance room of **Leonora E. Piper** (1857–1950), the medium whom many psychical researchers would later declare the greatest mental medium of all time. Taking such precautions as identifying himself with a false name, the psychologist came away from the sitting completely baffled as to how the medium's **spirit control** had been able to provide accurate information on all the subjects about which he had queried. Although he was never greatly impressed by the phenomena produced by the physical mediums, James began a lengthy study of mental mediums, whom he hoped would be able to exhibit as much genuine phenomena as Piper.

James served as vice president of the American Society for Psychical Research (ASPR) from 1890 to 1910 and as president from 1894 to 1895. Although he was a stalwart champion of the scientific research of paranormal phenomena, he never quite found the proof in survival after death which he had hoped to discover through the study of mediumship. William James died on August 26, 1910, at his summer home in Chocurua, New Hampshire.

✤ DELVING DEEPER

Burkhardt, Frederic, and Fredson Bowers, eds. *The Works of William James: Essays in Psychical Research.* Cambridge, Mass.: Harvard University Press, 1986.

Myers, Gerald E. *William James: His Life and Thought.* New Haven, Conn.: Yale University Press, 1986.

SIR OLIVER LODGE (1851–1940)

Sir Oliver Joseph Lodge was a world-renowned British physicist whose first experiences in psychical research date back to 1881, when Malcolm Guthrie, the owner of a drapery shop, invited him to join his investigations in thought transference in Liverpool. Lodge was quite amazed with the results, and he began to conduct his own tests. Shortly thereafter, he joined the **Society for Psychical Research** (SPR).

In 1889, Lodge invited the famous Boston medium **Leonora E. Piper** (1857–1950) to England for tests and saw that she was made comfortable in his own home. Ever the exacting researcher, he took every conceivable precaution to eliminate any possibility of foreknowledge or fraud on Piper's part. He went so far as to temporarily dismiss all of his servants and replace them with others who knew absolutely nothing about any member of the Lodge family or Piper. Although a guest in the Lodge home, the medium was kept incommunicado and was constantly watched by experienced professional detectives. With Piper's permission, her private mail was opened and read. Every possibility of her communicating with others and receiving any type of information was completely eliminated, yet Piper's **spirit guides** provided accurate communication in every test that Lodge devised, which helped convince the researcher that spiritistic phenomena were real.

Sir Oliver Lodge (1851–1940). (THE LIBRARY OF CONGRESS)

vent her from resorting to trickery, Lodge was impressed with what he had witnessed. "Things hitherto held impossible do actually occur," the physicist concurred. "Certain phenomena usually considered abnormal do belong to the order of nature, and as a corollary from this, that these phenomena ought to be investigated and recorded by persons and societies interested in natural knowledge."

Oliver Lodge was knighted in 1902 while he was serving as president of the Society for Psychical Research (SPR). In 1913, he was elected president of the British Association for the Advancement of Science. His fascination with **Spiritualism** did nothing to prevent him from accomplishing highly regarded work with electricity and with early forms of radio before Guglielmo Marconi (1874–1937).

In August 1915, Lodge received what he considered proof of survival after death when, in Boston, Leonora Piper relayed what he considered to be convincing messages from Fredric Myers, who had died in 1901, and Edmund Gurney, who had passed on in 1888—two close friends and associates. Such dramatic assurances of life in the spirit world helped to prepare Lodge for the death of his son Raymond, who was killed on September 14, 1915, in his capacity as a medical officer of the Second South Lancers.

"The messages received tend to render certain the existence of some outside intelligence or control," he said. "My sittings convinced me of survival. I am as convinced of continued existence on the other side of death as I am of existence here…I say this on distinct scientific grounds. I say it because certain friends of mine who have died still exist, because I have talked with them."

Five years later, in 1894, Lodge's first encounters with physical **mediumship** took place when he and **Fredric W. H. Myers** (1843–1901) traveled to the summer home of the French psychical researcher Charles Richet (1850–1935) to investigate the extraordinary **Eusapia Palladino** (1854–1918). Although Palladino had to be observed carefully to pre-

On September 25, Lady Lodge sat with medium Gladys Osborne Leonard (1882–1968), who described a photograph that had been taken of Raymond with a group of fellow officers. Lady Lodge knew of no such photograph. The medium said that Raymond's spirit was insistent that he should tell Lady Lodge that in this particular photograph, Raymond was holding his walking stick under his arm. The Lodges had numerous photographs of their son, but they did not possess a single one depicting a group of medical officers in which Raymond would be included. Lodge was impressed with the emphasis that the medium had placed upon Raymond's insistence that they should locate such a photograph.

Then, according to Sir Oliver's report on the case (*Proceedings*, S.P.R. Vol. XXIX), on November 29, a letter was received from a Mrs. Cheves, who was a stranger to the Lodges, but who was the mother of a friend of Raymond's. Cheves informed the Lodges that she had half a dozen photographs from a sitting by a group of medical officers in which Raymond and her son were present. Cheves inquired if the Lodges would like a copy of the photograph.

Although Lodge and his wife responded immediately and enthusiastically, the photograph did not arrive until the afternoon of December 7. In the interim, Lady Lodge had gone through Raymond's diary, which had been returned from the front, and had found an entry dated August 24 which told of such a photo having been taken. In his report for the Society for Psychical Research (SPR), Lodge noted that the photograph had been taken 21 days before their son's death. "Some days may have elapsed before [Raymond] saw a print, if he ever saw one," he wrote. "He certainly never mentioned it in his letters. We were, therefore, in complete ignorance of it."

While the Lodges were awaiting the photograph from Cheves, they visited another medium through whose spirit control Raymond gave them additional details concerning the group picture. Now, it seemed, Raymond was not so certain he held his walking stick, but he confirmed that there were a considerable number of men in the photograph, including two who were friends of his. These two men were prominently featured standing behind Raymond, one of whom annoyed him by leaning on his shoulder.

When the photograph was delivered to the Lodge home, Sir Oliver and Lady Lodge noticed at once that it offered a poor likeness of Raymond, but provided excellent evidence that their son had communicated to them from beyond the grave. The walking stick was there, though not under Raymond's arm, as the first medium had said. The fellow officers Raymond had named through the second medium were in the photograph and the general arrangement of the men was as both mediums had described it.

"But by far the most striking piece of evidence is the fact that some one sitting behind Raymond is leaning or resting a hand on his shoulder," commented Lodge in his report. "The photograph fortunately shows the actual

occurrence and almost indicates that Raymond was rather annoyed with it, for his face is a little screwed up, and his head has been slightly bent to one side out of the way of the man's arm. It is the only case in the photograph where one man is leaning or resting his hand on the shoulder of another."

Lodge once again contacted Cheves and learned where he might obtain prints of other photographs that had been taken at the same time. Upon examination of all accessible prints, Lodge found that the basic group pose had been repeated with only slight variations for three different photographs. The Lodges felt the evidential value of the communication had been greatly enhanced by the fact that one medium had made a reference to the existence of Raymond's last photograph, and another medium, unknown to the first, had supplied the details of the photograph in response to Lodge's direct question. In his *My Philosophy* (1933), he wrote: "I am absolutely convinced not only of survival, but of demonstrated survival, demonstrated by occasional interaction with matter in such a way as to produce physical results."

Among the books written by Sir Oliver Lodge are such titles as: *Man and the Universe* (1908); *Science and Religion* (1914); *Raymond or Life and Death* (1917); *Raymond Revisited* (1922); *Science and Human Progress* (1927); *Why I Believe in Personal Immortality* (1928); *The Reality of a Spiritual World* (1930); and *My Philosophy* (1933).

❋ DELVING DEEPER

Jolly, W. P. *Sir Oliver Lodge*. London: Constable, 1974.

Tabori, Paul. *Pioneers of the Unseen*. New York: Taplinger, 1973.

FREDRIC W. H. MYERS (1843–1901)

Fredric William Henry Myers was born in 1843 in Keswick, Cumberland, England, into the family of a clergyman. He was educated at Cheltenham and Trinity College, Cambridge. In 1865, he became a lecturer in the classics at Cambridge, but in 1872, he resigned that position to become a school inspector. Myers published several volumes of poetry, though it was as an essayist that he became known (*Essays, Classical and Modern* [1885]).

Intrigued by the possibility of ghosts, spirits, and the survival of the soul since he was very young, Myers began sitting with mediums in 1872, often in the company of his friends, Henry Sidgwick (1838–1900) and Edmund Gurney (1847–1888). In 1882, he was one of the original group, together with Sidgwick and Gurney, who founded the British Society for Psychical Research (BSPR) and remained until the end of his life one of its most active and productive members, serving as the society's secretary from 1888 to 1899 and its president in 1900.

Although he was never a skeptic toward the paranormal, Myers deemed many of the manifestations of spirit mediums to be simplistic and puerile. In his opinion, the greatest evidence for survival of the human personality after death was to be found in what he called the "subliminal consciousness," that mysterious realm that lies beneath the threshold of ordinary consciousness wherein exist the faculties of **telepathy, clairvoyance, psychokinesis,** and **precognition.** All the phenomena of mediumism and the seance room Myers attributed to the manifestations of the subliminal consciousness.

Myers investigated one of the most evidential cases suggestive of the survival of human personality beyond the death experience recorded in the early annals of psychical research. The report, which has come to be known as "The Case of the Scratch on the Cheek."

In 1876 Mr. F. G., a traveling salesman, was sitting in a hotel room in St. Joseph, Missouri. It was high noon and he was smoking a cigar and writing out sales orders. Suddenly conscious of someone sitting on his left with one arm resting on the table, the salesman was startled to look up into the face of his dead sister, a young lady of 18 who had died of cholera in 1867. "So sure was I that it was she," he wrote in an account to the American Society for Psychical Research (ASPR) (*Proceedings,* S.P.R., VI, 17), "that I sprang forward in delight, calling her by name."

As he did so, the image of his sister vanished, and Mr. F. G. resumed his seat, stunned by the experience. The cigar was still in his mouth, the pen was still in his hand, and the ink was still moist on his order blank. He was satisfied that he had not been dreaming, but was wide awake. He had been near enough to touch her, "had it been a physical possibility." He had noted her features, expression, and details of dress. "She appeared as if alive," he stated. "Her eyes looked kindly and perfectly naturally into mine. Her skin was so lifelike that I could see the glow of moisture on its surface, and, on the whole, there was no change in her appearance."

Mr. F. G. was so impressed by the experience that he took the next train home to tell his parents about the remarkable visitation. But his mother nearly fainted when he told them of "a bright red line or scratch on the right-hand side" of his sister's face. With tears streaming down her face, his mother told him that he had most certainly seen his sister's spirit since only she was aware of a scratch that she had accidentally made while doing some little act of kindness after the girl's death. Feeling terrible over what had occurred, his mother had carefully "obliterated all traces of the slight scratch with the aid of powder" and had never mentioned the unfortunate occurrence to a single person from that day onward until F. G. had mentioned seeing it on the spirit form of his sister.

It seems a bit more than coincidence when the anonymous narrator, F. G., adds: "A few weeks later my mother died, happy in her belief that she would rejoin her favorite daughter in a better world."

In discussing this case, Fredric W. H. Myers wrote that, in his opinion, the spirit of the daughter had perceived the approaching death of her mother and had appeared to the brother to force him into the role of message bearer. Also, by prompting F. G. to return home unexpectedly at that time, the spirit had enabled him to have a final visit with his mother. Myers was further intrigued by the fact that the spirit figure appeared not as a corpse, but as a girl full of health and happiness "with the symbolic red mark worn simply as a test of identity." Myers discounted the theory that the spirit figure could have been a projection from the mother's mind. "As to the spirit's own knowledge of the fate of the body

Frederic W. Myers
(1843–1901). (FORTEAN
PICTURE LIBRARY)

after death, other reported cases show that this specific form of post-mortem perception is not unusual," he concluded. "This case is one of the best attested, and in itself one of the most remarkable that we possess...It certainly seems probable that recognition was intelligently aimed at."

The Reverend Arthur Bellamy told Myers about the "lady" he saw one night sitting by the side of the bed where his wife lay sound asleep. Bellamy stared at the strange woman for several minutes, noting especially the elegant styling of her hair, before the lady vanished.

When Mrs. Bellamy awakened, the reverend described her mysterious caller. He was startled to learn that the description fit that of a schoolgirl friend of his wife's with whom she had once made a pact that the first one to die should appear after her death to the survivor. The astonished clergyman then asked his wife if there was anything outstanding about her friend, so they might be certain it had been she. "Her hair," she answered without hesitation. "We girls used to tease her at school for devoting so much time to the arrangement of her hair." Later, Bellamy identified a photograph of his wife's friend as being the likeness of the specter that had appeared at her bedside.

The results, speculations, and conclusions of Frederic W. H. Myers's many years of research were published posthumously in *Human Personality and Its Survival of Bodily Death* (coauthored with Edmund Gurney and Frank Podmore, 1903). Myers died in Rome in 1901 and was buried in Keswick.

❋ Delving Deeper

Gauld, Alan. *The Founders of Psychical Research*. London: Routledge & Kegan Paul, 1968.

Oppenheim, Janet. *The Other World: Spiritualism and Psychical Research in England*. Cambridge: Cambridge University Press, 1985.

Spence, Lewis. *An Encyclopedia of Occultism*. New Hyde Park, N.Y.: University Books, 1960.

Society for Psychical Research (SPR)

In 1882, a distinguished group of Cambridge scholars founded the British Society for Psychical Research (BSPR) for the purpose of examining allegedly paranormal phenomena in a scientific and unbiased manner. The first president of the society was Professor Henry Sidgwick (1838–1900), and the council numbered among its members Edmund Gurney (1847–1888), Frank Podmore (1856–1910), **Fredric W. H. Myers** (1843–1901), and Professor William Barrett (1844–1925). The initial major undertaking of the newly formed society, the first of its kind in the world, was to conduct a census of hallucinations by means of a circulated questionnaire that asked its respondents:

> Have you ever, when believing yourself to be completely awake, had a vivid impression of seeing or being touched by a living being or inanimate object, or of hearing a voice; which impression, so far as you could discover, was not due to any external physical cause?

The SPR received answers from 17,000 people, 1,684 of whom answered "yes." From this, the committee which was conducting the census estimated that nearly 10 percent of the population had experienced some kind of visual or auditory "hallucination." Those people who indicated that they had experienced some paranormal appearance or manifestation were sent forms requesting details.

The census of hallucinations enabled the researchers to arrive at a number of basic premises concerning ghosts and apparitions, which were strengthened by subsequent research. The committee was able to conclude, for example, that although apparitions are associated with other events besides death, they are more likely to be linked with death than anything else. Visual hallucinations were found to be the most common (1,087). This seemed especially important to note because psychologists have found that auditory experiences are most common among the mentally ill. Of the visual cases reported, 283 had been shared by more than one witness. This was also noted to be of great importance because critics of psychic phenomena have always argued that the appearance of a "ghost" is an entirely subjective experience. Those who answered the committee's follow-up form indicated that they had not been ill when they had witnessed the phenomena they reported, and they insisted that the "hallucinations" were quite unlike the bizarre, nightmarish creatures which might appear during high fevers or high alcoholic consumption. Of the 493 reported auditory hallucinations, 94 had occurred when another person had been present. Therefore, about one-third of the cases were collective—that is, experienced by more than one witness at the same time.

After the findings of the census of hallucinations were made public, the SPR began to be flooded by personal accounts of spontaneous cases of ghosts and apparitions. In order to aid an appointed committee in the handling of such an influx of material, the SPR worked out a series of questions that could be applied to each case that came into their offices:

1. Is the account firsthand?
2. Was it written or told before the corresponding event was known?
3. Has the principal witness been corroborated?
4. Was the percipient awake at the time?
5. Was the percipient an educated person of good character?
6. Was the apparition recognized?
7. Was it seen out of doors?
8. Was the percipient anxious or in a state of expectancy?
9. Could relevant details have been read back into the narrative after the event?
10. Could the coincidence between the experience and the event be accounted for by chance?

Later, committee member J. Fraser Nichol established three points of critique that could be used by the investigator of spontaneous phenomena:

1. That the experience be veridical—that is, that it relate to an actual event that was occurring, had occurred, or would occur;
2. That there be an independent witness who testifies that the percipient related his experience to him before he came to know, by normal means, that the experience had been veridical; and
3. That no more than five years have passed between the experience and the written account of it.

The American Society for Psychical Research (ASPR), first organized in 1885 with astronomer Simon Newcomb (1835–1909) as president, later became a branch of the British Society of Psychical Research (BSPR) and functioned in Boston under the guidance of Richard Hodgson (1855–1905), formerly of Cambridge University, until his death in 1905. The ASPR became independent of the BSPR and relocated to New York City in 1906 with James Hervey Hyslop (1854–1920), Professor of Logic and Ethics at Columbia University, as its secretary and treasurer. For the next 14 years, until his death in 1920, Hyslop expanded the scope of the society's work.

A GROUP *of Cambridge scholars founded the British Society for Psychical Research for the purpose of examining allegedly paranormal phenomena in a scientific and unbiased manner.*

At the ASPR all-day ESP forum held on November 20, 1965, in New York City, Dr. Gardner Murphy (1895–1979), president of the ASPR, told assembled parapsychologists and representatives from other scientific disciplines that "...Progress in parapsychology in the direction of science calls for major, sustained effort...devoted to the building of theories and systematic models. The primary need is not for lots and lots of further little experiments, but for bold and sound model building."

Murphy concluded his address, "Advancement of Parapsychology as a Science," by stating that the future of parapsychology as a science is going to depend on multidisciplinary cooperation between the psychical researcher and "...the medical man, the anthropologist, the sociologist, the physicist, the biologist, the psychologist, and a great many other kinds of people working together within a broad perspective and giving each other mutual support."

MAKING THE CONNECTION

automatic writing Writing that occurs through either an involuntary, or unconscious, trance-like state with the source being the writer's own unconscious self, from a telepathic link with another, or from a deceased spirit wishing to communicate a message.

dogma A principle, belief, or set of beliefs considered to be absolutely true, whether religious, political, or philosophical.

ecclesiasticism Principles, practices, activities, or body of thought that is all-encompassing and adhered to in an organized church or institution.

elemental spirits A lower order of spirit beings, said to be usually benevolent and dwell in the nature kingdom as the life force of all things in nature, such as minerals, plants, animals, and the four elements of earth, air, fire and water; the planets, stars, and signs of the zodiac; and hours of the day and night. Elves, brownies, goblins, gnomes, and fairies are said to be among these spirits.

knockings/rappings Tapping sounds said to be coming from deceased spirits in an attempt to communicate with or frighten the living.

materialization Something that appears suddenly, as if out of nowhere. In the paranormal it might be a ghost or spirit that suddenly appears to take on a physical form.

medium In the paranormal, someone who is able to convey messages between the spirits of the deceased and the spirits of the living.

messiah A leader who is regarded as a liberator or savior. In Christianity, the Messiah is Jesus Christ (c. 6 B.C.E.–c. 30 C.E.), in Judaism, it is the king who will lead the Jews back to the Holy Land of Israel and establish world peace.

near-death experience A mystical-like occurrence or sensation that individuals on the brink of death or who were dead, but brought back to life, have described which includes leaving their physical body and hovering over it as though they were a bystander.

parapsychologist One who studies mental phenomena, such as telepathy or extrasensory perception, the mind/body connection, and other psi or paranormal factors that cannot be explained by known scientific principles.

phenomena Occurrences, persons, or things that are strange, extraordinary, or considered to be unusual and significant.

precognition The ability to foresee or to know what is going to happen in the future, before it occurs, especially if based on extrasensory perception.

psychokinesis The ability to make objects move or to in some way affect them without using anything but mental powers.

schizophrenia A severe psychiatric disorder which can include symptoms of withdrawal or detachment from reality, delusions, hallucinations, emotional instability, and intellectual disturbances or illogical patterns of thinking to various degrees. The term comes from Greek words meaning "split mind."

seance A meeting or gathering of people in which a spiritualist makes attempts to communicate with the spirits of deceased persons, or a gathering to receive spiritualistic messages.

shaman A religious or spiritual leader, usually possessing special powers such as that of prophecy, and healing, and acts as an intermediary between the physical and spiritual realms.

spirit control The guide that mediums contact to receive messages from deceased spirits, or another name for spirit guide as used in mediumship.

spirit guide A nonphysical being or entity which possibly can be an angel, the higher self, the spirit of a deceased person, a higher group mind, or a highly evolved being whose purpose is to help, guide, direct, and protect the individual.

stigmata Marks on a person's body resembling the Crucifixion wounds suffered by Jesus Christ (c. 6 B.C.E.–c. 30 C.E.) during his Crucifixion on the cross.

telepathy Communication from one person's mind to another without the use of speech, writing, or any other signs or symbols, but through extrasensory means.

totem An animal, bird, plant, or any other natural object that is revered as a personal or tribal symbol.

transference The process of change that happens when one person or place is transferred to another.

CHAPTER 3
RELIGIOUS PHENOMENA

This chapter will explore a number of the phenomena that surround a great variety of religious beliefs, from the veneration of sacred objects to the expectation of miracles, from the power of prayer to heal to the judgment of ecclesiastical tribunals to cause suffering.

ANTICHRIST

APOCALYPSE

APPARITIONS OF HOLY FIGURES

ARMAGGEDON

COSMIC CONSCIOUSNESS

DEMONS

DEVIL'S MARK

ECSTASY

EXORCISM

FAITH HEALING

GUARDIAN ANGELS

ILLUMINATION

INQUISITION

MIRACLES

POSSESSION

POWER OF PRAYER

THE RAPTURE

SHROUD OF TURIN

666

SNAKE HANDLING

STIGMATA

VIRGIN OF GUADALUPE

VISIONS

WEEPING STATUES AND ICONS

Introduction

In recent years there has been a tremendous surge of interest in both organized religion and expressions of individual spirituality. People speak freely of their **guardian angels,** their belief in life after death, their efforts to elevate their consciousness, and the **power of prayer.** Others are concerned about being under psychic attack by **demons** when they learn from the mainstream media that the number of **exorcisms** of those who are suffering demonic **possession** has been rising steadily. In a Gallup poll released on June 10, 2001, the administrators of the survey found that 54 percent of Americans believe in spiritual or **faith healing;** 41 percent acknowledge that people can be possessed by the devil; 50 percent accept the reality of ESP, or **extrasensory perception;** 32 percent believe in the power of **prophecy;** and 38 percent agree that **ghosts** and **spirits** exist.

In a recent survey, it was revealed that 41 percent believe people can be possessed by the devil and 38 percent believe ghosts and spirits exist.

In the fall of 1988 the editors at *Better Homes and Gardens* conducted a survey of their readers' spiritual lives. The editors were astonished when the subject drew more than 80,000 responses, and more than 10,000 people attached thoughtful letters expressing remarkable strength of feeling. Of the 80,000 readers who responded to the survey: 86 percent believed in miracles; 89 percent in eternal life; 30 percent in a spirit world; and 13 percent accepted the possibility that beings in the spirit world can make contact with the living.

In December 1997, the editors of *Self* magazine published the results of a similar survey conducted with their readership: 91 percent believed in miracles; 87 percent, angels; 85 percent, spirits; 82 percent, heaven; 65 percent, hell; and 65 percent, the devil.

Some observers of the contemporary scene attribute this great spiritual questing to the advent of the millennium and the concerns of certain Christians about an approaching **Apocalypse,** when people will be called to account for their misdeeds. Others say that large masses of people have become disillusioned with the tenets of science and the tools of technology that promised an earthly paradise, but cannot answer the basic questions of why humans are here and what they are to do with themselves in their allotted time on the planet.

In *Why Religion Matters: The Future of Faith in an Age of Disbelief* (2001), Huston Smith states that a people with only science to guide them are morally lost. Smith readily grants that the scientific method is "nearly perfect" for understanding the physical aspects of human life. "But it is a radical [rather] limited viewfinder in its inability to offer values, morals, and meanings that are at the center of our lives," Smith says. The practice of science can deepen the understanding of the physical world, "but it can never answer the questions about our moral universe that have troubled our ancestors since the beginning of time—who are we, why are we here, and how should we behave while we are here?"

Why should there be such a dramatic spiritual awakening at this time? Dr. Walter Houston Clark, professor emeritus at Andover Theological Seminary, saw it beginning in the early 1970s. At that time (c. 1972) he said, "I think the best explanation is the obvious starvation of humankind's nonrational needs over many decades. Materialism, competition, power politics, and human exploitation can be endured only so long before they begin to make nonsense to sensitive natures jaded by the persistent denial of their essential longing, the longing for a living God and a vital religious experience."

All of the highly varied religious phenomena described in this chapter have one thing in common: They all involve human beings responding to an individual mystical experience. Whether one is soaring to the heart of the universe after receiving **cosmic consciousness,** standing in awe before a **weeping statue** of Mother Mary, or strengthening the spirit to resist the temptations of the fallen angels, a true blending of the phenomenon with the

I n the U.S., some clergypersons believe Satan and his demons appear to be busier than ever in the new millennium—and they admit that the ancient rites of exorcism are being performed in increasingly large numbers to combat the evil machinations of the powers of darkness.

While the Roman Catholic Church is most noted for conducting exorcisms, their clergy is actually extremely cautious in approving the rites. Once official approval has been granted to conduct an exorcism, the rites themselves may take hours, days, or weeks to complete. But in spite of their careful scrutiny of all claims of satanic possession, the church has admitted to having ten official exorcists on duty in the United States today; ten years ago, they had only one.

Most experts agree the majority of exorcisms currently being conducted in the Americas are being performed by Protestant churches and sects. Approximately 600 evangelical exorcism ministries are in operation, in addition to numerous exorcisms being conducted by Pentecostals and other Christian sects. These religious bodies see Satan as an active force. They perceive a heightened campaign of evil in what they believe are the fast-approaching End-Times before the Second Coming of Christ. They believe the devil and his demonic hordes must put in overtime to lead as many people astray as possible before the Lord conquers Satan and casts him into the pit of fire.

In some of these exorcisms, little more is done than prayers for deliverance of the afflicted and the laying on of hands to heal the victim of demonic influences. In others, the so-called exorcism may be a kind of counseling session in which the troubled individual is advised how best to escape the lures of the demons of lust, greed, anger, and so forth. In still other instances, those accused of being possessed might be tied to chairs and subjected to teams of exorcists praying and screaming for the demons to retreat. Some observers have compared the techniques of some of the more elaborate exorcisms to a kind of psychodrama in which the possessed is able to enact a kind of release of guilt and feel reborn and freed of sin.

DEMONIC INVASIONS

While not all contemporary clergypersons believe in the possibility of demon possession, but prefer to speak of mental health problems that may trouble certain parishioners, most still concede that there appears to be an intelligence of some kind that directs evil in the world. They caution that those who suspect possession in themselves or others are not gullible or that they open themselves to the suggestion of demonic possession when other mundane explanations may exist.

SOURCES:

Cuneo, Michael W. *American Exorcism: Expelling Demons in the Land of Plenty.* New York: Doubleday, 2001.

individual psyche occurs during the awesome splendor of a mystical experience.

In his *Varieties of Religious Experience* (1902), **William James** (1842–1912) states his view that personal religion has its origin in the mystical consciousness. "The mother sea and fountainhead of all religions lie in the mystical experiences of the individual, taking the word mystical in a very wide sense. All theologies and all ecclesiasticisms are secondary growths superimposed."

At the same time that men and women are examining various aspects of religious phenomena and evaluating them in terms of their own spiritual quest, scientists around the world are assessing the individual mystical experience and asking whether spirituality cannot be explained in terms of neural transmitters, neural networks, and brain chemistry. Perhaps that feeling of transcendence that mystics describe could be the decreased activity in the brain's parietal lobe, which helps regulate the sense of self and physical orientation. Perhaps, these neurotheologians theorize, the human brain is wired for God.

And the great mystery will always remain. Is it the wiring of the human brain that creates God and the mystical experience? Or was it God who created this brain wiring so humans might experience the splendor within and all religious phenomena?

ANTICHRIST

The Antichrist, as the word implies, is one who opposes Christ or who falsely presents himself or herself as Christ. Although the word is most commonly associated with the apocalyptic New Testament book of Revelation, the word "Antichrist" is nowhere to be found within its text. In 1 John 2:18, the epistle writer declares that the "enemy of Christ" has manifested and that many false teachers have infiltrated the Christian ranks. In verse 22, John names as the Antichrist anyone who would deny Jesus as the Christ and the Father and the Son, and in 2 John verse 7 he declares that there are many deceivers already at work among the faithful.

The concept of an earthly opponent or antagonist of the Messiah also appears in the Old Testament. The earliest form of the Antichrist is probably the warrior King Gog, who appears in the Book of Ezekiel and who reappears in Revelation along with his kingdom of Magog, representing those earthly minions of Satan who will attack the people of God in a final great battle of good versus evil. In Jewish eschatology, writings about the "end of days" state that the armies of Gog and Magog will eventually be defeated and the world will finally be at peace.

Throughout the Bible the Antichrist bears many titles: Son of Perdition, Man of Sin, Man of Lawlessness, the Prince of Destruction/Abomination, and the Beast. The prophet Daniel describes the man in great detail: He shall be an evil king who will "...exalt himself and magnify himself above every god and shall speak outrageous things against the God of gods, and shall prosper until the indignation is accomplished: for that which has been determined shall come to pass. Neither shall he regard the God of his fathers, nor the desire of women, nor regard any god: for he shall magnify himself above all. But in his estate he shall (secretly) honor a god of forces and a god whom his fathers never knew. To these he will worship with gold and silver and with precious stones and pleasant things. Thus shall he do in his fortress with a strange god, whom he shall acknowledge and increase with glory; and he shall cause them to rule over many and shall divide the land for gain" (Daniel 11:36).

St. Paul, writing in 2 Thessalonians 2:3, had a similar vision concerning the arrogant and evil king: "The man of sin...who opposes and exalts himself above all that is called God or that is worshipped; so that he as God sits in the temple of God, displaying himself as if being God...for the mystery of lawlessness is already at work in the world: only he who now restrains (the coming of the Antichrist) will do so.... And then shall that Wicked [one] be revealed, whom the Lord will consume with the spirit of his mouth.... Destroying him whose coming is in harmony with the working of Satan with all power and signs and false miracles...."

In both the prophecies of Daniel and John the Revelator, the evil king, the Antichrist, is associated with 10 rulers who give their power and allegiance to him in order to form a short-lived empire of bloodshed and destruction. "And the ten horns of this kingdom are ten kings that shall arise: and another shall rise after them, and he shall be diverse…and speak great words against the most high God and shall wear down the saints of the Highest One and think to make changes in times and laws: and they shall be given into his hand for three and one half years" (Daniel 7:24). "And there are seven kings: five are fallen, and one is, and the other is not yet come; and when he comes, he must continue only for a short time" (Revelation 17:10).

In Matthew 24:3–44, Jesus (c. 6 B.C.E.–c. 30 C.E.) speaks to his disciples at great length concerning the false Messiahs and prophets who will deceive many people with their rumors about the end of the world. He makes reference to the prophet Daniel and his warnings concerning the end times and the Antichrist, and he admonishes the disciples not to chase after false teachers who will produce great miracles and signs to trick God's chosen ones. No one knows when the Son of Man shall appear again coming on the clouds of heaven, Jesus tells them, not even the angels.

Although Jesus makes it clear that no one knows the hour or day of his Second Coming, for many centuries now certain Christian clergy and scholars have steadfastly associated the rise of the Antichrist to earthly power as a kind of catalyst that would set in motion **Armageddon,** the last final battle between good and evil, the ultimate clash between the armies of Jesus Christ and Satan. Throughout the centuries, Christians have attempted to determine the Antichrist from among the powerful and ruthless leaders of their day. Ever since the Protestant Reformation, the pope has been a favorite of Evangelicals for the ignominious title. While many of the pontiffs in the Middle Ages did exercise great power over the rulers and the people of the emerging European nations, contemporary popes wield little political influence, surely none that would place them in world-threatening positions.

Aleister Crowley (1875–1947) of the Order of the Golden Dawn. (CORBIS CORPORATION)

There have been such men as **Aleister Crowley** (1875–1947), who actually appeared to seek the position by calling himself the Beast and **666.** The numerical value of Franklin Delano Roosevelt's (1882–1945) name reportedly added up to 666, and since he held the office of president of the United States for 12 years—and during the Great Depression and World War II—many of his conservative Christian critics began thinking of him as the Antichrist. And even the former President Ronald Wilson Reagan (1911–), had certain dissenters calling attention to the fact that he had six letters in each of his three names—6-6-6.

In recent decades, the term of Antichrist has been applied to so many individuals in popular culture that it has lost much of its meaning and its sense of menace. During the Gulf War in 1992, Saddam Hussein (1937–) received many votes for the title of the Beast, especially when he announced plans to begin to restore the ruins of Babylon to a splendor that would approximate the wicked city's former glory. Before Hussein, there were many nominations for the Ayatollah Khomeini (1900–1989) to don the mantle. But later when certain extremists named President Reagan, former U.S. Secretary of State Henry Kissinger (1923–), and even the children's television icon Barney the Dinosaur as the Antichrist, the word began losing its threat for the general population. However, those Christians who believe strongly in the coming time of Tribulation, the Apocalypse, the **Rapture,** and the great final battle of good versus evil at Armageddon, firmly believe that the title of Antichrist maintains its fear factor and that those signs and warnings of the Beast as prophesied in the book of Revelation should be seriously heeded.

❧ Delving Deeper

Crim, Keith, gen. ed. *The Perennial Dictionary of World Religions*. San Francisco: HarperSanFrancisco, 1989.

Lindsey, Hal, with C. C. Carlson. *The Late Great Planet Earth*. New York: Bantam Books, 1978.

McGinn, Bernard. *Antichrist: Two Thousand Years of the Human Fascination with Evil*. San Francisco: HarperSanFrancisco, 1994.

Unterman, Alan. *Dictionary of Jewish Lore and Legend*. New York: Thames and Hudson, 1991.

Apocalypse

In apocalyptic visions, prophets see ahead to the end time. Humankind's salvation lies in the future, and the meaning of the present is obscured in the chaos of survival on the Earth's plane. In apocalyptic thought, humankind's destiny is viewed as steadily unfolding according to a great design of God. The present is a time of trial and tribulation, and its meaning will only be made clear in the last days before the final judgment occurs. Placing the ultimate revelation of God at the end time seems to imply a history for God, as well as for his creation—or at least an evolution, or transformation, from one sphere of activity to another.

In the Jewish tradition, apocalyptic thought presupposes a universal history in which the Divine Author of that history will reveal and manifest his secrets in a dramatic end time that with finality will establish the God of Israel as the one true God. The "end of days" (*acharit ha-yamin*) is bound up with the coming of the Messiah, but before his appearance governments will become increasingly corrupt, religious schools will become heretical, the wisdom of the scribes and teachers will become blasphemous, young people will shame their elders, and members of families will turn upon one another. Then, just prior to the arrival of the Messiah, the righteous of Israel shall defeat the armies of evil that have gathered under the banner of Gog and Magog, and the exiles shall return to the Holy Land. The world will be at peace and all people will recognize the one true God. With the advent of the Messiah will come the great Day of Judgment in which the dead shall rise from their graves to begin a new life. During the period known as the World to Come (*Olam Haba*), the righteous will join the Messiah in partaking of a great banquet in which all foods, even those previously judged impure, shall be declared kosher. All the many nations of the world will communicate in one language; the Angel of Death will be slain by God; trees and crops will produce fresh harvests each month; the warmth of the sun shall heal the sick; and the righteous will be nourished forever by the radiance of God.

To most orthodox Christians, the profound meaning of the New Testament is that Jesus Christ (c. 6 B.C.E.–c. 30 C.E.) will one day return in the Last Days and his Second Coming will prompt the resurrection of the dead and the Final Judgment. The heart of the gospels is eschatological, or end-oriented. The essential theme of Jesus and the apostles is that the last stage of history, the end time, was being entered into with his appearance. In Matthew 24:3–44,

Jesus speaks to his disciples at great length concerning false Messiahs and prophets who will deceive many people with their rumors about the end of the world. He makes reference to the prophet Daniel and his warnings concerning the end times and the **Antichrist,** and he admonishes the disciples not to chase after false teachers who will produce great miracles and signs to trick God's chosen ones. No one knows when the Son of Man shall appear again coming on the clouds of heaven, Jesus tells them, not even the angels.

As in Jewish apocalyptic tradition, Christians also recognize that there must come the terrible time when the Antichrist, summoning great powers of evil, will triumph for a period over the righteous believers and that there will be one last awful clash between the forces of good under the banner of Christ and his angels and the minions of evil under the banner of Satan. Before that final battle in the valley of **Armageddon,** the faithful may look for various signs to alert them that the end time, the Apocalypse, has begun. Drawing upon the apocalyptic traditions of his Jewish background, John the Revelator, presents in Revelation, the last book in the New Testament, a guidebook for the Christian on what to expect during the Apocalypse, the time of Tribulation. Specifically, the book was written for the members of the churches of Ephesus, Smyrna, Pergamum, Thyatira, Sardis, Philadelphia, and Laodicea in order to prepare them for what John believed to be a fast-approaching time of persecution and the return of Jesus Christ.

The first of Seven Seals to be opened (Revelation 6:1–2) by the Lamb (Christ) discloses a conquering king astride a white horse, the first of the Four Horsemen of the Apocalypse. Scholars disagree whether this triumphant king represents Christ returning to do battle with Satan or the Antichrist emerging to summon the forces of evil to oppose Christ and his angelic army. The Second Seal (6:3–4) reveals the red horse, representing civil war; the third, the black horse, symbolizing famine (6:5–6); the fourth, the pale horse, representing the suffering that follows war and famine. The Fifth Seal to be opened by the Lamb yields a vision of the persecution of the

Church throughout history and during the Last Days. When the Sixth Seal is revealed, it displays the coming signs of a great Day of Wrath at hand when there will be Earthly upheavals, a darkened sun, stars falling from the heavens, mountains and islands removed, and more strife and revolution throughout the nations. The Seventh and final Seal releases seven trumpets that sound the triumphant blast signaling the approach of the final and everlasting victory of Christ over the kingdoms of the world.

But rising out of the abyss to block Christ's triumph at Armageddon is a monstrous army of demons, some resembling locusts and scorpions, others a repulsive mixture of humans, horses, and lions. These demons are soon joined by 200,000 serpentine-leonine horsemen capable of belching fire, smoke, and brimstone. Led by Satan, the once-trusted angel who led the rebellion against God in Heaven, the Prince of the World sets his legions upon the faithful to make their lives as miserable as possible in the end time. To make matters even more complex for those who serve God, the Antichrist appears on the scene pretending to be the Lamb, the Messiah. John the Revelator is told that this man, this beast in lamb's clothing, can be recognized by a name, the letters of which, when regarded as numbers, total 666.

The Four Riders of the Apocalypse. (FORTEAN PICTURE LIBRARY)

Although the term "Antichrist" is frequently used by those Christians who adhere to the New Testament book of Revelation as a literal guide to the end of days which they feel is here, the word is nowhere to be found within its text. Traditionally, it was believed for many centuries that the apostle John, the one especially loved by Jesus, was the author of Revelation. Contemporary scholarship generally disputes that St. John was the lonely visionary on the Island of Patmos who foresaw the time of great tribulation. It is, however, likely that the apostle John is the first to mention the Antichrist. In 1 John 2:18, he declares that the "enemy of Christ" has manifested and that many false teachers have infiltrated the Christian ranks. In verse 22, John names as the Antichrist anyone who would deny Jesus as the Christ and the Father and the Son as the Antichrist, and in 2 John verse

7 he declares that there are many deceivers already at work among the faithful.

According to Revelation, Christ and his angelic armies of light destroy the forces of darkness at Armageddon in the final battle of good versus evil. Babylon, the False Prophet, and the Beast (the Antichrist) are dispatched to their doom, and Satan, the Dragon, is bound in a pit for a thousand years. With Satan imprisoned and chained, the Millennium, the Thousand Years of peace and harmony, begins.

Although Christ's Second Coming is said to be mentioned over 300 times in the New Testament, the only references to the Millennium are found in Revelation 20:2–7. Christian scholars disagree whether or not there will be an initial resurrection of the just at the advent of the Millennium and a second one a

thousand years later immediately prior to the Final Day of Judgment. While many Christian theologians link Christ's Second Coming, the Resurrection, and Judgment Day all occurring after the defeat of Satan and the beginning of the thousand years of peace and harmony, others maintain that the resurrection of the dead and the final judgment of God will not take place until after the Millennium has come to a close.

For some rather incomprehensible reason, Satan is released from the pit at the conclusion of the Millennium; and true to his nature, he makes a furious attempt to regain his earthly kingdom. His former allies, the Beast (the Antichrist), the False Prophet, and the hordes of Babylon, were destroyed at Armageddon, but there were some demons who escaped annihilation at the great battle who stand ready to serve their master. In addition to these evil creatures, Satan summons Gog and his armies of the Magog nations to join them in attacking the saints and the righteous fol-lowers of God. Although the vast multitude of vile and wicked servants of evil and grotesque monsters quickly surround the godly men and women, God's patience with the rebellious angel has come to an end. Fire blasts down from heaven, engulfing and destroying the satanic legions and the armies of Gog and Magog. Satan himself is sent to spend the rest of eternity in a lake of fire.

ALTHOUGH *Christ's Second Coming is said to be mentioned more than 300 times in the New Testament, the only references to the Millennium are found in Revelation 20:2–7.*

And now (Revelation 20:11–15) comes the Final Judgment, the time when God shall judge the secrets of all men and women (Romans 2:16). This Judgment will be complete. Every person from every age and nation will be there. And there shall only be classes: the Saved and the Lost. The Book of Life will have the names of the Saved. For those whose names do not appear on those heavenly records, there is the final doom: to be sentenced to join Satan and his angels in the place where the fire is never quenched. When the Judgment has been completed, the first heaven and Earth shall pass away and a new heaven and new Earth shall be established for those Saved to occupy with their glorified, incorruptible, spiritual bodies.

❖ DELVING DEEPER

Abanes, Richard. *End-Time Visions.* Nashville, Tenn.: Broadman & Holman, 1998.

Cohn, Norman. *The Pursuit of the Millennium.* New York: Oxford University Press, 1970.

Goetz, William R. *Apocalypse Next.* Camp Hill, Penn.: Horizon Books, 1996.

Shaw, Eva. *Eve of Destruction: Prophecies, Theories and Preparations for the End of the World.* Chicago: Contemporary Books, 1995.

Unterman, Alan. *Dictionary of Jewish Lore and Legend.* New York: Thames and Hudson, 1991.

Wheeler, John Jr. *Earth's Two-Minute Warning: Today's Bible-Predicted Signs of the End Times.* North Canton, Ohio: Leader Co., 1996.

APPARITIONS OF HOLY FIGURES

I n the twelfth century, St. Francis of Assisi (1181–1226) was credited with seeing an apparition of Jesus Christ (c. 6 B.C.E.–c. 30 C.E.). St. Catherine of Siena (1347–1380) reported seeing Jesus in the fourteenth century. The Catholic devotion to the Sacred Heart as a symbol of love was begun in the seventeenth century after an apparition of Jesus Christ had been seen by the French nun St. Margaret Mary (1647–1690).

At the height of his illness in December 1954, Pope Pius XII (1876–1958) had a vision of Jesus in which the Savior spoke to him in "His own true voice." The Vatican kept Pius's revelation secret for nearly a year, then through the "affectionate indiscretion" of one of the Holy Father's close friends, the magazine *Oggi* broke the story in its November 19, 1955, issue. On December 12, the Vatican confirmed the remarkable disclosure, declaring the vision not to have been a dream. Sources near to the pope said that he had been wide awake and lucid.

Vatican authorities said that there had not been a more vivid or specific vision of Jesus since the days of the Apostles than that reported by the pontiff. According to Church records, Christ had appeared to a pope only once before, and that was in the fourth century, when Pope Sylvester (d. 335) consecrated the mother church of St. John Lateran in Rome after Emperor Constantine had ended the brutal persecutions of the Christians.

Although devout Christian laypersons occasionally report apparitions of various saints and the image of Jesus, by far the greatest number of apparitions of religious figures are those of Mother Mary. Pope John Paul II (1920–) has proclaimed his firm belief that it was a number of significant apparitions of Mother Mary that brought about the end of communism in the former Soviet Union, thus fulfilling a prophetic pronouncement to one of the three children to whom she appeared six times between May 13 and October 13, 1917, in Fatima, Portugal.

In his book *Russia Will Be Converted* (1950), John Haffert detailed a series of apparitions of Mary in the 1940s that began eroding communist doctrine and converting thousands to Roman Catholicism. In one instance, a young girl was said to have beheld the apparition of a beautiful lady who told her to return to the same spot for 15 days. After having received visions on each of these successive days, the girl was presented with the materialization of seven perfect rose petals. It was claimed that the petals did not fade or lose their fragrance. It was also said that a botanist declared that the petals could not have come from an ordinary Earth rose.

Ann Matter, a specialist in the history of Christianity at the University of Pennsylvania, has commented that contemporary times constitute the most active age of devotion to Mother Mary, not the twelfth century or the

On April 2, 1968, two mechanics working in a city garage across the street from St. Mary's Church of Zeitoun, Egypt, were startled to see what appeared to be a nun dressed in white standing on top of the large dome at the center of the roof. Fearful that something might happen to the sister, one of the men ran into the church to get a priest, the other telephoned for a police emergency squad.

When the priest ran from the church to look up at the dome, he was the first to recognize it as a manifestation of Mother Mary. The image of the Blessed Mother remained in full view of the priest, the two mechanics, and a growing crowd of excited witnesses for several minutes, then disappeared.

The news of the Holy Mother's visitation spread rapidly from Zeitoun, a suburb of Cairo, to the greater metropolitan population of over six million. While the religious makeup of Cairo is largely Muslim, there is a fairly large Coptic Catholic minority. Thousands began to gather at the majestic church of Zeitoun at Tomanbey Street and Khalil Lane to see for themselves the place where the Queen of Heaven had come to Earth.

Amazingly, for the next three years, the visions of the Holy Mother manifested sporadically atop the dome of the church. Millions claimed to witness the visitations, and numerous photographs of the spiritual phenomenon can be found on the Internet.

Although thousands of people claimed miraculous cures as they looked upward at the glowing figure of the Holy Mother, no one announced receiving any special messages from her. No visionaries ever claimed to have received any warnings of impending disasters or relayed any admonitions from Mother Mary to repent or to cease sinning.

MOTHER MARY APPEARS IN EGYPT

SOURCES:

Apparitions of Virgin Mary. http:// www.geocities.com/Athens /7084 /stmaridx. htm, 11 October 2001.

Our Lady of Zeitoun. http://www.zeitoun.org/, 11 October 2001.

Zeitoun Apparition. http://www.science-frontiers.com, 11 October 2001.

Virgin Mary and Jesus
vision in Hungary.
(KAROLY LIGETI/FORTEAN
PICTURE LIBRARY)

Paris, France: The Holy Mother appeared to a nun in 1830 and asked her to fashion a medal to commemorate the Immaculate Conception.

La Salette, France: A weeping, sorrowful Mary manifested to two peasant children on September 19, 1846, and instructed them to do penance for their sins.

Lourdes, France: Identifying herself as the Immaculate Conception, Mary appeared 18 times to 14-year-old Bernadette Soubrious between February 11 and July 16, 1858. The waters of the miraculous spring that appeared according to Mary's promise are world famous for their healing powers.

Fatima, Portugal: Mother Mary appeared to three children near Fatima, instructing them to say their rosary frequently. During her six visits between May 13 and October 13, 1917, Mary issued a number of prophecies, many of which are said to be held secret by the Vatican.

Beauraling, Belgium: Between November 29, 1932, and January 3, 1933, five children at a convent school experienced a remarkable 33 encounters with Mother Mary in the school garden.

Banneaux, Belgium: Mother Mary appeared to an 11-year-old girl eight times between January 15 and March 2, 1933, in the garden of her parents' humble cottage.

In addition to the above listed Vatican-recognized meetings with Mother Mary, there are a number of other encounters with her that have been highly publicized and may even be better known than many of those on the approved roster.

Village of Knock, County Mayo, Ireland: In 1879, in the midst of terrible famine, devout villagers gathered in their church to ask for deliverance from hunger. Then, at one end of the church, a glowing light began to form that soon revealed the figures of Mother Mary, St. Joseph, St. John, and a lamb surrounded by golden stars. A short time after the villagers had reported their collective vision, many ill, diseased, or crippled people who visited the church began to claim miraculous cures as they knelt at the statue of Mother Mary. Since that

ninth century, but "right now." Matter stated that the interest in apparitions of the Holy Mother has been building for the past 150 years, "with more and more reports of visions of Mary in more and more places."

In the past few decades, apparitions of Mother Mary and her attending angels have been seen in places as varied as Betania, Venezuela; Cuapa, Nicaragua; Akita, Japan; Damascus, Syria; San Nicholas, Argentina; Cairo, Egypt; Naju, Korea; and Hrouchiv, Ukraine. In spite of an increasing number of apparitions around the world, the Roman Catholic hierarchy officially recognizes only seven appearances of Mother Mary:

Guadalupe, Mexico: In 1531, a Native American named Juan Diego saw Mother Mary four times and was given a miraculously created serape as evidence of her heavenly visitation.

Virgin Mary appearing before Bernadette Soubirous (1844–1879) at Lourdes. (FORTEAN PICTURE LIBRARY)

time, the small village of Knock has come to be called the "Irish Lourdes."

Garabandal, Spain: A series of ecstatic visions of Mother Mary began for four children one Sunday after Mass in 1961. The visitations continued until 1965 and produced numerous accurate prophecies and astonishing **miracles.**

THE *Roman Catholic hierarchy officially recognizes only seven appearances of Mother Mary.*

Zeitoun, Egypt: As many as a million witnesses may have glimpsed the figure of the glowing Madonna standing, kneeling, or praying beside a cross on the roof of St. Mary's Coptic Church. Miraculous cures manifested among the pilgrims from 1968 to 1971.

Medjugorje, Yugoslavia: In 1981, six children saw Mother Mary holding the infant Jesus near the village. The holy figure appeared on an almost daily basis for five months, leaving behind a continuing legacy of miraculous healings.

Bayside, New York: From 1970 to the present day, the "Bayside Seeress," Veronica Lueken, issues pronouncements from Mother Mary against the spiritual abuses of contemporary society.

Conyers, Georgia: Since 1987, Nancy Fowler has been receiving daily messages from Mother Mary. On the thirteenth of each month, beginning in 1990, apparitions of Mary and Jesus began to appear. By 1993 as many as 50,000 pilgrims could be expected to gather for each month's demonstration of the divine.

Hollywood, Florida: A devout Catholic who had fled to Florida from Castro's Cuba in 1967, Rosa Lopez was left bedridden after a series of painful surgeries in 1982. In 1992, after making a pilgrimage to Conyers, Georgia, Lopez received a healing miracle; and in 1993, Jesus manifested to her and proclaimed that she, too, had been chosen to be a messenger for Mother Mary. Soon the Divine Mother began conveying messages to Rosa Lopez to be

shared with the thousands of faithful who gather outside her modest home.

Roman Catholic scholarship holds that there are two kinds of visions: One is the imaginative vision, in which the object seen is but a mental concept or symbol, such as Jacob's Ladder leading up to heaven. St. Teresa of Avila (1515–1582) had numerous visions, including images of Christ, which Church authorities have judged were of this symbolic kind of vision. The other is the corporeal vision, in which the figure seen is externally present or in which a supernatural power has so modified the retina of the eye so as to produce the effect of three-dimensional solidarity.

By no means are Roman Catholics the only Christians who have religious visions and see apparitions of holy figures. In October of 2000, a Lutheran minister and a sociologist in Minnesota released their study that more than 30 percent of 2,000 Christians surveyed said that they had had dramatic visions, heard heavenly voices, or experienced prophetic dreams.

In April 2001, details of research conducted at the University of Wales detected a common core to religious experiences that crosses boundaries of culture and faith. An analysis of 6,000 such experiences revealed that Christians may describe a religious experience as an encounter with Jesus, Mary, or an angel; Muslims often interpret the phenomenon as the presence of an angel; and Jews describe the event as a sign of insight or an experience of God.

With all the interest in spiritual experiences, scientists have begun asking if spirituality can be better explained in terms of neural networks, neurotransmitters, and brain chemistry. Philadelphia scientist Andrew Newberg, who wrote the book *Why God Won't Go Away* (2001), says that the human brain is set up in such a way as to have spiritual and religious experiences. Michael Persinger, a professor of neuroscience at Laurentian University in Sudbury, Ontario, conducts experiments with a helmet-like device that runs a weak electromagnetic signal around the skulls of volunteers. Persinger claims that four in five people report a mystical experience of some kind when they don his magnetic headpiece. Matthew Alper,

author of *The "God" Part of the Brain* (1998), a book about the neuroscience of belief, goes so far as to declare that dogmatic religious beliefs that insist particular faiths are unique, rather than the results of universal brain chemistry, are irrational and dangerous.

In his book *The Faith of Biology and the Biology of Faith* (2000), Robert Pollack concedes that religious experience may seem irrational to a materialistic scientist, but he argues that irrational experiences are not necessarily unreal. In fact, he states, they can be just as real, just as much a part of being human, as those things that are known through reason. Lorenzo Albacete, a Roman Catholic priest, a professor of theology at St. Joseph's Seminary in Yonkers, writes in the *New York Times Magazine* (December 18, 2000) that he is somewhat nervous about the new efforts of science to explain human spirituality: "If the religious experience is an authentic contact with a transcendent Mystery, it not only will but should exceed the grasp of science. Otherwise, what about it would be transcendent?"

Daniel Batson, a University of Kansas psychologist who studies the effect of religion on people, states that the brain is the hardware through which religion is experienced. "To say that the brain produces religion is like saying a piano produces music," he commented.

Numerous believers in the transcendent and in the possibility of experiencing religious apparitions argue that if God created the universe, wouldn't it make sense that he would wire our brains so it would be possible to have mystical experiences?

✤ DELVING DEEPER

Begley, Sharon. "Religion and the Brain." *Newsweek*, 7 May 2001, pp. 50–57.

Cranston, Ruth. *The Miracle of Lourdes*. New York: McGraw-Hill, 1955.

Delaney, John J, ed. *A Woman Clothed with the Sun*. Garden City, N.Y.: Doubleday, 1961.

Vietnamese Roman Catholic nuns in a commemorative anniversary procession of the Virgin Mary apparition in Vietnam. (AP/WIDE WORLD PHOTOS)

Kirkwood, Annie. *Mary's Message of Hope*. Nevada City, Calif.: Blue Dolphin Publishing, 1995.

Sparrow, Scott G. *I Am with You Always: True Stories of Encounters with Jesus*. New York: Bantam Books, 1995.

Steiger, Brad, and Sherry Hansen Steiger. *Mother Mary Speaks to Us*. New York: Dutton, 1996; Signet, 1997.

ARMAGEDDON

In Revelation 16:16, the battlefield designated where blasphemers, unclean spirits, and devils join forces for the final great battle of the ages between their evil hordes and Christ and his faithful angelic army is Armageddon, "the mound of Megiddo." The inspiration for such a choice of battlegrounds was quite likely an obvious one for John the Revelator, for it has been said that more blood has been shed around the hill of Megiddo than any other single spot on Earth. Located 10 miles southwest of Nazareth at the entrance to a pass across the Carmel mountain range, it stands on the main highway between Asia and Africa and in a key position between the Euphrates and the Nile rivers, thus providing a traditional meeting place of armies from the East and from the West. For thousands of years, the Valley of Mageddon, now known as the Jezreel Valley, had been the site where great battles had been waged and the fate of empires decided. Thothmes III, whose military strategies made Egypt a world empire, proclaimed the taking of Megiddo to be worth the conquering of a thousand cities. During World War I in 1918, the British general Allenby broke the power of the Turkish army at Megiddo.

Most scholars agree that the word "Armageddon" is a Greek corruption of the Hebrew *Har-Megiddo*, "the mound of Megiddo," but they debate exactly when the designation of Armageddon was first used. The city of Megiddo was abandoned sometime during the Persian period (539 B.C.E.–332 B.C.E.), and the small villages established to the south were known by other names. It could well have been that John the Revelator, writing in the Jewish apocalyptic tradition of a final conflict between the forces of light and darkness, was well aware of the bloody tradition of the hill of Megiddo and was inspired by the ruins of the city on its edge; but by the Middle Ages, theologians appeared to employ Armageddon as a spiritual concept without any conscious association with the Valley of Megiddo. Armageddon simply stood for the promised time when the returning Christ and his legions of angels would gather to defeat the assembled armies of darkness. During that same period, those church scholars who persisted in naming an actual geographical location for the final battle between good and evil theorized that it might occur at places in the Holy Land as widely separated as Mount Tabor, Mount Zion, Mount Carmel, or Mount Hermon.

In the fourteenth century, the Jewish geographer Estori Ha-Farchi suggested that the roadside village of Lejjun might be the location of the biblical Megiddo. Ha-Farchi pointed out that Lejjun was the Arabic form of Legio, the old Roman name for the place. In the early nineteenth century, American biblical scholar Edwin Robinson traveled to the area of Palestine that was held at that time by the Ottoman Empire and became convinced that Ha-Farchi was correct in his designation of the site as the biblical Megiddo. Later explorers and archaeologists determined that the ruins of the ancient city lay about a mile north of Lejjun at what had been renamed by the Ottoman government as the mound of Tell el-Mutasellim, "the hill of the governor."

Today, tourists visit Tel Megiddo in great numbers, attracted by the site's apocalyptic mystique and the old battleground's significance as the place where the fate of ancient empires was decided with the might of sword and spear. The Israel National Parks Authority works in close coordination with the Megiddo Expedition and the Ename Center for Public Archaeology of Belgium in offering visitors a dramatic perspective of the history of Armageddon.

❋ DELVING DEEPER

Bloomfield, Arthur E. *Before the Last Battle—Armageddon*. Minneapolis: Dimension Books, Bethany Fellowship, 1971.

Goetz, William R. *Apocalypse Next*. Camp Hill, Penn.: Horizon Books, 1996.

Shaw, Eva. *Eve of Destruction: Prophecies, Theories and Preparations for the End of the World*. Chicago: Contemporary Books, 1995.

Silberman, Neil Asher, Israel Finkelstein, David Ussishkin, and Baruch Halpern. "Digging at Armageddon." *Archaeology*, November/December 1999, pp. 32–39.

Unterman, Alan. *Dictionary of Jewish Lore and Legend*. New York: Thames and Hudson, 1991.

Cosmic Consciousness

In his classic work, *Cosmic Consciousness* (1901), Dr. Richard Maurice Bucke (1837–1902) did not presume to place himself in the company of the illumined individuals whose lives he examined in his book, but he did relate—in the third person—the account of his own experience. It was in the early spring at the beginning of Bucke's 36th year. He and two friends had spent the evening reading selections from such poets as William Wordsworth, Percy Bysshe Shelley, John Keats and Robert Browning, with a special emphasis on Walt Whitman. The young men had become so enraptured by their readings that they didn't part until midnight, and Bucke faced a long ride home in a horse-drawn hansom cab. He recalled that his mind was still deeply under the influence of the many inspirational ideas, images, and emotions that had been provoked by the reading and discussions of the evening. He was feeling calm and peaceful when, without any warning of any kind, "he found himself wrapped around as it were by a flame-colored cloud." For an instant, he thought of a great fire somewhere in the city, then "he knew that the light was within himself."

Upon this realization, Bucke experienced a great sense of exultation, of joyousness, "immediately followed by an intellectual illumination quite impossible to describe." It seemed as if there streamed into his brain "one momentary lightning-flash of the Brahmic Splendor" which would henceforth forever lighten his life. He saw and knew that the cosmos is not dead matter but a living presence, that the soul of man is immortal, that the universe is so built and ordered that without peradventure all things work together for the good of each and all, that the foundation principle of this world is what we call love and that the happiness of everyone is in the long run absolutely certain. Bucke would ever after insist that he learned more within the few seconds during which the illumination experience lasted than in previous years of study—and "he learned much that no study could ever have taught."

Among those historic individuals whom he saw as definitely having attained cosmic consciousness, Bucke included Gautama the Buddha (c. 563–c. 483 B.C.E.), Jesus Christ (c. 6 B.C.E.–c. 30 C.E.), Paul (d. 62–68 C.E.), Plotinus (205–270 C.E.), Muhammed (c. 570–632 C.E.), Dante (1265–1321), Francis Bacon (1561–1626), Jakob Behmen (1575–1624), William Blake (1757–1827), and his own idol, Walt Whitman (1819–1892). It is apparent from the above listing that Bucke saw such illumination occurring more often to men than to women. In added chapters, he named a number of other individuals whom he considered lesser, imperfect, or doubtful recipients of cosmic consciousness—men such as Moses (fourteenth–thirteenth century B.C.E.), Gideon, Isaiah (eighth century B.C.E.), Socrates (c. 470–399 B.C.E.), Spinoza (1632–1677), **Emanuel Swedenborg** (1688–1772), Ralph Waldo Emerson (1803–1882), Henry David Thoreau (1817–1862), and Ramakrishna Paramahansa (1836–1886).

In order for one to achieve cosmic consciousness, Bucke maintains that he or she must first belong to the "top-layer of the world of Self-Consciousness." One must have a good intellect, a good physique, good health, but above all "...he must have an exalted moral nature, strong sympathies, a warm heart, courage, strong and earnest religious feelings." Bucke's extensive study of those whom he considered possessed of cosmic consciousness led him to consider the approximate age of 36 as the most propitious time in one's life to achieve this elevated state of consciousness. In summation, he found the marks of the "Cosmic Sense" to be the following:

1. Subjective light: The person suddenly finds himself or herself immersed in flame, or a rose-colored cloud, or "perhaps a sense that the mind is itself filled with such a cloud of haze."

2. Moral elevation: The recipient is bathed in an emotion of "joy, assurance, triumph, 'salvation.'" But, Bucke explains, it is not "salvation" in its usual context of deliverance from sin, but it is the realization that "no special 'salvation' is needed, the scheme upon which the world is built being itself sufficient."

3. Intellectual illumination: The recipient does not merely come to *believe*, "but he sees and knows that the cosmos, which to the self-conscious mind seems made up of dead matter, is in fact far otherwise—is in very truth a living presence."

4. Sense of immortality.

5. Loss of the fear of death.

6. Loss of the sense of sin.

7. Instantaneousness of the illumination.

8. Previous character of high intellectual, moral, and physical degree.

9. Age about 36.

10. Added charm of the illumined personality.

11. Transformation or change of appearance: Although this change may gradually pass away, Bucke writes, "In those great cases in which the illumination is intense, the change in question is also intense and may amount to a veritable transfiguration."

Bucke's primary thesis is that during the centuries of humankind's evolutionary development as a species there have been three forms of consciousness. First, there was simple consciousness, our instinctual awareness. Next came a self-consciousness, a self-awareness that allowed human beings to realize themselves as distinct individuals. And now, developing among the human species, are those individuals possessed of cosmic consciousness, a new faculty of consciousness, that will lead humankind to the pinnacle of human evolution.

Such spiritual prophets as **Rudolf Steiner** (1861–1925) also foretold that humankind is entering a "fullness" of time in which a new consciousness shall emerge. Steiner termed the new awareness "Christ consciousness," a transformative energy that would transcend orthodox Christianity. In his view, "the rest of humanity must now, in imitation of Christ, gradually develop what was present for 33 years on the Earth in one single personality."

Steiner acknowledged that spiritual history is replete with many sincere and insightful prophets and teachers who lived before the Master Jesus, but, in his opinion, they could only speak to their fellow humans by using the faculties transmitted through their earthly natures. They used the energy and the wisdom of Earth. Jesus, however, tapped into an awareness of that higher energy that comes from the realm of the Divine. He knew that a speck of this energy no larger than a mustard seed could exalt the human psyche. He knew that even the slightest infusion of this energy into a man or a woman would transform the individual into a citizen of a higher dimension of reality, the "Kingdom of God." And, at the same time, he taught that the doorway to enter such a wondrous kingdom lay within the heart of each sincere pilgrim who sought to join him there.

Author/philosopher John W. White (1939–   ) also sees Jesus as an evolutionary forerunner of the higher race that will inherit the Earth, a "race of people that will embody Cosmic Consciousness, the Christ Consciousness on a species-wide basis, rather than the sporadic individual basis seen earlier in history when an occasional avatar, such as Buddha or Jesus, appeared." White gives the name of *Homo Noeticus* (pertaining to higher consciousness) to this evolving form of humanity. "Because of their deepened awareness and self-understanding, the traditionally imposed forms, controls, and institutions of society are barriers to their full development," White says. "Their changed psychology is based on expression, not suppression, of feeling. Their motivation is cooperative and loving, not competitive and aggressive. Their sense of logic is multilevel, integrated, simultaneous.… Their identity is sharing-collective, not isolated-individual.… The conventional ways of society do not satisfy them. The search for new ways of living concerns them."

In the 1950s, Albert Einstein (1879–1955) strongly advised people that humankind had to develop a new way of thinking if they were to survive as a species. Since that time, the great genius physicist has not been alone in suggesting that humanity must develop an inner road to salvation involving a synthesis of rational understanding with the mystical experience of oneness, of unity.

In his *Mystics as a Force for Change* (1981), Dr. Sisirkumar Ghose argues that throughout the evolution of humankind, the mystics have always been among people as evidence of transitional forms within the species. Instead of accusing mystics of being dropouts and escapists, Ghose insists that "it might be fairer to say that in breaking the illusions of the cave dwellers they have been more responsible to reality and to the race…. They have been the true scientists of catharsis and conversion…. The only radical thinkers, they alone go to the root of the matter, beyond the various shaky schemes of mundane perfection, swaying between the worship of the Fatted Calf and the horror of the Organization Man."

Since many saints, prophets, and mystics have seemingly achieved a state of cosmic consciousness and/or **illumination, William James** (1842—1910), writing in his classic work *Varieties of Religious Experience* (1902), lists the features that he believes form a composite picture of "universal saintliness, the same in all religions:"

1. A feeling of being in a wider life than that of this world's selfish little interests; and a conviction, not merely intellectual, but as it were sensible, of the existence of an Ideal Power….

2. A sense of the friendly continuity of the ideal power with our own life, and willing self-surrender to its control.

3. An immense elation and freedom, as the outlines of the confining selfhood melt down.

4. A shifting of the emotional center toward loving and harmonious affections, towards "yes-yes" and away from "no," where the claims of the self-ego are concerned.

Many contemporary researchers use the term "peak experience" when referring to cosmic consciousness. In her *Ordinary People as Monks and Mystics* (1986), Marsha Sinetar writes that the peak experience is "critical to any discussion of the mystic's journey, since through it and because of it the individual gains an overarching and penetrating view into what he is at his best, into what he is when he simply 'is.' The peak experience means that the person experiences himself 'being,' rather than becoming." Sinetar goes on to state that the person undergoing such an expansion of consciousness is able to have a direct experience with "the transcendent nature of reality." The person then "enters into the Absolute, becoming one with it, if only for an instant…a life-altering instant." The peak experience expands "the individual's field of consciousness to include everything in the universe…he feels he has everything because he experiences everything within."

In his *Watcher on the Hills* (1959), Dr. Raynor C. Johnson sets forth the following three criteria to test the validity of mystical experience, those moments when one feels that he or she has touched "the transcendent nature of reality":

1. The pragmatic test. Has it led to well-balanced, happy, serene living of an enhanced quality?

2. Is it consistent with the well-established findings of reason? (This need not imply that it is supported by reason.)

3. Is it unifying and integrative, or isolating and destructive so far as the individual's relationship to an all-embracing whole is concerned?

Johnson contends that it is obvious that "…all psychotic products resulting in obsessional feeling-states cannot pass the first criterion." It is also clear, he writes, that "all allegedly religious people who…have only intolerance in common and are sure that if people only believed as they do, all would be well, are ruled out by the third criterion."

❧ **DELVING DEEPER**

James, William. *Varieties of Religious Experience*. Garden City, N.Y.: Masterworks Program, 1963.

Johnson, Raynor C. *Watcher on the Hills*. London: Hodder & Stoughton Ltd., 1959.

Otto, Rudolf. *Mysticism East and West*. New York: Macmillan, 1970.

Tilby, Angela. *Soul: God, Self and the New Cosmology*. New York: Doubleday, 1993.

Underhill, Evelyn. *Mysticism*. New York: Dutton, 1961.

Demons

In the teachings and traditions of all world religions, demons are spiritual entities without physical bodies that roam the Earth seeking to torment whomever attracts them through a wide variety of means—from weakness to wizardry. According to these ancient traditions, demons have supernatural powers; they are numerous; and they are organized. They can inflict sickness and mental disorders on their victims. They can possess and control humans and animals. Demons lie and deceive and teach false and misleading doctrines of spirituality. They oppose all teachings and actions that seek to serve the good and God.

Demons are spiritual entities without physical bodies that roam the Earth seeking to torment whoever attracts them.

According to the great teachers of the world religions, the main tasks of demons are to disseminate error among humans and to seduce believers into forsaking good for evil. Since they are such skilled deceivers, it is nearly impossible to develop an adequate litmus test that will unfailingly distinguish between good spirits and bad ones. Unless one is truly pure in heart, mind, and soul and has the ability to maintain only clean thoughts and good habits, it is very difficult to discern with unfailing accuracy the true nature of demon spirits.

Theologians remind their followers that as mortal beings they are in the midst of a great spiritual warfare between the angels of light who serve God and the fallen angels who serve the forces of darkness—and that their souls may be the prize for the victors. Accomplished spiritual teachers of all faiths advise their congregants that the good spirits will never try to interfere with the free will of humans or seek to possess their bodies. On the other hand, the evil spirits desire the physical host body of a human being. In fact, they must have such a vehicle if they are to experience earthly pleasures. When a demon invades a human body, it is said that **possession** has occurred and an **exorcism** by a priest or shaman may be required to free the victim from the evil spirit's grasp.

Demonic entities are credited with will and intellect, but these attributes are invariably directed toward evil as they exert their malevolent powers. When these evil spirits penetrate the material world and the circumstances of human life, they conceal themselves in every aspect of human existence.

In many instances, the gods of the old religions become the demons of the new. The *Asuras*, a race of gods in the early *Vedas* (sacred Hindu texts composed around 1500 to 1200 B.C.E.), are transmuted to powerful evil beings with the advent of the new deities of Indra and Vishnu. The *raksasas* are a class of entities who attack humans with the intended goal of driving them insane or causing them material ruin. As in many theologies, there is an ambivalence concerning certain deities. In Hinduism, the most terrifying of the gods, such as Kali, Durga, and Shiva, although seemingly demonic and destructive, often perform deeds that ultimately turn out to be good.

In the scriptures of the world religions, the chief of the legions and hordes of demons is known by various names: Satan, Lucifer, Iblis, Mara, and Angra Mainyu, among others. The word "devil" is derived from the Greek *diabolos*, which means "accuser" or "slanderer," and is one of the names for Satan. *Daimon*, the Greek word from which "demon" is derived, originally meant a tutelary spirit or a **spirit guide**, but it is frequently, and incorrectly, translated as "devil" or "demon."

In the traditions of Christianity, Islam, and Judaism, the animosity between demons (the fallen angels) and the human race can be traced to the moment when God granted his earthly creations of dust and clay with the priceless gift of free will. In the biblical and qur'anic traditions are found references to the jealousy that afflicted certain angels regarding the attention that God displayed toward his human creation. In the Qur'an (17:61–64), Iblis (Satan), the leader of the rebellious angels, refuses to bow to a creature that God has created of clay, and he threatens to make existence miserable for the descendants of the being that the Creator has honored above them. Because of the declared animosity of the fallen angels against those heavenly beings who remain faithful to the Creator and against those mortals who seek to follow the higher teachings of revealed truth, the epistle writer Paul (d. 62–68 C.E.) gave counsel when he warned that humans not only engage in spiritual warfare with those of flesh and blood who serve evil, "but against the principalities, against the powers, against the world rulers of this present darkness, against the spiritual hosts of wickedness in the heavenly places" (Ephesians 6:12).

Although Buddhism generally rejects a cosmological dualism between good and bad, angels and demons, there is an aspect within the traditional lives of the Buddha which echoes the jealousy motif of various entities toward humans. Mara, who tempted the Awakened One on the night of his enlightenment, is said to be an *asura* or a Deva (a being of light) who was jealous of the power that was about to be bestowed on a human, for to become a Buddha would be to achieve spiritual status greater than they possessed. Tibetan Buddhism borrows its demons from Hinduism and adds a number of indigenous entities, who are ambivalent toward the inhabitants of the Himalayas, sometimes appearing as fierce and malevolent creatures, other times manifesting as teachers of enlightenment.

Various scriptures state firmly that regardless of their strength, power, and majesty, angels are not to be worshiped, and religious teachers advise that true heavenly beings will immediately discourage any humans from attempting to bow their knees to them. On the other hand, the fallen angels, the demons, are motivated by their own selfish goals and delight in corrupting humans. They encourage mortals to express greed and to seek the acquisition of material, rather than spiritual, treasures. As a general spiritual law, these negative entities cannot achieve power over humans unless they are somehow invited into a person's private space—or unless they are attracted to an individual by that person's negativity or vulnerability.

According to certain Christian teachers, there was an outburst of demonic activity upon the occasion of Jesus' coming to Earth, which was perceived as a great threat to Satan's material kingdom. Other church scholars state that another such outburst is expected just before the Second Coming of Christ. Some fundamentalist Christians believe that that time has begun.

THE word "devil" is derived from the Greek diabolos, which means "accuser" or "slanderer."

Regardless of the general view of the vast majority of contemporary scientists and psychologists—and even many members of the clergy—to regard a belief in demons as a superstitious holdover from the past and to attribute the traditional accounts of possession by evil spirits as primitive ways of describing mental illness, there are professional caregivers and clerics who maintain that these evil creatures are as much a part of the twenty-first-century world as they were in the Middle Ages. And the results of a Gallup poll released in June 2001 reveal that 41 percent of adult Americans believe that people can be possessed by the Devil or his demons.

Professor Morton Kelsey, an Episcopal priest, a noted Notre Dame professor of theology, and the author of *Discernment—The Study of Ecstasy and Evil* (1978), states that demons are real and can invade the minds of humans. "Most people in the modern world consider themselves too sophisticated and too intelligent to be concerned with demons," he commented. "They totally ignore the evidence around them.

But in thirty years of study, I have seen the effects of angels and demons on humans."

Kelsey insists that a demon is not a figment of the imagination. "It is a negative, destructive spiritual force. It seeks to destroy the person and everyone with whom that person comes into contact. The essential mark of the demon—and those possessed by demons—is total self-interest to the exclusion of everyone and everything else."

Agreeing with many other contemporary religious scholars, Kelsey expressed his concern that most people in today's world offer little challenge for demons. "They find it easy to enter and operate in the unconscious parts of the mind, taking control of the person and his character," he said. In offering advice for those who may fear themselves to be under demonic attack, Kelsey said that they should not despair. They must focus their thoughts on God, and "try to reach out to Him and find His light."

There are numerous admonitions in the New Testament to be cautious of any manifesting entity and to test it to determine its true motives. "Beloved, do not believe every spirit, but test the spirits to see whether they are of God" (1 John 4:1).

While such a passage is easily quoted, its admonition is much more difficult to put into practice when warned in 2 Corinthians 11:14, "Even Satan disguises himself as an angel of light."

Dr. Wilson Van Dusen is a university professor who has served as chief psychologist at Mendocino State Hospital in California. Based upon his decades of research, Van Dusen has stated that many patients in mental hospitals may be possessed by demons and that people who hallucinate may often be under the control of demonic entities. Van Dusen also affirms that he has been able to speak directly to demons that have possessed his patients. He has heard their own guttural, otherworld voices, and he has even been able to administer psychological tests to these tormenting entities.

An accomplished psychologist, Van Dusen has lectured at the University of California, Davis; served as professor of psychology at

John F. Kennedy University; and published more than 150 scientific papers and written several books on his research, such as *The Presence of Other Worlds: The Psychological/ Spiritual Findings of Emanuel Swedenborg* (1974) and *The Natural Depth in Man* (1974).

In a landmark research paper, the clinical psychologist noted the "striking similarities" between the hierarchy of the unseen world described by the Swedish inventor-mystic Emanuel Swedenborg (1688–1772) and the alleged hallucinations of his patients in a state mental hospital. Van Dusen began to seek out those from among the hundreds of chronic schizophrenics, alcoholics, and brain-damaged persons who could distinguish between their own thoughts and the products of their hallucinations. He would question these other supposed entities directly and instruct the patient to give a word-for-word account of what the voices answered or what was seen. In this manner, he could hold long dialogues with a patient's hallucinations and record both his questions and the entity's answers.

On numerous occasions the psychologist found that he was engaged in dialogues with hallucinations that were above the patient's comprehension. He found this to be especially true when he contacted the higher order of hallucinations, which he discovered to be "symbolically rich beyond the patient's own understanding." The lower order, Van Dusen noted, was composed of entities that were consistently antireligious, and some actively obstructed the patient's religious practices. Occasionally they would even refer to themselves as demons from hell, suggest lewd acts, then scold the patient for considering them. They would find a weak point of conscience and work on it interminably. They would invade "every nook and cranny of privacy, work on every weakness and credibility, claim awesome powers, lie, make promises, and then undermine the patient's will."

Van Dusen also found that the "hallucinations" could take over a patient's eyes, ears, and voice, just as in traditional accounts of demon possession. The entities had totally different personalities from his patients' normal dispositions, which indicated to him that they were not simply products of his patients' minds. Some of the beings had **ESP** and could predict the future. Often they would threaten a patient and then cause actual physical pain. The demons were described in a variety of shapes and sizes, but generally appeared in human form, ranging from an old man to alleged space aliens, but any of them could change form in an instant. Some were so solid to the victims that they could not see through them. At times the patients would become so angry at the apparitions that they would strike at them—only to hurt their hands on the wall.

Van Dusen made detailed studies of 15 cases of demonic possession, but he dealt with several thousand patients during his 20 years as a clinical psychologist. In his opinion, the entities were present "in every single one of the thousands of patients." He even admitted that some of the entities knew far more than he did, even though he tried to test them by looking up obscure academic references.

One of Van Dusen's conclusions was that the entities took over the minds of people who were emotionally or physically at a low ebb. The beings seemed to be able to "leech on those people because they had been weakened by strains and stresses with which they could not cope."

Considering once again some of the implications of Swedenborg's thoughts and works, Van Dusen commented that it was curious to reflect that, as Swedenborg has suggested, human lives may be "the little free space at the confluence of giant higher and lower spiritual hierarchies." The psychologist finds a lesson in such a consideration: "Man freely poised between good and evil, is under the influence of cosmic forces he usually doesn't know exist. Man, thinking he chooses, may be the resultant of other forces."

✤ **DELVING DEEPER**

Crim, Keith, ed. *The Perennial Dictionary of World Religions*. San Francisco: HarperSanFrancisco, 1989.

Karpel, Craig. *The Rite of Exorcism: The Complete Text*. New York: Berkley, 1975.

Kinnaman, Gary. *Angels Dark and Light*. Ann Arbor, Mich.: Servant Publications, 1994.

Mack, Carol K., and Dianah Mack. *A Field Guide to Demons, Fairies, Fallen Angels, and Other Subversive Spirits*. New York: Owl Book, Henry Holt, 1999.

Montgomery, John Warwick. *Powers and Principalities*. Minneapolis: Dimension Books, 1975.

Van Dusen, Wilson. *The Psychological/Spiritual Presence of Other Worlds: The Findings of Emanuel Swedenborg*. New York: Harper & Row, 1974.

Devil's Mark

During the time of the **Inquisition** of the Middle Ages, it was believed that the Devil placed upon his human brides, the witches, a special mark that was insensitive to pain. Because it was supposed that such a mark might be well hidden somewhere on the witch's body, one of the first of the many degrading and painful ordeals of the Inquisition began when the accused woman was turned over to the torturers to have her body shaved in search of the "Devil's Mark."

Once the alleged spot—which could well have been a mole or a birthmark—was found, the torturers would insert long, sharp pins into the victim's flesh or sear the mark with red-hot branding irons in order to test its resistance to pain. The fact that the suspected area gave no indication of being immune to pain did nothing to absolve the woman accused of witchcraft from later being burned at the stake.

In 1486, Malleus Maleficarum ("A Hammer for Witches") became the handbook of the professional witch hunters.

In 1486, two devout priests, Jakob Sprenger and Heinrich Kramer, published *Malleus Maleficarum* (A Hammer for Witches), the book that became the handbook of the professional witch hunters. Charles Williams, writing in his *Witchcraft*, believes that Sprenger and Kramer proceeded with great care to examine the nature of witchcraft and to ana-

The Spanish Inquisition was ordered to rid Europe of heretics. By 1257, the Church officially sanctioned torture as a means of forcing witches, sorcerers, and shapeshifters to confess their alliance with Satan. (FORTEAN PICTURE LIBRARY)

lyze the best methods of operating against its menace. They perceived the witches as making use of their unholy alliance with Satan to corrupt the generative powers of humankind. In addition, they believed that witches sought to depopulate Christendom by demanding the sacrifice of children and babies.

The tribunal judges of the Inquisition examined, tried, and tortured female witches over male witches at a ratio of (depending upon the authority) 10 to 1, 100 to 1, or 10,000 to 1. And beginning with the brutal search for the Devil's Mark, the inquisitors directed their tortures toward the private parts of the body.

Once a woman accused of witchcraft found herself in prison through the testimonies of witnesses who had seen her alleged evil powers at work (these could be a neighbor woman jealous of her beauty, a suitor disappointed at her rejection of his love, a relative who sought her share of an inheritance), she was often as good as condemned. At the height of the witch hunt mania, an accusation was the equivalent of guilt in the eyes of

judges. And few lawyers would dare defend an accused witch for fear that he would himself be accused of witchcraft or heresy if he pled her case too well.

The common justice of the Inquisition demanded that a witch should not be condemned to death unless she convict herself by her own confession. Therefore, the judges had no choice other than to order her to be examined for the Devil's Mark and to turn her over to the torturers to extract a confession from her. In a bizarre rationalization and paradox of justice, the law insisted that the tribunal could not use torture to wring a confession from an accused witch, so they turned her over to black-hooded torturers to burn, stretch, starve, and beat her until she confessed. Once this confession had been accomplished, the accused was made to stand once again before the judges (usually standing of one's own volition was impossible at this stage, so the woman was supported by priests) and confess of her "own free will without torture." Once the confession was properly recorded, the victim of the Inquisition would be led directly from the courtroom to be burned at the stake.

✤ DELVING DEEPER

Russell, Jeffrey Burton. *Witchcraft in the Middle Ages.* Ithaca, N.Y.: Cornell University Press, 1972.

Seligmann, Kurt. *The History of Magic.* New York: Pantheon Books, 1948.

Trevor-Roper, H. R. *The European Witch-Craze.* New York: Harper & Row, 1967.

ECSTASY

"All that the soul knows when it is left to itself is nothing in comparison with the knowledge that is given it during ecstasy. When the soul is raised aloft, illumined by the presence of God, when God and it are lost in each other, it apprehends and possesses with joy good things which it cannot describe. The soul swims in joy and knowledge." (Angela da Foligno, mystic, quoted by Father A. Poulain in *The Graces of Interior Prayer* [1910])

Many students of spirituality describe the ecstatic experience as the mystic state *par*

The city of Jerusalem contains some of the most venerated sites in the Muslim, Christian, and Jewish religions. To name only a few, the Muslims built the Dome of the Rock over the place from which Muhammad ascended to heaven; the Jews revere the Wailing Wall, all that remains of the great Temple of Solomon destroyed by the Romans; and the Christians flock to the Church of the Holy Sepulchre, built around the tomb from which Jesus rose from the dead. Because of the extreme emotionality and religious fervor which exists around such sacred sites, a bizarre psychological condition known as "Jerusalem Fever" plagues certain visitors to the city, causing them to believe that they are on a mission from God and that they must carry out His will.

Thousands of pilgrims come each year from all over the world to experience the sacred sites of Old Jerusalem. The visitors are able to walk the streets where many of their biblical heroes and heroines trod. In Jersusalem, citizens of our modern, fast-paced technological society can meditate under the shade of olive trees and reflect upon the divine inspiration that guided the ancient prophets, teachers, and kings to write the psalms, sermons, and scriptures. The pilgrims can leave the city and travel through the same landscapes where the great figures of the bible and the Qu'ran sought God and heard His messages.

Such a total immersion in the places and events recounted in scripture overpowers some visitors with a desire to bring about a oneness of all religions and all people on Earth. They develop a deep sense of sadness for all the religious wars and crusades that have been waged over earthly possession of the Holy City; they want to do whatever they can to bring together all believers. At the other end of the spectrum, other pilgrims are struck with a paranoia that makes them think the End-Times are near and that they must prepare at once for Armageddon—the last great conflict between good and evil and the precursor to Christ's Second Coming and the Final Judgment.

Both psychological conditions are clinically identified as "Jerusalem Fever." While these peculiar psy-

JERUSALEM FEVER

chological symptoms are usually fleeting, they can occasionally be severe enough to result in bizarre behavior and acts of violence against others.

SOURCES:

Jerusalem Syndrome. http://www.jerusalemsyndrome.com/jsint. htm, 12 October 2001.

excellence. Mystics from all traditions agree in regarding ecstasy as a wonderful state—the one in which the human spirit is swept up and into an immediate union with the divine. As Evelyn Underhill points out in her *Mysticism* (1961), the word has become synonymous with joyous exaltation: "The induced ecstasies of the Dionysian mysteries, the metaphysical raptures of the Neoplatonists, the voluntary or involuntary trance of Indian mystics and Christian saints—all these, however widely they may differ in transcendental value, agree in claiming such value, in declaring that this change of consciousness brought with it a valid and ineffable apprehension of the Real."

Ecstasy differs from meditation—one of the stages that may precede it—both in character and development. In all the lengthy preliminary training of the mystical consciousness, a constant exertion of the will is required. But when at last the new and long-desired experiences come to the mystic "like a flash" into the psyche, he or she knows that there is nothing more to do than to accept that which has been given.

In *a state of ecstacy, the human spirit is swept up and into an immediate union with the divine.*

Fredric W. H. Myers (1843–1901) observed that the evidence for ecstasy is stronger than the evidence for any other religious belief. "Of all the subjective experiences of religion, ecstasy is that which has been most urgently, perhaps to the psychologist most convincingly asserted; and it is not confined to any one religion," Myers said. "From the medicine man…up to St. John, St. Peter, and St. Paul, with Buddha and Mahomet on the way, we find records which, though morally and intellectually much differing, are in psychological essence the same."

Evelyn Underhill states that ecstasy "represents the greatest possible extension of the spiritual consciousness in the direction of Pure Being: the blind intent stretching here receives its reward in a profound experience of

Eternal Life. In this experience, the consciousness of 'I-hood,' of space and time…all that beings to the World of Becoming and our own place therein…are suspended. The vitality which we are accustomed to split amongst these various things, is gathered up to form a state of pure apprehension…a vivid intuition of the Transcendent."

Underhill goes on to explain that in the perfect unity of consciousness that comes in a state of ecstasy, the mystic is so concentrated on the Absolute that his or her faculties are suspended and he or she ceases to think of himself or herself as separate from the "All That Is." The mystic becomes so immersed in the Absolute that "as the bird cannot see the air which supports it, nor the fish the ocean in which it swims, [the mystic] knows all, but think naught, perceives all, but conceives naught."

In addition to the passive nature of the ecstasy, another characteristic of its content is its relative unity and the narrowness of its conscious field. To a large extent, the outside world is shut out, and the five senses are completely closed to external stimuli. Every other thought, feeling, or emotion is pushed out of the mind but the idea of God and the emotions of joy and love. These fill the mind to the exclusion of nearly everything else, and are themselves blended into a single whole. The mystic does not *believe* God to be present; he or she *feels* God united with his or her soul, so that this intense awareness and its strong emotional accompaniment leave no room in his or her consciousness for anything else.

A story is told that St. Ignatius (1491–1556) was seated at the side of a road, looking at the stream that crossed it, absorbed in contemplation, when the eyes of his soul were opened and inundated with light. He was able to distinguish nothing with his five senses, but he comprehended marvelously a great number of truths pertaining to the faith or to the human sciences. The new concepts and ideas were so numerous and the light so bright that St. Ignatius seemed to enter into a new world. The amount of this new knowledge was so great that, according to Ignatius, all that he had learned in his life up to his 62nd year, whether supernatural or through laborious study, could not be compared to what he had learned at this one ecstatic experience.

The knowledge that one receives while in a state of ecstasy is immediate and leaves the percipient with a complete sense of the noetic, an inner knowing and awareness that what was shown to him or her in the ecstatic vision is the way things truly are. The knowledge received in such a state often has very little to do with conceptual or representative knowledge about things. To the mystic, true reality does not lie in such knowledge. Only in an immediate experience, a visionary ecstatic experience, which stands for itself alone, can one find true reality—and most certainly of all, there alone can one find the ultimate reality with God.

St. Teresa of Avila (1515–1582), the esteemed Spanish Carmelite nun, mystic, and writer, referred in her last great work, the *Interior Castle* (1577), to four degrees of the mystic union with God:

1. the incomplete mystic union that comes with a quieting of the mind;

2. the semi-ecstatic union;

3. the ecstatic union;

4. the transforming union of complete oneness with God.

Perhaps the most dramatic characteristic of the ecstatic experience is the occasional phenomenon of visions, often of Christ, Mary, various saints, or angels. Since so many of these visionary encounters are compatible with the ecstatic's religious beliefs, certain researchers maintain that the visions of the mystics are determined in content by their spiritual orientation and are set in motion by the imagination working in dreamlike fashion upon the mass of theological material which fills the mind. Some researchers also find it likely that the vision, much like a normal dream, originates from some sensational stimulus which the imagination proceeds to interpret and elaborate.

Mystic ecstasy, to the percipient of the experience, reveals a genuine truth. He or she is brought face-to-face with ultimate reality that is experienced with emotions and intuition. A transcendence of the self is achieved.

The mystic returns from the experience with the certainty of having been somewhere else where a revelation of some remarkable truth was given, a truth such as reality is unitary and divine; even ordinary human experiences are phenomenal; the soul, which is the key to reality, may rise to oneness with God; that God's presence may be found everywhere hidden in the midst of daily life.

In her *Ecstasy: A Study of Some Secular and Religious Experiences* (1961), Marghanita Laski lists five principal manifestations of the ecstatic mystical experience:

1. The feelings of loss: i.e., loss of time, of place, of worldliness, of self, of sin, and so on.

2. The feelings of gain: i.e., gain of a new life, of joy, of salvation, of glory, of new knowledge, and so on.

3. Ineffability: experiences which the person finds impossible to put into words at all.

4. Quasi-physical feelings: i.e., reference to sensations suggesting physical feelings, which may accompany ecstatic experiences, such as floating sensations, a feeling of swelling up, an impression of a shining light, and so on.

5. Feelings of intensity or withdrawal: i.e., a feeling of a 'winding up,' an accumulation of force to the point at which it is let go, whereas withdrawal is the opposite—an ecstatic condition reached 'not by accumulation but by subtraction,' a feeling of withdrawal of force and energy.

Laski states that ecstatic experiences can never be satisfactorily explained if it is suggested that ecstasies are "...only this or only that—only a phenomenon of repressed sexuality or only a concomitant of some or other morbid condition." In her examination of the recipients' convictions of the value of the ecstatic experience, she came to believe that such manifestations must be "treated as important outside religious contexts, as having important effects on people's mental and physical well-being, on their aesthetic preferences, their creativity, their beliefs and philosophies, and on their conduct...." To ignore or to deny the importance of ecstatic experiences, Laski contends, is "to leave to the irrational the interpretation of what many people believe to be of supreme value."

❋ DELVING DEEPER

Bach, Marcus. *The Inner Ecstasy*. New York, Cleveland: World Publishing, 1969.

James, William. *Varieties of Religious Experience*. Garden City, N.Y.: Masterworks Program, 1971.

Otto, Rudolf. *The Idea of the Holy*. New York: Galaxy Books, 1958.

Suzuki, D. T. *Mysticism, Christian and Buddhist*. New York: Perennial, 1971.

Tart, Charles T. *Altered States of Consciousness*. New York: John Wiley & Sons, 1969.

Underhill, Evelyn. *Mysticism*. New York: Dutton, 1961.

EXORCISM

On September 11, 2000, newspapers around the world carried the story about how Satan had invaded the Vatican in Rome and screamed insults at Pope John Paul II (1920–   ) through the agency of a teenage girl, reported to have been a "splendid girl in terms of purity and goodness" before being possessed by the devil at the age of 12. The 19-year-old began shouting in a "cavernous voice" during a general papal audience in St. Peter's Square. Despite the efforts of the pope to quiet the attack, the Prince of Darkness laughed at the Holy Father's efforts to drive him away. When Vatican guards attempted to constrain the girl, she violently pushed them back in a display of superhuman strength.

THE *practice of performing an exorcism on candidates for baptism was first recorded by the church father Hippolytus (c. 170–c. 235) in third-century Rome.*

Vatican exorcist Father Gabriele Amorth said that he and another exorcist, Father Giancarlo Gramolazzo, had previously worked with the girl and that the pope had spent half an hour with her the day before the incident and had also exorcised the teenager. However, it soon became apparent when the girl began insulting the pope and speaking in unknown tongues during the papal audience that neither of the exorcisms had managed to banish Satan. Vatican sources were quick to remind the media of Pope John Paul II's successful exorcism of an Italian woman named Francesca Fabrizzi in 1982.

Later in September 2000, Reverend James Le Bar, an exorcist for the Archdiocese of New York, commented that there had been a "large explosion" of exorcisms in recent years. In New York alone, he said, the number had accelerated from none in 1990 to a total of 300 in the last 10 years. Reverend Le Bar said that as men and women have diminished self-respect for themselves and decreased reverence for spirituality, for other human beings, and for life in general, one of Satan's **demons** can move in and "attack them by possessing them and rendering them helpless."

On November 26, 2000, an Associated Press story datelined Mexico City, Mexico, stated that a steady procession of men and women believing themselves to be possessed pass through the doors of the city's Roman Catholic parishes seeking exorcism from the eight priests appointed by the archbishop to battle Satan and his demons. Reverend Alberto Juarez told of seeing a young woman who began to speak in a man's voice and then growl like a dog. Father Enrique Maldonado spoke of houses where he witnessed locked doors open and objects move about the rooms. Reverend Daniel Gagnon stated that he had once considered himself scientific, pragmatic, but he had changed his mind. "Psychology is where you begin, but there is an area that science cannot explain," he said.

The casting out of demons and the healing of the sick and the lame were two of the great facets of the apostolic commission that Jesus (c. 6 B.C.E.–c. 30 C.E.) gave to his followers, but the practice of performing an exorcism on candidates for baptism was first recorded by the church father Hippolytus (c. 170–c. 235) in third-century Rome. The priest or layman instructing those who would join the church was instructed to lay his hands upon the heads

MOTHER TERESA'S EXORCISM

Mother Teresa (1910–1997), winner of the Nobel Peace Prize in 1979, had led such an exemplary life as a nun devoted to healing the poor of India that, shortly after her death on September 5, 1997, Pope John Paul II (1920–) waived the customary five-year-waiting period and began the process to consider her for possible sainthood. On September 5, 2001, on the fourth anniversary of her death, the Archbishop of Calcutta, Henry D'Souza, revealed that Mother Teresa had an exorcism performed on her while she was hospitalized in 1997. Because the Roman Catholic Church performs exorcisms only when someone is believed to be possessed by the devil, the world was shocked by such a disclosure.

According to D'Souza, shortly before her death at the age of 87, Mother Teresa was admitted to a hospital because of heart trouble. D'Souza happened to be a patient in the same hospital during her stay, and he learned that the nun was having difficulty sleeping. When it was determined that there was no medical reason to account for such problems, it occurred to him that some evil spirit might be trying to disturb her during the night.

With the nun's consent, D'Souza arranged for a priest to perform an exorcism as a precautionary measure. Mother Theresa participated with the priest in a prayer for protection and slept peacefully after the ritual had been completed. Not wishing to tarnish Mother Teresa's sanctity, immediately after he had made the disclosure of her exorcism, D'Souza insisted that she had not been satanically possessed, and he was firm in his assertion that the exorcism should in no way affect her candidacy for sainthood.

SOURCES:

"Archbishop: Mother Theresa underwent Exorcism." http://www.cnn.com/2001/WORLD/asiapcf/south/09/04/mother.theresa.exorcism/. 7 September 2001.

---

of the catechumens and pray. It was then supposed that it would be impossible for a demonic entity to remain quiet and unnoticed at this time, thereby betraying its presence and presenting the unfortunate human host for the process of exorcism.

According to the September 1, 2000, issue of the *National Catholic Reporter,* the first mention of "exorcist" as an office in the Roman Catholic Church exists in a letter of Pope Cornelius in 253. Historian Jeffrey Burton Russell states that in the early medieval liturgies, there were three kinds of common exorcisms—the exorcism or blessing of houses or objects, of those about to receive baptism, and of people believed to be possessed by demons. In various parts of Europe, the priest conducting the exorcism might also use the rites to banish such pre-Christian deities as Thor and Odin.

Accounts of demonic possession were commonplace in ancient Egypt, Babylonia, and Persia from the earliest times. Although there are no accounts of demonic possession or of exorcism in the Old Testament, the casting out of demons is an integral part of Jesus' ministry and it is an important aspect of the earthly assignments that he gives to his followers. ("Then he called together his twelve apostles and sent them out two by two with power over evil spirits" [Mark 6:7]. "Finally, Paul…turned and said to the spirit, 'In the name of Jesus Christ, I order you to leave this girl alone!'" [Acts 16:18]. The New Testament also refers to Jewish exorcists who begin to cast out demons in Jesus' name (Mark 9:38–40): "'Teacher, we saw a man using your name to force demons out of people. But he wasn't one of us, and we told him to stop.' Jesus said to his disciples: 'Don't stop him! No

Perry King in the 1972
movie *The Possession of
Joel Delaney.* (THE
KOBAL COLLECTION)

one who works miracles in my name will soon turn and say something bad about me. Anyone who isn't against us is for us.'"

Neither Jesus nor those who cast out demons in his name is called an "exorcist" in the New Testament, and the word "exorcise" is never used anywhere in the Bible in the context of banishing demons. By contrast to shamanic exorcisms of evil spirits in tribal cultures, which can last for hours or days; the rituals of demonic banishment in ancient Egypt or pagan Europe, which were dramatic ordeals of lengthy duration; or the rites of exorcism of the Roman Catholic Church, which can go on for many days, months, even years, Jesus' exorcisms consisted of his/her simple and direct command to the demon to leave its unwilling host body.

In the Kabbalist tradition, the exorcist demands to know the nature of the sin that led the demon to attach itself to a human body so that after expulsion the soul can be rectified and placed at rest.

When Jesus triumphs easily and immediately over the evil beings that have infested a human body and soul in the many encounters described in the gospels, the possessing enti-

ties are always demons, never Satan himself. Although these are victories that diminish Satan's earthly powers, it may be that the great showdown between Jesus, the Son of God, and Satan, the Lord of the Earth, is building for the great final battle between good and evil at **Armageddon** at the time of the **Apocalypse.**

Although accounts of exorcism are not to be found in the Old Testament, later Jewish tradition employs a ritual that involves the sounding of the shofar, the reciting of prayers, and the anointing of the afflicted person with oil and water over which passages from Psalms have been read. As in Christian exorcism, it is important that the true identity of the demon be learned so that it can be addressed by name and ordered out of the body of its victim. In the Kabbalist tradition, the exorcist also demands to know the nature of the sin that led the demon to attach itself to a human body so that after expulsion the soul can be rectified and placed at rest.

John L. Allen, Jr., a staff writer for the *National Catholic Reporter,* acknowledged (September 1, 2000) that in a few well-publicized cases "failure to make a careful assessment of possible brain dysfunction before performing exorcism has resulted in disaster." Allen then mentions a 1976 case in which two Bavarian priests were convicted of negligent homicide when medical treatment for a 23-year-old epileptic was discontinued in favor of exorcism and the young woman died. He also refers to a 1996 case in which a Korean Protestant exorcist in California was convicted of involuntary manslaughter and sentenced to four years in prison for inadvertently trampling a woman to death during a four-hour exorcism.

Vatican exorcist Gabriele Amorth said that he always asks for a person's medical history and consults a psychiatrist if he feels such information will be useful before beginning an exorcism. He argues, however, that only performing an exorcism can provide certainty, because it is in the response to the rites that one can detect the presence of a demon.

While many priests appear to have the attitude that a little exorcism could never hurt anyone, Father Joseph Mahoney, a Catholic chaplain in Detroit who works with individuals suffering from multiple personality disorder, sees it quite differently. He believes that an exorcism can be "extremely destructive" when applied to patients with undiagnosed multiple personality disorders, and he refers to research carried out by the Royal Ottawa Hospital in Canada, which concluded that the process of exorcism could create new personalities in such subjects.

In January 1999, the Vatican issued a revised Catholic rite of exorcism for the first time since 1614, reaffirming the existence of Satan and revamping his image for the millennium. Officials stressed that the church was not revising scriptural references to the Devil or suggesting that people should cease believing in the Evil One. But priests who conduct exorcisms should now deal with evil as a force lurking within all individuals, rather than one that threatens people from without.

Father Malachi Martin, a Jesuit who served as an advisor to three popes, has authored a number of books dealing with demon possession and exorcism, including *Hostage to the Devil*. When he was asked why there has been such a spectacular rise in the number of people possessed by demons and in need of exorcism, he replied that it was as St. Paul (d. 62–68 C.E.) had declared: "There is a spiritual war on, a war with the spirits…a war with the invisible forces that want men's souls."

Describing the process of exorcism, Martin explained that an exorcism was a confrontation, not a mere exercise in prayer. The exorcist was at war with the demon. Once begun, the process must be finished. If the exorcist should stop the rites for any reason, the demon will pursue him.

The exorcism continues with a kind of conversation between the demon and the exorcist, who is attempting to learn as quickly as possible the demon's name. Often the entity's name is a reflection or a symbol of that demon's function, and it must be forced to admit it.

The demon systematically ridicules human love and faith and constantly probes the exorcist for any signs of weakness, any area of his

Linda Blair in the popular 1973 film *The Exorcist*. (THE KOBAL COLLECTION)

past that might be open to reproach. Objects in the room may move, windows shatter, doors open and close. "At a certain moment," Martin told journalist Wen Smith, "everybody in the room knows there's *something* in the room that wants you dead. It's a horrible feeling knowing that unless something happens, you are going to die—now."

Martin freely admitted that not all exorcisms end in triumph for the exorcist. Sometimes the demon remains in control and the victim remains possessed. Even when the demon is expelled from its unwilling human host, it may still wander about seeking other vulnerable men and women to inhabit. And the exorcist himself may continue to pay a price for interfering in the demon's possession of its host body. Martin said that he had been flung out of bed, knocked off stools, and had his shoulder broken—reminders that the demon was still around and very angry with him.

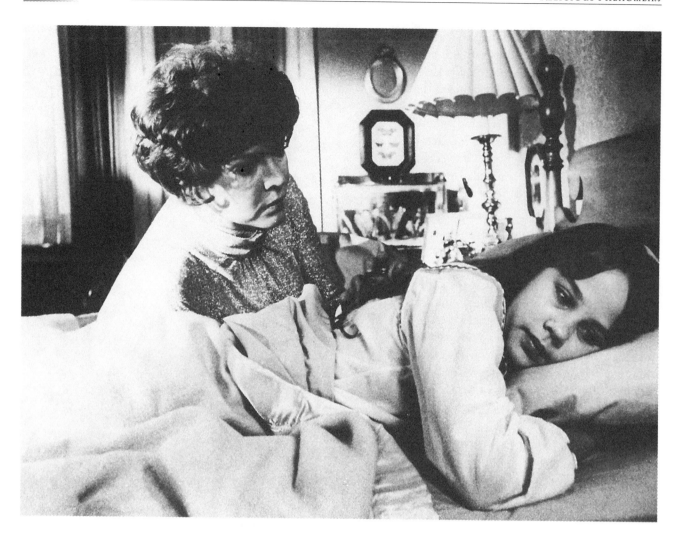

Ellen Burstyn and Linda Blair in a scene from *The Exorcist.* **(CORBIS CORPORATION)**

On September 22, 2000, the 1973 horror film *The Exorcist* was rereleased with added footage that had been excised from the original, and priests across the nation braced themselves for a tidal wave of cases of alleged demonic possession. Arguably the most frightening movie ever made, the film was based on the best-selling novel by William Peter Blatty and was directed by William Friedkin. As many motion picture reviewers and commentators have discussed, the film presentation of demonic possession touched a kind of collective primal fear in its audiences that was made all the more horrible by the fact that the victim was a smiling, cherubic, innocent young girl. Demons became all the more real when people realized that possession could occur to their child, to their spouse, even to them. Father Merrin, the exorcist in the film, uses the actual Roman Ritual of exorcism that was created by the Roman Catholic Church in

1614, and the repetitious chanting of the actors performing the rites gave the presentation an added aura of reality and of participation in a supernatural event.

Reverend Bob Larson, an evangelical preacher and author who runs an exorcism ministry in Denver, told the *New York Times* (November 28, 2000) that he had 40 exorcism teams across the country and that his goal was that "no one should ever be more than a day's drive from a city where you can find an exorcist." Larson could not see why anyone would be "freaked out" over the idea of an exorcism: "It's in the Bible. Christ taught it."

Michael W. Cuneo, a Fordham University sociologist, has been studying the subject of exorcisms for many years. His research indicates that as recently as the 1960s, exorcism in the United States was nearly completely abandoned as a church rite. Then, in 1973, the motion picture *The Exorcist* changed that. By the mid-1980s, there was a "proliferation of exorcisms being performed by evangelical Protestants." In the 1990s, Cuneo says that there is an "underground network" of exorcists numbering in the hundreds, and a "bewildering variety of exorcisms being performed."

Reverend Martin Marty, a Lutheran minister and an analyst of religious trends and customs in the United States, commented that exorcisms were "all over the place" and the driving out of evil spirits has a long and varied history. Marty noted that the godparents at the baptismal service in many Christian faiths are asked, on behalf of the child they sponsor, if they renounce the devil and all his works and ways. That, he explained, is a mild version of exorcism. And exorcism is a smaller part of modern Western religions than it was in ancient Babylon, Egypt, and Greece. There are witchdoctors in African societies who perform exorcisms, medicine people among Native American tribes who are exorcists, and shamans throughout Asia who banish evil spirits.

As long as there are human beings who believe in supernatural powers, there will be exorcists who will be summoned to rid the innocent of the demons who have possessed them. A survey of its readers conducted by *Self* magazine in 1997 revealed that 65 percent of those surveyed believed in the Devil; and the results of a Gallup poll released in June 2001 indicated that 41 percent of adult Americans believe that the Devil or his demons can possess humans.

❀ DELVING DEEPER

Bamberger, Bernard J. *Fallen Angels*. New York: Jewish Publication Society, Barnes & Noble, 1995.

Blatty, William Peter. *The Exorcist*. New York: Bantam Books, 1972.

Dickason, C. Fred. *Demon Possession & The Christian*. Westchester, Ill.: Crossway Books, 1989.

McGinn, Bernard. *Antichrist: Two Thousand Years of the Human Fascination with Evil*. San Francisco: HarperSanFrancisco, 1994.

Oesterreich, T. K. *Possession: Demonical & Other Among Primitive Races, in Antiquity, the Middle Ages, and Modern Times*. New Hyde Park, N.Y.: University Books, 1966.

FAITH HEALING

Faith healing refers to the termination of an illness or a debilitating physical condition through supernatural means, such as the **power of prayer** or an intervention of God through a **miracle.** In the New Testament, one of the principal facets of Jesus' (c. 6 B.C.E.–c. 30 C.E.) earthly ministry was the healing of those who sought surcease of pain and suffering. Throughout the gospels, Jesus heals the lame, the blind, the diseased, and those **possessed** by **demons,** and he charges his apostles to go out into the world to do as he has done in their presence.

The early churches included a time for the healing of its members within the formal service, a practice which many contemporary Christian congregations still maintain, as a prayer for the sick if not as an actual time for the laying on of hands. The pattern for such a procedure within the church service was set forth in the epistle of James (5:14–16): "Is any one of you sick? He should call upon the elders of the church to pray over him and anoint him with oil in the name of the Lord. And the prayer offered in faith will make the sick person well; the Lord will raise him up. If he has sinned, he will be forgiven. Therefore confess your sins to each other and pray for each other so that you may be healed. The prayer of a righteous man is powerful and effective."

The May 1, 2000, issue of *Newsweek* magazine released the results of a survey that its staff had conducted regarding such miracles as faith healing. According to its statistics, 71 percent of all Christians said that they had prayed for miracles regarding the healing of the terminally ill. A national Gallup poll released in June 2001 revealed that 54 percent of adult Americans of all faiths believed in spiritual healing and the power of the mind through prayer to heal the body.

Many people of faith find that a pilgrimage to a holy shrine or icon can accomplish miracles of healing. Among the most famous in the world is the healing Grotto of Bernadette at Lourdes, France, which was constructed on the spot where Bernadette

According to the Gallup Poll, belief in God has always been very high in the United States, ranking in the mid-90 percent range over the last sixty years. Interestingly, while 95 percent of Americans believe in God, only eight in ten envision that the Supreme Being is one who watches over them and answers their prayers. And even fewer, six in ten, recently declare their complete trust in God.

When the Gallup Poll asked Americans how important religion was in their lives, six in ten (about 58.7 percent) say it is very important. In fifty years of measurement, the highest percentage regarding the importance of religion (75 percent) was registered in 1952; the lowest (52 percent) in 1978.

According to a 2000 Gallup poll, 64.9 percent of respondents believed that religion has the ability to answer today's problems. This particular statistic has ranged from a high of 81 percent in 1957 to a low of 53 percent in 1993.

Church membership reached a high of 76 percent in both 1943 and 1947 and dropped to a low of 65 per-

Ninety-Five Percent of Americans Believe in God

cent in 1988 and 1990. In 1939, when Gallup first began measuring church attendance, 41 percent of Americans claimed to attend weekly worship services. The high point for weekly observance of religious faith was reached in the mid- and late 1950s, when 49 percent of the adult population said that they attended church or synagogue once a week.

SOURCES:

Gallup, George Jr. "Americans More Religious Now Than Ten Years Ago, but Less So Than in 1950s and 1960s." Gallup News Service, 29 March, 2001. http://www.gallup.com/poll/releases/pr010329.asp. 17 October 2001.

Soubrious (1844–1879) had the vision of Mother Mary in 1858. Since the time the miracle occurred to the young miller's daughter, pilgrims have journeyed to Lourdes to seek healing and salvation from the waters of the natural spring that appeared in the hillside after the apparition of the Holy Mother appeared to Bernadette. Consistently, for decades, an average of 200,000 people visited the shrine every year. During the centennial celebration of Lourdes in 1958, more than two million people came to the tiny community in southern France seeking a healing. In recent years, annual attendance has risen to over five million.

Thousands of pilgrims have left their crutches and canes at the shrine. Thousands more have been cured of such fatal diseases as advanced stages of cancer. Hundreds of

thousands of cures have been claimed by men and women who immersed themselves in the cold spring waters of the shrine, but the Lourdes Medical Bureau has established certain criteria that must be met before it will certify a cure as an example of miraculous faith healing:

1. The affliction must be a serious disease. If it is not classified as incurable, it must be diagnosed as extremely difficult to cure.

2. There must be no improvement in the patient's condition prior to the visit to the Lourdes shrine.

3. Medication that may have been used must have been judged ineffective.

4. The cure must be totally complete.

5. The cure must be unquestionably definitive and free of all doubt.

The results of a *Time*/CNN poll (*Time*, June 24, 1996) stated that 82 percent of those surveyed believed in the personal power of prayer to heal; 73 percent believed that their prayers could heal others of their illness; 77 percent expressed their faith that God could sometimes intervene to heal people with a serious illness; and 65 percent indicated that a doctor should join their patients in prayer if so asked. Interestingly, with all these high percentages indicating a belief in faith healing, only 28 percent of those polled believed in the ability of faith healers to make people well through their personal touch. It would seem that in matters of faith healing, the great majority of individuals prefer a cooperative union between themselves and God.

Since Dr. Herbert Bensen's seminal research at Harvard in 1972 demonstrating the influence that the mind can have over the body, 92 of 125 medical schools offer courses in nontraditional healing methods. In his *The Relaxation Response* (1975), Bensen showed how patients could successfully battle a number of stress-related illnesses by practicing a simple form of meditation. Bensen, president of the Mind/Body Medical Institute of Boston's Deaconess Hospital and Harvard Medical School, has suggested that 60 percent to 90 percent of all visits to doctors are in the mind-body, stress-related area and that the traditional medical ways of treating such patients through prescription medicines or surgeries are not effective in such chronic cases. Perhaps, more and more researchers are discovering, faith can make a sick person well.

Dr. Jeffrey Levin, of Eastern Virginia, and Dr. David Larson, a research psychiatrist with the National Institute for Healthcare Research, have located more than 200 studies that touch directly on the role that faith and religion may have in the healing process. Among such research studies were a 1995 study at Dartmouth-Hitchcock Medical Center which found that heart-surgery patients who drew comfort and strength from religious faith were more than three times more likely to survive; a 30-year study on blood pressure that showed that churchgoers have lower blood pressure than non-churchgoers, even when adjusted for smoking and other risk fac-

tors; a 1996 National Institute on Aging study of 4,000 elderly which found that those who attend religious services are less depressed and physically healthier than those who don't attend or who worship at home; and numerous studies in which non-churchgoers have been found to have a suicide rate four times higher than regular churchgoers and much higher rates of depression and anxiety-related illnesses.

NATIONAL *Institute on Aging study found that those who attend religious services are less depressed and physically healthier than those who don't attend or who worship at home.*

In *Timeless Healing* (1996), Herbert Benson states that those patients who claim to feel the intimate presence of a higher power have generally better health and chances for much more rapid recoveries. He writes that the human genetic blueprint has made a belief in an Infinite Absolute a part of human nature in order to offset the uniquely human tendency to ponder one's own death: "To counter this fundamental angst, humans are also wired for God."

✸ DELVING DEEPER

Benson, Herbert. *Timeless Healing*. New York: Scribner, 1996.

Cranston, Ruth. *The Miracle of Lourdes*. New York: McGraw-Hill, 1955.

Humphrey, Nicholas. *Science, Miracles and the Search for Supernatural Consolation*. New York: Basic Books, 1996.

Lewis, C. S. *Miracles*. New York: Macmillan, 1970.

Villoldo, Aberto, and Stanley Krippner. *Healing States*. New York: Fireside, Simon & Schuster, 1987.

GUARDIAN ANGELS

An old tradition says that guardian angels are appointed to children at the time of their birth. The seventeenth-century mystic Amos Komensky (1592–1670) declared that each child has an angel "given to him by God and ordained to be his guardian, that [the angel] might guard him, preserve him, and protect him against all dangers and snares, pits, ambushes, traps, and temptations."

Those men and women who claim to have seen their guardian angels generally describe them as appearing youthful, commanding, beautiful of countenance, and often majestic and awesome. Manifestations of light often accompany them, which lend to the grandeur of their appearance and the feelings of profound reverence that suffuse those who encounter angelic beings.

Not all angels appear as blond, blue-eyed entities in flowing white robes. Angels are thought to have the ability to appear in a variety of forms and with a wide range of physical characteristics. They seem completely capable of shaping reality in the three-dimensional world to suit their heavenly purposes. In certain cases, they may even reveal themselves as beings of pure light.

According to a poll conducted by *Time* magazine and published in the December 27, 1993, issue, 69 percent of Americans believed in the existence of angels, and 46 percent were certain that they had their own guardian angels to watch over them and to guide them. Of those men and women polled by the news magazine, 32 percent claimed that they had personally felt the presence and/or guidance of ethereal entities in their lives; and 15 percent believed that the heavenly helpers who ministered to them were the benevolent spirits of humans who had died, rather than higher spiritual beings with special powers. A similar poll conducted by *Self* magazine for its December 1997 issue found that 87 percent of readers believed in angels.

All religions have some tradition of a guardian angel or type of **spirit guide** assigned to each individual human soul. In the ancient Sanskrit texts of the Vedas, the word for angel is *angira*; in Hebrew, *malakh*, meaning "messenger," or *bene elohim*, for God's children; in Arabic, *malakah*; and in India, multiwinged angels or beings are

called *garudas*. As early as the third millennium B.C.E., the written records of ancient Egypt and Mesopotamia recognized a hierarchy of supernatural beings that ruled over various parts of the Earth, the universe, and the lives of human beings. They also believed in lower levels of entities that might be either hostile or benign in their actions toward humans. The Mesopotamians wanted to be certain that they were well protected by their spiritual guardians, the *shedu* and the *lamassu*. The *lamassus* were portrayed in art as grotesque creatures that looked like lions or bulls with human heads and large wings, and they were often represented by statues at the entrances of temples to ward off evil. The people of Mesopotamia considered them to be guardian spirits. An ancient magical text of the Mesopotamians invokes the good *shedu* to walk on one's right hand and the good *lamassu* to walk on the left.

In nearly all stories of angels, the beings appear to be paraphysical—that is, they are both material and nonmaterial entities. Although they originate in some invisible and nonphysical dimension, they are often seen to manifest as solidly in human reality as those humans whose lives they affect. There is no question that in both the Old and New Testaments angels are considered fully capable of becoming quite physical and material—at least long enough to accomplish their appointed mission of rescue, healing, or guidance. Throughout the Bible there are accounts of angels who wrestle with stubborn shepherds, guide people lost in the wilderness, and free persecuted prophets from fiery furnaces and dank prisons. Jesus (c. 6 B.C.E.–c. 30 C.E.) himself was fed by angels, defended by angels, and strengthened by angels.

Although popular culture has for centuries perpetuated the idea that humans become angels when they die, the holy books of the great world religions are in agreement that angels are an earlier and separate order of creation from human beings. According to these ancient teachings, humans were created a "little lower than the angels," and mortal men and women do not join their guardian spirits in the heavenly realm until after death—or, in some traditions, until after the Final Judgment. But even though humans are "lower than the angels" and made of material, physical substance in comparison with their ethereal, heavenly spirits, the scriptures of various faiths state firmly that the angels are not omnipresent, omnipotent, or omniscient—and neither are they immune to falling into temptation or into error: "Even in his servants he puts no trust, and his angels he charges with error" (Job 4:18).

A number of religious traditions teach that each human individual has a good and a bad angel that remain with him or her throughout his or her entire earthly lifespan. Others maintain that there are two unseen angels that hover near each person, and it is the task of the one to record the good deeds; the other, the bad. The American poet Henry Wadsworth Longfellow (1807–1882) gave expression to this concept in his poem "The Golden Legend" (1851):

> He who writes down the good ones,
> after each action closes his volume and
> ascends with it to God. The other
> keeps his dreadful day-book open until
> sunset, that we may repent.

The sacred writings of Islam also proclaim that every human is guarded by two angels—one taking the day watch, the other, night duty. As in Longfellow's poem, these two vigilant guardians record their human's good and bad deeds for Judgment Day.

In addition to their task as guardians, the benevolent unseen companions have as a considerable portion of their earthly mission, the task of guiding their humans toward spiritual awareness and leading their human wards to a clearer understanding of their true role in the cosmic scheme of things. Episcopal bishop Philip Brooks once observed that there is nothing clearer or more striking in the Bible than "the calm, familiar way with which from end to end it assumes the present existence of a world of spiritual beings always close to and acting on this world of flesh and blood.... From creation to judgment, the spiritual beings are forever present. They act as truly in the drama as the men and women who, with their unmistakable humanity, walk the sacred stage in successive scenes. There is nothing of hesitation about the Bible's treatment of the spiritual world. There is no reserve, no vagueness that would leave a chance for the whole system to be explained away in dreams and metaphors. The spiritual world, with all its multitudinous existence, is just as real as the crowded cities and the fragrant fields and the loud battlegrounds of the visible, palpable Judea, in which the writers of the sacred books were living."

The teachings of Islam state that there are three distinct species of intelligent beings in the universe: first, the angels, a high order of beings created of Light, the *malakh*; second, the *al-jinn*, ethereal, perhaps even multidimensional entities; and then human beings, fashioned out of the stuff of Earth and born into physical bodies. On occasion, the *al-jinn* can serve as helpful guides or guardians, but they can also be tricksters.

There are numerous admonitions in the New Testament to be cautious of any manifesting entity and to test it to determine its true motives. "Beloved, do not believe every spirit, but test the spirits to see whether they are of God." (1 John 4:1) While such a passage is easily quoted, its admonition is much more difficult to put into practice when people are warned in 2 Corinthians 11:14, "Even Satan disguises himself as an angel of light."

A general admonition mentioned by several spiritual teachers is never to enter meditation or prayer with the sole thought of obtaining ego aggrandizement or material gain. Selfish motivation may risk one becoming easily affected by those spirit beings who rebelled against God and became ensnared in their own selfish lust for power.

On December 12, 2000, the *London Times* reported on the two-year study of the phenomenon of guardian angels that was conducted by Emma Heathcote, a Birmingham University researcher. Heathcote's study, the first academic research into the subject of angels, examined the stories of over 800 Britons who claimed encounters with heavenly beings. Almost a third of those who contacted the researcher reported seeing a traditional angel with white gown and wings.

Another 21 percent saw their guardian angel in human form. Others experienced the sensation of a force around them or being engulfed in light.

In one of the more dramatic accounts in Heathcote's research, an angel appeared during a baptism at a village church in Hertfordshire in front of 30 witnesses, including the rector, churchwarden, and organist. Confirming the story for journalist Carol Midgley, the rector said that he was baptizing a 22-year-old woman who was about to be married but had never been christened. Suddenly there appeared before the rector "a man, but he was totally different from the rest of us. He was wearing something long, like a robe, but it was so white it was almost transparent." The angelic figure didn't have wings, and he simply stood there silently, looking at those assembled for the baptismal service. Children came forward with their mouths open. People said later that they felt as if "warm oil" had been poured over them. Then, in a few seconds, the angel was gone. But, the rector stated, the appearance of the angel had changed the lives of everyone present that day.

Other witnesses of angelic activity told Heathcote stories of seeing guardian angels at hospital beds and deathbeds, ministering to the ill or manifesting to escort souls to heaven. A good number of accounts reported the appearance of majestic beings to allay people's fears, to let them know that they were not alone in dangerous or stressful situations.

Rather than external entities presenting themselves to provide assurance of a celestial helping hand, psychotherapist Dr. Susan Blackmore theorizes that angel sightings are merely apparitions created by the brain in times of crisis in order to provide comfort. Though she might agree with Blackmore that certain angel sightings might be "crisis apparitions," Heathcote returns to the baptism in the church in Hertfordshire as an incident to give the staunchest critic pause to wonder: "I interviewed a lot of people about that angel," she said, "and everybody told the same story. Their descriptions were totally consistent."

Emma Heathcote said that although humans have been preoccupied with angels for centuries, humankind may now be going through an increased period of interest in the heavenly beings because "people are feeling a spiritual shortage and angels fill the gap." In her opinion, men and women in contemporary times fashion their own faiths in what often seems like a "spiritual supermarket" of choices available to them. "They might take a bit of Christianity, a bit of Judaism and Buddhism, together with a belief in angels to create their own eclectic religion," she said.

�֍ DELVING DEEPER

Burnham, Sophy. *A Book of Angels*. New York: Fawcett Columbine, 1995.

Hastings, Arthur. *With the Tongues of Men and Angels*. Ft. Worth, Tex.: Holt, Rinehart, Winston, 1991.

Moolenburg, H. C. *Meetings with Angels*. New York: Barnes & Noble, 1995.

Pruitt, James. *Angels through the Ages: All You Need to Know*. New York: Avon Books, 1995.

Steiger, Sherry, and Brad Steiger. *Angels around the World*. New York: Fawcett Columbine, 1996.

ILLUMINATION

The Buddha (c. 563–c. 483 B.C.E.) had spent one week in *samadhi*, a state of deep awareness when, on the morning of December 8, 528 B.C.E., he looked up at Venus, the morning star, beheld its brilliance, and exclaimed in a state of enlightenment, "That's it! That's me! That's me that's shining so brilliantly!"

Rinzai Zen master Shodo Harada Roshi (1940–   ) writes, in *Morning Dewdrops of the Mind: Teachings of a Contemporary Zen Master* (1993), that Buddha, in the rebirth of his consciousness, looked around and saw how wondrous it was that all beings were shining with the brilliance of the morning star. From such a deep illumination of the mind of Buddha, all of Buddha's wisdom was born and all of Zen was held within the deep impression of Buddha's mind at that moment. Therefore, each year as the eighth of December approaches, Zen monks anticipate the *rohatsu sesshin* (intensive meditation retreat) and vow to experience the brilliance of such a deep realization.

In *An Introduction to Zen Buddhism* (1934), D. T. Suzuki (1870–1966) describes satori, the state of illumination attained by reaching a higher level of consciousness, as the state that the masters of Zen call the mind of Buddha, the knowledge whereby humans experience enlightenment or Prajna, the highest wisdom. "It is the godly light, the inner heaven, the key of all the treasures of the mind, the focal point of thought and consciousness, the source of power and might, the seat of goodness, of justice, of sympathy, of the measure of all things," Suzuki states. "When this inmost knowledge is fully awakened, we are able to understand that each of us is identical in spirit, in being, and in nature with universal life."

The Hindu scripture Bhagavad Gita's instruction on how best to practice Yoga ends with the promise that "...when the mind of the Yogi is in harmony and finds rest in the Spirit within, all restless desires gone, then he is a Yukta, one in God. Then his soul is a lamp whose light is steady, for it burns in a shelter where no winds come."

In the chapter on "Basic Mystical Experience" in his *Watcher on the Hills* (1959), Dr. Raynor C. Johnson (1901–1987) places "the appearance of light" at the top of his list of illumination characteristics:

1. *The Appearance of light.* This observation is uniformly made, and may be regarded as a criterion of the contact of soul and Spirit.

2. *Ecstasy, love, bliss.* Directly or by implication, almost all the accounts [of mystical experience] refer to the supreme emotional tones of the experience.

3. *The Approach to one-ness.* In the union of soul with Spirit, the former acquires a sense of unity with all things.

Johnson lists other aspects of the illumination as profound insights given to the recipient of the experience; a positive effect on the person's health and vitality; a sense that time has been obscured or altered; and a positive effect on the individual's lifestyle. Johnson quotes a recipient of the illumination experience who said, "Its significance for me has been incalculable and has helped me through sorrows and stresses."

In her autobiographical work *Don't Fall Off the Mountain* (1970), actress/author Shirley MacLaine (1934–) tells of the night that she lay shivering in a Bhutanese hut in the Paro Valley of the Himalayas, wondering how she might overcome the terrible cold. Suddenly she remembered the words of a Yoga instructor in Calcutta who had told her that there was a center in her mind that was her nucleus, the center of her universe. Once she would find this nucleus, neither pain, fear, nor sorrow, could touch her. He had instructed her that it would look like a tiny sun. "The sun is the center of every solar system and the reason for all life on all planets in all universes," he had said. "So it is with yours."

With her teeth chattering, she closed her eyes and searched for the center of her mind. Then the cold room and the wind outside began to leave her conscious mind. Slowly in the center of her mind's eye a tiny, round, orange ball appeared. She stared and stared at it. Then she felt as though she had become the little orange ball. Heat began to spread down through her neck and arms and finally stopped in her stomach. She felt drops of perspiration on her midriff and forehead.

MacLaine writes that the light grew brighter and brighter until she finally sat up on her cot with a start and opened her eyes, fully expecting to find that someone had turned on a light. "I lay back," she said. "I felt as though I was glowing.... The instructor was right; hidden beneath the surface there was something greater than my outer self."

Parapsychologist Dr. W. G. Roll has commented that "It is true that this light phenomenon does occur. Some people believe it's a sort of quasi-physical light. When we get into these areas, it becomes difficult to distinguish between the physical and the spiritual worlds. What we call the spiritual, the physical, and the mental, are probably all the same thing."

Dr. Walter Houston Clark speaks of the phenomenon of the blinding light of illumination in connection with those who have undergone revelatory experiences as "...a kind of symbol of the new and freeing insight into the nature of the subject's existence. However, I am inclined to think that the profundity and excitement of the experience causes some kind of nervous activity that produces the light. Of course, in some sense, this may have a cosmic origin."

Writing in *Psychiatry* (Vol. 29, 1966), Dr. Arthur J. Deikman refers to the mystical perceptions of encompassing light in terms of his hypothesis of a "sensory translation," which he defines as "the perception of psychic action (conflict, repression, problem solving, attentiveness, and so forth) via the relatively unstructured sensations of light, color, movement, force, sound, smell or taste…. 'Sensory translation' refers to the experience of nonverbal, simple, concrete perceptual equivalents of psychic action." In Deikman's theory, "light" may be more than a metaphor for mystical experience: "Illumination may be derived from an actual sensory experience occurring when, in the cognitive act of unification, a liberation of energy takes place, or when a resolution of unconscious conflict occurs, permitting the experience of 'peace,' 'presence,' and the like. Liberated energy experienced as light may be the core sensory experience of mysticism."

According to research conducted at the University of Wales, Christians, Jews, and Muslims have similar experiences in which they describe an intense light and a sense of encompassing love. The research-in-progress, funded by the Sir Alister Hardy Trust, has collected 6,000 accounts of religious experiences from people of all ages and backgrounds. About 1,000 of these describe a light which enters the room, and others tell of being enveloped or filled with light. Most people are alone when they have such an experience, but the researchers have collected accounts of a number of individuals witnessing the same light.

Sir Alister Hardy (1896–1985) formed the Religious Experience Research Unit, Manchester College, Oxford, in 1969 and began the program by studying a more general kind of spiritual awareness—the feeling of being in touch with some "transcendental power, whether called God or not, which leads to a better life." Although the researchers stressed their interest in collecting these kinds of reports, they immediately received an almost equal number "of the more ecstatic mystical type," which included experiences with the light phenomenon that accompanied illumination.

In his book *The Divine Flame* (1966) Hardy suggested that science should "entertain the possibility that the rapture of spiritual experience…may…be a part of natural history…and that perhaps it may have only developed as religion when man's speech enabled him to compare and discuss this strange feeling of what [Rudolf] Otto called the numinous…[and] what I am calling a divine flame as an integral part of the creative evolutionary process which man, with his greater perceptive faculties, is now becoming aware."

Hardy concedes that science can no more be concerned with the "inner essence" of religion than it can be with the nature of art or the poetry of human love. But he does maintain that "an organized scientific knowledge—indeed one closely related to psychology—dealing with the records of man's religious experience…need not destroy the elements of religion which are most precious to man—any more than our biological knowledge of sex need diminish the passion and beauty of human love."

With the advent of the twenty-first century, many scientists are involved in research projects dealing with religious, spiritual, and mystical experiences. *Varieties of Anomalous Experiences* (2000), edited by Etzel Cardena, of the University of Texas Pan American in Edinburg, Steven J. Lynn, of the State University of New York at Binghamton, and Stanley Krippner, of the Saybrook Graduate School in San Francisco, examines the scientific evidence for altered states of consciousness associated with mystical experiences and other so-called anomalous events. According to *Science News* (February 17, 2001), the three psychologists "see no reason to assume that supernatural worlds…exist outside of the minds of people who report them. Instead [they] want to launch a science to study the characteristics of human consciousness that make mystical experiences possible. Their focus on a spectrum of consciousness defies the mainstream notion that there's a single type of awareness...."

David M. Wulff, a psychologist at Wheaton College in Norton, Massachusetts, has said that mystical experiences occur on a continuum: "Even if they are not religiously inspired, they can be striking, such as the transcendent feelings musicians sometimes get while they perform. I have colleagues who say they've had mystical experiences, although they have various ways to explain them."

Other scientists pursuing the study of mystical experiences suggest that the transcendent feelings noted by musicians, actors, and artists; the claims of two-thirds of American adults who claim to have been in touch with a force or spirit outside of themselves; and even the illumination of Buddha or the heavenly voices heard by Moses (14th–13th century B.C.E.), Muhammed (c. 570C.E.–632C.E.), and Jesus (c. 6 B.C.E.–c. 30 C.E.) were nothing more than the decreased activity of the brain's parietal lobe, which helps regulate the sense of self and physical orientation. And what of the feelings of unconditional love and overwhelming compassion for all living things that come over so many of those who claim illumination? These scientists argue that perhaps prayer, meditation, chanting, or some other religious or spiritual practice could have activated the temporal lobe, which imbues certain experiences with personal significance.

Other scientists testing the boundaries of the human psyche and the wonders of illumination are more open to the reality of the individual mystical experience. While researchers like Matthew Alper, author of *The "God" Part of the Brain* (1998), argue that human brains are hardwired for God and religious experiences, others, such as Daniel Batson, a University of Kansas psychologist, respond that the "brain is the hardware through which religion is experienced."

Duke psychiatrist Roy Mathew told the *Washington Post* (June 18, 2001) that too many of the contemporary neuroscientists and neurotheologians are "taking the viewpoints of the physicists of the last century that everything is matter. I am open to the possibility that there is more to this than what meets the eye. I don't believe in the omnipotence of science or that we have a foolproof explanation."

🜊 **Delving Deeper**

Bach, Marcus. *The Inner Ecstasy*. New York, Cleveland: World Publishing, 1969.

James, William. *Varieties of Religious Experience*. Garden City, N.Y.: Masterworks Program, 1902.

Otto, Rudolf. *The Idea of the Holy*. New York: Galaxy Books, 1958.

Suzuki, D. T. *Mysticism, Christian and Buddhist*. New York: Perennial, 1971.

Tart, Charles T. *Altered States of Consciousness*. New York: John Wiley & Sons, 1969.

Underhill, Evelyn. *Mysticism*. New York: Dutton, 1961.

Inquisition

When Christianity became the state religion of Rome in the fourth century, those who held dissenting or differing views from the established church were condemned as heretics and excommunicated from church membership. Most of the early church fathers, such as St. Augustine (d. 604), were displeased by any action taken by the state toward heretics, but the clergy generally gave their reluctant approval, stressing that the church abhorred any kind of physical mistreatment of dissenters.

In 906, the *Canon Episcopi* by Abbot Regino of Prum (d. c. 915) condemned as heretical any belief in witchcraft or in the power of sorcerers to transform people into animals. The consensus of the Christian clergy was that those individuals who believed that they could fly through the air or work evil magic on another person were allowing Satan to deceive them. The clergy was more concerned with stamping out all allegiance to the goddess Diana and any other regional deities, and they regarded as primitive superstition any suggestion that witches possessed any kind of magical powers. In 1000, Deacon Burchard (d. 1025), later archbishop of Worms, published *Corrector*, which updated Regino's *Canon Episcopi* and stressed that God alone had the kind of power that the untutored masses were attributing to witches. In 1022 there occurred the first fully attested burning of a heretic, in the city of Orleans.

By the twelfth century, the **Cathar** sect had become so popular among the people that Pope Innocent III (1160 or 1161–1216) considered it a greater menace to Christianity than the Islamic warriors who pummeled the crusaders and who threatened all of Europe. To satisfy his outrage, he ordered the only Crusade ever launched by Christians against fellow Christians, declaring as heretics the Albigensians, as the Cathars of southern France were known.

The Inquisition came into existence in 1231 with the *Excommunicamus* of Pope Gregory IX (c. 1170–1241), who at first urged local bishops to become more vigorous in ridding Europe of heretics, then lessened their responsibility for determining orthodoxy by establishing inquisitors under the special jurisdiction of the papacy. The office of inquisitor was entrusted primarily to the Franciscans and the Dominicans, because of their reputation for superior knowledge of theology and their declared freedom from worldly ambition. Each tribunal was ordered to include two inquisitors of equal authority, who would be assisted by notaries, police, and counselors. Because they had the power to excommunicate even members of royal houses, the inquisitors were formidable figures with whom to reckon.

In 1257, the church officially sanctioned torture as a means of forcing witches, sorcerers, shapeshifters, and other heretics to confess their alliance with Satan.

In 1246 Montsegur, the center of Albigensian resistance, fell, and hundreds of Cathars were burned at the stake. The headquarters of the Inquisition was established in Toulouse, and in 1252, Pope Innocent IV (d. 1254) issued a papal bull that placed inquisitors above the law. Another decree within the bull

demanded that all civil rulers and all commoners must assist the work of the Inquisition or face excommunication. In 1257, the church officially sanctioned torture as a means of forcing witches, sorcerers, shapeshifters, and other heretics to confess their alliance with Satan.

The inquisitors would stay in a particular location for weeks or months, from which they would bring suit against any person suspected of heresy. Lesser penalties were levied against those who came forward of their own volition and confessed their heresy than against those who ignored the summons and had to be placed on trial. The tribunal allowed a grace period of about a month for the accused to come to them and confess before the heretic would be arrested and brought to trial. The penances and sentences for those who confessed or were found guilty during the trial were pronounced by the inquisitors at a public ceremony known as the *sermo generalis* or *auto-da-fe* and might consist of a public whipping, a pilgrimage to a holy shrine, a monetary fine, or the wearing of a cross. The most severe penalty that the inquisitors could pronounce was life imprisonment; therefore, when they turned over a confessed heretic to the civil authorities, it was quite likely that person would be put to death at the stake.

The wealthy and powerful **Knights Templar** were accused of heretical acts, such as invoking Satan and worshipping demons that appeared as large black cats. In spite of a lengthy trial and 573 witnesses for their defense, the arrested Templars were tortured *en masse*, burned at the stake, and their order was disbanded by Pope Clement V (c. 1260–1314). In 1313 as he was being burned to death on a scaffold built for the occasion in front of Notre Dame Cathedral, Jacques de Molay (1243–1314), the Knights Templar grand master, recanted the confession produced by torture and proclaimed his innocence to the pope and the king—and he invited them to meet him at heaven's gate. When both dignitaries died soon after de Molay's execution, it seemed to the public at large to be a sign that the grand master had been innocent of the charges of heresy.

With the Albigensian heresy destroyed, the Inquisition began to direct more of its attention toward witches. In 1320 Bernard Gui (c. 1261–1331) published *Practica*, an influential instructional manual for inquisitors, in which he urged them to pay particular heed to arresting those women who cavorted with the goddess Diana. Four years later, in 1324, Ireland's first witchcraft trial convened when Alice Kyteler was found guilty of consorting with a demon.

Separate from the Inquisition that extended its jurisdiction over all the rest of Europe, in 1478, at the request of King Ferdinand II (1452–1516) and Queen Isabella I (1451–1504), papal permission was granted to establish the Spanish Inquisition. More a political, than a religious, weapon, this Inquisition persecuted the Marranos or conversos, those Jews suspected of insincerely converting to Christianity; converts from Islam, similarly thought to be insincere in practicing the Christian faith; and, in the 1520s, those individuals who were believed to have converted to Protestantism. The support of Spain's royal house enabled Tomas de Torquemada (1420–1498) to become the single grand inquisitor whose name has become synonymous with the Inquisition's most cruel acts and excesses. Torquemada is known to have ordered the deaths by torture and burning of thousands of heretics and witches.

In 1484, Pope Innocent VIII (1432–1492) became so angered by the apparent spread of witchcraft in Germany that he issued the papal bull *Summis Desiderantes Affectibus* and authorized two trusted Dominican inquisitors, Heinrich Institoris (Henry Kramer) (1430–1505) and Jakob Sprenger (c. 1435–1495), to stamp out demonology in the Rhineland. In 1486, Kramer and Sprenger published *Malleus Maleficarum*, the "Hammer for Witches," which quickly became the "bible" of heretic and witch hunters. The book earnestly refuted all those who would claim that the works of demons existed only in troubled human minds. Certain angels fell from heaven, and to believe otherwise was to believe contrary to the true faith. And now these fallen angels, these demons, were intent upon destroying the human race. Any persons who consorted with demons and became witches must recant their evil ways or be put to death.

By the late sixteenth century, the power of the Inquisition was beginning to wane. In 1563, Johann Weyer (Weir) (1515–1588), a critic of the Inquisition, managed to publish *De praestigus daemonum*, in which he argued that while Satan does seek to ensnare and destroy human beings, the charge that accused witches, werewolves, and vampires possessed supernatural powers was false. Such abilities existed only in their minds and imaginations. As if to provide an antidote to Weyer's call for a rational approach to dealing with accusations of witchcraft, in 1580 the respected intellectual Jean Bodin (1530–1596), often referred to as the Aristotle of the sixteenth century, wrote *De La demonomanie des sorciers*, a book that caused the flames once again to burn high around thousands of heretics' stakes.

BY *the late sixteenth century, the power of the Inquisition was beginning to wane.*

With the spread of Protestantism throughout Europe, in 1542 Pope Paul III (1468–1549) established the Congregation of the Inquisition (also known as the Roman Inquisition and the Holy Office), which consisted of six cardinals, including the reformer Gian Pietro Cardinal Carafa (1476–1559). Although their powers extended to the whole church, the Holy Office was less concerned about heresies and false beliefs of church members than they were with misstatements of orthodoxy in the academic writings of its theologians. When Carafa became Pope Paul IV in 1555, he approved the first *Index of Forbidden Books* (1559) and vigorously sought out any academics who were prompted any thought that offended church doctrine or favored Protestantism.

Although organized **witchcraft trials** continued to be held throughout Europe, and even the American colonies, until the late seventeenth century, they were most often civil affairs and the Inquisition had little part in such ordeals. However, the Holy Office continued to serve as the instrument by which the papal government regulated church order and doctrine, and it did try and condemn Galileo (1564–1642) in 1633. In 1965, Pope Paul VI (1897–1978) reorganized the Holy Office and renamed it the Congregation for the Doctrine of the Faith.

✤ DELVING DEEPER

Netanyahu, B. *The Origins of the Inquisition*. New York: Random House, 1995.

Russell, Jeffrey Burton. *Witchcraft in the Middle Ages*. Ithaca, N.Y.: Cornell University Press, 1972.

Seligmann, Kurt. *The History of Magic*. New York: Pantheon Books, 1948.

Trevor-Roper, H. R. *The European Witch-Craze*. New York: Harper & Row, 1967.

MIRACLES

According to a Gallup poll taken in 1988, 88 percent of the people in the United States believed in miracles. In the results of a survey on spirituality published in the December 1997 issue of *Self* magazine, 91 percent of the readers who responded answered that they believed in miracles. In that same month and year, a poll commissioned by the Pew Research Center found that 61 percent of Americans believed in miracles and that such acts originate from the power of God. The May 1, 2000, issue of *Newsweek* carried the result of that news magazine's poll that stated 84 percent of American adults said they believe that God performs miracles and 48 percent claimed to have witnessed one.

MIRACLES *have been defined as physical events that defy the laws of nature.*

Jon Butler, a Yale University professor of American history who specializes in American religion, defined miracles as physical events that defy the laws of nature. "Most miracles have some physical manifestation that is evi-

dent not only to the individuals involved, but may be evident to the people around them," he said. "The catch is, how do you explain it?"

Father James Wiseman, associate professor of theology at Catholic University, said that there are always going to be some people "who see immediately the hand of God in every coincidence, and those who are going to be skeptical of everything. And there is a great in-between."

Miracle stories are found in all the world religions, and while accounts of wonder-working saints and sages and the ancient acts of divine intervention in human affairs are celebrated regularly by the faithful who gather in churches, synagogues, and mosques throughout the world, contemporary Buddhists, Christians, Hindus, Jews, and Muslims still pray for and expect miraculous occurrences in their own lives today. And, according to the *Newsweek* survey, 43 percent of those polled who belonged to no religious body at all admitted that they had on occasion prayed for God's intervention.

Both the Old and New Testaments of the Bible are filled with miracles and wonders performed by prophets, angels, and God. So, too, does the Qur'an contain accounts of countless miracles, thus enabling the contemporary followers of Islam to expect such occurrences as proof of the validity of their faith. Islamic theologians have established two basic kinds of miracles: the *mu'jizat*, or prophetic miracles; and the *karamat*, those wonders performed by holy people and saints.

The Roman Catholic tradition contains many healing miracles performed by saints and popes—both alive and in spirit. Early in 1967 the *Irish Independent* of Dublin carried the account of a miracle healing that had brought a dying nun "from death's door to a healthy normal life" after the spirit of Pope John XXIII (1881–1963), who had died in 1963, appeared and spoke to her.

Sister Caterina Capitani (b. 1943 or 1944), a nun of the Sisters of Charity of St. Vincent de Paul, suffered from varicose veins of the esophagus, a condition thought to be incurable and surgically inoperable. However, because the unfortunate sister endured con-

I n Italy alone there are 190 blood samples of various saints that are venerated by the faithful as important religious relics. In a number of cases, these vials of clotted blood become liquefied in a paranormal manner, especially during religious ceremonies, thus exalting the sample from relic to a supernatural miracle.

Perhaps the most celebrated of such relics is the vial of blood said to be that of St. Januarius (c. 272–305), an early bishop of Benevento, who was beheaded during the persecutions of the Christians by Emperor Diocletian (245–316) in 305. Once or twice a year since 1389, St. Januarius' dried blood has liquefied in full view of the pilgrims who arrive to pay tribute to his memory in Naples.

The blood of St. Lorenzo (d. 258) rests in a small flask in the right wing of the church of St. Maria in Amaseno. Lorenzo was martyred on August 10, 258 under the order of the Emperor Valerian (d. 260), and although he was condemned to be burned to death on a grill, some of his blood was caught and preserved by his fellow Christians. Each year on the anniversary of his martyrdom, the vial is brought near the altar and locked in a glass cabinet. There, in full view of the assembled worshippers at St. Maria, the transformation of the centuries-old clotted blood to liquid occurs.

Psychical researcher Luigi Garlaschelli has proposed that a process called "thixotropy" might explain how the blood of St. Januarius might liquefy each year. Thixotropy "denotes the property of certain gels to liquefy when stirred or vibrated, and to solidify again when left to stand." It is Garlaschelli's theory that the very act of handling the relic during the religious ceremony, the motions of a priest repeatedly checking the progress of the blood in the vial, might well provide the necessary movement to prompt the liquefaction of the saint's blood.

But the investigator is cautious about applying his theory to explain the liquefied blood of St. Lorenzo, which is only moved once on August 10 from its place of safekeeping to the altar, or the large vial containing the blood of St. Panatleone, which becomes liquefied

LIQUEFIED BLOOD OF SAINTS

on July 27 and is never moved from its resting place behind a grating.

Garlaschelli speculates that the overall look of the substances in the vials, together with their observed properties of softening and liquefying when near the warming effect of altar candles and human touch, then returning to solid once removed from the warmth, suggest that the relics may consist of fats or waxes and an oil-soluble red dye. While the rational mind insists that the substance in the vials of the saints cannot possibly be blood, until church authorities permit scientists to withdraw actual specimens from the receptacles, the question remains a puzzle to scientists and a miracle of faith to believers.

SOURCES:

Garlaschelli, Luigi, Ramacine, F. and S. Della Sala. "Working Bloody Miracles," *Nature,* Vol. 353, 1991, p. 507.

———. "A Miracle Diagnosis," *Chemistry in Britain,* Vol. 30, 1994, p. 123.

tinual hemorrhages, physicians decided to attempt an operation at Medical Missionaries of Mary of the Clinca Mediterranea in Naples, Italy. Two surgeries were performed, but they were unsuccessful; and when the incision on her stomach opened, Sister Caterina's condition steadily worsened to the point where she collapsed. Desperate to attempt any new therapy, her doctors sent the nun south for a change of air, but she was soon returned to Naples when it was decided that she had only a brief time to live.

Sister Caterina lay in her room alone. She had turned on her side when she felt someone place a hand on her stomach. Summoning all her strength, she turned to see Pope John XXIII standing beside her bed. He was not attired in his papal robes, but she easily recognized him. In a quiet yet authoritative voice, the ethereal image of the pope, who had died on June 3, 1963, spoke words of great comfort: "Sister, you have called to me so many times…that you have torn out of my heart this miracle. Do not fear. You are healed."

VARIOUS *committees of the Roman Catholic Church takes serious steps to authenticate a miracle.*

The spirit of Pope John then told Sister Caterina to call in the sisters and the doctors so that a test could be performed. But before she did so, he assured her once again that no trace of her illness would remain. Just before the image vanished, he told Sister Caterina to come to Rome and pray at his tomb.

The moment the spirit of the deceased pope disappeared, Sister Caterina rose from her bed and was elated that she felt no pain. When she summoned the sisters and doctors into her room, they were astonished to find that the scar on her abdomen, which had been open and bleeding, was now completely healed. No other physical sign indicated that moments before there had been a gaping wound. The sisters declared the healing a miracle. Sister Caterina had not been expected to

survive the day, yet that evening she was up and eating her supper with the community.

According to the *Irish Independent*, ever since her miracle healing by the apparition of Pope John XXIII, Sister Caterina lived a normal, healthy life in every way. "This is a phenomenon that cannot be explained in a human way," the account concluded.

Contrary to those skeptics who suggest that the Roman Catholic Church is likely to accept nearly all claims of miracles as genuine, many serious steps are taken by various committees to authenticate a miracle. Father Frederick Jelly, professor of systematic theology at Mount Saint Mary's Seminary in Emmitsburg, Maryland, has served on miracles committees and has listed the questions asked to authenticate a miracle as the following: What is the psychological state of the person claiming the miracle? Is there a profit motive behind the miracle claim? What is the character of the person who is claiming the miracle? Does the miracle contain any elements contrary to scripture or faith? What are the spiritual fruits of the miracle—does it attract people to prayer or to acts of greater charity?

Once these questions have been determined and reviewed, the committee makes its decision as to whether or not the event was heaven-inspired. If the committee decides the event is miraculous and its implications have national or international effect, the case may be referred to the Vatican's Sacred Congregation for the Doctrine of the Faith in Rome. The Sacred Congregation has the authority to institute a new investigation and make its own ruling and recommendation to the pope, who is the final arbiter of the validity of miracles.

Rather than miracles, Philip Hefner, professor of systematic theology at the Lutheran School of Theology in Chicago, stated in an essay in *Newsweek* (May 1, 2000) that he would rather talk about blessings. "We receive blessings, often quite unexpectedly, and we want to praise God for them. We know we cannot claim the credit for these blessings. Even though we cannot predict their arrival, nor understand why so much of human life involves sorrow and evil, we can be grateful and render praise."

✤ DELVING DEEPER

Glynn, Patrick. *God: The Evidence—The Reconciliation of Faith and Reason in a Postsecular World.* Rocklin, Calif.: Prima Publishing, 1997.

Humphrey, Nicholas. *Science, Miracles and the Search for Supernatural Consolation.* New York: Basic Books, 1996.

Lewis, C. S. *Miracles.* New York: Macmillan, 1970.

Schroeder, Gerald L. *The Science of God: The Convergence of Scientific and Biblical Wisdom.* New York: Free Press, 1997.

Steiger, Sherry Hansen, and Brad Steiger. *Mother Mary Speaks to Us.* New York: Dutton, 1996; Signet, 1997.

POSSESSION

In February 2001, a 53-year-old Oklahoma woman who had no history of mental illness, drug or alcohol abuse, or domestic strife, began working a **Ouija board** with her daughter and two granddaughters. Later that night, claiming to be possessed by a spirit from the Ouija board that told her to kill, the woman stabbed to death her son-in-law, who was sleeping in another room, and attempted to kill other members of her family. Police later apprehended the woman, who was hiding in a wooded area, and commented how unbelievable it was that she could have allowed a Ouija board to "consume her life."

International newspapers carried an account in March 2001 describing how demands for **exorcisms** were soaring in Brazil due to the fact that demonic possession was on the rise. A priest was quoted as saying that he believed the number of evil spirits among the populace could only mean that the **Apocalypse** would soon be manifesting.

In April 2001, Croatian newspapers reported that the Roman Catholic clergy were desperately looking for exorcists to deal with the large numbers of men and women who gave evidence of being possessed by Satan.

In June 2001, a new Gallup poll of adult Americans indicated that 41 percent believe that people can be possessed by the devil or his minions.

The majority of healthcare professionals discount possession by spirits as superstitious nonsense and believe such claims to be primitive responses to a variety of mental illnesses, and there are few contemporary clergymen who will acknowledge the existence of demons and the possibility of demonic or spirit possession. However, Dr. Morton Kelsey, an Episcopal priest and a noted Notre Dame professor of theology, has this to say to those who protest that demon possession is a superstitious throwback to the Middle Ages: "Most people in the modern world consider themselves too sophisticated and too intelligent to be concerned with demons. But in thirty years of study, I have seen the effect of demons upon humans."

A MAJORITY *of healthcare professionals discount possession by spirits as superstitious nonsense and believe such claims to be primitive responses to a variety of mental illnesses.*

Kelsey maintains that demons are real and can invade the minds of humans. Demons are not the figment of the imagination, but are negative, destructive spiritual forces that seek to destroy the possessed host body and everyone with whom that person comes into contact. The most severe cases of possession can trigger suicide, Kelsey said, because the demon is trying to destroy people any way it can.

Among those traits which the Roman Catholic Church might find indicative of possession, rather than mental illness, are exhibition of superhuman strength; knowledge of languages outside of a person's education or training; demonstration of hidden insights into a person's private life or past indiscretions; and aversion to all things spiritual—holy water, the mass, a crucifix, or the name of Jesus.

While the skeptical might argue that LeBar is a priest, an exorcist, and that his theological training has conditioned him to believe in demons, they may wish to take into serious consideration the comments of Dr. Ralph Allison, senior psychiatrist at the California state prison in San Luis Obispo: "My conclusion after 30 years of observing over one thousand disturbed patients is that some of them act in a bizarre fashion due to possession by spirits. The spirit may be that of a human being who died. Or it may be a spirit entity that has never been a human being and sometimes identifies itself as a demon, an agent of evil."

Dr. Wilson Van Dusen, a university professor who has served as chief psychologist at Mendocino State Hospital, is another health care professional who has stated his opinion that many patients in mental hospitals are possessed by demons.

"I am totally convinced that there are entities that can possess our minds and our bodies," Van Dusen said. "I have even been able to speak directly to demons. I have heard their own guttural, other-world voices."

And all too often, some researchers say, those hellish guttural voices have commanded their possessed hosts to kill, to offer human sacrifice to Satan.

In a recent report released by the American Psychological Evaluation Corporation, Dr. Andrew Blankley, a sociologist, issued statements about the rise in contemporary sacrificial cults, warning that society at large might expect a "serious menace" to come. According to Blankley, human sacrifice constitutes an alarming trend in new religious cults: "Desperate people are seeking dramatic revelation and simplistic answers to complex social problems. They are attracted to fringe groups who provide the ritualistic irrationality that they crave. In the last ten years, fringe rituals often include the sacrifice of a human being."

Dr. Al Carlisle of the Utah State Prison System has estimated that between 40,000 and 60,000 humans are killed through ritual homicides in the United States every year. In the Las Vegas area alone, Carlisle asserts, as many as 600 people may die in demon-inspired ceremonies each year.

Based on a synthesis of the studies of certain clergy and psychical researchers, following is a pattern profile of what may occur when someone has become the unwilling host of an uninvited spirit presence and become possessed:

The possessed may begin to hear voices directing him/her to do antisocial or perverse acts that he/she had never before considered. He/she will claim to see the image of a spirit or demonic presence. In the weeks and months that follow, he/she may fall into states of blacked-out consciousness, times of which he/she later has absolutely no memory. On occasions, he/she will fall into a trance-like state. The possessed will be observed walking and speaking differently, and acting in a strange, irrational manner. He/she will begin doing things that he/she has never done before. In the worst of cases, the possessing spirit or demon will consume the victim's life. It may reach to a climax where the possessed commits murder, suicide, or some violent antisocial act.

Healthcare professionals will point out that many of the above "symptoms" of possession may also indicate the onset of stress, depression, and certain mental illnesses.

Dr. Adam Crabtree, a psychotherapist in Toronto, has stated his view that the spirits of the deceased can possess their living relatives. Crabtree, who is a former priest and Benedictine monk, said that entities from beyond the grave usually seek a living person's mind and body because they have unfinished business on Earth. Crabtree has encountered such cases when emotionally disturbed patients came to him complaining that they seemed to feel a "presence" in them that was different from their usual mental awareness. Crabtree discovered that these people were adopting traits and characteristics that were not their own. They complained of hearing voices that told them what to do, and they saw mental images of dead relatives who were dictating their actions.

While more conventional psychotherapists might provide a different diagnosis from Crabtree's, in his opinion because the spirits were related to the living person and were emotionally tied to them, their physical relationship made possession easier to accomplish. The reasons for such possession vary. According to Crabtree's research, sometimes the dead simply do not realize that they have changed planes of existence and wish to maintain their relationship with their relatives. In other cases, the spirits want to take care of unfinished business and have no compunction about using their living relatives to attain their goals.

Dr. C. Fred Dickason, chairman of the Theology Department at Moody Bible Institute in Chicago, relates a number of cases of demonic possession through ancestral lines in his book *Demon Possession and the Christian* (1987). In one case, a Chicago-area pastor consulted Dickason to receive his advice concerning his father, who had been invaded by demonic spirits because his mother (the pastor's grandmother) had been heavily involved in occult practices. The entities had begun to enter the pastor's young daughter, but alert to possession, he prayed with his wife that the spirits be dismissed from her.

Dickason is of the firm opinion that demons, who are nonmaterial entities that may exist for thousands of years, feel that they have the right to enter any man or woman—regardless of how innocent he or she may be—whose ancestors were involved in occult and demonic activities.

✢ DELVING DEEPER

Crim, Keith, ed. *The Perennial Dictionary of World Religions*. San Francisco: HarperSanFrancisco, 1989.

Harpur, Patrick. *Daimonic Reality*. London: Penguin Group, 1994.

Karpel, Craig. *The Rite of Exorcism: The Complete Text*. New York: Berkley, 1975.

Kinnaman, Gary. *Angels Dark and Light*. Ann Arbor, Mich.: Servant Publications, 1994.

Mack, Carol K., and Dinah Mack. *A Field Guide to Demons, Fairies, Fallen Angels, and Other Subversive Spirits*. New York: Owl Book, Henry Holt, 1999.

Montgomery, John Warwick. *Powers and Principalities*. Minneapolis: Dimension Books, 1975.

Van Dusen, Wilson. *The Presence of Other Worlds: The Findings of Emanuel Swedenborg*. New York: Harper & Row, 1974.

POWER OF PRAYER

Prayer is a basic element of religious expression. According to a survey taken by Lutheran Brotherhood and reported in *USA Today* (February 7, 1997) Americans are great practitioners of prayer: 24 percent of those polled said that they prayed more than once a day; 31 percent prayed every day; 16 percent, several times a week; 10 percent, several times a month; 9 percent, several times a year.

PRAYER *is a basic element of religious expression.*

For Christians worldwide the "perfect prayer" is the one that Jesus (c. 6 B.C.E.–c. 30 C.E.) gave to his apostles and which has been known for centuries as the Lord's Prayer: "And…as [Jesus] was praying in a certain place, when he ceased, one of his disciples said unto him, Lord, teach us to pray as John [the Baptist] also taught his disciples. And he said unto them, "When ye pray, say,

> Our Father which art in heaven, Hallowed be thy name. Thy kingdom come. Thy will be done, as in heaven, so on Earth. Give us this day our daily bread. And forgive us our sins; for we also forgive everyone that is indebted to us. And lead us not into temptation; but deliver us from evil" (Luke 11: 1–4, King James Version). [Matthew 6:13 adds: "For thine is the kingdom and the power and the glory, forever. Amen."]

The Lord's Prayer has long been esteemed as without equal or rival as a prayer. "Short and mysterious," the seventeenth-century bishop Jeremy Taylor (1613–1667) declared, "and like the treasures of the Spirit, full of wisdom and latent senses."

Jesus prayed a great deal throughout the gospels. In addition to his giving of the well-known prayer quoted above, he prayed at his baptism (Luke 3:21), before he chose the Twelve (Luke 6:12), before his invitation to all humankind to "come unto" him (Matthew 11:25–27), at the feeding of the 5,000 (John 6:11), before his Transfiguration (Luke 9:28–29), for little children (Matthew 19:13), at the Last Supper (Matthew 26:26–27), in

The phenomenon of speaking in tongues during ecstatic religious experiences is also known as glossolalia, and began among the first Christians.

Described in Acts 2:1–18, the Holy Spirit granted to the apostles the ability to speak in the languages of the foreigners who had assembled in Jerusalem for the observance of Pentecost. The visitors were amazed they could speak with them in their native language.

While Holy Spirit allowed the apostles to converse suddenly in a foreign language, later references implied that glossolalia was a kind of religious ecstasy or unintelligible babbling. In I Corinthians, Paul lists the variety of spiritual gifts that might be received by Christians; he writes that one such blessing is the ability to interpret what another speaking in tongues might be saying. Paul states that those who speak in a tongue that only God can understand might well be pleasing themselves, but they deliver no edification to others in the church. He concludes that, if one speaks in unknown tongues and no one can interpret the speech, then "let him keep silence in the church and speak to himself and to God."

Paul's denigration of the act of speaking in tongues set the standard for Christians down through the centuries. Various church fathers advised against the practice, and St. John of Chrysostom (c. 347–407) believed that the usefulness of glossolalia for the Christian ended in the first century. St. Augustine (354–430) denied that any special ability, such as speaking in tongues, prophesy, and so forth, proved one's faith. With the advent of the Protestant Reformation, leaders such as Martin Luther (1483–1546) dismissed glossolalia as unnecessary to the Christian faith.

In the eighteenth century, however, certain new visionary sects, such as the Shakers and the Catholic Apostolic Church, began to consider speaking in tongues as one of the special gifts given to true believers. Then, in the early 1900s, Pentecostalism declared that "Spirit-baptism" brought with its indwelling power the ability to speak in tongues. In the 1960s, glossolalia became suddenly popular even among the more mainstream churches.

SPEAKING IN TONGUES

While the movement spread in the 1970s, the position largely taken by the mainstream church bodies was that, while it may be legitimate gift from the Holy Spirit, glossolalia was hardly the normative expression for Christians and did not denote a superiority over those who did not practice it. However, today's approximately 500,000 practicing Pentecostals continue to believe in the power of the Holy Spirit to bring about a baptism of the spirit like that received by the apostles that enabled them to speak in tongues.

SOURCES:

Dyer, Luther B. *Tongues*. Jefferson City, Mo.: Le Roi, 1971.

Rosten, Leo. *Religions of America*. New York: Simon & Schuster, 1975.

Sherrill, John L. *They Speak with Other Tongues*. New York: Pyramid Books, 1965.

Gethsemane (Matthew 26: 36–44), and on the Cross (Luke 24:30) to name only some of the most significant prayers recorded by the gospel writers. But as often as Jesus declared that prayer could work mysteries and wonders, he also admonished his followers concerning the secret nature of the act of praying:

> "When thou prayest, thou shalt not be as the hypocrites are, for they love to pray standing in the synagogues and in the corners of the streets that they may be seen of men.… But thou, when thou prayest, enter into thy closet, and when thou hast shut thy door, pray to the Father which is in secret; and thy Father which seeth in secret shall reward thee openly. But when ye pray, use not vain repetitions, as the heathen do, for they think they shall be heard for their much speaking. Be not ye therefore like unto them: for your Father knoweth what things ye have need of before ye ask him" (Matthew 6: 5–8, King James Version).

In Islam prayer, *salat* is one of the five Pillars of Islam, and the true believer must say his prayers (*salla*) five times a day, as well as on special occasions. The set schedule of prayers—dawn, noon, afternoon, sunset, and nighttime—is strictly prescribed and regulated. There is another category of prayer, the *du'a*, which permits spontaneous expressions of supplication, petition, and intercession. The *du'a* may also be allowed after the uttering of the formal *salat*.

While many religions suggest that their supplicants fold their hands, bow their head, close their eyes, and so forth, the followers of Islam have many exact procedures that must be observed in their prayers. Before prayer, there is the ritual purification (*tahara*), which at the very least requires washing the face and the hands to the elbows, rubbing the head with water, and bathing the feet to the ankles. In addition, the mouth, nose, and teeth must receive a thorough cleansing. If water should be unavailable to someone on a journey or away from home, clean earth or sand may be substituted in an abbreviated ritual exercise of cleansing.

Believing in the power of prayer, a group of Muslims pray for rain in Kabul, Afghanistan. (AP/ WIDE WORLD PHOTOS)

In a city or village, the call to prayer (*Adhan*) is announced from a minaret or tall building by a muezzin, a crier. When the worshippers have assembled, another crier issues the *iqama* in a rapid, but more subdued, voice, announcing that it is now time to begin the prayers. If the worshippers should be away from a city, a mosque, or a muezzin, they themselves may call out the two summons to prayer.

A TRUE *believer of Islam must say his prayers* (salla) *five times a day—dawn, noon, afternoon, sunset, and nighttime.*

While it is desirable to pray in a mosque, when the supplicants find themselves away from a formal place of worship, they must attempt to find as clean an area as possible.

A ccording to a 2001 survey on the prayer habits of Americans conducted by Yankelovich Partners for Lutheran Brotherhood, nine out of 10 adults responded by saying that they prayed regularly. When asked what they most often prayed for, 98 percent answered that they prayed most frequently for their own family members. Petitions for the children of the world were designated for 81 percent of the prayers; 77 percent for world peace, and 69 percent for the needs and concerns of their co-workers.

In an earlier survey (c. 1992), Andrew M. Greeley, the sociologist-novelist-priest, and his research center found that 78 percent of Americans pray at least once a week and 57 percent pray at least once a day. Combining the statistics of the Father Greeley research with those of a Gallup and Poloma poll, it was revealed that 91 percent of women pray, as do 85 percent of men. Twenty-six percent of those who pray say that they regularly sense the strong presence of God, and 32 percent feel a deep sense of peace.

THE MOST POPULAR PRAYERS OF AMERICANS

SOURCES:

"Snapshot." *USA Today,* 14 June 2001.

"Talking to God." *Newsweek,* 6 January 1992, pp. 39–44.

Prayer rugs (*saijada*) are carried by many Muslims, but they are not an essential aspect of the ritual. It is essential to properly cover the body: males, at least from the navel to the knees; females, the entire body except for face, hands, and feet. It is also of utmost importance that wherever they may be, they face the *Qiblah,* the precise direction of Mecca. And while it is always preferable to perform the *salat* in the company of others, it is permissible under certain conditions to pray in private—except for the Friday congregational *salat,* which may never be performed alone.

Before kneeling on their prayer rugs, however, it is of the utmost importance that the supplicants perform a required number of bending and bowing postures (*rak'as*) with the appropriate accompanying phrases. There must be two *rak'as* at dawn, four at

noon, four in the afternoon, three at sunset, and four at night.

Jewish liturgy did not begin to achieve its fixed form until the centuries after the destruction of the second temple, and the prayer book did not appear in its classical form until the Middle Ages. But spontaneous prayers are found throughout the Tanakh, the Hebrew Bible, and the Old Testament in the Christian Bible. To list only a few: the prayers of Abraham (Genesis 15:2–3), Isaac (Genesis 25:21–23), and Hannah (1 Samuel 1:9–13) petitioning God for an heir; Moses' prayers for plagues on the Egyptians (Exodus 8:12), for the Red Sea to part its waters (Exodus 14:21), for a glimpse of God's glory (Exodus 33:18), for Aaron's forgiveness after his sin of making the gold calf (Deuteronomy 9:20); Samson's prayer for strength to bring the columns down upon the Philistines (Judges 16:28–31); David's prayer to be forgiven for his immorality with Bathsheba (Psalms 51); Job's prayer to be forgiven for pride (Job 40:3–4; 42:6); Solomon's prayer for wisdom (1 Kings 3:5–9); Elijah's prayer for fire to consume the altars of Baal (1 Kings 18:36–37); Jabez's prayer for prosperity in his work (1 Chronicles 4:10).

There is a rich Jewish tradition that envisions angels carrying human prayers to heaven, and there is a belief that the entreaties of the righteous can more effectively intercede with God than ordinary mortals. As in the Christian and Islamic traditions, there are strict warnings against worshipping the angelic intercessors. God alone must be the sole and ultimate focus of all prayer.

In recent years, more and more doctors and scientists have begun to study the power that many religious men and women claim may be achieved by focusing their prayers upon God and asking healing for themselves or others. Dr. Larry Dossey (1940–   ), author of *Healing Words: The Power of Prayer and the Practice of Medicine* (1993), recalled when he was doing his residency at Parkland Memorial Hospital in Dallas, Texas, and had his first patient with a terminal case of cancer. Whenever he would stop by the man's hospital room, Dossey found him surrounded by visitors from his church, praying and singing. Dossey thought this was appropriate since they would soon be singing and praying at the man's funeral, because the cancer had spread throughout both lungs. A year later, when he was working elsewhere, Dossey learned from a colleague that the terminally ill patient was alive and well. When he had an opportunity to examine the man's X-rays, Dossey was stunned to see that his lungs were completely clear. There was no trace of cancer. Although Dossey had long since given up the faith of his childhood, it seemed to him that prayer had healed this man of his terminal cancer.

Intrigued, but devoted to the power of modern medicine, Dossey became chief of staff at a large urban hospital. He observed that many of his patients prayed, but he put little trust in the practice until he came across a study done in 1983 by Dr. Randolph Byrd, a cardiologist at San Francisco General Hospital, in which half of a group of cardiac patients were prayed for and half were not. Those who were prayed for did better in a significant number of ways. Dossey could no longer ignore the evidence. The Byrd study had been designed according to rigid criteria. It had been a randomized, double-blind experiment—neither the patients, nurses, nor doctors knew which group the patients were in.

Inspired to search for other such experiments, Dossey was astonished to find more than 100 serious and well-conducted studies exhibiting the criteria of good science. About half demonstrated that prayer could bring about significant changes in those suffering from a variety of illnesses. Dossey has since given up the practice of medicine to devote himself full time to researching and writing about prayer and how it affects human health. His extensive studies have produced the following discoveries:

THE *Jewish prayer book did not appear in its classical form until the Middle Ages.*

1. The power of prayer does not diminish with distance. It can be as effective from the other side of the world as it is from the next room.

2. There is no right way to pray. There is no difference in the effectiveness of the various religious methods of praying.

3. Rather than asking for a specific healing for a particular health problem, the nonspecific prayer, "Thy will be done," works as well or better as attempting to specify the outcome.

4. Love added to prayer increases its power.

5. Prayer is outside of time. It can be answered even before it is made.

6. Prayer is a reminder that we are never alone.

In June 2000, researchers at Duke University Medical Center in Durham, North Caroli-

na, presented the results of a six-year study in the *Journal of Gerontology* in which nearly 4,000 mostly Christian men and women 65 and older were asked about health problems and whether they prayed, meditated, or read the Bible. Dr. Harold Koenig, one of the researchers, stated that this was one of the first studies showing that people who pray live longer. Relatively healthy seniors who said that they rarely or never prayed ran about a 50 percent greater risk of dying during the six-year study, compared with those who prayed at least once a month. People who prayed even once a month appeared to get the same protection as those who prayed more often.

Critics of such studies accuse the researchers of making subjective judgments concerning patients or of injecting hope into the equation. Others say that the results of people praying for the sick are no greater than random chance.

But, in general, Americans believe that the power of prayer is beneficial for their health. A 1999 CBS News poll found that 80 percent of adult Americans believe prayer improves recovery from disease. In June 2001, a Gallup Poll revealed that 54 percent of adult Americans believed in spiritual healing.

The contemporary mystic Harold Sherman was firm in stating that one should never pray out of a sense of duty or obligation or habit. One should not make a ritual of getting a prayer over with as quickly as possible. Nothing is accomplished by rapidly mumbling a prayer without thought or feeling behind it. It is the feeling behind a prayer, Sherman advised, not the words thought or spoken, which gets through to God, to the **cosmic consciousness** level of the mind. In his book *How to Solve Mysteries of Your Mind and Soul* (1965), Sherman presented "Seven Secrets for Successful Prayer":

1. Remove all fears and doubts from your mind before you start to pray.

2. Make your mind receptive so it is prepared to receive guidance and inspiration.

3. Picture clearly in your mind what it is that you desire to bring to pass in your life.

4. Have unfaltering faith that with God's help what you are picturing will come true.

5. Repeat your visualization and your prayer... until what you have pictured becomes a reality.

6. Review each day's activities and constantly strive to improve your mental attitude, so your mind can become a clearer channel attuned to the God Power within.

7. Realize that if your thinking is right and if you persist with faith and put forth every effort in support of your prayer, then that which you create in your mind must eventually come to pass.

❋ DELVING DEEPER

Benson, Herbert. *Timeless Healing*. New York: Scribner, 1996.

Dossey, Larry. *Healing Words: The Power of Prayer and the Practice of Medicine*. San Francisco: HarperSanFrancisco, 1993.

Guideposts Associates. *The Unlimited Power of Prayer*. Carmel, N.Y.: Guideposts, 1968.

Humphrey, Nicholas. *Science, Miracles and the Search for Supernatural Consolation*. New York: Basic Books, 1996.

Steiger, Sherry Hansen. *The Power of Prayer to Heal and Transform Your Life*. New York: Signet, 1997.

THE RAPTURE

According to the beliefs of the born-again Christians concerning the end times, the Rapture is an event when Christians will be taken up into the air to meet Christ in the sky. Many believe that the Rapture will happen unexpectedly and that those Christians of special merit will be lifted suddenly from their homes, their automobiles, even from their passenger seats on airliners. The Rapture is a literal, physical occurrence, rather than a spiritual transformation. Those who are taken up by Christ may leave behind their clothing on the streets and their cars crashing into trees, but they will be lifted body and soul into the sky.

Most of humankind will be left behind, including those Christians whose faith requires strengthening. It is believed that the Rapture will cause great confusion and chaos. A time of tribulation will begin, making the world easy pickings for the advent of a charismatic savior who appears to have all the best ways, financial means, and power to make things right again. This individual shall rise to international domination and deceive many before he is revealed as the **Antichrist.**

Although those Christians who believe in the Rapture are certain that it will occur in association with the time of tribulation (the seven-year period of disasters, famine, and illness during which the Antichrist will be in power), there are differences of opinion whether it will come about just before the tribulation begins, midway through the seven-year reign of the Antichrist, or at the end of the time of tribulation. There is, however, general agreement that when this awful time of lawlessness and corruption has passed, Christ will return to Earth with his army of angels, defeat the forces of evil in a great final battle at **Armageddon,** and begin his 1,000-year reign, during which time there will be nothing but justice, peace, and joy on Earth. When this millennial reign comes to an end, history will end and Christ shall establish a new heaven and a new Earth.

Those Christians who believe in the Rapture maintain that it was Jesus (c. 6 B.C.E.–

c. 30 C.E.) himself who established the format for such an event in the end times:

> "Immediately after the tribulation of those days shall the sun be darkened, and the moon shall not give her light, and the stars shall fall from heaven, and the powers of the heavens shall be shaken. And then shall appear the sign of the Son of man in heaven and then shall all the tribes of the Earth mourn, and they shall see the Son of man coming in the clouds of heaven with power and great glory. And he shall send his angels with a great sound of a trumpet, and they shall gather together his elect from the four winds, from one end of heaven to the other" (Matthew 24:29–31, King James Version).

In Mark 13:24–27, the prediction of Jesus concerning the end times is essentially the same: "There will be an end to the time of tribulation; the sun and moon will be darkened and stars will fall; the Son of man will be seen in the clouds coming with great power and glory; angels will be sent to gather the elect from every part of the heavens and the Earth."

In two of his epistles, St. Paul speaks of the return of Christ and what many Christians believe to be the Rapture, when those who are believers shall be caught to meet the Lord in the air: "For the Lord himself shall descend from heaven with a shout, with the voice of the archangel, and with the trump of God: and the dead in Christ shall rise first: Then we which are alive [and] remain shall be caught up together with them in the clouds, to meet the Lord in the air: and so shall we ever be with the Lord" (1 Thessalonians 4:16–18). In 1 Corinthians 15:51–53, the epistle writer tells of the mystery when "in the twinkling of an eye" those who believe in Christ shall be changed: "Behold, I shew you a mystery; We shall not all sleep, but we shall all be changed. In a moment, in the twinkling of an eye, at the last trump: for the trumpet shall sound, and the dead shall be raised incorruptible, and we shall be changed. For this corruptible must put on incorruption, and this mortal must put on immortality."

Although not all Christians accept the scenario of the Rapture, many Christians and non-Christians alike find the premise intriguing and read the books in the "Left Behind" series as exciting science fiction. By June 2001, the first six volumes in the series based on the events of the Rapture by fundamentalist minister Tim LaHaye and professional writer Jerry Jenkins have sold over 12 million copies. Number seven in the series of planned 12 volumes, *The Indwelling* (2000), had an initial print run of two million and appeared on the bestseller lists a few days after its publication. In addition, a complementary "Left Behind" series for children has sold three million copies, and, altogether, over 18 million various products related to the series have been purchased.

✤ DELVING DEEPER

Abanes, Richard. *End-Time Visions*. Nashville, Tenn.: Broadman & Holman, 1998.

Goetz, William R. *Apocalypse Next*. Camp Hill, Penn.: Horizon Books, 1996.

Lindsey, Hal, with C. C. Carlson. *The Late Great Planet Earth*. New York: Bantam Books, 1978.

McGinn, Bernard. *Antichrist: Two Thousand Years of the Human Fascination with Evil*. San Francisco: HarperSanFrancisco, 1994.

Shaw, Eva. *Eve of Destruction: Prophecies, Theories and Preparations for the End of the World*. Chicago: Contemporary Books, 1995.

Wheeler, John Jr. *Earth's Two-Minute Warning: Today's Bible-Predicted Signs of the End Times*. North Canton, Ohio: Leader Co., 1996.

SHROUD OF TURIN

In the fall of 1978, the ancient Shroud of Turin was exhibited publicly for the first time since 1933, thus rekindling the fires of controversy that have raged intermittently around this **icon** since the first century C.E. Is this cloth truly the authentic burial shroud of Jesus of Nazareth (c. 6 B.C.E.–c. 30 C.E.)? Is the full-sized human image impressed on its coarse fibers the actual physical representation of Jesus as he lay in the tomb after his death by crucifixion at the hands of Roman soldiers? When looking at the shroud, is one seeing a kind of supernatural photograph of Jesus that can accurately depict his actual human appearance?

The fourteen-by-four-foot shroud has been kept under guard in a Roman Catholic chapel in Turin, Italy, since 1452, and it has been previously examined by technical investigators in 1973 and 1978. Although at that time the researchers were unable to date the cloth with certainty, scientists at the Los Alamos Scientific Laboratory in New Mexico announced that the burial shroud appeared to be authentic, woven of a type of linen typically used in Jewish burials in the Holy Land about 30 C.E., thus approximating the date of Jesus' Crucifixion. As for the remarkable image imprinted on the shroud, Los Alamos chemist Ray Rogers, stated his opinion that the impression had been formed by "a burst of radiant energy—light, if you will."

Such a view is in harmony with gospel references to a brilliant light from heaven and the process of transformation undergone by Jesus at the moment of his Resurrection after three days in the tomb. A statement issued by the Los Alamos Laboratory, operated by the University of California for the U.S. Department of Energy, explains one hypothesis that draws a parallel between the mysterious images on the shroud "and the fact that images were formed on stones by fireball radiation from the atomic bomb at Hiroshima."

Many of the experts who have examined the shroud insist that the image was not painted on the cloth, for the portrait is not absorbed into the fibers. Neither could the image have been placed on the shroud by any ordinary application of heat, they argue, or the fibers would have been scorched.

The gospel accounts of Jesus' Crucifixion state that he was whipped and beaten by Roman soldiers, who placed a crown of thorns on the head of the man who was identified as the "King of the Jews." The beating completed completed, Jesus was marched through the streets of Jerusalem bearing the wooden cross on his back before he was nailed to its horizontal bar at the place of execution. After his apparent death, a spear was thrust into his side by a Roman soldier.

Certain researchers have declared the front and the back images on the Shroud of Turin to be anatomically correct if the cloth

had been used to wrap a crucified man in its folds. The impressions on the shroud are of a tall man with a beard, his hands crossed with the imprints of nails through the wrists and feet. The right side of the man's chest was pierced. In addition, the image is said by investigators to bear the marks of whip lashes on the back. The man's right shoulder is chafed, as if from having borne a rough, heavy object. A number of puncture wounds appear around the head, and one cheek displays a pronounced bruise. The chest cavity is expanded, as if the victim had been trying desperately to draw air into the lungs, a common occurrence and a typical physical response during crucifixion.

Since its second examination in 1978, the Shroud of Turin has been hailed by some as physical proof of Jesus' Resurrection from the dead and his triumph over the grave, while others have condemned it as a hoax crafted by medieval monks who sought to create the ultimate in holy relics for spiritual pilgrims to venerate. Ray Rogers is one of a number of scientists who believes that the burial cloth is truly the shroud of Jesus Christ. In his view—and in that of many others—the Shroud of Turin answers the eternal question of whether humans can achieve immortality. "If Christ was resurrected from the dead," Rogers stated, "then the gospels are true, and eternal life is offered to all."

THE *Shroud of Turin has been hailed by some as physical proof of Jesus' Resurrection, while others have condemned it as a hoax crafted by medieval monks.*

In October 1978, the Shroud of Turin Research Project, the U.S. scientific group that examined the shroud, unanimously reported that "the image on the cloth is not the result of applied materials." In their estimation, the man on the shroud was not painted on the cloth and that an unknown event of oxidation selectively darkened certain fibrils of the threads so as to make a superficial image of a man with accurate details valid when magnified 1,000 times. Through some paranormal occurrence the body image is much like a photographic negative.

During the September/October 1978 exhibition of the shroud in Turin, more than three and a half million people viewed the relic. The viewing was followed by a Sindonological Congress of experts on October 7 and 8, and on October 8–13, a detailed, around-the-clock, 120-hour scientific examination of the shroud that included more than 30,000 photographs of various kinds. The latter effort was conducted primarily by scientists from the United States who had brought 72 crates of equipment weighing eight tons.

Also in 1978, Ian Wilson published *The Shroud of Turin: The Burial Cloth of Jesus Christ?* in which he presented the results of his historical research which brought continuity, from 33 C.E. to 1204 C.E., to the story of the shroud and its travels. Wilson concluded that the "Face of Edessa" and the "Mandylion of Constantinople" were but other designations for the Shroud of Turin. He also postulated a **Knights Templar** connection for the so-called missing years of the shroud from 1204 to 1357 which indicates that the relic was in Athens and Bescancon, France, during that period. It may well have been, Wilson suggested, that the extensive copying of the face on the shroud by the Knights Templar could have led to the papal revocation of their charter, which was later followed by the execution of their leaders by the French ecclesiastical court. The Templar involvement appeared to be validated by the discovery of a matching shroud face that was found behind the false ceiling of an outbuilding in Templecombe, southern England, on grounds that had once served as a Templar recruitment and training center.

From its earliest years, in legends and in art, there have been claims of **miracles** and healings through the shroud. Four credible witnesses reported that in 544 when Edessa was threatened with siege by a Persian army, the image was rushed to the top of the city wall and prominently displayed; the army turned and abandoned the attack. Eusebius and others state that King Agabar V of Edessa was mortally ill and was instantly healed when shown the face on the cloth. While the shroud was being carried to Constantinople in 944, it was said that a man possessed of **demons** was cleansed when he touched it.

In 1954, in a small village of Gloucestershire, England, 11-year-old Josie Wollam was in the hospital dying of a severe bone disease, osteomyelitis, in hip and leg, plus lung abscesses. The doctor advised that there was no hope for Josie, and she was given the last rites of the church. However, Josie had learned that retired RAF Group Captain Leonard Cheshire (1917–1992) was giving lectures in the area on the Shroud of Turin, and she told her mother that she was certain she would be able to walk again if she could only see the shroud. At Josie's urging, her mother wrote Captain Cheshire and his office sent a photograph of the shroud face. Merely holding the photograph appeared to accomplish a partial remission of the bone disease, and two weeks later, Josie was sent home from the hospital.

The girl was still unable to walk, and she continued to declare that if she could actually see the shroud and be in its presence, she knew that she would be completely healed. Cheshire was so impressed by Josie's faith that he took her with him to Portugal to see former King Umberto II (1904–1983), the shroud's owner, to ask permission for a rare private session with the shroud. Umberto readily granted their request, and Cheshire and Josie traveled on to Turin, where the rolled shroud was placed across the arms of her wheelchair. Cautiously, respectfully, the girl reached a hand into the end of the roll to touch gently the inner surface.

At the 1978 public exhibition of the shroud 24 years later, Josie, now 35, walked into the cathedral at Turin, once again accompanied by Cheshire but no longer in a wheelchair. The child who had been given last rites in 1954 had been allegedly healed completely by being in the presence of the shroud. She met Father Peter Rinaldi while at Turin and told him that after her healing she had matured normally through childhood and adolescence, married, had a daughter, and was gainfully employed.

While many scientists urged increased usage of carbon-dating techniques to determine once and for all the true age of the shroud, other experts warned that an accurate carbon dating might not be technically possible with present-day laboratory techniques and practices. In the 1970s, two researchers independent of each another suggested that the 1532 fire at Chambery, France, which caused the silver reliquary to drip molten silver onto the cloth, also may have created a "pressure-cooker effect" of driving known contaminants on the cloth into the molecules of the cloth, so that the carbon content would be skewed. At the Rome Symposium of 1993, and subsequently, Dmitri Kouznetsov of the Sedov Laboratory in Moscow asserted that during the 1532 fire the molten silver acted as a catalyst for carboxylation of the cellulose, so that subsequently the cloth became enriched with carbon, thus making it appear to be younger than it may actually be. In spite of such protests regarding carbon-dating techniques, laboratory tests conducted in 1985 reported that 1320 was the median date that the shroud cloth had been woven.

As might be expected, large numbers of diligent researchers object to the date of 1320 and the suggestion that some talented artisan in the Middle Ages had created the image on the shroud as a work of piety or as an instrument of deception. Those who champion the authenticity of the shroud point out that the scalp punctures and blood rivulets as seen on the forehead of the man of the shroud have the characteristics and proper location for both veinous and arterial blood flow, and yet, if the shroud were a hoax created in approximately 1320, circulation of human blood was not discovered until 1593. The cloth-to-body distance correlates so precisely that the image perfectly encapsulates three-dimensional data perfectly. When the shroud image is fed into NASA's VP-8 image analyzer, it produces a bas-relief of the man of the shroud with no distortion. No other image, drawing, painting, or photograph has this quality—only star maps and the shroud image; everything else distorts.

Other researchers who claim the shroud is authentic point out that the 70 varieties of pollen found on the burial cloth come from the Near East and 38 varieties come from within 50 miles of Jerusalem—and 14 of them grow nowhere else.

Among other significant data which would seem to testify to the shroud's authenticity are such items as the following:

- The Z-twist thread and 3-to-1 herringbone-twill weave used in forming the shroud were known only to the Near East and Asia until recent centuries. The cotton fibers in the shroud linen could have come only by weaving on looms of the Near East.

- Microscopes were perfected in the period between 1590 to 1610, and yet meaningful data in the shroud image has been found by magnifications up to 1,200 times. How could an artist working in the 1300s have fashioned such details?

- The feet of the man of the shroud bears smudges of actual dirt that contain travertine aronite, a rare form of calcium that matches the spectral properties of this limestone substance found in caves near Jerusalem's Damascus Gate. No other source is known.

- One oddity of the shroud image is that it can be seen only in an optimum viewing distance of six to 15 feet. Closer or farther and the image fades out of view. Did the supposed hoaxer paint the man on the shroud by holding a six-foot brush at arm's length?

Even the most recent translations of the gospels state that Jesus was nailed to the cross by his hands. But the shroud correctly displays a medical truth: He was nailed through the "space of Destot" in the wrist, because a nail in the soft flesh of the hands would not support a man's weight. Another medical fact is that a spike driven through the "space of Destot" in the wrist will lacerate the median nerve, causing the thumb to flex sharply into the palm. The man of the shroud has no discernible thumbs. Would an artist in the Middle Ages have known such medical idiosyncrasies?

The man was crowned with a *cap* of thorns, typical of the Near East Judeans, not the Greek-style wreath so often depicted in artists' renderings of Jesus' "crown of thorns."

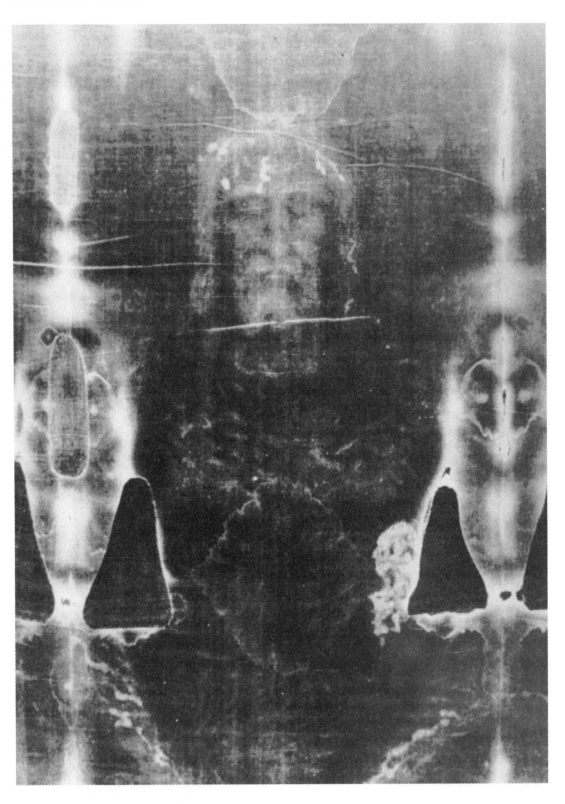

The bloodstains on the shroud are precisely correct, both biblically and anatomically. If the shroud had been lifted off the man, one of two things would have happened: If the blood was still wet the stain on the cloth would smear; if the blood was dry it would have bro-

ken the crusted blood that had soaked into the weave. Neither occurred, thus leading some researchers to believe that the body must somehow have dematerialized without the removal of the shroud. If the shroud merely collapsed and was not thrown back, then the story of Peter and John's arrival at the tomb after Jesus' Resurrection (John 20:1–10) makes better sense when Peter saw "the linen cloths lying" and John "saw and believed."

Although the shroud had some contact with Jesus' body, for scientists have decreed the bloodstains on the cloth to have been made by real blood, the body-image is described by some of the researchers as "made through space" by an "image-making process" which they have named "flash photolysis," because the images are not pressure sensitive in that the back and front images of the man have the same shadow and lack of saturation characteristics. If contact with the bleeding physical body was the only factor, the man's lying on his back should have made the image darker and different.

Many of the critics of the authenticity of the shroud and its images argue that it is nothing more than a finely executed medieval painting. Some skeptics have even claimed that the shroud images were painted by Leonardo da Vinci (1452–1519). Such an argument was quickly dissolved by pointing out that the great artist was born in 1452, nearly one hundred years after the shroud had been on exhibit in Lirey in 1357. At the scientific symposium on the shroud conducted in Rome in 1993, Isabel H. Piczek of Los Angeles presented her conclusions that the controversial cloth is not and cannot be a painting of any sort, technique, or medium. Piczek is a professional artist with degrees in physics who has won international awards for painting and figurative draftsmanship. She has personally executed art works in every ancient and modern technique known, including nearly 500 giant-size items in public buildings throughout the world. In her opinion, Piczek cautions that the shroud must not be conserved as a painting would be, "or else we may destroy the only object on Earth which is the blueprint of the future of our cosmos."

There have always been critics, skeptics, and disbelievers when it comes to the authenticity of the shroud. Even King Abgar's second son, Manu V, was a doubter, in spite of his father's alleged cure after viewing the face on the shroud. The sons of the Byzantine emperor were also skeptics. Bishop Henri de Poitieres of Troyes (fl. mid-fourteenth century) vacillated between praising the exhibition in Lirey, then trying to have it closed down. His successor, Bishop Pierre D'Arcis (fl. late-fourteenth century), attempted to stop later showings of the burial cloth in Lirey, but the pope ordered him to cease such efforts or face excommunication.

Critical researchers in the twentieth century found an alleged memo from Bishop D'Arcis written in 1389 and presumably intended for the pope in which the bishop claimed to know the identity of the painter who was responsible for creating the shroud images. The French scholar Ulysee Chevalier (1841–1923) believed in the testimony of the memo and so did the Jesuit Herbert Thurston (1856–1939). Dr. John A. T. Robinson, the English theologian, also accepted the document at first, but he later rejected its allegations and accepted the shroud as genuine. In the 1990s, Parisian researchers determined that the so-called "D'Arcis memo" was no memo at all, but merely a clerk's draft in poor Latin, never dated nor signed nor sent to the Vatican, and with no official copy in either Troyes or the Vatican archives.

In sharp contrast to those critical researchers who attempt to diminish the shroud's credibility are those scientists of faith who are personally convinced that the shroud is truly the one that briefly enveloped the body of Jesus Christ and that the images on its cloth were made by a supernatural energy as part of a spiritual event that Christians call the Resurrection. At the Rome Symposium of 1993, Dr. Gilbert R. Lavoie of the Fallon Clinic, Worcester, Massachusetts, demonstrated that the blood and body images on the burial cloth are of a man who had been suspended upright as if hanging on a cross. According to tradition, the body of Jesus hung on the cross from 9 A.M. until 3 P.M., and he was not placed on his back within the folds of a burial cloth until about 5 P.M. Thus, according to Lavoie, a truly spiritual image resulted on the shroud in order for the image to show Jesus as if hanging on the cross.

Pope John Paul II (1920–   ) authorized public exhibitions of the shroud for April 18 to

May 31, 1998, and for April 29 to June 11, 2000. Among the latest findings prompted by the most recent showings was the report by two Israeli scientists who stated in June 1999 that plant imprints and pollen found on the shroud supported the premise that it originated in the Holy Land. Avinoam Danin, a botany professor at the Hebrew University of Jerusalem, said that the shroud contained images of some plants, such as the bean caper (*Zygophyllum dumosum*), which grows only in Israel, Jordan, and Egypt Sinai desert. The rock rose (*Cistus creticus*) which grows throughout the Middle East was also detected, along with the imprint of a coin minted in the reign of the Roman Emperor Tiberius (42 B.C.E.–37 C.E.), who ruled at the time of the Crucifixion.

Clearly, while a number of scientists debate the accuracy of the radiocarbon dating results—some insisting that the most reliable results date the shroud to 1260–1390—and others defend the authenticity of the burial cloth and argue that it was the one that wrapped Jesus' crucified body until the cosmic event of the Resurrection, one can only echo the words of Archbishop Severino Poletto, the shroud's custodian: "The last word has not yet been said."

❁ DELVING DEEPER

Riggi, Giovanni. *The Holy Shroud.* Roman Center for Shroud Studies, 1981.

Shroud of Turin Research at McCrone Research Institute. http://www.mcri.org/Shroud.html. 14 August 2001.

Shroud of Turin. http://www.shroud.com. 14 August 2001.

Tribbe, Frank. *Portrait of Jesus?—The Illustrated Story of the Shroud of Turin.* New York: Stein & Day, 1983.

Wilson, Ian. *The Shroud of Turin: The Burial Cloth of Jesus Christ?* New York: Doubleday, 1978.

666

The association of the number 666 with the **Antichrist** is derived from Revelation 13:18 in which John the Revelator is told in his apocalyptic vision that the number of the Beast is 666 and that the number stands for a person. In John's world of the first century, the Beast that ruled the Earth would have been the emperor, the caesar, of the Roman Empire, Nero (37 C.E.–68 C.E.). Using the Hebrew alphabet, the numerical value of "Caesar Nero," the merciless persecutor of the early Christians, is 666.

Although Jesus (c. 6 B.C.E.–c. 30 C.E.) made it clear when speaking to the apostles that no one will know the exact hour or day of his Second Coming, for many centuries certain Christian theologians have associated the rise of the Antichrist to power and his achievement of a seven-year reign over all the Earth as a kind of catalyst that would set in motion **Armageddon,** the last final battle between good and evil—the ultimate clash between the armies of Jesus Christ and Satan.

Ever since the Protestant Reformation, the pope has been a favorite of certain Evangelicals for the ignominious title. Many of the pontiffs in the Middle Ages did exercise great power over the rulers and the people of the emerging European nations; and consequently, there were numerous embittered princes and fiery Protestant leaders who did seek to affix the blame for a large number of repressive social and religious programs on the Vatican. However, contemporary popes have wielded little political influence, surely none that would place them in world-threatening positions. There have been such men as **Aleister Crowley** (1875–1947), who actually appeared to covet and campaign for the position by calling himself the Beast and 666.

Hollywood has capitalized on the fascination of certain Christians and horror movie fans with the menacing evil of the Antichrist and depicted him in a number of motion pictures. In *Rosemary's Baby* (1968), an unsuspecting young wife (Mia Farrow) is selected to bear the Antichrist after her husband (John Cassavetes) makes a pact with Satan. *The Omen* (1976) spawned a series of three films that follow the Antichrist from early childhood to his position of wealth, power, and charismatic mastery as an adult. In the first of these films, Gregory Peck, as the unsuspecting surrogate father of the Antichrist, is warned of his son's true identity by a number of priests and other individuals who all meet untimely ends. Although initially he considers such warnings as the babble of the demented, he is later shocked to discover the numerals "666" on his son's scalp and he resolves to do whatever must be done to stop Satan's will from being accomplished. In spite of a valiant effort on the part of the father, who now concludes rightfully that his true son was killed and supplanted by the disciples of the Antichrist, the demon seed continues his destructive path to world domination in two additional films. In the *The Chosen* (1977), Kirk Douglas plays another unaware father, an industrialist specializing in building nuclear power plants, who comes to realize that his son (Simon Ward) is the Antichrist. In *Lost Souls* (2000), a devout teacher played by Winona Ryder must convince an unsuspecting young journalist that he is the Antichrist before the fated hour when his newly awakened demonic awareness will seize control of his consciousness. Arnold Schwarzenegger is challenged by the almost impossible mission of preventing Satan (Gabriel Byrne) from fathering the Antichrist in *End of Days* (2000). In *Stigmata* (2000), Byrne switches sides and plays a priest who fights to thwart satanic interference toward a young stigmatist, a woman who bears the bleeding wounds of Christ's crucifixion. *Bless the Child* (2000) portrays a desperate mother (Kim Basinger) who must somehow prevent her specially gifted and blessed child from becoming the human sacrifice that would grant the Antichrist his full-powered entry into the world.

Christians who believe completely that the end times drama will play out according to certain scriptural references maintain a wary eye for signs of the Antichrist and the onset of the **Apocalypse,** but not all Christians accept the warnings of the advent of the Beast with his telltale numerical designation of 666 or believe that the traditional scenario of the Antichrist and his seven-year reign has any real relevance to the actual "signs in the sky" that will precede the Second Coming of Christ. In today's world the term "antichrist" lost much of its power to provoke fear after the concept entered the popular mass culture. For millions of modern secular men and women, the Beast 666 has become merely a sinister, but always defeated, villain in horror movies, and his once dreaded title is often loosely applied in an offhanded manner to everything from cartoon figures to a wide range of men and women in a vast spectrum of modern society.

✦ DELVING DEEPER

Abanes, Richard. *End-Time Visions*. Nashville, Tenn.: Broadman & Holman, 1998.

Goetz, William R. *Apocalypse Next*. Camp Hill, Penn.: Horizon Books, 1996.

McGinn, Bernard. *Antichrist: Two Thousand Years of the Human Fascination with Evil*. San Francisco: HarperSanFrancisco, 1994.

Shaw, Eva. *Eve of Destruction: Prophecies, Theories and Preparations for the End of the World*. Chicago: Contemporary Books, 1995.

Unterman, Alan. *Dictionary of Jewish Lore and Legend*. New York: Thames and Hudson, 1991.

SNAKE HANDLING

In the sixteenth chapter of the gospel of Mark, the resurrected Jesus (c. 6 B.C.E.–c. 30 C.E.) appears to his disciples and, before ascending to heaven, sends them forth into the world to preach the gospel. Jesus promises that all who believe in him shall cast out devils and shall speak with new tongues. In addition, believers "shall take up serpents; and if they drink any deadly thing, it shall not hurt them" (Mark 16:17–18).

In 1909, Reverend George Went Hensley (c. 1870s–1955) of the Church of God in Grasshopper, Tennessee, began to teach that those verses in Mark should be taken literally. If believers truly had the Holy Spirit within them, he argued from the pulpit, they should be able to handle rattlesnakes and any number of other venomous serpents. They should also be able to drink poison and suffer no harm whatsoever. Snake handling as a test or demonstration of faith became popular wherever Hensley traveled and preached in the small towns and backwaters of Tennessee, Kentucky, the Carolinas, Virginia, Ohio, and Indiana.

For a time, the Church of God defended the innovation of snake handling that had

been injected into the prescribed order of service by Hensley, but in 1922, it disavowed the practice. Other Pentecostal churches followed suit and discouraged their members from testing the Holy Spirit by picking up venomous snakes or drinking poison. Undaunted, Hensley established the Church of God with Signs Following.

Some researchers of the religious snake handling phenomenon state that the practice sprang up independently on Sand Mountain, Alabama, around 1912 without any assistance from George Hensley. Within a couple decades, snakes were being handled openly in outdoor worship services in east Birmingham. However, in 1950, the Alabama Legislature, reacting to a number of highly publicized snake fatalities, passed an act making it illegal to "display, handle, use, or exhibit any poisonous snake or reptile in such a manner as to endanger the health of another."

Those who have investigated snake handling have found that it is a popular misconception that the snakes won't bite the snake handlers in their religious ritual or that, if bitten, the handlers, under the direction of the Holy Spirit, won't die. Although exact records are difficult to substantiate, at least 71 people have been killed by poisonous snakebites during religious services in the United States. And that number includes the founder of the snake handling movement, George Went Hensley, who, it has been estimated, had been bitten over 400 times before his death in 1955. While some might consider such deaths as strong reasons to discontinue the practice of actually handling poisonous snakes during services, devout snake handlers say that it is a good thing that one of their members occasionally dies as a result of a snake bite. Such fatalities only prove to skeptics and nonbelievers that they are truly using dangerous snakes in their worship services.

In those rural churches in the Appalachian highlands where snake handling remains popular, no members of the congregations are required to handle the snakes, and in most churches, no one under the age of 18 is permitted to pick up the serpents. The American Civil Liberties Union has defended the religious freedom of snake handlers against various attempts to have the practice abolished. In Thomas Burton's *Serpent-Handling Believers* (1993), Burton states that snake handling is a complex traditional religious belief of a group of American Christians which should be respected for what it is.

✤ DELVING DEEPER

Burton, Thomas. *Serpent-Handling Believers*. Knoxville, Tenn.: University of Tennessee Press, 1993.

Crim, Keith, gen. ed. *The Perennial Dictionary of World Religions*. San Francisco: HarperSanFrancisco, 1989.

Farnell, Kathie. "Snakes and Salvation." *Fate*, December 1996, pp. 28–32.

STIGMATA

Stigmata are spontaneous bleeding wounds which appear in various places on the body, such as the hands, the feet, the back, the forehead, and the side, and, in the Christian context, are considered to be manifestations of the suffering endured prior to, and during, Jesus' (c. 6 B.C.E.–c. 30 C.E.) Crucifixion. While theologians debate whether or not St. Paul himself may have been a stigmatic (Galatians 6:17—"I bear on my body the marks of Jesus"), St. Francis of Assisi (1181–1226) suddenly bore the wounds of Christ while praying outside a cave after a 40-day retreat in 1224, thereby becoming the first stigmatic recorded in the annals of church history. St. Francis is also the only stigmatic on whom the wounds in the feet and the hands actually bore representations of nails.

In 1275, a Cistercian nun named Elizabeth received stigmata on her forehead, representing Christ's crown of thorns, after she witnessed a vision of the Crucifixion. Church tradition has it that St. Catherine of Siena

(1347–1380) was visited with the marks of Christ's suffering, but through her great humility she prayed that they might become invisible, and, though the pain of the wounds remained, her entreaty was granted and the blood no longer flowed. The *Catholic Encyclopedia* states that the suffering that stigmatics endure is the "essential part of visible stigmata; the substance of this grace consists of pity for Christ, participation in his sufferings, sorrows, and for the same end—the expiation of the sins unceasingly committed in the world." If the stigmatics did not suffer, the wounds would be "but an empty symbol, theatrical representation, conducing to pride." And if the stigmata truly issue from God, it would be unworthy of his wisdom to participate in such futility, "and to do so by a miracle."

While not yet blessed with sainthood, Padre Pio (1887–1968), one of the most well-known stigmatics of the twentieth century, saw a vision of a mysterious person whose hands, feet, and side were dripping blood on August 20, 1918. After Padre Pio was delivered from such a terrifying sight, the priest suffered the first of the stigmata which would cause his wounds to bleed daily for 50 years.

Therese Neumann (1898–1962) was also a stigmatic who became familiar to the general public. Born between Good Friday and Easter at Konnersreuth, Bavaria, Neumann suffered a series of serious accidents that brought blindness, convulsions, and paralysis. Her eyesight was restored on the day of the beatification of St. Therese of Lisieux (1873–1897), April 29, 1923, and on the day of St. Therese's canonization on May 17, 1925, her mobility returned. Then, after a vision of Jesus on March 4, 1926, the stigmata began, and she would suffer bleeding from all the wounds, including shoulders and knees, on Fridays, especially during the church season of Lent. It is claimed that from Christmas 1926 until her death in 1962, Neumann didn't eat or drink anything except daily Communion.

For those saints who were also stigmatics or for those stigmatics who may be authentic, the church has issued three qualifications regarding the production of the phenomena on their bodies:

I n 1997, Michael Drosnin's book *The Bible Code* claimed that the Hebrew Bible contains a complex code that had predicted events which occurred thousands of years after the ancient texts were first written.

Drosnin's book was based on the work of Dr. Eliyahu Rips, an Israeli mathematician, who discovered the codes along with Doron Witzman and Yoav Rosenberg. The mathematicians first arranged the 304,805 Hebrew letters of the Bible into a large array, removing all spaces and punctuation and running the words together one after another. Then a computer searched for matches in all directions for names, words, and hidden phrases. According to Rips, only the Hebrew Bible may be used, because God gave the Hebrew characters to Moses one at a time, with no spaces or punctuation. The colleagues published a peer reviewed paper in the *Statistical Science Journal* in 1994 regarding their findings when they applied the code to the book of Genesis. Since then, research has indicated that the hidden code exists throughout all the books of the Tanakh in the original Hebrew.

Rips and his associates tested the book of Genesis to see if the code could pick out the names of the 66 Rabbis who had the longest entries in various Jewish annals. The Bible code revealed all 66 names, together with either the Rabbis' birth date or death date. In test after test, the Bible code found people, places, and inventions that did not come into being until 3,000 years after the ancient Hebrew texts had been recorded.

Drosnin, an agnostic, states that his belief in the Bible code was confirmed when Israeli Prime Minister Yitzhak Rabin was assassinated in 1995. Drosnin states that he had seen the forecast in the code a year earlier and even warned Rabin of the danger.

While Drosnin is reluctant to state that the Bible code proves that God is its author, others have firmly stated their belief that God guided the ancient scribes and directed them to place the prophecies within the texts.

To test the claims of the Bible code, skeptical mathematicians have downloaded the texts of the

IS THERE A HIDDEN CODE IN THE BIBLE?

Hebrew Bible and the King James Version. In the opinion of these researchers, hidden messages and prophetic statements made about famous politicians, inventors, military men, musicians, and so forth can also be located.

SOURCES:

Drosnin, Michael. *The Bible Code.* New York: Simon & Schuster, 1997.

Thomas, David E. "Hidden Messages and the Bible Code." *Skeptical Inquirer,* November 1997. http://www.csicop.org/si/9711/bible-code.html. 11 October 2001.

Wiztum, Doron, Eliyahu Rips, and Yaov Rosenburg. "Equidistant letter sequences in the Book of Genesis." *Statistical Science Journal* 1994, Vol. 9, No. 3, pp. 429–438.

1. Physicians could not succeed in curing the wounds with their remedies.

2. Unlike long-lasting wounds in others, those of stigmatics give off no foul or fetid odor.

3. Sometimes the wounds of the stigmatics emit the odor of perfumes.

In April 1998, various media carried the story of a priest who began to manifest stigmata in his side, hands, and feet while serving a parish in Antigua, West Indies. Reverend Gerard Critch was flown to New York to be treated by medical specialists. Dr. Joseph John was quoted as saying that no treatment he had given Critch had worked or been effective. According to Critch's parishioners, they were thrown to the floor by an invisible force or felt their injuries healed when he blessed them. R. Allen Stanford, a banker from the United States who flew Critch to New York City on his private jet, said that oil was oozing from the marks on the priest's feet, as it did from

Jesus. "The wounds were real," Stanford said (*Evening Telegram*, April 11, 1998).

The Roman Catholic Church does not see the onset of stigmata as bringing with it any increase of holiness, so its clergy recognizes the real possibility of conscious or unconscious fraud in some of the cases of stigmata reported almost annually. The church also acknowledges the role that psychosomatic medicine might play in explaining many instances of the spontaneous wounds that mimic those of Christ's Crucifixion. Some people who suffer from stigmata report having felt sadness, depression, a general malaise, and physical pain prior to the bleeding. Many stigmatics could be so emotionally involved with the passion of Christ that their imagination could somehow manifest the physiological phenomena of the bleeding wounds. Perhaps those who enter deep states of trance or religious **ecstasy** might trigger a mind-body link capable of

Gabriel Byrne portrays a priest in the movie *Stigmata.* (KEVORK DJANSEZIAN/ AP/WIDE WORLD PHOTOS)

producing stigmata. And the phenomenon is
not exclusively a Christian one. Cases are
also known of Muslim stigmatics who bear
wounds that correspond to those known to
have been suffered by Muhammed (c. 570
C.E.–632 C.E.) while doing battle.

❋ DELVING DEEPER

Carty, Rev. Charles M. *Padre Pio the Stigmatist*.
    Dublin: Clonmore and Reynolds, 1955.

Crim, Keith, gen. ed. *The Perennial Dictionary of
    World Religions*. San Francisco: HarperSanFran-
    cisco, 1989.

Steiner, Johannes. *Therese Neumann*. New York: Alba
    House, 1967.

Wilson, Ian. *Stigmata*. New York: Harper & Row,
    1989.

VIRGIN OF GUADALUPE

In Mexico, December 12, Virgin of
Guadalupe Day, is a national holiday, and
often as many as five million Mexicans—
many crawling on bloodied knees—make
their annual pilgrimage to the country's most
venerated shrine, a basilica for the Virgin
Mary in Mexico City. In 1996, eight people
were killed and 15 were injured in the press of
pilgrims gathered around the site.

The story of the Virgin of Guadalupe is
one of a mystery within a miracle. In 1531, a
57-year-old Aztec Indian named Juan Diego
(1474–1548), whose native name Cuauhtla-
toatzin means "eagle that sings" (or in some
translations, "eagle that talks"), claimed to
have encountered the Blessed Virgin Mary on
four occasions in desolate regions outside of
Mexico City. At first she appeared as a beautiful, dark-skinned 14-year-old Mexican Indian
girl, who then revealed herself as the "ever-
virgin Mary, Mother of God." During later
appearances, Mother Mary told Diego that she
wished a church built to her in the place
where she appeared to him–Guadalupe, the
river of the wolf. As proof of her holy appearances, the Queen of Heaven projected an
image of herself upon his *tilma* (cloak). It is
that artifact that brought Bishop Juan de
Zumarraga (1468–1548) of Mexico City and
his entire household to their knees when he
asked for some kind of tangible sign from the
Holy Mother. It is that same image on the
tilma, set in gold at the center of an elaborate
altar, that still awaits today's pilgrim at the
basilica of the Virgin of Guadalupe.

It has been said that the dark-skinned
image of Mother Mary as a virginal Native
American girl helped the Spanish priests convert millions of Mexican Indians to Catholicism. After an extensive examination, the
committee from the Holy See in Rome
declared the apparitions seen by Juan Diego to
be authentic, thus making the miracle one of
seven appearances of Mother Mary officially
recognized by the Vatican.

Then, in 1929, an image was discovered
within the right eye of the image of the Virgin
on Juan Diego's *tilma*. Alfonso Marcue, official

photographer of the old Basilica of Guadalupe in Mexico City, discovered what appeared to be a clear image of a bearded man reflected within the right eye of the Virgin. At first doubting his own senses, Marcue made many black-and-white photographs of the image; and after he had examined them exhaustively, he went to the authorities of the basilica with his incredible finding. He was told to remain silent about his discovery, and out of respect for the church officials, he did.

On May 29, 1951, Jose Carlos Salinas Chavez was examining a particularly good photograph of the face of the Virgin and rediscovered what clearly appeared to be the image of a bearded man reflected in both the right and left eyes of Mother Mary. Since that time, more than 20 experts, including a number of ophthalmologists, have carefully inspected the eyes and the mysterious image.

On March 27, 1956, Dr. Javier Torroella Bueno, a prestigious ophthalmologist, certified the presence of the triple reflection (Samson-Purkinje effect) characteristic of all live human eyes and stated that the resulting images of the bearded man were located precisely where they should be according to such an effect. Bueno also pointed out that the distortion of the images agreed with the normal curvature of the cornea.

In that same year, another experienced ophthalmologist, Dr. Rafael Torrija Lavoignet, using an ophthalmoscope, studied the apparent human figure in the corneas of both eyes, with the location and distortion of a normal human eye, and found that the Virgin's eyes appeared "strangely alive" when he examined them.

While working at IBM in 1979, Dr. Jose Aste Tonsmann, a graduate of environmental systems engineering of Cornell University, scanned a photograph of the Virgin's face on the *tilma* and was astonished to discover what he believed to be other human figures reflected in the eyes. Aste Tonsmann has since theorized that Our Lady of Guadalupe not only left a miraculous image as proof of her apparition to Juan Diego, but may also have left some important messages hidden in her eyes that could not be revealed until new technologies would permit them to be discovered.

On December 12, many Mexicans celebrate the Virgin of Guadalupe Day by visiting the basilica. This painting is by Juan de Villegas. (ARTE PUBLICO PRESS)

Another mystery that had puzzled academic researchers into the phenomena surrounding the Virgin of Guadalupe was how the colored image of the apparition could have been impressed upon the simple *tilma* of a poor Aztec tribesman and how it could have lasted for centuries without falling apart. As early as the eighteenth century, scientists discovered that it was impossible to paint such an image in a fabric of such texture. The *ayate* fibers used by the Aztecs at that time deteriorated after 20 years. Richard Kuhn (1900–1967), a Nobel Prize winner in chemistry, stated in his report of the *tilma* that it had not been painted with natural, animal, or mineral colorings. Since there were no synthetic colorings in 1531, the possibility of a native artist accomplishing a hoax seems out of the question.

In January 2001, Dr. Jose Aste Tonsmann, now with the Mexican Center of Guadalupan Studies, revealed at a conference at the Pontifical Athenaeum Regina Apostolorum in Rome that advances in digital photography now revealed that the images in the Virgin's eyes were those assembled with Bishop Juan de Zumarraga when Juan Diego first unfurled his *tilma* and displayed the miraculous image. By magnifying the iris of the Virgin's eyes 2,500 times and, through mathematical and optical procedures, Aste Tonsmann feels that he is able to identify all the people imprinted in the eyes. In other words, the Virgin's eyes bear a kind of instant photograph of what occurred the moment the image was unveiled before the bishop.

✤ DELVING DEEPER

Delaney, John J., ed. *A Woman Clothed with the Sun.* New York: Doubleday, Image Books, 1961.

Our Lady of Guadalupe. http://www.sancta.org/eyes.html. 14 August 2001.

"Science Stunned by Virgin of Guadalupe's Eyes: Engineer Sees a Reflection, Literally, from a Scene in 1531," *Zenit News Agency,* 15 January 2001.

Visions

A vision consists of something seen other than by ordinary sight. Throughout the centuries, mystics, prophets, and ordinary people from all religions have experienced visions from their deities or higher levels of consciousness that have informed them, warned them, or enlightened them. From Genesis to Revelation in the Bible, God uses visions and dreams as a principal means of communicating with his prophets and his people. In Numbers 12:6, God declares, "If there is a prophet among you, I the Lord make Myself known to him in a vision and speak to him in a dream." And in Joel 2:28: "And it shall come to pass afterward that I shall pour out my spirit upon flesh; and your sons and your daughters shall prophesy, your old men shall dream dreams, your young men shall see visions."

The great Jewish philosopher Maimonides (1135–1204) conceived of revelations received through visions as a continuous emanation from the Divine Being, which is transmitted to all those men and women who are endowed with a certain imaginative faculty and who have achieved a certain moral and mental standard. The revelatory transmission is filtered through the medium of the active intellect, first to the visionary's rational faculty, then to his or her imaginative faculty. In this way the distribution of prophetic **illumination** occurs in conformity with a natural law of emanation.

Roman Catholic scholarship holds that there are two kinds of visions. One is the imaginative vision, in which the object seen is but a mental concept of symbol, such as Jacob's Ladder leading up to heaven. St. Teresa of Avila (151–1582) had numerous visions, including images of Christ, which church authorities have judged were of this symbolic kind of vision. The other is the corporeal vision, in which the figure seen is externally present or in which a supernatural power has so modified the retina of the eye as to produce the effect of three-dimensional solidarity.

In 1976 an extensive survey conducted by the administrators of the Gallup Poll indicated that 31 percent of Americans had experienced an "otherworldly" feeling of union with a divine being. The survey was based on in-home interviews with adults in more than 300 scientifically selected localities across the nation, and a further breakdown of the percentages revealed that 34 percent of the women polled and 27 percent of the men admitted that they had had a "religious experience."

To refute the often-heard suggestion that people with little formal education are more likely to undergo such experiences, the poll disclosed little difference in the educational level of the respondents: college background, 29 percent; high school, 31 percent; grade school, 30 percent. According to the pollsters, "Whether one regards these experiences as in the nature of self-delusion or wishful thinking, the important fact remains that, for the persons concerned, such experiences are very real and meaningful. Most important, perhaps, is the finding that these religious experiences are widespread and not limited to particular groups [or] one's circumstances in life...rich or poor, educated or uneducated, churched or unchurched."

According to a press release issued by the Gallup office in Princeton, New Jersey, these kinds of experiences "appear to have a profound effect on the outlook and direction of a person's life." A 29-year-old office worker in Lynnwood, Washington, told a Gallup interviewer that she had been reading the Bible one night and was unable to sleep. A vision appeared to her that rendered her frozen, motionless. "I saw an unusual light that wasn't there—but was," she said. "There was a greater awareness of someone else being in that room with me. And ever since, it is as if someone else is walking with me."

A spokesperson for the Gallup Poll commented: "One of the most interesting aspects of these phenomena is that they happen to the nonchurched and the nonreligious as well as to persons who attend church regularly or who say religion plays an important role in their lives."

On January 23, 1994, *USA Today* published the results of an analysis of the most comprehensive data available at that time of private religious experience based on a national sociological survey conducted for the National Opinion Research Center, University of Chicago, which reveals that more than two-thirds of Americans claim to have had at least one mystical experience. According to Jeffrey S. Levin, an associate professor at Eastern Virginia Medical School, Norfolk, Virginia, such experiences as visions and the feeling of being connected to a powerful spiritual force that elevates one's consciousness are reported *less* by those people who are active in church or synagogue. All types of mystical experiences have been around since "time immemorial," Levin acknowledges, but "some kind of stigma" may have prevented people from reporting them. However, while only 5 percent of the population has such experiences somewhat regularly, such occurrences are becoming "more common with each successive generation."

As these many polls and surveys demonstrate, visions come to the religious, the nonreligious, and the antireligious alike. To the psychologist, these experiences may be revelations of the personal unconscious of the individual and attempts at psychic integration or psychic wholeness. Dr. Robert E. L. Masters and Dr. Jean Houston were among the first researchers to have recognized that throughout history people have sought altered states of consciousness as gateways "to subjective realities." At their Foundation for Mind Research, which they established in 1966, they concluded on the basis of hundreds of experiments with normal, healthy persons that the "brain-mind system has a built-in

contact point with what is experienced as God, fundamental reality, or the profoundly sacred." (*Time*, October 5, 1970).

At the beginning of the twenty-first century, scientists have begun asking if the "brain-mind system," with its built-in contact point with God or a greater reality that produces such mystical experiences as visions, can be better explained in terms of neural networks, neurotransmitters, and brain chemistry. Philadelphia scientist Andrew Newberg, who wrote the book *Why God Won't Go Away* (2001), says that the human brain is set up in such a way as to have spiritual and religious experiences. Michael Persinger, a professor of neuroscience at Laurentian University in Sudbury, Ontario, conducts experiments with a helmet-like device that runs a weak electromagnetic signal around the skulls of volunteers. Persinger claims that four in five people report a mystical experience of some kind when they don this magnetic headpiece. Matthew Alper, author of *The "God" Part of the Brain* (1998), a book about the neuroscience of belief, goes so far as to declare that dogmatic religious beliefs that insist that particular faiths are unique, rather than the results of universal brain chemistry, are irrational and dangerous.

Daniel Batson, a University of Kansas psychologist who studies the effect of religion on people, states that the brain may be the hardware through which religion is experienced, but for certain neurotheologians to say that the brain produces religion "is like saying a piano produces music." In his book *The Faith of Biology and the Biology of Faith* (2000), Robert Pollack concedes that religious experience may seem irrational to a materialistic scientist, but he argues that irrational experiences are not necessarily unreal. In fact, he states, they can be just as real, just as much a part of being human, as those things which are known through reason.

Numerous believers in the possibility of experiencing visions and religious apparitions argue that if God created the universe, wouldn't it make sense that he would wire the human brain so it would be possible to have mystical experiences?

Huston Smith (1919–), author of *The World's Religions* (first published as *The Religions of Man* in 1958), was six weeks short of earning his Ph.D. in naturalistic theism—a philosophical system that emphasizes science over religion—when he happened to read philosopher Gerald Heard's (1889–1971) sympathetic treatment of the mystical experience in *Pain, Sex and Time* (1939). Smith said that he experienced an epiphany when he read Heard's argument that mysticism is the true experience of God. He completed his degree in naturalistic theism, but for the next 45 years he has sought out the mystic path in every religion he has encountered. In *Why Religion Matters: The Future of Faith in an Age of Disbelief* (2001), Smith seeks to explain the differences between science and religion. Where science attempts to define reality through numbers, formulas, and facts, religion strives to know it through spiritual practice and devotion. "Scientism," the belief that only science has all the answers, ultimately fails when it attempts to answer the questions that have troubled humans since the beginning of human existence—who are we...why are we here, and how should we behave while we are here?

Writer Eddie Ensley believes that the visionary dimension of spirituality has the ability to transform a person and reconnect humanity to its innate yearning for God. Ensley, of Native American descent, states in *Visions: The Soul's Path to the Sacred* (2000), that human beings are "fashioned to see God" and nurture a "deep desire for this mystery and an ability to be open to it and receive it." Ensley, who has a master's degree in pastoral ministry from Loyola University in New Orleans, also says that the Christian, Jewish, and Native American ancestors "understood the subtle interrelationships of flesh and spirit more accurately than we do. When they received visions, they knew what to do with them."

Because sociological, psychological, and religious research have all discovered that visions are much more common than scholars once believed, Ensley is of the opinion that such experiences should be treated differently by both the church and society at large. "People who have mystical experiences are not

crazy," he said. "Some research suggests that they tend to be (mentally) healthier."

Numerous studies substantiate Ensley's high opinion regarding the mental health of visionaries. Among such studies is one conducted by psychologists at Carleton University of Ottawa, Canada, published in the November 1993 issue of the *Journal of Abnormal Psychology*, in which they reported that those individuals examined who had "seemingly bizarre experiences," such as mystical visions, missing time, and so forth, were just as intelligent and psychologically healthy as other people. Recognizing that their findings contradicted the previously held notion that such individuals had "wild imaginations" and could be "easily swayed into believing the unbelievable," the psychologists who had administered an extensive battery of psychological tests to the subjects found that they tended to be "white-collar, relatively well-educated representatives of the middle class."

Albacete, a Roman Catholic priest and a professor of theology at St. Joseph's Seminary in Yonkers, acknowledges that until recently psychiatric orthodoxy held the view that the more "sensational a person's religious experience (voices, visions...extraordinary missions), the more pathological the underlying conflict." Then, in 1994, the American Psychiatric Association softened its position and officially recognized the "religious or spiritual" as a normal dimension of life.

"As a believer and as a priest, as well as a former scientist," Albacete says that he finds himself "somewhat nervous about this blurring." He suggests that it is only right that psychiatrists and neurologists should find it difficult to incorporate the transcendent into scientific methodology and that they should look upon mystics and visionaries as if they were suffering mental disturbances. "If the religious experience is an authentic contact with a transcendent mystery, it not only will but should exceed the grasp of science," he reasons. "Otherwise what about it would be transcendent?"

Albacete quotes Monika Grygiel, who told him that as a psychiatrist, she experienced "great poverty before the mystery perceived in the religious experience." As a psychiatrist who was also a person of faith, she said that her hope was that she would not "destroy the patient's extraordinary experience, but help him or her integrate it into the rest of life as harmoniously as possible."

🕮 **DELVING DEEPER**

Alper, Matthew. The "God" Part of the Brain. Rogue Press, 2001.

Benson, Carmen. Supernatural Dreams & Visions. Planfield, N.J.: Logos International, 1970.

Ensley, Eddie. Visions: The Soul's Path to the Sacred. New Orleans: Loyola Press, 2001.

Newberg, Andrew, Eugene G. D'Aquili, and Vince Rause. Why God Won't Go Away: Brain Science and the Biology of Belief. New York: Ballantine, 2001.

Smith, Huston. Why Religion Matters: The Future of Faith in an Age of Disbelief. San Francisco: Harper San Francisco, 2001.

WEEPING STATUES AND ICONS

She was like thousands of other plaster Madonnas manufactured at a plant in Sicily and sold throughout the country for a few lira. This particular Madonna was sold as a wedding present from a friend who decided that such a statue would be an appropriate gift for Antionetta and Angelo Iannusco, who were married in Syracuse, Sicily, in the spring of 1953. Then, on the morning of August 29, 1953, as Antionetta prayed devoutly to the Blessed Mother to grant her surcease from the pains of her pregnancy, the statue began to weep.

At first her mother-in-law and sister-in-law were skeptical, but then they witnessed a virtual torrent of tears flowing from the eyes of the plaster Madonna. Angelo, who prided himself on his atheistic philosophy and communistic politics, became so moved by the apparent supernatural manifestation that he left the Communist Party and assisted the priest as he said mass over the weeping Madonna.

Doubting neighbors, cynical journalists, and rational, scientific investigators were baffled by the phenomenon of the weeping statue in the Iannusco household. When news of the miracle Madonna spread throughout Italy, thousands of people hurried to view it for themselves. The southeastern Sicilian community's hotels were quickly swamped with requests for accommodation.

Before the Iannusco's home could be crushed by the onslaught of curious pilgrims, the Syracuse Police Department agreed to remove the little Madonna to their headquarters for safekeeping. As the squad car moved through the streets, a patrolman carefully held the statue on his lap. Soon his jacket was drenched with tears. A skeptical detective caught several tears in a chemist's vial and, without identifying the liquid, sent the specimen to a police laboratory for analysis. The next morning the irritated director of the lab berated him for wasting his time analyzing such substances as human tears.

Hardly any time passed before the crippled, the lame, and the ill from all over Italy were soon gathering before the weeping Madonna. The tears were caught on a cloth and wiped on the bodies of the afflicted. A middle-aged man recovered the use of a crippled arm. A three-year-old girl stricken with polio was able to discard the stainless steel braces that had encased her twisted legs. An 18-year-old girl who had been struck dumb 11 years before began to speak. Hundreds of others claimed to have received a healing blessing from the tears of the little Madonna.

The Madonna's tears ceased to flow on the fourth day of the phenomenon, but exactly one month later, the statue was carried through the streets of Syracuse at the head of a procession of 30,000 people. Since that day, thousands of pilgrims have flocked to the shrine of the little Madonna, including more than a hundred bishops and archbishops and several cardinals. Her glassed-wall case, capped with a bronze cross, is surrounded by dozens of crutches and braces that have been left there as silent testimony of hundreds of miracle healings. Hopeful that their city would become known as the "Italian Lourdes," the citizens of Syracuse purchased a 12-acre site and constructed a lattice-type pagoda shrine for the Madonna. Large ramps lead up to the entrance and the 400-foot high walls.

A man named Fabio Gregori of Civitavecchia, near Rome, became extremely devout after surviving an automobile crash in 1993. To aid in his devotions, his priest Father Pablo gave him a 17-inch replica of the statue of the Madonna that now stands in Medjugorje, Bosnia. Father Pablo blessed the statuette with holy water and told Gregori that Mary would be his guardian. Reverently, Gregori placed the image in a niche in the backyard grotto that he had created for his family's prayers.

On February 2, 1995, Gregori and his wife were getting ready to attend church when their daughter ran into the house shouting that the statue was crying tears of blood. The statue of Mother Mary wept tears of blood for the next four days. Soon the grotto was overrun by thousands people. Many soaked handkerchiefs in the blood, and some claimed that they were healed of their afflictions after wiping the blood on their bodies.

When word of the miracle reached Bishop Girolamo Grillo, he requested that the statue be turned over to the church for scientific examination. Gregori willingly complied, and the commission assembled by Bishop Grillo conducted an extensive examination of the statue, which included X-rays and a CAT scan.

Bishop Grillo admitted his initial skepticism, but when the commission found no evidence of trickery and determined that the tears were composed of human blood, he had changed his mind.

After the examination, the tears of blood ceased. But thousands of pilgrims continued to seek healing and inspiration from the statuette, and it was placed in the St. Agostino church in Pantano, near Civitavecchia.

Bishop Grillo's conversion to the authenticity of the weeping Madonna did little to quiet the accusations of fraud that had begun to arise from skeptics. Amid the controversy, Fabio Gregori and his family were named often as the most likely instigators of the deception. In spite of his denials, skeptics continued their investigations of the weeping Madonna.

Later, a DNA examination of the bloodstains revealed that they were from a male, and researchers

TEARS OF BLOOD

argued that if the tears were the Madonna's blood, they should have come from a female. Gregori was suspected of placing drops of his own blood upon the statuette. Bishop Grillo said it had bled when it was far away from Gregori; he stated that the male blood was Jesus', not Mother Mary's, which resulted in the critics accusing Bishop Grillo of perpetrating a "pious fraud."

Although it will perhaps remain a subject of controversy, each year the statuette attracts thousands of pilgrims and is said to be responsible for scores of miracles.

SOURCES:

Kirsta, Alix. "The Crying Game." *The Guardian,* 18 December 2000.

Steiger, Brad and Sherry Hansen Steiger. *Mother Mary Speaks to Us.* New York: Dutton, 1996.

Weeping Statues Archive. http://www.mcn.org/1/miracles/weeping.html. 24 October 2001.

Thirty-six small chapels surround the shrine and await the devout.

In a message to the Sicilians in 1958, Pope Pius XII (1876–1958) said: "So ardent are the people of Sicily in their devotion to Mary that who would marvel if she had chosen the illustrious city of Syracuse to give a sign of her grace?"

While the skeptical explain weeping statues and icons of the Madonna, Jesus (c. 6 B.C.E.–c. 30 C.E.), or other holy figures as bizarre moisture condensation at best and as outright fraud at the worst, throughout the world and all of Roman Catholic Christendom, the ordinary statues or paintings become highly venerated objects of faith. As the old saying goes, "For those who believe, no explanation is needed. For those who do not believe, no explanation is possible."

Just before Christmas in 1996, a painting of Jesus was seen by hundreds of eyewitnesses to be weeping red tears. This painting was no ordinary icon, for it hangs in the Bethlehem Church of the Nativity, above the spot where Christian tradition maintains Jesus was born. A Muslim cleaning lady was the first to see a light that came from the painting just prior to the tears flowing from the eyes of Jesus. Since her sighting, thousands of Christians of all denominations, along with many Jews and Muslims, have witnessed the tears.

Among other recent manifestations of weeping statues and icons are the following:

Rooty Hill, near Sydney, Australia: Since 1994, tears have streamed from the eyes of a statue of Our Lady of Fatima in a small, private home.

Grangecon, Ireland: Three weeks after a retired postmaster and her daughter noticed tears and drops of blood tricking from the eye of a statue of the Madonna one day in 1994, 3,000 visitors from all over the world had arrived to witness the phenomenon for themselves.

The phenomena associated with the madonnas and the icons of various saints and holy figures that appear to issue tears are worldwide. To the skeptical, such phenomena can be easily explained as moisture gathering in the eye hollows of the statues due to condensation, sudden changes in humidity, or

Bleeding Rosa Mystica statue. (FORTEAN PICTURE LIBRARY)

outright fraud. The weeping of blood is dismissed as normal condensation colored by the reddish-hued paints so often used in the formation of religious statues. For the faithful, who point to dozens of dramatic healings, hundreds of mystical experiences, and thousands of religious conversions as their evidence that something supernatural is occurring around these icons, such phenomena as the weeping madonnas are likely to be interpreted as physical signs that the spiritual presence of the holy figure is with them.

✤ DELVING DEEPER

Delaney, John J. ed. A Woman Clothed with the Sun. Garden City, N.Y.: Doubleday, 1961.

Hayford, Jack. The Mary Miracle. Ventura, Calif.: Gospel Light, 1994.

Kirkwood, Annie. Mary's Message of Hope. Nevada City, Calif.: Blue Dolphin Publishing, 1995.

The weeping statue of Rosa Mystica in Maamechelen, Belgium.
(FORTEAN PICTURE LIBRARY)

Steiger, Brad and Sherry Hansen Steiger. *Mother Mary Speaks to Us: Life-Changing Encounters with the Virgin Mary.* New York: Dutton, 1997.

Weeping Statues Archives. http://www.mcn.org/1/Miracles/weeparchive.htm. 1 October 2001.

Zimdars-Swartz, Sandral. *Encountering Mary.* New York: Avon Books, 1992.

Making the Connection

Antichrist The antagonist or opponent of Jesus Christ (c. 6 B.C.E.–c. 30 C.E.), who is anticipated by many early as well as contemporary Christians to lead the world into evil before Christ returns to Earth to redeem and rescue the faithful. Can also refer to any person who is in opposition to or an enemy of Jesus Christ or his teachings, as well as to those who claim to be Christ, but in fact are false and misleading.

apocalypse From the Greek *apokalupsis,* meaning "revelation." In the Bible, the Book of Revelation is often referred to as the Apocalypse. Comes from many anonymous, second-century B.C.E. and later Jew-

ish and Christian texts that contain prophetic messages pertaining to a great total devastation or destruction of the world and the salvation of the righteous.

Armageddon From late Latin *Armagedon,* Greek and Hebrew, *har megiddo, megiddon,* which is the mountain region of Megiddo. Megiddo is the site where the great final battle between good and evil will be fought as prophesied and will be a decisive catastrophic event that many believe will be the end of the world.

Bhagavad Gita From Sanskrit *Bhagavadgi ta,* meaning "song of the blessed one." A Hindu religious text, consisting of 700 verses, in which the Hindu god, Krishna, teaches the importance of unattachment from personal aims to the fulfillment of religious duties and devotion to God.

cosmic consciousness The sense or special insight of one's personal or collective awareness in relation to the universe or a universal scheme.

cosmic sense The awareness of one's identity and actions in relationship to the universe or universal scheme of things.

demon possession When low-level disincarnate spirits invade and take over a human body.

eschatology Comes from the Greek word *eskhatos* meaning "last" and -logy literally meaning "discourse about the last things." Refers to the body of religious doctrines concerning the human soul in relation to death, judgment, heaven or hell, or in general, life after death and of the final stage or end of the world.

Five Pillars of Islam In Arabic, also called the *arkan,* and consists of the five sacred ritual duties believed to be central to mainstream Muslims' faith. The five duties are: the confession of faith, performing the five daily prayers, fasting during the month of Ramadan, paying alms tax, and performing at least one sacred pilgrimage to Mecca, the holy land.

guardian angel A holy, divine being that watches over, guides, and protects humans.

Mesopotamia Greek word, meaning "between two rivers." An ancient region that was located between the Tigris and Euphrates rivers in what is today, modern Iraq and Syria. Some of the world's earliest and greatest ancient civilizations such as Ur, Sumer, Assyria, and Babylonia were developed in that region.

Old Testament The first of the two main divisions of the Christian Bible that corresponds to the Hebrew scriptures.

omen A prophetic sign, phenomenon, or happening supposed to portend good or evil or indicate how someone or something will fare in the future.

Qur'an (Koran) The sacred text, or holy book, of Islam. For Muslims, it is the very word of Allah, the absolute God of the Islamic faith, as revealed to the prophet Muhammad (c. 570C.E.–632 C.E.) by the archangel Gabriel.

shamanic exorcism When a shaman, or tribal medicine-holy person, performs a ceremonial ritual to expel the disincarnate spirits from a person.

Tanakh (Also known as Tanach.) From the Hebrew *tenak*, an acronym formed from *torah*. It is the sacred book of Judaism, consisting of the Torah—the five books of Moses, *The Nevi'im*—the words of the prophets, and the *Kethuvim*—the writings.

tribulation Great affliction, trial, or distress. In Christianity, the tribulation refers to the prophesied period of time which precedes the return of Jesus Christ to Earth, in which there will be tremendous suffering that will test humanity's endurance, patience, or faith.

CHAPTER 4

MYSTERY RELIGIONS AND CULTS

Throughout the history of organized religion there have been congregants who became dissatisfied with the structure of orthodoxy. These people left to develop their own forms of worship. The new groups were considered heretical by the mainstream religions, and were branded as "cults." In other instances, those who practiced ancient forms of deity worship that were before the more recently established religions were identified as "devil-worshippers." In this chapter, a number of faith groups that have been called cults and heresies are examined.

Introduction

From the very beginnings of organized religion in Egypt, Sumer, and Babylonia (c. 3000 B.C.E.), certain members of the established or state religion have become dissatisfied with the structure of orthodox worship and have broken away from the larger group to create what they believe to be a more spiritually transcendent and personal form of religious expression. Sometimes these splinter groups are organized around the revelations and visions of a single individual, who is recognized as a prophet by his or her followers. Because the new revelator's teaching may seem unorthodox or heretical to the beliefs of the larger body of worshippers, its members are branded as cultists or heretics. In other instances, those practitioners of ancient wisdom who celebrate the rituals of a religion that existed long before the dominant faith had established itself are condemned as devil-worshippers. It has been observed that the god of the old religion often becomes the devil of the faith that has supplanted it.

Often, the members of cults are forced to meet in secret due to oppression by the established majority religion and the state or because of their own wishes to practice their faith in private. Because these groups often require their members to swear to maintain the strictest of silence and secrecy regarding the rites and rituals employed by their religion, the general term "mysteries" is often applied to them. The word "mystery" comes from the Greek word *myein*, "to close," referring to the need of the *mystes*, the initiate, to close his or her eyes and lips and to keep secret the rites of the cult.

In ancient times, the students who would be initiates of the mystery schools were well aware that they must undergo the rigors of disciplined study and the training of body, soul, and spirit. In order to attain the self-mastery demanded by the priests of the mysteries, the newcomers understood that they would undergo a complete restructuring of their physical, moral, and spiritual being. The priests, the hierophants, preached that only by developing one's faculties of will, intuition, and reason to an extraordinary degree could one ever gain access to the hidden forces in the universe. Only through complete mastery of body, soul, and spirit could one see beyond death and perceive the pathways to be taken in the afterlife. Many times these mysteries were taught in the form of a play and celebrated away from the cities in sacred groves or in secret temples.

In contemporary usage, the word "cult" generally carries with it very negative connotations and associations. Many men and women, who draw upon stereotypes created by sensationalism in the media, hear the word and immediately think of devil-worshippers sacrificing babies or black-swathed zealots, carrying bombs under their robes, intent on blowing up a church, synagogue, or mosque in order to appease their angry god of wrath. Too often, it seems, the word "cult" has become synonymous with "hate," and religious hatreds tend to have long memories.

Writing in the March 15, 1993, issue of *Time* magazine, Lance Morrow suggested that every cult is a kind of nationalism with citadels that "bristle with intolerant clarities and with high-caliber weapons." Scratch any aggressive tribalism or nationalism surface and one is likely to find "a religious core, some older binding energy of belief or superstition, previous to civic consciousness, previous almost to thought." Here, Morrow discovered, is the great paradox—God-love, the life-force, the deepest well of compassion "is capable of transforming itself into a death force, with the peculiar annihilating energies of belief."

A number of apocalyptic cults, such as AUM Supreme Truth, the **Branch Davidians,** and the **People's Temple,** have seen signs in contemporary society that they have interpreted as omens that the end-times are fast approaching. Because these groups want to isolate their members and prepare to defend themselves during **Armageddon,** they have frightened the general population by their stockpiling of arms and their occasional antisocial acts. The mass suicides carried out by members of **Heaven's Gate,** People's Temple, and **Order of the Solar Temple** have also presented negative and alarming images of what many believe to be typical cultist practice.

However, for every Heaven's Gate seeking to send its members to a "higher level" aboard a UFO, there is an **Aetherius Society,** wherein its members simply wish to convey the messages of hope and good will that they believe was given to them by the Space Brothers, extraterrestrial visitors in the skies. For every AUM Supreme Truth releasing poison gas in a crowded Japanese train station, there is a **Falun Gong** that trains its members to be emissaries of peace and champions of civil rights in China. Caution must be used in labeling any seemingly unorthodox group of religionists as a cult; what is regarded as antisocial or blasphemous expression by some may be hailed as sincere spiritual witness by others.

❦ DELVING DEEPER

Brandon, S. G. F. *Religion in Ancient History.* New York: Charles Scribner's Sons, 1969.

Gaster, Dr. Theodor H., ed. *The New Golden Bough.* New York: Criterion Books, 1959.

Morrow, Lance. "In the Name of God." *Time,* 15 March 1993, pp. 24–25.

Rosten, Leo, ed. *Religions of America.* New York: Simon & Schuster, 1975.

Steiger, Brad. *The Fellowship: Spiritual Contact Between Humans and Outer Space Beings.* New York: Doubleday, 1988.

EGYPTIAN MYSTERY SCHOOLS

For more than 3,000 years, the mystery schools of Egypt have epitomized the ultimate in secret wisdom and knowledge. As in ancient times, certain contemporary scholars and researchers insist that the great teachers who presided over the Egyptian mystery schools had to have come from some extraordinary place. Perhaps, it has been theorized, they were wise masters who survived the destruction of the lost continent of **Atlantis** and made their way to the early civilization of Egypt, where they helped elevate it to a greatness far in advance of other cultures of that era. Some have even suggested that the entity known as the god **Osiris** was an extraterrestrial astronaut from the Pleiades, who first visited Egypt in prehistoric times when it was composed of barbaric tribes. Because he came from

EGYPTIAN GODS AND GODDESSES

- *Amen:* A creation-deity

- *Anubis:* God of the dead

- *Bast:* Cat goddess

- *Bes:* God to guard against evil spirits and misfortune

- *Chons:* God of the moon

- *Dua:* Protector of the stomach of the dead

- *Geb:* God of the Earth

- *Hathor:* Cow goddess

- *Isis:* Mother goddess

- *Ka:* God for the vital force of life

- *Maat:* Goddess of truth and justice

- *Min:* Egyptian fertility god

- *Mut:* Wife of Amen, mother of Khons

- *Nephthys:* Goddess of the dead

- *Nut:* Goddess of the sky and of the heavens

- *Osiris:* God of the underworld and of vegetation

- *Qetesh:* Goddess of love and beauty

- *Ra:* God of the sun

- *Selket:* Goddess of childbirth

- *Set:* God of chaos

- *Shu:* God of the air

- *Sobek:* Crocodile god

- *Taweret:* Hippopotamus goddess and protective deity of childbirth

- *Wepwawet:* God of war and of funerals

SOURCE:
"Social Science Data Lab: Egyptian Gods Theme." http://sobek.colorado.edu/LAB/GODS/index.html. 12 November 2002.

an advanced extraterrestrial culture, say the proponents of this theory, he was considered a god and became the founder of the mystery schools and raised the primitive Egyptians' standard of living to a remarkable degree.

Even many conservative scholars of the history of religion have a sense that the mystery schools of Egypt contain within their teachings a particular knowledge that came, if not from prehistoric times, from ancient times. The earliest human records legible, the **Pyramid Texts of Egypt** (c. 3000 B.C.E.), contain many prayers that are quoted from a far more ancient period, and it is apparent that the prayers were used in the texts as magical formulas and spells.

THE *earliest, legible human records, known as the* **Pyramid Texts of Egypt** *(c. 3000 B.C.E.), contained many prayers which were used as magical formulas and spells.*

The mysterious first initiator into these sacred doctrines was known as Toth and later to the Greeks by his more familiar name of Hermes. Hermes-Toth is a generic name that designates a man, a caste, and a god at the same time. As a man, Hermes-Toth is the originator of a powerful system of magic and its first initiator; as a caste, he represents the priesthood, the repository of ancient wisdom; as a god, Hermes becomes Mercury for the Greeks, the god who delivers messages to mortals from the Olympiad and the god who initiates mortals into transcendent mysteries. Later, the Greek disciples of this secret tradition would call him **Hermes Trismegistus** (three times great), and he would be credited for originating the material contained in 42 books of esoteric science.

In the time of the Ramses (c. 1300 B.C.E.), Egypt shone as a beacon light of civilization throughout the known world, and while the leaders of foreign nations sought to barter for the empire's rich produce in order to avert local famines and to make treaties with pharaoh in order to avert his military might, seekers of the divine sciences came from the distant shores of Asia Minor and Greece to study in the sanctuaries with magi and hierophants who they believed could give them the secrets of immortality. The students who would be initiates of the mystery schools were well aware that they must undertake the rigors of disciplined study and the training of body, soul, and spirit. They had heard from former initiates that in order to attain the mastery demanded by the priests of the mysteries that the newcomers would undergo a complete restructuring of their physical, moral, and spiritual being. According to the credo of the mysteries, only by developing one's faculties of will, intuition, and reason to an extraordinary degree could one ever gain access to the hidden forces in the universe. Only through complete mastery of body, soul, and spirit could one see beyond death and perceive the pathways to be taken in the afterlife. Only when one has conquered fate and acquired divine freedom could he or she, the initiate, become a seer, a magician, an initiator.

The Greek philosopher **Pythagoras** (c. 580–c. 500 B.C.E.) learned the secret doctrine of numbers, the heliocentric system of the universe, music, astrology, astronomy, mathematics, and geometry from the powerful Egyptian Magi. Before he established his own school of philosophy in southern Italy, Pythagoras spent 22 years in the temples of Egypt as an initiate in the ancient mysteries.

A particularly interesting aspect of the Egyptian mystery schools is that for centuries the pharaohs themselves were the pupils and instruments of the hierophants, the magicians, who presided over the temples and cults of **Isis** and **Osiris.** Each pharaoh received his initiation name from the temple, and the priests were honored with the roles of counselors and advisors to the throne. Some have even referred to the rule of ancient Egypt as government of the initiates.

Although the ancient Egyptians never appeared to produce a philosophical system in the manner of the Greeks or the Romans, the mysteries produced a remarkable number of systematized theologies that dealt with the essential questions about the true nature of humankind and its relationship to the cosmos. The hierophants created theological constructs and formulated esoteric answers that brought initiates and aspirants to the great religious cities of Heliopolis, Memphis, Hermopolis magna, Abydos, and Thebes.

✤ DELVING DEEPER

Brandon, S. G. F. *Religion in Ancient History*. New York: Charles Scribner's Sons, 1969.

Cotterell, Arthur, ed. *Encyclopedia of World Mythology*. London: Dempsey Parr Book, 1999.

Crim, Keith, ed. *The Perennial Dictionary of World Religions*. San Francisco: Harper Collins, 1989.

Ferm, Vergilious, ed. *Ancient Religions*. New York: Philosophical Library, 1950.

Grimal, Nicolas. *A History of Ancient Egypt*. Cambridge: Blackwell Publishers, 1994.

AKHENATEN

Some scholars credit the pharaoh Amenhotep IV, who ruled Egypt (c. 1358–1340 B.C.E.), with being an astonishing visionary who conceived of monotheism in a time when multiple gods flourished. Amenhotep IV chose to call himself Akhenaten. Because of his revolutionary religious views, his contemporaries chose to call him "heretic," and he remains a controversial historical figure to this day.

During the so-called Old Kingdom period of Egyptian history (c. 2700–2185 B.C.E.), pharaohs were considered to be divine, representatives of the many gods of ancient Egypt, and the earthly incarnation of the "Great God," the sun god, Ra. During the Middle Kingdom (c. 2000–1785 B.C.E.) when the Egyptian power base shifted from Heliopolis, near the junction of Upper and Lower Egypt, to Thebes in Upper Egypt, the Theban god "Amun" became combined with Ra to become Amun-Ra. Although he was generally depicted in human form, Amun-Ra was still considered the Great God/Creator Being and still identified with the sun, and since Egypt under the Theban kings entered into a period of great power and posterity, he was esteemed as a mighty and benevolent god.

When Amenhotep IV became pharaoh about the year 1367 B.C.E., he inherited his

Pharoah Akhenaten.

(CORBIS CORPORATION)

father's name, as well as his throne. Amenhotep means "Amun is content," but the young ruler neglected his responsibility to Amun and paid special attention to the "aten," the representation of the sun's disc and a symbol of the sun god Ra. While there is evidence that the pharaoh's mother, Queen Tiye, may have been associated with a cult of the Aten and may have been influential in her son's growing belief in a single god; his spiritual path was established at an early age. Choosing to call himself Akhenaten (It is pleasing to the Aten), the pharaoh declared that there was only one god, his father Aten. By his royal decree, the worship of Amun was to be suppressed and his very name was to be chiseled away from any statues, monuments, temples, or city walls throughout all of Egypt. Likewise, images of all of the ancient representations of the Egyptian gods—Osiris, Horus, Isis, and so forth—were to be destroyed. Even the centuries-old Osirian funerary rites were to be abandoned and the name of Osiris was to be replaced in the mortuary texts by prayers to the Aten. Aten also directed Akhenaten to disassociate himself with the city sacred to Amun, and to establish a new holy city, a new capital for Egypt, called Akhetaton or Amarna (known today as Tell el-Amarna), 300 miles north of Thebes. The mystically enlightened Akhenaten stayed true to tradition only in that he, as pharoah, was the single most unique son of the sun god on Earth and only through his physical being could other mortals approach the Great God.

Akhenaten insisted upon naturalism in all of Egyptian life, including its artistic represen-tation of the pharoah and his family. Such a command to portray only truth in art gave pos-terity a unique portrait of this religious reformer who so jarred history. While the portraits and the famous statue of his queen, Nefertiti, have allowed her to be recognized as one of the great beauties of the ages, the king himself appears to have been far from majestic in appearance. Narrow-shouldered and pear-shaped in body, his head is abnormally elongated with a droop-ing jaw. Only in his mysterious, pensive eyes does one glimpse a fleeting shadow of the soul that sought to persuade a kingdom to under-stand his belief in monotheism.

For the 17 or so years of his reign, Akhen-aten was so absorbed in preaching his new faith that he sought to conquer no new terri-tories—nor did he heed the reports of his mili-tary commanders and allies to shore up the defenses of Egypt's borders. To the dismay of those who had grown wealthy with the expan-sion of the Egyptian empire, Akhenaten was not the great warrior-pharoah that so many of his predecessors to the throne had been. Nei-ther was he an effective missionary, for the angry, dispossessed priests of Amun and the outcast servants of the many other gods only bided their time to resume control of the spiri-tual needs of the Egyptian people. While some scholars maintain that Akhenaten's experi-ment in monotheism has had lasting effect upon the religions of today, the cult of Aten appeared to have had no real lasting effect upon the religious framework of Egypt.

Recent scholarship has suggested that about the twelfth year of his reign, Nefertiti and Akhenaten became estranged and that he may have taken another queen who might bear him a son. Others have argued he elevat-ed his son-in-law Smenkhkare to share the throne with him in a kind of co-rulership

capacity. Still other scholars have debated that Nefertiti herself ascended the throne after Akhenaten died a natural death or was killed by those who condemned him as a heretic. All that is certain is that the son-in-law who suc-ceeded Akhenaten soon changed his name from Tutankhaten to Tutankhamun, thereby indicating his allegiance to the Theban god of Amun, rather than Aten, the god of Akhenat-en. It is also evident that the priests and fol-lowers of Amun achieved their revenge on the heretic pharoah by obliterating his name and the name of his god from all monuments, stat-ues, temples, and city walls throughout Egypt.

In 1907, a mummy was found in a violated tomb in the Biban-el-Moluk that some Egyptol-ogists theorized might well contain the remains of Akhenaten. While such claims have not yet been verified, perhaps modern pathology might one day solve another controversy that has been provoked by the mystical pharoah.

✴ DELVING DEEPER

Aldred, Cyril. *Akhenaten: King of Egypt*. London: Thames and Hudson, 1989.

Assmann, Jan. *Moses the Egyptian: The Memory of Egypt in Western Monotheism*. Cambridge: Har-vard University Press, 1997.

Brandon, S. G. F. *Religion in Ancient History*. New York: Charles Scribner's Sons, 1969.

Ferm, Vergilious, ed. *Ancient Religions*. New York: Philosophical Library, 1950.

Grimal, Nicolas. *A History of Ancient Egypt*. Cam-bridge: Blackwell Publishers, 1994.

ISIS

Around the year 2000 B.C.E. Egypt was invaded and partially conquered by bands of shepherd-kings from Asia called *Hyksos*, who occupied the areas of the Delta and Middle Egypt. The invaders brought with them a culture that was corrupt by Egyptian standards, and for a time it seemed as though the life and soul of Egypt was threatened. However, the priesthood that kept alive the ancient knowledge of Hermes with-drew to hidden sanctuaries and temples and practiced the secret mysteries. While they out-wardly bowed to the foreign gods, they main-tained their old traditions and believed in a time when the dynasties of Egypt would be restored in all their magnificence.

It was during this time that the priests began to propagate the legend of Isis, goddess of enchantment and magic, and her husband **Osiris,** father of the great war god Horus, finally conqueror of northern Upper Egypt. Osiris came into conflict with Set, who killed and dismembered him, scattering his body parts in the Nile. Death didn't eliminate Osiris, for Isis, incarnation of the divine mother goddess, used her magic to put him back together. Osiris and his doctrines were concerned with the problems of life, death, resurrection, and an afterlife.

The initiate who wished to attain mastery over the mysteries of life after death would be sent to knock at the door of the great temple of Thebes or of Memphis. Here, he had been told, the priests could teach what Isis and Osiris knew. If the newcomer were admitted, the priest of Osiris would question him about the place of his birth, his family lineage, and the temple where he had received his elementary instruction. In a brief but revealing interrogation, if the student was found unworthy of the mysteries, he would be sent quickly away. If the seeker appeared to be one who sincerely desired to learn the truth of the mysteries, he would be led through a corridor to an underground crypt where a large statue of Isis hid the doorway to an inner sanctuary. The goddess's face was veiled, with an inscription that advised all initiates that no mortal could ever lift her veil and look upon her true features until the moment of death.

Within the hidden sanctuary were two columns, one colored black, the other red. The priest explained to the novice that the red column represented the ascension of the spirit into the light of Osiris, while the black one signified the captivity of the spirit in physical matter. Whoever sought the mysteries risked madness or death, the initiate was warned. Once the door closed behind him, he would no longer be able to turn back.

Those novices who chose to go forward were assigned a week of menial tasks working with the temple servants and forced to observe a strict silence. When the evening of the ordeals arrived, two *neocoros,* assistants of the hierophant, led the candidate to the secret sanctuary, a dark room where statues of the

Isis. (ARCHIVE
PHOTOS, INC.)

ancient gods and goddesses, entities with human bodies and animal heads, appeared foreboding and threatening in the flickering torchlight. On the far side of the room, a hole in the wall, flanked by a human skeleton and a mummy, appeared just large enough for someone to enter on hands and knees. Here, the novice was given another opportunity to turn back. Or, if he had the courage, he was to crawl into the tunnel and continue on his way.

With only a small lamp to drive back the shadows of the cramped corridor, the novice crawled on his hands and knees, hearing over and over a deep sepulchral voice warning that fools who coveted knowledge were certain to perish in the tunnel. As the initiate proceeded forward, he eventually found himself in a wider area where he began to descend an iron ladder. But as he reached the lowest rung, he saw below him only a gaping abyss. There seemed no choice left to him. He could not go back, and he could surely die if he stepped off the ladder into what might be a drop of thousands of feet into the blackness below him.

It was at this point that the fortunate initiate, if the oil in his small lamp had held out, would notice a staircase carved into a crevice to his right. Stepping into the crevice and ascending the spiral staircase, he would find himself entering a great hall and being congratulated by a magician called a *pastophor,* a guardian of sacred symbols, for having passed the *first* test.

Before the next ordeal, the *pastophor* explained the sacred paintings and the 22 secret symbols on the walls of the great hall. These represented the 22 first mysteries and the alphabet of their secret science, the universal keys, the source of all wisdom and power. Each letter and each number given in the language of the mysteries had its repercussion in the worlds of the divine, the intellectual, and the physical.

The second test involved passing through a great furnace of flames. Those initiates who refused, protesting that to enter such a wall of fire could only result in death, never got close enough to see that it was all a clever optical illusion and that there was a safe pathway through the middle. Following the trial by fire was the trial by water, which offered no illusion, but only a walk through a chest-high dark and stagnant pool.

Two assistants helped pull the novice from the dank pool, escorted him to a room with a tub filled with warm and perfumed water, then left him to dry off and to dress in fine linens while awaiting the hierophant. Exhausted from his ordeals, the initiate could enjoy the bath, and later lie on a soft bed to relax while awaiting the priest.

Soon music sounded from an invisible group of musicians, and within a few moments, a lovely young woman, appearing much like the goddess Isis herself, entered the room where the initiate lay resting upon the bed. Heavy with perfumes, moving in rhythm to the sounds of harp, flute, and drum, the personification of Isis would do her best to tempt and seduce the novice.

If she succeeded, the initiate failed. He would be sent away from the temple with the admonishment that he had triumphed over death, fire, and water, but he had not learned to conquer himself. He had succumbed to the first temptation of the senses that he encountered after the tests, and he fallen into the abyss of matter.

If, however, the initiate had resisted the seductress, 12 *neocoros* would enter the room to lead him in triumph into the sanctuary of Isis, where the priests awaited him beneath a massive statue of the goddess. Beneath this representation of Isis, a gold rose at her breast, wearing a crown of seven rays, and holding her son Horus in her arms, the aspirant would take oaths of silence and submission as a disciple of Isis. From that day forward, he would be a recipient of the mysteries of Isis.

❧ Delving Deeper

Brandon, S. G. F. *Religion in Ancient History.* New York: Charles Scribner's Sons, 1969.

Imel, Martha Ann, and Dorothy Myers. *Goddesses in World Mythology.* New York: Oxford University Press, 1995.

Schure, Edouard. *The Great Initiates.* New York: Harper & Row, 1961.

Stone, Merlin. *When God Was a Woman.* New York: Barnes & Noble Books, 1993.

Walker, Barbara G. *The Woman's Encyclopedia of Myths and Secrets.* San Francisco: Harper & Row, 1983.

Young, Dudley. *Origins of the Sacred.* New York: St. Martins, 1991.

Osiris

The god Osiris appears in the **Pyramid Texts** (c. 2400 B.C.E.), the earliest of Egyptian records, as the deity of the royal mortuary ritual. The ancient myths proclaim that Osiris first received renown as a good king, a peaceful leader of a higher culture in the eastern Delta, then as a powerful lord over all the Delta. Although Osiris was eventually slain by an evil being called Set, it was believed that the great king's power conquered the grave and enabled him to be resurrected. Henceforth, beginning with the pharoahs and later to all who could afford mummification, all those who paid homage to Osiris would gain eternal life.

Down through the centuries, Osiris was transformed into a veritable god of the Nile and its vegetation, growth, life, and culture. He was the husband of Isis, goddess of enchantment and magic; father of the great war god Horus; and conqueror of northern Upper Egypt with his principal city at Abydos.

The cult of Osiris was established at Abydos, where he became known as the Lord of the

Death or Lord of the West, referring to his mastery over all those who had traveled "west" into the sunset of death. An initiate into the cult would be led at dusk into the lower crypt of the temple by four priests carrying torches. In a corner of the crypt was an open marble sarcophagus supported by four pillars placed upon four **sphinxes.** The chief priest of the mystery would advise the aspirant that no man could ever escape death, but every soul who died was also destined to be resurrected and to receive life anew. Those who would be a priest of Osiris must enter the tomb alive and await his light. He must spend the night in the coffin and enter through the door of fear to achieve mastery.

The initiate would lie down in the open sarcophagus and be left alone in the crypt. The priests would leave him a small lamp which would soon use up its reservoir of oil. From somewhere outside the tomb, he would be able to hear priests chanting his funeral song. Then he would be alone in the darkness, feeling the cold of the grave close in upon him.

Perhaps the initiate would experience a life review or begin to see colors and lights appear around him. This illumination, he believed, was the light of Osiris come to bring him visions. Some aspirants might claim to have had conversations with Isis or Osiris. Others might visualize themselves in the land of the dead, walking and talking with departed spirits and receiving special teachings from Osiris.

Those who survived the night alone in the sarcophagus were awakened by the priests who proclaimed the initiate's resurrection and who brought him refreshing food and drink. Later, at an appropriate time in the temple of Osiris, the newly initiated member of the cult would be asked to describe any visions that he experienced or any prophetic messages that he received while on the journey of light with Osiris.

The theology of Osiris that promised resurrection soon overshadowed that of the sun god Ra (Re). Ra was a creator god, fundamentally solar, a king by nature, whose theology concerned itself with the world—its origin, creation, and the laws that governed it. Osiris and his doctrines were concerned with the problems of life, death, resurrection, and an after-

Osiris, god of the Underworld, is considered to be a symbol of resurrection. (ARCHIVE PHOTOS, INC.)

life. The connection between the two deities was Horus, who was a sky god of the heavens and also the dutiful son and heir of Osiris.

OSIRIS *became known as the Lord of the Death or Lord of the West, referring to his mastery over all those who had traveled "west" into the sunset of death.*

The cosmology of Osiris may be divided into two periods. The earliest period extended to the time of the **Pyramid Texts** (c. 3000 B.C.E.). He was known as a peaceful political power, an administrator of a higher culture, the unifying factor in bringing the Delta and northern Upper Egypt into one realm, the ideal husband and father, and after his death, the god of resurrection. The second period extended from the time of the Pyramid Texts to the common era when he was primarily god of the dead and king of the underworld.

According to the scholar E. A. W. Budge, "[Osiris] was the god-man who suffered, and died, and rose again, and reigned eternally in heaven. They [the Egyptians] believed that they would inherit eternal life, just as he had done." When an ancient Egyptian died, the deceased expected to appear before Osiris, who would be sitting upon his throne, waiting to pass judgment on him or her. The deceased would be led into a room by the jackal-headed god Anubis, followed by the goddess Isis, the divine enchantress, representing life, and the goddess of the underworld Nephthys, representing death. There were 42 divine judges to assess the life of the one who stood before them, and the deceased would be allowed to deny 42 misdeeds. Once the deceased had presented his or her case, Osiris indicated a large pair of balances with the heart of the deceased and the feather of truth, one in each of the pans. The god Thoth read and recorded the decision.

THE *gods of Ancient Greece possessed the same vices and virtues as the humans who prayed to them for guidance.*

Standing in the shadows was a monstrous creature prepared to devour the deceased, should the feather of truth outweigh his or her heart. In those instances when the heart outweighed the feather—and few devout Egyptians could really believe that their beloved Osiris would condemn them—the deceased was permitted to proceed to the Fields of Aalu (or Iahru), the real world, where the gods lived. Because humans were the offspring of the gods, the Fields of Aalu (also known as Kherneter) offered an eternal association and loving companionship with the deities. The ancient Egyptians had no doubts about immortality. In their cosmology, an afterlife under the watchful eye of Osiris was a certainty.

❀ **DELVING DEEPER**

Ferm, Vergilious, ed. *Ancient Religions*. New York: Philosophical Library, 1950.

Grimal, Nicolas. *A History of Ancient Egypt*. Cambridge: Blackwell Publishers, 1994.

Schure, Edouard. *The Great Initiates*. New York: Harper & Row, 1961.

Stone, Merlin. *When God Was a Woman*. New York: Barnes & Noble Books, 1993.

Walker, Barbara G. *The Woman's Encyclopedia of Myths and Secrets*. San Francisco: Harper & Row, 1983.

GREEK MYSTERY SCHOOLS

The origin and substance of the state religion of ancient Greece was a sophisticated kind of nature worship wherein natural elements and phenomena were transformed into divine beings who lived atop Mount Olympus. Like the humans who worshipped them, the Olympians lived in communities and had families, friends, and enemies and were controlled by the same emotions, lusts, and loves. The pantheon of the gods of ancient Greece were not cloaked in the mysterious, unfathomable qualities of the deities of the East, but possessed the same vices and virtues as the humans who sought their assistance. Although the Olympians could manifest as all-powerful entities, none of them were omnipotent. Although they were capable of exhibiting wisdom, none of them were omniscient. And they often found themselves just as subject to the whims of Fate as the humans who prayed to them for their guidance.

The Olympians were worshipped by the Greeks most often in small family groups. There existed no highly organized or formally educated priesthood, no strict doctrines, no theologians to interpret the meaning of ambiguous scriptural passages. The followers of the state religion could worship the god or gods of their choosing and believed that they could gain their favor by performing simple ritual acts and sacrifices.

In addition to the state religion into which every Greek belonged automatically at birth, there were the "mystery religions," which required elaborate processes of purification and initiation before a man or woman could qualify for membership. The mystery religions were concerned with the spiritual welfare of the individual, and their proponents believed in an orderly universe and the unity of all life with God. The relationship of the *mystes*, the initiate, was not taken lightly, as in the official state religion, but was considered to be intimate and close. The aim and promise of the mystical rites was to enable the initiate to feel as though he or she had attained union with the divine. The purifications and processions, the fasting and the feasts, the blazing lights of torches, and the musical liturgies played during the performances of the sacred plays, all fueled the imagination and stirred deep emotions. The initiates left the celebration of the mystery knowing that they were now superior to the problems that the uninitiated faced concerning life, death, and immortality. Not only did the initiates know that their communion with the patron god or goddess would continue after death, but that they would eventually leave Hades to be born again in another life experience.

The early mystery schools of the Greeks centered around a kind of play or ritual reenactment of the life of such gods as **Osiris, Dionysus,** Demeter—divinities most often associated with the underworld, the realm of the dead, the powers of darkness, and the process of rebirth. Because of the importance of the regenerative process, the rites of the mysteries were usually built around a divine female as the agent of transformation and regeneration. While the initiates of the mystery cult enacted the life cycle of the gods who triumphed over death and who were reborn, they also asserted their own path of wisdom that would enable them to conquer death and accomplish resurrection in the afterlife, with rebirth in a new body in a new existence.

There is a general consensus that the most important mystery religions of Greece—the Eleusinian, the Dionysian, and the Orphic—were brought to that country from abroad sometime during the closing centuries of the Prehistoric Era (c. 2000 B.C.E.). The oldest of the mysteries, the Dionysian, was probably developed in Thrace, in the eastern Balkans, and introduced to the Greeks. Once the mysteries were accepted by the Greek initiates, the passion plays of Demeter and Dionysus became popular in the sixth century B.C.E. and

again in the Hellenistic Age in the fourth century B.C.E. This was when individualism was encouraged and the old gods of Olympus fell into disregard. Perhaps the time of greatest popularity for the mysteries occurred during the closing centuries of pagan worship practices and the advent of the Christian Era. The early Christian Fathers regarded the rites in the sacred groves as strong rivals for their faith, and in the Middle Ages (500–1500 C.E.), the Christian clergy would declare such mysteries as satanic.

✤ Delving Deeper

Brandon, S. G. F. *Religion in Ancient History.* New York: Charles Scribner's Sons, 1969.

Cotterell, Arthur, ed. *Encyclopedia of World Mythology.* London: Dempsey Parr Book, 1999.

Crim, Keith, ed. *The Perennial Dictionary of World Religions.* San Francisco: Harper Collins, 1989.

Ferm, Vergilious, ed. *Ancient Religions.* New York: Philosophical Library, 1950.

Larousse Dictionary of Beliefs and Religions. New York: Larousse, 1994.

Delphi

For centuries, the Temple of Apollo at Delphi in central Greece contained the most prestigious oracle in the Graeco-Roman world, a favorite of public officials and individuals alike. The oracle was said to relay prophetic messages and words of counsel from Python, the wise serpent son of the Mother-goddess Delphyne or from the Moon-goddess Artemis through their priestess daughters, the Pythonesses or Pythia. According to myth, the god Apollo murdered Delphyne and claimed the shrine and the Pythia for himself, imprisoning the serpent seer in the recesses of a cave beneath the temple.

The historian Plutarch (c. 46–120 C.E.), author of *Plutarch's Lives,* served for a time as high priest at the Delphic Oracle and explained why its oracles had remained popular while others had fallen into disrepute. In his opinion, the gods had declined to speak through the other oracles because their devotees had insulted them by asking too many blasphemous and trivial questions, such as advice concerning love affairs and disreputable business transactions.

Plutarch also described how the oracle worked. The priestess went into a small chamber called the adyton where she would inhale sweet-smelling fumes that issued from fissures in the rocks. The fumes, supposedly released by the serpent deep within the cave, would place the Pythia in a **trance** that would allow her to see the future and to make predictions. Plutarch asserted that such trance states occasionally deepened into delerium, even death.

While some researchers have touted the accuracy of the oracle at Delphi, other scholars have protested that the predictions of the Pythia were too often made in extremely ambiguous language, so that it could always be claimed that the petitioner had misinterpreted or misunderstood the true meaning of the prophecy. An oft-cited example of such ambiguity concerns the wealthy and powerful Croesus (d. 546 B.C.E.), king of Lydia, who sought counsel regarding his plans to attack Cyrus the Great (c. 600–529 B.C.E.), king of Persia. The oracle told Croesus that if he went to war with Cyrus, he would thereby destroy a mighty kingdom. Encouraged by such a prophecy, Croesus went to war and was soundly defeated by the Persians. The Greek king had fulfilled the prophecy by destroying his own kingdom. In response to his bitter complaint, the Pythia reminded him that their seership had been accurate. Croesus was told that he should have thought first to ask whose kingdom would be destroyed before he set about waging war against the Persians.

The Oracle at Delphi was a major religious site for 2,000 years until it was closed by the Christian emperor Theodosius I (346?–395). Later, Arcadius ordered the temple destroyed.

THE *Oracle at Delphi was a major religious site for 2,000 years.*

In the summer of 2001, Jelle de Boer of Wesleyan University in Connecticut and co-workers discovered a previously unknown geological fault passing through the sanctuary of the Temple of Apollo. According to de Boer, the fault crosses the previously known Delphi fault directly below the temple. This crossing makes the bitumen-rich limestone much more permeable to gases and groundwater. The researchers speculated that seismic activity on the faults could have heated such deposits, releasing light hydrocarbon gases, such as ethylene. Ethylene is a sweet-smelling gas that was once used in certain medical procedures as an anesthetic. Although fatal if inhaled in large quantities for too long a period of time, in small doses ethylene stimulates the central nervous system and produces a sensation of euphoria and a floating feeling—according to Jelle de Boer, just what oracles need to prompt visions.

❋ DELVING DEEPER

Ball, Philip. "Oracle's Secret Fault Found." Nature News Service/ Macmillan Magazines, Ltd. 17 July 2001.

Cotterell, Arthur, ed. *Encyclopedia of World Mythology*. London: Dempsey Parr Book, 1999.

De Boer, J. Z., J. R. Hale, and J. Chanton. "New Evidence of the Geological Origins of the Ancient Delphic Oracle." Geology, 29 (2001): 707–710.

Piccardi, L. "Active Faulting at Delphi, Greece: Seismotectonic Remarks and a Hypothesis for the Geologic Environment of a Myth." Geology 28 (2001): 651–54.

Gaskell, G. A. *Dictionary of All Scriptures & Myths*. Avenel, N.J.: Gramercy Books, 1981.

DIONYSUS

Next to the Eleusinian mysteries in importance and popularity was the Dionysian, which was centered around Dionysus (Bacchus), a god of life, vegetation, and the vine, who, because all things growing and green must one day decay and die, was also a divinity of the underworld. Those initiates who entered into communion with Dionysus drank heavily of the fruit of the vine and celebrated with feasts that encouraged them to dress themselves in leaves and flowers and even to take on the character of the god himself, thereby also achieving his power. Once the god had entered into union with the initiates, they would experience a new spiritual rebirth. This divine union with Dionysus marked the beginning of a new life for the initiates, who, thereafter, regarded themselves as superior beings. And since Dionysus was the Lord of Death, as well as the Lord of Life, the initiates believed that their union with him would continue even after death and immortality was now within their grasp.

The earlier rites of Dionysus were conducted on a much lower level than those of Eleusis, and often featured the sacrifice of an animal— usually a goat— that was torn to pieces by the initiates, whose savagery was meant to symbolize the incarnation, death, and resurrection of the divinity. Although the cult was not looked upon with high regard by the sages and philosophers of the day, amulets and tablets with fragments of Dionysian hymns upon them have been found dating back to the third century B.C.E. These magical symbols were buried with the dead and meant to protect the soul from the dangers of the underworld.

Orpheus may have been an actual historic figure, a man capable of charming both man and beast with his music, but god or human, he modified the Dionysian rites by removing their orgiastic elements. According to some traditions, he was said to be the son of a priestess of Apollo, gifted with a melodious voice, golden hair, deep blue eyes, and a powerful magnetism that exerted a kind of magic upon all those with whom he came into contact. Then, so the legend goes, he disappeared, and many presumed him dead. In reality, he had traveled to Memphis, where he spent the next 20 years studying in the **Egyptian mystery schools.** When he returned to Greece, he was known only by the name that he had received in the initiation rites, Orpheus of Arpha, "the one who heals with light."

Orpheus next changed the cult of Bacchus/Dionysus and set about restructuring the spiritual soul of Greece, recreating the mysteries by blending the religion of Zeus with that of Dionysus. Orpheus taught that Dionysis Zagreus, the horned son of Zeus and Persephone, the great god of the Orphic mysteries, was devoured by the evil Titans while Zeus was otherwise distracted. Athena managed to save Dionysus Zagreus's heart while the enraged Zeus destroyed the Titans with his thunderbolts. Zeus gave the heart of his beloved son to the earth goddess Semele who

dissolved it in a potion, drank thereof, and gave birth to Dionysus, the god of vegetation, whose cycle of birth, death, and rebirth reflects the cycle of growth, decay, and rebirth seen in nature.

Orpheus preached that humankind was created from the ashes of the Titans who devoured Dionysus Zagreus; therefore, the physical bodies of humans are formed from the evil of the Titans, but they also contain within them a tiny particle of the divine essence. Within this duality a constant war rages, so it is the duty of each human to repress the Titanic element and allow the Dionysian an opportunity to assert itself. The final release of the divine essence within, the redemption of the soul, is the utmost goal of the Orphic process. This process may best be obtained by the soul reincarnating in a number of physical bodies in different life experiences.

THE *gods Apollo and Dionysus were two representations or revelations of the same divinity.*

In Orphic thought, the gods Apollo and Dionysus were two representations or revelations of the same divinity. Dionysus represented the mysteries of life, the secrets of past and future incarnations, the true relationship between spirit and body—truths that could only be accessible to the initiates of the mystery school. Dionysus was the expression of the evolving soul in the universe. Apollo personified those same truths as they could be applied to humans in their earthly existence. Apollo gave inspiration to those who would be artists, poets, doctors, lawyers, and scientists through divination, such as that which issued from his priestesses at **Delphi.**

One of the essential aspects of the Orphic initiation was the process of the initiate absorbing the healing light of Orpheus and purifying the heart and spirit. Among the truths that Orpheus had learned in the Egyptian sanctuaries was that God is One, but the gods are many and diverse. Orpheus had descended into hell, the underworld, and braved its challenges and subdued the demons of the pit. The disciples of the Orphic/Dionysus schools were promised the celestial fire of Zeus, the light retrieved by Orpheus, that enabled their souls to triumph over death. These things would all be enacted in the mystery play that depicted Orpheus descending into Hades and observing Persephone, the queen of the dead, being awakened by Dionysus and being reborn in his arms, thus perpetuating the cycle of rebirth and death, past and future, blending into a timeless immortality.

While other schools of reincarnation see the process of rebirth as an evolving of the soul ever higher with each incarnation, the Orphic concept introduces the aspect of the soul being gradually purged or purified through the sufferings incurred during each physical rebirth. As the soul inhabits the body, it is really doing penance for previous incarnations, a process that gradually purifies the soul. Between lifetimes, when the soul descends to Hades, it can enjoy a brief period of freedom that can be pleasant or unpleasant. Then it must return to the cycle of births and deaths. How many lifespans must the soul endure before the process of purification is completed and its final release is obtained? Plato envisioned three periods of a thousand years each as a possible answer.

According to Orphic teachings, the only way out of the "wheel of birth," the "Great Circle of Necessity," was through an act of divine grace that could possibly be obtained by the supplicant becoming immersed in the writing, ritual acts, and teachings of Orpheus and receiving initiation into the mysteries of the cult. Although there are no available texts clearly setting forth the process of initiation, it is likely that they included fasting, rites of purification, and the reciting of prayers and hymns. It also seems quite certain that the initiates would have enacted a play depicting the life, death, and resurrection of Dionysus Zagreus. In addition, records suggest that a horned bull was sacrificed and the initiates partook of a sacramental feast of its raw flesh as a holy act that brought them in closer union with the god. Once this had been accomplished, the initiates were given secret formulas that would enable them to avoid the snares awaiting the unwary soul as it descended to Hades and would ensure them a blissful stay while they awaited a sign that their participation in the Great Circle of Necessity had ended.

❈ DELVING DEEPER

Brandon, S. G. F. *Religion in Ancient History*. New York: Charles Scribner's Sons, 1969.

Crim, Keith, ed. *The Perennial Dictionary of World Religions*. San Francisco: Harper Collins, 1989.

Ferm, Vergilious, ed. *Ancient Religions*. New York: Philosophical Library, 1950.

Sullivan, Lawrence E., ed. *Death, Afterlife and the Soul*. New York, Macmillan, 1989.

Young, Dudley. *Origins of the Sacred*. New York: St. Martins, 1991.

ELEUSIS

The sacred Eleusinian mysteries of the Greeks date back to the fifth century and were the most popular and influential of the cults, and it has been said that nowhere did the ancient mysteries appear in such human, vital, and colorful form. The cult of Eleusis centered around the myth of Demeter (Ceres), the great mother of agriculture and vegetation, and her daughter Persephone, queen of the Greek underworld, the original name of the goddess of death and regeneration. The drama enacted for the initiates symbolized the odyssey of the human soul, its descent into matter, its earthly sufferings, its terror in the darkness of death, and its rebirth into divine existence. Some contemporary students of the mysteries have portrayed the myth as the story of the Fall of humankind and its Redemption as expressed in the religion of the Eleusinians. In the temples and in the groves where the mysteries were celebrated, the candidates were told that life was a series of tests and that after death would be revealed the hopes and joys of a glorious world beyond and the opportunity for rebirth.

The rites of the mysteries took place near Eleusis, a small community 14 miles west of Athens, but it was the ruler of Athens, together with a specially selected committee, who was in charge of the general management of the annual event. Although the Dionysian and Orphic rites could be celebrated at any time, the Eleusinian rites were held at a fixed time in the early fall after the seeds had been entrusted to the fields and were conducted by a hereditary priesthood called the Eumolpedie, the "singers of gracious melodies."

Sometime in the month of September, the Eumolpedie removed the Eleusianian holy objects from Eleusis and carried them to the sacred city of Athens where they were placed in the Eleusinion. Three days after the holy relics had been transported, the initiates gathered to hear the exhortations of the priests, who solemnly warned all those who did not consider themselves worthy of initiation to leave at once. Women and even slaves were permitted to join the mysteries of Eleusis, providing they were either Greeks or Romans, but it was required that all those wishing to be considered as initiates had first undergone the lesser mysteries held in Agrae, a suburb of Athens, six months before in March. After the rites of purification had been observed, the initiates bathed in the sea and were sprinkled with the blood of pigs as they emerged. A sacrifice was offered to the gods, and a procession began the journey to Eleusis, where, upon the arrival of the priests, the initiates were received by the high priest of Eleusis, the *hieroceryx*, or sacred herald, who was dressed in a manner suggesting the god Hermes (Mercury), holding the caduceus, the entwined serpents, as a symbol of his authority. Once the aspirants had assembled, the sacred herald led them to a sanctuary of the goddess Persephone hidden in a quiet valley in the midst of a sacred grove. Here, the priestesses of Persephone, crowned with narcissus wreaths, began chanting, warning the newcomers of the mysteries that they were about to perceive. The initiates would learn that the present life that they held so dear was but a tapestry of illusion and confused dreams. After a stern admonition that the aspirants be careful not to desecrate the mysteries in any way lest the goddess Persephone pursue them forever, they were allowed to partake of food and drink.

For the next several days, the initiates fasted and participated in cleansing rituals and prayers. On the evening of the last day of the celebration of the mystery, the candidates gathered in the most secret area of the sacred grove to attend the *Rape of Persephone*. The Eleusinian drama reenacted the myth of the rape, abduction, and marriage of Persephone (Kore) by Hades, god of the underworld, and her separation from her mother, Demeter (Ceres), the goddess of grain and vegetation. When, in her despair, Demeter refuses to allow the earth to bear fruit and causes a time of blight and starvation that threatens to bring about the extinction of both humans and the gods, Zeus recalls Persephone from Hades. Filled with joy at the reunion with her daughter, Demeter once again allows the earth to bear fruit. Persephone, however, will now divide her time between her husband Hades in the underworld and her mother on Earth, ensuring a bountiful harvest.

Essentially, the rites imitated the agricultural cycles of planting the seed, nurturing its growth, and harvesting the grain, which, on the symbolical level, represented the birth of the soul, its journey through life, and its death. As the seed of the harvest is planted again and the agricultural cycle is perpetuated, so is the soul harvested by the gods to be resurrected. Membership in the mysteries of Eleusis was undertaken for the purpose of the initiates ensuring themselves a happy immortality. They returned to their customary occupations as mystics, ones who had been endowed with the ability to open their inner eyes to perceive a world of light beyond the darkness of their ordinary lives.

✣ **DELVING DEEPER**

Cotterell, Arthur, ed. *Encyclopedia of World Mythology*. London: Dempsey Parr Book, 1999.

Ferm, Vergilious, ed. *Ancient Religions*. New York: Philosophical Library, 1950.

Fox, Robin Lane. *Pagans and Christians*. New York: Alfred A. Knopf, 1989.

Gaskell, G. A. *Dictionary of All Scriptures & Myths*. Avenel, N.J.: Gramercy Books, 1981.

Young, Dudley. *Origins of the Sacred*. New York: St. Martins, 1991.

CHRISTIAN MYSTERY SCHOOLS, CULTS, HERESIES

The Christian Mystery Schools were largely condemned by the early Church Fathers because of the fear that their practitioners were consciously or unconsciously continuing the old pagan ways. As it was, nearly all of the Christian holy days coincided with pagan holidays, from Christmas and the Roman feast of Saturnalia to Easter and the fertility rites of the goddess Eastre. The Church patriarchs were not at all willing to encourage any additional blendings of Christianity with the Old Religions.

NEARLY *all of the Christian holy days coincided with pagan holidays.*

Christianity was a young religion when compared to the worship of the Greek, Roman, Egyptian, and other Middle Eastern and Eastern deities. The mystery schools kept alive the practice of magic and the belief that secret rituals and sacred relics could command the presence of divinity. The ancient mystery rites dedicated to such gods as **Osiris, Isis,** and **Dionysus,** together with the magical formulas discovered by **Hermes Trimegistus** and other masters of the art of theurgy, compelled the gods to manifest and share their powers. The myths of the old gods and the holy scriptures of the Christians, the secret experiences of the ancients and the revelations of the apostles, the personal sense of God developed by the pagan cults, and the promise of the Church Fathers that one could know God through his son—all seemed to some individuals to be harmonious. The rich inheritance of the pagan world seemed too valuable to abandon when such mysteries could be so easily adapted and kept alive in the new rituals.

The Church Fathers disagreed sharply with the devotees of the Christian mystery schools who sought their approval. In their unanimous opinion, those who sought to blend the old pagan rituals with the new revelation of Christ were members of secret cults who were to be condemned as heretics. In response to the rejection of the church establishment, the heretical members of the Christian mystery schools simply became less open

and more secretive in the expression of their religious practices.

Originally, the word "heresy" was an unemotional term that meant to engage in the act of choosing a course of action or a set of principles. In contemporary culture, to be called a heretic may be considered something of a compliment, suggesting that one is an independent or adventurous thinker. However, in the epistles of St. Paul, heretics were condemned as being those dangerous teachers who sought to distort or corrupt the teachings of Jesus (c. 6 B.C.E.–c. 30 C.E.). Ironically, it was in Antioch, the city where those who followed Jesus of Nazareth were first called Christians, that Bishop Ignatius (c. 40–107) became the first of the Church Fathers to use the term "heretic" to condemn those he believed were altering the true understanding of Christ.

It was rather easy to be labeled a heretic by the early Church Fathers. Originally composed of a small group of Jews who had followed the teachings of their rabbi until his death on the cross, the first members of that sect—or cult—were sharply divided in what it was that they believed. Was Jesus of Nazareth a great prophet or was he truly the long-awaited Messiah of the Jews? The early Christians had no established doctrines regarding the resurrection of their teacher from the dead or his alleged divinity. They were even uncertain if they should continue to follow the Jewish religious laws. When Gentiles were allowed to join the small Jewish sect, the arguments concerning the true revelation of Jesus the Christ only escalated. Eventually, as the Christians solidified their beliefs, established their doctrines, became recognized as a church, and held councils to establish more rigid creeds and ecclesiasticisms, it became much easier to identify those men and women who were heretics and who truly departed from the established beliefs of the church.

There is often confusion between the terms "cult" and "sect." Generally speaking, if a cult becomes accepted by the mainstream culture, some of its original enthusiasm will eventually cool and it will steadily become more organized and structured until it matures into a "religious organization." Later, as some

Although Mithraism, the most popular religion among the soldiers in the Roman legions, became Christianity's greatest rival in the early centuries of the church, it was not, as is often incorrectly cited, a Christian heresy. While it is true that the worshippers of the Persian god Mithras spoke of the adoration of their deity by a group of shepherds at his miraculous birth, observed a baptismal ritual that must be observed by those who wished to follow him, participated in a communal meal of bread and water which resembled the Eucharist, and celebrated his birthday on December 25, Mithraism had been established throughout the Persian Empire at least 500 years before the birth of Jesus Christ in 6 B.C.E. Mithraism had been spread throughout the then-known world by a group of **magi**, who preached an **apocalyptic** scenario in which Mithras, greatly associated with solar symbolism, would return at the end of a 7,000-year cycle to renew the world and to reestablish his earthly reign.

In Rome, Mithras had appeal to both the foot soldier and his ranking officers. Mithraism was a macho religion for men only—no women allowed. After baptismal rites had been conducted, the rugged legionnaires passed through graded ranks, such as Crow, Soldier, Lion, Courtier of the Sun, and, ultimately, Father. Boys as young as seven could begin their initiation as Crow, and neither military rank nor class distinctions differentiated those who followed Mithras. Those who declared themselves to be practicing Mithraists were valued as disciplined and temperate soldiers who had formed an unbreakable bond with their fellow worshippers. And those men who faced death in battle were assured that the rites of Mithras would guide them securely into a peaceful afterlife.

The powerful effects of Emperor Constantine's (d. 337) conversion to Christianity in the fourth century had a great influence on vast numbers of the Roman legions, and thousands of soldiers followed his example and converted to the teachings of Jesus of Nazareth (c. 6 B.C.E.–c. 30 C.E.) and the Christian Church. Mithraism gradually faded into obscurity by the end of the fourth century, retaining only small

MITHRAS IN THE ROMAN LEGIONS

pockets of followers scattered throughout what had once been the Persian Empire.

SOURCES:

Clifton, Chas S. *Encyclopedia of Heresies and Heretics*. New York: Barnes & Noble, 1998.

Fox, Robin Lane. *Pagans and Christians*. New York: Alfred A. Knopf, 1989.

Spence, Lewis. *Encyclopedia of Occultism*. New Hyde Park: N.Y.: University Books, 1960.

of the orgnization's members become dissatisfied with the religious routine and yearn for a more passionate expression of faith, they break off into a splinter group of the church and become a "sect." As the sect becomes more organized and is regarded more seriously by the mainstream culture, it becomes known as a "denomination."

The various Christian mystery schools, cults, and heresies that have influenced millions of individuals for two millennia. From the earliest days of Christianity, there were basically two opposing interpretations of Jesus:

1. Jesus, a rabbi of Nazareth, was a powerful teacher and prophet, a devout man divinely inspired by God.

2. Jesus of Nazareth was the Christ, the Messiah, the true Son of God made flesh to serve as a sacrificial lamb for the sins of humankind.

From these two metaphysical expressions with their vast essential differences, there arose centuries of theological arguments and interpretations of the gospels. What was heresy to some was sacred belief to others. And so it continues to this day.

❋ DELVING DEEPER

Brandon, S. G. F. *Religion in Ancient History*. New York: Charles Scribner's Sons, 1969.

Clifton, Charles S. *Encyclopedia of Heresies and Heretics*. New York: Barnes & Noble, 1992.

Ferm, Vergilious, ed. *Ancient Religions*. New York: Philosophical Library, 1950.

BLACK MADONNA

Of the more than 400 images of the Black Madonna or Black Virgin known worldwide, the image of Our Lady in Czestochowa, Poland, has received the most recent recognition because of the personal devotion displayed toward this religious icon by Pope John Paul II (1920–   ). The pope, a native of Poland, prayed before the Madonna of Czestochowa in 1979, several months after his election to the Chair of Peter, and he is known to have made subsequent visits in 1983 and in 1991. The reports of miracles and healings attributed to Our Lady of Czestochowa (also known as Our Lady of Jasna Gora) through the centuries are

numerous. They include Our Lady greatly enhancing the ability of a small group of Polish defenders to protect her sanctuary from an army of Swedish invaders in 1655 and her holy apparition appearing to disperse an invading army of Russians in 1920. Records of such spectacular acts of intervention and dramatic cures are kept in the archives of the Pauline Fathers at Jasna Gora, the monastery site in which the portrait was housed for six centuries.

The Black Madonna of Czestochowa is of such antiquity that its origins are unknown. Tradition has it that St. Luke, the "beloved physician," painted the portrait of Jesus's mother on the cedar wood table at which she took her meals. Two centuries later, during her visit to the Holy Land, St. Helena (c. 248–c. 328), the Queen-Mother of Emperor Constantine (d. 337), is said to have discovered the portrait and brought it to Constantinople in the fourth century. Five centuries later, determined to save the image of the Madonna from the repeated invasions of the Tartars, St. Ladislaus (1040–1095) took the portrait to Opala, Poland, the city of his birth, for safekeeping. Regretfully, not long after its move, a disrespectful Tartar arrow managed to find its way to the Madonna's throat, inflicting a scar that still remains visible. In 1430, Hussite thieves stole the portrait and broke it into three pieces.

Contemporary scholar Leonard Moss has argued against a vast antiquity for the Black Madonna of Czestochowa, claiming that the figure of the woman in the portrait was painted in a distinctly thirteenth- or fourteenth-century Byzantine style. Janusz Pasierb, another scholar who examined the portrait, counters such an assertion, stating that the image was "painted virtually new" in 1434 because of the extensive damage that the portrait had suffered at the hands of vandals.

Another aspect of the mystery of Our Lady of Czestochowa and all the other Black Madonnas that has puzzled many individuals is why they are portrayed with such dark skin tones. Some scholars answer this by stating that it wasn't until the onset of the Renaissance in the fourteenth century that Jesus, Mary, and Joseph began being portrayed with pale skin, blue eyes, and blond or reddish-blond hair. Prior to that period, the Holy Fam-

Pope John Paul II
praying at the Black
Madonna Shrine in
Czestochowa, Poland, in
1999. (AP/WIDE
WORLD PHOTOS)

ily and the apostles were most often depicted as semitic people whose dark skin tones reflected the hot arid climate in which they lived. If the Black Madonna of Czestochowa was truly a portrait of Mary that had been painted from life by the apostle Luke, he would surely have captured a woman with olive or dark brown skin and black or brown hair.

Other researchers into the mystique of the Black Madonna state that the reasons that the Roman Catholic Church in general has not warmly embraced such depictions of the Holy Mother or Virgin Mary are because they fear that such representations are actually paying tribute to the ancient goddesses and Earth mothers and that these images perpetuate strains of pagan worship of the female principle. For example, church scholars point out that St. Germain de Pres, the oldest church in Paris (Par-isis, the Grove of Isis), was built in 542 on the site of a former temple dedicated to Isis. Isis had been the patron goddess of Paris until Christianity replaced her with St. Genevieve. Within the church of St. Germain de Pres, however, parishioners worshipped a black statue of Isis until it was destroyed in 1514.

Christianity warred against goddess worship from the days of the apostles when St. Paul (d. 62–68 C.E.) found to his great frustration that his message was being shouted down by the crowds at Ephesus who pledged their obeisance to Diana. Until they had been romanized and westernized, Diana/Artemis, together with the other two preeminent goddesses of the East, Isis and Cybele, were first represented as black madonnas. And before the people of the East bent their knees to Diana, Isis, and Cybele, they had worshipped the Great Mother as Inanna in Sumeria, as Ishtar in Babylonia, and as Astarte among the Hebrews. Most scholars agree that among the first images of the Black Madonna and her son were representations of Isis and Horus.

The Black Madonna may also refer to Mary Magdalene, who, in the traditions of many Christian sects, such as the **Gnostics,** was the wife of Jesus (c. 6 B.C.E.–c. 30 C.E.) In this interpretation of the events that occurred after Jesus' death at the hands of the Romans, Mary brought the cup used at the Last Supper—the Holy Grail—from Palestine to southern France, where it would eventually be guarded by the **Knights Templar.**

There is also a belief that Mary arrived in France carrying within her womb a child fathered by Jesus of Nazareth, who then became the progenitor for the royal family of France. For those who hold such beliefs, the Holy Grail is but a metaphor for Mary Magdalene's womb, which carried the true blood of Jesus in the person of his unborn son. Therefore, many of the depictions of the Black Madonna and child throughout the regions of southern France and Spain may be regarded as images of Mary Magdalene carrying the infant son of Jesus rather than the Virgin Mary carrying the infant Jesus.

✤ DELVING DEEPER

Baigent, Michael, Richard Leigh, and Henry Lincoln. *Holy Blood, Holy Grail.* New York: Dell Publishing Co., 1983.

Clifton, Charles S. *Encyclopedia of Heresies and Heretics.* New York: Barnes & Noble, 1992.

Dorese, Jean. *The Secret Books of the Egyptian Gnostics.* New York: MJF Books, 1986.

Duricy, Michael P. "Black Madonnas: Our Lady of Czestochowa," maintained by the Marian Library/International Marian Research Institute. [Online] http://www.udayton.edu/mary/meditations/olczest.html. 23 January 2002.

Imel, Martha Ann, and Dorothy Myers. *Goddesses in World Mythology.* New York: Oxford University Press, 1995.

Matthews, Caitlin. *Sophia Goddess of Wisdom: The Divine Feminine from Black Goddess to World-Soul.* London: Aquarian Press, 1992.

Sjoo, Monica, and Barbara Mor. *The Great Cosmic Mother.* San Francisco: Harper and Row, 1987.

CATHARS

In 1208, Pope Innocent III (c. 1161–1216) declared the Cathars, a sect of Christianity (also known as the Albigenses), to be heretical and condemned the citizens of Beziers, Perpignan, Narbonne, Toulouse, and Carcassone to death as "enemies of the Church." Simon de Montfort (c. 1165–1218), an accomplished military leader, was appointed to conduct a crusade against fellow Christians, cultured men and women of what is today southern France, who the pope had deemed a greater threat to Christianity than the Islamic warriors who had pummeled the Crusaders. Although it took him nearly 20 years of warfare against the beleaguered Albigenses, de Montfort managed to exterminate 100,000 men, women, and children, before he himself was killed during the siege of Toulouse in June 1218.

According to many contemporary scholars, the Cathars' or Albigenses' real offense, their "heresy," was their opposition to the sacramental materialism of the medieval church. The group had no fixed, religious doctrine, and was known by various names. They called themselves the True Church of God, and most of the few manuscripts that survived the flames of siege were all written in Proven-

Annie Besant and the Theosophical Society

nnie Besant was a social reformer and Theosophist who advocated for the independence and religious rights of women. Born to William and Emily Wood in 1847 England, Annie married a young clergyman, Frank Besant, at 19; they had two children. She questioned the extreme traditional religious views of her husband, and in response he ordered her out of the church, home, and family.

Besant preached a different kind of religion: free thought. She began working with Charles Bradlaugh (1833–1891), leader of the secular movement in Britain and editor of the radical paper *National Reformer*. They coauthored a book, *The Fruits of Philosophy*, which advocated the use of birth control, buttressed by such arguments as financial distress and overcrowding. Their writings caused them to be arrested in 1877 on charges of immorality, for which they served six months before the sentence was appealed and overturned. Not intimidated, Besant wrote another book advocating the use of birth control, *The Laws of Population*.

During the 1880s Besant attacked unhealthy working conditions and low wages for women factory workers, leading the Match Girls' Strike in 1888. A popular speaker on women's rights, Besant was elected to the London School Board and earned a science degree from London University. She continued to urge the legalization of birth control, and produced other writings defending free thought and atheism while criticizing Christianity. An 1887 pamphlet, "Why I Do Not Believe in God," coauthored with Bradlaugh, added to her notoriety.

In 1887, Besant met Spiritualist Helena Petrovna Blavatsky (1831–1891), who in 1885 had founded the Theosophical Society. Besant embraced Blavatsky's beliefs, which seemed to ignite a religious awakening within her. The Theosophical Society split into two branches after Blavatsky's death in 1891, with Annie Besant as president of one of them.

Besant emigrated to India, where she founded the Central Hindu College in 1898. She established the Indian Home Rule League in 1916 and became its president; in 1917, she became president of the Indian National Congress, but would break ties with Ghandi. Besant remained in India until her death in 1933, but returned to England in 1926–1927 with her protege, Jiddu Krishnamurti, whom she announced as the new Messiah.

SOURCES:

Besant, Annie Wood. *Annie Besant, An Autobiography*. London: T. Fisher Unwin, 1893. Reprint Adgar: The Theosophical Press, 1939.

———. *Avatares*. London: Theosophical Press, 1923.

———. *H. P. Blavatsky and the Masters of the Wisdom*. London: Theosophical Publishing House, 1918.

cal, the old language of southern France, with even fewer written in Latin. Albi was the town in the province of Languedoc in which an ecclesiastical church council condemned them as heretics, hence the Albigenses designation. The cultural life of the Albigenses far out-shone that of any other locality in the Europe of their day. In manners, morals, and learning, objective historians state the Albigenses deserved respect to a greater extent than the orthodox bishops and clergy. It is now generally conceded among researchers that the court of Toulouse before the ravages of Simon de Montfort's siege was the center of a higher type of civilization than existed anywhere else in Europe at that time.

Most experts on this historical period agree that the nearly 40 years of warfare against the Cathars ruined the most civilized nation in thirteenth-century Europe. The pitiless cruelty and brutal licentiousness, which was habitual among the Crusaders, achieved new depths of inhumanity against the Albigenses. No man was spared in their wrath. No woman was spared their violence. It has been observed that no Roman, Hunnish, Muslim, or Mongol conqueror ever annihilated a Christian community with greater savagery.

Since most of the Albigensian communities were first sacked, then burned, their records and their libraries were destroyed. Because the testimony of exactly what the Cathars really believed was wrung out under extreme pain from those who survived the massacres and endless sieges long enough to be tortured and burned at the stake, it has been difficult to gain access to their true belief structure until recent times. Research now indicates that far from the devil-worshipping heretics that Pope Innocent III decreed warranted extermination, the Albigenses were devout, chaste, tolerant Christian humanists, who loathed the material excesses of the medieval church. They were metaphysicians, spiritual alchemists, herbalists, healers, and social activists with a pragmatic turn of mind. Similiar expressions of their belief concepts may be found in the Gnostic Gospels, in the Essenic teachings discovered at Qumran, and in the **Egyptian mystery schools.**

It would appear that the greatest heresy to the Christian Church lay in the Cathars' denial that Christ ever lived as a man, but was a being of spirit, much like an angel. They also believed that it was Satan who created the material world after his expulsion from heaven when God the Father, taking pity on his once bright star Lucifer, allowed him seven days to see what he might create. The bodies of Adam and Eve were animated by fallen angels and directed by Satan to beget children who would follow the ways of the serpent. To counter the lust of the flesh inspired by the devil, the Cathars preached abstinence before marriage, chastity, vegetarianism, and nonviolence. They believed in a progressive doctrine of reincarnation with the spirits of animals evolving into humans. In their view, it was a dualistic universe, with good and evil having equal strength, and they considered their time in the world as a struggle to resist Satan's power.

In 1244 Montsegur, the last center of Albigensian resistance, fell, and hundreds of Cathars were burned at the stake. The headquarters of the Inquisition was now established in the once highly cultured Albigensian city of Toulouse, and the few Cathars who had managed to escape death during the bloody decades of the crusade that had been launched against them were now at the mercy of the relentless witch and heretic hunters.

Monument memorial in Field of the Burned in Montsegur, Cathar country, France. (F. C. TAYLOR/FORTEAN PICTURE LIBRARY)

from the Greek "gnosis," meaning "to know," and the adherents of Gnosticism unabashedly declared that members of their form of religious expression "knew" from firsthand experience the truths that other beliefs had to accept on faith.

THE *Gnostics sought direct experience with the divine by uttering secret words of wisdom.*

Many of the Gnostic sects blended elements of Christianity with the **Eleusianian mysteries,** combining them with Indian, Egyptian, and Babylonian magic, and also bringing in aspects of the Jewish Kabbalah as well. Whatever the expression of the various Gnostic belief structures, they all emphasized a detachment from the material world and an elaborate series of spiritual hierarchies through which those initiates who had achieved personal knowledge of divinity could arise. The Christian Church Fathers branded the Gnos-

❋ DELVING DEEPER

Baigent, Michael, Leigh, Richard, and Lincoln, Henry. *Holy Blood, Holy Grail.* New York: Dell Publishing Co., 1983.

Clifton, Charles S. *Encyclopedia of Heresies and Heretics.* New York: Barnes & Noble, 1992.

Delaforge, Gaetan. *The Templar Tradition.* Putney, Vt.: Threshold Books, 1987.

Lea, Henry Charles. *The Inquisition of the Middle Ages.* New York: Citadel Press, 1963.

Trevor-Roper, H. R. *The European Witch-Craze.* New York: Harper & Row, 1967.

GNOSTICISM

Several cults with widely differing beliefs all bearing the label of "Gnostic" arose in the first century, strongly competing with the advent of Christianity. The term Gnostic is derived

Simon Magus: The earliest known Gnostic. Magnus construed that the Garden of Eden, the exodus from Egypt, and the Red Sea crossings were symbols.

Marcion (85–160 C.E.): Organizer of Gnostic congregations. These eastern Mediterranean congregations lasted into the third century C.E. Christian leaders from Rome excommunicated Marcion for writing a book called Antitheses. He believed the death of Christ was a hallucination, because Jesus did not have a physical body.

Valentinus: Founder of the largest Gnosticism school which lasted into the fourth century C.E. He taught that groups of Aeons made up the fullness of the High God. The groups were divided into three parts: the Ogoad—Depth, Silence, Mind, Truth, Word, Life, Man and Church; the Decad (10) and Dodecad (12); and the Docecad—Wisdom, also called Sophia.

Carpocrates (c.140 C.E.): Teacher of reincarnation. He believed an individual had to live many lives and adsorb a full range of experiences before being able to return to God.

MAIN LEADERS OF GNOSTICISM

SOURCE:

"Gnosticism: Ancient and Modern." [Online]. http://www.religioustolerance.org/gnostic.htm.

tics as heretics just as soon as they had developed enough power within the Roman Empire to do so, and the cult continued to be anathema to the Church down through its variations in the **Cathars,** the Albigensis, and the **Knights Templar.**

The first Gnostic of importance would seem to be Simon Magus (fl. c. 67 C.E.), a Samarian sorcerer, a contemporary of the apostles, who was converted to Christianity, then strongly rebuked by Peter when he sought to purchase the wonder-working power of the Holy Spirit (Acts 8:9–24). Those Gnostic Christians influenced by such charismatic individuals as Simon Magus believed that there was a secret oral tradition that had been passed down from Jesus that had much greater power and authority than the scriptures and epistles offered by the orthodox teachers of Christianity. The Gnostics, like the initiates of the Greek and Egyptian mysteries, sought direct experience with the divine and they believed that this communion could be achieved by uttering secret words of wisdom that God had granted to specially enlightened teachers. The Gnostics considered themselves much more spiritually advanced than the larger community of Christians, whom they regarded as ignorant plodders and easily led sheep.

Nearly everything that was known about the Christian Gnostics prior to the discovery of the Nag Hammadi library in 1945 was taken from the highly prejudiced writings of such Church Fathers as Irenaeus, Hippolytus, and Epiphanius, who condemned the Gnostics as heretics and devil-worshippers. The library that was found in Upper Egypt consists of 12 books, plus eight leaves removed from a thirteenth book and tucked inside the front cover of the sixth. These eight leaves make up the complete text of a work that has been taken out of a volume of collected works. Each of the books, except the tenth, consists of a collection of brief works, such as "The Prayer of the Apostle Paul," "The Gospel of Thomas," "The Sophia of Jesus Christ," "The Gospel of the Egyptians," and so on. Although the Nag Hammadi library is written in Coptic, the texts were originally composed in Greek and contain many references to Egyptian sites and beliefs. And although the work is ascribed to Christian Gnostics, there are many essays within the library that do not seem to reflect much of the Christian tradition. While there are references to a Gnostic Savior, his presentation does not seem to be based on the Jesus found in the New Testament. On those occasions when Jesus does appear in the texts, he often appears to be criticizing those orthodox Christians who have confused his words and his teachings. By following the true way and thus achieving transcendence, Jesus says in "The Apocalypse of Peter," every believer's "resurrection" becomes a spiritual reality.

Throughout the Nag Hammadi library there are admonitions to resist the lures and traps of trying to be content in a world that has been corrupted by evil. The world created by God is good. The evil that has permeated the world, although alien to its original design, has risen to the status where it has become the ruler of Earth. Rather than perceiving existence as a battle between God and the devil, the Gnostics envisioned a struggle between the true, most high, unknowable God and the lesser god of this Earth, the "Demiurge," that they associated with the angry, jealous, rule-giving deity of the ancient Hebrews. They believe that all humans have the ability to awaken to the realization that they have within themselves a spark of the divine. By attuning to the mystical awareness within them, they may transcend all earthly entrapments and regain their true spiritual home. Jesus had been sent by God as a guide to teach humans how to free themselves from the control of the Demiurge and to under-

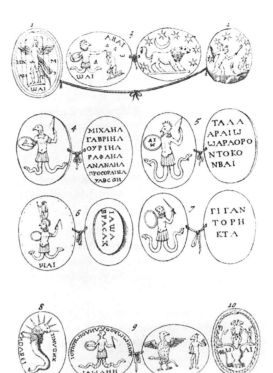

Illustrations of Gnostic gems from *Mensa Isaica* (1669) by Lorenzo Pignoria. FORTEAN PICTURE LIBRARY)

stand that the kingdom of God was within, a transcendental state of consciousness, rather than a future reward.

As if the theology of the Gnostics was not enough to have them branded as heretics by the orthodox Christian establishment, their doctrines and their scriptural texts often utilized feminine imagery and symbology. Even more offensive to the patriarchal Church Fathers was the Gnostic assertion that Jesus had close women disciples as well as men. In *The Gospel of Phillip* it is written that the Lord loved Mary Magdalene above all the other apostles, and he sharply reprimanded those of his followers who objected to his open displays of affection toward her.

GNOSTICISM *ceased to be a threat to the Christian Church by the fourteenth century.*

Gnosticism ceased to be a threat to the organized Christian Church by the fourteenth century, but many of its tenets of belief have never faded completely from the thoughts and writings of many scholars and intellectuals down through the centuries. Elements of the Gnostic creeds surfaced again in the New Age movement of the late twentieth century. An impetus to study the writings of the Gnostic texts was provided by psychologist Carl Gustav Jung (1875–1961), who perceived value in the writings of Valentinus, a prominent Gnostic teacher. In Jung's opinion, Gnosticism's depiction of the struggle between God and the false god represented the turmoil that existed among various aspects of the human psyche. God, in the psychologist's interpretation, was the personal unconscious; the Demiurge was the ego, the organizing principle of consciousness; and Christ was the unified self, the complete human.

✤ DELVING DEEPER

Clifton, Charles S. *Encyclopedia of Heresies and Heretics*. New York: Barnes & Noble, 1992.

Crim, Keith, ed. *The Perennial Dictionary of World Religions*. San Francisco: Harper Collins, 1989.

O'Grady, Joan. *Early Christian Heresies*. New York: Barnes & Noble, 1985.

Robinson, James, ed. *The Nag Hammadi Library*. San Francisco: Harper & Row, 1981.

MANICHAEISM

Mani (c. 216–277), a self-proclaimed "apostle of Christ" who spoke in Syrian, a version of the Aramaic language in which Jesus (c. 6 B.C.E.–c. 30 C.E.) taught, proclaimed that his church would preach a universal religion that would be for all people, regardless of nationality or tongue. The well-educated child, born to a Persian family that lived near Babylon and who worshipped with the Elkesaites, fell under the influence of Gnostic teaching and began to devise a philosophy that saw life on Earth as a constant struggle between good and evil. When he was only 12, Mani experienced his first religious vision and perceived an angelic being who declared itself his heavenly twin and who promised always to be Mani's helper and protector. When he was 24, the twin appeared again, and he instructed the young visionary that it was now time to leave the Elkesaite community and to begin his public ministry.

Mani believed that his visions qualified him to preach a new gospel that combined the words and works of Jesus with other great messianic teachers. He sought to pattern his life after that of St. Paul (d. 62–68 C.E.), and he called himself an apostle through the will of Christ before he set out on his extensive missionary travels. However, unlike Paul, Mani believed, as did so many Christian heretics, that as the Son of God Jesus could not have been born of a woman and he would never have subjected himself to a death upon a cross. In true apostle fashion, however, Mani did heal the sick and the lame, and he did perform miracles. In addition, he wrote seven holy texts, ranging from a collection of his letters to his "Living Gospel" and his own version of the "Acts of the Apostles."

According to Mani's theology, in the beginning of the universe the powers of good and evil, light and dark, were placed in two different spheres. The Father of Greatness personified the principle of goodness and light, the divine and the spiritual. The Prince of Darkness represented the principle of evil and the material. Over time, the world became a place of constant struggle and turmoil between an evil kingdom of darkness and the particles of light and goodness that had eventually become ensnared in matter. To assist him in the great battle, the Father of Greatness created the Mother of Life, who produced Primordial Man as an instrument of light to combat the powers of darkness. With the assistance of the Living Spirit, a second divine personage fashioned by the Father of Greatness, Primordial Man fought the forces of the Prince of Darkness. In the process of the great struggle, the physical Earth was created as a kind of by-product of the raging cosmic energies. Although Primordial Man was defeated by the Prince of Darkness and his children devoured by the monster, enough of their light leaked out to enable the Third Messenger, another creation of the Father of Greatness, to rescue them. Humans were later produced by the mating of demons who had inadvertently swallowed particles of light, and it would be Jesus who would at last awaken human beings to the spiritual realization that they each contained a spark of the divine light within them.

Mani taught that continued spiritual warfare was an unpleasant fact of life on Earth,

B orn on June 16, 1880, in Manchester, England, Alice Ann La Trobe Bateman was a devoted missionary worker and Sunday school teacher. She later became known as a writer of the occult. Many refer to her as the mother of the modern form of the New Age Movement.

One Sunday, Alice was alone in her room reading, when the door opened and a stranger entered. Terrified, she listened as the man dressed in European clothing with a large turban on his head informed her that there was a plan for her to do some work in the world, if she chose to; however, her disposition would have to change. If she could learn to exercise self-control and become a more pleasant, trustworthy person, she would travel throughout the world and do the "master's work." Promising to check on her in several-year intervals, he paused, looked at her one last time, and walked out.

Thinking the stranger to be Jesus Christ (c. 6 B.C.E.–c. 30 C.E.) and deeply affected by his message, she worked to become a nice person, so much so that her family was concerned that she was ill. In 1915, nearly five years later, when several English women introduced Alice to **Helena Petrovna Blavatsky** (1831–1891) and Theosophy, her studies of Blavatsky's Secret Doctrines revealed that the man was the Master Koot Hoomi. In 1919, another "teacher" appeared to Alice, identifying himself as Tibetan Master Djwhal Khul.

Alice Bailey wrote a series of Ageless Wisdom books of teachings from Djwhal Khul that became lauded as classics in occult teaching. In an unfinished autobiography, Bailey expressed her love and compassion for her teachers, declaring them hard-working disciples of the world and of the Christ.

In 1923, she established *The World Goodwill Centers,* to assist those in need, and *The Arcane School* for the education and development of spiritual disciplines and techniques, such as meditation. In order to offer the school activities and courses free of charge, Bailey established *The Lucis Trust,* a publishing company and funding organization, which in 1924 published Bailey's popular Great Invocation Prayer, and

ALICE BAILEY

would eventually publish 24 other works in 50 languages. Baily's writings continue to be a main influence of "New Agers" or those interested in the occult or deeper spiritual mysteries.

SOURCES:

Bailey, Alice A. *The Unfinished Autobiography.* New York: Lucis Trust Publishing, 1951.

Three Remarkable Women. Flagstaff, Ariz.: Altai Publishing, 1986.

and it was being conducted daily in the hearts and minds of all human beings. By responding to Mani's Gospel of Light, a person could awaken to the persistent earthly dualism of good and evil and activate the particles of goodness trapped within his or her own fleshly bodies. Once these elements of light had been released, the newly awakened individuals could hope to progress to a higher existence in the afterlife. While they remained in their bodies on Earth, however, they must accept their state of sin and acknowledge that they would never be able to conquer the state of wickedness that encompassed the physical world. Those whom Mani deemed "the Elect" would rise directly to the kingdom of light when they died; those "hearers," individuals who had merely heard the Gospel of Light being preached, would have the opportunity of experiencing additional incarnations before achieving such elevation. All disbelievers, those who rejected Mani's gospel, were destined to hell when Jesus returned to bring about the end of the world.

In *the Middle Ages, the term "Manichaean" was used interchangeably with "heretic."*

Manichaeans were taught that the particles of light and goodness remained trapped in evil matter and that all living things, including plant life, were sentient beings to be respected. Hunting and meat-eating were forbidden, and Manichaeans were strict vegetarians. Later, when Mani had a vision of vegetables screaming as they were about to be pulled from the ground, gardening and farming were also discouraged. To solve the dilemma of what food his followers might partake for nourishment, he advised the eating of melons, fleshless vegetables of concentrated goodness and light, that separated themselves from the parent vine when they were mature.

Mani first traveled to India with his new Gospel of Light, then turned back to Persia at the summons of Emperor Shapur I (d. 272), who became a strong adherent of the young

man's universal religion, gave Mani permission to preach throughout his kingdom. In spite of the support of Shapur I, the Magi, the official Zoroastrian clergy who had unrivaled supremacy in Persia for many centuries, detested Mani and believed his "new" religion to be nothing more than an amalgamation of Zoroastrianism, Christianity, Buddhism, and a wide assortment of other doctrines. At the instigation of the Magi, Persia's next ruler, Bahram I, who ruled from 273–276, ordered Mani arrested, interrogated, then executed, his head impaled on the city gates and his body thrown to the dogs.

Mani's death did little to thwart the zeal of the ever-growing number of new Manichaean missionaries, and his religion came to be preached in eleven languages and spread from North Africa to China; there it continued to thrive as a living faith from the T'ang dynasty (618–907) to the 1930s. In Europe, Manichaeism remained quite strong in Sicily, Spain, and southern France until the sixth century. Although the sect posed little threat to the Christian Church in the Middle Ages, the term "Manichaean" was used interchangeably with "heretic." Elements of Manichaeism have survived in minor ways in various secret societies, most frequently in its symbolism.

✤ DELVING DEEPER

Brandon, S. G. F. *Religion in Ancient History*. New York: Charles Scribner's Sons, 1969.

Clifton, Charles S. *Encyclopedia of Heresies and Heretics*. New York: Barnes & Noble, 1992.

Ferm, Vergilious, ed. *Ancient Religions*. New York: Philosophical Library, 1950.

Fox, Robin Lane. *Pagans and Christians*. New York: Alfred A. Knopf, 1989.

O'Grady, Joan. *Early Christian Heresies*. New York: Barnes & Noble, 1985.

TRIBAL MYSTERIES

The tribal cults that have emerged in the past 500 years offer a blend of Christianity—the majority religion of the conqueror and the slave owner—and the aboriginal belief structures of the Native American or African tribes that were subjugated or enslaved. While the early Christian missionaries, ministers, and priests were sincere in preaching what they considered to be the authentic word of God to the tribes of North and South America and Africa, they regarded their culture, customs, and religion as innately superior. Thus, a deeper understanding and respect between the missionaries and the tribal peoples was difficult to achieve.

"Lost in the dark the heathen doth languish," bemoans a familiar missionary hymn, soundly implying that there is but a single source of illumination. When the Christian clergy set forth on their spiritual journeys to convert the tribal peoples, they established themselves in the parental role and widened the gap of understanding between religious traditions.

On the North American continent, the Christian missionaries were intrigued to discover that tribe after tribe across the length and width of the continent had legends and myths which closely paralleled so many of the accounts found in Genesis and in other books of the Old Testament. The Delaware, to cite only one example, told the story of the Creation and the Great Deluge in pictographs. Some missionaries dealt with the mystery in the same manner that the early Spanish priests who accompanied the conquistadores had dealt with the Aztec myths that told stories similiar to those found in the Bible—they declared that the native people had been told these stories by Satan.

In a study of the aboriginal peoples of the United States written by a theologian in the late 1800s, Dr. John Tanner fulminated against such accounts related by the tribal priests and declared: "If the Great Spirit had communications to make, he would make them through a *white* man, not an Indian!"

Other Christian scholars and missionaries were not so certain, and, in an effort to explain the similarity between so many of the tribal legends and rites to the Judeo-Christian traditions, a theory was formulated that argued that the aboriginal peoples of the New World were the descendants of the Lost Tribes of Israel. To add an intriguing credence to this theory was the enigma of the Mandan tribe—

blue-eyed, fair-complexioned native people of the central plains. Christian clergymen set out with renewed vigor to reclaim the scattered Israelite tribes, lost to the fold for so long, denied the opportunity to accept Jesus Christ (c. 6 B.C.E.–c. 30 C.E.) as the Messiah, condemned to wander a strange and pagan land with their holy traditions but dim memories.

In recent decades, the term "cult" has become negative, quickly applied to religious expressions that may seem different from the order of service in more conventional church bodies. In the twenty-first century, one should always be mindful that what seems to be a strange cult to one person is likely to be a sincere and serious form of worship to another; just because this "strange religious practice" may be an eclectic blend of several traditions does not make it any less serious to its practitioners.

✦ DELVING DEEPER

Crim, Keith, ed. *The Perennial Dictionary of World Religions*. San Francisco: Harper Collins, 1989.

Harvey, Graham. *Indigenous Religions*. New York: Cassell, 2000.

Rosten, Leo, ed. *Religions of America*. New York: Simon & Schuster, 1975.

Sharma, Arvind, ed. *Women in World Religions*. Albany: State University of New York Press, 1987.

GHOST DANCE

In 1890 Jack "Wovoka" Wilson (1856–1932), a Paiute who worked as a ranch hand for a white rancher, came down with an illness accompanied by a terrible fever. For three days, the Native American lay as if dead. When he returned to consciousness and to the arms of his wife Mary, he told the Paiute who had assembled around his "dead" body that his spirit had left his body and had walked with God, the Old Man, for those three days. As if that were not wonder enough, the Old Man had given him a powerful vision to share with the Paiute people.

Wovoka's vision had revealed that Jesus (c. 6 B.C.E.–c. 30 C.E.) moved again upon the Earth Mother and that the dead of many tribes were alive in the spirit world, just waiting to be reborn. If the native people wished the buffalo to return, the grasses to grow tall, the rivers to

run clean, they must not injure anyone; they must not do harm to any living thing; they must not make war. On the other hand, they must lead lives of purity, cease gambling, put away the alcohol, and guard themselves against all lusts and weaknesses of the flesh.

To perform the Ghost Dance was to insure that God's blessings would be bestowed upon the Paiute tribe.

The most important part of the vision that God gave to Wovoka was how to perform the Ghost Dance. The Paiute prophet told his people that the dance had never been performed anywhere on Earth. It was the dance of the spirit people of the Other World. To perform this dance was to insure that God's blessings would be bestowed upon the tribe, and

many ghosts would materialize during the dance to join with the living in celebration of the return of the old ways. Wovoka said that the Old Man had spoken to him as if he were his son, and God had assured him that many miracles would be worked through him. In his heart and in his life, Wovoka, also known in his tribe as "the Cutter," became Jesus; Mason Valley, Nevada became Galilee; and the Native American people received a messiah.

Wovoka's father had been the respected holy man Tavibo and his grandfather had been the esteemed prophet Wodziwob. And now he, too, had spent his time in imitation of death, lying in a trance-like state for three days, receiving his spiritual initiation in the Other World. Wovoka had emerged as a holy man and a prophet, and history would forever know him as the Paiute Messiah.

Soon, many representatives from various tribes visited the Paiute and saw them dance Wovoka's vision. They saw the truth of the Ghost Dance, and they began calling Wovoka,

Jesus. His fame spread so far that newspaper reporters from St. Louis, New York, and Chicago came to see the Ghost Dance Messiah and record his words. Whites were pleased that Wovoka did not speak of war, only of the importance of all people living together in harmony.

Chief Big Foot (1825?–1890) of the Sioux traveled from the camp in South Dakota to Nevada to see the Ghost Dance, and he returned to tell Sitting Bull (c. 1831–1890) about Wovoka's promise that the dead from many tribes would soon be joining the living in a restored world that would once again be filled with plentiful game, herds of buffalo, and the tall grasses of the prairie. All those whites who interfered with this would be swallowed up by the earth, and only those who practiced the ways of peace would be spared.

Sitting Bull, the great Sioux prophet and holy man, was impressed by Big Foot's report, but rather noncommittal toward the teachings of the Paiute Messiah. While he did not wholeheartedly endorse the Ghost Dance, neither did he prevent those Sioux who wished to join in the ritual from doing so.

Sometime during the fall of 1890, the Ghost Dance spread through the Sioux villages of the Dakota reservations with the addition of the Ghost Shirts, special shirts that could resist the bullets of the bluecoats, the soldiers who might attempt to stop the rebirth of the old ways. As the Sioux danced, sometimes through the night, believing they were hastening the return of the buffalo and their many relatives who had been killed in combat with the pony soldiers, the settlers and townsfolk in the Dakota territory became anxious. And when the Sioux at Sitting Bull's Grand River camp began to dance with rifles, it becme apparent to the white soldiers that the Ghost Dance was really a war dance after all.

After a nervous Indian agent at Pine Ridge wired his superiors in Washington that the Sioux were dancing in the snow and were acting crazy, it was decided that Sitting Bull and other Sioux leaders should be removed from the general population and confined in a military post until the fanatical interest in the Ghost Dance religion had subsided. Sitting Bull was killed by Sioux reservation police on December 15, 1890,

and Big Foot and 350 of his people were brought to the edge of Wounded Knee to camp.

On December 28, Sioux police, Fouchet's Cavalry, and Drum's Infantry moved against the Sioux camp at Grand River. The aggressors also brought with them Hotchkiss multiple-firing guns and mountain howitzers. A shot rang out. The Sioux scattered to retrieve rifles that had been discarded or hidden. From all around the camp, fire from the automatic rifles, violent eruptions from the exploding shells, and volleys of bullets destroyed the village. As they were being slaughtered by two battalions of soldiers, the Sioux sang Ghost Dance songs, blended with their own death chants. Within a short period of time, approximately 300 Sioux had been killed, Big Foot among them, and 25 soldiers had lost their lives. The massacre at Wounded Knee ended the Native American tribes' widespread practice of the Ghost Dance religion and ended the Indian Wars.

It was said that Wovoka wept bitterly when he learned the fate of the Sioux at Wounded Knee. Jack Wilson, the Cutter, the Paiute Messiah, died in 1932.

✦ Delving Deeper

Brown, Dee. *Bury My Heart at Wounded Knee*. New York: Bantam Books, 1972.

Harvey, Graham. *Indigenous Religions*. New York: Cassell, 2000.

La Barre, Weston. *The Ghost Dance*. New York: Delta Books, 1972.

Macumba

The Macumba religion (also known as Spiritism, Candomble, and Umbanda) is practiced by a large number of Brazilians who cherish the ages-old relationship between a **shaman** and his or her people. In its outward appearances and in some of its practices, Macumba resembles **voodoo** ceremonies. Trance states among the practitioners are encouraged by dancing and drumming, and the evening ceremony is climaxed with an animal sacrifice.

Macumba was born in the 1550s from a compromise between the African spirit worship of the slaves who had been brought to Brazil and the Roman Catholicism of the slaveholders. Although they were forced to honor an array of Christian saints and the God of their masters, the native priests soon realized how complementary the two faiths could be—especially since, unlike the slaveowners in the United States, the Brazilians allowed the slaves to keep their drums. The Africans summoned their gods, the Orishas, with the sound of their drums and the rhythm of their dancing. From the melding of the two religious faiths, the Africans created the samba, the rhythm of the saints. The African god, Exu, became St. Anthony; Iemanja became Our Lady of the Glory; Oba became St. Joan of Arc; Oxala became Jesus Christ; Oxum became Our Lady of the Conception, and so on.

During this same period, Roman Catholic missionaries were attempting to convince the Native American tribes in Brazil to forsake their old religion and embrace Christianity. In many instances, Macumba provided the same kind of bridge between faiths for the indigenous people as it had for the Africans imported to the country by the slave trade. While they paid homage to the religious practices of the Europeans, they also could worship their nature spirits in the guise of paying homage to the Christian saints.

The ancient role of the shaman remains central to Macumba. He (it is most often a male) or she enters into a **trance** state and talks to the spirits in order to gain advice or aid for the supplicants. Before anyone can participate in a Macumba ceremony, he or she must undergo an initiation. The aspirants must enter a trance during the dancing and the drumming and allow a god to possess them. Once the possession has taken place, the shaman must determine which gods are in which initiate so the correct rituals may be performed. The process is assisted by the sacrifice of an animal and the shaman smearing blood over the initiates. Once the initiates have been blooded, they take an oath of loyalty to the cult. Later, when the trance state and the possessing spirit has left them, the aspirants, now members of the Macumba cult, usually have no memory of the ritual proceedings.

❋ DELVING DEEPER

Huxley, Francis. *The Invisibles*. New York: McGraw-Hill, 1966.

"Macumba," *Occultopedia*. [Online] http://www.occultopedia.com/m/ macumba.htm. 23 January 2002

Middleton, John, ed. *Magic, Witchcraft, and Curing*. Garden City, N.Y.: Natural History Press, 1967.

Sharma, Arvind, ed. *Women in World Religions*. Albany: State University of New York Press, 1987.

Villodo, Alberto, and Stanley Krippner. *Healing States: A Journey into the World of Spiritual Healing and Shamanism*. New York: Fireside Books, 1987.

SANTERIA

In April 1989, the religion of Santeria was dealt a negative blow to its image that has been difficult to overcome in the public consciousness. Police officials digging on the grounds of Rancho Santa Elena outside of Matamoros, Mexico, brought up a dozen human corpses that had all suffered ritual mutilations. And when it was learned that Adolfo de Jesus Constanzo, the leader of the drug ring responsible for the murders, had a mother who was a practitioner of Santeria, a media frenzy swept across both Mexico and the United States. Santeria was most often defined in the media as an obscure cult that was a mixture of **Satanism, voodoo, witchcraft,** and demon-worship, rather than a religious amalgamation that evolved from a blending of African slaves' spirit worship with their Spanish Catholic masters' hierarchy of intercessory saints.

Constanzo, a drug smuggler, had created his own cruel concept of a cult and declared himself its high priest. He was joined by Sara Maria Aldrete, an attractive young woman, who led a bizarre double life as a high priestess and as an honor student at Texas Southmost College in Brownsville. Although, on the one hand, it seemed that the cruel executions were used as a disciplinary tool by the drug boss, as in all instances of ritual sacrifice it was learned from surviving gang members that Constanzo had promised his followers that they would be able to absorb the spiritual essence of the victims.

While Santeria's rites are controversial in that they may include the sacrifice of small animals, it is essentially a benign religion. Once a serious investigation was made of Constanzo's grotesque and gory version of a cult of human sacrifice, it was learned that he had combined aspects of Santeria, voodoo, and an ancient

Aztec ritual known as *santismo* with elements of his own personal bloody cosmology. Mexican police officials had discovered the grisly handiwork of the drug ring by following one of its members to a large black cauldron in which a human brain, a turtle shell, a horseshoe, a human spinal column, and an assortment of human bones had been boiled in blood.

Subsequent investigation revealed that Constanzo's drug ring was actually composed of individuals who belonged to a number of religious groups common to the area, including Roman Catholicism, Santeria, and Palo Mayombe. Many members of the gang insisted that the true inspiration for the human sacrifices came from Constanzo's demand that each of them watch the motion picture *The Believers* (1987) 14 times. This thriller, starring Martin Sheen, Jimmy Smits, and Robert Loggia, took certain elements of Santeria, added numerous concepts foreign to the faith—including a malevolent high priest with incredible supernatural powers—then climaxed these powerful ingredients with human sacrifice.

In spite of such public relations low points as the murders at Matamoros and negative depictions in motion picture and television presentations, Santeria continues to grow among Hispanics in Florida, New York City, and Los Angeles. Some estimates state that there are more than 300,000 practitioners of Santeria in New York alone. Although it was suppressed in Cuba during the 1960s, lessening of restrictions upon religious practices in the 1990s saw the practitioners of Santeria in that country increase in great numbers. While the rites remain secret and hidden from outsiders, a few churches have emerged that provide their members an opportunity to practice Santeria freely. The Church of the Lukumi Babalu Aye was formed in southern Florida in the early 1970s and won a landmark decision by the Supreme Court to be allowed to practice animal sacrifice. The African Theological Archministry, founded by Walter Eugene King in South Carolina, now reports approximately 10,000 members. The Church of Seven African Powers, also located in Florida, instructs its members how to use spells in their daily lives.

Santeria originated in Cuba around 1517 among the slaves who combined elements of the Western African Yoruba and Bantu religions with aspects of Spanish Catholicism. When they were forced to accept the religious practices of their masters, the African slaves were at first greatly distressed that they could no longer pay homage to their worship of the Orishas, their spiritual guardians. Since they were in no position to protest for the freedom to practice their native religion, their resourceful priests quickly noticed a number of parallels between the Yoruba religion and Catholicism. While paying respect and homage to various Christian saints, the Africans found that they could simply envision that they were praying to one of their own spirit beings. A secret religion was born—Regla de Ocha, "The Rule of the Orisha," or the common and most popular name, Santeria, "the way of the saints."

Santeria *originated in Cuba around 1517.*

In Santeria, the principal God, the supreme deity, is referred to as *Olorun* or *Olodumare*, "the one who owns heaven." The lesser guardians, the Orisha, were the entities who were each associated with a different saint: Babalz Ayi became St. Lazaurus; Oggzn became St. Peter; Oshzn became Our Lady of Charity; Elegba became St. Anthony; Obatala became the Resurrected Christ, and so forth. Priests of the faith are called Santeros or Babalochas; priestesses are called Santeras or Iyalochas. The term Olorisha may be applied to either a priest or a priestess.

Although little is known of the rites of Santeria, from what can be ascertained each celebration usually begins with an innovation of Olorun, the supreme deity. Dancing to the strong African rhythms continues until individuals are possessed by a particular Orisha and allow the spirits to speak through them. The ritual is climaxed with the blood sacrifice, usually a chicken.

❖ **Delving Deeper**

Middleton, John, ed. *Magic, Witchcraft, and Curing.* Garden City, N.Y.: Natural History Press, 1967.

"Santeria," *Alternative Religions*. [Online] http://www. religioustolerance. org/santeri.htm. 23 January 2002.

Sharma, Arvind, ed. *Women in World Religions*. Albany: State University of New York Press, 1987.

Villodo, Alberto, and Stanley Krippner. *Healing States: A Journey into the World of Spiritual Healing and Shamanism*. New York: Fireside Books, 1987.

SATANIC CULTS

The scriptures of all religions acknowledge the existence of demonic beings. Some, including Christianity, Islam, and Zoroastrianism, regard the power of evil entities to be real and perceive them as rivals to the dominion of God. Others, such as Buddhism, consider them to be manifestations of ignorance and illusion. Those religions that testify to demonic powers also recognize that these negative beings are subject to the commands of a leader, known by various names: Satan, Lucifer, Beelzebub, Iblis, Mara, and Angra Mainyu, among others.

THE *Qur'an warns that "whoever follows the steps of Satan will assuredly be bid to indecency and dishonor."*

While rationalists in the present age of science and technology find it difficult to accept the concept of demons tempting men and women to commit acts of wickedness under the direction of a central embodiment of evil, such as Satan, other serious-minded philosophers and theologians call attention to the diverse horrors of the twentieth century and the seemingly endless capabilities of humans to inflict evil upon their fellow beings in the beginning of the twenty-first century and argue that such perversities transcend the bounds of reason. The Qur'an warns that "whoever follows the steps of Satan will assuredly be bid to indecency and dishonor." The prophet Zoroaster (c. 628 B.C.E.–c. 551

B.C.E.) blamed the Evil One for spoiling the plan of life and depriving humans of the "exalted goal of Good Thought." Hinduism envisions the gods and the demons as cosmic rivals for humankind. The demons are self-centered and interested in their own gain while the gods are generous and willing to share their bounty with others. The epistle writer Paul (d. 62–68 C.E.) informs Christians in Ephesians 6:12 that they are not fighting against creatures of flesh and blood, "but against the principalities, against the powers, against the world rulers of this present darkness, against the spiritual hosts of wickedness in the heavenly places."

While it is one thing to recognize the human capacity for inflicting acts of incredible evil upon their fellow men and women, it is quite another to fear rumors of organized cults of thousands of Satan worshippers who allegedly plot horrid deeds against the members of other religions in the name of their cloven-hoofed and horned god. Contrary to the beliefs of certain conservative Christians, Satanism as an actual religion is composed of a few small groups, which according to census figures in the United States and Canada probably number less than 10,000 members. Such religious cults as **Santeria, Wicca, voodoo,** and various neopagan groups are regularly and incorrectly identified as satanic, and it has been suggested by some that the statistics often quoted by certain Christian evangelists, warning of millions of Satan worshippers, quite likely consider all non-Christian religions as satanic, including Buddhism, Hinduism, and Islam.

In the 1980s and 1990s, a widespread fear swept across the United States that there were dozens of secret satanic cults involved in satanic ritual abuse and sacrificing hundreds of babies, children, and adults. Television and radio talk shows featured people who claimed to be former members of such demonic cults and those who had allegedly recovered memories of satanic abuse. For a time, certain communities developed a near-hysteria and a fear of Satanists that recalled the time of the **Salem witchcraft trials.** Even at its most alarming peak of irrational belief in such murderous cults, however, few accused such religious Satanists as Anton LaVey (1930–1997) and his **Church of Satan** in San Francisco as condoning ritual human sacrifices. After exhaustive police investigations on both local and national levels failed to produce any hard evidence to support such frightening accounts, allegations of satanic ritual abuse faded to the status of a kind of Christian **urban legend.**

There are many kinds of free-form Satanism, ranging from that which is merely symptomatic of sexual unrest and moral rebellion among young people to those mentally unbalanced serial killers who murder and sacrifice their victims to their own perverse concept of satanic evil. Teenagers and young adults may be mistaken for Satanists, because they dress in dark gothic clothes, read occult literature, or play with a **ouija board** with friends—but most of them are merely role-playing and quietly protesting the conformity they wish to resist. Other young people are drawn into a transient attraction toward Satanism by a number of heavy-metal bands who merely pretend to be practicing Satanists to shock parents and to provoke publicity in the highly competitive field of contemporary music.

Each year, hundreds of homicides are thought to have been satanically or ritually inspired. However, federal, state, and local law enforcement has never proven the existence of an organized satanic movement that has been responsible for these deaths, or that those murderers who were apprehended for the homicides were members of any satanic religious group. Some serial killers have claimed to be Satanists, but in each of these cases, police investigations have revealed that the murderers were not actually members of any of the satanic religious groups. Even such a high-profile "devil-worshipper" as Richard Ramirez (1960–), the infamous "Night Stalker" of Los Angeles, who committed a series of brutal night-time killings, robberies, and sexual attacks, was never found to be a member of any formal satanic group. Although Ramirez scrawled an inverted pentagram (a symbol traditionally associated with satanic rituals) in the homes of some of his victims and shouted, "Hail, Satan!" as he was being arraigned on charges of having murdered 14 people, he was strictly a lone-wolf worshipper of evil.

Individuals, primarily teenagers and young adults, may for a time dabble in the occult, ceremonial magick, and other freelance rituals and declare themselves as Satanists. Their numbers are difficult to assess with any degree of accuracy, for they are essentially faddists, generally inspired by a current motion picture or television series that popularizes Satanism or witchcraft, and their interest in Satanism is short-lived. Some of these satanic dabblers may go so far as to sacrifice a small animal and spray-paint satanic symbols on houses and sidewalks, but their commitment to a lifestyle dominated by dedication to Satan soon dissipates.

Although Satanism and **witchcraft** have become synonymous in the popular mind for many centuries, they constitute two vastly divergent philosophies and metaphysical systems. Generally speaking, witchcraft, the Old Religion, has its origins in primitive nature worship and has no devil or Satan in its cosmology. While some traditional witches seek to control the forces of nature and elemental forces in both the seen and unseen worlds, others are contented to work with herbs and healing. In essence, what many have described as the "power" of witchcraft throughout the ages may be the effective exercise of mind over matter, those abilities in the transcendent level of mind that today we term psychic or mental phenomena. True Satanism—although manifesting in a multitude of forms and expressions and having also originated in an ancient worship of a pre-Judeo-Christian god—is today essentially a corruption of both the nature worship of witchcraft and the formal Christian church service, especially the rites of the Roman Catholic Church.

Some scholars argue that in a real sense, the Christian Church itself "created" the kind of Satanism it fears most through the excesses of the **Inquisition,** which made an industry out of hunting, persecuting, torturing, and killing those men and women accused of being doctrinal heretics and those practitioners of the Old Religion who were condemned for worshipping the devil through the practice of witchcraft. Then, in the sixteenth century, a jaded and decadent aristocracy, weary of the severity of conventional morality legislated by the church, perversely began to convert the primitive belief structures of serf and peasant into an obscene rendering of the rites of traditional paganism with the ritualistic aspects of Christian worship.

In contemporary times, many of those who openly claim to be Satanists and to belong to organized satanic groups insist that they do not worship the image of the devil condemned by Christian and other religions because the word "Satan" does not specify a being, but rather a movement or a state of mind. What Satanists do worship, these individuals explain, is a spirit being commonly known as Sathan in English and Sathanas in Latin. They do not believe Satan to be the Supreme God, but they believe him to be the messenger of God in that he brought to Eve the knowledge of God. Satanists believe that there is a God above and beyond the "god" that created the cosmos. The most high God takes no part in the affairs of the world; thus Satanists believe their faith to be the only true religion, insofar as revealed religion to mortals can be understood.

ANTON *Szandor LaVey started the rebirth of Contemporary Satanism on Walpurgisnacht (May 1), 1966 with the Church of Satan.*

Satanism, according to certain of its exponents, is the oldest of all world religions, and it is the only one that by doctrine lays claim to having its origin in the Garden of Eden. Adam's firstborn son, Cain, is thought to have celebrated the first Satanic Mass, and today, any lone Satanist can celebrate a valid Mass if the occasion arises. In the case of established covens, an ordained priest performs the office of the liturgy. Satanism, they maintain, is also the oldest form of worship according to discoveries made by archaeologists, who have discovered drawings of the Horned God (Sathan) in caves of Europe dating to prehistoric times.

The following signs and symbols are among the most common expressions of Satanism, both among individual Satanists and those self-proclaimed "high-priests and priestesses" who have established small covens of 13 or fewer members:

The Pentagram: The traditional five-pointed star, most often shown within a circle.

Goat's Head within a Pentagram: *The sigil of Baphomet, the symbol for Anton LaVey's Church of Satan.*

Number 666: The number of the beast in the Book of Revelation, considered by many Christians to represent Satan.

Upside-Down Cross: A mockery of Jesus' death on the cross. Sometimes the cross is shown with broken "arms."

Upside-Down Cross Incorporating an Inverted Question Mark: The cross of confusion, questioning the authority and power of Jesus.

Quarter Moon and Star: Represents the Moon Goddess Diana and Lucifer, the "Morning Star." When the moon is reversed, it is usually satanic.

Classic Peace Symbol of the 1960s: The sign of peace carried by protestors of the Vietnam War in the 1960s has allegedly been appropriated by Satanists who now use it to denote an upside-down cross with broken arms, thus signifying the defeat of Christianity.

Inverted Swastika: The swastika is another once-honorable symbol that simply represented the perpetual progression of the four seasons, the four winds, the four elements, and so forth. Already perverted when the Nazis claimed it as their symbol, Satanists are said to invert it to show the elements of nature turned against themselves and out of harmony with God's divine plan of balance.

Ritual Calendar: Satanism adopted the traditional calendar of witchcraft and celebrates eight major festivals, known as *Sabbats:*

• February 1 Candelmas

• March 21 Spring Equinox

• April 30 Walpurgisnacht

• May 1 Beltane

• June 21 Summer Solstice

• August 1 Lammas

• September 23 Fall Euinox

• October 31 Samhain

*• December 21 Winter Solstice

Contemporary Satanism is said to have experienced its rebirth on Walpurgisnacht (May 1), 1966, when Anton Szandor LaVey brought into being San Francisco's Church of Satan. The kinds of Satanism in vogue at various times in the centuries before LaVey's revival expressed itself in many ways—some reflected the Dark Gods of antiquity, but most mirrored the dark side of the human imagination. Generally speaking, the kind of Satanism championed by LaVey and others preaches indulgence in personal pleasure, and it has never pretended to be other than a counterculture alternative to the civil and religious establishments and a relentless foe of conventional morality. But none of the satanic cults, such as the **Church of Satan** or the **Temple of Set,** have many points in common with the conservative Christian concept of Satan. They do not worship a Satan that commands demons and seduces human souls into hell. To most of the satanic cultists, Satan represents a force of nature that inspires their own individual expressions of virility and sexuality.

✵ **DELVING DEEPER**

Cristiani, Leon. *Evidence of Satan in the Modern World.* New York: Avon, 1975.

Freedland, Nat. *The Occult Explosion.* New York: Berkley, 1972.

LaVey, Anton Szandor.*The Satanic Bible.* New York: Avon, 1969.

———. *The Satanic Rituals.* New York: Avon, 1972.

Lyons, Arthur. *Satan Wants You: The Cult of Devil Worship in America.* New York: Mysterious Press, 1989.

THE RISE OF SATANISM IN THE MIDDLE AGES

For the common folk of Europe, the Middle Ages (c. 500–c. 1500) were a time of fear, oppression, and despair, thus providing fertile soil for the seeds of the old pagan practices to take root and flourish anew. The ancient rituals and nature rites that were practiced with joy and abandon by the peasants came to be feared by the Medieval Church as demonic witchcraft that worshiped Satan and sought to destroy Christendom, which was at that time the official religion of all European

countries. According to a number of scholars, the Church itself may have been greatly responsible for the revival of the Old Religion by its having increasingly exercised extremely repressive regulations upon the private lives of the common people. Then, once excessive doctrines and dogmas had provoked a rebirth of paganism, the Church saw the nature-worshipping rituals of the common people as a threat to its authority and condemned these men and women as being practitioners of an organized satanic religion that never really existed.

An analysis of the Medieval Church's sexual code reveals that its basic law was that the act of sexual intercourse was to be performed as seldom as possible. Stern-faced Church authorities encouraged their flocks to avoid cohabitation completely, even if married. In the eyes of the Church there was no love, only desire. To have feelings toward a member of the opposite sex, even though no actual physical intimacy took place, was inherently sinful. And the holy state of matrimony provided no sanctuary for love. To love, or desire, one's lawful marriage partner was considered sinful. One of the Church's defenders stated that if a man loved his wife too passionately, he had committed a sin worse than adultery.

In his *Sex in History* (1954), G. Rattray Taylor summarized the strict system of Church morality as it was set forward in a series of penitential books. Every imaginable misdeed and every conceivable misdemeanor is discussed and analyzed at great length and appropriate penalties are set forth for each sexual misstep. Taylor explains that the basic code of the Church was composed of three main propositions:

1. All who could were urged to accept the ideal of complete celibacy;

2. An absolute ban was placed on all forms of sexual expression other than intercourse between married persons, and prohibitions were drawn up to thwart an exhaustive list of sexual activity, the violation of which resulted in terrible penitential acts;

3. The days per year upon which even married couples might consummate the sex act were decreased in number.

The frustrated populace were left with the equivalent of about two months of the year during which they might, for the purpose of procreation alone and without invoking any sensations of pleasure, engage in sexual connection. If a child had been born to them and had been delivered at a particular time of the year which would fit in a certain manner in the Church calendar, the anxious parents might be prevented by their faith from having intercourse for a year or more.

The penitential books developed the mystical concept that all virgins were the brides of Jesus Christ (c. 6 B.C.E.–c. 30 C.E.). Therefore, any man who seduced a virgin was not only committing fornication, but, at the same time, the more serious sexual crime of adultery. Christ was cast into the role of the indignant and outraged husband, and Mother Church, as his earthly representative, was thereby empowered to exact the terrible penance which the angered deity demanded. The maiden, unless she had been forcibly raped, was also held to be in mortal sin, for she had committed adultery against her husband, Christ.

F⊙R *the common folk of Europe, the Middle Ages were a time of fear, oppression, and despair.*

Chastity was honored as the Church's sexual ideal and the virtuous wife was the one who would deny herself to her husband. It was not only the sexual act for which the penitentials prescribed prohibitions and penance. Kissing and fondling also brought down severe penalties.

It was, according to Taylor, in a spirit of desperation to save the souls of weaker brethren that the Church passed such ruthless codes of personal behavior and repeatedly distorted and falsified the pronouncement of biblical texts in order to obtain justification for its laws. Such an extreme asceticism was certainly not preached by Christ, and such a sexual code is supported by neither the Old nor New Testaments.

The Middle Ages had become a time of intolerable sexual frustration and sexual obsession. In its attempt to eradicate sin by means of enforced sexual repression, the Church inadvertently created fertile ground for the rebirth of the dormant Old Religion. With the sanctioned state of Holy Matrimony open to only a few, the stories of the old ways, the old customs, and the old mysteries with their emphasis on fertility and communal sex rites became appealing to the common folk.

In the early days of Christianity, the Church Fathers permitted women to preach, cure, exorcise, and baptize. By the Middle Ages, women had lost all vestiges of any legal rights whatsoever, and the Church regarded them as responsible for all sexual guilt. It was woman who had precipitated the Fall by tempting man, who would otherwise have surely remained pure. Women were considered a necessary evil. In the Old Religion, she would once again be elevated to the status of priestess, healer, and a respected symbol of fertility.

The loss of civil rights, the tyranny of the feudal lords, and the imposition of sexual repression by the Church provided the fresh fuel for the smoldering sparks of the Old Religion among the common people. But the Church and the feudal establishment would soon move to combat the "evil" influence of the resurrected Pan, god of fertility, nature, and freedom. Church scholars would soon consult the ancient manuscripts to determine how best to deal with the formidable adversary who had returned from the past. The feudal lords would soon lose all patience with the rebellious serfs and set about to slay them as methodically as a farmer sets out to remove noxious weeds from his fields of grain, and the Church would ignite a flame which would eventually destroy thousands of innocents in the Inquisition. Pan, the horned and goat-hoofed god of the ancient mystery rites, had been transformed into Satan, the enemy of the Church, Christ, and all good.

In *The History of Magic*, (1948), Kurt Seligmann offered what seems to be an astute analysis of the situation: "…the ancient survivals, the amusements of serfs, the most innocent stories, were henceforth Satanic, and the women who knew about the old legends and magic traditions were transformed into witches....the traditional gatherings, the Druid's Festival on the eve of May Day, the Bacchanals, the Diana feasts, became the witches' sabbath...the broom, symbol of the sacred hearth...became an evil tool. The sexual rites of old, destined to stimulate the fertility of nature, were now the manifestations of a forbidden carnal lust. Mating at random, a survival of communal customs...now [were] an infringement of the most sacred laws."

To the Church, the devils solidified into one—Satan, enemy of Christ's work here on Earth. To the people, who could not really care about the philosophical dualism of an evil adversary for the Christ of the Feudal Lords and the Church, the Old Religion offered release from oppression and unrelenting drudgery.

According to Seligmann, the peasants of the Middle Ages did not view their Old Religion as a perversion, but as "...primitive and innocent customs. At the sabbat [the peasant] was free to do as he pleased. He was feared also; and in his lifelong oppression, this gave him some dignity, some sense of freedom."

It was in his enjoyment of the excitement and vigor of the Old Religion that the peasant could allow himself the luxury of experiencing pleasure without the interference of Mother Church, which sought to control and repress even human emotions. But it was in rebellion against church and state that provoked the feudal and church establishments to denounce the Old Religion as satanic and to declare its practitioners witches, Satan's willing servants. And it was in that same time of unrest, despair, and fear of demons that "woman" and "witch" became largely synonymous. St. Augustine (d. 604) had declared that humankind had been sent to destruction through one woman (Eve) and had had salvation restored to it through another woman (Mary). But, as many writers have since commented, woman had, to the medieval and Renaissance man, become almost completely dualistic.

❀ DELVING DEEPER

Hunt, Morton. *The Natural History of Love*. New York: Anchor, 1994.

Russell, Jeffrey Burton. *Witchcraft in the Middle Ages*. Ithaca, N.Y.: Cornell University Press, 1972.

Seligmann, Kurt. *The History of Magic*. New York: Pantheon Books, 1948.

Taylor, G. Rattray. *Sex in History*. New York: Vanguard Press, 1952.

Trevor-Roper, H. R. *The European Witch-Craze*. New York: Harper & Row, 1967.

BLACK MASS

In 1966, when Anton Szandor LaVey (1930–1997), high priest of the **Satanic Church of America,** joined socialite Judith Case and freelance writer John Raymond in the bonds of matrimony, he performed the rites over the naked body of Lois Murgenstrumm, who served as the living altar. Later, when LaVey explained the ritual significance of the living altar to reporters, he remarked that an altar shouldn't be a cold, unyielding slab of sterile stone or wood. It should be a symbol of unrestrained lust and indulgence.

All in all, it was quite a wedding for the first public marriage ceremony ever held in the United States by a devil-worshipping cult. The bride shunned the traditional white gown to appear in a bright red dress. The groom wore a black turtleneck sweater and coat. The satanic high priest stole the show, however, in a black cape lined with scarlet silk and a close-fitting blood-red hood from which two white horns protruded.

The cynical might point out that LaVey's San Francisco-based church headquarters was once a brothel; the purists among the Satanists might grumble about how LaVey's showbiz approach has demeaned the esoteric allure of their secret rituals; but it is difficult to be dogmatic about the precise rites and liturgies of the Black Mass.

EARLY *Sabbats were held well away from the cities and villages on large areas of flat ground.*

Most authorities agree that the early Sabbats were held well away from the cities and villages on large areas of flat ground. Many covens preferred hilly ground, even mountainsides; but wherever the rituals were held, it was essential that one end of the worship area be wooded. This grove, according to tradition, served as the choir and sanctuary. The open area served as the equivalent of the nave in an orthodox church. At the far end of the wooded grove, the worshippers erected an altar of stones. Upon the altar was placed a large, wooden image of Satan, which many contemporary scholars agree was quite likely intended to be a representation of the nature god Pan, rather than the Prince of Darkness.

Even in its most polished form, this effigy did not resemble the sleek, mustachioed popular conception of a long-tailed devil in red tights. The idol's torso was human, but its bottom half was that of a goat. Its head, too, was more often goat-like than that of a clearly discernible human physiognomy. The entire image was stained black, and in some locales, bore a small torch between its horns. The central feature of all such idols was said to be a prominent penis of exaggerated proportions, emphasizing the rites of fertility in which the ancient rituals originated.

A COVEN *is traditionally comprised of no more than 12 members.*

The tortures of the Inquisition brought forth all manner of obscene versions of the Black Sabbat, and perhaps the great majority of such testimony is suspect. It must be pointed out that descriptions of the Black Mass were derived from confessions achieved by torture, as well as from accounts of medieval Christians who observed pagan celebrations of the solstices, midsummer, and so forth and who collectively designated the participants as "satan-worshippers." However, numerous scholars of witchcraft, sorcery, and Satanism generally agree on the following order of service for the observance.

The Sabbat began with the ceremonial entrance of the participants, led by the high priest or high priestess of the coven. (A coven is traditionally comprised of no more than 12 members.) Christian observers of the Sabbat were quick to compare this ceremonial entrance to the orthodox introit, but there is no evidence that the witches referred to the procession by this name or even intended a comparison to the Christian order of service. According to contemporary reports of Sabbat gatherings in the Middle Ages (c. 500–c. 1500), several hundred, and in some cases, several thousand, people attended the ritual observances.

The chief officiant was called "The Ancient One," a purely symbolic title, as in many Sabbats, the priestess might be an adolescent girl. At the priestess' signal, the celebrants touched their torches to the flame burning between the dark image's horns and received the transference of Lucifer's light. The office was opened with the priestess chanting: "I will come to the altar. Save me my Holy Lord Satan from the treacherous and the violent." The ceremonial procession and opening prayer completed, the priestess next delivered the ceremonial kiss to the hindquarters of the image.

The only real steadfast rule of the Sabbat was that there must be an equal number of both sexes. Each participant must have a mate. Under torture, many witches told their confessors that Satan would conjure up demons to take the place of either sex if human company should run short.

Each initiate and each member in attendance was required to bring food and drink for the banquet. In the state of poverty and deprivation in which so many peasants lived, it is easy to see why they looked forward to these smorgasbords during the Sabbats. Wine, beer, and cider were all known by the twelfth century, and attendees were encouraged to drink as well as eat their fill.

It seems, in the opinion of many scholars, that the celebrants may have sprinkled liberal dosages of trance-inducing herbs into the communal brew. Undoubtedly, such an action was designed to break down the last vestiges of inhibitions that some newcomers might maintain. It was most important that everyone be congenial by the hour when it was time for the Sabbat Dance, or, as it is commonly known, the Witches' Round.

The round was performed with the dancers in a back-to-back position with their hands clasped and their heads turned so that they might see each other. A lively dance such as this, which was essentially circular in movement, would need little help from drugged drinks to bring about a condition of vertigo in the most hearty of dancers. In his *The Satanic Mass* (1965), H. T. F. Rhodes writes: "The result of the dance was an ecstatic condition wherein, as the movement progressed, officiants and congregation were united as if in one body."

In the sixteenth century, Florin de Raemond described the rites of the Sabbat then extant (translation from Rhodes, *The Satanic Mass*): "The presiding deity is a black goat with two horns. A man dressed as a priest is attended by two women servers. A young initiate is presented to the goat who makes the sign of the cross with the left hand and commands those present to salute him with…the kiss upon the hind-quarters. Between his horns the creature carries a black lighted candle from which the worshippers' tapers are lighted. As each one adores the goat, money is dropped into a silver dish." De Raemond goes on to state that the new witch is initiated by giving Satan a lock of her hair, and by "going apart with him into a wood." Then, according to de Raemond, "The Sabbat dance follows in the familiar back-to-back positions and the Mass proper then begins. A plain black cape is worn by the celebrant. A segment of turnip, dyed black, is used in place of the Host for the elevation. On seeing it above the priest's head, the congregation cry, 'Master, save us!' Water replaces wine in the chalice. Offensive material is used as a substitute for holy water."

The simplest ring dance practiced by witches is that of a plain circle with men and women alternating with joined hands. Sometimes the men face in and the women face out. In certain cases, upright poles may be placed on the perimeter of the dance circle so that the dancers might weave their way through the staves. As the witches become more accomplished, the dance patterns may become more sophisticated, but most authorities feel that nearly all of the dances may be traced from ancient designs, such as the **swastika,** which represents the horns of four beasts turning a mill or a wheel.

Perhaps the climax of the traditional Witches Round came with the priestess becoming the living altar and lying there, naked, to receive the material offerings of the group. Token gifts of wheat, fruit, and in some cases, small animals, may have been offered on the human altar. This part of the Sabbat seems to have been a most important facet of the fertility rites, which, in primitive times, was probably the primary motivation for the observance.

By the time of the Middle Ages with its grim repression of pleasure and sex, it appears to be a point of general agreement that a mass sexual communion was followed by wild and ecstatic dancing. Such accounts must always be evaluated by considering the source: women and men under torture and death at the stake. It seems certain from the perspective in the twenty-first century, that the old mystery religions took on a completely different interpretation when observed by Christian witnesses.

It was during the sixteenth and seventeenth centuries that the mold became set for the ritual patterns which many today commonly think of as Satanism. It was then that the practitioners of the Old Religion went completely underground with their worship ceremonies while the decadent aristocracy seized upon the Black Mass as a kind of hedonistic parlor game in which one might express his sexual fantasies on living altars and cavort about in the nude. Unrestrained immorality was the order of the day as Parisians followed the example of their Sun King, Louis XIV (1638–1715). Satanism was perhaps developed to its highest estate, as the jaded aristocrats began to adapt the witchcraft rituals to suit their own sexual fantasies. The enlightened sophisticate's mockery of the primitive customs had been converted to a serious interest by the tension and insecurity of the times. Although the Inquisition still consumed its quota of witches, the France of King Louis XIV was a high-living, low-principled era, and lords and ladies began to pray in earnest to Satan to grant them high office and wealth. Whether or not their wishes for elevation in the society of their day was granted, it would seem that the majority of these high-born Satanists paid cursory homage to the Horned God only as a means of indulging their baser passions.

❖ DELVING DEEPER

O'Keefe, Daniel Lawrence. *Stolen Lightning: The Social Theory of Magic*. New York: Vintage Books, 1983.

Rhodes, H. T. F. *The Satanic Mass*. London: Arrow Books, 1965.

Taylor, G. Rattray. *Sex in History*. New York: Vanguard Press, 1952.

Trevor-Roper, H. R. *The European Witch-Craze*. New York: Harper & Row, 1967.

Williams, Charles. *Witchcraft* . New York: Meridian Books, 1960.

CATHERINE MONTVOISIN

At her trial in Paris in 1680, Catherine Deshayes, "La Voisin" (c. 1640–1680), boastfully stated that she had sacrificed more than 2,500 children who had their throats slit at her Black Sabbats. She also claimed that her poisonous potions brought about the deaths of many more jealous husbands, unfaithful wives, and unwanted parents than all the other professional poisoners of Paris combined.

> LA *Voisin convinced a learned tribunal that her approach to astrology was completely acceptable to the Church.*

In 1647, the little girl who would become one of history's most infamous Satanists was just another barefooted beggar who had been sent out into the streets to tell fortunes for a few coins from the passersby. By coincidence, many of the waif's "predictions" came true, and she cultivated a clientele who swore by her "God-given powers." But the appealing little prophetess with the smudged nose soon discovered that Satan's wages were much higher than the ones offered by the angry wives who suspected their husbands of infidelity or the frustrated young women who wanted to know when they would get a husband.

When she was 20, Catherine married Antoine Montvoisin, who, as far as can be determined, never contributed any money toward her well-being. Innately resourceful, she had soon established herself as a midwife, a beautician, and an herbalist, and was supporting both Antoine and his daughter by a former marriage in handsome style.

It was when the enterprising La Voisin included palmistry, prophecy, and astrology among her stock-in-trade that she incurred the wrath of the established Church. Instead of being flayed alive by a grand inquisitor, the young woman convinced a learned tribunal composed of the vicars general and several doctors of theology from the Sorbonne that her approach to astrology was completely acceptable to the Church.

The effect that her release had upon her already flourishing trade as an herbalist and her ever-increasing reputation as a seer was remarkable. People reasoned that La Voisin had secured the Church's blessing on her magic. She was soon surrounded by many wealthy clients.

La Voisin received her supplicants in a darkened chamber wherein she appeared in an ermine-lined robe emblazoned with two hundred eagles embroidered in gold thread on purple velvet. For the right price, the high priestess would officiate at a special Black Mass for a troubled seeker of satanic solace. If the supplicant were female, then the client herself, regardless of how high-born she might be, would serve as the Black Mass's living altar.

The high priestess kept a secret list of more than 50 Roman Catholic priests who would celebrate the Black Mass at her bidding. Her great favorite was Abbe Guilborg (d. 1680), who, in spite of the fact that he held a number of public and private ecclesiastical offices, was always in need of extra money to maintain his mistresses he kept closeted about Paris. His skill as a chemist was also put to good use by La Voisin for her clients who wished effective poisons, and Guilborg managed to cut down on housekeeping expenses with his mistresses by selling his many illegitimate children to La Voisin for use as satanic sacrifices during her Black Masses.

Babies for sacrifice cost the high priestess a good deal of money, but she had learned to economize in the Paris streets. She established a home for unwed mothers, which saw the girls through their pregnancies and relieved them of the responsibility of caring for an unwanted child. Girls without financial means were provided for at no charge. The bills presented to the women of the aristocracy were large enough to cover the operating expenses for the entire home. The young pampered aristocrats, who inconveniently found themselves in a family way, were, however, offered the bonus of having a punitive potion secretly administered to the rogue who had been so careless in his seduction. With moral laxity the order of the day in Louis XIV's (1638–1715) France, the shrewd La Voisin's home for unwed mothers always managed to provide her with a stockpile of sacrificial infants.

The Black Mass was held deep in the bowels of La Voisin's high-walled house in the region lying south of St. Denis, which, in seventeenth-century Paris, was called Villeneuve. The supplicant approached the altar in complete nudity and lay upon its black surface. A black-robed acolyte stepped forward to place a flickering black candle in each of her upturned palms. At this point, Abbe Guilborg (d. 1680) appeared and positioned himself at the living altar. He wore vestments of an orthodox shape made of white linen. The chasuble (outer vestment worn by celebrant at Mass) and the alb were embroidered with black pine cones, the ancient Greek symbol of fertility. The priest placed the chalice upon the supplicant's stomach, kissed her body, and officiated the ceremony. The prayer book was bound in human skin; the holy water was urine; and the host was usually a toad, a turnip, or on occasion, true host stolen from a church and desecrated with filth.

The rituals completed, it was time for the offering. Abbe Guilborg stretched out his arms to receive the infant delivered there by the black-robed acolyte, intoning the dark entities Astaroth and Asmodeus to accept the sacrifice of the child so the supplicants at the Black Mass might receive the things that they asked.

The child was raised aloft and the priest deftly slashed its throat.

Marguerite, La Voisin's stepdaughter, often assisted at the Black Mass in the capacity of clerk to the celebrating priest. When Marguerite happened to find herself with child as the result of a flirtation with a married neighbor, she became alarmed when she found her stepmother casting appraising eyes at the bulge of her pregnancy. When the child was born, Marguerite, in spite of herself, found that a maternal instinct existed within her. Since she was quite aware that La Voisin had no interest in becoming a grandmother, Marguerite had sent her child away to be brought up in the country.

While she was becoming wealthy from her performance of the satanic rites, La Voisin was unaware that a police official named Desgrez, a detective who had arrested Madame de Brinvilliers (1630–1676), an aristocratic Satanist who specialized in poisons, was closing in on her Black Sabbats. When his men reported the number of the high-ranking and the high-born who were frequenting the Satanist's subterranean chambers, Desgrez found himself faced with quite a decision. It would not benefit him to anger so many important people by suggesting that the activities in which they were engaging were wrong. If he arrested La Voisin, he would, at least indirectly, be criticizing the members of the aristocracy who regularly attended her Sabbats and who relied upon her talents as a seeress and a priestess.

As Desgrez struggled with this dilemma, one of his officers came to him trembling with fear. He had recognized the crest on one of the coaches waiting before La Voisin's walls as belonging to none other than Madame de Montespan (1641–1707), the mistress of King Louis XIV. The officer told him that the royal mistress had served as the naked, living altar at one of La Voisin's Sabbats.

Desgrez brought his evidence and the list of names to his superior, La Reynie, head of the Chambre Ardente. King Louis had pledged himself to support the Chambre, but the rank of the names on the list, including that of his own mistress, placed him in a politically explosive situation. His advisors cautioned him that a hasty exposure of the decadence of court life would lead to a revolution or encourage England to launch an invasion against a morally corrupt and internally torn France.

After the arrest of La Voisin, several planted rumors caused some of the court favorites involved to flee the country on extended trips abroad. After they were safely out of the country, the king saw to it that evidence against highborn court figures, including his indiscreet mistress, was suppressed. La Voisin herself was treated to a rather pleasant stay in jail, until King Louis had seen to it that all those of high position had been protected. Then La Voisin was delivered to the grand inquisitor.

Catherine Montvoisin endured four six-hour ordeals in the torture chamber before she was brought to the stake on February 23, 1680. By the king's order, only testimony concerning those Satanists who had already been condemned was allowed to be recorded. The former fortuneteller from the streets of Paris went to her death singing offensive songs and cursing the priests who sought her final confession.

✤ DELVING DEEPER

Cavendish, Richard. *The Black Arts.* New York: Capricorn Books, 1968.

Rhodes, H. T. F. *The Satanic Mass.* London: Arrow Books, 1965.

Seligmann, Kurt. *The History of Magic.* New York: Pantheon Books, 1948.

Williams, Charles. *Witchcraft.* New York: Meridian Books, 1960.

GILLES DE RAIS (1404–1440)

In 1415, as a boy of 11, Gilles de Rais became heir to the greatest fortune in France. At 16, he increased his net worth by marrying the extremely wealthy Catherine de Thouars. Although he was known as a devout Christian with a mystical turn of mind, and is described by his contemporaries as a man of rare elegance and almost angelic beauty, he was far from an ascetic. He was highly skilled in the arts of warfare, and when he had barely turned 20 he rode by the side of Joan of Arc (c. 1412–1441) and served as her chief lieutenant, fighting with such fierce merit that King Charles VII (1403–1431) later awarded de Rais the title of Marshal of France.

Gilles de Rais was a man so noted for his devotion to duty and his personal piety that he came to be regarded as a latter-day Lancelot. But, like Lancelot, de Rais entered into an ill-fated love affair that destroyed him. Although it was undoubtedly an affair that was conducted entirely on a spiritual plane, de Rais became the platonic lover of Joan of Arc, the strange young mystic whose "voices" dictated that she save France. He became her guardian and protector, but when Joan was captured and burned at the stake, de Rais felt as though his years of serving God and the good had been for naught. After the maid of Orleans was betrayed by the Church, he became transformed into a satanic fiend of such hellish and unholy proportions that his like may be unequaled in the annals of perverse crimes against society. Many scholars who have examined the life of this pietist turned monster in depth have agreed that de Rais's crimes and acts of sacrilege were quite likely inspired by what he considered God's betrayal of God's good and faithful servant, Joan of Arc.

Although she had given him a child, Gilles de Rais left his wife, vowed never to have sexual intercourse with another woman, and secreted himself in his castle at Tiffauges. The young man who had once surrounded himself with priests and supported dozens of chapels throughout France, now welcomed profligates, broken-down courtiers, sycophants, and wastrels to his castle, and his family gold supported several rounds of lavish orgies. At last, even the vast wealth of the de Rais was depleted, and Gilles decided to try his hand at alchemy, the dream of transmuting base metals into gold, as a means of replenishing his fortune.

Within a short time, he had converted an entire wing of his castle into a series of extensive alchemical laboratories. Alchemists and sorcerers from all over Europe flocked to Tiffauges. Some came to freeload on the feasts and to fleece the young nobleman out of a few bags of gold. Others came to seek final answers and resolution to the persistent, haunting quest of the alchemist. Although de Rais himself joined the alchemists and magicians in work sessions that went nearly around the clock, all of their experiments counted for naught.

It was the Italian alchemist/sorcerer Antonio Francisco Prelati, a former priest, who told him that a mortal cannot hope to achieve the transmutation of base metals into gold without the help of Satan. And the only way that an alchemist or a sorcerer could hope to arouse Satan's interest in his work was by dedicating the most abominable crimes to his name.

Under Prelati's direction, de Rais set about to commit his first abominable crime. He lured a young peasant boy into the castle and into the chambers that he provided for Prelati. Under the alchemist's instruction, de Rais brutally killed the boy and used his blood for writing of evocations and formulas. Satan did not appear and no base metals were transmuted into gold, but Gilles de Rais no longer cared. He had discovered an enterprise far more satisfying than the alchemist's quest. He had discovered sadistic satisfaction and pleasure in the torture and murder of children.

On September 13, 1440, Jean the Bishop of Nantes signed the legal citation which would bring the Baron Gilles de Rais to trial. Among the charges levied on him were the killing, strangling, and massacring of innocent children. In addition to such horrors, he was also charged with evoking demons, making pacts with them, and sacrificing children to them.

Etienne Corillaut, one of de Raises's personal servants, later testified at his master's trial when the Marshal of France was accused of having slain as many as 800 children.

Rather than be put to the question by the court, de Rais chose to confess every sordid and gory deed. Such a confession would spare him the ordeals by torture awaiting those who protested their innocence. Because of his high position in the court of France, Gilles de Rais was granted the mercy of being strangled before being burned. The tribunal conveniently looked the other way after his execution, however, and the de Rais family was permitted to remove his corpse after it had been given only a cursory singeing. The mass murderer of hundreds of innocent children was interred in a Catholic ceremony in a Carmelite churchyard. Antonio Francisco Prelati and the other professing Satanists were given, at most, a few months in prison for their part in the murders.

"It is thought likely by some historians that this was their reward for testifying against their master," Masters and Lea reflect, "and that both ecclesiastical and civil authorities were far more interested in obtaining Gilles' money and properties, which were still considerable, than in punishing him for his crimes."

🕮 **DELVING DEEPER**

Lyons, Arthur. *The Second Coming: Satanism in America*. New York: Award Books, 1970.

Masters, R. E. L. and Eduard Lea. *Perverse Crimes in History*. New York: Julian Press, 1963.

Trevor-Roper, H. R. *The European Witch-Craze*. New York: Harper & Row, 1967.

Williams, Charles. *Witchcraft*. New York: Meridian Books, 1960.

ANTON LAVEY'S FIRST CHURCH OF SATAN

On Walpurgisnacht, April 30, 1966, Anton Szandor LaVey (1930–1997) of San Francisco shaved his head, donned clerical clothing, complete with white collar, and proclaimed himself Satan's high priest. Concurrently, LaVey announced the establishment of the First Church of Satan in America. A short time later, LaVey published *The Satanic Bible* (1969), affirming in bold language the teachings of the Church of Satan and proclaiming that Satan ruled the earth. This was the dawn of the Age of Satan, he announced—the morning of magic and undefiled wisdom.

Worship of the Prince of Darkness is at least as old as the Judeo-Christian tradition, and there was nothing new about a belief in magical powers. What was new was LaVey's use of the term "church" as part of his organization's title. While some accused him of blasphemy, he pointed out that the word itself came from the Greek and applied to any group that feels it has been "called out" of society's rank-and-file for a special purpose. And there seemed little question that LaVey seriously considered his church to be quite special. In addition to ceremonies and rituals devoted to the Prince of Darkness, there were weddings, funerals, and children baptized in the name of Satan.

Church of Satan founder
Anton Szandor La Vey
(1930–1997). (CHURCH OF
SATAN ARCHIVES)

LaVey's *The Satanic Bible* listed nine declarations that defined Satanism for a new age:

1. indulgence, instead of abstinence;

2. vital existence, instead of spiritual pipe dreams;

3. undefiled wisdom, instead of hypocritical self-deceit;

4. kindness to those who deserve it, instead of love wasted on ingrates;

5. vengeance, instead of turning the other cheek;

6. responsibility to the responsible, instead of concern for psychic vampires;

7. man as just another animal…more often worse than those that walk on all fours, who because of his divine spiritual and intellectual development, has become the most vicious animal of all;

8. all of the so-called sins, as they lead to physical, mental, or emotional gratification;

9. Satan is the best friend the Church has ever had, as he has kept it in business all these years.

In *The Satanic Bible*, LaVey revealed and explained the credos of Satanism as proclaimed by the Church of Satan. In his introduction to the work, he described Satanism as being "dedicated to the dark, hidden force in nature responsible for the workings of earthly affairs for which science and religion had no explanation." He explained that he was moved to establish the Church of Satan when he saw the need for a church that would "recapture man's body and carnal desires as objects of celebration." The Church of Satan preaches a religious system that endeavors to overcome the repressions and inhibitions of human instinctual behavior it believes has been fostered by the Judeo-Christian tradition.

The First Church of Satan does not recognize the existence of Satan as an actual being, but as a symbol representing materialism. The church emphasizes that the figure of Satan stands for an inner attitude, and it is never to be regarded as an object onto which human powers are projected in order to worship what is only human in an externalized form. In *The Satanic Bible*, Satanists are charged to Asay unto thine own heart, 'I am my own redeemer.'" (Book IV, line 3.)

The Satanic Bible is divided into four sections, or books, each corresponding to one of the four hermetic elements of fire, air, earth, and water. The first section is entitled *The Book of Satan*, and its introduction advises the reader that the "ponderous rule books of hypocrisy are no longer needed," it is time to relearn the Law of the Jungle. The second section, *The Book of Lucifer*, explains how the Roman god Lucifer, the light bearer, the spirit of enlightenment, was made synonymous with evil through Christian teachings. *The Book of Belial*, the third section, is a basic text on materialistic magic, a book of ritual and ceremonial magic expressed in satanic terms. The fourth section, *The Book of Leviathan*, stresses the importance to successful magic of the spoken word.

The Satanist doctrine celebrates man the animal. It exalts sexual lust above spiritual love, claiming that the latter is but a sham and a cover-up. Satanism declares that violence must be met with violence and that to love one's neighbor is a utopian unreality. "Hate your enemies with a whole heart," *The Satanic Bible* advises. "And if a man smite you on one cheek, smash him on the other! Smite him hip and thigh, for self-preservation is the highest law!" (Section III, paragraph 7).

Satanists condemn prayer and confession as vain, futile gestures, believing that the way

to achieve what one wants is through magic and aggressive effort—and that the best method of ridding oneself of guilt is not to assume it in the first place. If Satanists make a mistake, they recognize sincerely that to err is human; and instead of involving themselves in efforts to cleanse themselves, they examine the situation in order to determine exactly what happened and how to prevent its happening again.

Satanists regard the Christian preoccupations with otherworldliness as subterfuge, with self-denial as depravity, and with piety as a sign of weakness. To Satanists, the Christian way of life is a colorless, odorless, and tasteless encounter with stagnation and boredom. Worshippers of Satan believe that the way to greater levels of personal perfection and an exploration of the deeper mysteries of life is through study and the performance of rituals emphasizing the sensual nature of humankind and directing this power toward the release of psychic or emotional energy.

ANTON LaVey's The Satanic Bible *was published in 1969.*

Because Christian churches, especially the Roman Catholic, are considered anathema to the Prince of Darkness, Satanists use parodied versions of their rituals and symbols in their ceremonies. The cross is used, but it is worn or displayed with the long beam pointing downward. Satanists may on occasion use the pentagram or five-pointed star, traditionally used by the practitioners of Wicca or witchcraft, but as with the cross, it is inverted, resting upon a single point, rather than two. Satanists insist that their parodying and inversion of other religions' rites and symbols are not done strictly for purposes of blasphemy. It is their belief, they maintain, that such use appropriates the power inherent in the rite or symbol and inverts it for Satan's purposes.

Satanists believe their doctrine and belief system is of the here and now. Acting on that premise, they look for their rewards in their

Anton LaVey, the founder of the First Church of Satan in San Francisco, ran away from home at the age of 17 to work as a cage boy for the circus lion tamer Clyde Beatty. Later, LaVey became a carnival mentalist and hypnotist, then an organ player for the dancers and strippers in the sideshows. On Sunday mornings he had an extra job playing the organ for an evangelist who conducted revival meetings in a large tent on the neighboring lot.

In the 1950s, LaVey became a San Francisco Police Department crime scene photographer, but he maintained the same fascination for magic that had driven him to perform as a stage mentalist, hypnotist, and magician in the carnivals and circuses of his youth, and he soon included a widening circle of devotees in his Magic Circle discussion group. In the late 1960s, when he founded the First Church of Satan, LaVey became immediately popular in the media, often allowing reporters to attend certain rituals that he conducted over the living altar of a woman's naked body in his church, the famous "Black House," said to have been a brothel. Then in a sudden rush came the books, the attention from movie stars, the position as technical advisor to such motion pictures as *Rosemary's Baby*, (1968), and the hostility of millions of devout Christians, who saw LaVey as a kind of **antichrist.** By the 1970s, the death threats and the harassment had become oppressive, and LaVey went underground, ceased all public ceremonies, and recast his church as a secret society.

In February 23, 1986, *The Washington Post Magazine* carried Walt Harrington's account of a visit with LaVey in which the journalist noted that the satanic high priest, like anyone else, loved his friends, wife, and children, but there was a venom that went beyond his claim that Satanism was a parody of Christianity: "Anton LaVey is not a cartoon Satan," Harrington wrote. "He's far less frightening than you would imagine, because he is admittedly a carnival hustler. Yet he is still terrifying, because he touches, if not the mystical darkness, then the psychological darkness—the hate and fear—in us all."

present life and in this world. "Life is the great indulgence—death the great abstinence. Therefore, make the most of life here and now!" (Book IV, line 1.)

As a supplement to *The Satanic Bible*, LaVey published *The Satanic Rituals* (1972), in which he explained the Church of Satan's rituals and ceremonies in greater detail. *Rituals* includes the actual text of the **Black Mass** and the ritual for the satanic baptism of adults and children.

In 1991, LaVey lost ownership of the "Black House" when a judge ordered him to sell the satanic temple, along with such mementos as a shrunken head and a stuffed wolf, and split the proceeds with his estranged wife, Diane Hagerty.

Anton Szandor LaVey died on October 30, 1997, the day before Halloween, and soon after his death, what remained of his estate became the object of a legal struggle between his oldest daughter Karla and Blanche Barton, his longtime consort and the mother of his son Xerxes. At the same time, LaVey's younger daughter Zeena, who renounced the Church of Satan in 1990 and became a priest in the *Temple of Set*, began proclaiming what she claimed was the truth about the Church of Satan, listing, among other charges, that it had never been intended to be a spiritual movement, but was created solely as a money-making venture. Such denouncements are unlikely to damage severely the reputation of the First Church of Satan, which continues today under the direction of the High Priestess Blanche Barton and the Magister Peter H. Gilmore.

✤ DELVING DEEPER

Church of Satan web page. [Online] http://www. churchofsatan.org/main.html. 26 January 2002.

Freedland, Nat. *The Occult Explosion*. New York: Berkley, 1972.

Harrington, Walt. "The Devil in Anton LaVey," *The Washington Post Magazine*, February 23, 1986. [Online] http://www.churchofsatan.com/Pages/ WaPost/html. 26 January 2002.

LaVey, Anton Szandor. *The Satanic Bible*. New York: Avon, 1969.

———. *The Satanic Rituals*. New York: Avon, 1972.

TEMPLE OF SET

The ancient Egyptians were perhaps the first to personify evil as a distinct force in the universe, but they retained a concept of unity by representing the evil god Set as a brother of Horus, prince of light and goodness. Although Set was actually the younger brother of **Osiris**—who, with **Isis,** his wife, and Horus, his son, comprised the Egyptian trinity—he was represented as Horus's brother, because Set stood for the opposing forces of evil and darkness. Set was jealous of

Osiris's power and sought to seize the throne from him. In ensuing struggle, Osiris was dismembered, leaving Horus to oppose his evil brother/uncle. In the war between the two that ensued, Horus and the forces of good prevailed. In the story of Set's insurrection can be seen a parallel with the Hebrew tradition of Lucifer's rebellion, his defeat by Michael and the angels, and his subsequent expulsion from heaven. Set, therefore, is clearly an early forerunner of Christianity's and Islam's irreconcilably and absolutely evil Satan.

The Temple of Set maintains, however, that regardless of how evil Set may be portrayed, his "essential function" of "expanding the borders of existence and then returning that Chaotic energy to the center" has continued to the present day. In the temple's cosmology, Set stands separate and apart from the forces of the natural universe.

In 1975, Michael Aquino (1946–   ), one of **Anton LaVey**'s followers, left the Church of Satan after a disagreement and organized the Temple of Set in San Francisco. Aquino had been the editor of the Church of Satan newsletter, and when it appeared to him that LaVey was merely "selling" priesthoods, he lodged a firm protest with the Black Pope. In Aquino's view, priesthoods in satanic orders should be conferred solely on the basis of magical achievement. Unimpressed with Aquino's argument, LaVey dismissed the matter by explaining that he considered the degrees he issued as merely symbolic of the member's status in the outside world. In protest, Aquino resigned his priesthood in the Church of Satan and with Lilith Sinclair, head of the New York Lilith Grotto, formed the Temple of Set.

Aquino, a former lieutenant in Army Intelligence, specializing in psychological warfare, had joined the Church of Satan together with his first wife in 1968. An enthusiastic member of the church, he was ordained a satanic priest after he had returned from serving in Vietnam in 1970; and he envisioned his mission in life as one of destroying the influence of conventional religion in human affairs. Filled with missionary zeal, Aquino made it clear that he did not wish to convert everyone to Satanism, but he did wish to remove the shadow of fear and superstition that he believed had been perpetuated by organized religion.

On the eve of the summer solstice on June 21, 1975, after his split with LaVey, Aquino performed a magical ritual and sought to summon Satan to appear to him to advise him how best to proceed in his earthly mission. According to Aquino, the Prince of Darkness appeared to him in the image of Set and declared to his disciple the dawning of the Aeon of Set. It was revealed that Set appeared to **Aleister Crowley** (1875–1947) in Cairo in 1904 in the image of Crowley's guardian angel, Aiwass. At this time, Crowley was declared the herald for the advent of the Aeon of Horus and assumed the title of "The Beast." In 1966, Anton LaVey had ushered in the Aeon of Satan, an intermediary stage that was designed to prepare the way for the Aeon of Set, an age that would bring forth enlightenment. Aquino was delighted and honored to assume the mantle of "The Second Beast," and he even had "**666,**" the number of the Beast in the book of Revelation tattooed on his scalp. At the same time, he also assumed Crowley's Golden Dawn degree of Ipsissimus as his own.

In Aquino's view, the Temple of Set offers its followers an opportunity to raise their consciousness and to apprehend what exists in each individual to make him or her unique. Such awareness, according to the precepts of the Temple of Set, will permit its members to use this gift of expanded consciousness to make themselves stronger in all facets of their being. To accomplish this, they state, they "preserve and improve the tradition of spiritual distinction from the natural universe, which in the Judeo/Christian West has been called Satanism," but they choose to call "the Left-Hand Path." To follow such a path, they promise, is to enter a process that will create "an individual, powerful essence that exists above and beyond animal life. It is thus the true vehicle for personal immortality."

The Temple of Set emphasizes the employment of black magic of a sort that focuses on "self-determined goals." While this form of magic may be utilized to accomplish everything from healing one's ill friends or relatives to obtaining a better paying position, the tem-

ple stresses that the practitioner must first learn to develop a system of ethics and discernment before putting such power to use. Using magic for "impulsive, trivial, or egoistic desires" is not considered to be Setian. Black magic is the means by which Setian initiates "experience being gods, rather than praying to imaginary images of gods."

The Temple of Set does not tolerate congregations of docile Setians. Those who attend must be considered "cooperative philosophers and magicians." According to their general information distributed to those who inquire about the temple, executive authority is held by the Council of Nine, which is responsible for appointing both the high priest and the executive director. There are six degrees of initiates: Setian 1, Adept II, Priest/Priestess of Set III, Magister/ Magistra Templi IV, Magus/Maga V, and Ipsissimus/Ipissima VI. To be recognized as an Adept II, one must demonstrate that he or she has successfully mastered and applied the essential principles of black magic. Reading materials available to the initiates include the newsletter *Scroll of Set* and the encyclopedias entitled the *Jeweled Tablets of Set*.

The Temple of Set emphasizes that the black arts may be as dangerous to the newcomer as volatile chemicals may become to the inexperienced lab technician. It cautions that the practice of magic is not for unstable, immature, or emotionally weak-minded individuals. And it also stresses that the process offers to those who seek their "evolutionary product of human experience" is the kind of activity that no enlightened, mature intellect would regard as "undignified, sadistic, criminal, or depraved."

✦ **DELVING DEEPER**

Lyons, Arthur. *Satan Wants You: The Cult of Devil Worship in America*. New York: Mysterious Press, 1989.

———. *The Second Coming: Satanism in America*. New York: Award Books, 1970.

Temple of Set. [Online] http://www.xeper.org/pub/tos/infoadms/html. October 31, 2001.

UFO CULTS

n November 20, 1952, George Adamski (1891–1965) walked into the night near Desert Center, California, and when he returned, he claimed to have communicated with the pilot of a Venusian spaceship through telepathic transfer. The entity was benign and seemed extremely concerned with the spiritual growth of humankind. He was what George Adamski called a "space brother." Just as the prophets of old had retreated into the desert wilderness to receive their inspiration from a higher source, so had Adamski, by some prearranged cosmic signal, gone to meet his space brother in the desert.

Adamski was the first of a long line of UFO contactees who would claim to have communicated with extraterrestrial intelligences. Many, like Adamski, became New Age UFO prophets, sharing the cosmic sermonettes that they said were given to them by wise beings from the stars. These men and women said they were not at all frightened by the extraterrestrial entities with whom they had come into contact. On the contrary, such a contact with the space brothers and sisters had enabled them to undergo a kind of **cosmic consciousness** experience. Throughout his career as a UFO prophet, Adamski's believers steadfastly declared him to be one of the most saintly of men, completely devoted to the teachings of universal laws.

After Adamski's contact experience in 1952, there were individuals like George Van Tassel (1910–1978), George Hunt Williamson, Truman Bethurum, Daniel Fry (1908–1992), Cedric Allingham, Orfeo Angelucci, Franklin Thomas, Buck Nelson, Gloria Lee (d. 1962), and Howard Menger, who claimed to have touched souls and, in some cases, bodies with space beings. Their accounts were circulated most often in privately printed books, which became scrolls of wisdom for thousands of questing seekers. The contactee literature ranges from reports of fanciful adventures in other worlds, in which the UFO contactee appears as some modern-day Gulliver being escorted through awesome alien cultures by a benevolent extraterrestrial guide, to works which concern themselves with more philosophical, religious, and moral information.

George Van Tassel (1910–1978) published his first booklet in 1952 and introduced the world to "Ashtar, commandant of station Schare." Those who visited Van Tassel's headquarters at Giant Rock, California, soon became aware that "Schare" was one of several flying saucer stations in Blaau, the fourth sector of Bela, into which our solar system is moving. "Shan" was the name that Van Tassel's space brother had given for Earth. Commandant Ashtar also decreed the universe to be ruled by the Council of Seven Lights, which had divided the cosmos into sector systems and sectors. Van Tassel found the Ministry of Universal Wisdom based on his revelations from the space brothers. This ministry teaches the universal law that operates in seven states: *gender*, male and female; the Creator as *cause*; *polarity of negative and positive*; *vibration*; *rhythm*; *relativity*; and *mentality*.

Daniel Fry (1908–1992) established Understanding Incorporated in 1955 as a means of better spreading the teachings of space brother A-Lan, whom Fry claimed to have met on his first trip in a UFO. In that same year, George King (1919–1997) claimed to have been named the "Primary Terrestrial Mental Channel" by Master Aetherius of Venus. King was later declared an agent for the Great White Brotherhood and a channel for both Aetherius and Master Jesus. Members of the **Aetherius Society** are earnestly engaged in the war being waged by the brotherhood against the black magicians, a group they feel seeks to enslave the human race.

By the 1960s, few people were claiming the direct kind of physical contact that Adamski had alleged he had experienced out in the California desert, and the psychic-channeling flying saucer groups were becoming increasingly popular among the faithful followers of the UFO prophets. Gloria Lee (d. 1962), a former flight attendant and the wife of aircraft designer William H. Byrd, sighted a UFO in the 1950s. In 1953, she began to receive telepathic communications from an entity on the planet Jupiter who revealed himself only as "JW." As she came to place more confidence in her space being, she became a well-known figure among UFO cultist groups as a lecturer and a channel.

JW revealed that on Jupiter vocal cords had gone out of use, so he began to channel a book through Gloria Lee. He also prompted her to found the Cosmon Research Foundation, dedicated to the spreading of his teachings and the bringing about of humankind's spiritual development in preparation for the New Age. Through JW's direction and the persistence of Gloria Lee on the lecture circuit, the foundation became a thriving organization.

Then, tragically, Lee starved herself to death after a 66-day fast instituted upon the instructions of her mentor from Jupiter. The fast was carried out in the name of peace, in a Gandhi-like effort to make the United States government officially investigate and study plans for a spacecraft that she had brought with her to Washington. On September 23, 1962, Lee secured herself in a hotel room. On December 2, with still no word from any government official—or from her extraterrestrial advisor—the 37-year-old UFO prophet died.

Shortly after her passing, the Mark-Age Metacenter in Miami, Florida, announced that they were receiving messages from the spirit of Gloria Lee. Her etheric form told the group that she was now able to discover how the method of interdimensional communication actually worked. As the Metacenter took notes for a booklet Gloria Lee's publisher would later issue to the faithful and the curious, Gloria's spirit spoke through the channel Nada Yolanda, explaining how her conscious intelligence had been transferred to another frequency and another body of higher vibrational rate.

The death of George Adamski on April 12, 1965, by no means stilled the heated controversy which had always swirled around the prolific and articulate founder of the Flying Saucer Movement, for his followers quickly resurrected him. In the book *Scoriton Mystery* (1967) by Eileen Buckle, a contactee named Ernest Bryant claims to have met three spacemen on April 24, 1965, one of whom was a youth named Yamski, whose extraterrestrial body already housed the spirit of George Adamski.

Often those men and women who join UFO cults are, by their own admission, individuals who have become disillusioned with existing religious institutions and dissatisfied by the manner in which the political estab-

lishment is dealing with social and economic injustices. As in the accounts of the prophets and seekers of old, the contemporary UFO cultists are looking for a more intimate relationship with a source of strength and inspiration outside of themselves. And they cannot seek much farther outside of themselves than outer space.

When such world-weary pilgrims encounter a charismatic man or woman who tells a marvelous story of having received direct spiritual enlightenment from beings from beyond the stars, the potential cultists feel that they have found a teacher who can now truly answer their questions. Their quest has come to an end. They, too, will now willingly become messengers for a new gospel from outer space, for the UFO prophet has not only made contact with a godlike being from another world, but he or she is offering a blend of science and religion that offers a theology that seems more applicable to the problems of modern humankind.

There is a New Age coming, the UFO prophets tell their followers. It will be an age wherein humankind will attain a new consciousness, a new awareness, and a higher state—or frequency—of physical vibration. The UFO beings themselves come from higher dimensions all around us which function on different vibratory levels, just as there are various radio frequencies operating simultaneously in our environment. The space brothers and sisters have come to Earth to reach and to teach those humans who will respond to the promise of a larger universe.

According to the UFO prophets, the space beings have advanced information which they wish to impart to their weaker cousins on Earth. They want humankind to join an intergalactic spiritual federation. They are here to teach, to help awaken the human spirit, to help humankind rise to higher levels of vibration so that the people of Earth will be ready to enter new dimensions. Such a goal, according to the UFO prophets, was precisely what Jesus (c. 6 B.C.E.–c. 30 C.E.), the Buddha (c. 563–c. 483 B.C.E.), the prophets in the Bible, and the other leaders of the great religions sought to teach humanity. In fact, Jesus, known to Mark-Age and others in the Flying

Saucer Movement as "Sananda," has been in orbit around the planet since 1885 and will take on material form as Earth's transition to a higher consciousness is made.

Humankind stands now in the transitional period before the dawn of a New Age, according to the UFO prophets. If earthlings do not raise their vibrational rate within a set period of time, severe earth changes and major cataclysms will take place. Such disasters will not end the world, but shall serve to eliminate the unreceptive members of the human species. However, those who die in such dreadful purgings of the planet will be allowed to reincarnate on higher levels of development so that their salvation will be more readily accomplished through higher teachings on a higher vibratory level.

For thousands of men and women throughout the world, the UFO has become a symbol of religious awakening and spiritual transformation. Some envision the UFO as their deliverer from a world fouled by its own inhabitants, and the presence of UFOs proves to them that humans are not alone in the universe. Because humans are not alone, then life does have meaning, for humans are therefore part of a larger community of intelligences. All humans have become evolving members in a hierarchy of cosmic citizenship.

Although certain UFO cults such as **Heaven's Gate** and **Order of the Solar Temple** acquired a dark side that eventually led to the mass suicide of many of its members, the great majority of these groups are benign; and as many scholars of contemporary religious movements have noted, may be the heralds of a New Age religion, a blending of technology and traditional religious concepts. Dr. Gordon Melton, director of the Institute for the Study of American Religion, has commented that such groups are best understood as "an emerging religious movement with an impetus and a life of their own."

❋ DELVING DEEPER

Clark, Jerome. *The UFO Book*. Detroit: Visible Ink Press, 1998.

Godwin, John. *Occult America*. New York: Doubleday, 1972.

Steiger, Brad. *The Fellowship: Spiritual Contact Between Humans and Outer Space Beings*. New York: Doubleday, 1988.

Story, Ron, ed. *The Encyclopedia of Extraterrestrial Encounters*. New York: New American Library, 2001.

Sutherly, Curt. *Strange Encounters*. St. Paul, Minn.: Llewellyn Publications, 1996.

AETHERIUS SOCIETY

In 1954 while he was in a deep meditative trance, George King (1919–1997) claimed that he received a message from an outer space being who told him to prepare himself to become the human voice of the Interplanetary Parliament. While such a command might have startled one unqualified to receive such communication, the 35-year-old Englishman had been immersed in spiritual studies since he was young. Beginning with an intense study of orthodox Christianity, King became interested in exploring psychic phenomena and spiritual healing. When he was to be the primary mental channel for the cosmic masters, King intensified his practice of yoga, which included the yogic sciences of raja, gnani, and kundalini. This permitted him to attain the state of samadhi—the union of spirit with the superconscious, which allowed communication with the masters in other energy spheres. Soon, King was to discover that the voice that had contacted him belonged to the master Aetherius, a 3,500-year-old Venusian whose name, loosely translated, meant "one who comes from outer space."

By 1955, King had received a number of teachings from the cosmic masters that he felt compelled to share with others. With a number of men and women who had been drawn to his **channeling** of the messages from outer space, King formed the Aetherius Society in London, England, in 1956, relinquishing all of his other spiritual research and his materialistic enterprises to focus his life completely on the transmissions from the cosmic masters.

According to what King had learned from his contact, Aetherius and the other cosmic mentors came from a world or a dimension that was far more technologically advanced than Earth. While they arrive in crafts referred to as UFOs, their advanced technology allows them to remain invisible to Earth's radar and other scientific detection devices until they permit themselves to be seen just often enough to provoke controversial sightings and signs to the people of the planet. In spite of their superior scientific knowledge, the outer space beings choose to visit Earth because they are benevolent entities who wish to guide humankind in its spiritual evolution. Essentially, the masters are the planet's **spirit guides,** and they can appear to earthlings from time to time in physical bodies simply by lowering their vibratory rate.

As well as seeking to guide earthlings spiritually, the cosmic masters have also protected Earth on numerous occasions from both external and internal forces, King claimed. They have intervened and prevented ecological disasters from occurring. Their spacecraft have, from time to time, blocked the invasion of the planet from hostile interplanetary imperialists who wish to colonize Earth. The outer space masters have even gone so far as to erect an invisible barrier around the planet to protect it from invasion by the "black magicians," evil aliens who wish to enslave the people of Earth.

As with a number of UFO contactees, King linked the masters from extraterrestrial worlds with the ancient metaphysical legend of the Great White Brotherhood, the light beings who are said to belong to a multidimensional, intergalactic organization that dedicates itself to serving the divine cosmic plan in the universe. Among the ascended masters who have been historical figures on Earth, the contactees include Jesus (c. 6 B.C.E.–c. 30 C.E.), **St. Germain,** Krishna, and Lord Buddha (c. 563–c. 483 B.C.E.). By benefit of his crucial role in the relaying of transmissions from Aetherius, George King, in the view of the members of the Aetherius Society, had been elected by the brotherhood to become the next great spiritual prophet.

To further assist his fellow brothers and sisters of Earth to welcome the wisdom and knowledge of the outer space beings, King began to publish *The Cosmic Voice*, a transcript of the communications that he had received from the cosmic masters. He also began giving public demonstrations of his channeling of the extraterrestrial teachers and presenting lectures to audiences of the curious and the true believers in the spiritual teachings from wise mentors from outer space. On May 21, 1959, King went into samadhic trance while being interviewed on the BBC, and thousands of radio listeners in the United Kingdom were able to hear for themselves the warnings and the counsel of the cosmic masters. In recognition of his devotion to his extraterrestrial assignment as the principal terrestrial contact for the masters, King's followers bestowed upon him the titles of Sir George King, O.S.P., Ph.D., Th.D., D.D., Metropolitan Archbishop of the Aetherius Churches, Prince Grand Master of the Mystical Order of St. Peter, and HRH Prince De George King De Santori.

By 1960, King and his Aetherius Society had spread their Cosmic Gospel throughout the British Isles, as well as to the United States, and an American headquarters was established in Hollywood, California. Soon there would be branches in Detroit, Michigan; Australia; and West Africa.

The Aetherius Society warned that matters were serious in the view of the cosmic masters. Two previous terrestrial civilizations, **Atlantis** and **Lemuria,** had destroyed themselves in a nuclear war in prehistory, and the Intergalactic Council was concerned that such a catastrophe could take place once again. The members of humankind were regarded as the problem children of the solar system, and various masters and adepts were forced to give Earth special attention. To this end, a grand master plan would see the arrival of a cosmic master in a spacecraft in a time in the near future. When this event occurs, the people of Earth will be given the choice of following the laws of the Most High God and entering a new era of peace and enlightenment, or rejecting the divine laws and pass through the gateway of death to be placed on a planet where they will have the opportunity to relearn the lessons of the universe.

❖ DELVING DEEPER

Aetherius website. [Online] http://www.aetherius.org. 28 January 2002.

Godwin, John. *Occult America.* New York: Doubleday, 1972.

King, George, and Richard Lawrence. *Contacts with the Gods from Space: Pathway to the New Millennium.* Hollywood, Calif.: Aetherius Society, 1996.

Steiger, Brad. *The Fellowship: Spiritual Contact Between Humans and Outer Space Beings.* New York: Doubleday, 1988.

Story, Ron, ed. *The Encyclopedia of Extraterrestrial Encounters.* New York: New American Library, 2001.

HEAVEN'S GATE

When the bodies of the 39 men and women were found in rooms throughout the spacious Rancho Santa Fe mansion outside of San Diego, California, on March 26, 1997, their deaths by suicide enabled the media to transform them from members in a UFO cult previously known as Human Individual Metamorphosis to the Heaven's Gate suicide cult. According to what could be learned about the deceased in letters and videotapes that they had left behind, they had interpreted the arrival of the Hale-Bopp comet as the sign for which they had been waiting. When the comet passed overhead, they would hasten their "graduation from the human evolutionary level" through self-administered poison and hitch a ride to their "Father's Kingdom" on the extraterrestrial spacecraft that they believed followed in the wake of the comet's tail.

The cosmology of what has come to be known as the Heaven's Gate cult was born in the minds of Marshall Herff Applewhite (1931–1997) and Bonnie Lu Trousdale Nettles (1927–1985) sometime around 1972 when they formed the Christian Arts Center in Houston for the declared purpose of helping to make humans more aware of their spiritual potential by sponsoring lectures in comparative religion, mysticism, meditation, and astrology. Applewhite, the son of a Presbyterian minister, had served with the Army Signal Corps in Salzburg, Austria; studied sacred music at Union Theological Seminary in Richmond, Virginia; directed musicals for the Houston Music Theatre; and from 1966 to 1971 taught music at the University of St. Thomas in Houston. Nettles, an astrology enthusiast, was a graduate of the Hermann Hospital School of Professional Nursing in 1948 and worked as a nurse in the Houston

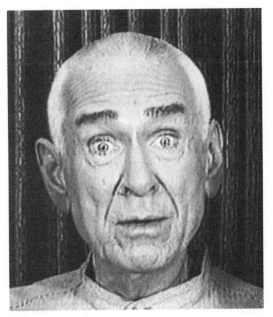

Marshall Herff Applewhite, Jr. (1931–1997), leader of the Heaven's Gate cult, convinced his followers to commit a mass suicide, because he believed a spaceship following the Hale Bopp Comet would take them to their "new world destination." (AP/WIDE WORLD PHOTOS)

area. Although they had each been previously married to others, in 1974, when Applewhite and Nettles were creating their philosophical blend of apocalyptic Christianity and UFOlogy, they said that they were not married, but were living together "by spiritual guidance." Espousing the highest principles, the couple stated that they had renounced sex in preparation for their journey to the Father's Kingdom.

MARSHALL *Herff Applewhite and Bonnie Lu Trousdale Nettles were also known as "Bo and Peep."*

Applewhite and Nettles began to call themselves "Bo" and "Peep," and they proclaimed that they had awakened to their true extraterrestrial origins and earthly mission. They had come to the planet to acquaint humankind with the basic methods by which a human might leave his or her humanity and make the graduation to an entirely different consciousness. As benevolent aliens, they had come to Earth to demonstrate, if need be, by their own deaths and resurrection in three and a half days, how the human body could undergo a dramatic metamorphosis, just as the chrysalis changed from caterpillar to butterfly.

Bo and Peep claimed to have originated from the same level as Jesus (c. 6 B.C.E.–c. 30 C.E.), asserting that they were the two witnesses referred to in the Book of Revelation who would be the harbingers of a great harvest time for humanity: [Revelation: 11:3–13] "And I will give power to two witnesses, and they shall prophesy....And when they have finished their testimony, the beast that ascendeth out of the bottomless pit shall...overcome them and kill them. And their dead bodies shall lie in the street of the great city...three days and a half....And after three days and a half the spirit of life from God entered them and they stood upon their feet...And they heard a great voice from heaven saying to them, Come up hither. And they ascended to heaven in a cloud...and the remnant were affrighted and gave glory to the God in heaven."

It has long been one of the major tenets of Christianity that if one aspires to a higher level beyond death, one will achieve such a state in spirit form, not in the physical body. However, Bo and Peep insisted that spiritual seekers must begin their butterfly-like apprenticeship by leaving the ways of their human caterpillar family and friends behind and attain the higher level in an actual physical body. The kingdom of heaven and all those who occupy it, according to the two, were literally physical in form. No spirits were permitted in their father's kingdom. If one stays at the human level, Bo and Peep warned, whether incarnate or discarnate, one still has all ties with this garden Earth.

Bo and Peep achieved national media attention after a UFO lecture in Waldport, Oregon, on September 14, 1975, when they were said to have mysteriously whisked away 20 members of the audience aboard a flying saucer. Concerned family members of the vanishing Oregonians were not convinced that extraterrestrials had kidnapped their relatives. They feared that it was more likely that their missing kin had been murdered. Law enforcement officials tried their best to squelch rumors that satanic sacrifice was involved in the mysterious disappearances. However, it would soon be revealed that a good number of the UFO enthusiasts who had attended the

lecture had chosen of their own free will to join Bo and Peep on their spiritual pilgrimage.

The two did not promise an easy path to higher awareness. They instructed their followers that they must walk out the door of their human lives and take with them only what would be necessary while they were still on the planet. Newcomers were advised that the process worked best if they had a partner and that they would be paired with another for a time. However, the only bond that was to exist between them would be a mutual desire to raise their vibrational levels so they might ascend to the next realm. Bo and Peep admitted they didn't know where their father would lead them or when their assassinations and subsequent demonstration overcoming death might occur. But those who felt they must accompany them, they were to bring with them a car, a tent, a warm sleeping bag, utensils, and whatever money they could carry with them. Those who joined the Human Individual Metamorphosis (HIM) group would be camping out a lot in order to take the word to others who might be seeking it.

In spite of painting such a bleak picture of a nomadic existence, traveling from city to city as Bo and Peep spread the word, within a few months a remarkable number of highly educated professionals left high-salaried jobs, expensive homes, and loving spouses and children to follow the two on a journey of faith that would have them living hand-to-mouth and sleeping under the stars. Bo and Peep stated firmly that they found no need to defend themselves against any charges of kidnapping or of brainwashing their followers into any kind of organized cult activity. The only kind of conversion experience that the two were interested in was that of the physical—the biological and chemical changeover from human-level creatures to creatures on the next evolutionary level. Just as a caterpillar has to cease all of its caterpillar activities in order to achieve its chrysalis, they instructed their followers, so must the same thing happen to a human who wished to make the transition. All human desires and activities must be left behind so one could emerge as an individual capable of entering a realm that is altogether different from the human.

Applewhite and Nettles warned their followers and the members of their lecture audiences that Earth was fast approaching "that season" when humans could enter the process that would enable them to graduate to a higher level. They insisted that they were not speaking of anything "etheric." They were talking about actually leaving the Earth's atmosphere. Those who took the trip would no longer be associated with the human kingdom, but with the next level of existence. They will have graduated from Earth.

Many members of the HIM inferred from various pronouncements by Bo and Peep that it was quite likely that they would be assassinated sometime around June 1976. They told a number of their followers that they would lie in state for three-and-a-half days, then rise to the next level in full view of the media, thereby proving that they were the two spoken of in the Book of Revelation.

When such a convincing demonstration of their true identity was delayed because of the two's dissatisfaction with certain media representations of their mission, a large number of disillusioned followers dropped out of the group, leaving Bo and Peep and their most faithful members to resume their nomadic lifestyle and to go underground with their ministry. In 1985 Bonnie Nettles, who at that time called herself "Ti," died of cancer, and, in the words of an ardent follower, "returned to the next level." Applewhite, now "Do," carried on their mission of informing humans that salvation hovered overhead in a spaceship. Sometime in 1993, there were signs that the group was active under the new name of the Total Overcomers, and still under the leadership of Applewhite, who now warned earthlings that their planet was at the mercy of alien star gods, the "Luciferians," who had fallen away from the Father's Kingdom many thousands of years ago.

In 1995, renaming the group Heaven's Gate, Applewhite and his most devoted disciples moved to San Diego and established a computer business, Higher Source, which specialized in designing computer websites. In October 1996, the group, which had seemingly chosen to live quietly and avoid extensive media exposure, moved into the mansion at Rancho Santa Fe.

Five months later, on March 26, 1997, news media around the world carried the startling announcement of the mass suicide. Apparently Applewhite had become convinced that he had at last found the narrow window of opportunity for graduation to the higher level provided by a spacecraft bound for heaven, the father's kingdom. Tragically, he took 38 loyal followers with him.

✦ Delving Deeper

Jackson, Forest, and Rodney Perkins. *Cosmic Suicide: The Tragedy and Transcendence of Heaven's Gate*. Dallas, TX: Pentaradial Press, 1997.

Heaven's Gate website. [Online] http://www.web-coast.com/heavensgate.com. 28 January 2002.

Steiger, Brad, and Hayden Hewes. *Inside Heaven's Gate: The UFO Cult Leaders Tell Their Story in Their Own Words*. New York: Signet, 1997.

Story, Ron ed. *The Encyclopedia of Extraterrestrial Encounters*. New York: New American Library, 2001.

Wessinger, Catherine Lowman. *How the Millennium Comes Violently: From Jonestown to Heaven's Gate*. New York: Chatham House, 2000.

THE RAELIANS

On December 13, 1973, Claude Vorilhon (1946–), a French sports journalist and former race car driver, claimed to have been contacted by an extraterrestrial being while climbing the Puy de Lassolas volcanic crater near Clermond-Ferrand, France. Vorilhon was astonished when he spotted a metallic-looking object in the shape of a flattened bell about 30 feet in diameter descend from the sky. A door opened in the side of the craft, and what appeared to be a humanlike being about four feet in height approached in a peaceful manner. Vorilhon soon believed that the being was a member of the Elohim—the "gods" who made humans in their own image. The primitive ancestors of modern humankind had interpreted the extraterrestrial visitors from the stars as gods, because to them any beings arriving from the heavens could only be divine. It was the extraterrestrials, the Elohim, who created *Homo sapiens* in their image in their laboratories, utilizing deoxyribonucleic acid (DNA), just as contemporary Earth scientists are at the point of creating "synthetic" humans in the same manner.

Then, Vorilhon said, the extraterrestrial being explained that in a manner similar to the Greek legend of Pygmalion who created a statue so beautiful that he fell in love with it, so did certain of the Elohim find the products of their laboratory artistry compellingly irresistible. The results, Vorilhon said, were recorded in Genesis 6:4: "...When the sons of God came in unto the daughters of men...they bare children to them, the same became mighty men which were of old, men of renown."

The extraterrestrial told Vorilhon that the Elohim had sent great prophets, such as Moses (c. 14th–13th century B.C.E.), Ezekial (sixth century B.C.E.), the Buddha (c. 563–c. 483 B.C.E.), and Muhammad (c. 570–632 C.E) to guide humankind. Jesus (c. 6 B.C.E.–c. 30 C.E.), the fruit of a union between the Elohim and Mary, a daughter of man, was given the mission of making the Elohim's messages of guidance known throughout the world in anticipation of the Age of Apocalypse—which in the original Greek meant the "age of revelation," not the "end of the world." It is in this epoch, which the people of Earth entered in 1945, that humankind will at last be able to understand scientifically that which the Elohim accomplished aeons ago in the Genesis story.

Claude Vorilhon said that the Elohim renamed him "Rael," which means "the man who brings light." Shortly after his encounter with the extraterrestrial, he created the Raelian Movement, which soon acquired more than a thousand members in France. In 2001, according to figures produced by the Raelians, their membership included 55,000 individuals in 85 different countries.

Rael claimed that on October 7, 1975, the Elohim physically contacted him again, and this time he was invited aboard a spacecraft and taken to their home planet. During this extraterrestrial contact experience, Rael learned that after the nuclear explosions in 1945, the Elohim believed that humans had entered the Age of Apocalypse. However, they cannot return in large numbers until the inhabitants of Earth begin to display a greater

ability to live together in peace, love, and brother/sisterhood. And the Elohim are awaiting some evidence that the planet can be governed with intelligence and spirit before they fully reveal themselves to Earth at large.

Because the Elohim feel that many members of humankind are now able to understand their extraterrestrial creators without mystifying or worshipping them, they asked Rael to establish an embassy wherein they will be able to meet with Earth's leaders. Although the Elohim feel strongly that a mass landing would bring about disastrous political, religious, social, and economic consequences throughout the world, the neutrality provided by such an embassy would enable them to demonstrate the love and respect that they hold for humankind.

Rael maintains that he has established the Raelian Movement according to the instructions given to him by the Elohim. Its aims are to inform humankind of the reality of the Elohim "without convincing," to establish the embassy where the Elohim would be welcome, and to help prepare a human society adapted to the future. In the years since his first contact experience, he has written a number of books that may be obtained directly from the Raelians. The titles include *The Message Given by Extraterrestrials,* (detailing his first messages from the Elohim, said to have sold one million copies and to be printed in 22 languages), and *Let's Welcome Our Fathers from Space.*

In July 2001, the Raelian Movement made headlines around the world when one of its members, Brigitte Boisselier, a 44-year-old scientist with doctorates from universities in Dijon and Houston, announced that Clonaid, her team of four doctors and a technician, would soon produce the first human clone. Defying opposition from President George W. Bush, the U.S. Congress, Secretary of Health Tommy Thompson, and the Food and Drug Administration, Boisselier refused to disclose the location of Clonaid's two laboratories, other than to state that one was in the United States and the other abroad. Clonaid, established by Rael in 1997, is funded in part by $500,000 from an anonymous couple who want a child cloned from the DNA of their deceased 10-month-old son.

In Rael's opinion, such cloning will demonstrate the methods employed by the Elohim in their creation of the human species. As it was told to him, many centuries ago on a distant planet, scientific teams set out to create life on more primitive worlds. On one such planet, Earth, their laboratories created the life forms that became human beings.

✤ Delving Deeper

Ellison, Michael. "Cult Determined to Clone Humans," *The Guardian.* July 19, 2001. [Online] http://www.guardian.co.uk/Print/ 0,3858, 4224163,00.html. 28 January 2002.

Raelian Revolution website. [Online] http://www.rael. org. 28 January 2002.

Story, Ron, ed. *The Encyclopedia of Extraterrestrial Encounters.* New York: New American Library, 2001.

Twentieth-Century Spiritual Expression

Although millennial thought dates back to the ancient Persian philosophers and was sustained through the centuries by Christian, Jewish, and Muslim teachers, Americans especially seem always to have been fascinated by the horror of a certain apocalyptic vision that includes plagues, earthquakes, and cataclysmic volcanic eruptions. Christopher Columbus was a devout student of biblical prophecies who believed that the world would end in 1650. He perceived that his personal mission was to find a new continent that would be a special refuge for those who survived the purging of Armageddon, the final battle between the armies of Christ and Satan, that he believed would occur during the mid-seventeenth century.

Scores of American preachers and mystics from colonial times through the Civil War and up to the present day have continued the precedent set by Columbus and occupied themselves with predicting the exact time of Christ's return and the subsequent final battle between Good and Evil.

Of course such obsessions with apocalyptic teachings and personal quests for spiritual ful-fillment are by no means limited to Americans. By the twentieth century, many formerly loyal followers of organized religious bodies throughout the world were beginning to become impatient with doctrinal rules of order and began to blend the new discoveries of science with the faith of their forefathers. In the West, many spiritual seekers chose to combine the teachings of Eastern religions with those aspects of western science which they felt supported their spiritual beliefs, including meditation, biofeedback, and extrasensory perception as means of attaining higher awareness.

These amalgamations of science, conventional Christianity, and such eastern religions as Hinduism and Buddhism offended many individuals who deemed themselves to be the true followers of the revelations disclosed in the Bible; and these apocalyptic groups, such as the Branch Davidians set themselves apart to prepare for the time of judgment that they believed was imminent.

While members of organized church bodies, as well as the general public, were quick to brand these various splinter groups as cults, in contemporary language usage such a term is considered negative and judgmental. Although the beliefs practiced by some of these groups may seem strange to certain of the more conventionally religious, the sincerity of the members of such evolving spiritual bodies cannot be so readily discounted by those who have not carefully examined what may be a blending of several traditions and a serious attempt to achieve enlightenment.

It may be that many of the spiritual experiments of the twentieth century will be assessed by more conventional students of theology as modern expressions of the Christian Mystery Schools that combined elements of the occult within their dogma. Unfortunately, far too many of these newly emergent groups began with visions of peace and love and ended with the mass suicides and deaths of their followers. In the United States, The Peoples' Temple began with Pastor James Jones expanding the teachings of a liberal Protestant denomination into a doomsday cult and later revealing himself to group as being the reincarnation of Jesus and the Bud-

THE RESTORATION OF THE TEN COMMANDMENTS

The cult of the Restoration of the Ten Commandments appears to have had its origins in the late 1970s when a group of schoolchildren claimed to have received visions of the Virgin Mary on a soccer field in the town of Kibeho, Rwanda. A cult of the Virgin, combining Roman Catholicism with aboriginal religious traditions, formed and spread to southwest Uganda. It was here that Credonia Mwerinde, a store proprietor and brewer of banana beer, said that the Virgin Mary appeared to her in 1984.

In 1989, Mwerinde met Joseph Kibwetere, a school administrator and politician, and informed him the Virgin required his aid in spreading a message: people must restore value to the Ten Commandments and strictly follow their admonitions if they were to escape damnation at the end of the world. And the end was near: According to Mwerinde's visions, the world would end on December 31, 1999/January 1, 2000.

The convictions of Mwerinde and the newly inspired Kibwetere proved to be convincing, and membership in Uganda swelled to 5,000. The rules for the program dictated by the Virgin Mary through Mwerinde were extremely strict. Cult members were forbidden to communicate other than through sign language. They were to labor in the fields to grow their own food, and had to fast regularly. On Mondays and Fridays they were allowed only one meal. Soap, a sinful indulgence, was forbidden.

The continued existence of the world after January 1, 2000, caused dissension to grow in the ranks of the cult. Many members, having followed the command to sell their property and belongings and give all proceeds to the cult, wanted their money back.

On March 15, 2000, the cult held a great party in the town of Kanungu, roasting three bulls and providing 70 crates of "soft drinks" for their members. Although facts remain unclear, apparently more than 1,000 were poisoned or otherwise murdered, doused with sulphuric acid, and set on fire. The bodies of Credonia Mwerinde and Joseph Kibwetere were not found among the charred remains of their faithful members. A witness in Kanungu told police that he had caught sight of the two leaving the festivities with suitcases in hand and wondered at the time why they would leave before their party had ended.

SOURCES:

Fisher, Ian. "Exploring the Deadly Mystique Surrounding a Uganda Cult." *New York Times on the Web,* April 1, 2000.

Sieveking, Paul. "Shallow Grave." *Fortean Times,* July 2000, 34–38.

dha. In Jonestown, Guyana, on November 14, 1978, Jones joined 638 of his adult followers and 276 of their children in a mass suicide. In Rwanda, Credonia Mwerinde combined a cult of the Virgin Mary and Roman Catholicism with aboriginal religious traditions and allowed the heavenly messages to end the lives of over 1,000 members by mass murder on March 15, 2000. In Switzerland, The Order of the Solar Temple sought to prepare humankind for the return of Christ through the wisdom of occult and extraterrestrial masters, but when the illusion of immortality faded, a series of mass suicides of cult members took place in Switzerland, France, and Quebec, from October 1994 to March 1997.

Many of the new spiritual groups combine aspects of Christianity with the "new gospels' that they claim to have obtained from extraterrestrial Masters. Members of some of these UFO groups call Jesus by what they believe to be his true name of Sananda and recognize him as an extraterrestrial who is circling Earth in a spaceship, awaiting the proper time for his Second Coming. While UFO cults such as Heaven's Gate, the Raelians, and the Order of the Solar Temple developed sensational or negative images, there are many UFO groups who seek to develop a new religion that will blend science and more traditional religious concepts.

Falun Gong, although branded an evil cult by the Chinese government in 1999, claims to have 100 million members worldwide. Li Hongzhi, the founder of the movement who lives in the United States, insists that his group is not a religion, but a series of five daily exercises by which individuals may activate the higher abilities of mind, body, and spirit.

The Church of Scientology is classified as a cult by its detractors, but its members assert that Scientology is a new religion that was founded by L. Ron Hubbard in the twentieth century and has its roots in the deep beliefs and ancient wisdom that go back more than 50,000 years. By combining with the physical sciences, Scientology offers an application of scientific methodology to spiritual questions and allows individuals to approach their lives with more confidence.

As the world continues to shrink and millions of pulpits on the Internet become available to new mystics and visionaries, it remains for the individual reader to judge which groups contain the precepts, the truths, and the moral values to survive into the twenty-first century and beyond.

Branch Davidians

The Branch Davidian religious group had its origins when Victor Houteff (1885–1929) separated from the Seventh-Day Adventist Church in 1929 to form the Shepherds Rod, Branch Seventh-Day Adventist. In 1935, with 11 of his followers, Houteff founded the Mount Carmel Center near Waco, Texas. In 1942 he changed the name of his group to the Davidian Seventh-Day Adventist Association.

Houteff died in 1955, and his wife, Florence Houteff, focused the group with her vision that Judgment Day would occur on April 22, 1959. Her prophecy having failed, she sold Mount Carmel in 1965 to Benjamin Roden, who named his faction the Branch Davidian Seventh-Day Adventist Association. After Roden's death in 1978, his wife, Lois Roden, declared herself the Sixth Angel in Revelation and a prophet speaking through the feminine aspect of the Holy Spirit.

A young man named Vernon Howell joined the Branch Davidians in 1981 and almost immediately caught Lois Roden's eye as the group's next prophet. Howell assumed control of the Davidians in 1988 and changed his name to David Koresh in 1990. He pronounced himself the Lamb of Revelation, who would open the seven seals of the scroll and interpret the secrets that would immediately bring about the Second Coming of Jesus Christ.

Koresh believed that the final struggle between good and evil would begin in the United States, rather than Israel, so the community of believers stockpiled food, water, and weapons. In 1992, Koresh renamed the Mount Carmel commune "Ranch Apocalypse."

Rumors began to circulate that the Branch Davidians were abusing children and storing large amounts of illegal firearms and explosives. On February 28, 1993, Bureau of Alcohol, Tobacco, and Firearms (BATF) agents

David Koresh, founder of
the Branch Davidian.
(AP/WIDE WORLD PHOTOS)

raided Ranch Apocalypse, resulting in ten deaths and 25 wounded. The FBI took over, and the ensuing siege lasted 51 days. On April 14, Koresh had a vision that instructed him to write his translation of the seven seals in Revelation and then surrender. But the encircling forces had grown tired of his biblical babblings and apocalyptic pronouncements. On April 19, the FBI attacked and ended the stand-off at Ranch Apocalypse.

Koresh and 75 of his followers, including 21 children, died in the fire that swept through the entire compound. Prior to the siege at Ranch Apocalypse, there were about 130 members of the Branch Davidians. After the destruction of the compound, there were estimates of 30 to 50 members who had managed to leave the commune before the final days or who had escaped the inferno. Accusations circulated that the FBI was responsible for starting the fire with incendiary tear gas cartridges.

❋ DELVING DEEPER

Neville, Leigh. "We Didn't Start the Fire." *Fortean Times*, April 2000, 34–38.

Kantrowitz, Barbara, with Peter Annin, Ginny Carroll, and Bob Conn. "Was It Friendly Fire? In the Bungled Waco Raid, Federal Agents May Have Been Shot by Their Own Men." *Newsweek*, April 5, 1993, 50–51.

Rainie, Harrison, with James Popkin, Dan McGraw, Brian Duppy, Ted Gest, Jo Ann Tooley, and David Bowermaster. "Armageddon in Waco: The Final Days of David Koresh." *U.S. News and World Report*, May 3, 1993, 24–34.

Reavis, Dick J. *The Ashes of Waco: An Investigation.* Syracuse, N.Y.: Syracuse University Press, Reprint, 1998.

ECKANKAR

Those who follow the alternative religion of Eckankar say that theirs is the religion of the Light and Sound of God. The Light of God is the ECK, known to many saints and mystics as the Holy Spirit. The Sound of God is the rushing wind that the disciples of Jesus (c. 6 B.C.E.–c. 30 C.E.) heard on that first Pentecost.

Eckists believe that they follow ancient wisdom teachings that were revived in 1965 for modern men and women by the Living ECK Master Paul Twitchell (1910?–1971). According to Twitchell and such masters from higher planes as Rebazar Tarzs, whose teachings he relayed, the soul is on a journey of self- and god-realization. To assist the individual soul to achieve contact with the ECK, the Divine Spirit, the Mahanta, the Living ECK Master, provides spiritual exercises and guidance available to all sincere seekers.

Because the Mahantas emphasize that Eckankar is a living faith that changes constantly, Eckists must pay close attention to the teachings and revelations of the Living Master, who comes from a long line of masters from the Vairagi Order, whose spiritual essences reside in the Golden Temple of Wisdom on higher dimensions of being. The Living Master is never worshipped, but he is highly revered by all Eckists. According to official Eckankar records, there are approximately 50,000 members in more than 100 countries.

Shortly before Twitchell's death in 1971, critics accused him of fabricating the religious origins of Eckankar, borrowing concepts from other spiritual groups, and plagiarizing ideas from previously published works. A firm denial by Twitchell did little to quench the controversy, and Twitchell's successor, Darwin Gross, became involved in an internal struggle that resulted in his expulsion from Eckankar and his founding of the Ancient Teachings of the Masters, which he claimed perpetuated the true teachings of Twitchell.

The present Living ECK Master, Harold Klemp, who claims to be the 973rd initiated Mahanta, became the spiritual leader of Eckankar in 1981. At the present time, the spiritual home of Eckankar is the Temple of ECK in Chanhassen, Minnesota.

Twitchell from Eckankar standing before the Stardust Hotel podium in Las Vegas. (ARCHIVES OF BRAD STEIGER)

❁ DELVING DEEPER

Eckankar: The Religion of Light and Sound. [Online] http://religiousmovements.lib.virginia.edu/nrms/ecka.html.

Klemp, Harold. The Art of Spiritual Dreaming. Minneapolis: Eckankar, 1999.

Lane, David. The Making of a Spiritual Movement: The Untold Story of Paul Twitchell and Eckankar. Del Mar, Calif.: Del Mar Publishing, 1978.

Main Site of Eckankar, Religion of Light and Sound of God. [Online] http://www.eckankar.org.

Twitchell, Paul. Eckankar: The Key to the Secret Worlds. New York: Lancer Books, 1969. Reprint, Minneapolis: Eckankar, 1989.

FALUN GONG

For 13 hours on April 25, 1999, 15,000 members of the Falun Gong qigong sect, five or six rows deep, stretching for more than a mile along the Avenue of Everlasting Peace in central Beijing, China, protested their negative treatment in the state media and demanded official recognition for their sect and the freedom to publish their texts. The protest managed to get the State Council of China to agree to negotiate with the Falun Gong. However, in July 1999, Chinese officials branded the Falun Gong an evil cult, claiming that it had caused the deaths of 1,500 of its members. The Chinese government banned the practice of the cult and sent more than 50,000 adherents to prisons, labor camps, and mental hospitals.

Falun Gong means the "Practice of the Wheel of the Dharma." (Dharma is a complex Hindu and Buddhist concept that translates in a broad sense to "law," especially to the natural order of personal ethics and principles of conduct, equivalent to what is commonly referred to as "religion.") The founder of the movement, Li Hongzhi, a former Chinese government grain clerk now residing in the United States, claims to have been born on May 13, 1951, the supposed birthday of Siddhartha Gautama, the Buddha (c. 563–c. 483 B.C.E.), but government records list his birthday as July 7, 1952. Hongzhi also claims that Falun Gong has 100 million members worldwide, 80 million of whom are in China. The Chinese government says the number in their country is closer to two million.

Founded in 1992, the movement prescribes five daily exercises are to activate the higher abilities of mind, body, and spirit, and contribute to an individual's self-examination and self-knowledge. If practiced properly, Hongzhi promises, Falun Gong will enable one to attain enlightenment and to master many supernatural powers, including levitation, **psychokinesis,** and **telepathy.**

Hongzhi has often stated that he believes that Earth has been quietly invaded by evil aliens from extraterrestrial worlds who have come to undermine humans' spirituality by contributing to the rapid expansion of technology. In his opinion, humankind would be much better off without computers and all

other machines that seek to replicate human activity and to supplant human productivity.

✤ Delving Deeper

"Beijing, Falun Gong Group in New War of Words," *Yahoo! Finance/DowJones,* January 6, 2001. [Online] http://sg.biz.yahoo.com/news/ international/article.html?s =sgfinance/news/010106/.

"Falun Gong." *Religious Movements Homepage.* [Online] http:// religiousmovements.lib.virginia.edu/nrms/falun-gong.html.

Falun Gong Official Website. [Online] www.falundafa.com/.

Order of the Solar Temple

The Order of the Solar Temple claims a spiritual heritage from the **Order of the Knights Templar** (founded c. 1118 and dissolved in 1307). Among its declared goals are helping Earth to prepare for the return of Christ in solar glory and assisting humankind through a time of transition as spirituality assumes primacy over materiality. Although the group claims it is descended from the original Templars, the Order of the Solar Temple was founded in 1984 by Joseph Di Mambro (1924–1994) and Luc Jouret (1947–1994). By 1989, the cult had gathered about 500 members, most of them in Switzerland, France, and Canada.

Joseph Di Mambro, of Pont-Saint-Espirit, France, had a fascination with the occult dating back to his childhood. In 1976, he became a self-appointed spiritual master, and by 1978, he had established the Golden Way Foundation in Geneva. About then he made a hard assessment of own appeal, deciding that if his cult was to expand, he needed to find a more charismatic individual to share its leadership.

In 1981, Luc Jouret, a physician who had been grand master of the Renewed Order of the Temple, another group that combined concepts of the Knights Templar and the Rosicrucians, left that order over a policy dispute. Di Mambro appealed to him to jointly form a new order. Jouret agreed, and the two founded the Order of the Solar Temple.

Jouret's credentials as a physician and his dynamic platform personality drew large crowds to his lectures. From 1984 to about 1990, Jouret convinced many that the time of the **apocalypse** was drawing near and the best way to survive was in the safety of the Order of the Solar Temple.

But by 1992, Jouret and Di Mambro had made too many unfulfilled predictions and promises. Even Di Mambro's son Elie declared that he doubted the existence of the masters who were allegedly guiding his father and Jouret, and he went so far as to expose some of the illusions his father employed to create certain phenomena during demonstrations.

With the structure of the Order crumbling, Di Mambro and Jouret began preparing for their transition to another world. Those who remained faithful to the teachings also began their own transitions.

When authorities from Chiery, Switzerland, investigated a fire in a farmhouse on October 4, 1994, they discovered a secret room containing 22 corpses, many of them wearing ceremonial capes. On October 5, three adjacent houses burning in the village of Granges-sur-Salvan yielded the bodies of 25 more members of the Order. Six charred bodies found in Morin Heights, Quebec, a day earlier, were also members. In December 1995, 16 more members were found dead in France, and in March 1997, five killed themselves in Quebec. Joseph Di Mambro and Luc Jouret had convinced at least 74 of their followers to join them in mass suicide.

❋ DELVING DEEPER

Hall, John, and Philip Schuyler. "The Mystical Apocalypse of the Solar Temple." In *Millennium, Messiahs, and Mayhem*. Edited by Thomas Robbins and Susan J. Palmer. New York: Routledge, 1997, 285–311.

Mayer, Jean Francois. "Apocalyptic Millennialism in the West: The Case of the Solar Temple." *Critical Incident Analysis Group*. [Online] http://faculty.virginia.edu/ciag/apoc_bkg.html.

"Order of the Solar Temple." *Religious Movements homepage*. [Online] http://religiousmovements.lib.virginia.edu/nrms/solartemp.html.

THE PEOPLE'S TEMPLE

Although James Jones (1931–1978) held degrees from Indiana University and Butler University, he had received no formal training in theology when he was invited to speak at the Laurel Street Tabernacle, an Assemblies of God Pentecostal church, in Indianapolis in September 1954. Following his powerful sermon on racial equality, many members left the congregation to follow Jones and to form a new church, the Wings of Deliverance, which was renamed the People's Temple. Within a short period of time, Jones's gospel of equality and love attracted more than 900 members. In 1965 the temple moved to Ukiah, California, where Jones believed racial equality could be preached with greater openness and less fear of retaliation. Seventy families moved with him. A second congregation was added in San Francisco in 1972.

In 1977, following various exposes directed at the temple, Jones moved his community to the South American nation of Guyana, where he had acquired a lease from the Guyanese government for 4,000 acres of land to be used for colonization. The new community was called the People's Temple Agricultural Project, and eventually more than 900 men, women, and children would follow their charismatic leader to Jonestown.

Members were required to labor 11 hours per day, six days per week, and eight hours on Sunday, clearing land for agriculture, planting crops, and erecting buildings. They ate primarily of rice and beans, and their evenings were filled with required meetings before they were allowed to get some rest. Jones claimed to be

Jim Jones, founder of the People's Temple. (CORBIS CORPORATION)

receiving messages from extraterrestrials that described a process called "Translation," in which he and his followers would all die together and their spirits would be taken to another planet to enjoy a life of bliss. Jones directed rehearsals of a mass suicide, having followers pretend to drink poison and fall to the ground.

On November 14, 1978, California congressman Leo Ryan and several representatives of the media visited Jonestown to investigate claims of civil rights violations that had reached the United States. On November 18, a temple member made an attempt on Ryan's life, and the visitors decided to leave Jonestown immediately. While they were boarding two planes on the jungle airstrip, some heavily armed members of the temple's security guards arrived and began firing on the group. Ryan and four others were killed and 11 were wounded before the planes could get into the air.

Jones decreed that it was time to put "Translation" into effect. Some members of the temple committed suicide by ingesting cyanide-laced Kool-Aid, and others injected poison directly into their veins or were shot. An investigation revealed that 638 adult

Actor John Travolta (center) standing with actress Jenna Elfman (left) and wife Kelly Preston (right) while attending a Scientology conference. (AP/WIDE WORLD PHOTOS)

members of the community died, together with 276 children. A few fled into the jungle and survived.

Various investigations continue into the reasons why such a tragedy could have occurred and what appeal James Jones could have had to cause so many individuals to take their own lives. Conspiracy theorists argue that the deaths at Jonestown in November 1978 eliminated evidence of a CIA experiment gone bad. Others suggest that Jones subjected his followers to mind-control experiments of his own and lost control of the situation. And then there are those who insist that Jones was mentally ill and complicated his mental imbalance with drug abuse.

✤ DELVING DEEPER

Jonestown: Examining the People's Temple. [Online] http://www.owlnet.rice.edu/~reli291/Jonestown/Jonestown.html.

Maaga, M. McCormick, and Catherine Wessinger. *Hearing the Voices of Jonestown.* Syracuse, N.Y.: Syracuse University Press, 1998.

Wright, Lawrence. "Orphans of Jonestown." *The New Yorker,* November 22, 1993, 66–89.

SCIENTOLOGY

Some have called Scientology a cult of celebrity because of the number of well-known entertainers who ascribe to its teachings. In spite of endorsements regarding the

benefits of Scientology from various well-known persons, the organization is often in the center of controversy. Richard Behar, writing in *Time* magazine, stated that rather than being a religion or a church, Scientology "…is a hugely profitable global racket that survives by intimidating members and critics in a Mafia-like manner."

The founder of the church, Lafayette Ronald Hubbard (1911–1986), known to Scientologists as "L. Ron," is said to have studied many Eastern philosophies as he journeyed to the various countries of their origins. When injuries suffered during service as a naval officer during World War II (1939–1945) left him crippled and blind, Hubbard claimed that his ability to draw upon mental insights allowed him to cure himself of his disabilities. He called this process Dianetics, and outlined its central elements in an article for the May 1950 issue of *Astounding Science Fiction* magazine. Shortly thereafter Hubbard published *Dianetics: The Modern Science of Mental Health.*

Dianetics deals with what it terms the Analytical and the Reactive components of the mind. The Reactive mind absorbs and records every nuance of emotional, mental, and physical pain. Hubbard called the impressions or "recordings" made by the Reactive mind during moments of trauma "engrams," and while the conscious, Analytical mind may remain unaware of their presence, they can cause debilitating mental and physical problems and inhibit one's full potential. The Dianetics process enables a person to explore and be "cleared" of such impediments by an "auditor"—a minister of Scientology—clearing the way to a state of freedom from all the constraints of matter, energy, space, and time and a transcendent level of near-perfection.

In August 1952 the *Journal of Scientology* began publication, and in 1954 the first Church of Scientology was founded in Los Angeles. Increasing demand for more information about Scientology led to the establishment of the Founding Church of Scientology and the first Academy of Scientology in Washington, D.C., in 1955. Today, Scientology claims a worldwide membership of around eight million and more than 3,000 churches.

✤ DELVING DEEPER

Behar, Richard. "The Thriving Cult of Greed and Power." *Time*, May 6, 1991, 50–57.

"Church of Scientology." *Religious Movements*. [Online] http://religiousmovements.lib.virginia.edu/nrms/scientology.html.

Frantz, Douglas. "Scientology Faces Glare of Scrutiny after Florida Parishioner's Death." *New York Times*, December 1, 1997.

Hubbard, L. Ron. *Dianetics: The Modern Science of Mental Health*. Bridge Publications, 1985.

Scientology: Applied Religious Philosophy. [Online] http://www.scientology.org/scn_home.htm.

MAKING THE CONNECTION

aboriginal Refers to a people that has lived or existed in a particular area or region from the earliest known times or from the beginning.

abyss From late Latin *abyssus* and Greek *abussos*, which literally means "bottomless," stemming from *bussos*, meaning "bottom." A gorge or chasm that is unfathomably deep, vast or infinite, such as the bottomless pit of hell or a dwelling place of evil spirits.

Anti-Christ From the Greek *antikhristos*. Any antagonist, opponent, or enemy of Jesus Christ, whether a person or a power. A false Christ.

black magick The use of magic for evil purposes, calling upon the devil or evil spirits.

blasphemy Something said or done which shows a disrespect for God or things that are sacred.

conquistadores From the Latin *conquirere* meaning "to conquer." Spanish soldiers or adventurers, especially of the sixteenth century who conquered Peru, Mexico, or Central America.

coven From the Anglo-Norman, mid-seventeenth century "assembly" and from *convenire* meaning convene.

dogma From Greek stem word *dogmat*, meaning "opinion" or "tenet," and from *dokein*, "to seem good." A belief or set of beliefs, either political, religious, philosophical, or moral and held to be true.

hierophant From the Latin *hierophanta* and Greek *hierophantes*, meaning literally a "sacred person who reveals something." An ancient Greek priest who revealed or interpreted the sacred mysteries, or holy doctrines, at the annual festival of Eleusis.

incarnation A period of time in which a spirit or soul dwells in a bodily form or condition. One of a series of lives spent in a physical form.

indigenous From a mid-seventeenth century word *indigena*, literally meaning "born-in," and from *gignere*, meaning "to beget." Inborn, intrinsic, or belonging to a place, such as originating, growing, or living in an area, environment, region, or country.

left-hand path In occult tradition, a practitioner who practices black magick.

L. Ron Hubbard (1911–1986), the founder of the Church of Scientology. (AP/WIDE WORLD PHOTOS)

neophyte From the Latin *neophytus* and Greek *neophutos* or *phuein*, "to plant" or "cause to grow"—literally meaning "newly planted." A beginner or novice at a particular task or endeavor. Somebody who is a recent convert to a belief. A newly ordained priest, or someone who is new to a religious order, but who has not yet taken their vows, so is not yet a part of the order.

Pan In Greek mythology the god of nature or of the woods, fields, pastures, forests, and flocks. Is described as having the torso and head of a human, but the legs, ears, and horns of a goat.

pharaoh From the Hebrew *par'oh*, Egyptian *pr-'o*, and Latin and Greek *Pharao*, meaning literally "great house." An ancient Egyptian title for the ruler or king of Egypt, often considered a tyrant and one who expected unquestioning obedience.

physiognomy From *phusis* meaning "nature, character" and *gnomon*, "to judge." The art of judging a person's character or temperament by their physical features, especially facial features.

reincarnation The reappearance or rebirth of something in a new form. Some religions or belief systems state that the soul returns to live another life in a new physical form and does so in a cyclical manner.

resurrection The act of rising from the dead or returning to life. In Christian belief, the Resurrection was the rising of Jesus Christ from the dead after he was crucified and entombed. Resurrection also refers to the rising of the dead on Judgment Day, as anticipated by Christians, Jews, and Muslims.

right-hand path In occult tradition, a practitioner who practices white magic.

Sabbath From the Greek *sabbaton*, and the Hebrew *sabba*, both meaning "to rest." Sunday is observed as the Sabbath, or day of rest from work and for religious worship in Christianity, and Saturday is the Sabbath as observed by Judaism and some Christians.

Santeria From Spanish *santeria* meaning "holiness". A religion which originated in Cuba by enslaved West African laborers that combines the West African Yoruba religion with Roman Catholicism and recognizes a supreme God as well as other spirits.

sarcophagus From the Greek *sarkophogos*, which literally means "flesh-eater" and probably refers to the kind of limestone that was used in the making of coffins thought to decompose bodies rapidly.

spell A formula or word believed to have magical power. A trance or a bewitched state.

vision From the Latin *vis*, to see. Faculty of sight or a mental image produced by imagination. Can refer to a mystical experience of seeing as if with the eyes, only through a supernatural means such as in a dream, trance, or through a supernatural being, and one which often has religious, revelatory, or prophetic significance.

voodoo From Louisiana French, *voudou* or *vodu*, meaning "fetish." A religion mainly practiced in the Caribbean countries, especially Haiti, that is comprised of a combination of Roman Catholic rituals and animistic beliefs involving fetishes, magic, charms, spells, curses, and communication with ancestral spirits.

white magick The use of magic for supposed good purposes such as to counteract evil.

GLOSSARY

abductee Someone who believes that he or she has been taken away by deception or force against his/her will.

aboriginal Refers to a people that has lived or existed in a particular area or region from the earliest known times or from the beginning.

abyss From late Latin *abyssus* and Greek *abussos*, which literally means "bottomless," stemming from *bussos*, meaning "bottom." A gorge or chasm that is inconceivably deep, vast or infinite, such as the bottomless pit of hell or a dwelling place of evil spirits.

alchemy From Greek, *khemeia* to Arabic, *alkimiya* via medieval Latin *alchimia* and Old French, fourteenth century *alquemie*, meaning "the chemistry." A predecessor of chemistry practiced in the Middle Ages and Renaissance principally concerned with seeking methods of transforming base metals into gold and the "elixir of life."

alien A being or living creature from another planet or world.

amnesia The loss of memory which can be temporary or long term and usually brought on by shock, an injury, or psychological disturbance. Originally from the Greek word *amnestos*, literally meaning not remembered and from a later alteration of the word *amnesia* forgetfulness.

anomalous Something strange and unusual that deviates from what is considered normal. From the Greek *anomalos*, meaning uneven.

anthropology The scientific study of the origins, behavior, physical, social, and cultural aspects of humankind.

Antichrist The antagonist or opponent of Jesus Christ (c. 6 B.C.E.–c. 30 C.E.), who is anticipated by many early as well as contemporary Christians to lead the world into evil before Christ returns to Earth to redeem and rescue the faithful. Can also refer to any person who is in opposition to or an enemy of Jesus Christ or his teachings, as well as to those who claim to be Christ, but in fact are false and misleading.

anthroposophy A spiritual or religious philosophy that Rudolph Steiner (1861–1925), an Austrian philosopher and scientist, developed, with the core belief centering around the human accessibility of the spiritual world to properly developed human intellect. Steiner founded the Anthroposophical Society in 1912 to promote his ideas that spiritual development should be humanity's foremost concern.

apocalypse From the Greek *apokalupsis,* meaning "revelation." In the Bible, the Book of Revelation is often referred to as the Apocalypse. Comes from many anonymous, second-century B.C.E. and later Jewish and Christian texts that contain prophetic messages pertaining to a great total devastation or destruction of the world and the salvation of the righteous.

apothacary From the Greek *apotheke* meaning "storehouse." A pharmacist or druggist who is licensed to prescribe, prepare and sell drugs and other medicines, or a pharmacy—where drugs and medicines are sold.

apparition The unexpected or sudden appearance of something strange, such as a ghost. From the Latin *apparitus,* past participle of *apparere,* meaning to appear.

archaeologist A person who scientifically examines old ruins or artifacts such as the remains of buildings, pottery, graves, tools, and all other relevant material in order to study ancient cultures.

archipelago From the Greek *arkhi,* meaning "chief or main" and *pelagos* meaning "sea." Any large body of water that contains a large number of scattered islands.

Armageddon From late Latin *Armagedon,* Greek and Hebrew, *har megiddo, megiddon,* which is the mountain region of Megiddo. Megiddo is the site where the great final battle between good and evil will be fought as prophesied and will be a decisive catastrophic event that many believe will be the end of the world.

astral self Theosophical belief that humans possess a second body that cannot be perceived with normal senses, yet it coexists with the human body and survives death.

astronomy The scientific study of the of the workings of the universe—of stars, planets, their positions, sizes, composition, movement behavior. Via the Old French and Latin from Greek *astronomia,* meaning literally star-arranging.

automatic writing Writing that occurs through either an involuntary, or unconscious, trance-like state with the source being the writer's own unconscious self, from a telepathic link with another, or from a deceased spirit wishing to communicate a message.

banal Boring, very ordinary and commonplace. From the French word *ban,* originally used in the context of a mandatory military service for all or common to all.

barter The exchange or the process of negotiating certain goods or services for other goods or services.

Bedouin A nomadic Arabic person from the desert areas of North Africa and Arabia. Via Old French *beduin,* ultimately from Arabic *badw,* or desert, nomadic desert people.

betrothal The act of becoming or being engaged to marry another person.

Bhagavad Gita From Sanskrit *Bhagavadgi ta,* meaning "song of the blessed one." A Hindu religious text, consisting of 700 verses, in which the Hindu god, Krishna, teaches the importance of unattachment from personal aims to the fulfillment of religious duties and devotion to God.

bipedal Any animal that has two legs or feet. From the Latin stem *biped,* meaning two-footed.

birthstone Each month of the year has a particular precious gemstone or a semi-precious stone associated with it. It is believed that if a person wears the stone assigned their birth month, good fortune or luck will follow.

bitumen Any of a variety of natural substances, such as tar or asphalt, containing hydrocarbons derived from petroleum and used as a cement or mortar for surfacing roads.

black magick The use of magic for evil purposes, calling upon the devil or evil spirits.

blasphemy Something said or done which shows a disrespect for God or things that are sacred. An irreverent utterance or action showing a disrespect for sacred things or for God.

cadaver A dead body that is usually intended for dissection. From the Latin *cadere*, meaning to fall or to die.

charlatan From the Italian *ciarlatano*, via seventeenth-century French *ciarlare*, meaning "to babble or patter" or "empty talk." Someone who makes elaborate claims or who pretends to have more skill or knowledge than is factual, such as a fraud or quack.

chieftain The leader of a clan, tribe, or group.

clairvoyance The ability to visualize or sense things beyond the normal range of the five human senses. From the French word *clairvoyant*, meaning clear-sighted and *voyant*, the present participle of *voir* to see.

conjurations The act of reciting a name, words or particular phrases with the intent of summoning or invoking a supernatural force or occurrence.

conquistadores From the Latin *conquirere* meaning "to conquer." Spanish soldiers or adventurers, especially of the sixteenth century who conquered Peru, Mexico, or Central America.

consciousness Someone's mind, thoughts or feelings, or can be referring to the part of the mind which is aware of same. The state of being aware of what is going on around you, either individually or the shared feelings of group awareness, feelings or thoughts.

conspiracy A plan formulated in secret between two or more people to commit a subversive act.

contactee Someone who believes to have been or is in contact with an alien from another planet.

cosmic consciousness The sense or special insight of one's personal or collective awareness in relation to the universe or a universal scheme.

cosmic sense The awareness of one's identity and actions in relationship to the universe or universal scheme of things.

cosmology The philosophical study and explanation of the nature of the universe or the scientific study of the origin and structure of the universe.

cosmos From the Greek *kosmos* meaning "order, universe, ornament." The entire universe as regarded in an orderly, harmonious and integrated whole.

coven From the Anglo-Norman, mid-seventeenth century "assembly" and from *convenire* meaning convene. An assembly of or a meeting of a group of witches, often 13 in number.

cryptomensia A state of consciousness in which the true source or origin of a particular memory is forgotten or is attributed to a wrongful source or origin.

cryptozoology The study of so-called mythical creatures such as the Yeti or Bigfoot, whose existence has not yet been scientifically substantiated.

cubit From the Latin *cubitum*, meaning forearm or elbow. An ancient unit of length, based on the distance from the tip of the middle finger to the elbow which approximated 17 to 22 inches.

deity From late Latin *deitas* "divine nature," and *deus* "god." A divine being or somebody or something with the essential nature of a divinity, such as a god, goddess. When the term is capitalized, it refers to God in monotheistic belief or religions.

demarcation The process of setting borders, limits or marking boundaries. From the Spanish *demarcacion*, literally meaning, marking off.

demon possession When low-level disincarnate spirits invade and take over a human body.

desecration When something sacred is treated in a profane or damaging manner.

discarnate The lack of a physical body. Coined from *dis-* and the Latin stem *carn*, meaning *flesh*.

The Dispersion From the Greek *diaspora* meaning to scatter or disperse. Refers to the period in history when the Jewish people were forced to scatter in countries outside of Palestine after the Babylonian captivity.

dogma From Greek stem word *dogmat*, meaning "opinion" or "tenet," and from *dokein*, "to seem good." A belief or set of beliefs, either political, religious, philosophical, or moral and considered to be absolutely true.

druid Someone who worships the forces of nature as in the ancient Celtic religion. Can also refer to a priest in the Celtic religion.

ecclesiasticism Principles, practices, activities, or body of thought that is all-encompassing and adhered to in an organized church or institution.

ecstatic Intense emotion of pleasure, happiness, joy or elation.

electrodes Two conductors through which electricity flows in batteries or other electrical equipment.

electroencephalograph A device or machine that through the use of electrodes placed on a person's scalp, monitors the electrical activity in various parts of the brain. These are recorded and used as a diagnostic tool in tracing a variety of anything from brain disorders, tumors or other irregularities to dream research.

electroencephalographic dream research Researching dreams using a electroencephalograph to aid the researcher in the brain activity of the one being studied.

electromagnetic Of or pertaining to the characteristics of an electromagnet, which is a device having a steel or iron core and is magnetized by an electric current that flows through a surrounding coil.

elemental spirits A lower order of spirit beings, said to be usually benevolent and dwell in the nature kingdom as the life force of all things in nature, such as minerals, plants, animals, and the four elements of earth, air, fire and water; the planets, stars, and signs of the zodiac; and hours of the day and night. Elves, brownies, goblins, gnomes, and fairies are said to be among these spirits.

elixir Something that is a mysterious, magical substance with curative powers believed to heal all ills or to prolong life and preserve youthfulness. From the Arabic *al-iksir* and the Greek *xerion*, meaning dry powder for treating wounds.

enchantments Things or conditions which possess a charming or bewitching quality such as a magical spell.

encode To convert a message from plain text into a code. In computer language, to convert from analog to digital form, and in genetics to convert appropriate genetic data.

enigma From Greek *ainigma* "to speak in riddles" and *ainos*, meaning "fables." Somebody or something that is ambiguous, puzzling or not easily understood and might have a hidden meaning or riddle.

ephemerality Refers to the state of something living or lasting for a markedly short or brief time. The nature of existing or lasting for only a day, such as certain plants or insects.

eschatology Comes from the Greek word *eskhatos* meaning "last" and *-logy* literally meaning "discourse about the last things." Refers to the body of religious doctrines concerning the human soul in relation to death, judgment, heaven or hell, or in general, life after death and of the final stage or end of the world.

evocation The act of calling forth, drawing out or summoning an event or memory from the past, as in recreating.

exorcism The act, religious ceremony, or ritual of casting out evil spirits from a person or a place.

extraterrestrial Something or someone originating or coming from beyond Earth, outside of Earth's atmosphere.

false memory Refers to situations where some therapies and hypnosis may actually be planting memories through certain suggestions or leading questions and comments; thereby creating memories that the patient or client believes to be true, but in reality they are not.

fanatical Extreme enthusiasm, frenzy, or zeal about a particular belief, as in politics or religion.

Five Pillars of Islam In Arabic, also called the *arkan*, and consists of the five sacred ritual duties believed to be central to mainstream Muslims' faith. The five duties are the confession of faith, performing the five daily prayers, fasting during the month of Ramadan, paying alms tax, and performing at least one sacred pilgrimage to Mecca, the holy land.

foo fighter A term coined by pilots who reported sightings of unconventional aircraft that appeared as nocturnal lights during World War II. A popular cartoon character of the time, Smokey Stover, often said "Where there's foo there's fire" and it became the saying to describe the strange phenomena.

frieze From the Latin *phrygium (opus)*, meaning work or craftmanship. A decorative architectural band, usually running along a wall, just below the ceiling, often sculpted with figurines or ornaments.

fulcrum From the Latin *fulcire*, meaning "to prop up or support." The part of something that acts as its support.

Geiger counter An instrument named after its inventor, German physicist Hans Geiger (1882–1945), that is used to measure and detect such things as particles from radioactive materials.

geoglyphics Lines, designs, or symbols left in the earth, such as those in Egypt, Malta, Chile, Bolivia, and Peru with a mysterious, ancient, and puzzling origin.

Gestalt therapy A type of psychotherapy that puts a emphasis on a person's feelings as revealing desired or undesired personality traits and how they came to be, by examining unresolved issues from the past.

Gnostic From the Greek, *gnostikos*, meaning "concerning knowledge." A believer in Gnosticism, or relating to or possessing spiritual or intellectual knowledge or wisdom.

guardian angel A holy, divine being that watches over, guides, and protects humans.

hallucinations A false or distorted perception of events during which one vividly imagines seeing, hearing or sensing objects or other people to be present, when in fact they are not witnessed by others.

haruspicy A method of divining or telling the future by examining the entrails of animals.

heresy The willful, persistent act of adhering to an opinion or belief that rejects or contradicts established teachings or theories that are traditional in philosophy, religion, science, or politics.

heretic From the Greek *hairetikos*, meaning "able to choose." Someone who does not conform or whose opinions, theories, or beliefs contradict the conventional established teaching, doctrines, or principles, especially that of religion.

hieroglyphics A writing system of ancient Egypt that uses symbols or pictures to signify sounds, objects, or concepts. Can also refer to any writing or symbols that are difficult to decipher. The word comes from an ancient Greek term meaning "sacred carving."

hierophant From the Latin *hierophanta* and Greek *hierophantes*, meaning literally a "sacred person who reveals something." An ancient Greek priest who revealed or interpreted the sacred mysteries, or holy doctrines, at the annual festival of Eleusis.

hoax An act of deception that is intended to make people think or believe something is real when it is not.

Homo sapiens Mankind or humankind, the species of modern human beings.

horoscope From Greek *horoskopos*, literally meaning "time observer" and from *hora* meaning "time, or hour," referring to the time of birth. A diagram or astrological forecast based on the relative position in the heavens of the stars and planets in the signs of the zodiac, at any given moment, but especially at the moment of one's birth.

hypnagogic Relating to or being in the state between wakefulness and sleep where one is drowsy. From the French *hypnagogique* meaning literally leading to sleep.

hypnopompic Typical of or involving the state between sleeping and waking. Coined from *hypno* and Greek *pompe*, meaning a sending away.

hypnosis The process of putting or being in a sleeplike state, although the person is not sleeping. It can be induced by suggestions or methods of a hypnotist.

hypothesis A theory or assumption that needs further exploration, but which is used as a tentative explanation until further data confirms or denies it. From the Greek *hupothesis* meaning foundation or base.

Ice Age Any of the periods of extreme cold or glacial epochs in the history of Earth when temperatures fell, resulting in large areas of Earth's surface covered with glaciers; the most recent one occurring during the Pleistocene epoch.

incantation From fourteenth-century French, *cantare*, meaning "to sing" via Latin—*incantare*—"to chant." The chanting, recitation or uttering of words supposed to produce a magical effect or power.

incarnation A period of time in which a spirit or soul dwells in a bodily form or condition. One of a series of lives spent in a physical form.

indigenous From a mid-seventeenth century word *indigena*, literally meaning "born-in," and from *gignere*, meaning "to beget." Inborn, intrinsic, or belonging to a place, such as originating, growing, or living in an area, environment, region, or country.

Inquisition Fourteenth century, from Latin *inquirere* via Old French *inquisicion*, meaning "to inquire." In the thirteenth century, Roman Catholicism appointed a special tribunal or committee whose chief function was to combat, suppress and punish heresy against the church. Remaining active until the modern era, the official investigations were often harsh and unfair.

insurrectionist Someone who is in rebellion or revolt against an established authority, ruler, or government.

intergalactic Something that is located, or is moving, between two or more galaxies.

Invocation The act of calling upon or appealing to a higher power such as a deity, spirit, or God for assistance. A form of prayer, that invites God's presence, at the beginning of a ceremony or meeting. In black magick, can be the casting of a spell or formula to invite an evil spirit to appear.

ions An atom or group of atoms that are electrically charged through the process of gaining or losing one or more electrons. From the Greek *ion* meaning moving thing; and from the present participle of *ienai* meaning to go —from the movement of any ion toward the electrode of the opposite charge.

jinni In Islamic or Muslim legend, a spirit that is capable of taking on the shape of humans or animals in order to perform mischievous acts or to exercise supernatural power and influence over humans. From the Arabic *jinn*, which is the plural of *jinni*.

Kabbalah body of mystical Jewish teachings based on an interpretation of hidden meanings contained in the Hebrew scriptures. Kabbalah is Hebrew for "that which is received," and also refers to a secret oral tradition handed down from teacher to pupil. The term Kabbalah is generally used now to apply to all Jewish mystical practice.

karmic law Karma is the Sanskrit word for "deed." In the Eastern religions of Buddhism and Hinduism all deeds of a person in this life dictate an equal punishment or reward to be met in the next life or series of lives. In this philosophy, it is a natural moral law rather than a divine judgment which provides the process of development, enabling the soul into higher or lower states, according to the laws of cause and effect to be met.

knockings/rappings Tapping sounds said to be coming from deceased spirits in an attempt to communicate with or frighten the living.

left-hand path In occult tradition, a practitioner who practices black magic.

leprous From the Greek, *lepros,* meaning "scale." Something resembling the symptoms of or relating to the disease of leprosy, which covers a person's skin with scales or ulcerations.

loa A spirit that is thought to enter the devotee of the Haitian voodoo, during a trance state, and believed to be a protector and guide that could be a local deity, a deified ancestor or even a saint of the Roman Catholic Church.

lupinomanis Having the excessive characteristics of a wolf, such as being greedy or ravenously hungry.

lycanthropy The magical ability in legends and horror stories of a person who is able to transform into a wolf, and take on all of its characteristics.

magus A priest, wizard, or someone who is skilled or learned, especially in astrology, magic, sorcery, or the like.

manitou A supernatural force, or spirit that suffuses various living things, as well as inanimate objects, according to the Algonquian peoples. In the mythology of the Ojibwa of the eastern United States, Manitou is the name of the supreme deity, or God, and means "Great Spirit."

manna The food miraculously supplied to the Israelites by God, according to the Old Testament, as they wandered in the wilderness during their flight from Egypt. Spiritual nourishment or something of value received of divine origin or unexpectedly.

materialization Something that appears suddenly, as if out of nowhere. In the paranor-

mal it might be a ghost or spirit that suddenly appears to take on a physical form.

medium In the paranormal, someone who is able to convey messages between the spirits of the deceased and the spirits of the living.

megalith A very large stone that is usually a part of a monument or prehistoric architecture.

Mesopotamia Greek word, meaning "between two rivers." An ancient region that was located between the Tigris and Euphrates rivers in what is today, modern Iraq and Syria. Some of the world's earliest and greatest ancient civilizations such as Ur, Sumer, Assyria, and Babylonia were developed in that region.

messiah A leader who is regarded as a liberator or savior. In Christianity, the Messiah is Jesus Christ (c. 6 B.C.E.–c. 30 C.E.), in Judaism, it is the king who will lead the Jews back to the Holy Land of Israel and establish world peace.

metaphysical Relating to abstract thought or the philosophical study of the nature of existence and truth.

metrology The scientific system or study of measurements. From the Greek *metrologie,* meaning theory of ratios and *metron,* or measure.

mortician An undertaker or one who prepares dead bodies for burial and funerals.

narcolepsy A condition where a person uncontrollably falls asleep at odd times during daily activities and/or for long extended periods of time. Hallucinations and even paralysis might also accompany this condition.

near-death experience A mystical-like occurrence or sensation that individuals on the brink of death or who were dead, but brought back to life, have described which includes leaving their physical body and hovering over it as though they were a bystander.

neo-paganism Someone who believes in a contemporary or modernized version of the religions which existed before Christianity, especially those with a reverence for nature over the worship of a divine or supreme being.

neophyte From the Latin *neophytus* and Greek *neophutos* or *phuein*, "to plant" or "cause to grow"—literally meaning "newly planted." A beginner or novice at a particular task or endeavor. Somebody who is a recent convert to a belief. A newly ordained priest, or someone who is new to a religious order, but who has not yet taken their vows, so is not yet a part of the order.

neuron The basic functional unit of the nervous system a cell body that consists of an axon and dendrites and transmit nerve impulses. A neuron is also called a *nerve cell*. Via German from Greek *neuron*, meaning sinew, cord, or nerve.

Novena of Masses In the Roman Catholic Church, the recitation of prayers or devotions for a particular purpose, for nine consecutive days. From the Latin *nus*, meaning nine each and from *novem*, meaning nine.

Old Testament The first of the two main divisions of the Christian Bible that corresponds to the Hebrew scriptures.

omen A prophetic sign, phenomenon, or happening supposed to foreshadow good or evil or indicate how someone or something will fare in the future—an indication of the course of future events.

oracle Either someone or something that is the source of wisdom, knowledge or prophecy. Can also refer to the place where the prophetic word would be given. Via French from the Latin *oraculum*, from *orare* to speak.

paleoanthropology The study of humanlike creatures or early human beings more primitive that Homo Sapiens, usually done through fossil evidence.

paleontology The study of ancient forms of life in geologic or prehistoric times, using such evidence as fossils, plants, animals, and other organisms.

Pan In Greek mythology the god of nature or of the woods, fields, pastures, forests, and flocks. Is described as having the torso and head of a human, but the legs, ears, and horns of a goat.

paranormal Events or phenomena that are beyond the range of normal experience and not understood or explained in terms of current scientific knowledge.

parapsychologist One who studies mental phenomena, such as telepathy or extrasensory perception, the mind/body connection, and other psi or paranormal factors that cannot be explained by known scientific principles.

parapsychology The study or exploration of mental phenomena that does not have a scientific explanation in the known psychological principles.

Passover The seven or eight days of a Jewish festival that begins on the fourteenth day of Nissan and commemorates the exodus of the Hebrews from their captivity in Egypt. From the Hebrew word *pesa*, meaning to pass without affecting.

pharaoh From the Hebrew *par'oh*, Egyptian *pr-'o*, and Latin and Greek *Pharao*, meaning literally "great house." An ancient Egyptian title for the ruler or king of Egypt, often considered a tyrant and one who expected unquestioning obedience.

pharmacologist The study of or science of drugs in all their aspects, including sources, chemistry, production, their use in treating ailments and disease, as well as any known side effects.

phenomena Strange, extraordinary, unusual, even miraculous events, or happenings to persons or things. From the Greek *phainomenon*, that which appears, from the past participle of *phainein*, to bring to light.

philanthropist Someone who is benevolent or generous in his or her desire or activities to improve the social, spiritual or material welfare of humankind. From the late Latin, ultimately, Greek *philanthropos*, humane; *philos*; loving and *anthropos*, human being.

philanthropy From the Greek *philanthropos*, meaning "humane," and from *philos*, meaning "loving." An affection or desire to help improve the spiritual, social, or material welfare of humanity through acts of charity or benevolence.

physiognomy From *phusis* meaning "nature, character" and *gnomon*, "to judge." The art of judging a person's character or temperament by their physical features, especially facial features.

physiology The study of the functioning and internal workings of living things, such as metabolism, respiration, reproduction and the like. From the Latin word *physiologia* and the Greek *phusiologia*, and *phusis* meaning nature.

precognition The ability to foresee what is going to happen in the future, especially if this perception is gained through other than the normal human senses or extrasensory.

predator Any organism or animal that hunts, kills, and eats other animals. Can refer to a ruthless person who is extremely aggressive in harming another. From the Latin *praedator* and *praedari*, meaning to seize as plunder.

psi The factor or factors responsible for parapsychological phenomena. Derived from the Greek letter *psi* which is used to denote the unknown factor in an equation.

psyche The soul or human spirit or can refer to the mental characteristics of a person or group or nation. Via Latin from Greek *psukhe* meaning breath, soul, mind and from *psukhein* to breathe.

psychiatrist A doctor who is trained to treat people with psychiatric disorders.

psychoanalysis The system of analysis regarding the relationship of conscious and unconscious psychological aspects and their treatment in mental or psycho neurosis.

psychoanalyst One who uses the therapeutic methods of psychiatric analysis, such as dream analysis and free association, as developed by Sigmund Freud (1856–1939) to treat patients in order to gain awareness of suppressed subconscious experiences or memories that might be causing psychological blocks.

psychokinesis The ability to make objects move or to in some way affect them without using anything but mental powers.

pulsar A star generally believed to be a neutron star and that appears to pulse as it briefly emits bursts of visible radiation such as radio waves and x-rays.

putrefy Causing something to decay, usually indicating a foul odor. From the Latin stem, *putr*, meaning rotten, plus *facere*, to make.

Qur'an The sacred text, or holy book, of Islam. For Muslims, it is the very word of Allah, the absolute God of the Islamic faith, as revealed to the prophet Muhammad (c. 570 C.E.–632 C.E.) by the archangel Gabriel.

rectory The house or dwelling that a rector (clergyman) lives in.

reincarnation The reappearance or rebirth of something in a new form. Some religions or belief systems state that the soul returns to live another life in a new physical form and does so in a cyclical manner.

resurrection The act of rising from the dead or returning to life. In Christian belief, the Resurrection was the rising of Jesus Christ from the dead after he was crucified and entombed. Resurrection also refers to the rising of the dead on Judgment Day, as anticipated by Christians, Jews, and Muslims.

retrocognition The mental process or faculty of knowing, seeing, or perceiving things, events, or occurrences of things in the past, especially through other than the normal human senses as in extrasensory.

right-hand path In occult tradition, a practitioner who practices white magic.

rite Originally from an Indo-European base meaning "to fit together" and was the ancestor of the English words *arithmetic* and *rhyme* via, the Latin *ritus*. A formal act or observance as a community custom, such as the rite of courtship. Often has a solemn, religious or ceremonial meaning, such as the rite of baptism.

Sabbath From the Greek *sabbaton*, and the Hebrew *sabba*, both meaning "to rest." A day of rest from work and for religious worship. In Christianity, Sunday is the observed day of worship while Saturday is observed in Judaism and some Christian denominations.

Sanskrit Sanskrit is an ancient Indo-European language and the language of traditional Hinduism in India. Spoken between the fourteenth and fifth centuries B.C.E., it has been considered and maintained as a priestly and literary language of the sacred Veda scriptures and other classical texts.

Santeria From Spanish *santeria* meaning "holiness." A religion which originated in Cuba by enslaved West African laborers that combines the West African Yoruba religion with Roman Catholicism and recognizes a supreme God as well as other spirits.

sarcophagus From the Greek *sarx* meaning "flesh," and Greek *sarkophogos*, literally meaning "flesh-eater." Originally a kind of limestone that had properties to aid in the rapid decomposition of the deceased bodies and was used in the making of coffins. Eventually came to mean any stone coffin, especially one with inscriptions or decorated with sculpture and used as a monument.

sauropod Any of various large semi-aquatic plant-eating dinosaurs that had a long neck and tail and a small head. From the suborder *Sauropoda*, a Latin word meaning lizard foot.

schizophrenia A severe psychiatric disorder which can include symptoms of withdrawal or detachment from reality, delusions, hallucinations, emotional instability, and intellectual disturbances or illogical patterns of thinking to various degrees. The term comes from Greek words meaning "split mind."

seance A meeting or gathering of people in which a spiritualist makes attempts to communicate with the spirits of deceased persons, or a gathering to receive spiritualistic messages.

semidivine Possessing similar or some of the characteristics, abilities, or powers normally attributed to a deity and/or existing on a higher spiritual level or plane than common mortals yet not completely divine.

shaman A religious or spiritual leader, usually possessing special powers, such as that of prophecy, and healing, and acts as an intermediary between the physical and spiritual realms.

shamanic exorcism When a shaman, or tribal medicine-holy person, performs a ceremonial ritual to expel the disincarnate spirits from a person.

shapeshifter A supposed fictional being, spirit or something that is able to change its appearance or shape.

shofar A trumpet made of a ram's horn, blown by the ancient and modern Hebrews during religious ceremonies and as a signal in battle.

soothsayer From Middle English, literally meaning "somebody who speaks the truth." Someone who claims to have the ability to foretell future events.

soul The animating and vital principal in human beings, credited with the faculties of will, emotion, thought and action and often conceived as an immaterial entity, separate from the physical body. The spiritual nature of human beings, regarded as immortal, separable from the body at death, and susceptible to happiness or misery in a future state. The disembodied spirit of a dead human being.

spell A formula or word believed to have magical power. A trance or a bewitched state.

spirit control The guide that mediums contact to receive messages from deceased spirits, or another name for spirit guide as used in mediumship.

spirit guide A nonphysical being or entity which possibly can be an angel, the higher self, the spirit of a deceased person, a higher group mind, or a highly evolved being whose purpose is to help, guide, direct, and protect the individual.

spittle Something that looks like or is saliva, which is secreted from the mouth.

stigmata Marks on a person's body resembling the wounds inflicted on Jesus Christ (c. 6 B.C.E.–c. 30 C.E.) during his Crucifixion on the cross.

subversive To cause the ruin or downfall of something or to undermine or overthrow principles, an institution, or a government.

supernatural Relating to or pertaining to God or the characteristics of God; a deity or magic of something that is above and beyond what is normally explained by natural laws.

superstition The belief that certain actions and rituals have a magical effect resulting in either good or bad. From the Latin stem *superstition*, and *superstes*, meaning standing over or in awe.

taboo Something that is forbidden. In some cases can refer to something being sacred, therefore forbidden, such as in Polynesian societies. From the Tongan *tabu*, said to have been introduced into the English language by Captain James Cook in the late eighteenth century.

talisman An object such as a gemstone or stone, believed to have magical powers or properties. From the Greek *telesma*, meaning something consecrated, *telein*, to complete, and *telos*, result.

Tanakh From the Hebrew *tenak*, an acronym formed from *torah*. It is the sacred book of Judaism, consisting of the Torah—the five books of Moses, *The Nevi'im*—the words of the prophets, and the *Kethuvim*—the writings.

telepathy Communication of thoughts, mental images, ideas, feelings, or sensations from one person's mind to another's without the use of speech, writing, signs, or symbols.

theory of evolution The biological theory of the complex process of living organisms, how they change and evolve from one generation to another or over many generations.

therianthropic Used to describe a mythological creature that is half human and half animal. Coined from the Greek *therion*, meaning small wild animal, and *anthropo*, meaning human being.

totem An animal, bird, plant, or any other natural object that is revered as a personal or tribal symbol.

transference The process of change that happens when one person or place is transferred to another.

transience A state of impermanence, or lasting for only a brief time. Remaining in a place only for a short time, or the brief appearance of someone or something.

transmutation The act of transforming or changing from one nature, form, or state into another.

tribulation Great affliction, trial, or distress. In Christianity, the tribulation refers to the prophesied period of time which precedes the return of Jesus Christ to Earth, in which there will be tremendous suffering that will test humanity's endurance, patience, or faith.

UFO Literally an unidentified flying object, although the term is often used by some to refer to an alien spacecraft.

UFOlogist Someone who investigates the reports and sightings of unidentified flying objects.

Valhalla In Norse mythology, when the souls of heroes are killed in battle, they spend eternity in a great hall, which is called Valhalla. From the Old Norse *valhall*, literally meaning hall of the slain.

Valkyrie One of the 12 handmaids of Odin in Norse mythology who ride their horses over the battlefield as they escort the souls of slain heroes to Valhalla. From the Old Norse *Valkyrja*, meaning literally chooser of the slain.

vision From the Latin *vis*, to see. Faculty of sight or a mental image produced by imagination. Can refer to a mystical experience of seeing as if with the eyes, only through a supernatural means such as in a dream, trance, or through a supernatural being, and one which often has religious, revelatory, or prophetic significance.

voodoo From Louisiana French, *voudou* or *vodu*, meaning "fetish." A religion mainly practiced in the Caribbean countries, especially Haiti, that is comprised of a combination of Roman Catholic rituals and animistic beliefs involving fetishes, magic, charms, spells, curses, and communication with ancestral spirits.

white magick The use of magic for supposed good purposes such as to counteract evil.

Wiccan Someone who is a witch, a believer or follower of the religion of Wicca.

wizard A variant of the fifteenth century word *wisard*, meaning "wise." Someone professing to have magical powers as a magician, sorcerer, or a male witch. In general, someone who is extremely knowledgeable and clever.

zoology The scientific branch of biology that studies animals in all their characteristics and aspects. From the Greek *zoologia*, literally the study of life and from *zolion*, or life form.

Zoroaster A Persian prophet (c. 628 B.C.E.– c. 551 B.C.E.) and the founder of an ancient religion called Zoroastrianism whose principal belief is in a supreme deity and of the existence of a dualism between good and evil. Derived from the Greek word *Zarat* or *Zarathustra*, meaning camel handler.

The Cumulative Index, found in each volume, is an alphabetic arrangement of all people, places, images, and concepts found in the text. Names of publications, movies, ships, television programs, radio broadcasts, foreign words, and cross-references are indicated by italics.

The page references to the subjects include the Arabic volume number as well as the page number. Main entries are designated by bold page numbers while images are denoted by italics.

Cumulative Index

The Others (film), 3:50

The Others (TV program), 3:51

Ouija boards, 1:85, **1:85–86**

Our Lady of Czestochowa. *See* Black Madonna

Our Lady of Jasna Gora. *See* Black Madonna

Out-of-body experiences, 3:12, 158, 170–171

    See also Autoscopy

Out-of-body experiences, research in,
    3:170–174

Out on a Limb (film), 1:96

Owen, Robert Dale, 3:11

P

Paganism, popularity of, 2:94

Page (tarot). *See* Knave (tarot)

Paiens, Hugues des, 2:19–20

Pain relief, 3:139, 147–148

Paiute Messiah. *See* Wilson, Jack

The Palantine (ship), 3:10

Palladino, Eusapia, **1:120–122**, *121*, 168

Palm reading. *See* Palmistry

Palmistry, **2:147–150,** *148, 149*

Pan (Greek deity), 2:123

Panatleone, St., 1:221

Panchen Lama, 1:*44*

Panic disorders, 3:137

Paracelsus (German physician), 2:41, 43,
    47–48, *48*, 57, 3:146

Paranormal photography. *See* Psychic
    photography

The Parapsychological Association, Inc., 1:145

Parapsychologists, 3:157–158

    See also Researchers of clairvoyance;
        Researchers of ESP (Extrasensory
        perception); Researchers of
        psychokinesis; Researchers of spirit
        contact; Researchers of telepathy

Parini, Giuseppi, 1:*118*

Paris (France) holy apparitions, 1:188

Parker, Alice, 2:106

Parker, Walter E., Sr., 3:9

Parks, Carl, 2:193

Parks, Jo Ann, 2:193

Parris, Betty, 2:104, 105

Parris, Samuel, 2:104

Parzeval (Eschenbach), 2:205, 206

Pasierb, Janusz, 1:272

Passivity, in consciousness, 1:145

Past-life therapy, **1:67–69**

Past lives, **1:57–70**

Patience (tarot). *See* Temperance (tarot)

"Patience Worth" (spirit control). *See* Curran,
    Pearl Leonore

Patrick, St., 3:225

Patterson, Roger, 3:61, 62

Paul, St.

    on afterlife, 1:8

    on the Antichrist, 1:180

    on fight against forces of evil, 1:288

    on glossolalia, 1:226

    possible stigmata of, 1:241

    on The Rapture, 1:231

    on soul, 1:8–9

Paul III, Pope, 1:219, 2:96–97, 125

Paul IV, Pope, 1:219, 2:97

Paul VI, Pope, 1:220, 2:97

Peace symbols, 1:290

Pearls, 3:195

"Peep." *See* Nettles, Bonnie Lu Trousdale

Pennsylvania State Police, hoax warnings from,
    3:228, 229

Pennsylvania thunderbird sightings, 3:97, 99

Pentagrams, 1:290

Pentecostalism, glossolalia and, 1:226

People's Temple, 1:313, 315, **319–320**

Peretti, Felice. *See* Sixtus V, Pope

Perkins, Thomas H., 3:94

Perls, Fritz, 3:128

Perntz, Anders, 3:178

Persephone (mythic figure), 1:34, 268, 269

Persia, dog superstitions, 3:193

Persinger, Michael, 1:190, 247

Peter, St., 2:69

Peter of Abano, 2:144

Petroglyphs, 3:97–98, *248*

Peuckert, Erick-Will, 3:153

Peyramale, Father, 2:249

Phantasms. *See* Apparitions

"Phantom hitchhiker" urban legend,
    3:234–235

Phantoms, 3:2, 4, **14–18**

    See also Apparitions; Ghosts and ghostly
        beings

Pharaohs, role in religion, 1:258

Pharos of Alexandria (Egypt), 2:243

The Phenomena of Astral Projection (Carrington,
    Muldoon), 3:172

Philadelphia Experiment (1943), **3:298–301**

Philbin, Regis, 3:48

Philip IV (King of France), 2:22–23, 24

Philippines, food kinship custom, 3:216